INDEX TO BRITISH
LITERARY BIBLIOGRAPHY

I

BIBLIOGRAPHY OF BRITISH LITERARY BIBLIOGRAPHIES

T. H. HOWARD-HILL

OXFORD
AT THE CLARENDON PRESS
1969

Oxford University Press, Ely House, London W. 1

GLASGOW NEW YORK TORONTO MELBOURNE WELLINGTON
CAPE TOWN SALISBURY IBADAN NAIROBI LUSAKA ADDIS ABABA
BOMBAY CALCUTTA MADRAS KARACHI LAHORE DACCA
KUALA LUMPUR SINGAPORE HONG KONG TOKYO

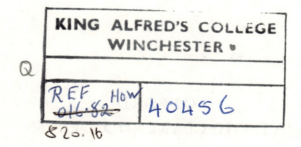

PREFACE

THE first selection of entries for this and the further volumes started in New Zealand in 1959. I am truly grateful for the help and advice of my friends and colleagues in New Zealand libraries, particularly the Alexander Turnbull library, the General Assembly library, and the National Library Centre, Wellington, to whom, if this book were to be dedicated, I would make more formal acknowledgement. A large part of the labours fell unavoidably on the library assistants in the Upper Reading Room, Bodleian Library, whose ready co-operation I continue to enjoy and appreciate. For advice and encouragement in the early stages, I am indebted to Sir Frank Francis, Secretary of the Bibliographical Society, and to Mr. John C. Wyllie, then Secretary of the University of Virginia Bibliographical Society. My greatest and more recent obligation is to Mr. John S. G. Simmons, Fellow of All Souls, who was generous with time, counsel, and encouragement when it was most needed.

My debt to Mr. Alan Eager's work on the bibliography of Ireland is obvious; I received similar considerable aid from the Modern Humanities Association's annual bibliographies, without which my task would have been overwhelming.

I am grateful, too, to the Delegates of the Oxford University Press for accepting this work for publication, and for the compositors, proofreaders, and editors who have saved me from many an error. I must acknowledge my responsibility for remaining errors and misprints from which I could not be protected.

I hope that a second edition will be called for in due course and would be greatly obliged by readers kind enough to send me, care of the publishers, notes of any omissions and errors they may discover.

T. H. H.

'Trevenny', Noke, Oxford
June, 1968

CONTENTS

INTRODUCTION

THE *Bibliography of British Literary Bibliographies* forms the first volume of the *Index to British Bibliography* which is intended to cover books, substantial parts of books, and periodical articles written in English and published in the English-speaking Commonwealth and the United States after 1890, on the bibliographical and textual examination of English manuscripts, books, printing and publishing, and any other books published in English in Great Britain or by British authors abroad, from the establishment of printing in England, except for material on modern (post-1890) printing and publishing not primarily of bibliographical or literary interest.

The second volume will record the bibliographies of the work of Shakespeare (which have been excluded from the present volume) and bibliographical and textual discussions of them. The final volume, the *Bibliography of British Bibliography and Textual Criticism*, will list material not included in the prior volumes, according to the statement of coverage outlined in the first paragraph above. Although each volume will be separately indexed and may be used separately, it is hoped that the inclusion of a comprehensive index in the third volume will serve to justify the comprehensive title.

THE BIBLIOGRAPHY OF
BRITISH LITERARY BIBLIOGRAPHIES

I. SCOPE. This bibliography records all publications in English which list the printed works of British writers, which list and describe the works published in Britain from 1475 to the present day, whether generally or classified by period, or literary form or genre, or which describe English works dealing with particular subjects. (The obvious provisos to this general statement are discussed under the relevant heading below.) In general, no material published before 1890 has been included though I have felt free to depart from this and other general principles in particular cases when it has seemed that the exceptional material would substantially aid the user. The date was decided on largely because modern British bibliographical studies may be thought to have originated with the foundation of the Bibliographical Society, London, in 1892 (the Edinburgh Bibliographical Society was founded in 1890), and the conception of the 'new' bibliography in its descriptive as well as its analytic aspect is central to the idea of this bibliography. I have tried to list everything which will give the user information on the physical description of a book or class of books associated with a period, place, subject, form, or genre related to English literature. It has not been my task to compile a bibliography of bibliographies of English publications in general; only those lists which are potentially useful to a student of English literature have been included, and, more specifically, those contributions which are both enumerative and descriptive. In brief, this is a bibliography for all those people who are interested in publication in English as *literature*.

Much of the material listed here will be familiar to the practised scholar; some of it is of little intrinsic usefulness and has been included only because it is all that exists on a particular subject, but every item here has been examined by the compiler, who has had constantly before him Bowers's views on what an enumerative bibliography should be. Obviously there are very few lists included here which would embody the best modern standards, but I mention this to illuminate the guiding principle behind the compilation of this list. I have recorded every literary bibliography (handlist, catalogue, checklist, and so on) which has satisfied the general criteria, and for authors, the list which most approaches the ideal has been singled out by annotation. One might say, then, that the items listed here are enumerative bibliographies with varying amounts of descriptive information. Finally, this is not a bibliography for readers interested in alchemy, conjuring, or any of the other subjects listed under the particular subject headings, but a bibliography for people interested in the *books* published in English in Britain on those subjects.

Exclusions. It has been impossible to find a proper basis for the exclusion of material on the grounds of form. Although Professor Bowers and other recent writers on 'what is bibliography' quite properly distinguish amongst bibliographies, bibliographical catalogues, hand- and check-lists, the literature of bibliography itself is not capable of clear-cut classification, despite the claims of the individual item in its title to be one or the other of the various types of bibliographical listing. Accordingly it has been impossible to draw a line appropriately to exclude mere checklists and short-title catalogues, and the general concepts outlined above have been my sole aid in determining the propriety of including any particular item.

In addition, for convenience though not, one hopes, to any great detriment to the usefulness of the list, certain types of material have not been considered for inclusion; these categories were:

(*a*) Catalogues of *manuscripts*, and of
(*b*) *Letters*,

(*c*) Lists of *incunabula* in the U.S.A., save for the editions of the Bibliographical Society of America's *Census*. Since incunabula in general does
not properly fall within the scope of this list, but since on the other hand
it would be difficult to list the English incunabula in catalogues of English
collections, and as there is some advantage in a list of catalogues of English
collections of incunabula, I have included all general catalogues of incunabula, with the exception of those that are specifically of non-English
incunabula and the booksellers' catalogues of not specifically English
incunabula.

(*d*) *Library accession lists*, save when they are avowedly to collections of
English literature, or have had exhibition catalogues prepared from
them.

(*e*) *Theses*. The reader will find means of access to the bibliographies of
theses on English literature by consulting the appropriate general guides
listed in the first section. The London University School of Librarianship
and Archives bibliographies are so comprehensive and generally useful that
they have been listed briefly in exception to my general practice.

(*f*) *Exhibition catalogues*, and similar ephemera, have been excluded when
less than 10 pages in length, depending on how extensive otherwise the
literature is.

(*g*) *Library catalogues of general literature* such as the British Museum
catalogue: such catalogues demonstrate neither definite English literary
bias nor descriptive bibliographical information and the user is recommended to consult the general guides in the first section for details of them.

(*h*) *Booksellers' catalogues*: some have, however, been included when
devoted to a particular class of English material, and when they have come
to have a certain standing in the literature.

(*i*) *Auction and sale catalogues*: some have been listed, selectively and
perhaps capriciously: those I have known about I have tended to include,
those I have not known about I have tended to exclude. In general, the
auction catalogues of the less well known or minor collections have been
discarded.

(*j*) *Retrospective catalogues of private English libraries*: since they are
usually not predominantly of English literature, such compilations as
Harrison and Laslett's *The library of John Locke* (Oxford, 1965) have been
left to find their proper place in a further volume of this bibliography.

Certain other limitations on coverage of material are mentioned in the
notes on the classification of entries.

II. STYLE OF ENTRY. (*a*) *Main entry*. English practice has been followed
in the entry of works by noble authors under the family name. Hyphenated

names have been entered under the last part, and the appropriate references have been provided.

An item published first in a periodical and then issued separately and generally within a short time as a monograph has usually been entered here as if it had first appeared in monograph form, since it is in that form it will generally be consulted and referred to in the literature. On the other hand, I have not listed at all the mere offprints from periodicals.

(b) *Titles*: when a book contains a bibliographical list, the title of that list provides the first part of the entry under the name of the author, whether personal or corporate, followed by the short title and short imprint of the work in which the list is contained. For such a work no collational details have been given. When, however, a work contains two or more lists, the main work forms the substantial entry and the bibliographical lists are noted underneath the collation. The titles of monographs have usually been shortened to provide only the information useful for the identification of the book and an understanding of its scope and contents.

(c) *Periodical citations*: full citation of the names of periodicals is typographically wasteful and unnecessary; on the other hand, over-concise abbreviation which forces the user to the table of abbreviations for nearly every item is inefficient. Accordingly I have adopted a system which abbreviates most of the most frequently occurring parts of periodical names (e.g. N = Notes; Q = Quarterly; R = Review) and leaves in fullest form the least frequent—and presumably least familiar—names. Consequently most proper nouns (e.g. Rutgers, Harvard, Princeton) are given in full. It is hoped that the abbreviations will be readily expanded without recourse to the table on p. xxiii–xxv which has been provided to ensure accuracy in difficult cases.

The order of items in the periodical citations is (a) abbreviated title of periodical; (b) series; (c) volume number; (d) part number when the month of publication has not been given; when the separate issues of a periodical are dated, the part number has been omitted from the reference. Moreover no use has been made of such terms as 'Spring', 'Fall', and 'Summer'; (e) inclusive pagination; (f) date (usually month) and year of publication.

(d) *Collations*: normal modern Anglo-American library practice has been followed save that especial notice has been made of facsimiles. In some cases I have not mentioned illustrations not related to the item's bibliographical content.

(e) *Annotations*: the annotations are intended to help the user towards some idea of the nature of the particular bibliographical list before he decides to inspect a copy of it himself. Consequently I have noted for each item not only the various points which have not been clearly revealed in its title but also the absence of such features as indexes which otherwise the user might reasonably have expected to find. The annotations are informative to the extent that they convey further facts about the item, descriptive in that they describe the extent and arrangement of entries. They are rarely critical, for it seemed doubtful whether useful specific criticisms could be made within the efficient limits of the entry, and unlikely that any compiler of a work of such wide coverage could be considered competent to annotate critically. Readers intending to rely greatly on a particular bibliographical list are recommended to consult the reviews listed at the end of the appropriate entries.

In annotating I have endeavoured to convey information about the following points: (1) *Arrangement of entries*, whether chronological by date of publication or printing, alphabetical by titles or authors' names or both, or classified by subject or form. 'Dictionary' form refers to a single alphabetical sequence of authors' names, titles, and subject headings. Quite obviously, the arrangement of entries appropriate to particular types of material differs, and a bibliography will often have different arrangements in separate sections; bibliographies of the work of an author, for example, often present the monograph and periodical works in separate sequences, arranged in different ways. Although for the principal author lists I have tried to give some fuller account of the arrangement (especially if it appears to be unusual), for the lists in the preceding sections, I have usually noted only the arrangement of the main sequence.

(2) *Type of list*: generally the title of the particular list makes its pretensions to coverage and detail fairly clear, and in such a case, no further annotation has been made. Other items have been described in terms of a hierarchy of bibliographical compilation drawn largely from modern writings on this subject, but as I have commented above, such descriptive nomenclature as 'descriptive bibliography', 'bibliographical catalogue', 'bibliographical checklist', 'catalogue', and 'checklist' can rarely be applied exactly and justly to the items listed in the present compilation.

(3) *Content of bibliographical descriptions*: I have noted when the individual compilation contains details of (*a*) the *title-page*; by 'quasi-facsimile transcription' is meant that the type-founts have been distinguished, the line-endings marked, ornaments reproduced or noted, and all matter transcribed; 'TP transcriptions' means something less, but usually an extended transcription, accurate for the matter given without differentiating the founts but generally marking the line-endings; 'short-title' means a non-discriminating listing of the barest essentials for identification of the particular item referred to. (*b*) *Collations*, a term which may include the listing of pagination and contents to varying fullness. (*c*) *Bibliographical*

notes, a term embracing miscellaneous and various information about types, ornaments, illustrations, bindings, circumstances of publication and the like. (*d*) *Bibliographical references* is used to indicate that references have been given to other standard bibliographical lists. (*e*) *Locations of copies* means that the list notes where copies of the various items listed may be located. (*f*) *Indexes* have usually been specifically noted only when they provide access to unusual forms of material or are unusually extensive, but the absence of indexes where they might reasonably have been expected has been noted.

(*f*) *Reviews*: short references to reviews have been provided only when they have come to hand without prolonged searching and only for items which are themselves bibliographies; no reviews have been noted for publications in which the bibliographical list is only a minor part of the whole work, or for works in the first section, or for items since superseded listed under *Authors*.

III. ARRANGEMENTS OF ENTRIES. The 'List of contents' on p. vii–x shows that the entries have been classified in six main sections; the following comments will clarify the further principles which have determined the selection and arrangement of the entries under their respective headings.

Within each section and subsection the entries have been arranged chronologically by date of publication. When a work has gone into several editions, a reference has been made from the date of first publication to that of the last edition where the main annotated entry may be found. Reprints have been recorded under the date of the main entry. In general, each separate contribution to the bibliography of English literature has been listed in one place only in the list; in many cases there can be legitimate argument about the best classification of an item, but I hope to have mitigated the force of any objections by having indexed every item under each heading in the index appropriate to it. Hence, subject lists of books of a particular period (say, Kelso on 'treatises on the gentleman and related subjects . . . to 1625') though entered in the bibliography itself under the subject heading are indexed under the proper period heading.

(1) *Bibliographies of bibliography*: in general, bibliographies of bibliographies pertinent to the subjects contained in the present list precede the entries under the relevant subject heading. The entries in this section have been provided for readers who might require access to additional material beyond the scope of this list. This is the only section for which items have been 'selected' from the range of possible entries.

(2) *General and period bibliographies: period subdivisions*: publication of Pollard and Redgrave's and Wing's short-title catalogues, and the adop-

tion of 1475 as the arbitrary starting-date for English publication, has virtually enforced 1640 and 1700—together with 1500 for incunabula—as universal termini for the period catalogues of English books. I have attempted to use the same period divisions for all types of publication, although they obviously do not fit say, newspapers and novels, as neatly as they do general catalogues. More literary divisions by centuries often overlap the narrower divisions, and a special effort has been made to isolate the bibliography of the eighteenth century which lacks a modern general short-title catalogue. Within the period divisions the items have been placed where they best fit, a list covering books to 1705, for instance, being located under a heading ending at 1700. There is no fear that the user will be led to miss relevant material since the index provides appropriate references and will in addition lead him from general period headings to material located more specifically in the bibliography under form or subject. Similarly, a list entered in the bibliography under a heading divided by a period which the scope of the list substantially exceeds will be indexed again under the additional period.

Arrangement: the arrangement of the entries for books published in Wales, Scotland, or Ireland is unavoidably awkward, and I have been obliged to refer users from the general lists divided by country to the further entries under *Regional bibliographies* and *Presses and Printers*; other regional divisions occur with headings in the *Forms and genres* section. The index brings the regional headings together so the user should find little difficulty in locating the material he requires on, say, Irish publication. The rationale of the period divisions has been discussed above.

For the subheading 'British books published abroad', the works of individual English authors have been entered as appropriate in the *Authors* section. Accordingly, this heading records general lists only. The heading 'Foreign books published in English in Britain' is an especially intractable category, and one must doubt whether in fact it is very useful save for referring the user to items of which he must have known before in any case. I have not attempted a bibliography of bibliographies of translations but merely listed those compilations I have come across which seem to offer some aid to the bibliographer or literary scholar. Lists of foreign translations of English works such as C. A. Rochedieu's *Bibliography of French translations . . . 1700–1800* have been excluded on the principle that whereas English translations of foreign literature have usually been printed or at least published in the British Isles and thence provide a minimum guide to a class of British publication, lists of English works in translation generally serve no such purpose.

(3) *Regional bibliographies*: it is important to note that no attempt has

been made here to cover lists of books associated with the regions and places of the British Isles; the items listed under the above heading cover only publications printed at a certain place or written by natives of that place. Generally, regional bibliography is underdeveloped and this section is hardly satisfactory, but I have attempted to bring out in the annotations those parts of general regional bibliographies which will guide the user to local printing and publication. I have been unable to examine all the early periodical publications on this subject which are mostly to be found in the proceedings of archaeological societies not widely held other than in the largest libraries (and all too frequently not even there: even the Bodleian and British Museum libraries' holdings are patchy in this field) and in general I have concentrated on the more widely available monographs which, with the general bibliographies listed at the head of each division of this section, will refer the reader to the smaller items. A supplement to Humphreys would be a useful project.

The bibliography of Irish printing is largely the work of E. R. McC. Dix whose writings I have after prolonged searching been unable to view completely. I beg the reader's indulgence for those entries for which I have had to note 'Not seen'. A collected volume of Dix's minor papers would be a significant addition to Irish bibliography especially as the newspapers in which much of his earlier material first appeared are not widely held. However, it seems fair to remark that Dix's monograph publications summarize most of the important early material. The inclusion at all of material on Irish literature was long debated as its particularly national, not to say nationalistic, nature seemed to set much of it apart even from similar Welsh or Scottish material, but in the end, despite the inadequacy of the coverage mentioned above, it was decided to include it to avoid the necessity of decisions about what lists and author bibliographies to include or exclude, with which readers might find even less satisfaction. I have similarly avoided distinction between the literature of Eire and Northern Ireland.

(4) *Presses and printers*: for many of the private presses the only checklists of publications are those they issued themselves, often in limited numbers and of ephemeral nature; it has been impossible to locate copies of all of them, or even to find satisfactory references to them—many of the entries in standard bibliographies such as Haas seem to be 'ghosts'. This section is headed by a list of general bibliographies of printing. Bigmore and Wyman has not been listed here as it is useful for the whole field of descriptive and historical bibliography and it has been entered in the first section; that a more comprehensive bibliography of printing in more modern times does not exist points to a further gap requiring to be filled.

It should be noted that items on any individual printer who was also an author (e.g. Caxton) are listed in this section rather than in *Authors* where, however, references have been provided. Publishers and booksellers such as Curll and Dodsley also find their natural places here.

(5) *Forms and genres*: 'Illustrated books' may justly be considered a special form of printing but the literature of this category often has not narrowed itself to treat exclusively of English items; this has led me to include a selection of items more general in coverage. For books of 'emblems' as previously with 'incunabula' the principles of inclusion have been relaxed somewhat, though the inclusion of these more general items should not be taken as precedents for the inclusion of others considered but excluded.

It might be thought that the heading 'Maps', here listed as a special form of British printing and publication with the entries classified by place, might more reasonably have been placed in the regional section. However, its location under *Forms and genres* serves to exemplify the distinction made earlier about the *subject content* and the *printed works* on a particular theme. Lists of estate and local parish maps have not been included. 'Music' like 'Maps' is a special type of publication and belongs in this section rather than under subject; I have not attempted a general bibliography of music in Britain. 'Newspapers and periodicals' have been listed under the one heading as have 'Novels' and 'Fiction' together under 'Fiction' because the existing bibliographies are so inconsistent and various in their coverage. The items listed under 'Bible' are more general than desirable though this may be excused perhaps since most catalogues and lists of Bibles cover principally the English versions.

(6) *Subjects*: a few general lists have strayed into this section because if not avowedly English in emphasis or coverage, they provide a large amount of English material usually inaccessible otherwise. I doubt whether I could have brought myself to exclude the magnificent Arents tobacco catalogue, or the Wellcome Historical Medical Library's general catalogue under any principle of coverage, though I must refer the reader to Besterman for details of other general lists. There seems to have been some unconscious bias in my mind when I selected the subject lists, as the user will agree when observing how many of the subject headings relate to traditional British concerns and activities.

(7) *Authors*: although the authors listed in this section do not include Old or Middle English writers, there are occasional references for early writers when lists have been prepared of the later editions of their work; however, no particular search was made for such items as it was not envisaged as part of the work's scope to cover them.

Originally classification of the authors' names by period commended itself, but it was decided that one alphabetical sequence would not only avoid difficult decisions of classification but would be easier for the uninformed user. The entries in this section are arranged to lead the user to the standard (generally, the most recent) list for each author and have been arranged chronologically to that end. Each author entry commences with a note of any bibliographies of works, criticism, etc., *about* the author, and thereafter follow the entries for the bibliographical description and/or enumeration of his published work. I do not apologize for the inclusion in this section of many simple checklists which in no way approach the descriptive standards advocated by Professor Bowers, for I felt that for authors, something, however inadequate, is better than nothing, and an inadequate list noted here might stimulate bibliographers to produce more satisfactory replacements. On the other hand, there are for the major authors many simple lists in collected and other editions of their works, and I have not attempted either to track them all down or to list them. Bibliographical lists superseded by modern descriptive bibliographies may seem a matter for mere record, and that is mainly how they have been treated, but, however, not all users have ready access to all the bibliographies they might require and in many cases may have to make do with the bibliography that is available rather than the one that is best. Accordingly, earlier bibliographical lists are noted with entries full enough for the items to be identified and to some extent evaluated, though such entries have been annotated only when for an author there is no bibliography of agreed superiority but only a number of lists reflecting various aspects of his bibliography. Similarly, I have annotated entries published after the publication of the principal bibliography and thence to some extent complementing it.

As this is a list for literary-minded users, bibliographies of pseudonymous authors have been listed under the pseudonym; references in this section will ensure that the user finds his way. I do regret, however, that the principle of entering noble authors under their family names has led to the location of authors such as Rochester more familiar by their titles where the user will not generally look first.

IV. INDEX. The *Index* covers the headings of the main bibliography, the names of the authors contributing the items therein and the names of compilers, editors, authors of books in which the bibliographical lists form a part, names of major collectors whose books are in public collections, and distinctive titles under which access might be sought. Authors of reviews are not listed in the Index. The *Index* includes all references for noble authors and authors with compound names, and care has been taken to provide copious references to the given form of entry for such corporate authors as the Sutro Library and other organizations which might be sought under place or name. When an index entry corresponds to a subject heading in the bibliography the item numbers corresponding to the entries under the main heading are printed in bold face.

The user should note that since each item has been placed only once in the bibliography, subject headings repeated in the index will record additional references to material listed under other headings in the bibliography (e.g. many of the items listed under 'English books printed abroad' are indexed as well under 'Catholic books') and the headings divided by period and place have been reclassified. The user therefore would be well advised to commence his inquiry with the *Index* but this I fear is a counsel of perfection. Nevertheless, in the event of the bibliography failing by its classification to yield suitable material, the reader should not then conclude that there is nothing on the subject of his search, but should consult the *Index*.

Finally, it should be noted that only the information recorded in the bibliography has been indexed; other details given in the books themselves or their title-pages but not relevant to the subject of this compilation (and so not noted in the entries) have not been indexed.

TABLE OF ABBREVIATIONS

Abstr	Abstract/s
Acad	Academy
Afric	Africa/n
Ag	August
Am	America/n
Ann	Annual
Angl	Anglia; Anglaise
Antiqu	Antiquarian
Ap	April
Assn	Association
Archæol	Archæology; Archæological
Atlan	Atlantic
Beibl	Beiblatt
Bib	Bibliographical; Bibliography
bibliogr.	bibliographical; bibliography
Biblioth	Bibliotheck
Biog	Biographical; Biography
Bk	Book
Bkmns	Bookman's
Bks	Books
Bod	Bodleian
Brit	Britain; British
Bull	Bulletin
c.	*circa*
Cent	Century
Chron	Chronicle
cm.	centimetres
col.	coloured; column/s
Coll	Collector; Collector's; College
Coloph	Colophon
Comp	Comparee
comp.	compiled; compiler/s
Congreg	Congregational
Crit	Criticism; Critical
C.U.P.	Cambridge University Press
D	December
Dept.	Department
diagr/s.	diagram/s
Doc	Documentation
ed.	edited; edition/s; editor/s
Educ	Education/al
Eng	English
Engl	Englische
enl.	enlarged
F	February
facsim/s.	facsimile/s

Fict	Fiction
Fleur	Fleuron
fold.	folded
Fortn	Fortnightly
Gaz	Gazette
Germ	Germanic
graph.	graphic
Grol	Grolier
Guildh	Guildhall
Hisp	Hispanic
Hist	Historical; History
H.M.S.O.	His (or Her) Majesty's Stationery Office
Hndbk	Handbook
ib.	*ibidem* (i.e. in the same place)
illus.	illustration/s; illustrated
Inst	Institute
J	Journal
Ja	January
Je	June
Jl	July
Keats–Sh	Keats–Shelley
l.	leaf, leaves; line/s
Lang	Language
Lib	Library
Libn	Librarian
Libs	Libraries
Lit	Literary; Literature
Lond	London
Mag	Magazine
Mar	Mariner's
Merc	Mercury
Mirr	Mirror
Misc	Miscellany
Mod	Modern
Mr	March
Mthly	Monthly
Mus	Music
My	May
N	Note/s; November
N&Q	Notes and Queries
Nat	National; Natural
Neophilol	Neophilologus
Ninet	Nineteenth
no/s.	number/s
Notebk	Notebook
N.Y.	New York
N.Z.	New Zealand
Oc	October
O.U.P.	Oxford University Press
p.	page/s
Pa	Paper/s
Pam	Pamphlet/s
Philobib	Philobiblon

Philol	Philological; Philology
Philos	Philosophical; Philosophy
port/s.	portrait/s
pr.	press
Print	Printer/s; Printing
Priv	Private
Proc	Proceedings
pt/s.	part/s
ptd.	printed
ptr.	printer
Pub	Public; Publisher/s'
Pubs	Publications
Q	Quarterly
R	Review; Revue
Rec	Record
Renaiss	Renaissance
repr.	reprinted
Repub	Republic
Res	Research
rev.	revised
rf.	refer
Roy	Royal
S	September
Sat	Saturday
Scot	Scottish
ser.	series
Sevent	Seventeenth
Sh	Shakespeare
Signat	Signature
Soc	Society; Societies
Statesm	Statesman
STC	Short-title catalogue, comp. by Pollard and Redgrave
Sth	South
Stud	Studies; Study; Studien
Suppl	Supplement
Surv	Survey
Theat	Theatre
TLS	Times Literary Supplement
TP	title-page
Trans	Transactions
Transit	Transition
Univ	University
U.P.	University Press
v.	volume/s
Vict	Victorian
Wkly	Weekly

INDEX TO BRITISH
LITERARY BIBLIOGRAPHY

I

Bibliography of
British literary bibliographies

GENERAL BIBLIOGRAPHIES OF
AND GUIDES TO
BRITISH LITERATURE

1 **Dobrée, Bonamy,** *ed.* Introductions to English literature. Rev. ed. London, Cresset pr., 1950–8. (First pub. 1938–40) 5v. 21cm.

Contents: 1. Renwick, William L. and H. Orton. The beginnings of English literature to Skelton. (1952).—2. Pinto, Vivian de S. The English renaissance, 1510–1688. 3d. ed., rev. 1966—3. Dyson, Henry and J. Butt. Augustans and romantics, 1689–1830. (1950).—4. Batho, Edith C. and B. Dobrée. The victorians and after, 1830–1914. (1950).—5. Daiches, David. The present age, after 1920. (1958). (Replaces Muir, Edwin. The present age from 1914. (1939)).

2 **National book league.** Writers and their work; general ed. T. O. Beachcroft. [1– .] London, Longmans, 1950– . v. 21cm. (Formerly Bibliographical supplements to British book news.)

Monographs devoted largely to lives and works of British authors, with select bibliogrs.

3 **Saul, George Brandon.** 'An introductory bibliography in Anglo-Irish literature' *in* Stephens, Yeats, and other Irish concerns. New York, 1954. p.12–18.

Repr. from N.Y. Pub Lib Bull 57:429–35 S '54.

4 **Kennedy, Arthur Garfield** and **D. B. Sands.** A concise bibliography for students of English. 4th ed. Stanford, Calif., Stanford U.P. [1960]. (First pub. 1940) xi,467p. 22cm.

'Journalistic art, periodical and newspaper bibliographies, and publication rights' (p.304–23); 'Printing, the book trade, and library science' (p.324–46); 'General bibliographical guides' (p.347–92).

5 **Altick, Richard Daniel.** Selective bibliography for the study of English and American literature. 2d ed. New York [1963]. (First pub. [1960]) x,149p. 18cm.

6 **Bateson, Frederick Wilse.** A guide to English literature. [London] Longmans [1965]. xii,260p. 22cm.

7 **Watson, George Grimes,** *ed.* The concise Cambridge bibliography of English literature, 600–1950. 2d ed. Cambridge, C.U.P., 1965. (First ed. 1958) xi,269p. 21cm.

See CBEL: no. 349.

The following lists arranged by period are useful for supplementary material:

8 **Read, Conyers,** *ed.* Bibliography of British history: Tudor period, 1485–1603. 2d ed. Oxford, Clarendon pr., 1959. (First pub. 1933) xxviii,624p. 24cm.

9 **Davies, Godfrey,** *ed.* Bibliography of British history: Stuart period, 1603–1714. Oxford, Clarendon pr., 1928. x,459p. 24cm.

10 **Morgan, William Thomas.** A bibliography of British history, 1700–1715. Bloomington, Ind., 1934–42. 5pts. 26cm. (Indiana university Studies, 94–5, 114–24.)

11 **Pargellis, Stanley** and **D. J. Medley,** *ed.* Bibliography of British history: the eighteenth century, 1714–1789. Oxford, Clarendon pr., 1951. xxvi,642p. 24cm.

12 **Grose, Clyde Leclare.** A select bibliography of British history, 1660–1760. Chicago, Ill., University of Chicago pr. [1939]. xxv,507p. 23cm.

13 **Wales. University. Board of Celtic studies. History and law committee.** A bibliography of the history of Wales. 2d ed. Cardiff, University of Wales pr., 1962. xviii,330p. 25cm.

14 —— [Same]: Supplement I (1963). Bull Board Celtic Stud 20:126–64 My '63.
First ed. by Wales. University. Guild of graduates. Welsh history section. 1931.

ENGLISH LITERATURE—SERIAL BIBLIOGRAPHIES

15 **Fisher, John Hurt.** Serial bibliographies in the modern languages and literatures. Pub Mod Lang Assn 66:138–56 Ap '51.

16 **White, William.** One man's meat; societies and journals devoted to a single author. Am Bk Coll 8:22–4 N '57.
Serial bibliographies about individual authors have been listed under the names of the respective authors.

17 **Gerstenberger, Donna Lorine** and **G. Hendrick.** Directory of periodicals publishing articles in English and American literature and language. Denver, A. Swallow [1959]. 178p. 23cm.

18 —— [Same]: 1960 Supplement. Twent Cent Lit 7:80–3 Jl '61.

19 —— [Same]: 1961 Supplement. *ib.* 8:83–5 Jl '62.

20 —— [Same]: 1962 Supplement. *ib.* 9:89–92 Jl '63.

21 —— [Same]: 1963 Supplement. *ib.* 10:77–9 Jl '64.

SERIAL BIBLIOGRAPHIES ARRANGED BY PERIOD COVERED—GENERAL

25 **Abstracts of English studies**; an official publication of the National council of teachers of English. 1– . Boulder, Col., 1958– .
Numbered abstracts of articles in English and American literary periodicals; each part and volume indexed.

26 **Annual bibliography of English language and literature,** 1920– . 1– . Cambridge. Modern humanities research association, 1921– .
See especially 'II. (*a*) Bibliography, (*b*) Book production, selling, collecting; librarianship, (*c*) Typography.'

27 'MLA international bibliography of books and articles on the modern languages and literatures' *in* **Publications of the Modern language association of America.** (Transactions, 1884/5–8.) 1– . Baltimore, 1886– .

Annually in May issue. ('American bibliography for 1921–[55]' 1922–56, annually in March issue; 1930–   as Supplement; 'Annual bibliography for 1936–[63]', 1957–64.

28 **Year's work in English studies** [1919–   ] London, English association, 1921– .

Classified annual review articles, with bibliogr. refs.

———PERIOD

29 'Recent literature of the renaissance' *in* **Studies in philology.** 1– . Chapel Hill, Philological club, University of North Carolina, 1906– .

Annually in April issue; formerly entitled 'Recent literature'.

30 'English literature, 1600–1800; a current bibliography' *in* **Philological quarterly**; a journal. . . . 1– . Iowa city, Iowa, University of Iowa, 1922–   .

Annually in July issue; Oc 1926– , Ap 1927– , Jl 1950– •

31 **English literature, 1660–1800**; a bibliography of modern studies compiled for Philological quarterly by Ronald S. Crane [and others] Princeton, Princeton U.P., 1950– . v. 23cm. VI. 1926–1938.—2. 1939–1950.—3. 1951– 1956.—4. 1957–1960.

Repr. from annual compilations in Philol Q; various editors.

32 'The romantic movement, a current selective and critical bibliography for 1936[–48]' *in* **ELH**, a journal of English literary history. 1– . Baltimore, Tudor and Stuart club, Johns Hopkins university, 1934– .

Annually in March issue, v.4–16, 1937–49.

33 'The romantic movement, a selective and critical bibliography for 1949–   ' *in* **Philological quarterly,** a journal. . . . 1–   . Iowa city, Iowa, University of Iowa, 1922– .

Annually in April issue; v.19– , 1950– •

34 'Current bibliography [of Keats, Shelley, Byron, Hunt, and their circles, 1950–]' *in* **Keats–Shelley journal.** 1–   . New York, Keats–Shelley association of America, 1952– .

Annually, 1952– •

35 **Keats–Shelley journal.** Keats, Shelley, Byron, Hunt, and their circles, a bibliography: July 1, 1950–June 30, 1962. Edited by David Bonnell Green and Edwin Graves Wilson; compiled by David Bonnell Green [and others]. Lincoln, Neb., University of Nebraska pr., 1964. 323p. 24cm. (Not seen.)

Repr. of the annual compilations, with a general index.

36 'Victorian bibliography for 1932[–56]' *in* **Modern philology,** a quarterly journal. . . . 1– . Chicago, University of Chicago pr., 1903–

Annually in May issue, 1933–57.

37 **Templeman, William Darby,** *ed.* Bibliographies of studies in victorian literature . . . 1932–1944. Urbana, University of Illinois pr., 1945. ix,450p.
24cm.
Reprints of annual lists in Mod Philol.

38 **Wright, Austin,** *ed.* Bibliographies of studies in victorian literature . . . 1945–
1954. Urbana, University of Illinois pr., 1956. vii,310p. 24cm.
Reprints of annual lists in Mod Philol.

38a **Slack, Robert C.,** *ed.* Bibliographies of studies in victorian literature . . . 1955–
1964. Urbana, University of Illinois pr., 1967. xvi,461p. 24cm.
Reprints of annual lists in Mod Philol.

39 'Victorian bibliography for 1957[–]' *in* **Victorian studies,** a quarterly
journal of the humanities, arts, and sciences. 1– . Bloomington, Ind., Indiana
university, 1957– .
Annually in June issue, 1no4 '58– .

40 'The year's work in victorian poetry: 1963[–]' *in* **Victorian poetry,** a critical
journal of victorian literature. 1– . Morgantown, W.Va., West Virginia
university, 1963– .
Annual review article in summer issue.

41 'Current bibliography' *in* **Twentieth century literature,** a scholarly and
critical journal. 1– . Denver, Col., Swallow, 1955– .
Annually in April issue.

BIBLIOGRAPHY—BIBLIOGRAPHIES

45 **Bigmore, Edward Clements** and **C. W. H. Wyman.** A bibliography of printing.
London, B. Quaritch, 1880–6. (Repr. New York, P. Duschnes, 1945. 2v.)
3v. illus., ports., facsims. 21cm.
Remains useful for access to early bibliogr. studies; alphabetical author–subject arrangement; annotations.

46 **Reed, Talbot Baines.** A list of books and papers on printers and the art of
printing, under the countries and towns to which they refer. Bib Soc Trans
3pt1:81–152 '95.

47 **Peddie, Robert Alexander.** A list of bibliographical books published since the
foundation of the Bibliographical society in 1893. Bib Soc Trans 10:235–311
Oc–Mr '08/9.

47a **Gray, George John.** The writings of Charles Sayle. Library ser4 6:82–9
Je '25.

48 **Northup, Clark Sutherland.** A register of bibliographies of the English language and literature by Clark Sutherland Northup, with contributions by
Joseph Quincy Adams and Andrew Keogh. New Haven, Yale U.P.; London,
H. Milford, O.U.P., 1925. (Repr. 1962) 507p. 25cm.
'General' (p.9–34) arranged by author; 'Individual authors and topics' (p.34–417)
arranged alphabetically under the author or subject heading; 'Additions and corrections'
(p.419–49). *See also* no.53.

49 **O'Leary, John Gerard.** [A bibliography of bibliographies of English literature and English writers . . .] *in* English literary history and bibliography. London, Grafton, 1928. p.133–62.

50 **Cole, George Watson.** A survey of the bibliography of English literature, 1475–1640, with especial reference to the work of the Bibliographical society of London. Chicago, 1930. 95p. 25cm.

Repr. from Pa Bib Soc Am 23pt2 '39.

Useful for the entertaining accounts of the earlier English bibliographers and their works.

51 **Hart, Horace.** Bibliotheca typographica, a list of books about books. Dolphin 1:161–94 '33.

52 —— Bibliotheca typographica in usum eorum qui libros amant; a list of books about books. Rochester, N.Y., L. Hart, 1933. xi,142p. 23cm.

53 **Van Patten, Nathan.** An index to bibliographies and bibliographical contributions relating to the work of American and British authors, 1923–1932. Stanford university, Calif., Stanford U.P.; London, H. Milford, O.U.P., 1933. vii,324p. 23cm.

Unacknowledged extension of Northup (no.48), arranged alphabetically under authors' names; 'Additional titles' (p.281–4); 'Selected list of general works' (p.285–94) is a short subject and general list, arranged by author.

54 **Vail, Robert William Glenroie.** The literature of book collecting, a selective bibliography prepared for the Washington Square college book club of New York university. [2d ed.] New York, Privately ptd. for the Book club, 1936. (First pub. 1936) 50p. 23m.

55 **Webber, Winslow Lewis.** Books about books, a bio-bibliography for collectors. Boston, Hale, Cushman and Flint, 1937. 168p. 26cm.

Contents: Book collecting and books about books.—Bio-bibliography, the text books of the collector.—Magazine reference, a bibliography, 1900–37.—Glossary.

Fulsomely annotated.

56 **[Esdaile, Arundell James Kennedy]** *comp.* 'Bibliographies' *in* Bateson, Frederick W., *ed.* Cambridge bibliography of English literature. Cambridge, 1940–57. V.1, p.3–9.

57 **[Pollard, Graham]** *comp.* 'Book production and distribution' *in* Bateson, Frederick W., *ed.* Cambridge bibliography of English literature. Cambridge, 1940–57. V.1, p.345–62; 2, p.82–107; 3, p.70–106.

58 **Francis, sir Frank Chalton.** A list of the writings of Ronald Brunlees McKerrow. Library ser4 21:229–63 D–Mr. '40/1.

59 **Bibliographic index,** a cumulative bibliography of bibliographies. [Cumulations, 1937– .] New York, H. W. Wilson, 1945– . v. 26cm.

Current subject list covering both monographs and periodical articles; a useful complement to Besterman (no.248).

60 **Francis, sir Frank Chalton.** A list of dr. Greg's writings. Library ser4 26:72–97 Je '45.

See also no.245a.

62 **Francis, sir Frank Chalton.** The catalogues of the British museum. 1. Printed books. J Doc 4:14–40 Je '48.

63 **Grolier club,** NEW YORK. List of publications, exhibition catalogues, and other items issued by the Grolier club, 1884–1948. New York, 1948. 24p. 24 cm.

Comp. by Will Ransom; earlier lists repr. from the Grolier club's Officers, committees, members, pub. in 1906, 1917, and 1928.

64 **London. University. School of librarianship and archives.** List of bibliographies and theses accepted for part III of the University of London Diploma in librarianship between 1936 and 1950. [London, 1951] 10p. 22cm.

65 —— **[Same]:** 1951 and 1952, with some earlier ones not previously listed. [London, 1954] 5p. 22cm.

66 —— **[Same]:** Cumulated list . . . 1946–1960. [London, 1960] 37p. 22cm.

67 —— **[Same]:** Bibliographies, calendars and theses . . . 1961–1962. [London] 1963. 9p. 22cm.

Annual lists appear in London. University. Library. Theses and dissertations accepted for higher degrees, 1 October, 19— –30 September, 19—. London, University of London, 19—. The following is a selected alphabetical list of contents:

70 **Abel, Lola L.** A bibliography of some eighteenth-century books on architecture (British Palladians) 1715–1780. 1950.

71 **Adams, R. E.** A bibliography of the critical and editorial works of Hugh Blair. 1962.

72 **Albu, K. M.** John and Thomas Martyn; a bibliography. 1956.

73 **Allford, J. M.** Bibliography of the published works of John Lindley, 1799–1865. 1953.

74 **Arnett, Muriel.** Angliæ notitiæ, a bibliography. 1936.

75 **Ayres, F. H.** Robert Hooke, a bibliography. 1951.

76 **Barker, J. R.** A Liverpool printer; an attempt at a bibliography of works printed in Liverpool, 1792–1805, by John M'Creery, with an account of his life and a brief survey of the previous history of printing in Liverpool. 1951.

77 **Barnecut, H.** A bibliography of the Tracts for the times. 1952.

78 **Barnes, Ann P.** Bibliography of festschriften composed by members of the University of Cambridge between 1587 and 1640, based on examination of copies held in the British museum. 1948.

79 **Barr, C. B. L.** Texts and translations of Greek and Latin ancient mediæval writers printed in Scotland to 1700. 1964.

80 **Barr, John R.** The writings of victorian architects, a guide to certain periodicals. 1964.

81 **Barrett, Helen M.** A bibliography of Charles Kingsley. 1936.

82 **Bayley, D. J.** Ambrose Philips, a bibliography of writings by and about him. 1952.

83 **Bennett, N. E.** A bibliography of printed material relating to Belfast up to 1820. 1963.

84 **Bickle, Catherine H. W.** A bibliography of zoological works by British authors or printed in Great Britain, 1477–1550. 1948.

85 **Birley, Pauline.** The early printed editions of the works of Laurence Sterne, a select bibliography. 1939.

86 **Bishop, Leila R. M.** A bibliography of the English translations, editions and criticism of the works of madame de la Fayette. 1948.

87 **Blackstock, C. M.** The translations and criticism in English of the works of Gustave Flaubert. 1958.

88 **Bloomfield, Barry C.** W. H. Auden, a trial checklist with some bibliographical notes. 1957. (*See* no.2359.)

89 **Bowyer, Tony H.** The letters of Junius; a bibliographical examination of the earliest editions, 1769–1775. 1952. (*See* no.3899.)

90 **Burdess, James N.** A bibliography of the literary works published by Barnaby Bernard Lintott. 1938.

91 **Burton, M. E.** Charles Robert Darwin, 1809–1882; a list of his published writings. 1964.

92 **Butler, P. M.** Catullus, a bibliography of editions and English translations published in this country to December, 1951. 1952.

93 **Butterworth, M.** Select bibliography of works on William Caxton, the first printer at Oxford, the St. Albans printer, and John Siberch of Cambridge. 1951.

94 **Canney, Margaret B. C.** A bibliography of George Savile, marquis of Halifax, 1633–1695. 1948.

95 **Caro, A. E.** William Blake, 1757–1827, a bibliographical continuation to the Grolier bibliography of 1921. 1964.

96 **Carter, Margaret J.** A bibliography of the English miracle and popular morality plays printed to 1945. 1950.

97 **Christophers, Richard A.** A bibliography of George Abbot, archbishop of Canterbury. 1960. (*See* no.2300.)

98 **Clarke, D. A.** A handlist of books said to have been printed by John Day before 1557. 1950.

99 **Clarke, Stella M.** A bibliography of mrs. Barbauld (Anna Lætitia Aikin...). 1949.

100 **Clitheroe, Barbara M.** A bibliography of editions of Carlyle's Sartor resartus. 1937.

101 **Colquhoun, Jean.** A bibliography of Margaret Cavendish, duchess of Newcastle, 1623–1673. 1950.

102 **Cook, D. F.** The first 200 years in print of st. Anselm, archbishop of Canterbury: a survey of the works attributed to him, 1474–1675. 1955.

103 **Crook, Ronald H.** A bibliography of Joseph Priestley, 1733–1804. 1965. (*See* no.4442).

104 **Curnow, A.** David Gascoyne, a bibliography. 1956.

105 **Cutler, C. V.** A select bibliography of the writings of Thomas Hughes. 1950.

106 **Davies, A. M. E.** Ifor Williams, a check-list of his writings. 1960.

106a **Davis, Robin J.** A bibliography of Samuel Beckett. 1966.

107 **Dawson, N. F.** A bibliography of published works by and on viscount Grey of Falloden. 1953.

108 **Day, A. E.** J. B. Priestley, an interim bibliography. 1959.

109 **Dieneman, W.** A bibliography of John Toland, 1670–1722. 1953.

110 **Doughty, D. W.** A bibliography of sir Thomas Wyatt, 1503–1542. 1939.

111 **Downward, M. E.** Bibliography of the Buxton family. 1957.

112 **Drake, S.** A bibliography of books and articles relating to Thomas Chatterton, from 1916 to the present day. 1947.

113 **Dudley, Eveline.** Samuel Richardson, a bibliography. 1937.

114 **Duffy, E. M. T.** Henry Morley, 1822–1894, a bibliography of works in print. 1952.

115 **Dyson, G.** The manuscripts and proof sheets of Scott's Waverley novels, a bibliography. 1956.

116 **Eddy, J. A.** A list of books printed before 1700 with illustrations showing an interest in machines. 1964.

117 **Edmonston, Mary E.** Richard Hooker's Laws of ecclesiastical polity, a bibliography of the early editions. 1939.

118 **Egoff, Sheila A.** A bibliography and survey of children's periodicals of the 19th century. 1949. (*See* no.1560.)

118a **English, David J.** A bibliography of works by and about Thomas Mann published in Great Britain. 1966.

119 **Fanstone, R. I.** Books for girls published in the British Isles, 1800–1850, a bibliography. 1949.

120 **Fawcett, T. C.** The writings of Richard Walter Sickert, a bibliography. 1961.

121 **Ferguson, V. A.** A bibliography of the works of Richard Mead. . . . 1959.

122 **Fifoot, Erik R. S.** Sitwelliana, 1915–1950, a tentative bibliography of the first publications of the writings of Edith Sitwell, Osbert Sitwell, and Sacheverell Sitwell. 1951. (*See* no.4694.)

123 **Flanagin, Isobel E.** A bibliography of the works of William Barnes. 1939.

124 **Freeman, E. J.** Bibliography of sir Thomas Elyot, 1490?–1546. 1962.

125 **Fung, S-K. S.** A bibliography of the writings of Edmund Charles Blunden. 1961.

126 **Gibb, I. P.** A bibliography of the works of George Farquhar, 1678–1707. 1952.

127 **Gibson, J.** A partial bibliography of mainly 17th century pamphlets contained in St. George's chapter library, Windsor. 1955.

128 **Giffard, N. D.** A bibliography of the published writings of Edmund Selous, ornithologist. 1951.

129 **Gocking, W. E.** Wordsworth, a supplementary bibliography, 1926–1950 [to J. V. Logan's Wordsworthian criticism]. 1952.

130 **Goy, J. R.** George Campbell, 1719–1796, and Alexander Gerard, 1728–1795, a bibliography of their published works. 1964.

131 **Gregory, A. D.** Griffith Jones, Llanddowror, 1683–1761, a bibliography. 1939.

132 **Griffin, J. M.** Scores of British operas composed and published during the period 1801–1850, in the library of the British museum. 1963.

133 **Griffiths, J. M. I.** A bibliography of sir Edward Burne-Jones. 1937.

134 **Guyatt, E. J.** A bibliography of the printed works of Thomas Hearne. 1952.

135 **Halls, C. M. E.** Bibliography of Elizabeth C. Gaskell. 1957.

136 **Hares, R. R.** Shakespeare glossaries and concordances; bibliography. 1960.

137 **Hargreaves, Joan M.** Bibliography of Thomas Hobbes. 1949. (*See* no.3668.)

138 **Harington, J.** Henry Lawes, printed editions of his work and sources of information thereon; a bibliography. 1957.

138a **Harrison, Elizabeth M.** A bibliography of works about Katherine Mansfield. 1958.

139 **Heley, Joan.** Susannah Gunning, a bibliography, to include her sister, Margaret Minifie. 1938.

140 **Hinton, V. H. F. A.** William Motherwell, 1797–1835, a bibliography. 1960.

141 **Hoare, J.** Mark Pattison, 1813–1884, a bibliography of his published works. 1953.

142 **Holder, Cecilia E.** A bibliography of the works of sir Victor Horsley. 1949.

143 **Holiday, J. P.** Humphry Repton, English landscape gardener, 1752–1818. 1953.

144 **Huddy, E. J.** Early printed topographical maps of the counties of England and Wales; a descriptive catalogue. 1960.

145 **Hutchins, W. J.** Hauptmann in England, a bibliography of editions, translations and criticism of Gerhart Hauptmann's works in England from 1890 to 1962. 1964.

146 **Jeffreys, Alan E.** Michael Faraday, a list of his lectures and published writings. 1958. (*See* no.3282.)

147 **Jolley, L. J.** A bibliography of the ode, 1700–1725. 1936.

148 **Jones, J. M.** H. E. Bates, a bibliography. 1964.

149 **Kemp, J. A.** The venerable Bede; editions of his works printed before 1700. 1953.

150 **Ker, C. S.** A bibliography of Richard Lovelace. 1949.

151 **Kerr, Margaret M.** A bibliography of Robert Herrick. 1936.

152 **King, C. M. (Key).** A bibliography of contemporary material on the popish plot. 1958.

153 **King, Shirley E. A.** A bibliography of sir St.Clair Thomson. 1950.

154 **Kirkpatrick, Brownlee J.** A bibliography of Virginia Woolf. 1948. (*See* no.5159.)

155 **Lawes, Fay T.** Bibliography of sir Henry Irving. 1949.

156 **Legg, C. M.** A bibliography of the books printed at Reading during the eighteenth century. 1961.

157 **Lilley, G. P.** John Middleton Murry, 1889–1957, a bibliography of his writings published before the end of 1929. 1964.

158 **Loney, C. E.** A bibliography of Mary Russell Mitford, 1787–1855. 1948.

159 **Lord, H. M.** John Wilkins, 1614–1672, bishop of Chester and fellow of the Royal society; a bibliography. 1957.

160 **Loveday, A. J.** Cyril William Beaumont, historian of ballet and publisher; a stage towards a complete bibliography of his published writings, and including a bibliography of the Beaumont press. 1951.

161 **Lust, J.** Bibliography of James Harrington, 1611–1677. 1950.

162 **McIvor, R. M.** Scottish drama from 1900, a bibliography. 1939.

163 **McLorn, M. E. R.** Freya Madelaine Stark, a bibliography. 1957.

164 **MacPhail, Ian S.** A bibliography of the books printed at Trinity college, Dublin, 1734–1875. 1956.

165 **MacRobert, T. M.** English translations and criticisms of Calderon, a bibliography. 1950.

166 **Marsh, A. S.** Edward Gordon Duff, 1863–1924, a bibliography. 1953.

167 **Marshallsay, D. M.** A checklist of works printed by Thomas Baker of the High street, Southampton, 1774–1805. 1955.

168 **Matthews, D. A.** Notes towards a bibliography of George Crabbe, 1754–1832. 1954.

169 **Middlemast, K.** A bibliography of Theodore Watts-Dunton. 1950.

170 **Middleton, Joyce.** A bibliography of Matthew Gregory Lewis. 1948.

171 **Miles, P. J.** A short-title catalogue of books printed before 1550 in Wells cathedral library. 1956.

172 **Milligan, Edward H.** Darton imprints of the eighteenth century, a preliminary checklist. 1950.

173 **Morgan, N.** Bibliography of Dorothea and Richard Baxter Townshend. 1950.

174 **Morris, J.** Cambridge printing, 1740–1766, a short-title list. 1961.

175 **Muizz, Mohammed Abdul-.** Bibliography of Walter Bagehot's works. 1939.

176 **Mulcahy, B.** A bibliography of J. M. Synge. 1951.

177 **Nairn, A.** Alexander Bain; bibliography. 1960.

178 **Palmer, J. E. C.** Railway periodicals of the 19th century published in the British Isles; a bibliographical guide. 1959.

179 **Parsons, K. O.** A bibliography of the separately published works of mr. Walter de la Mare. 1949.

180 **Perkin, M. J.** The novels and short stories of Arnold Bennett. 1964.

181 **Perkin, M. R.** The works of Abraham Cowley. 1964.

182 **Phillips, R.** Oliver Simon at the Curwen press; a bibliographical handlist of their book-production from 1917 to 1955. 1964.

183 **Philpot, V. J.** Christopher Isherwood, a bibliography of his writings to the year 1956. 1957.

184 **Pinnock, C. L.** Sir Frederick Treves; a bibliography of his published writings and reported speeches. 1952.

185 **Playfair, J. K. H.** James Grant, 1822–1887, a select bibliography of his separately published works. 1957.

186 **Plincke, E. M.** David Masson, 1822–1907, a bibliography. 1952.

187 **Polak, Rose-Lida.** Bibliography of G. R. Gissing; his works and a selection of biography and criticism. 1950.

188 **Powell, D.** A bibliography of the writings of John Clare, with a selection of critical material after 1893. 1953.

189 **Price, Ursula E.** The maps of Buckinghamshire, 1574–1800; a bibliography. 1948. (*See* no.1175.)

189a **Ralph, Brenda A.** William Law, 1686–1761: a select bibliography of published works by and about William Law. 1966.

190 **Riding, J.** A bibliography of sir Philip Sidney, 1587–1931. 1948.

191 **Rodger, Elizabeth M.** Printed maps of Cornwall, 1576–1800; bibliography. 1956.

192 **Rodgers, F.** James Thomson, 1700–1748; a bibliography of his minor work to the year 1800. 1952.

193 **Russell, June.** Bibliography of Barbara Hofland. 1950.

194 **Scarlett, O. W.** Arthur Symons, 1865–1945; the published and privately printed works. 1958.

195 **Sheldon, Peter.** Printing in Derbyshire to 1800; a bibliography. 1949.

196 **Shipway, I. M.** A contribution to a bibliography of 18th century courtesy and conduct books. 1951.

197 **Simpson, Jean M.** (i.e. Lefèvre, J. M. S.) Bibliography of John Home, 1722–1808. 1957.

198 **Sinnhuber, A. M. W.** Herbert John Fleure, a bibliography. 1954.

199 **Skerl, M.** The writings of mrs. Craik; a select bibliography. 1949.

200 **Skipper, Jean.** A bibliography of Hampshire authors, 1640–1799. 1948.

201 **Smith, A. H.** A bibliography of John Nichols, 1745–1826. 1958.

202 **Smith, R. S.** Sir William Petty, a bibliography. 1950.

203 **Sopher, A.** A handlist of works printed by Thomas East. 1959.

204 **Sopher, R.** John Dowland, a bibliography. 1959.

205 **Spencer, E. M.** The medical works of sir Henry Thompson, a bibliography. 1957.

206 **Spurrell, J.** The writings of sir Francis Bacon published between 1750 and 1850. 1955.

207 **Stallybrass, O. G. W.** Edward Morgan Forster, a checklist of his writings. 1958.

208 **Starbuck, P. R.** Ralph Vaughan Williams, O.M., 1872–1958; a bibliography of his literary writings and criticism of his musical works. 1962.

209 **Statham, M. H.** H. H. Statham, 1839–1924, architect, editor, and critic of the arts; a bibliography. 1957.

210 **Steiner, J. H.** A bibliography of the works of saint John Fisher, cardinal bishop of Rochester. 1952.

211 **Stevenson, E. E. D.** Sir Walter Scott, a bibliography of the contemporary editions of the chief poems. 1936.

212 **Stirling, M. V.** Bibliography of the writings and speeches of viscount Cecil of Chelwood. . . . 1959.

213 **Stott, F.** A bibliography of the English romances of Guy of Warwick and Bevis of Hampton. 1950.

214 **Sutherland, F. M.** A bibliography of the separately published works of G. K. Chesterton. 1949.

215 **Sutton, Enid.** A bibliography of the detention of Charles I at Carisbrooke castle . . . 1648. 1948.

216 **Sutton, H. B.** First editions of literary works by medical men in the eighteenth century; a bibliography. 1961.

217 **Symons, L. E.** A bibliography of English–French and French–English dictionaries to 1800. 1949.

218 **Taylor, Nancy E.** A bibliography of Thomas Dekker's prose works. 1936.

219 **Thomas, Beryl E.** A bibliography of the works of Roger Ascham. 1949.

220 **Thomas, M. M. A. A.** The Gregynog press, Newton, Montgomeryshire; miscellaneous publications, 1921–1941, in the collection of the National library of Wales, Aberystwyth; a bibliography. 1956.

221 **Thomas, N. M.** Froissart in England; a bibliography of English translations and criticisms of the work of Jean Froissart. 1948.

222 **Thurley, R. L.** A bibliography of modern writings, 1900–1939, on Laurence Sterne. 1939.

223 **Tolfree, M. P. G.** A bibliography of Mary Webb. 1956.

224 **Truman, Joan.** Books printed in Anglo-Saxon, 1600–1800. 1949.

225 **Watkins, A. E.** Bibliography of the London pharmacopœia. 1954.

226 **Watkins, Diana G.** Bibliography of the Taylor family of Ongar. 1936.

227 **Watson, Barbara.** A bibliography of sir Kenelm Digby, 1603–1665. 1938.

227a **West, Charles B.** A bibliography of the works of E. H. W. Meyerstein. 1966.

228 **Whalley, Joyce I.** A bibliography of Ernest Christopher Dowson, 1867–1900. 1950.

229 **White, B. E. Grove-.** Bibliography of part of the work of Arnold Bennett. 1964.

230 **Whitmee, Dorothy E.** Bibliography of John Skelton, poet laureate, ?1460–1529. 1939.

231 **Whitmore, Phyllis.** A bibliography of the works of Robert Bloomfield. 1937.

232 **Williams, Eileen A.** A bibliography of Giraldus Cambrensis, c.1147–c.1223. 1960.

233 **Williams, Joan.** Sir Napier Shaw, F.R.S., a bibliography. 1947.

234 **Willison, Ian R.** George Orwell, some materials for a bibliography. 1953.

235 **Wines, J. M.** A bibliography of the writings of V. Sackville-West. 1958.

236 **Wing, H. J. R.** A bibliography of dr. Thomas Willis, 1621–1675. 1962.

237 **Wingate, H. E.** Gertrude Lowthian Bell, a bibliography. 1956.

238 **Wright, G. M.** A bibliography of a collection of sermons of the 17th and early 18th centuries in the Chapter library of St. George's chapel, Windsor. 1960.

239 **Yeo, C. M.** Sir John Suckling, a bibliography. 1948.

240 **Ziman, E. R.** George Grote, 1794–1871; a bibliography of his writings, together with a selection of critical works and reviews. 1954.

241 **Marsh, A. S.,** 1953; no.166.

242 **Freer, Percy.** Bibliography and modern book production; notes and sources for student librarians, printers, booksellers, stationers, book-collectors. Johannesburg, Witwatersrand U.P., 1954. xiv,345p. 21cm.
Handbook to bibliogr. studies, with useful annotated lists.

243 **Foxon, David Fairweather.** The technique of bibliography. [London] Published for the National book league at the C.U.P., 1955. 20p. 21cm.
Annotated list of basic books.

244 **Scotland. Scottish central library,** EDINBURGH. A classified list of catalogues and bibliographies in the library, compiled by S. T. H. Wright and I. McKinlay. Edinburgh, 1955. iv,63p. 27cm. (Duplicated typescript.)

245 **Peet, William H.** and **F. A. Mumby,** *comp.* 'Bibliography of publishing and bookselling' *in* Mumby, Frank A. Publishing and bookselling, a history from the earliest times. [4th rev. ed.] London [1956]. p.373–415. (First pub. 1930.)

245a **McKenzie, Donald Francis.** The writings of sir Walter Greg, 1945–1959. Library ser5 15:42–6 Mr '60.
Continuation of no.60.

246 **W., N.** Book collecting, with particular reference to early printed books. Manchester R 9:226–32 '61.

247 **Lefanu, William Richard,** *comp.* 'A list of the writings of sir Geoffrey Keynes compiled by permission from his own register' *in* Geoffrey Keynes; tributes on the occasion of his seventieth birthday. [London] 1961. p.27–61.

248 **Besterman, Theodore Deodatus Nathaniel.** A world bibliography of bibliographies and of bibliographical catalogues, calendars, abstracts, digests, indexes, and the like. 4th ed., rev. and greatly enl. Lausanne, Societas bibliographica [1965–6]. 5v. 28cm.
The 3d ed. (1955–6, 4v.) remains useful; this list does not include bibliographies published in periodicals or as part of separate works.

BIBLIOGRAPHY—SERIAL BIBLIOGRAPHIES

250 'A selective check list of bibliographical scholarship, 1949–   ' *in* **Studies in bibliography.** 3– . Charlottesville, Va., 1950– .
Annually, except for 1955, which was included in

251 **Selective** check lists of bibliographical scholarship, 1949–1955. Charlottesville, Va., Bibliographical society of the University of Virginia, 1957. viii, 192p. 26cm.
Part 1. Incunabula and early renaissance, by Rudolf Hirsch. [Derek A. Clarke, 1963– .].
—2. Later renaissance to the present, by Lucy Clark and Fredson Bowers. [Howell J. Heaney, 1950– .]. This cumulation is indexed.

252 **Oxford bibliographical society.** Bibliography in Britain, a classified list of books and articles published in the United Kingdom. 1– , 1962– . Oxford, 1963– . v. 25cm. (Duplicated typescript.)
Ed. by John S. G. Simmons.

BIBLIOGRAPHY—PRINCIPAL CUMULATED INDEXES

255 **Bibliographical society,** LONDON. Transactions. General index, volumes I–X, 1893–1909. London, Ptd. for the Bibliographical society by Blades, East, & Blades, 1910. 101p. 19cm.

256 —— The Library . . . Fourth series, volumes I–X: general index. London, O.U.P., H. Milford, 1932. viii,101p. 19cm.

257 **Cole, George Watson.** An index to bibliographical papers published by the Bibliographical society and the Library association, London, 1877–1932. Chicago, Ill., Published for the Bibliographical society of America at the University of Chicago pr. [1923]. ix,262p. 22cm.

258 **Bibliographical society of America.** Index to the publications of the Bibliographical society of America and of the Bibliographical society of Chicago, 1899–1931. Chicago, Ill., University of Chicago pr., 1931. v,43p. 24cm.

259 —— Index to the Papers . . . volumes 26–45, 1932–1951; a supplement to Index, volumes 1–25, 1899–1931. . . . New York, 1954. 84p. 24cm.

260 **Book collector.** . . . Index 1952–1961, volume Ino1 to volume Xno4, compiled by Enid D. Nixon. [London, Shenval pr., 1965]. 59p. 23cm.

261 **Edinburgh bibliographical society.** General index to Publications, v.I–XV, compiled by Marryat Ross Dobie. Edinburgh, 1936. viii,37p. 25cm.
Repr. from Edinburgh Bib Soc Pub 15pt3:87–128 '35.

262 **Simon, Oliver.** 'Appendix. Index to Signature, 1935–40' *in* Printer and playground, an autobiography. London [1956]. p.[141]–7.

BIBLIOGRAPHY—LIBRARY CATALOGUES

(Arranged by date of publication; other library catalogues are listed under the subject-headings to which they most particularly refer, e.g. *Presses and printers.*)

265 **British museum. Dept. of printed books.** List of bibliographical works in the reading room of the British museum 2d ed. rev. [London] Ptd. by order of the trustees, 1889. xi,103p. 22cm.

Revision by George K. Fortescue of the Hand-list, 1881, comp. by George W. Porter.

266 **Bibliographical society, LONDON. Library.** Hand list of books in the library of the Bibliographical society, March, 1935. [Oxford] Ptd. at the O.U.P. for the Bibliographical society, 1935. 67p. 23cm. (First pub. [1907].)

267 **National book league. Library.** Books about books; catalogue of the library of the National book league. [5th ed., rev. and enl.] London, Published for the National book league by the C.U.P., 1955. x,126p. 22cm.

Earlier ed. by the National book council in 1933, 1935, 1938, 1944, and 1948 (Supplement).

268 **Library association, LONDON. Library.** Catalogue. London, 1958. vii,519p. 26cm.

Ed. by D. C. Henrik Jones.

269 **British library of political and economic science, LONDON.** Classified catalogue of a collection of works on publishing and bookselling in the British library of political and economic science. London, London school of economics, 1961. vi,186p. 24cm. (First pub. 1936.)

270 **Newberry library, CHICAGO. John M. Wing foundation.** Dictionary catalogue of the history of printing from the John M. Wing foundation. Chicago, 1962. 6v.(6074p.) 36 cm. (Not seen.)

'The John M. Wing foundation . . . is a collection of some 20,000 volumes on the history of printing. Books and journals descriptive of the graphic arts, national and regional printing histories, works on papermaking, binding, book design and illustration ancilliary to printing, and books on bookselling and collecting comprise half the collection.'—Advt.

BIBLIOGRAPHY—PERIODICALS (SELECT LIST)

275 American book collector. 1–6. Plainfield, N. J., 1932–35; 1– . Chicago, 1950– .

276 An Leabharlann. (Journal of the Library association of Ireland) new ser 1– . Dublin, 1930– .

277 Bibliographica. 1–3. London, 1895–7.

278 Bibliographical society, London. Transactions. 1–15. London, 1892–1919.

279 Bibliographical society of America. Proceedings and papers. 1–3. New York, 1904–6/8; Papers 4– . 1910– .

280 Bibliographical society of Ireland. Publications. 1– . Dublin, 1918/20– .

281 Bibliotheck; a journal of bibliographical notes and queries mainly of Scottish interest. 1– . Glasgow, Scottish group, University and research section, Library association, 1956– .

282 Black art. 1– . London, 1962– .

283 Bodleian library record. 1– . Oxford, 1938– . (Formerly Bodleian quarterly record, 1–8, 1914–37/8)

284 Book collector. 1– . London, 1952– . (Formerly Book handbook)

285 Book collector's quarterly. 1–17. London, First edition club, 1930–5.

286 Book handbook; an illustrated quarterly. . . . 1–2. Bracknell, 1947–51.

287 Bookman. 1–87. London, 1891–1934.

288 Boston public library quarterly. 1– . Boston, 1949— .

289 Bulletin of bibliography and dramatic index. 1– . Boston, Mass., F. W. Faxon, 1897– .

290 Bulmer papers. 1– . Wylam, 1960– .

291 Cambridge bibliographical society. Transactions. 1– . Cambridge, 1949– .

292 Colby library quarterly. 1– . Waterville, Me., 1943– .

293 Colophon, a book collectors' quarterly. 1–5; new ser 1–3; new graphic ser 1. New York, 1930–40.

294 Durham philobiblon. 1– . Durham, Durham university library, 1949– .

295 Edinburgh bibliographical society. Publications. 1–15. Edinburgh, 1890–1935; Transactions. 1– . 1935/6– .

296 English literature in transition. 1– . West Lafayette, Ind., Purdue university, 1957– . (Formerly English fiction in transition, 1957–62.)

297 Fleuron; a journal of typography. 1–7. London, 1923–30.

298 Glasgow bibliographical society. Records. 1– . Glasgow, 1912– .

299 Harvard library bulletin. 1–14. Cambridge, Mass., Harvard university, 1947–60, 1967– . (Formerly Harvard university library notes. 1–32. 1920–42.)

300 Huntington library quarterly. 1– . San Marino, Calif., Henry E. Huntington library and art gallery, 1937– . (Formerly Huntington library bulletin. 1–11. Cambridge, Mass., 1931–7.)

301 Irish book. 1– . Dublin, Bibliographical society of Ireland, 1959– .

302 Irish book lover; a monthly review of Irish literature and bibliography. 1–32. Dublin, 1909–57.

303 John Rylands library bulletin. 1– . Manchester, 1903– .

304 Journal of the Printing historical society. 1– . London, 1965– .

305 Library. (Transactions of the Bibliographical society, second series) 1–10; new ser 1–10; ser3 1–10; ser4 1–26; ser5 1– . London, 1889– .

306 More books, the Bulletin of the Boston public library. 1– . Boston, 1926– .

307 National library of Wales. Journal. 1– . Aberystwyth, 1939– .

308 New York public library bulletin. 1– . New York, 1897– .

309 Newberry library bulletin. 1– . Chicago, Newberry public library, 1944– .

310 Oxford bibliographical society. Proceedings and papers. 1–7; new ser 1– . Oxford, 1922/6–46; 1947– . (Publications, 6– .)

311 Princeton university library chronicle. 1– . Princeton, N.J., 1939– .

312 Printing and graphic arts. 1– . Lunenburg, Vt., 1953– . (Formerly Notes on printing and the graphic arts, 1. 1953.)

313 Private library. 1– . North Harrow, Private libraries association, 1957– .

314 Rutgers university library journal. 1– . New Brunswick, N.J., 1937– .

315 Signature; a quadrimestrial of typography and graphic arts, &c. 1–15; new ser 1–18. London, 1935–40, 1946–54.

316 Studies in bibliography. 1– . Charlottesville, Va., Bibliographical society of the University of Virginia, 1948– . (Formerly Papers. . . .)

317 University of Pennsylvania library chronicle. 1– . Philadelphia, Pa., 1933– .

318 University of Texas library chronicle. 1– . Austin, Tex., 1944– .

319 Welsh bibliographical society. Journal. 1– . Aberystwyth, 1910– .

320 Yale University library gazette. 1– . New Haven, Conn., 1926– .

GENERAL AND PERIOD
BIBLIOGRAPHIES

PERIOD DIVISIONS (entries arranged by date of publication)

1475–	[general catalogues]
1475–1500	[incunabula only]
1475–1640	[STC period]
1475–1700	[STC and Wing books; 'early' books]
1641–1700	[Wing period]
1701–1800	
1801–1900	
1901–	

See also period divisions under *Drama, Newspapers and periodicals, Poetry, Fiction, Pamphlets.*

See also Regional bibliographies.

BOOKS—1475–

325 **Gosse, sir Edmund William.** A catalogue of a portion of the library of Edmund Gosse, by R. J. Lister. London, Privately ptd., Ballantyne pr., 1893. xxi,195p. 26cm.

Alphabetical short-title catalogue of collection strong in restoration dramatists and presentation copies; *see* no.343.

Rev: [A. W. Pollard] Bibliographica 1:125–8 '95; Library 6:257–8 '94.

326 **John Rylands library,** MANCHESTER. Catalogue of the manuscripts, books, and bookbindings exhibited at the opening of the John Rylands library . . . 1899. Manchester, R. Gill, ptr. [1899]. 41p. 22cm.

327 **Grolier club,** NEW YORK. An exhibition of selected works of the poets laureate of England. [New York, 1901]. xv,80p. 19cm.

328 —— **[Same]:** [2d rev. and enl. ed.] with title: Catalogue of an exhibition of selected works. . . . New York, 1901. xix,81p. 23cm.

Chronol. catalogue of 89 works from Chaucer to Austin, with bibliogr. notes.

329 **Cambridge. University. Library.** Catalogue of a collection of early printed and other books bequeathed to the library by John Couch Adams. Cambridge, 1902. 203p. 17cm.

Checklist repr. from Cambridge Univ Lib Bull extra ser 10, 1894, with index.

330 **Grolier club,** NEW YORK. One hundred books famous in English literature, with facsimiles of the title-pages. . . . New York, 1902. iii,200p. facsims. 28cm.

331 —— Bibliographical notes on One hundred books famous in English literature . . . compiled by Henry W. Kent. New York, 1903. xii,227p. 28cm.
See also no.368.

332 **Wise, Thomas James.** The Ashley library; a catalogue of printed books, manuscripts and autograph letters collected by Thomas James Wise. London, Ptd. for private circulation only, 1905–8. 2v. port., facsims. 29cm.
Only 12 copies printed; *see* no.342.

333 **Oaten, Edward Farley.** 'A list of Anglo-Indian works . . .' *in* A sketch of Anglo-Indian literature. London, 1908. p.199–211.
Classified checklist.

334 **Karslake, Frank.** Notes from Sothebys, being a compilation of 2,032 notes from catalogues of book-sales . . . 1885–1909. London, Karslake, 1909. 392p. ports. 22cm.
Author catalogue, with various notes.

335 **Drummond castle,** PERTH. **Library.** Catalogue of the rare and most interesting books, . . . compiled by George P. Johnston. Edinburgh, Privately ptd., 1910. 96p. 25cm.
Alphabetical checklist.

336 **John Rylands library,** MANCHESTER. . . . Catalogue of an exhibition of original editions of the principal English classics. . . . Manchester, Ptd. by order of the governors, 1910. xv,85p. 23cm.
Comp. by Henry Guppy.

337 **[Lindsay, James Ludovic, 26th earl of Crawford]** . . . Catalogue of the printed books preserved at Haigh Hall, Wigan . . . [Aberdeen] Aberdeen U.P., 1910. 4v. 36cm. (Bibliotheca Lindesiana.)
'List of collected works which have been analysed and the parts thereof catalogued separately' (v.1, col.xxi–xxx).—'List of subject-headings' (col.xxxiii–c).—etc. Short-title general catalogue with full descriptions of early books.

338 **Harvard university. Library. Widener collection.** A catalogue of the books and manuscripts of Harry Elkins Widener, by A. S. W. Rosenbach. . . . Philadelphia, Privately ptd., 1918. 2v. illus., port. 29cm.
Alphabetical catalogue with some bibliogr. notes; no index.

339 **Texas. University. John Henry Wrenn library.** A catalogue of the library of the late John Henry Wrenn, compiled by Harold B. Wrenn, edited by Thomas J. Wise. Austin, University of Texas, 1920. 5v. port. 27cm.
Author catalogue of 5,300 vols., with collations and bibliogr. notes. 'Aside from all the impostures, the hybrids in flashy bindings, and the refuse from Wise's own collection, every third description is misleading and every other attribution false.' (*See* no.5140, p.5.)
Rev: J. W. Draper Mod Lang N 37:237–43 '22.

340 **De Ricci, Seymour Montefiore Roberto Rosso.** The book collectors' guide; a practical handbook of British and American bibliography. Philadelphia, Rosenbach, 1921. xviii,649p. 24cm.
Short-title list by author of 'collectable' books, with notes of sales and prices, some locations of copies; no title index.

341 **Clark, William Andrews.** The library of William Andrews Clark, jr. Index to authors and titles, compiled and arranged by Robert Ernest Cowan [and others]. San Francisco, Ptd. by J. H. Nash, 1922–30. 2v. 27cm.

Indexes volumes covering Cruikshank, Dickens, Pickwick club, early and modern English literature, Kelmscott and Doves presses.

342 **Wise, Thomas James.** The Ashley library; a catalogue of printed books, manuscripts and autograph letters, collected by Thomas James Wise. London, Ptd. for private circulation only, 1922–36. 11v. ports., facsims. 27cm.

Indexes to v.9 (for v.1–9) and v.11. The collection, principally of 18th- and 19th-century authors, is now in the BM; the catalogue must be used with caution.

Rev: v.1 W. G. Partington Bkmns J 6:82–4 '22; Lit R 8 Jl '22:799; v.2 W. G. Partington Bkmns J 8:25–6 '23; TLS 10 My '23:312; v.3 TLS 18 Oc '23:691; W. G. Partington Bkmns J 8:197–201 '23; v.4 W. G. Partington Bkmns J 10:8–11 '24; TLS 15 My '24:303; v.5 W. G. Partington Bkmns J 11:103–7 '24; v.6 TLS 10 S '25:580; v.7 TLS 29 Ap '26:319; v.8 TLS 17 Mr '27:182; v.9 TLS 29 Mr '28:237; v.11 TLS 19 S '36:749.

343 **Gosse, sir Edmund William.** The library of Edmund Gosse, being a descriptive and bibliographical catalogue, of a portion of his collection, compiled by E. H. M. Cox, with an introductory essay by mr. Gosse. London, Dulau, 1924. 300p. port. 23cm.

Alphabetical catalogue with short collations of early items; no index. The collection was sold in 1928–9: *see* no.399.

Rev: N&Q 146:334 '24; TLS 21 F '24:106; A. W. P[ollard] Library ser4 5:100–2 '24; I. A. Williams Lond Merc 9:641–4 '24; H.G. Bkmns J 10:62 '24.

344 **Southwark. Public libraries and Cuming museum.** Catalogue of four and a half centuries of printing showing a book for every year from 1472 to 1927 from the private collection of Thomas A. Gilbert. . . . [London, Southwark public libraries and museum committee] 1927. 36p. 23cm.

345 **Schwartz, Jacob.** 'English authors' *in* 1100 obscure points; the bibliographies of 25 English and 21 American authors. London [1931]. p.1–42.

Author checklists with TP transcr. and some bibliogr. notes.

346 **Baxter, James Houston, C. Johnson** and **J. F. Willard.** An index of British and Irish Latin writers, A.D. 400–1520. Paris, 1932. 115p. 25cm.

Author checklist by period, of 900 entries; repr. from Bull du Cange, v.7 '32.

347 **[Miller, Sydney Richardson Christie-]** The Britwell handlist; or, Short-title catalogue of the principal volumes from the time of Caxton to the year 1800 formerly in the library of Britwell court, Buckinghamshire. London, B. Quaritch, 1933. 2v.(1067p.) ports., facsims. 26cm.

Alphabetical catalogue comp. from the sale catalogues, 1916–27, with references to them, edited by Herbert Collmann and completed by G. A. P. Brown.

Rev: TLS 2 N '33:756; [A. W. Pollard] Library ser4 14:359–60 '33.

348 **Annals** of English literature, 1475–1950. Oxford, 1935. *See* no.364.

349 **Bateson, Frederick Wilse.** The Cambridge bibliography of English literature. Cambridge, C.U.P., 1940–57. 5v. 24cm.

350 —— [**Same**]: New York, Macmillan; Cambridge, C.U.P., 1941. 4v. 25cm.

Contents. 1. 600–1660.—2. 1660–1800.—3. 1800–1900.—4. Index.—5. Supplement: A.D. 600–1900, ed. by G. G. Watson.

CBEL is being revised by G. G. Watson.

Rev: TLS 1 F '41:60; *ib.* 22 F '41:91; *ib.* 1 Mr '41:103; 8 Mr '41:117; 17 Mr '41:127; D. Cook *ib.* 14 Je '41:292; C. J. Sisson Mod Lang R 36:247–9 '41; J. R. Sutherland R Eng Stud 17:490–4 '41; J. B. Hubbell Am Lit 13:183–5 '41; D. G. Wing Yale R 31:208– 9 '41; W. A. Jackson Pub Wkly 139:1676–7 '41; G.L.M. Pa Bib Soc Am 35:163–5 '41; H. S. V. Jones J Eng Germ Philol 40:564–6 '41; A. B. Shepperson Virginia Q R 17:597– 600 '41; C. Gauss Sat R Lit 33:7–8 '41; N. I. White Sth Atlan Q 40:298–300 '41; D. Roberts Nation 153:76–7 '41; A. Friedman Lib Q 11:521–4 '41; H. L. Binsse Common- weal 33:568 '41; M. Sadleir Ninet Cent 130:51–60 '41; H. Hobson Chri Sci Mon 15 F '41: 11; H. Hodson Spect 27 D '40:695; E. Kellett New Statesmn 8 Mr '41:254; W. Macmillan New Statesmn 22 Mr '41:308; S. Pargellis Yale R 30:860 '41; L. Roth N.Y. Herald-Trib Bk R 5 Oc '41:32; Coll Eng 3:210 '41; N&Q 180:89–90 '41; H. Craig Coll Eng 3:422–4 '42; D. F. Bond Mod Philol 39:303–12 '42 (important addenda); L. N. Broughton Mod Lang N 57:285–8 '42; R. Wellek Philol Q 21:251–6 '42; F. C. Francis Library ser4 22:250–5 '42; *Supplement*: C. E. Jones Bull Bib 22:104–5 '57; L. W. Hanson Library ser5 13:208–10 '57; J. Hayward Bk Coll 7:82,85 '57; G. L. McKay Pa Bib Soc Am 52:68–70 '57; H. Cahoon Lib J 83:61 '57; TLS 4 Oc '57:600; L. B. Etudes Angl 11:155 '58; G. J. Kolb Mod Philol 56:197–203 '59; R. Juchhoff Angl 79:214–16 '61; G. T. Senn Archiv 196:92–3 '60.

351 **Cambridge. University. Fitzwilliam museum.** Catalogue of an exhibition of printing at the Fitzwilliam museum. . . . Cambridge, C.U.P., 1940. [2d impression [corr.] 1940.] xi,136p. 24cm.

Checklist with descriptive notes of 641 items, and 'List of lenders' (p.ix–xi).

353 **Wigan. Public library.** The foundations of glory; a victory exhibition of first or early editions . . . from Chaucer to Stevenson. . . . Wigan, 1945. 15p. 22cm. Covertitle.

354 **Smith, Margaret S.,** *comp.* 'Printed catalogues of books and manuscripts in cathedral libraries: England and Wales' *in* Hands, M. S. G. The cathedral libraries catalogue. Library ser5 2:1–13 Je '47. p.11–13.

355 **New York. Public library. Berg collection.** Anniversaries, an exhibition of books . . . published in 1648–1748–1848. New York, New York public library, 1948. 13p. 25cm.

Annotated chronol. list.

356 —— First fruits, an exhibition of first editions of first books by English authors. By John D. Gordan. New York, New York public library, 1949. 36p. 25cm.

Annotated chronol. list.

357 **France. Bibliothèque nationale,** PARIS. Le livre anglais; tresórs des collec- tions anglaises. Paris, 1951. xxiv,251p.+15 illus., facsims. 21cm.

Annotated chronol. author catalogue of 377 books, with bibliogr. refs. and locations of copies.

358 **National book league,** LONDON. The Festival of Britain; exhibition of books arranged by the National book league at the Victoria & Albert museum. London, Published for the National book league by the C.U.P., 1951. 224p. 21cm.

Classified and annotated short-title catalogue comp. by John Hadfield.

359 **London. University. Library.** The Sterling library; a catalogue of the printed books and literary manuscripts collected by sir Louis Sterling and presented by him to the University of London. Privately printed. [Cambridge, C.U.P. for London university] 1954. xiv,612p. illus., port., facsims. 26cm.

Chronol. catalogue comp. by Margaret Canney, with bibliogr. notes; in 5 pts: 1. Printed books, fifteenth to nineteenth century.—2. Printed books, twentieth century.—3. Private presses and limited editions.—4. Illustrated and extra-illustrated books.—5. Literary manuscripts.

Rev: TLS 13 Ag '54:520; D. Holland Bk Coll 3:234–6 '54; sir G. L. K[eynes] Library ser5 10:72–3 '55.

360 **National book league,** LONDON. Fine books from famous houses; an exhibition of printed books and manuscripts from National Trust houses, organised by Robert Gathorne-Hardy. London [1958]. 48p. 22cm.

Short-title annotated catalogue of 200 items, with incunabula described in greater detail.

361 **New York. Public library. Berg collection.** Landmarks in English literature in first or early editions, 1490–1900; an exhibition from the Berg collection, by John D. Gordan. New York, New York public library, 1959. 25p. facsim. 25cm.

Repr. from N.Y. Pub Lib Bull 64:105–9 F '60; annotated chronol. list.

362 **Plume library,** MALDON. Catalogue of the Plume library at Maldon, Essex, compiled by S. G. Deed with the assistance of Jane Francis. Maldon, Plume library trustees, 1959. xvi,192p. 24cm.

Short-title author catalogue with bibliogr. refs.

Rev: TL S 11 D '59:732; J. Crow Bk Coll 9:215219 16–, '60.

363 **Tinker, Chauncey Brewster.** The Tinker library; a bibliographical catalogue of the books and manuscripts collected by Chauncey Brewster Tinker. Compiled by Robert F. Metzdorf. New Haven, Yale university library [1959]. xxvi,530p. port., facsim. 26cm.

Author catalogue of 2,368 items with TP transcrs.,'collations, and bibliogr. notes and refs., now located in the Sterling memorial library, Yale university.

Rev: L. S. Thompson Pa Bib Soc Am 53:351 '59; F. B. Adams Bk Coll 9:223–4,227–8 '60; R. Paulson J Eng Germ Philol 54:560–1 '60; S. C. Roberts Library ser5 15:71–3 '60; L. S. Thompson Am Bk Coll 10:29 '59; TLS 8 Ja '60:24.

364 **Annals** of English literature, 1475–1950; the principal publications of each year together with an alphabetical index of authors and their works. 2d ed. Oxford, Clarendon pr., 1961. vi,380p. 17cm. (First pub. 1935.)

Rev. by Robert W. Chapman.

365 **Texas. University. Humanities research center.** Prize books; awards granted to scholars, 1671–1935; in the schools and colleges of England, Scotland, Wales, Ireland. . . . [Catalogue to an exhibition held in October, 1961. Austin, 1961.] 1v.(unpaged) illus. 13 × 17cm.

Annotated checklist comp. by William B. Todd mainly from his own collection.

366 **Wales. University. University college of North Wales,** BANGOR. **Library.** Catalogue of the Bangor cathedral library, now deposited in the University college . . . compiled by E. Gwynne Jones and J. R. V. Johnston. Bangor, 1961 [i.e., 1962]. xxiv,172p. 16 × 24cm. (Duplicated typescript.)

'Incunabula, described by V. Scholderer' (p.xxiii–xxiv): 4 items; 'English and continental presses' (p.1–150): includes over 1,000v. printed before 1700; 'Welsh books' (p.151–72). Alphabetical short-title catalogue, with bibliogr. refs.; no index.

Rev: TLS 17 My '63:364.

367 **Scotland. National library,** EDINBURGH. English literature; catalogue of the exhibition. [Edinburgh] 1962. 33p. 23cm.

Classified and annotated checklist, prepared by William Park.

Rev: TLS 16 N '62:880.

368 **Grolier club,** NEW YORK. Grolier; or, 'Tis sixty years since; a reconstruction of the exhibit of 100 books famous in English literature, originally held in New York, 1903. . . . [Bloomington, Ind.] Indiana university library, 1963. 48p. 28cm.

Annotated catalogue, with bibliogr. notes on Lilly library copies. *See also* no.330.

369 **Keynes, sir Geoffrey Langdon.** Bibliotheca bibliographici, a catalogue of the library formed by Geoffrey Keynes. London, Trianon pr., 1964. xxiii,444p. illus., facsims. 29cm.

Short-title author catalogue of 4,316 entries, with 'numeration of all engraved plates contained in the books (other than those printed in the texts) and transcription of most of the signatures of former owners and of inscriptions . . .'; 'Index of owners and donors' (p.435–44).

Rev: B. Juel-Jensen Library ser5 20:71–4 '65; H. R. Archer Pa Bib Soc Am 59:334–8 '65.

370 **Southampton. Public libraries.** A catalogue of the Pitt collection. Southampton, City of Southampton public libraries committee, 1964. 133p. 23cm.

Rev: TLS 17 D '64:1152.

371 **Skipton. Public library. Petyt library.** A catalogue of the Petyt library. Gargrave, Colthurst trust, 1965. 417p. 28cm.

Short-title author catalogue; no title index.

Rev: TLS 11 F '65:116; P. Morgan Library ser5 20:162–3 '65.

BOOKS—1475– . SALE CATALOGUES (arranged by date of publication)

Not all the following selection of sale catalogues of important collections have been seen. Other catalogues predominantly of a particular period, genre, subject, or author are entered appropriately; they are indexed under the heading *Sale catalogues*.

380 **Marshall, Francis Albert.** Catalogue of the dramatic, Elizabethan and miscellaneous library of the late Frank A. Marshall . . . to which is added the library of E. L. Blanchard, sold by auction by messrs. Sotheby, Wilkinson & Hodge. . . . London, Dryden pr., J. Davy [1890]. 134p. 25cm. (Not seen.)

381 **Elton, Charles Isaac** and **M. A. Elton.** A catalogue of a portion of the library of Charles Isaac Elton and Mary Augusta Elton. London, Quaritch, 1891. 222p. illus. 26cm.

Comp. assisted by Alfred W. Pollard; 'A collection of small books' (p.[212]–22).

382 **Foote, Charles Benjamin.** Catalogue of the . . . collection made by Charles B. Foote . . . sold at auction . . . by Bangs & co. . . . [New York, 1894–5]. 3pts. in IV. facsims. 25cm.

Contents: First editions of American authors.—English literature, ancient and modern.—First editions of modern English and American authors.

383 **Ashburnham, Bertram, 4th earl of Ashburnham.** The Ashburnham library; catalogue of the magnificent collection of printed books . . . sold by auction by messrs. Sotheby, Wilkinson & Hodge. . . . [London, 1897–8.] 3pts. in IV. facsims. 26cm. 4,075 lots.

384 **Eames, Wilberforce.** Catalogue of the library of Wilberforce Eames . . . for sale at auction . . . by the Anderson auction company . . . New York. [New York, D. Taylor, 1905–7.] 5v. 26cm.

6,522 titles; pt. 2 only: 'England, Ireland, the Isle of Man, Scotland, and Wales.'

385 **Amherst, William Amhurst Tyssen-, 1st baron Amherst of Hackney.** A hand-list of a collection of books and manuscripts belonging to . . . lord Amherst of Hackney. Compiled by Seymour de Ricci. Cambridge, C.U.P., 1906. 433l. facsims. 29cm.

Checklist of 1,103 items arranged chronol. under subject, with indexes of authors and subjects, books bearing royal arms, and previous owners.

386 **Van Antwerp, William Clarkson.** Catalogue of the . . . collection . . . of William C. Van Antwerp comprising the rarest editions of classical English authors from Chaucer to Tennyson . . . sold by auction, by messrs. Sotheby, Wilkinson & Hodge. . . . [London] Dryden pr., J. Davy [1907]. viii,59p. 25cm. 243 lots.

387 **Church, Elihu Dwight.** A catalogue of books consisting of English literature and miscellanea including many original editions of Shakespeare, forming a part of the library. . . . Compiled and annotated by George Watson Cole. New York, Dodd, Mead, 1909. 2v.(viii,1153p.) facsims. 28cm.

Chronol. list of 748 items arranged by author, fully descr. with bibliogr. discussion and refs., locations of other copies, extensive facsims., and index. The collection is now in the Huntington library.

Rev: W. N. C. Carlton Pa Bib Soc Am 7:41–50 '13.

388 **Hoe, Robert.** Catalogue of the library of Robert Hoe of New York . . . to be sold by auction . . . by the Anderson auction company. . . . [New York, D. Taylor, 1911–12.] 8v. in 4. illus., facsims., plan. 24cm.

389 —— Priced list of the Robert Hoe library. . . . [New York, 1911–12.] 4v. 23cm. Caption title.
The bulk of the 14,585 lots, which realized $1,932,056.60 is in the Huntington library.

390 **Huth, Henry.** A short handlist of the rarer & most important books in the Huth library, compiled by Bernard Quaritch. [London, G. Norman, ptrs.] 1911. 111p. 25cm.

391 —— Catalogue of the famous library of printed books, illuminated manuscripts, autograph letters and engravings collected by Henry Huth and since maintained and augmented by his son Alfred H. Huth. The printed books . . . sold at auction by messrs. Sotheby, Wilkinson & Hodge. London, Dryden pr., J. Davy [1911–20]. 9v. plates (part col., part fold.), facsims. (part fold.) 26cm.
Alphabetical catalogue of 8,357 items, with bibliogr. descrs. of varying fullness, based on the catalogue pub. in 5v. in 1880. This catalogue was also issued without the illustrations.

392 —— The Huth library. Catalogue of books unsold or returned as imperfect. . . . [London] Dryden pr., J. Davy [1922]. 54p. 25cm. 232 lots.

393 **Hagen, Winston Henry.** Catalogue of the library of the late Winston Henry Hagen. New York, Anderson galleries [1918]. 272p. port., facsims. 23cm. (Not seen.) 1,466 entries.

394 **De Vinne, Theodore Low.** The library of the late Theodore Low De Vinne. New York, Anderson galleries, 1920. 170p. port. 23cm. (Not seen.)
Introduction by Henrietta C. Bartlett; 1,945 entries.

395 **Wallace, Walter Thomas.** Illustrated catalogue of the literary treasures . . . to be sold. . . . New York, American art association [1920]. IV.(unpaged) facsims. 24cm. 1,560 items.

396 **Chew, Beverley C.** The library . . . to be sold. . . . New York, Anderson galleries, 1924. ?pts. port., facsims. 22cm.
Pt.1. English literature before 1800. 474 items.

397 **Adam, Robert Borthwick.** Printed only for a few friends. [Catalogue of books not by Johnson, Boswell, or Goldsmith in the library of R. B. Adam.] Buffalo, N.Y., Buffalo volksfreund ptg. co., 1925. 186p. 33cm.
Descr. catalogue arranged in no discernible order, without index.

398 —— English literature from the library of mr. R. B. Adam, Buffalo, N.Y., . . . to be sold by auction. . . . New York, Anderson galleries, 1926. 132p. facsims. 24cm. (Not seen.) 433 entries.

399 **Gosse, sir Edmund William.** The Gosse library . . . catalogue of . . . the library of the late sir Edmund Gosse . . . which will be sold by auction by messrs. Sotheby and co. London, Ptd. by J. Davy [1928–9]. 5v. in 4. illus., facsims. 26cm.

400 **Kern, Jerome David.** The library of Jerome Kern, New York city . . . to be sold by his order. . . . New York, Anderson galleries, 1929. 2v. illus., facsims. 26cm.

The sale of 1,482 entries realized over $1,700,000.

401 **Perry, Marsden Jasiel.** The library of the late Marsden J. Perry . . . Public sale. . . . [New York] American art association, Anderson galleries, 1936. 337p. illus., facsims. 28cm. (Not seen.)

565 titles, including collection of Kelmscott press books.

402 **Newton, Alfred Edward.** Rare books, original drawings, autograph letters and manuscripts collected by the late A. Edward Newton . . . For public sale . . . at the Parke-Bernet galleries. . . . [New York, 1941.] 3v. illus., ports., facsims. 27cm.

585 entries including substantial Blake and Johnson collections.

403 **Hogan, Francis Joseph.** The Frank J. Hogan library, sold by order. . . . New York, Parke-Bernet galleries, 1945–6. 4pts. port., facsims. 26cm. (Not seen.)

Rev: TLS 28 Jl '45:360; *ib.* 4 Ag '45:372.

404 **Wilmerding, Lucius.** The notable library of the late Lucius Wilmerding. Public auction sale. New York, Parke-Bernet galleries, 1950–1. 3v. illus. 26cm.

Comp. by Marion Caming; pt.1 (November '50) lists English literature.

BOOKS—1475–1500—BIBLIOGRAPHIES

410 **Peddie, Robert Alexander.** Fifteenth century books; a guide to their identification . . . and an extensive bibliography of the subject. London, Grafton, 1913. 89p. 18cm.
'Catalogues of collections of incunabula' (p.53–89).

411 **Besterman, Theodore Deodatus Nathaniel.** Early printed books to the end of the sixteenth century; a bibliography of bibliographies. London, B. Quaritch [1940]. 309p. 23cm.

412 —— [Same]: 2d ed., rev. and much enl. Genève, Societas bibliographica, 1961. 344p. 23cm.
Rev: Sir F. C. Francis Library ser4 22:91–7 '41; J. B. Childs Pa Bib Soc Am 56:121–3 '62.

BOOKS—1475–1500

415 **Copinger, Walter Arthur.** Supplement to Hain's Repertorium bibliographicum. Or, Collections towards a new edition of that work . . . London, H. Sotheran, 1895–1902. 2v. in 3. 24cm.
Includes Burger's Index.

416 —— [Same]: Berlin, J. Altmann, 1926.

417 —— [Same]: Milano, Görlich [1950]. 2 pts. in 3v. 22cm.

418 **Proctor, Robert George Collier.** An index to the early printed books in the British museum from the invention of printing to the year 1500. . . . With notes on those in the Bodleian library. London, K. Paul, Trench, Trübner, 1898–1903; B. Quaritch, 1938. 4v. facsims. 29cm.
See also no.462.

419 —— [Same]: Supplements [1898–1902] London, Ptd. at the Chiswick pr., 1900–3. 5pts. 26cm.

420 —— Register to the four Supplements . . . by Konrad Burger. [London, Ptd. at the Chiswick pr., 1906] (Repr. London, 1960). 15p. 26cm.

421 **Bristol. Public libraries.** Early printed books and manuscripts in the city reference library, by Norris Mathews. . . . Bristol, Ptd. for the Libraries committee by W. C. Hemmons, 1899. xiii,84p. illus., facsims. 25cm.
Incunabula (p.1–10); later books, to 1628, principally foreign.

423 **Bennett, Richard.** A catalogue of the early printed books and illuminated manuscripts collected by Richard Bennett. [Guildford, Billings, ptr.] 1900. ii,55p. 25cm.
Author checklist; various indexes. *See* no.427.

424 **St. Bride foundation institute,** LONDON. **Technical reference library.** List of early printed books. London, 1904. [4]p. 25cm.
Checklist of about 100 items in Proctor order, comp. by Robert A. Peddie.

425 **Dublin. University. Trinity college. Library.** Catalogue of fifteenth-century books in the library of Trinity college, Dublin, and in Marsh's library, Dublin, with a few from other collections. By T. K. Abbott. . . . Dublin, Hodges, Figgis, 1905. vi,225p. 11pl. (part col.) 23cm.

Short-title author catalogue of 606 items, with bibliogr. notes and refs.; indexes.

Rev: Library ser2 7:105–6 '06.

426 **Minns, Ellis Hovell,** *comp.* 'Early printed books to the year 1500' *in* Cambridge. University. Pembroke college. Library. A descriptive catalogue of the manuscripts in the library . . . by Montague Rhodes James. . . . Cambridge, 1905. p.281–99.

Short-title catalogue of 110 items in Proctor order, with bibliogr. refs.; author index.

427 **Morgan, John Pierpont.** Catalogue of manuscripts and early printed books from the libraries of William Morris, Richard Bennett, Bertram fourth earl of Ashburnham, and other sources, now forming portion of the library of J. Pierpont Morgan. London, Chiswick pr., 1906–7. 4v. facsims. (part col.) 39cm.

Contents: 1. Manuscripts.—2. Early printed books. Xylographica, Germany and Switzerland.—3. Italy and part of France.—4. France (cont.), the Netherlands, Spain, & England [and Indexes].

The English incunabula were catalogued by Edward G. Duff, the Horae by Alfred W. Pollard, the general ed.

428 **Society of writers to H.M. Signet,** EDINBURGH. **Library.** Catalogue of early printed books in the library. Edinburgh, Ptd. by T. and A. Constable, 1906. x,27p. 29cm.

Short-title catalogue in Proctor order, comp. by John P. Edmond, with bibliogr. refs. and indexes.

429 **John Rylands library,** MANCHESTER. . . . Catalogue of the selection of books and broadsides illustrating the early history of printing, exhibited on the occasion of the visit of the Federation of master printers and allied trades. . . . Manchester, Ptd. by order of the governors, 1907. v,34p. 22cm.

Annotated exhibition catalogue.

430 **Stanford, sir Charles Thomas-.** Catalogue of a loan collection of early printed books, the property of C. Thomas-Stanford. [Brighton, 1907] 46p. illus., facsims. 22cm.

Catalogue of 101 items in Proctor order.

431 **British museum. Dept. of printed books.** Catalogue of books printed in the XVth century now in the British museum. London, Ptd. by the trustees, 1908– . v. facsims. 36cm.

Early parts cover foreign incunabula; British part yet to appear. Repr. lithographically, London, 1963—.

432 **Cambridge. University. King's college. Library.** A list of the incunabula in the library of King's college, Cambridge. Cambridge, C.U.P., 1908. iv,80p. 28cm.

Short-title catalogue of 198 items in Proctor order, with bibliogr. notes and refs.; ed. by George Chawner, with indexes of printers, publishers, authors, ex libris, and biographical notices of donors.

433 **Cambridge. University. Trinity hall. Library.** Early printed books to the
year 1500 in the library of Trinity hall, Cambridge. Cambridge, C.U.P.,
1909. 7p. 28cm. Covertitle.

Short-title catalogue of 28 items in Proctor order, with bibliogr. refs.

434 **Peddie, Robert Alexander.** Fifteenth century books, an author index. Lib
World new ser 11:43–53, 82–90, 144–52, 166–74, 209–17, 267–71, 288–300,
335–43, 374–82, 427–35, 454–62 Ag '08–Je '09; 12:10–18, 66–74, 101–9,
143–51, 192–200, 236–40, 280–92, 324–32, 364–72, 436–44, 472–6 Jl '09–Je
'10.

A–Cicero only; *see* no. 436.

435 **Cambridge. University. Queens' college. Library.** Early printed books to the
year 1500 in the library of Queens' college, Cambridge. Cambridge, C.U.P.,
1910. 8p. 27cm. Covertitle.

Short-title catalogue of 30 items in Proctor order, with bibliogr. refs.; comp. by Francis
G. Plaistowe.

436 **Peddie, Robert Alexander.** Conspectus incunabulorum; an index catalogue
of fifteenth century books. . . . London, Libraco, 1910–14. 2v. 25cm.

Contents: pt1. A–B.—pt2. C–G, incomplete.

Authors and ed. according to Hain with refs. to bibliogrs. in which descriptions and
facsims. given; partly repr. from Lib World: *see* no. 434.

437 **Worcester. Cathedral. Library.** Worcester cathedral library incunabula.
[Cambridge, C.U.P., 1910.] 8p. 21cm.

Checklist of 35 items in Proctor order, comp. by Cosmo Gordon, with bibliogr. refs.;
no index.

438 **Cambridge. University. Emmanuel college. Library.** Early printed books to
the year 1500 in the library. . . . Cambridge, C.U.P., 1911. 14p. 26cm.
Covertitle.

439 —— [Same]: Addenda. 1913. 4p. 26cm.

Short-title catalogue in Proctor order with bibliogr. refs., comp. by Philip W. Wood.

440 **Cambridge. University. St. Catherine's college. Library.** Early printed books
in the library of st. Catherine's college, Cambridge. Cambridge, C.U.P.,
1911. vi,38p. illus. 28cm.

Catalogue of 75 items in Proctor order with bibliogr. notes and refs. with indexes of
authors, printers, artists, binders, and biographical notices of donors; comp. by J. D.
Bilderbeck.

Rev: M. Radin Lib J 38:234–5 '13.

441 **Cambridge. University. St. John's college. Library.** Incunabula. . . . Cambridge, 1911. 17p. 21cm.

Short-title catalogue of 265 items in Proctor order, comp. by E. W. Lockhart and Charles
E. Sayle; repr. from the Eagle Mag., 1910.

442 **Edinburgh. Bibliographical society.** Lists of fifteenth century books in
Edinburgh libraries, by members of the Edinburgh bibliographical society.
Edinburgh, 1913. viii,107p. 25cm.

Contents: (9pt2) University library, by Frank C. Nicholson.—Advocate's library, by

William K. Dickson and miss J. M. G. Barclay.—Signet library, by John P. Edmond.—
United free church college library, by William Cowan.—(9pt3) The Crawford library,
Royal observatory, by George P. Johnston.—Library of the royal college of physicians,
by T. H. Graham.—St. Mary's cathedral library.—The Scottish episcopal church theo-
logical hall.—The Forbes library in the Theological hall.—The library of the Church of
Scotland.—The public library.—Additions to Advocate's library list.—Corrigenda.—
Index.

Numbered checklists in Proctor order, with bibliogr. refs. Repr. from Edinburgh Bib
Soc Pa 9:91–203 Ag/Oc '12/13.

443 **Cambridge. University. Peterhouse. Library.** Early printed books to the
year 1500 in the library of Peterhouse, Cambridge. Cambridge, C.U.P.,
1914. 10p. 26cm. Covertitle.

Checklist of 54 items in Proctor order with bibliogr. refs., and some bibliogr. notes;
comp. by C. G. (Cosmo Gordon?).

444 **Cambridge. University. Fitzwilliam museum.** Catalogue of the early printed
books bequeathed to the Museum by Frank McLean, by C. E. Sayle.
Cambridge, C.U.P., 1916. xx,173p. illus., facsims. 28cm.

Short-title catalogue of 338 items in Proctor order, with bibliogr. notes and refs.; 'List
of illustrated books' (p.139–42); 'Fifteenth century books from sources other than the
McLean bequest' (p.107–38).

Rev: Athenæum Je '17 : 301.

445 **Duff, Edward Gordon.** Fifteenth century English books; a bibliography of
books and documents printed in England and of books for the English
market printed abroad. London, Ptd. for the Bibliographical society at
the O.U.P., 1917. (Repr. Oxford, Clarendon pr., 1965) ix,136p. facsims.
29cm.

Short-title author checklist of 431 entries, with 'Typographical index' (p.125–36), collations, and locations of copies.

Rev: J. P. R. Lyell Lib World 20:176–7 '18.

446 **Stocks, E. V.** Incunabula. Durham Univ J new ser 21 : 472–4 Je '18; 22 : 21–3
D '18; 22 : 57–9 Ap '19.

Checklist of 258 items in Proctor order; includes books at Durham cathedral, Cosin's
library, St. Oswald's vicarage, and H. S. Squance's collection.

447 **Bibliographical society of America.** Census of fifteenth century books owned
in America; compiled by a committee of the Bibliographical society of
America. New York, 1919. xxiv,245p. 28cm.

Repr. with additions from N.Y. Pub. Lib Bull 1918–19.

Introduction signed by George P. Winship; later ed. by M. B. Stillwell, 1940: no. 463, and
F. R. Goff, 1964: no. 483.

448 **Cambridge. University. Clare college. Library.** Early printed books . . . in
the library of Clare college library, Cambridge. Cambridge, C.U.P., 1919.
8p. 27cm. Covertitle.

Short-title catalogue of 35 items in Proctor order, with bibliogr. refs.

449 **Oxford. University. Oriel college. Library.** [Incunabula. . . . Oxford, 1919.]
4p. 21cm.

Short-title checklist of 34 items, with bibliogr. refs., comp. by W. D. Ross.

450 **Gaselee, sir Stephen.** A list of the early printed books in the possession of Stephen Gaselee. Cambridge, C.U.P., 1920. 40p. illus. 27cm.

Checklist of 300 items in Proctor order, with bibliogr. refs.

451 **Cambridge. University. Corpus Christi college. Library.** The early printed books in the library of Corpus Christi college, Cambridge; a hand-list arranged in order of country, town & press, with short references to Proctor's Index and other bibliographical works, comp. by Stephen Gaselee. Cambridge, C.U.P., 1921. 38p. 27cm.

296 entries.

Rev: Library ser4 3:61–2 '22.

452 **Cambridge. University. Sidney Sussex college. Library.** Early printed books to the year 1500 in the library of Sidney Sussex college, Cambridge. Cambridge, C.U.P., 1922. 8p. 27cm. Covertitle.

Short-title catalogue of 36 items in Proctor order, with bibliogr. refs.

453 **Dunn, George.** A list of the incunabula collected by George Dunn, arranged to illustrate the history of printing, by Francis Jenkinson. [Oxford] Ptd. at the O.U.P. for the Bibliographical society, 1923. xx,83p. 23cm.

Checklist of 1,358 items in Proctor order, with bibliogr. refs.

454 **Aberdeen. University. Library.** A list of fifteenth century books in the university library of Aberdeen. [Aberdeen] Ptd. for the University of Aberdeen, 1925. vii,85p. facsims. 26cm.

455 —— **[Same]**: [Edinburgh] Ptd. for the Edinburgh bibliographical society, 1925.

Repr. from Aberdeen Univ Lib Bull 5:381–418, 509–48 '23–5. Checklist of 200 items in Proctor order, ed. by Ethel M. Barnett.

456 **Lincoln. Cathedral. Library.** Incunabula in the Lincoln cathedral library. Lincoln, 1925. 12p. 22cm.

Checklist of 97 items in Proctor order, with bibliogr. refs. and author index; comp. by James Bell and W. H. Kynaston.

457 **Cambridge. University. Gonville and Caius college. Library.** A descriptive catalogue of the incunabula in the library . . . comp. by G. A. Schneider. Cambridge, C.U.P., 1928. iv,45 [2]p. 27cm.

Catalogue of 101 items in Proctor order.

458 **John Rylands library, Manchester.** English incunabula in the John Rylands library; a catalogue of books printed in England and of English books printed abroad between the years 1475 and 1500, with chronological index, index of printers and stationers, subject index and sixteen facsimiles. Manchester, Manchester U.P., 1930. xv,102p. facsims. 31cm.

Alphabetical catalogue with TP transcrs., collations, and bibliogr. notes and refs.

Rev: TLS 26 Mr '31:248; A. W. P[ollard] Library ser4 11:511–12 '31.

459 **Milltown Park college, Dublin. Library.** A catalogue of the incunabula in the library at Milltown park, Dublin, by Paul Grosjean and Daniel O'Connell. Dublin, At the sign of the three candles, 1932. xii,53p. 24cm.

Collection of 177 items bequeathed by William O'Brien, in Gesamtkatalog order, with indexes.

460 **John Rylands library,** MANCHESTER. Descriptive catalogue of an exhibition of printed book illustrations of the fifteenth century. . . . Manchester, Manchester U.P., 1933. ix,90p. facsims. 27cm.

Ed. by Henry Guppy.

461 **Cambridge. University. Selwyn college. Library.** List of incunabula. . . . [Cambridge, 1934.] 8p. 27cm.

Checklist of 35 items, with Hain and Proctor numbers, comp. by Charles W. Phillips.

462 **Isaac, Frank Swinton.** An index to the early printed books in the British museum. Part II. MDI–MDXX. Section II. Italy. Section III. Switzerland and eastern Europe. London, B. Quaritch, 1938. xv,286p. 28cm.

Continuation of Proctor's Index; no. 418.

463 **Bibliographical society of America.** Incunabula in American libraries; a second census of fifteenth-century books owned in the United States, Mexico, and Canada, edited by Margaret Bingham Stillwell. New York, 1940. xlv,619p. 25cm.

Latest ed. by Frederick R. Goff, 1964: no. 483.

464 **Wales. National library,** ABERYSTWYTH. Hand-list of incunabula in the National library of Wales, comp. by Victor Scholderer. [Aberystwyth, Ptd. at the private pr. of the National library of Wales] 1940. viii,44p. facsims. 25cm. (Nat Lib Wales J Supplement ser1, no1.)

Short-title catalogue of 120 items in Proctor order, with bibliogr. notes and refs.

465 —— [**Same**]: Addenda & corrigenda 1 [Aberystwyth] 1941. 10p. facsims. 25cm. (Nat Lib Wales J Supplement ser1, no2.)

466 **Beattie, William.** Supplement to the Hand-list of incunabula in the National library of Scotland. Edinburgh Bib Soc Trans 11pt3:153–230 '44.

Annotated checklist of 326 items in Proctor order, with bibliogr. refs.; with chronol. index, and author and title index, to the whole collection, and 11 facsims.

467 —— [**Same**]: Second supplement. *ib.* 2pt4:331–44 '46.

Adds 26 items, with 4 facsims.

468 **Liverpool. University. Library.** Hand-list of incunabula in the University library, Liverpool, by David I. Masson. Liverpool, Privately ptd., 1949. 46p. 25cm.

Alphabetical checklist of 230 items, with index of printers and places; includes the Rylands bequest of 77 items.

469 —— [**Same**]: First supplement. [Liverpool] 1955. 8p. 25cm. (Duplicated typescript.)

Rev: D. A. Clarke Library ser5 5:152–3 '50.

470 **Gore, William George A. Ormsby-, 4th baron Harlech.** Incunabula at Brogyntyn. Nat Lib Wales J 6no4:329–37 '50.

471 **Morgan, Frederick Charles.** 'Appendix' [of early printed books] *in* Hereford cathedral library, including the chained library; its history and contents. Hereford, 1952. p.16–29.

See no. 481a.

472 **Cambridge. University. Library.** A catalogue of the fifteenth century printed books in the University library, Cambridge, comp. by J. C. T. Oates. Cambridge, C.U.P., 1954. xii,898p. illus., facsims., plan. 27cm.

Short-title catalogue of 4,227 entries in Proctor order ('England': nos. 4059–215) with bibliogr. notes and refs.

Rev: C. F. Buhler Pa Bib Soc Am 49 : 82–4 '55; TLS 4 F '55 : 80; N&Q 191 : 228–9 '55; W. White Bull Bib 21 : 128 '55; L. A. Sheppard Library ser5 10 : 218–22 '55; G. D. Painter Bk Coll 4 : 51–7 '55.

472a **Ramage, David** and **A. I. H. Doyle.** New incunabula. Durham Philobib 1:63–4 Mr '54.

Alphabetical checklist of 12 items with bibliogr. refs.

473 **Doyle, Anthony Ian H.** Early printed tracts. Durham Philobib 1:66–9 Mr '54.

Checklist of 15 early English books, some printed by de Worde, with bibliogr. notes and refs.

474 **Wellcome historical medical library,** LONDON. A catalogue of incunabula . . . [comp. by] F. N. L. Poynter. London, Published for the Wellcome historical medical museum by G. Cumberlege, O.U.P., 1954. xiv,159p. illus., facsims. 26cm.

Short-title author catalogue of 610 items, with bibliogr. notes and refs., indexes, and concordances of Osler and Klebs numbers.

475 **St. Andrews. University. Library.** Catalogue of incunabula. [St. Andrews?] University court of the University of St. Andrews, 1956. 101p. illus., facsims. 26cm.

Classified catalogue of 138 items, with bibliogr. notes and refs., and indexes; comp. by mrs. A. G. Scott.

Rev: G. D. Painter Bk Coll 6 : 302–5 '57.

475a **Morgan, Frederick Charles.** 'List of incunabula in the Vicars choral library' *in* Hereford cathedral: the Vicars choral library. Hereford, 1958. p.[32]

Alphabetical short-title catalogue of 6 items, with bibliogr. refs.

476 **Painter, George Duncan.** List of books acquired by the British museum from Chatsworth. Part 1: incunabula. Bk Coll 7n04:401–6 '58.

Author checklist with some bibliogr. notes and refs.

477 **[Hall, A. H.** and **W. Kellaway]** Fifteenth-century printed books in the Guildhall library. Guildhall Misc 1n010:63–75 S '59.

Short-title catalogue of 85 items in Proctor order, with bibliogr. notes and refs.; indexes.

Rev: G. D. Painter Bk Coll 9 : 219–20 '60.

478 **Donaldson, Robert.** Nine incunabula in the Cathcart White collection in the Edinburgh university library. Biblioth 2n02:66–9 '60.

Alphabetical catalogue with bibliogr. notes and refs.

479 **Birmingham. Public libraries.** Centenary exhibition of important acquisitions to the Reference library, 1861–1961, in the City art gallery. Birmingham, 1961. 32p. 20cm.

Checklist of 159 items including 24 incunables, and early Shakespeariana.

480 **Brighton. Public libraries.** Catalogue of manuscripts and printed books before 1500. Brighton, Royal pavilion, museums, and libraries committee, 1962. 22p. facsims. 24cm.

Annotated catalogue of 32 incunabula, most formerly in the collection of Leonard L. Bloomfield, with bibliogr. refs.; comp. by A. W. Ball.

Rev: Pa Bib Soc Am 60: 135 '66.

481 **Clark, Lilian G.** Collectors and owners of incunabula in the British museum; index of provenances for books printed in France, Holland and Belgium. Bath, Harding & Curtis, 1962. 75p. 20cm.

Rev: A. N. L. Munby Bk Coll 11: 494, 497 '62.

481a **Morgan, Frederick Charles.** [Appendix of early printed books] *in* Hereford cathedral library. . . . 3d ed., rev. [Hereford] 1963. p.18–31. (First pub. 1952)

482 **London. University.** Incunabula in the libraries of the University of London, a handlist. London, 1963 [i.e. 1964] iii,40p. 25cm.

Author list of 291 items in 328 copies held by 12 libraries, with bibliogr. refs., and index of printers and places; comp. by Margery F. Wild.

Rev: TLS 4 Je '64: 498; L. S. Thompson Pa Bib Soc Am 58: 205 '64.

483 **Bibliographical society of America.** Incunabula in American libraries, a third census of fifteenth century books recorded in North American collections, compiled and edited by Frederick R. Goff. New York, 1964. lxiii, 798p. 26cm.

Author list, with bibliogr. refs., of 12,599 ed., with index of printers and publishers, and concordances; 'Addenda' (p.795–8).

Rev: G. D. Painter Bk Coll 14: 373–4, 377 '65; TLS 7 Oc '65: 908; V.'Scholderer Library ser5 20: 247–9 '65.

484 **Rattey, Clifford C.** Catalogue of the library at Corbyns, Torquay, formed by Clifford C. Rattey. Block printing and incunabula. [Leamington Spa, Courier pr.] 1965. 56p. 24cm.

193 items in Proctor order, with bibliogr. notes and refs.

BOOKS—1475–1640

490 **[Craig, Hardin]** *comp.* 'Bibliographies . . .' *in* Bateson, Frederick W., *ed.* Cambridge bibliography of English literature. Cambridge, 1940–57. V.1, p.317–19.

491 **British museum. Dept. of printed books.** Catalogue of books in the library of the British museum printed in England, Scotland, and Ireland, and of books in English printed abroad, to the year 1640. . . . London, By order of the trustees, 1884. 3v. 24cm.

Alphabetical short-title catalogue, comp. by George Bullen and G. W. Eccles; title index (v.3, p.[1647]–1734), and index of printers, publishers and stationers.

492 **Cambridge. University. Trinity college. Library.** A catalogue of the English books printed before MDCI, now in the library of Trinity college, Cambridge, by Robert Sinker. Cambridge, Deighton, Bell, 1885. xii,488p. 23cm.

Arranged by place of publication and printer, with indexes of towns, printers, and books; short-title catalogue of 1,107 entries, with bibliogr. notes.

493 **Lampson, Frederick Locker-.** The Rowfant library; a catalogue of the printed books, manuscripts, autograph letters. . . . London, B. Quaritch, 1886. 232p. illus. 25cm.

Ed. by Alfred W. Pollard and R. H. Lister.

Pt.1. 1480–1700; alphabetical order by title under author.—Pt.2. 1700–1880; chronol. by date of first ed. under author. TP transcrs. with collations and some bibliogr. notes; no index. The collection was bought by E. D. Church, but later placed on the market and divided amongst R. Hoe, W. A. White, B. Chew, F. R. Halsey, H. E. Widener, and W. H. Hagen.

494 —— **[Same]:** An appendix. A catalogue of the printed books collected since . . . 1886. London, Chiswick pr., 1900. xvi,181p. illus. 26cm.

Author catalogue in three parts, English books to 1700, and after 1700, and foreign books; TP transcrs., collations and bibliogr. notes.

495 **Grolier club,** NEW YORK. A brief hand-list of original and earlier editions of some of the poetical and prose works of English writers from Langland to Wither, exhibited. . . . New York, 1893. 37p. 18cm.

See next item.

496 —— Catalogue of original and early editions of some of the poetical and prose works of English writers from Langland to Wither. . . . New York, 1893. (Repr. London, Holland pr., 1964) xiii,240p. illus., facsims. 25cm.

Descriptive catalogue of 272 items from the libraries of Grolier club members, arranged chronol. under authors, with extensive facsims.; no index.

Rev: Library 5:228 '93.

497 **London. Stationers' company.** A transcript of the registers of the Company of stationers of London, 1554–1640; ed. by Edward Arber. London, Privately ptd., 1875–7; Birmingham, 1894.

See no.568.

498 **John Rylands library,** MANCHESTER. Catalogue of books in the John Rylands library, Manchester, printed in England, Scotland and Ireland, and of books

in English printed abroad to the end of the year 1640. Manchester, J. E. Cornish, 1895. iii,147p. 30cm.

Author short-title catalogue, with entries arranged again under names of printers, ed. by Edward G. Duff.

499 **Liverpool. University. Library.** In memoriam Thomas Glazebrook Rylands; a catalogue of the books bequeathed . . . to the library of University college, Liverpool; compiled by John Sampson. [Liverpool] Liverpool U.P., 1900. ix,113p. 23cm.

'Early printed books', 1454–1536 (p. 20–37); short-title catalogue of 159 items, in Proctor order, with bibliogr. refs.

500 **Cambridge. University. Library.** Early English printed books in the University library, Cambridge, 1475 to 1640. Cambridge, C.U.P., 1900–7. 4v. 23cm.

Short-title list of 7,750 items arranged chronol. by printer, with indexes, including portraits, engravers, and 'bibliographica' in v.4; comp. by Charles E. Sayle.

501 —— [**Same**]: Appendix to volume III. Cambridge, C.U.P., 1907. p.1745–1804. 20cm.

502 **St. Edmund's college,** WARE. **Old hall library.** Catalogue of books in the libraries at st. Edmund's college, Old hall, printed in England, and of books written by Englishmen printed abroad to the year 1640. Compiled by Edwin Burton. Ware, Ptd. by Jennings & Bowley, 1902. v,94p. 22cm.

Chronol. catalogue of 235 entries, with index, including many books printed at foreign presses or secretly in England.

503 **Winchester. Cathedral.** Early printed books, 1479–1640. [Winchester, 1902] 28p. 23cm.

'Incunabula' (p.1); 'Early English books printed up to 1640' (p.2–9); short-title catalogue comp. by Francis T. Madge.

504 **Cambridge. University. Trinity college. Library.** Catalogue of the books presented by Edward Capell to the library . . . compiled by W. W. Greg. Cambridge, Ptd. for Trinity college at C.U.P., 1903. viii,172p. 20 cm.

Author catalogue, with TP transcrs., collations, and bibliogr. notes.

505 **Sheffield. University. Library.** Early-printed books in the library . . . English to 1640, foreign to 1600. Compiled by G. C. Moore Smith. . . . [Cambridge, C.U.P., 1909] 32p. 23cm.

Chronol. short-title catalogue of 191 English books to 1641, and 4 incunables.

506 **Oxford. University. Hertford college. Library.** Catalogue of books in the library . . . printed in the 15th and 16th centuries. Oxford, Ptd. for the librarian by Parker, 1910. 16p. 22cm.

Alphabetical short-title catalogue.

507 [**Pollard, Alfred William**] *comp.* 'Printed books' *in* British museum. Catalogue of the fifty manuscripts & printed books bequeathed to the British museum by Alfred H. Huth. London, 1912. p.21–32.

Alphabetical catalogue of 37 items, with full descriptions and TP facsims.; 'Index to printed books' (p.124–6).

508 **Bibliographical society, London.** Hand-lists of books printed by London printers, 1501–1556. By E. G. Duff, W. W. Greg, R. B. McKerrow, H. R. Plomer, A. W. Pollard, R. Proctor. London, Ptd. by Blades, East & Blades for the Bibliographical society, 1913. 4pts. in IV. illus., plates, facsims. 23cm.

Issued in parts, 1895–1913, each part with temporary TP: Hand-lists of English printers, 1501–1556.

510 **Duff, Edward Gordon,** *comp.* 'Early printed books to 1558' *in* [Tanner, Joseph R., and others] Bibliotheca Pepysiana, a descriptive catalogue. London, 1914–40. Pt.II (1914), p.1–82.

Author catalogue with TP transcrs., collations, and bibliogr. notes.

511 **White, William Augustus.** Hand-list of early English books, mostly of the Elizabethan period, collected by W. A. White, Brooklyn, N.Y.; digested from card catalogue made by miss Henrietta Bartlett. [New York, 1914.] 51p. 24cm.

See no. 525.

512 **Cambridge. University. Emmanuel college. Library.** A hand-list of English books in the library . . . printed before MDCXLI. [Cambridge] Ptd. for the Bibliographical society at C.U.P., 1915. viii,182p. 23cm.

Alphabetical checklist, with indexes, comp. by Philip W. Wood and G. H. Watts.

513 **Bonnard, Georges Alfred.** [Bibliography] *in* La contraverse de Martin Marprelate, 1588–1590. . . . Genève, 1916. p.[215]–37.

Chronol. checklist of 16 items, with locations of copies.

514 **Henry E. Huntington library and art gallery,** SAN MARINO, CALIF. Checklist or brief catalogue of the library of Henry E. Huntington; English literature to 1640. Compiled [by Philip S. Goulding] under the direction of George Watson Cole. New York, Privately ptd., 1919. 482p. 27cm.

515 —— [**Same**]: Additions and corrections, July, 1919–June, 1920. New York, Privately ptd., 1920. p.461–570. 26cm.

516 **Newberry library,** CHICAGO. Check list of books printed in English before 1641, compiled by Mae I. Stearns. Chicago, 1923. ix,198p. 26cm.

Author checklist, with 'Index of printers, booksellers, and stationers' (p.187–98).

517 **Clawson, John Lewis.** A catalogue of early English books in the library of John L. Clawson, by Seymour De Ricci. Philadelphia, Rosenbach, 1924. xvi,348p. facsims. 28cm.

Alphabetical catalogue of 926 items, with extensive TP facsims.

518 —— The splendid Elizabethan & early Stuart library of mr. John L. Clawson. . . . New York, Anderson galleries [1926] 2v. in 1. port., facsims. 28cm.

Sale catalogue based on De Ricci's catalogue.

Rev: I. A. Williams Lond Merc 10:639–40 '24; G. H. Sargent Bkmns J 11:21–4 '24.

519 **Harmsworth, sir Robert Leicester.** A short title catalogue of the printed books in the library of sir R. L. Harmsworth to the year 1640. [Bath] Ptd. for private circulation only, 1925. 372p. 27cm.

Alphabetical checklist, with notes of provenance, of collection now in Folger Shakespeare library.

520 **Haskell, Daniel Carl.** Check-list of early English printing, 1475–1640, in the New York public library. N.Y. Pub Lib Bull 29:484–512, 545–78 Jl, Ag '25.

Alphabetical checklist.

521 **Pollard, Alfred William** and **G. R. Redgrave.** A short-title catalogue of books printed in England, Scotland, & Ireland and of English books printed abroad, 1475–1640. Compiled by A. W. Pollard & G. R. Redgrave [and others] London, Bibliographical society, 1926. xvi,609p. 29cm.

522 —— [Same]: London, Ptd. by arrangement with the Bibliographical society for B. Quaritch, 1926. (Repr. lithographically in 1946, 1950, 1956, 1964.)

523 —— **Morrison, Paul Guerrant,** *comp.* Index of printers, publishers, and booksellers in A. W. Pollard and G. R. Redgrave, 'A short-title catalogue . . .'. Charlottesville, Bibliographical society of the University of Virginia; London, B. Quaritch, 1950. 82p. 27cm.

524 —— [Same]: 2d impression offset from the Secretary's copy, with a few corrections. Charlottesville, Va., Bibliographical society of the University of Virginia, 1961.

Rev: R. B. McK[errow] R Eng Stud 3:494–6 '27; TLS 7 Ap '27:247.

525 **White, William Augustus.** Catalogue of early English books, chiefly of the Elizabethan period, collected by William Augustus White and catalogued by Henrietta C. Bartlett. New York, Privately ptd., 1926. 170p. fold.facsim. 25cm.

Alphabetical short-title catalogue, with collations and bibliogr. notes, superseding the Hand-list of 1914.
Rev: TLS 16 S '26:620.

526 **Leach, Howard Seavoy.** Short-title catalogue of English books before 1640. Lib J 52:815–16 S '27.

Review containing list of Lehigh university library holdings and addenda; superseded by Bishop, no.539.

527 **Oxford. University. Magdalen college. Library.** Magdalen college library; with a list of books printed before 1641, not in the Bodleian library. Oxford Bib Soc Proc 2pt3:145–200 '29.

'List of books printed before 1641' (p.151–200).

528 **Oxford. University. Wadham college. Library.** A short catalogue of books printed in England and English books printed abroad before 1641 in the library . . . compiled by H. A. Wheeler, 1918. London, Longmans, Green, 1929. xv,101p. 23cm.

Short-title author catalogue.
Rev: R. B. McKerrow R Eng Stud 6:488–9 '30.

529 **Smith, David Baird,** *comp*. 'Topographical index of books printed before 1600' *in* Glasgow. University. Hunterian museum. Library. The printed books in the library of the Hunterian museum. . . . Glasgow, 1930. p.[vii]–xx.

The general collection is predominantly foreign; includes 534 incunabula.

530 **Leeds. University. Brotherton library.** The Brotherton library; a catalogue of ancient manuscripts and early printed books, collected by Edward Allen, baron Brotherton of Wakefield, compiled by John Alexander Symington. Leeds, Ptd. for private circulation, 1931. xv,300p. illus.(1 col.) 30cm.

Bibliogr. catalogue with facsims., and 'Index of incunabula' (p.199–267); index of printers.
Rev: TLS 15 Oc '31 : 804.

530a **Farnham, Willard.** The progeny of A mirror for magistrates. Mod Philol 29:395–410 My '32.

Discursive checklist, 1574–1629.

531 **Edmonds, Cecil Kay.** Huntington library supplement to the record of its books in the Short title catalogue of English books, 1475–1640. Huntington Lib Bull 4:1–151 Oc '33.

Author catalogue, with TP transcrs., and collations; 'Descriptions of titles . . . not recorded in the Short title catalogue' (p.111–[52]).
Rev: A. W. P[ollard] Library ser4 15:253–6 '34.

532 **Victoria, Australia. Public library, museums and national gallery,** MELBOURNE. **Library.** A catalogue of English books and fragments from 1477 to 1535 in the Public library of Victoria; compiled by Albert Broadbent Foxcroft. Melbourne, Ptd. for the trustees, 1933. xi,72p. facsims. 25cm.

Chronol. catalogue under names of printers, with bibliogr. notes and refs.

533 **Newberry library,** CHICAGO. English books & books printed in England before 1641 in the Newberry library; a supplement to the record in the Short title catalogue. Compiled by Gertrude L. Woodward. Chicago, 1939. vii,118p. 25cm.

No index.

534 **Miller, Clarence William.** Early English books at the University of Virginia; a short-title catalogue. Charlottesville, Alderman library, 1941. 29p. 23cm.

Chronol. catalogue, 1534–1640, with STC numbers.

535 **Allison, Antony Francis.** Early English books at the London oratory; a supplement to S.T.C. Library ser5 2:95–107 S '47.

Quasifacsim. TP transcrs., collations, bibliogr. notes, and STC addenda.

536 **Bishop, William Warner.** A preliminary checklist of American copies of Short-title catalogue books. Ann Arbor, 1941. v,173p. 27cm. (Duplicated typescript.)

537 —— A checklist of American copies of Short-title catalogue books. Ann Arbor, University of Michigan pr., 1944. xvi,250p. 28cm. (Duplicated typescript.) *See* no.539.

538 **Cunliffe, Rolf, baron Cunliffe.** Catalogue of the . . . library . . . . The first portion, English books published before 1640, which will be sold by auction by messrs. Sotheby. . . . [London, 1946] 79p. facsims. 26cm.

539 **Bishop, William Warner.** A checklist of American copies of Short-title catalogue books. 2d ed. Ann Arbor, University of Michigan pr., 1950. xi, 203p. 28cm.

'Additions to the Short-title catalogue' (p.187–201); 'Appendix: polyglot dictionaries' (p.203).

Rev: E. E. Willoughby Lib Q 21:60–1 '51.

540 **Georgetown university,** WASHINGTON, D.C. **Library.** Early English books in the Georgetown university library; a checklist of the 1540–1640 period [by] John Alden. Washington, 1952. 6l. 28cm.

STC supplement, with large proportion of English books printed abroad.

541 **Haverford college.** William Pyle Philips collection in the Haverford college library; an introductory essay and a descriptive catalogue to his rare books. Haverford, 1952. viii,133p. facsims. 24cm.

Contents:—Books of the renaissance, by R. M. Sargent.—A descriptive catalogue of the William Pyle Philips collection, by C. W. Miller.

The catalogue appears also *in* William Pyle Philips, 1882–1950. . . . (1952). Descr. catalogue of 58 entries, with locations.

542 **Jackson, William Alexander.** 'The "Lincolne nosegay" books' *in* Antiquarian booksellers' association. Books and the man. London, 1953. p.25–30.

'Appendix . . . the present location of the Nosegay books' (p.30): locations and STC numbers.

543 **Bristol. Public libraries.** A catalogue of books in the Bristol reference library printed in England and Ireland up to the year 1640 and of English books printed abroad during the same period. Bristol, Corporation of Bristol, 1954. 51p. illus. 26cm.

Alphabetical checklist of 350 titles, including 51 STC addenda; no index.

Rev: TLS 3 S '54: 564; J. C. T. Oates Library ser5 9: 278 '54.

544 **Shakespeare's birthplace trust,** STRATFORD-UPON-AVON. **Library.** English books published between 1500 and 1640 with S.T.C. references. [Stratford-upon-Avon] 1955 [i.e., 1956]. 19l. 26cm. (Duplicated typescript.)

545 **Francis Bacon foundation,** PASADENA, CALIF. Short title catalogue numbers in the library . . . compiled by Elizabeth S. Wrigley. Pasadena, Calif., 1958. iv.(unpaged) 28cm.

Alphabetical catalogue, chiefly of Baconiana, with TP transcrs. and collations; no index.

546 **MacPhail, Ian Shaw.** A short list of Elizabethan books in the library. Trinity Coll Dublin Ann Bull 3–7 '58.

Author checklist with STC numbers.

547 **Ramage, David [and others].** A finding-list of English books to 1640 in libraries in the British Isles (excluding the national libraries and the libraries of Oxford and Cambridge) based on the numbers in Pollard & Redgrave's Short title catalogue. . . . Durham, Council of the Durham colleges, 1958. xiv,101p. 28cm.

'Supplement: list of books not found in STC' (p.93–101).

Rev: A. N. L. Munby Bk Coll 7: 199–200 '58; TLS 11 Jl '58: 400; P. C. Clements *ib.* 25 Jl '58: 423; E. R. Wood *ib.* 1 Ag '58: 435; R. H. Bryan Pa Bib Soc Am 53: 76–7 '59.

548 **Allison, Antony Francis.** List of books acquired by the British museum from Chatsworth. Part II. English books 1501–1640. Bk Coll 8no1: 52–8 '59.

Annotated author checklist.

549 **Brand, Pamela.** STC items in Auckland public library. N.Z. Libs 24: 58–65 Ap '61.

550 **Watson, A. G.** Two unrecorded items of 1603. Library ser5 16: 299–302 D '61.

Facsims and descr. of 2 penitential pieces ptd. by Simon Stafford, 1603.

551 **Williams, Franklin Burleigh.** Index of dedications and commendatory verses in English books before 1641. London, Bibliographical society, 1962. xxvii, 256p. 26cm.

Provides key to contributors of commendatory verses and recipients of dedications, and other material in preliminary leaves, such as epistles by editor, printer, or bookseller; arranged with STC refs., in sequences for personal names, institutional and geographical, anonymous and bibliographical.

Rev: J. Crow Bk Coll 12: 236, 239–40, 243 '63; J. C. Maxwell N&Q 209: 40 '64; A. Fowler R Eng Stud new ser 15: 84–5 '64; A. Holaday J Eng Germ Philol 63: 336–7 '64.

552 **Pirie, Robert S.** Books and manuscripts from the collection of mr. & mrs. Robert S. Pirie; a catalogue of an exhibition at the Grolier club, . . . 1963. [New York, Grolier club, 1963?] 11p. illus. 23cm.

Alphabetical catalogue of 39 items, with bibliogr. notes and refs.

553 **Mitchell library, GLASGOW.** Catalogue of incunables and S.T.C. books in the Mitchell library, Glasgow. Glasgow, Corporation public libraries, 1964. 131p. 24cm.

Author checklist of 44 incunabula, and 590 STC books, with some bibliogr. notes; comp. by Anthony G. Hepburn.

554 **Maunsell, Andrew.** The catalogue of English books, 1595. [London, Gregg pr.; Archive pr., 1965] iv.(various pagings) facsims. 27cm. (English bibliographical sources, ser2, no1.)

Ed. by David F. Foxon from the BM copy.

555 **Williams, Franklin Burleigh.** Photo-facsimiles of STC books; a cautionary check list. Stud Bib 21:109–30 '68.

'Check list of STC facsimiles' (p.120–30)

BOOKS—1475–1700

568 **London. Stationers' company.** A transcript of the registers of the Company of stationers of London, 1554–1640; edited by Edward Arber. London, Privately ptd., 1875–7; Birmingham, 1894. 5v. illus. 30cm. (Repr. [New York, P. Smith, 1950].)

569 —— **[Same]**: . . . from 1640–1708. [Transcribed by H. Plomer and edited by G. E. B. Eyre] London [Roxburghe club] 1913–14. 3v. 36cm. (Repr. [New York, P. Smith, 1950].)

Unlike Arber, Plomer and Eyre is not indexed.

570 **Hodgkin, John Eliot.** Rariora; being notes of some of the printed books, manuscripts, historical documents . . . collected, 1858–1900. . . . London, S. Low, Marston [1902] 3v. illus., port., facsims. 29cm.

Profusely illustrated, discursive catalogue of incunabula and 15th century proclamations (v.2), English broadsides, and books on fireworks (v.3); each section separately indexed. The collections were sold by Sotheby, Wilkinson, and Hodge, 12–19 May, 1914.

571 **Lefferts, Marshall Clifford.** Catalogue of a splendid collection of English literature, including the works of the chief Elizabethan, Jacobean and restoration authors, all from the library of mr. Marshall C. Lefferts. . . . To be sold at auction . . . Bangs & co. . . . [New York, D. Taylor, 1902]. 228p. 25cm.

Alphabetical checklist of 1,460 titles; note also A checklist of the library . . . New York, G. H. Richmond, 1901. 96p. 24cm.

572 **Hoe, Robert.** Catalogue of books by English authors who lived before the year 1700, forming a part of the library of Robert Hoe. New York [Gillis pr.] 1903–5. 5v. illus., facsims. 23cm.

Author catalogue, with collations and some bibliogr. notes, comp. by James O. Wright and Carolyn Shipman; 'Appendix': v.5, p.[167]–417.

573 **International association of antiquarian booksellers.** Catalogue of an exhibition of books . . . illustrative of the history and progress of printing and bookselling in England, 1477–1800; held at Stationers' hall. . . . [London, Ptd. by W. Clowes] 1912. vi,216p. 22cm.

Arranged by printer and publisher; 'Printed books': 1–1028; 'Broadsides, proclamations, &c.': 1029–1064.

574 **Clark, William Andrews.** The library of William Andrews Clark, jr. Early English literature, 1519–1700, collated and compiled by Robert Ernest Cowan and William Andrews Clark. San Francisco, Ptd. by J. H. Nash, 1920–5. 4v. 27cm.

Author catalogue, with TP transcs., collations, bibliogr. notes and refs.; every vol. runs A–Z; no index. The collection now forms part of the University of California's William A. Clark library.

575 **Gray, William Forbes.** Catalogue of the library of John Gray, Haddington; with introduction and descriptive notes. Haddington, Haddington town council, 1929. 96p. 22cm.

Classified catalogue, with some annotation, of 968 items.

576 **Allen, Don Cameron.** A short-title catalogue of English books prior to 1700 in the library of the State college of Washington. Res Stud State Coll Washington 5 : 109–26 Je '37.

577 **Pforzheimer, Carl Howard.** The Carl H. Pforzheimer library; English literature, 1475–1700. New York, Privately ptd., 1940. 3v.(xli,1305p.) illus., ports., facsims. 31cm.

Quasifacsim. TP transcrs., full collations, and copious bibliogr. notes, refs., and locations of copies; 1,105 items; indexes of anonyma, provenance, bibliographica; comp. by Emma V. Unger and William A. Jackson.

Rev: C. F. Bühler Library ser4 23 : 140–2 '42.

577a **Hagedorn, Ralph.** Bibliotheca Thordasoniana: the sequel. Pa Bib Soc Am 44 : 29–54 '50.

'Appendix. Short-title catalogue' (p.51–3); 'Wing' (p.53–4). The collection is now in Wisconsin university library.

578 **Alexander Turnbull library,** WELLINGTON, N.Z. Holdings of early English printed books to 1700. Wellington, 1958. 4,14,2l. 27cm. (Duplicated typescript.)

Superseded by no. 585.

579 **Cameron, William James.** John Dryden in New Zealand; . . . together with a list of English books in the University of Auckland printed before 1700. . . . Wellington, Library school, National library service, 1960. 31p. 22cm.

580 **Cameron, William James** and **P. Brand.** Books printed in England before 1700; a tentative check-list of STC and Wing items in st. John's college, Auckland. N.Z. Libs 23 : 201–8 S '60.

581 **Esplin, David Grant.** STC and Wing STC books in Dunedin. N.Z. Libs 23 : 229–32, 254–63, 292–4 Oc, N, D '60.

582 **Hill, Trevor Howard Howard-.** Early English printed books in the General assembly library. N.Z. Libs 24 : 92–7 My '61.

583 **Natal. University. Library.** A short-title list of books printed before the year 1701. Durban, 1961. 24 [i.e. 59] p. facsims. 25cm.

Alphabetical list of 115 items with extensive TP facsims.

Rev: D. H. Varley Sth Afric Lib 29 : 38–9 '61; TLS 10 N '61 : 812.

584 **Tolley, Cyril W.** Early English printed books in Wellington public library. N.Z. Libs 24 : 117–18 Je '61.

585 **Alexander Turnbull library,** WELLINGTON, N.Z. English printed books to 1700. Wellington, N.Z., 1963. 104p. 25cm. (Duplicated typescript.)

Short-title author catalogue with bibliogr. refs. and title index; comp. by T. H. Howard-Hill.

586 **Royal college of surgeons of England.** English books printed before 1701 in the library. . . . Edinburgh, Published for the College by E. & S. Livingstone, 1963. 27p. 22cm.

Short-title author catalogue of 637 ed., comp. by William R. LeFanu, with bibliogr. refs.; no index.

Rev: E. J. Freeman Med Hist 9 : 197–8 '65.

587 **Tallon, Maura.** Hereford cathedral library . . . and . . . All saints church chained library, Hereford. [Athlone, 1963] 78p. illus., facsims. 23cm.
Discursive classified checklists.
Rev: TLS 9 Ja '64 : 33.

588 **Gt. Brit. Foreign office. Library.** A short title catalogue of books printed before 1701 in the Foreign office library, compiled by Colin L. Robertson. London, H.M.S.O., 1966. ix,177p. 25cm. (Not seen.)

589 **Bennett, Henry Stanley.** The Syndics' library at the University press. Cambridge Bib Soc Trans 4pt3:253–6 '66.

590 **London. Guildhall library.** A list of books printed in the British Isles and of English books printed abroad before 1701 in Guildhall library. London, Corporation of London, 1966. 2pts. 28cm.
Comp. by Kathleen I. Garrett.
Rev: Pa Bib Soc Am 61 : 153 '67.

BOOKS—1641–1700

595 The **Term** catalogues, 1668–1709, A.D.; with a number for Easter term, 1711 A.D. A contemporary bibliography of English literature in the reigns of Charles II, James II, William and Mary, and Anne. Edited from the very rare quarterly lists of new books and reprints . . . issued by the booksellers, etc. of London, by Edward Arber. London, Privately ptd., 1903–6. 3v. 30cm.

Contents:—v.1. 1668–1682.—2. 1683–1696.—3. 1697–1709, and Easter term, 1711; text and index.

595a **Plomer, Henry Robert.** Secret printing during the civil war. Library ser2 5:374–403 Oc '04.

'Bibliography' (p.395–403): checklists of the Coleman street pr.; the Martin Mar-priest pr.; the Goodman's fields pr.; and William Larner's pr.

596 **Grolier club,** NEW YORK. Catalogue of original and early editions of some of the poetical and prose works of English writers from Wither to Prior. . . . New York, 1905. 3v. illus., facsims. 25cm.

Descr. catalogue of 1,088 items taken mainly from the libraries of Grolier club members, arranged chronol. by author, with extensive TP facsims., and indexes of printers and booksellers, and of engravers.

597 **Dobell, Percy John.** The literature of the restoration; being a collection of the poetical and dramatic literature produced between the years 1660 and 1700, with particular reference to the writings of John Dryden, described and annotated. London, 1918. 101p. facsims. 22cm.

Bookseller's catalogue of 1,287 classified entries; no index; the Drydeniana was acquired by the Folger Shakespeare library.

598 —— Books of the time of the restoration, being a collection of plays, poems and prose works produced between the years 1660 and 1700, by the contemporaries of John Dryden; described and annotated. [London, P. J. & A. E. Dobell] 1920. 56p. 21cm.

Alphabetical bookseller's catalogue of 627 entries.

599 **Gerould, James Thayer.** Sources of English history of the seventeenth century, 1603–1689 in the University of Minnesota library. . . . Minneapolis, University of Minnesota, 1921. iv,563p. 26cm.

Classified chronol. checklist of 3,845 items, with 'Secondary works': items 3846–4447.

600 **Drury, George Thorn-.** Catalogue of the very extensive . . . library of English poetry, drama and other literature, principally of the XVII and early XVIII centuries, formed by the late George Thorn-Drury . . . which will be sold . . . by Sotheby. . . . London, Ptd. by J. Davy [1931–2]. 4 pts.(175p.) facsims. 25cm.

3,114 items, including important Drydeniana.

601 **Wing, Donald Goddard.** Short-title catalogue of books printed in England, Scotland, Ireland, Wales, and British America, and of English books printed in other countries, 1641–1700. New York, Index society, 1945–51. 3v. 29cm.

602 —— **Morrison, Paul Guerrant,** *comp.* Index of printers, publishers, and booksellers. . . . Charlottesville, University pr. for the Bibliographical society of the University of Virginia, 1955. 217p. 29cm.

Rev: E. E. Willoughby Lib Q 16:247–50 '46; A. T. Hazen Philol Q 25:129–32 '46; K. J. Holzknecht Pa Bib Soc Am 40:314–16 '46; W. G. Hiscock TLS 11 D '48:697; C. P. Rollins Sat R 16 Ag '52:21; E. E. Willoughby Lib Q 20:144–5 '50; K. J. Holzknecht Pa Bib Soc Am 46:400–6 '52; TLS 14 N '52:752; S. Pargellis Coll & Res Libs 14:98–9 '52; J. C. T. Oates Library ser5 10:225–6 '55; W. White Bull Bib 21:152 '55; E. E. Willoughby Lib Q 25:261–2 '55; TLS 20 My '55:274; J. Gerritsen Eng Stud 37:90 '55; Bk Coll 4:81 '55.

603 **Pennsylvania. University. Library.** English books, 1641–1700, acquired 1 July 1948 – 30 June 1949. Philadelphia [1949?] 20l. 28cm. (Duplicated typescript.)

Author catalogue with bibliogr. refs.; comp. by John Alden.

604 **Alden, John Eliot.** Pills and publishing; some notes on the English book trade, 1660–1715. Library ser5 7:21–37 Mr '52.

Addenda to Plomer's Dictionaries and Wing, in a list of advertisements for medicines (p.22–30), with indexes.

605 **Fry, Mary Isabel** and **G. Davies.** Supplements to the Short-title catalogue, 1641–1700. Huntington Lib Q 16:393–436 Ag '53.

Wing addenda in the library of Godfrey Davies, and the Huntington, and William Andrews Clark, U.C.L.A., libraries.

606 **Oxford. University. Christ church. Library.** The Christ church holdings in Wing's Short-title catalogue, 1641–1700, of books of which less than 5 copies are recorded in the United Kingdom. [Oxford] 1956. 165l. 33cm. (Duplicated typescript.)

Comp. by Walter G. Hiscock.

Rev: H. M. Adams Bk Coll 6:76,79–80 '57.

607 —— The Christ church supplement to Wing's Short-title catalogue 1641–1700, by W. G. Hiscock. Oxford, Ptd. for Christ church at the Holywell pr., 1956. 47p. 29cm.

'Errata to Wing's Short-title catalogue' (p.37–47).

Rev: H. M. Adams Bk Coll 6:76,79–80 '57.

608 **Oxford. University. Bodleian library.** English literature in the seventeenth century; guide to an exhibition held in 1957. Oxford, 1957. 167p. illus. 22cm.

Copiously annotated catalogue of 234 items, comp. by John Buxton and D. G. Neill.

Rev: J. W. Library ser5 13:148 '57.

609 **Alden, John Eliot.** Wing addenda and corrigenda; some notes on materials in the British museum. Charlottesville, Va., University of Virginia bibliographical society, 1958. 19p. 27cm. (Duplicated typescript.)

610 **Bristol. Public libraries.** A catalogue of books in the Bristol reference library printed in England, Scotland and Ireland, and of English books printed abroad, 1641–1700. [Bristol] Corporation of Bristol, 1958. vi,208p. illus. 25cm.

Alphabetical short-title catalogue; no title index.

611 **Francis Bacon foundation,** PASADENA, CALIF. **Library.** Wing (Short title catalogue 1641–1700) numbers in the library . . . Compiled by Elizabeth S. Wrigley. Pasadena, Calif., 1959. 186l. 29cm.

Alphabetical catalogue, chiefly of Baconiana, with full TP transcrs. and collations; no index.

612 **Philadelphia. Library company.** A check-list of the books in the library company of Philadelphia, in and supplementary to Wing's Short-title catalogue, 1641–1700, by Edwin Wolf. Philadelphia, 1959. viii,106p. 27cm.

'Provenance index' (p.99–106).

Rev: H. W. Winger Pa Bib Soc Am 54: 213–14 '60; L. V. Given Pennsylvania Mag Hist & Biog 84: 397–8 '60; W. G. Hiscock Bk Coll 9: 220, 223 '60; TLS 27 My '60: 344; J. M. Patrick Sevent Cent News 19: 10–11 '61; T. R. Adams New Eng Q 34: 130–1 '61.

613 **National book league,** LONDON. Restoration life and letters; an exhibition. . . . [London, 1960] 44p. 21cm.

Classified short-title catalogue, with descriptive notes.

614 **Cameron, William James.** Wing items in Auckland public library. N.Z. Libs 24: 6–15 Ja/F '61.

615 —— A short-title catalogue of books printed in Britain and British books printed abroad, 1641–1700, held in Australian libraries. . . . Sydney, Wentworth pr., 1962. xxi,154p. 26cm. (Duplicated typescript.)

Rev: W. Kirsop Aust Lib J 11: 91–5 '62; D. E. Kennedy Hist Stud 10: 395–6 '62; D. H. Borchardt Biblio-news 15: 4–6 '62.

616 —— [Same]: Wing books held in Australian libraries; supplement no. 1. Aust Lib J 11: 153–62 Jl '62.

617 —— [Same]: Wing books held in Australian libraries. . . . Supplement no. 2. A–E. Aust Lib J 12: 209–16 D '63.

617a **Bibliotheca annua** [or The annual catalogue for the year 1699. London, Gregg pr.; Archive pr., 1964] 2v. 25cm. (English bibliogr. sources, ser1, no4.)

Facsimile of British museum copy, to 1701, ed. by David F. Foxon.

Rev: TLS 15 Ap '65: 300.

618 **Clavel, Robert.** A catalogue of all the books printed in England since the dreadful fire of London, 1666. To the end of michaelmas term, 1672. (1673). [London, Gregg pr. in association with the Archive pr., 1965] 48,32p. facsims. 31cm. (English bibliographical sources, ser2, no3.)

Ed. by David F. Foxon from the Bodleian copy.

619 —— [Same]: To the end of trinity term, 1674. (1675). [London, Gregg pr. in association with the Archive pr., 1965] 119p. facsims. 31cm. (English bibliographical sources, ser2, no4.)

620 —— [Same]: To the end of trinity term, 1680. (1680). [London, Gregg pr. in association with the Archive pr., 1965] 191p. facsims. 31cm. (English bibliographical sources, ser2, no5.)

621 —— [Same]: To the end of michaelmas term, 1695. (1696). [London, Gregg pr. in association with the Archive pr., 1965] 127p. facsims. 31cm. (English bibliographical sources, ser2, no6.)

622 **London, William.** A catalogue of the most vendible books in England, 1657, 1658, 1660. [London, Gregg pr. in association with the Archive pr., 1965] 1v.(unpaged) facsims. 25cm. (English bibliographical sources, ser2, no2.)
Ed. by David F. Foxon from BM copies.

623 **Oxford university press.** A list of the books, pamphlets, broadsides, and leaflets in the Constance Meade memorial collection . . . printed . . . between 1640 and 1701 with reference to the Short-title catalogue of Donald G. Wing. Oxford, 1966. 32l. 33cm. (Duplicated typescript)

624 **Wing, Donald Goddard.** A gallery of ghosts; books published between 1641–1700 not found in the Short-title catalogue. [New York] Index committee, Modern language association of America, 1967. vi,225p. 27cm. (Duplicated typescript)

BOOKS — 1701–1800

625 **Ewen, Frederic.** Bibliography of eighteenth century English literature. New York, Columbia U.P., 1905. 28p. 19cm. (Not seen.)

626 **Tobin, James Edward.** 'Bibliographies of individual authors' *in* Eighteenth century English literature and its cultural background; a bibliography. New York, 1939. p.[65]–180. (Repr. New York, Biblo and Tannen, 1967.)(Not seen.)

627 **[Bernbaum, Ernest]** *comp.* 'Bibliographies'. . . . *in* Bateson, Frederick W., *ed.* Cambridge bibliography of English literature. Cambridge, 1940–57. V.2, p.3–4.

628 **Cordasco, Francesco G. M.** A register of 18th century bibliographies and references; a chronological quarter-century survey relating to English literature, booksellers, newspapers, periodicals, printing & publishing, aesthetics, art & music, economics, history & science; a preliminary contribution. Chicago, V. Giorgio, 1950. 74p. facsim. 23cm.
Chronol. list of some 500 entries.

629 **Hoe, Robert.** A catalogue of books in English later than 1700, forming a portion of the library of Robert Hoe. New York, Privately ptd., 1905. 3v. 23cm.
Short-title author catalogue of 4,118 titles, comp. by Carolyn Shipman, with some bibliogr. notes.

630 **London. Stationers' company.** Index of titles and proprietors of books entered in the Book of registry . . . from 28th April 1710 to 30th Dec. 1773. [London, Ptd. by Taylor and Francis, 1910.] 152p. 25cm.

631 **Griffith, Reginald Harvey.** The progress pieces of the eighteenth century. Texas R 5:218–33 Ap '20. (Not seen.)
'Check-list' (p.230–3).

632 **MacGeorge, Bernard Buchanan.** Catalogue of the . . . library of the late Bernard Buchanan MacGeorge . . . Glasgow . . . sold by auction by messrs. Sotheby, Wilkinson & Hodge. . . . London, Ptd. by J. Davy [1924] 168p. col.front., facsims.(2 fold., incl.port.) 25cm.
1,484 items.

633 **Williams, Iolo Aneurin.** Seven XVIIIth century bibliographies. London, Dulau, 1924. vii,244p. 23cm.
Contents: John Armstrong.—William Shenstone.—Mark Akenside.—William Collins.—Oliver Goldsmith.—Charles Churchill.—Richard Brinsley Butler Sheridan.—Index.
Chronol. descr. of 1st ed. for each author, with bibliogr. notes.
Rev: N&Q 146:315–16 '24; TLS 28 F '24:121; A. W. P[ollard] Library ser4 5:102–3 '24; Bkmns J 11:18 '24.

634 **Rothschild, Nathaniel Mayer Victor, baron Rothschild.** The Rothschild library; a catalogue of the collection of eighteenth-century printed books

and manuscripts. . . . Cambridge, Privately ptd. at the University pr., 1954. 2v.(xx,839p.) illus., facsims. 27cm.

Bibliogr. catalogue of 2,680 items arranged by author, with indexes, comp. by N. M. Shawyer. 'Appendix I: Poley collection of pamphlets' (p.761–75): checklist of contents of each of 20v.—'Appendix II: Rolle collection of plays' (p.776–80): checklist of 114 18th century ed.

Rev: H. Williams Library ser5 10: 284–7 '55; TLS 10 Mr '55: 172; H. Cahoon Pa Bib Soc Am 50: 95–7 '56; TLS 18 Mr '55: 172; A. T. Hazen Philol Q 34: 231–2 '55.

635 **Maslen, Keith Ian Desmond.** Eighteenth-century books in New Zealand libraries. N.Z. Libs 25:102–8 My '62.

Checklists of books printed by the William Bowyers, in various libraries.

641 **Monthly catalogue.** A catalogue of all books, sermons, and pamphlets published [1714–1730] . . . printed for Bernard Lintott. [London, Gregg pr.; Archive pr., 1964.] 3v. 29cm. (English bibliogr. sources, ser1, no1–2.)

Facsimile of London library copy, ed. by David F. Foxon, with index.

Rev: TLS 15 Ap '65: 300.

642 **A Register of books, 1728–1732** extracted from The monthly chronicle. [London] Gregg-Archive [1964] iv.(various pagings) 25cm. (English bibliogr. sources, ser1, no3.)

Facsimiles of various copies, ed. by David F. Foxon; no index.

643 **British magazine.** The lists of books from the British magazine, 1746–50, collected with annual indexes. London, Gregg pr. in association with the Archive pr., 1965. iv.(various pagings) facsims. 19cm. (English bibliographical sources, ser1, no8.)

Ed. by David F. Foxon from Bodleian copies.

643a **[Worrall, John]** The Annual catalogue, 1736–37. London, Gregg pr.; Archive pr., 1965. iv.(various pagings). 17cm. (English bibliographical sources, ser1, no5.)

Facsim. ed. by David F. Foxon from copy in Queens' college, Cambridge.

643b **Cameron, William James** and **D. J. Carroll,** *ed.* Short title catalogue of books printed in the British Isles, the British colonies and the United States of America and of English books printed elsewhere, 1701–1800, held in the libraries of the Australian capital territory. Canberra, National library of Australia, 1966. 2v.(xx,784p.) illus., port. 26cm. (Duplicated typescript)

643c The **Gentleman's magazine,** 1731–51; the lists of books, collected with annual indexes, and the annual index to the first twenty years compiled by Edward Kimber, 1752. [London, Gregg pr. in association with Archive pr., 1966] iv.(various pagings) facsims. 23cm. (English bibliographical sources, ser1, no6.)

Ed. by David F. Foxon from the London library copy.

644 **London magazine.** The monthly catalogues from the London magazine, 1732–66, with the index for 1732–58 compiled by Edward Kimber. London, Gregg pr.; Archive pr., 1966 [i.e.1967] [740]p. 24cm. (English bibliographical sources, ser1, no7.)

Ed. by David F. Foxon from own copy; index from BM copy.

650 **English association.** Short bibliographies of Wordsworth, Coleridge, Byron, Shelley, Keats. [London] 1912. 13p. 25cm. (English association Leaflet, no.23.) Covertitle.

The Wordsworth, Shelley and Keats lists comp. by A. C. Bradley; the Byron by F. S. Boas; and the Coleridge by A. A. Jack and A. C. Bradley.

651 **Muir, Percival Horace.** 'Some bibliographies of modern authors reviewed' *in* Points, second series, 1866–1934. London, 1934. p.45–57.

Annotated list of 85 items.

652 **Ehrsam, Theodore George [and others]** Bibliographies of twelve victorian authors, compiled by Theodore G. Ehrsam . . . and Robert H. Deily . . . under the direction of Robert M. Smith. New York, H. W. Wilson, 1936. 362p. 26cm.

Contents: Matthew Arnold.—Elizabeth Barrett Browning.—Arthur Hugh Clough.—Edward Fitzgerald.—Thomas Hardy.—Rudyard Kipling.—William Morris.—Christina Georgina Rossetti.—Dante Gabriel Rossetti.—Robert Louis Stevenson.—Algernon Charles Swinburne.—Alfred, lord Tennyson.

Checklists of critical works about the respective authors.

Rev: D. A. Randall Pub Wkly 129 : 1630 '36; J. I. Wyer Lib J 61 : 835 '36; Bklist 32:219 '36; TLS 4 Ap '36: 304; Wisconsin Lit Bull 32 : 46 '36; Lib J 61 : 835 '36; M. Ray Mod Lang N 52 : 458 '37; C. F. Harrold Mod Philol 34 : 331–2 '37; C. S. Northup J Eng Germ Philol 36 : 442–3 '37; K. A. Thompson Lib Q 7 : 161–2 '37; J. D. Cowley Mod Lang R 32:332–3 '37.

653 —— **[Same]:** A supplement, by Joseph G. Fucilla. Mod Philol 37:89–96 Ag '39.

654 **[Templeman, William Darby]** *comp.* 'Bibliographies' *in* Bateson, Frederick W., *ed.* Cambridge bibliography of English literature. Cambridge, 1940–57. V.3, p.3–4.

655 **Sadleir, Michael Thomas Hervey.** 'The development during the last fifty years of bibliographical study of books of the XIXth century' *in* Francis, sir Frank C., *ed.* The Bibliographical society, 1892–1942; studies in retrospect. London, 1949. p.146–58.

'Schedule of bibliographies, check lists, hints to collectors and so forth' (p.148–9).

656 **Smith, Simon Nowell-.** Michael Sadleir, a handlist. Library ser5 13 : 132–8 Je '58.

657 **Altick, Richard Daniel** and **W. R. Matthews.** Guide to doctoral dissertations in victorian literature, 1886–1958. Urbana, University of Illinois pr., 1960. vii,119p. 22cm. (Duplicated typescript.)

657a **Buckley, Jerome Hamilton.** Victorian poets and prose writers. New York, Appleton-Century-Crofts [1966] viii,63p. 24cm. (Goldentree bibliographies.)

657b **Fogle, Richard Harter.** Romantic poets and prose writers. New York, Appleton-Century-Crofts [1967] xvi,461p. 24cm. (Goldentree bibliographies.)

658 **Slater, John Herbert.** Early editions, a bibliographical survey of the works of some popular modern authors. London, K. Paul, Trench, Trübner, 1894. xii,339p. 23cm.

Checklists of victorian authors, with bibliogr. notes.

659 **Nicoll, sir William Robertson** and **T. J. Wise,** *ed.* Literary anecdotes of the nineteenth century; contributions towards a literary history of the period. London, Hodder & Stoughton; New York, Dodd, Mead, 1895–6. 2v. port., facsims. 22cm.

Partial contents: Materials for a bibliography of Robert Browning, v.1, p.361–627.— Elizabeth Barrett Browning and her scarcer books, a bio-bibliographical note [by Harry Buxton Forman], v.2, p.81–101.—The building of the Idylls, a study in Tennyson (including bibliographical descriptions), v.2, p.217–72.—A bibliographical list of the scarcer works and uncollected writings of Algernon Charles Swinburne, v.2, p. 291–374.

660 **London. Stationers' company.** Index of entries (literary) in the Book of registry of the Stationers' company . . . from 1st July, 1842 to [15 March, 1907] London, Harrison, 1896–1907. 4v. 42cm.

Title entries, with index of authors and publishers in v.2–4.

661 **Manchester. Public libraries.** Catalogue of the Alexander Ireland collection in the Free reference library; compiled by John Hibbert Swann. Manchester, Free reference library, 1898. 25p. facsims. 24cm.

Works by or relating to the Lambs, Hazlitt, Hunt, the Carlyles, and Emerson.

662 **[Keogh, Andrew]** *comp.* 'List of publications' *in* Phelps, William L. Essays on modern novelists. New York, 1910. p.261–93.

Includes chronol. checklists of R. D. Blackmore, William de Morgan, Hardy, Kipling, Stevenson, and mrs. Humphry Ward.

663 **Peddie, Robert Alexander** and **Q. Waddington,** *comp.* The English catalogue of books . . . books issued in the United Kingdom . . . 1801–1836. London, Low, Marston for the Publishers' circular, 1914. 655p. 26cm.

A retrospective compilation; from 1835 the English catalogue was issued currently.

664 **Clark, William Andrews.** The library of William Andrews Clark, jr. Modern English literature, collated and compiled by Robert Ernest Cowan and William Andrews Clark. San Francisco, Ptd. by J. H. Nash, 1920–8. 4v. 27cm.

Author catalogue of books printed after 1700, with full TP transcrs., collations, and bibliogr. notes and refs; every volume runs A–Z; no index. The collection now forms part of the University of California's William A. Clark library.

665 **Quinn, John.** The library of John Quinn. . . . To be sold. . . . New York, Anderson galleries, 1923–4. 5pts. ports., facsims. 24cm.

Sale catalogue of 12,096 titles, realising $226,000.

Rev: A. W. P[ollard] Library ser4 6 : 392–3 '26.

666 **Brett, Oliver Sylvain Baliol, 3d viscount Esher.** The modern library collected by viscount Esher at Watlington park. [Plaistow] Privately ptd. [at the Curwen pr.] 1930. xiv,320p. 25cm.

Alphabetical short-title catalogue; no index. A limited ed. of 20 copies was issued in 1925. The collection was sold at Sotheby's 25–6 Mr, 20–1 My, 18–20 N '46.

Rev: Bk Coll Q 1 : 23–5 '30.

667 **Muir, Percival Horace.** Points, 1874–1930; being extracts from a bibliographers note-book. London, Constable, 1931. xvii,167p. illus., facsims. 23cm.

Author checklists, with bibliogr. discussion; *see* no.670.

Rev: TLS 3 S '31 : 660; A. J. A. Symons Bk Coll Q 3 : 82–7 '31; A. W. P[ollard] Library ser4 12 : 362–3 '31.

668 **Block, Andrew.** The book collector's vade mecum. London, D. Archer, 1932. viii,375p. facsims. 23cm.

See no. 672.

669 **Targ, William.** Modern English first editions and their prices, 1931; a checklist of the foremost English first editions from 1860 to the present day. Chicago, Black archer pr., 1932. vii,108p. facsims. 17cm.

Chronol. author checklists, with some bibliogr. notes; no index.

670 **Muir, Percival Horace.** Points, second series, 1866–1934. London, Constable; New York, R. R. Bowker, 1934. xiv,155p. illus., facsims. 23cm.

Author checklists, with bibliogr. discussion; *see* no. 667.

Rev: TLS 24 Ja '35 : 52; R. E. Roberts Observer 17 F '35; A. J. A. S[ymons] Bk Coll Q 17 : 78–80' 35; M. J. MacManus Dublin Mag 10 : 62–3 '35; I. A. Williams Lond Merc 31 : 319–20 '35.

671 **Read, William Augustus.** The splendid library of . . . mr. and mrs. William A. Read . . . to be dispersed. . . . [New York] American art association, Anderson galleries, 1936. 287p. illus., port., facsims. 28cm. (Not seen.)

485 titles, mainly of victorian literature.

672 **Block, Andrew.** The bookcollector's vade mecum. [2d ed., rev. and corr.] London, Mitre pr., 1938. viii, 302p. facsims. 21cm.

Includes checklists of Scott, Hunt, Shelley, Keats, Byron, Dickens, Thackeray, Ainsworth, Browning, and Tennyson, based on the then standard bibliogrs. of the respective authors.

673 **Park, Julian.** A library of English first editions, mostly nineteenth century. Buffalo, 1960. 73p. Covertitle. (Not seen.)

674 **Fredeman, William Evan.** Pre-Raphaelitism, a bibliocritical study. Cambridge, Harvard U.P.; London, O.U.P., 1965. xix,327p. illus., ports., facsims. 25cm.

Classified checklists of ptd. and other works, and biogr. and criticism.

Rev: TLS 23 S '65 : 836.

BOOKS—1901–

680 **Danielson, Henry.** Bibliographies of modern authors. London, Bookman's journal, 1921. xi,211p. facsims. 18cm.

TP transcrs., collations, and bibliogr. notes, arranged by author; no index. Most material (except the bibliogr. of Symons) first appeared in Bkmns J; detailed citations are given under the names of the authors covered: Beerbohm, Brooke, Hubert Crackanthorpe, De la Mare, Drinkwater, Dunsany, J. E. Flecker, Gissing, Francis Letwidge, Compton Mackenzie, Masefield, Leonard Merrick, Richard Middleton, Symons, and Hugh Walpole.

Rev: I. A. Williams Lond Merc 5 : 181–2 '21.

681 **First edition club,** LONDON. A bibliographical catalogue of the first loan exhibition of books and manuscripts held by the First edition club, 1922. London, Privately ptd. [1922] 178p. facsims. 23cm.

Includes collections of the first ed. of J. D. Beresford, Norman Douglas, Chesterton, Aldous Huxley, and H. G. Wells, arranged alphabetically by author, with varying bibliogr. descrs.; no index.

682 **Stonehill, Charles Archibald** and **H. W. Stonehill.** Bibliographies of modern authors, second series. London, J. Castle [1925]. 162p. facsims. 21cm.

TP transcrs., collations, and bibliogr. notes on first ed. of John Davidson, Ernest Dowson, Katherine Mansfield, Alice Meynell, Pater, and Francis Thompson; no index. These bibliogrs. did *not* appear in Bkmns J.

Rev: A. W. P[ollard] Library ser4 6 : 399 '26.

683 **Fabes, Gilbert Henry.** Modern first editions: points and values. ([1st]–3d series). London, W. & G. Foyle [1929–32] 3v. 23cm.

Alphabetical checklists, with brief bibliogr. notes.

Rev: TLS 29 Ag '29:671; A. W. P[ollard] Library ser4 12:362–3 '31.

684 **Cutler, Bradley Dwyane** and **V. Stiles.** Modern British authors, their first editions. New York, Greenberg; London, G. Allen & Unwin [1930] xi,171p. 24cm.

Checklists, with some bibliogr. notes, of Baring, Barrie, Beerbohm, Brooke, Carroll, Conrad, John Davidson, De la Mare, Norman Douglas, Dowson, Doyle, Drinkwater, Dunsany, Firbank, Flecker, Galsworthy, Gissing, Hardy, Hewlett, W. H. Hudson, Aldous Huxley, Kipling, D. H. Lawrence, Le Gallienne, Machen, Mansfield, Masefield, Milne, George Moore, Pater, T. F. Powys, Shaw, Stephens, Stevenson, J. A. Symonds, F. Thompson, J. Thomson, Wells, Wilde, and Yeats.

Rev: TLS 1 Ja '31 : 11.

685 **Bibliographies of modern authors.** Third series. London, 1931. iv.(various pagings) facsims. 23cm.

Checklists, with some bibliogr. notes, each with separate TP and paging, first pub. as supplements to Bkmns J., of George Eliot, Hewlett, Firbank, by Percival H. Muir; Mark Rutherford, by Simon N. Smith; Leigh Hunt, by Alexander Mitchell. *See* notes under names of individual authors.

686 **Gawsworth, John,** *pseud.* Ten contemporaries; notes towards their definitive bibliography. London, E. Benn [1932] 224p. 19cm.

Checklists of Lascelles Abercrombie, Herbert E. Palmer, George Egerton, sir Ronald Ross, Stephen Hudson, Edith Sitwell, Wilfrid Gibson, Robert Nichols, Rhys Davies, and M. P. Shiel.

Rev: TLS 14 Jl '32 : 517; P. H. Muir Bk Coll Q 7 : 47–9 '32; I. A. Williams Lond Merc 27 : 164 '32.

687 —— Ten contemporaries; second series; notes toward their definitive bibliography. London, Joiner and Steele [1933] 240p. 19cm.

Checklists of Dorothy M. Richardson, Frederick Carter, Liam O'Flaherty, Stella Benson, Oliver Onions, E. M. Delafield, Thomas Burke, L. A. G. Strong, John Collier, and H. E. Bates.

Rev: J. Carter Pub Wkly 124: 508–9 '33.

688 **Manly, John Matthews** and **E. Rickert**. Contemporary British literature; a critical survey and 232 author-bibliographies, by Fred. B. Millett. 3d rev. and enl. ed., based on the 2d rev. and enl. ed. by. . . . New York, Harcourt Brace, 1948. (First pub. 1921.) xi,556p. 19cm.

689 **National book league,** LONDON. Modern books and writers; the catalogue of an exhibition held . . . 1951. [London] Published for the National book league by the C.U.P. [1951] 69p. 22cm. (Not seen.)

690 **English literature in transition.** 1– . West Lafayette, Ind., Purdue university, 1957– . (Formerly English fiction in transition, 1957–62.)

Contains occasional bibliogrs. of work by and about authors, 1880–1920, e.g. Arnold Bennett, J. D. Beresford, Walter Besant, John Buchan, Samuel Butler, Hubert Crackan-thorpe, Havelock Ellis, Ford Madox Ford, E. M. Forster, Galsworthy, W. L. George, Gissing, R. B. C. Grahame, Haggard, Hewlett, W. H. Hudson, Kipling, Rose Macaulay, Compton Mackenzie, Maugham, W. B. Maxwell, Leonard Merrick, C. E. Montague, George Moore, Arthur Morrison, H. H. Munro, G. L. Strachey, Sheila Kaye-Smith, Swinnerton, Walpole, Wells, and Richard Whiteing. Major accretions of these lists have been entered under the respective author's name.

GENERAL AND PERIOD BIBLIOGRAPHIES—WALES

See also Regional bibliographies—Wales, and subdivisions in *Forms and genres.* For fullest note of books printed in or otherwise relating to Wales, consult the Index.

BOOKS — WALES — 1475–

695 The **Hengwrt** library of printed books. Welsh Bib Soc J 1:78–83 D ʼ11; 1:123–8 Oc ʼ12.
Annotated checklist of rare Welsh items from Thomas Kerslake's catalogues.

696 **Wales. National library,** ABERYSTWYTH. . . . Catalogue of manuscripts & rare books exhibited in the Great hall of the library, 1916. Aberystwyth, Ptd. at the private pr. of the Library, 1916. 84p. facsims. 24cm.
See no.700.

697 **Davies, William Llewelyn.** Welsh books entered in the Stationers' registers, 1554–1708. Welsh Bib Soc J 2:167–74, 204–9 Ja, D ʼ21.
Chronol. list of Welsh entries in Arber's and Eyre's transcripts.

698 **B., K.P.** Grawn Sypian Canaan. Welsh Bib Soc J 2:320–1 Ag ʼ23.
Checklist of ed. of Welsh Calvinist hymnbook.

699 **Williams, Aneurin.** By-gone publishers and printers. Welsh Bib Soc J 3:57–60 Ja ʼ26.
Chronol. checklist of books by Welsh printers, 1543–1798.

700 **Wales. National library,** ABERYSTWYTH. Guide to the exhibition of manuscripts, books, prints, maps, broadsides, etc. . . . Aberystwyth, Ptd. at the private pr. of the National library, 1932. 59p. port. 21cm.
Principally Welsh books and books of Welsh interest, and fine printing.

701 **Lloyd, D. Myrddin.** Four centuries of Welsh printed literature; an exhibition. Welsh Bib Soc J 6:177–200 Jl ʼ47.
Classified checklist of 141 exhibits, with 4 TP facsims.

BOOKS — WALES — 1475–1700

702 **Short-title** list of Welsh books, 1546–1700. Welsh Bib Soc J 2:176–88, 210–28 Ja, D ʼ21; 2:254–69 Ag ʼ22.

703 —— [Same]: Supplement, by W. L. Davies. *ib.* 4:59–63 Ag ʼ32.
Chronol. checklist, with some bibliogr. notes and refs.

BOOKS — WALES — 1641–1700

704 **Wales. National library,** ABERYSTWYTH. Catalogue of tracts of the civil war and commonwealth period relating to Wales and the borders. Aberystwyth, 1911. ix, 85p. 22cm.
Chronol. catalogue of 264 items, 1640–61, with index.
Rev: A. W. Pollard Library ser3 2:441–2 ʼ11.

BOOKS — WALES — 1701–1800

705 **Short-title** list of eighteenth century Welsh books. Part 1: 1701–1710. Welsh
Bib Soc J 4:123–32 Ag '33.

Apparently all published; chronol. checklist, with some bibliogr. notes and locations of
copies.

GENERAL AND PERIOD BIBLIOGRAPHIES — SCOTLAND

See also Regional bibliographies—Scotland, and subdivisions in *Forms and genres.* For fullest note of books printed in or otherwise relating to Scotland, consult the Index.

BOOKS — SCOTLAND — BIBLIOGRAPHIES

710 **Printed** catalogues of Scottish university libraries. Aberdeen Univ Lib Bull 1:397–404 Oc '12.

710a **Linton, Marion P.** Special catalogues in the Department of printed books in the National library of Scotland. Biblioth 3n05:173–82 '62.

BOOKS — SCOTLAND — 1475-

711 **[Anderson, Peter John]** Catalogue of books in the Celtic department, Aberdeen university library. Aberdeen, Aberdeen U.P., 1897. 63p. 25cm.
Short-title dictionary catalogue.

712 **Aberdeen. University. Library.** MacBean collection; a catalogue of books, pamphlets, broadsides, portraits, &c. in the Stuart and Jacobite collection gathered together by W. M. MacBean; compiled by Mabel D. Allardyce. Aberdeen, Aberdeen U.P., 1949. xxvi,307p. illus., ports. 25cm.
Alphabetical catalogue; no index.
Rev: TLS 19 My '50:316.

BOOKS — SCOTLAND — 1475-1640

713 **Dickson, Robert** and **J. P. Edmond.** Annals of Scottish printing, from the introduction of the art in 1507 to the beginning of the seventeenth century. Cambridge, Macmillan & Bowes, 1890. xv,530p. illus., facsims. 30cm.
Discursive entries arranged by printer; TP transcrs., collations, locations of copies, and bibliogr. notes.
Rev: Library 3:157–8, 251–7 '91.

714 **Edmond, John Philip.** Bibliographical gleanings, 1890–1893; being additions and corrections to the Annals of Scottish printing. Edinburgh Bib Soc Proc 1:1–12 [i.e. 5–16] Oc '94.
Appendix of 50 items.

715 **Leith, William Forbes-.** Pre-reformation scholars in Scotland in the xvith century; their writings and their public services, with a bibliography . . . from 1500 to 1560. Glasgow, J. Maclehose, 1915. vi,155p. illus., ports. 23cm.
'Bibliography' (p. [23]–98): chronol. author checklist with notes and locations of copies.

BOOKS — SCOTLAND — 1475-1700

716 **Aldis, Harry Gidney.** A list of books printed in Scotland before 1700, including those printed furth of the realm for Scottish booksellers, with

brief notes on the printers and stationers. [Edinburgh] Ptd. for the Edinburgh bibliographical society, 1904. xvi,153p. 29cm.

A 'preliminary handlist' of 3,919 titles arranged chronologically, with topographical and alphabetical lists of printers, booksellers, and stationers, and general index.

Rev: A. W. Pollard Library ser2 6:223-4 '05.

BOOKS — SCOTLAND — 1641–1700

717 **Ogilvie, James D.** A bibliography of the resolutioner-protester controversy, 1650–1659. Edinburgh Bib Soc Pub 14pt1:57–86 Je '28.

'Bibliography' (p.79–86): chronol. list of 25 items, with collations and locations of copies.

718 —— The Cross petition, 1643. Edinburgh Bib Soc Pub 15pt2:55–76 Oc '34.

'Bibliography' (p.72–6): chronol. checklist of 17 items, with short collations, bibliogr. refs., and facsims.

719 —— A bibliography of the bishops' wars, 1639–40. Glasgow Bib Soc Rec 12:21–40 '36.

'Bibliography' (p.37–40): chronological checklist. Ogilvie's collection is now in the Glasgow university library.

719a **Scotland. National library,** EDINBURGH. . . . Shelf-catalogue of the Blaikie collection of Jacobite pamphlets, broadsides and proclamations. Boston, Mass., G. K. Hall, 1964. v,42l. 25cm.

754 items; no index.

BOOKS — SCOTLAND — 1701–1800

720 **Festival of Britain, 1951. Scottish committee.** Catalogue of an exhibition of 18th-century Scottish books at the Signet library, Edinburgh. [Edinburgh] Published for the Scottish committee of the Festival of Britain, 1951 and the National book league by the C.U.P., 1951. x,187p. illus., ports., facsims. 23cm.

Classified annotated short-title catalogue of 779 entries with index of authors, printers, and illustrators; comp. by R. O. Dougan.

721 **Duval, K. D., bksllr.,** FALKLAND, FIFE. A catalogue of eighteenth century Scottish books. Falkland, 1964. 119p. illus., facsims. 22cm.

Author catalogue of 988 items.

BOOKS — SCOTLAND — 1801–1900

723 **Dixon, James Main.** A survey of Scottish literature in the nineteenth century, with some reference to the eighteenth. Berkeley, Calif., 1906. 53p. 22cm.

BOOKS — SCOTLAND — 1901–

724 **Scottish chapbook.** 1no1–2no2. Montrose, 1922–3. 'Modern Scottish bibliographies' includes checklists of 1. John Ferguson (Ag '22); 2. James Kennedy (S '22); 3. James Joshua Guthrie (Oc '22); 5. George Reston Malloch (D '22); 8. Murdoch Maclean (My '23).

725 **Festival of Britain, 1951. Scottish committee.** Catalogue of an exhibition of 20th-century Scottish books at the Mitchell library, Glasgow. [Edinburgh] 1951. x,310p. illus. 23cm.

Classified annotated short-title catalogue, comp. by R. O. Dougan; including 'Scottish bookbinding' (p.270–4) arranged under binders' names.

726 **Duval, K. D., bksllr.,** EDINBURGH. The modern Scottish renaissance, 1920–1960; a catalogue of the period. Edinburgh [1961] lv.(unpaged) illus. 22cm.

'Hugh MacDiarmid', items 1–76; Neil M. Gunn, 77–120; Edwin Muir, 121–49; the other writers, 150–760 . . .'

See also Regional bibliographies—Ireland, and subdivisions in *Forms and genres*. For fullest note of books printed in or relating to Ireland, consult the Index.

BOOKS — IRELAND — 1475–

730 **Dottin, Georges.** Les livres irlandais imprimés de 1571 à 1820. R Celtique 31n03:294–9 '10.

Corrected resumé of Dix's list in An Claidheamh Soluis, 1904: no. 1174.

731 **Cambridge. University. Library. Bradshaw Irish collection.** A catalogue of the Bradshaw collection of Irish books in the University library, Cambridge. Cambridge, Ptd. for the University library and to be had of B. Quaritch, 1916. 3v. 26cm.

A catalogue of the collection presented in 1870 and 1886 was pub. in Cambridge Univ Lib Bull extra ser. '09.

Contents: v.1. nos. 1–4087. Books printed in Dublin by known printers, 1602–1882. List of printers and booksellers in Dublin.—v.2. nos. 4088–8743. Books printed in Dublin without printer's name. Provincial towns. The works of Irish authors printed elsewhere, arranged alphabetically . . . —v.3. Index.

Rev: Irish Bk Lover 8:101–3 '17; [J. S. Crone] *ib.* 8:104–5 '17.

732 **Cassedy, James.** Fictitious imprints on books printed in Ireland. Bib Soc Ireland Pubs 3n04:31–6 '27.

Discursive checklist, with 'Index of fictitious imprints' (p.36).

733 **Bourke, Francis Stephen.** A hand-list of books on Killarney. Bib Soc Ireland Pubs 6n02:25–34 '53.

Checklist of 73 items mainly published in Ireland, 1750–1948, with some bibliogr. notes.

BOOKS — IRELAND — 1475–1700

734 **Dix, Ernest Reginald McClintock.** Plays printed in Ireland before 1701. Irish Bk Lover 17:36–7 Mr–Ap '29.

Checklist of 5 items from 1635.

BOOKS — IRELAND — 1641–1700

735 **Alden, John Eliot.** Bibliographica Hibernica; additions and corrections to Wing. Charlottesville, Bibliographical society of the University of Virginia, 1955. 39p. 17cm. (Duplicated typescript)

GENERAL AND PERIOD BIBLIOGRAPHIES — BRITISH BOOKS
PUBLISHED ABROAD

740 **Gilbert, sir John.** Irish bibliography, two papers . . . with an introduction, notes, and appendices by E. R. McClintock Dix. Roy Irish Acad Proc Sect C 25:117–42 '04.

Appendix listing some important sixteenth- and seventeenth-century books printed abroad (p.126–33): chronol. checklists with locations of copies; 9 TP facsims.

741 **Leith, William Forbes-.** Bibliographie des livres, publiés à Paris et à Lyon par les savants écossais réfugiés en France an xvie siecle. R des Biblioth 21:241–68 '11. (Not seen)

742 **Steele, Robert Reynolds.** Notes on English books printed abroad, 1525–48. Bib Soc Trans 11:189–236 Oc '09–Mr '11.

'Bibliography [of the 'Marburg' press]' (p.208–12); '. . . a list of all English books prohibited by name during Henry VIII's reign' (p.214–17); 'Bale press' (p.232–6).

743 **Wilson, John Dover.** Richard Schilders and the English puritans. Bib Soc Trans 11:65–134 Oc '09–Mr '11.

'A descriptive list of the books . . .': (p.90–110): short-title chronol. list of 51 items 1579–1616, with collations, bibliogr. notes and refs., and locations of copies; TP and type-ornament facsims. (p.111–34).

744 **Murray, David.** Some old Scots authors whose books were printed abroad. Glasgow, Maclehose, Jackson, 1921. iv,41p. facsims. 21cm.

Repr. from Glasgow Archaeol Soc Trans new ser 7pt2:216–48 '20. Discursive checklist of works by 44 authors.

745 **Harris, James Kendel** and **S. K. Jones.** The Pilgrim press, a bibliographical and historical memorial of the books printed at Leyden by the Pilgrim fathers, with a chapter on the location of the Pilgrim press in Leyden, by Dr. Plooij. Cambridge, W. Heffer, 1922. 89p.+38 facsims., 2 plans. 23cm.

'Appendix II. Collations' (p.72–87); quasifacsim. TP transcrs. of 20 items, with TP facsims., collations, and locations of copies.

Rev: TLS 7 D '22:804.

747 **McNeill, Charles.** Publications of Irish interest published by Irish authors on the continent of Europe prior to the eighteenth century. Bib Soc Ireland Pubs 4n01:3–40 '30.

748 —— [**Same**]: Index, compiled by Rosalind M. Elmes. Bib Soc Ireland Pubs 4n02:45–8 '30.

749 **Isaac, Frank Swinton.** Egidius van der Erve and his English printed books. Library ser4 12:336–52 D '31.

Discussion and 'List of books printed in English . . .' (p.341–2): checklist with refs. and note of type.

750 **Baxter, James Houston** and **C. J. Fordyce.** Books published abroad by Scotsmen before 1700. Glasgow Bib Soc Rec 11:1–55 '33.

Alphabetical checklist with biographical notes.

751 **Books** about Ireland printed abroad. Belfast Municipal Mus Q N 52:2–7 Je '34.

Checklist of 51 items exhibited, largely by Irish authors.

752 **Price, Mary Bell** and **L. M. Price.** The publication of English literature in Germany in the eighteenth century. Berkeley, Calif., University of California pr., 1934. viii,288p. 23cm.

Short-title dictionary catalogue of 1,166 items.

753 —— The publication of English humaniora in Germany in the eighteenth century. Berkeley, University of California pr., 1955. xxxiii,216p. 23cm. (Duplicated typescript)

Author checklist, complementing the previous item.

754 **Brussel, Isidore Rosenbaum.** Anglo-American first editions. London, Constable, 1935–6. 2v. facsims. 23cm.

Contents: [pt.1] East to west [1826–1900] describing first editions of English authors whose books were published in America before their publication in England.—pt.2 West to east, 1786–1930, describing first editions of American authors. . . .
Checklists with TP transcrs., and extensive TP facsims., with descr. notes.
Rev: TLS 14 D '35:864; Lond Merc 32:585–6 '35; M. J. MacManus Dublin Mag 10:72–3 '35; J. Carter Pub Wkly 128:1548–50 '35; J. T. Winterich Sat R Lit 13:20 '35; TLS 28 N '36:1000; D. Flower Observer 22 N '36; J. Carter Pub Wkly 130:1151–2 '36; D. Flower Observer 10 Oc '37; M. J. MacManus Dublin Mag 12:68 '37.

755 **Johnson, Alfred Forbes.** The exiled English church at Amsterdam and its press. Library ser5 5:219–42 Mr '51.

'List of books printed by Thorp, 1604–1622' (p.225–30); 'List of books printed by Thorp's successors, 1623–35' (p.232–42); TP facsims., STC corrigenda and checklist, with bibliogr. notes.

756 —— J. F. Stam, Amsterdam and English bibles. Library ser5 9:185–93 S '54.

Annotated checklist and discussion of 19 items ptd. between 1635 and 1639, with facsims.

757 —— Willem Christiaans, Leyden, and his English books. Library ser5 10:121–2 Je '55.

Checklist with bibliogr. notes.

758 —— The 'Cloppenburg' press, 1640, 1641. Library ser5 13:280–2 D '58.

Discussion of the pr. associated with Jan Evertz. Cloppenburg (1581–1647) and checklist of 14 items.

759 **Barber, Giles.** J. J. Tourneisen of Basle and the publication of English books on the continent, c.1800. Library ser5 15:193–200 S '60.

'A list of English books published by J. J. Tourneisen' (p.198–200).

760 —— Galignani's and the publication of English books in France from 1800 to 1852. Library ser5 16:267–86 D '61.

'A list of English newspapers and magazines published in Paris, 1814–50' (p.284–6): chronol. checklist.

761 **Dorsten, Jan Adrianus van.** 'A checklist of works printed by Thomas Basson at Leiden, 1585–1612' *in* Thomas Basson, 1555–1613, English printer at Leiden. Leiden, 1961. p. [71]–101.

762 **Walsh, M. O'N.** Irish books printed abroad, 1475–1700; an interim checklist. Irish Bk 2no1:1–36 '62/3.

Checklist of 659 items, with 'Index of defendants of theses' (p.35–6)·

GENERAL AND PERIOD BIBLIOGRAPHIES—FOREIGN BOOKS
PUBLISHED IN ENGLISH IN BRITAIN

Note that the items listed in this section do not include all the bibliographies of foreign
works in English translation, but only those which fall strictly within the scope of the
heading, or of which a substantial number of the entries do.
    The entries under this heading are arranged by country, then author, and chrono-
logically thereafter.

—— GENERAL

770 **Harris, William James.** The first printed translations into English of the
great foreign classics; a supplement to text-books of English literature.
London, G. Routledge; New York, E. P. Dutton [1909] vii,209p. 17cm.
Author list, with title index.

771 **Bennett, Henry Stanley.** 'Trial list of translations into English printed between 1475–1560' *in* English books and readers, 1475 to 1557; being a study
in the history of the booktrade from Caxton to the incorporation of the
Stationers' company. Cambridge, 1952. p.277–319.
Author checklist, with STC numbers and names of translators.

771a **Ebel, Julia G.** A numerical survey of Elizabethan translations. Library
ser5 22:104–27 Je '67.
Chronol. table (p.106–22) listing translations, 1560–1603, by STC no. under language of
original.

—— CLASSICAL

772 **Palmer, Henrietta Raymer.** List of English editions and translations of
Greek and Latin classics printed before 1641. London, Ptd. for the Biblio-
graphical society by Blades, East and Blades, 1911. xxxii,119p. 23cm.
Author list with TP transcrs., and locations of copies; no index.
Rev: A. G. S. J[osephson] Lib J 37:524 '12; Athenaeum 13 Ap '12:409; *ib*. 20 Ap '12:535;
Nation 94:561–2 '12.

773 **Lathrop, Henry Burrowes.** 'Chronological list of translations' *in* Translations from the classics into English from Caxton to Chapman, 1477–1620.
Madison, 1933. p.311–18.
'Alphabetical list of translators' (p.319–24); 'Notes on miss Palmer's list of editions and
translations' (p.325–31).

774 **Nørgaard, Holger.** Translations of the classics into English before 1600.
R Eng Stud new ser 9no34:164–72 '58.
Addenda and corrigenda to Robert R. Bolgar's The classical heritage and its beneficiaries.
Cambridge, 1954. p.508–41.

—— —— GREEK

775 **Pollard, Alfred William,** *ed.* 'A bibliography of translations of Greek
dramatists into English verse' *in* Odes from the Greek dramatists, translated.
... London, 1890. p.[193]–208.
Chronol. checklist classified by Greek author.

776 **Foster, Finley Melville Kendall.** English translations from the Greek; a bibliographical survey. New York, Columbia U.P., 1918. xxix,146p. diagr. 21cm.

Chronol. checklist classified by Greek author; index of translators.

──── ──── ──── PLATO

777 **Evans, Frank B.** Platonic scholarship in eighteenth-century England. Mod Philol 41:103–10 N '43.

'A list of the editions and English translations of Plato from 1670–1804' (p.108–10): chronol. checklist, with locations of copies.

──── ──── LATIN. HORACE

778 **Benham, Allen R.** Horace and his Ars poetica in English; a bibliography. Classical Wkly 49:1–5 Oc '56.

Discursive checklist of 48 items from 1567.

──── ──── ──── LUCRETIUS

779 **Gordon, Cosmo Alexander.** Lucretius: list of editions. [Insch? 1954] 29p. 19cm. (Duplicated typescript)

800 ──── 'English translations' *in* A bibliography of Lucretius. London, 1962. p.169–92.

Items 330–59; TP transcrs., collations, and bibliogr. notes.

──── ──── ──── MARCUS AURELIUS

801 **Legg, John Wickham.** A bibliography of the Thoughts of Marcus Aurelius Antoninus. Bib Soc Trans 10:15–81 '09.

Chronol. checklist with TP transcrs., some TP facsims., and locations of copies.

──── DENMARK

802 **Bredsdorff, Elias Lunn.** 'A bibliography of Hans Christian Andersen's works in English translation and of books and articles relating to H. C. Andersen' *in* Danish literature in English translation. Copenhagen, 1950. p.[121]–94.

Author checklist; no index.

803 **Mitchell, Phillip Marshall.** A bibliography of English imprints of Denmark through 1900. Lawrence, University of Kansas libraries, 1960. 85p. 23cm.

Checklist of 394 items from 1553, with locations of copies, and some bibliogr. notes.

Rev: B. Juel-Jensen Library ser5 17:266–8 '62; P. Morgan Mod Lang R 57:148 '62.

──── FRANCE

804 **Upham, Alfred Horatio.** 'Translations' *in* The French influence in English literature from the accession of Elizabeth to the restoration. New York, 1908. p.471–505.

Chronol. checklist, 1556–1659.

805 **Tucker, Joseph Eagon.** English translations from the French, 1650–1700: corrections and additions to the C.B.E.L. Philol Q 21:391–404 Oc '42.

806 —— Wing's Short-title catalogue and translations from the French, 1641–1700. Pa Bib Soc Am 49:37–67 '55.

807 **Howard, Alison K. (Bee).** Montesquieu, Voltaire and Rousseau in eighteenth-century Scotland; a checklist of editions and translations of their works published in Scotland before 1801. Biblioth 2no2:40–63 '60.
Classified checklist of 80 items, deriving from London university School of librarianship thesis, 1955.

—— —— BAUDELAIRE

808 **Bandy, W. T.** Baudelaire in English; a check list. Bull Bib 23:106–9 My/Ag '61.
Checklist of 157 translated works.

—— —— LAMARTINE

809 **Lombard, C. M.** Lamartine in America and England, 1820–1876; a check list. Bull Bib 23:103–6 My/Ag '61.
Checklist of poems, book reviews, and critical and biogr. articles.

—— —— MOLIÈRE

810 **Jones, Claude Edward.** Molière in England to 1775; a checklist. N&Q 202: 383–9 S '57.
Checklist with author and title indexes.

—— —— D'OUTRE-MEUSE

811 **Cordier, Jean.** Jean de Mandeville. Leide, E. J. Brill, 1891. 38p. 25cm.
Classified chronol. checklist of English and foreign ed., with some bibliogr. notes, repr. from T'oung-Pao, v. 3.

812 **Letts, Malcolm Henry Ikin.** 'Bibliography II: printed editions, mainly before 1600' *in* Sir John Mandeville, the man and his book. London, 1949. p.177–81.

813 **Bennett, Josephine Waters.** 'Appendix II. The editions' *in* The rediscovery of sir John Mandeville. New York, 1954. p.335–85.
'English editions' (p.[346]–59): chronol. checklist of 59 items, 1496–1953, with short collations, locations of copies, and bibliogr. notes and refs.

—— —— ROUSSEAU

814 **Warner, James H.** A bibliography of eighteenth-century English editions of J.-J. Rousseau, with notes on the early diffusion of his writings. Philol Q 13:225–47 Jl '34.

815 —— [Same]: Addenda. Philol Q 19:237–43 Jl '40.
Chronol. checklist, 1739?–92, apparently comp. from secondary sources.

—— —— VOLTAIRE

816 **Evans, Hywel Berwyn.** 'A bibliography of eighteenth-century translations of Voltaire' *in* Studies in French language, literature, and history presented to R. L. Graeme Ritchie. Cambridge, 1949. p.48–62.
Classified checklist of the non-dramatic works.

817 —— 'A provisional bibliography of English editions and translations of Voltaire' *in* Besterman, Theodore D. N. Studies on Voltaire and the eighteenth century. Genève, 1959. V.8, p.1–121.
Classified list of 578 items, with quasifacsim. TP transcrs., collations, locations of copies, and some bibliogr. notes.

818 **Maslen, Keith Ian Desmond.** Some early editions of Voltaire printed in London. Library ser5 14:287–93 D '59.
Three additions to Bengesco (Bibliographie ses œuvres. Paris, 1882–90), printed by William Bowyer.

—— GERMANY

819 **Morgan, Bayard Quincy.** A bibliography of German literature in English translation. Madison, 1922. 708p. diagr., table, 25cm. (University Wisconsin Stud Lang Lit 26no16 D '22)

820 —— A critical bibliography of German literature in English translation, 1481–1927, with supplement embracing the years 1928–1935. 2d ed. completely rev. and greatly augmented. Stanford university, Stanford U.P.; London, H. Milford, O.U.P., 1938. (Repr. New York, Scarecrow pr., 1965) xi,773p. diagr., tables. 23cm.
Alphabetical checklist
Rev: A. Closs Angl Beibl 50:141–4 '39; H. A. Pochmann Am Lit 11:228–9 '39; H. Atkins Mod Lang R 34:629–31 '39; W. Süskind Die Lit 41:376–7 '39.

821 **Morgan, Bayard Quincy** and **A. R. Hohlfeld,** *ed.* German literature in British magazines, 1750–1860, by Walter Roloff [and others] Madison, Wisc., University of Wisconsin pr., 1949. 364p. 26cm. (Duplicated typescript)
Chronol. checklist.

—— —— GOETHE

822 **Frantz, Adolf Ingram.** 'Bibliography [of translations]' *in* Half a hundred thralls to Faust; a study based on the British and American translators of Goethe's Faust, 1823–1949. Chapel hill, 1949. p.[275]–98.
Alphabetical list by translator, with full titles.

—— —— MANN

822a **English, David John,** 1966: no.118a.

—— —— SCHILLER

823 **London. University. Institute of Germanic languages and literatures.** Schiller in England, 1787–1960, a bibliography compiled . . . under the direction of R. Pick. London, 1961. xi,123p. 23cm.
Chronol. checklist, with indexes; first issued as Eng Goethe Soc Pubs, v.30.

—— —— THOMAS À KEMPIS

824 **Copinger, Walter Arthur.** On the English translations of the Imitatio christi. Manchester, Privately ptd., 1900. xii,114p. 18cm.

Checklist of 33 original translations, adaptations, and paraphrases from 1502 to 1900, with discursive descr. notes.

825 **Evans, Albert Owen.** 'Welsh editions of the Imitation' *in* Thomas à Kempis and Wales. Carmarthen, 1932. p.30.

Chronol. checklist of 22 items, 1679–1908, with locations of copies; repr. from Welsh Bib Soc J 4:5–32 Mr '32.

—— HOLLAND. ERASMUS

826 **Devereux, E. James.** Some lost English translations of Erasmus. Library ser5 17:255–9 S '62.

Alphabetical checklist of 10 titles, with bibliogr. notes and discussion.

—— ITALY

827 **Scott, Mary Augusta.** Elizabethan translations from the Italian. Boston, H. Miflin, 1916. lxxxi,558p. 23cm.

Repr. in rev. form from Pub Mod Lang Assn 10:249–93 '95; 11:377–484 '96; 13:42–153 '98; 14:465–571 '99. Classified checklist of 466 items, with descr. and bibliogr. notes.

Rev: Nation 105:291–2 '17; Athenæum F '17:86; C. R. Baskervill Mod Philol 16:213–18 '18; J. de Perott Romanic R 9:304–8 '18.

827a **Sellers, Harry.** Italian books printed in England before 1640. Library ser4 5:105–28 S '24.

Checklist; facsims. of TPs and ornaments of Italian books printed between 1580 and 1600 by John Wolfe and John Charlewood, with bibliogr. discussion.

—— —— DANTE

827b **Gillum, W. J.** English translations of Dante. N&Q ser8 9:462–3 Je '96.

Checklist supplementing list in N&Q 1877.

828 **Toynbee, Paget Jackson.** Chronological list of English translations from Dante from Chaucer to the present day, 1380–1906. Boston, Ginn [1906] xix,111p. 22cm.

Appendix to Dante society. 24th annual report, 1905. Boston, 1906.

829 —— [Same]: *in* Dante studies. Oxford, 1921. p.[156]–280.

Chronol. classified checklist, with indexes; rev. and corr.

830 —— Britain's tribute to Dante in literature and art; a chronological record of 540 years, c.1380–1920. London, Published for the British academy by H. Milford, O.U.P. [1921] xvi,212p. 25cm. (British academy. Dante commemoration, 1921)

Chronol. checklist.

831 **Cunningham, Gilbert Farm.** The Divine comedy in English, a critical bibliography, 1782–1900. Edinburgh, Oliver and Boyd, 1965. xi,206p. 23cm.

Checklists of translations at ends of chapters.

Rev: C. P. Brand Bk Coll 14:567 '65.

—— —— GUAZZO

832 **Lievsay, John Leon.** 'Bibliographical finding list' *in* Stefano Guazzo and the English renaissance, 1575–1675. Chapel Hill, 1961. p.[277]–303.
Checklist of 126 items, with locations of copies.

—— —— PETRARCH

833 **Fucilla, Joseph Guerin.** Petrarchan translations in British periodicals. Bull Bib 18:39–40 S/D '43.
Checklist.

—— POLAND. MICKIEWICZ

834 **Coleman, Arthur Prudden** and **M. M. Coleman.** 'Tentative bibliography of translations into English from the Polish of Adam Mickiewicz' *in* Adam Mickiewicz in English. Schenectady, N.Y., 1940. p.31–43. (Not seen)

835 —— 'Additions and corrections to the Tentative bibliography . . .' *in* Mickiewiczana; articles, translations, bibliographies. . . . New York, 1946. p.41–54.

836 —— Adam Mickiewicz in English. Cambridge springs, Penn., Alliance college, 1954. 76p. illus., ports. 27cm. (Duplicated typescript)
Chronol. annotated checklist.

—— RUSSIA

837 **Ettlinger, Amrei** and **J. M. Gladstone.** Russian literature, theatre and art; a bibliography of works in English, published 1900–1945. London, Hutchinson [n.d., 1946?] 96p. 18cm.
Classified checklist; no index.

838 **Line, Maurice Bernard.** A bibliography of Russian literature in English translation (excluding periodicals). London, Library association, 1963. 74p. 22cm.
Alphabetical under authors' names, to 1900; chronol. index and index of translators.
Rev: [L. S. Thompson] Pa Bib Soc Am 58:81 '64.

—— SPAIN

839 **Underhill, John Garrett.** 'A bibliography of the Spanish works published in the original or in translation in the England of the Tudors' *in* Spanish literature in the England of the Tudors. New York; London, 1899. p.375–408.
Chronol. checklist, 1530–1602.

840 **Bourne, J. A.** Some English translations of seventeenth-century Spanish novels. Mod Lang R 31:555–6 Oc '36.
Annotated checklist.

841 **Pane, Remigio Ugo.** English translations from the Spanish, 1484–1943; a bibliography. New Brunswick, Rutgers U.P., 1944. vii,218p. 21cm.

Checklist of 2,682 items arranged by author, with index of translators.

Rev: N&Q 187:219–20 '44.

842 **Mathews, Ernest G.** English translations from Spanish; a review and a contribution. J Eng Germ Philol 44:387–424 Oc '45.

Addenda to Pane.

843 **Ungerer, Gustav.** The printing of Spanish books in Elizabethan England. Library ser5 20:177–229 S '65.

Discussion, with checklists including 'List of books in Spanish' (p.190–201); 'List of Anglo-Spanish primers, grammars, dictionaries, and dialogues' (p.201–9); 'Spanish books licensed to be printed' (p.215–18); 46 items with some bibliogr. notes.

—— —— CERVANTES

844 **Calvert, Albert Frederick.** 'English translations of Don Quixote' *in* The life of Cervantes. London, 1905. p.125–33.

Checklist of 126 items.

—— —— SAVONAROLA

845 **Butterworth, Charles C.** Savonarola's expositions on the fifty-first and thirty-first psalms. Library ser5 6:162–70 D '51.

Checklist, with bibliogr. notes and discussion, of Fratris hieronymi Ferrariensis in psalmos, 1534–5.

—— —— SWITZERLAND. LAVATER

845a **Graham, John.** Lavater's Physiognomy: a checklist. Pa Bib Soc Am 55: 297–308 '61.

'British publications' (p.299–302): classified checklist.

—— UNITED STATES. FLECKER

846 **Danielson, Henry.** Bibliographies of modern authors, no. II. James Elroy Flecker, 1884–1915. Bkmns J 1n02:34 '19.

TP transcrs., collations, and bibliogr. notes on 12 London-printed first ed.

847 —— 1921: no.680.

—— —— HARTE

848 **Gohdes, Clarence.** A check-list of Bret Harte's works in book form published in the British Isles. Bull Bib 18:19, 36–9 My/Ag, S/D '43.

Chronol. checklist.

—— —— LONGFELLOW

849 **Gohdes, Clarence.** A check-list of volumes by Longfellow published in the British Isles during the nineteenth century. Bull Bib 17:46 S/D '40; 17:67–9, 93–6 Ja/Ap, My/Ag '41.

Classified checklist.

—— —— POE

850 **Dedmond, Francis B.** A checklist of Edgar Allan Poe's works in book form published in the British Isles. Bull Bib 21:16–20 My/Ag '53.
Chronol. checklist, 1838–1949.

—— —— STOWE

851 **Talbot, William.** Uncle Tom's cabin; first English editions. Am Bk Coll 3:292–7 '33.
TP transcrs. and collations of 1852 English ed., with bibliogr. discussion.

REGIONAL BIBLIOGRAPHIES

Hereunder are listed items associated more with places than with periods or persons, divided by country and county.

REGIONAL BIBLIOGRAPHIES — ENGLAND

—— TOPOGRAPHY

855 **Anderson, John Parker.** The book of British topography; a classified catalogue of the topographical works in the library of the British museum relating to Great Britain and Ireland. London, W. Satchell, 1881. xvi,472p. 24cm.

856 **New York. Public library.** List of works relating to British genealogy and local history. New York, 1910. 366p. 26cm.

Repr. from N.Y. Pub Lib Bull v.14 Je–D '10.

857 **Spalding, John Tricks.** A bibliographical account of the works relating to English topography in the library. . . . Exeter, J. G. Commin, Privately ptd., 1912–13. 5v. ports. 25cm.

Contents: 1. General topography. Bedfordshire . . . Devonshire.—2. Dorsetshire . . . Lincolnshire.—3. London and Middlesex.—4. Monmouthshire . . . Sussex.—5. Warwickshire . . . Yorkshire; Ireland; Scotland; Wales; Heraldry, family history, etc. Index.

Full titles with discursive collations, arranged by author.

858 **Humphreys, Arthur Lee.** A handbook to county bibliography being a bibliography of bibliographies relating to the counties and towns of Great Britain and Ireland. London, 1917. x,501p. 25cm.

Checklist under county and place headings, with detailed and useful index; see 'Printing and private printing presses' (p.472–3).

859 **Webb, Sidney, baron Passfield.** Select bibliographies, no.17. Travellers' descriptions of Great Britain. Bull Brit Lib Pol Sci 16:16–21 N '21.

860 **Fussell, George Edwin** and **C. Goodman.** Travel and topography in eighteenth-century England; a bibliography of sources for economic history. Library ser4 10:84–103 Je '29.

860a **Fussell, George Edwin** and **V. G. B. Atwater.** Travel and topography in seventeenth-century England: a bibliography of sources for social and economic history. Library ser4 13:292–311 D '32.

861 **Cox, Edward Godfrey.** A reference guide to the literature of travel, including voyages, geographical descriptions, adventures, shipwrecks and expeditions. Seattle, University of Washington, 1935–49. (V.1 repr. by lithography, 1948; v.2 1950) 3v. 26cm.

Contents: 1. The old world.—2. The new world (with index of personal names to v.1–2).—3. Great Britain.

Classified chronol. checklist, with annotations containing bibliogr. information. 'Maps and charts' (v.3, p.571–607); 'Tours by natives' (v.3, p.1–66); '. . . by foreigners' (v.3, p.67–167).
Rev: G. B. Parks Mod Lang N 52:310 '37; J. I. Wyer Lib Q 9:355–7 '39; J. L. Mesick Am Lit 10:522–3 '40; R. W. Frantz Mod Philol 38:101–3 '40; W. H. Bonner J Eng Germ Philol 49:257–60 '50.

862 **Fussell, George Edwin.** The exploration of England; a select bibliography of travel and topography, 1570–1815. London, Mitre pr., 1935. 56p. 21cm.
First pub. in Bk Trade J no.5–13 '35. Chronol. checklist of 353 items, with index of names.

863 **Maggs bros., bksllrs.,** LONDON. Voyages and travels in all parts of the world; a descriptive catalogue. London, 1942–64. 5v. illus., facsims. 22cm.
Annotated alphabetical short-title catalogue with numerous facsims.; general and subject indexes in v.3–5.

—— DIRECTORIES

865 **Norton, Jane Elizabeth.** Guide to the national and provincial directories of England and Wales, excluding London, published before 1856. London, Royal historical society, 1950. vii,241p. 23cm.
National directories arranged chronol., local by place; short-title list of 878 items with bibliogr. notes and locations of copies; indexes.

—— PROVINCIAL PRESSES

866 **Allnutt, William Henry.** English provincial presses. Bibliographica 2:23–46, 150–80, 276–308 '96.

867 —— [**Same**]: Addenda. *ib.* 3:481–3 '97.
Checklist with discussion, arranged by place; no index. Supplemented by his Notes on the introduction of printing presses into the smaller towns of England and Wales after 1750 to the end of the eighteenth century. Library ser2 2:242–59 Jl '01.

868 **Duff, Edward Gordon.** 'List of books printed by provincial printers or for provincial stationers' *in* The English provincial printers, stationers and bookbinders to 1557. Cambridge, 1912. p.129–39.
Checklist arranged chronol. under place, with locations of copies.

—— ROADBOOKS AND ITINERARIES

870 **Fordham, sir Herbert George.** The roadbooks & itineraries of Great Britain, 1570 to 1850; a catalogue with an introduction and a bibliography. Cambridge, C.U.P., 1924. xv,72p. facsim. 23cm.
Second ed. rev. from Catalogue of the road-books and itineraries of Great Britain and Ireland to the year 1850, included in his Road-books and itineraries bibliographically considered, Bib Soc Trans 13:38–68 Oc '13–Mr '15, and also issued London, East & Blades, 1916.
Annotated chronol. list with TP transcrs., and some bibliogr. notes.
Rev: N&Q 146:182 '24; [A. W. Pollard?] Library ser4 5:103–4 '24; TLS 28 F '24:131; Bkmns J 10:63 '24.

—— BEDFORDSHIRE

872 **Conisbee, Lewis Ralph.** A Bedfordshire bibliography, with some comments and biographical notes. [Luton] Bedfordshire historical record society [1962] 333p. 25cm.
Classified short-title catalogue with index of authors and editors.
Rev: C. Hargreaves Lib Assn Rec 64:314 '62.

—— BERKSHIRE

873 **Reading. Public libraries.** Local collection catalogue of books and maps relating to Berkshire. Reading, 1958. 259p. 25cm.

Classified catalogue with author and subject indexes; 'Local authorship and book production' (p.28–52); includes 82 works pub. at the Golden cockerel press; 'Berkshire maps, 1574–1900' (p.251–8).

—— —— READING

874 **[Reading. University. Library]** Reading printing, 1736–1962; an exhibition. [Reading, 1963] 10p. 33cm. Caption title. (Duplicated typescript)

Annotated chronol. checklist of 31 items, 1736–1962.

—— BUCKINGHAMSHIRE. ETON. SCHOOL

875 **Harcourt, Lewis Vernon.** An Eton bibliography. London, S. Sonnenschein, 1898. 45p. 21cm.

876 —— **[Same]:** [Anr. ed.] London, A. L. Humphreys, 1902. 132p. 23cm.

Chronol. checklist, 1560–1901.

—— CAMBRIDGESHIRE

877 **Bowes, Robert.** A catalogue of books printed at or relating to the university, town & county of Cambridge from 1521 to 1893. Cambridge, Macmillan & Bowes, 1894. 2v. facsims. 24cm.

Chronol. bookseller's catalogue of 3,515 titles, mostly ptd. in Cambridge, with collations; 'Appendix IV: List of books printed at Cambridge, 1521–1650, by Francis Jenkinson' (p.505–16).

878 **Cambridge. University. Library.** Catalogue of the books and papers for the most part relating to the university, town, and county of Cambridge, bequeathed to the university by John Willis Clark, by A. T. Bartholomew. Cambridge, C.U.P., 1912. xiv,282p. port. 26cm.

Dictionary catalogue.

—— —— CAMBRIDGE

879 **Bumpus, John & Edward ltd., bksllrs., CAMBRIDGE.** Catalogue of an exhibition of Cambridge books and printing, held in the Old court house. . . . 1931. Cambridge, C.U.P., 1931. 51p. 21cm.

Annotated chronol. checklist, 1521–1895: 126 items; '1917–19: books designed by Bruce Rogers and printed by J. B. Peace' (items 127–38); 'Books printed at Cambridge by Walter Lewis for publishers and societies' (items 7923–31); no index.

880 **Birley, Robert.** Some unrecorded Cambridge books in the library of Eton college. Cambridge Bib Soc Trans 1pt5:441–3 '53.

TP transcrs. and collations of 4 items not in STC or Barnes (no.1278).

881 **Oates, John Claud Trewhard.** Cambridge books of congratulatory verses, 1603–1640. Cambridge Bib Soc Trans 1pt5:395–421 '53.

Checklist of 13 items, with bibliogr. notes (p.396–408).

—— —— —— UNIVERSITY. PETERHOUSE

882 **Walker, Thomas Alfred.** A Peterhouse bibliography; a list of books and manuscripts by or concerning Peterhouse men. Cambridge, C.U.P., 1924. vi,114p. 25cm.

Bio-bibliogr. lists by author; no index.

Rev: N&Q 147:220 '24; 'Biblio' Bkmns J 11:21 '24.

—— CHESHIRE

883 **Cooke, John Henry.** Bibliotheca Cestriensis; or, A biographical account of books, maps, plates, and other printed matter relating to, printed or published in, or written by authors resident in the county of Chester. . . . Warrington, Mackie, 1904. IV. (various pagings) illus., port. 39cm.

Chronol. checklist.

—— CUMBERLAND

884 **Sparke, Archibald.** A bibliography of the dialect literature of Cumberland and Westmorland, and Lancashire north-of-the-sands. Kendal, T. Wilson, 1907. vi,49p. 22cm.

Checklist of 158 items with much local printing.

—— DERBYSHIRE

885 **Taylor, Norman.** Derbyshire printing and printers before 1800. Derbyshire Archæol J 70:38–69 '50.

'A chronological list of printers, publishers, booksellers and bookbinders in Derby and other towns in the 18th and early 19th centuries' (p.58–69).

—— DEVONSHIRE

886 **Dredge, John Ingle.** A few sheaves of Devon bibliography . . . Not published. Plymouth, W. Brendon, ptrs., 1889–96. 5pts.(250l.) 22cm.

50 copies repr. from Devonshire Assn Trans 21:498–548 '89; 22:324–56 '90; 24:476–526 '92; 25:552–601 '93; 28:547–605 '96; '. . . with notes and additions by mrs. Frances B. Troup' 31:331–55 '99.

Contents: 'The first sheaf': George Hughes, Ralph Venning, Francis Fullwood, Alexander Grosse, Michael Jermin, George Kendall, Jasper Mayne, Zachary Mayne, John Rowe, William Sclater, William Stephens; 'The second sheaf': John Conybeare, Joseph Glanvill, George Hakewill, Edward Kellett, Robert Luck, Samuel Stoddon; 'The third sheaf': John Barlow, Martin Blake, Richard Burthogge, Samuel Hieron, William Kempe, John Quick, Nathanael Carpenter, John Cowell; 'The fourth sheaf': Bartholomew Ashwood, William Chilcott, John Chishull, William Easte, Simon Ford, Thomas Long, Thomas Trescot; 'The fifth sheaf': Samuel Bamfield, William Bartlett, Thomas Bowber, John Carpenter, Richard Carpenter, Thomas Easton, Thomas Foster, John Gauden, Josiah King, Francis Moore, John Shower, Richard Smyth, Francis Webber, Edward Wetenhall; 'The sixth sheaf': Thomas Baker, Roger Gostwyke, William Hole, Richard Hole, James Salter, elder and younger, John Seager, Anthony Sparrow, William Strode, Henry Tozer, Walter Wylshman.

Chronol. lists under each author of early ed., with transcrs. of imprints, collations, and locations of copies, each preceded by brief biography.

—— DURHAM. SURTEES SOCIETY

887 **Thompson, Alexander Hamilton,** *comp.* 'Publications of the Surtees society' *in* Surtees society, Durham. The Surtees society, 1834–1934. . . . Durham, 1939. p. [86]–216.

Annotated checklist of 152 items, 1835–1937, with some bibliogr. notes.

—— EAST ANGLIA

888 **East Anglian master printers' alliance.** Early print in East Anglia; an exhibition. Eastbourne, 1951. IV. (unpaged) facsim. 20cm.
Annotated catalogue comp. by Sydney F. Watson.

889 **Library association. Eastern branch.** East Anglian bibliography [a checklist of publications not in the British national bibliography. Norwich, 1960–] v. 21cm.
Classified checklist of books and pamphlets printed locally, or written by local authors or local editors, in Cambridgeshire, Isle of Ely, Huntingdonshire, Norfolk, and Suffolk.

—— ESSEX

890 **Leyton. Public libraries.** Essex literature: catalogue of books published in or relating to the county. Compiled by Z. Moon. Leyton, 1900. 11p. 19cm.
Classified checklist, with 'Authors connected with the county . . . whose works are in the library' (p.11).

891 **Havering. Public libraries.** South Essex authors: a check-list issued for National library week, 1966. Romford, Central library [1966] [24]p. 21 × 26cm. (Not seen)

—— GLOUCESTERSHIRE

892 **Hyett, Francis Adams.** Notes on the first Bristol and Gloucestershire printers. Bristol & Gloucestershire Archæol Soc Trans 20:38–51 '95/6.
Discursive checklist of 12 early Bristol books, with bibliogr. notes and locations of copies, and of early ptd. Gloucestershire books.

893 **Hyett, Francis Adams** and **W. Bazeley.** The bibliographer's manual of Gloucestershire literature: being a classified catalogue of . . . printed matter relating to the county of Gloucester or to the city of Bristol. . . . Gloucester, Ptd. for the subscribers by J. Bellows, 1895–7. 3v. 23cm.

894 —— [Same]: Biographical supplement . . . by F. A. Hyett. [Gloucester?] 1915. xlviiip. 26cm.

895 —— [Same]: Supplement . . . by F. A. Hyett and R. Austin. Gloucester, 1915–16. 2v. 23cm. (Not seen)
Classified checklist.

896 **Gloucester. Public library.** Catalogue of the Gloucestershire collection; books, pamphlets and documents in the Gloucester public library relating to . . . Gloucestershire, compiled by Roland Austin. [Gloucester, Ptd. by H. Osborne] 1928. xii,1236p. facsims. 26cm.
Classified catalogue with author, subject, and printers and booksellers indexes; 'Local writers; local printing' (p.1042–98); complements Hyett and Bazeley.

—— —— BRISTOL

896a **Bristol. Public libraries.** Bristol bibliography, a catalogue of the books, pamphlets, collectanea, etc. relating to Bristol . . . edited by E. R. Norris Mathews. Bristol, Ptd. by order of the Libraries committee, 1916. x,404p. 25cm.
'Bristol printed books having no reference to Bristol otherwise than topographically are not included'; see for Thomas Chatterton (p.57–82); 'Newspapers and periodicals' (p.264–71); 'Poetry' (p.295–303); 'Topography' (p.353–66), and works by Bristol authors.

—— HAMPSHIRE

897 **Edwards, F. A.** Early Hampshire printers. Hampshire Field Club Pa & Proc
2pt1:110–34 '91.
Checklist to 1800 by place (p.123–34).

—— HUNTINGDONSHIRE

898 **Norris, Herbert Ellis.** Catalogue of the Huntingdonshire books collected
by. . . . Cirencester, For private circulation, 1895. 51p. 19cm.
Classified checklist, with works by local authors and 'Newspapers' (p.8–9), 'Almanacs'
(p.9), 'County maps [1610–1899]' (p.18–19).

899 —— Huntingdonshire civil war tracts. N&Q 133:86–7, 105–7 Ja, F '16.
Chronol. checklist of 28 items, with TP transcrs.

—— ISLE OF MAN *see* MAN, ISLE OF

—— KENT

900 **Margate. Public library.** Catalogue of books, pamphlets, and excerpts dealing
with Margate, the Isle of Thanet and the county of Kent in the local collection . . . compiled by Archibald J. Gritten. Margate, Borough of Margate
public library committee, 1934. 166p. 22cm.
Classified short-title catalogue.

901 **Burch, Brian.** 'Newspapers'; 'Periodicals published in Bromley' *in* A bibliography of printed material relating to Bromley, Hayes, and Keston, in the
county of Kent. [Bromley] Public library, 1964. p.129–31.
Checklist of 14 items, with bibliogr. notes.

—— LANCASHIRE

902 **Sutton, Albert.** Bibliotheca Lancastriensis; a catalogue of books on the
typography & genealogy of Lancashire, with an appendix of Cheshire
books. [2d ed.] Manchester, 1898. (First pub. 1893) 87p. illus., facsims.
19cm.
Annotated bookseller's catalogue of 1,500 items arranged alphabetically under places.
'Bibliotheca Cestriensis' (p.[73]–87).

903 **Wigan. Public library.** Lancashire printed books; a bibliography of all the
books printed in Lancashire down to the year 1800 . . . compiled and edited
by Arthur John Hawkes. Wigan, Ptd. for the Public libraries committee by
J. Starr, 1925. xxviii,155p. 22cm.
Chronol. catalogue from 1604 under place headings, with some bibliogr. notes.
Rev: A. W. P[ollard] Library ser4 6:203–4 '25.

—— —— BOLTON

904 **Sparke, Archibald.** Bibliographia Boltoniensis; being a bibliography, with
biographical details of Bolton authors, and the books written by them from
1550 to 1912; books about Bolton, and those printed and published in the
town from 1785. Manchester, University pr., 1913. xvi,211p. 29cm.
Classified short-title catalogue; no index.

—— —— HEYWOOD

905 **Green, John Albert.** Bibliography of the town of Heywood. Heywood, Ptd. at the Advertiser office, 1902. 113p. 19cm.
Classified checklist; no index.

—— —— LIVERPOOL

906 **Jaggard, William.** Liverpool literature; a descriptive bibliography. . . . Liverpool, Shakespeare pr., 1905. 36l. 23cm.
Checklist of 796 items.

907 **Liverpool. Public libraries.** Liverpool prints and documents catalogue. . . . Liverpool, Library, museum, and arts committee, 1908. viii,374p. 25cm.
Classified checklist with subject index; 'Liverpool books to the year 1800' (p.333–44); 'Newspapers, magazines, periodicals' (p.344–53): chronol. checklists.

908 **[Williams, William, and others]** Liverpool books. Welsh Bib Soc J 7:94–113 Jl '51.
Chronol. checklist, 1767–1908, of books ptd. in Welsh in Liverpool.

909 **Lewis, Idwal.** Liverpool books. Welsh Bib Soc J 8:103 Jl '55.
Addenda to Williams.

—— —— MANCHESTER

910 **Manchester. Public libraries.** The Manchester press before 1801; a list of books, pamphlets and broadsides printed in Manchester in the 18th century. Manchester, Libraries committee, 1931. 30p. 25cm. Covertitle.
Chronol. checklist, comp. by Geoffrey R. Axon.

—— —— —— SPENSER SOCIETY

910a **Axon, William Edward Armytage.** The Spenser society and its work. Library 7:201–10 Jl '95.
'Note A [John Taylor's writings issued by the Society]' (p.207–9); 'Note B [George Wither's books reprinted by the Society]' (p.210).

—— —— —— WYTHENSHAWE

911 **Manchester. Public libraries.** Wythenshawe, a bibliography. Manchester, Private circulation, 1955. [12]p. map. 21cm. (Not seen)
Comp. by William H. Shercliff.

—— LEICESTERSHIRE

912 **Leicester. Public libraries.** Catalogue of the books, pamphlets . . . relating to Leicestershire . . . compiled by C. V. Kirkby. Leicester, Ptd. by Thornley and Waddington [1893] 94p. 20cm. Covertitle.
Author checklist.

—— LINCOLNSHIRE

913 **Lincoln. Public library.** Bibliotheca Lincolniensis; a catalogue of the books, pamphlets, etc. relating to the city and county of Lincoln, preserved in the Reference department . . . compiled by A. R. Corns. Lincoln, Ptd. by W. K. Morton, 1904. viii,274p. 25cm.
'Part VI: works on general subjects by local authors' (p.203–41): alphabetical checklist.

—— LONDON

914 **Goss, Charles William Frederick.** The London directories, 1677–1855; a bibliography with notes on their origin and development. London, D. Archer, 1933. x,146p. facsim. 22cm.

Chronol. checklist, with some bibliogr. notes, and locations of copies; no index.

Rev: TLS 5 Ja '33:20; A. Hayward Bk Coll Q 9:85–6 '33.

915 **Welch, Charles.** The city printers. Bib Soc Trans 14:175–241 '19.

Contains checklists of official pubs. of successive City printers.

916 **London. Guildhall library.** A select list of printed items in Guildhall library relating to pageants, entertainments, and other special occasions in the city of London. Guildh Misc 2:257–69 Oc '64.

916a A **list** of works in Guildhall library relating to the plague in London, together with the bills of mortality, 1532?–1858. Guildh Misc 2:306–17 S '65.

916b A **select** list of printed works relating to the great fire of 1666 and the rebuilding of London, from collections in Guildhall library. Guildh Misc 2:369–76 S '66.

—— —— CHARTERHOUSE SCHOOL

917 **[Tod, Alexander Hay]** Charterhouse bibliography. [n.p., Godalming, n.d., 1899] [6]p. 21cm.

Includes 'Miscellaneous publications by members of the school' (p.[3]).

—— —— GUY'S HOSPITAL

918 **Wale, William.** List of books by Guy's men in the Wills' library, Guy's hospital. [London, Ash, ptrs.] 1913. 69p. 25cm.

Author checklist; no index.

—— —— RAY SOCIETY

919 **Curle, Richard Henry Parnell.** The Ray society, a bibliographical history. London, Ptd. for the Ray society; sold by B. Quaritch, 1954. vi,101p. ports. 22cm.

Annotated classified checklist; no index.

—— —— ST. PAUL'S CATHEDRAL

920 **London. St. Paul's cathedral. Library.** S. Paul's cathedral library; a catalogue of bibles, rituals and rare books; works relating to London and especially to S. Paul's cathedral, including a large collection of Paul's cross sermons . . . by W. Sparrow Simpson. London, E. Stock, 1893. xxii,281p. front. 23cm.

Classified short-title catalogue.

Rev: Library 5:143–4 '93.

—— —— UNIVERSITY. JEWS' COLLEGE

921 **London. University. Jews' college.** Jews' college, London; centenary exhibition ... catalogue of an exhibition of books by members of the academic staff and alumni. London, 1955 14p. 22cm. Covertitle.
Comp. by Ruth P. Lehmann.

922 **Lehmann, Ruth Pauline.** 'Select bibliography of the works of past and present staff and students of Jews' college' *in* History of Jews' college library, 1860–1960. [London, 1960] p.10–26.

—— MAN, ISLE OF

923 **Cubbon, William.** A bibliographical account of works relating to the Isle of Man. . . . London, H. Milford, O.U.P., 1933–9. 2v. illus., ports., facsims., music. 22cm.
Annotated catalogue; 'Manx language and literature', 'Poetry and drama', 'Prose fiction', 'Printing, journalism, &c.' in v.2.

—— NORFOLK

924 **Quinton, John,** *comp.* Bibliotheca Norfolciensis; a catalogue of the writings of Norfolk men and of works relating to the county of Norfolk, in the library of mr. J. J. Coleman, at Carrow abbey, Norwich. Norwich, 1896. 591p. 27cm.
Alphabetical checklist; no index.
Rev: Library 9:114–15 '97.

—— NORTHUMBERLAND

925 **Heslop, Richard Oliver.** A bibliographical list of works illustrative of the dialect of Northumberland. London, Published for the English dialect society by H. Frowde, O.U.P., 1896. 40p. 23cm.
Alphabetical checklist.

926 **Newcastle-upon-Tyne. Public libraries.** Local catalogue of material concerning Newcastle and Northumberland. . . . Newcastle, 1932. vii,626p. illus. 26cm.
Edited by Basil Anderton.
Contents: Author list.—Classified list.—Appendix on Newcastle typography [designed to supplement Welford's Early Newcastle typography].—Index to Newcastle printers, 1639–1850.—Index to subject list.

—— —— ALNWICK

926a **Burman, Charles Clark.** An account of the art of typography as practised in Alnwick from 1748 to 1900. Hist Berwickshire Naturalists' Club 23:305–59 '16/18.
'Checklist of the Alnwick Burns, 1807–1828' (p.316–17); 'Books printed in Alnwick, 1748–1900' (p. 317–56): chronol. checklist with locations of copies; 'Alnwick journalism' (p.356–9).

—— —— NEWCASTLE

927 **Welford, Richard.** Early Newcastle typography. Archæologia Aeliana ser3 3:1–134 '06.

'Books printed in Newcastle, 1639–1800' (p.55–117): chronol. checklist with locations; lists also of broadsides, chapbooks, book auction catalogues, and newspapers and magazines.

—— NOTTINGHAMSHIRE

928 **Nottingham. Public libraries.** List of books in the Reference library. No.14. Nottinghamshire collection, compiled under the direction of J. Potter Briscoe. Nottingham, 1890. 95p. 25cm. Covertitle.

Partial contents: Directories and annuals (p.68–70).—Robin Hood collection (p.70–1).— Byron collection (p.72–9).—Kirke White collection (p.80).

929 —— Literary associations of Nottingham and Nottinghamshire . . . [an exhibition catalogue] Nottingham, 1951. 24p. ports., facsim. 22cm.

Annotated catalogue of 220 items, of exhibition arranged by Duncan Gray and others for the Festival of Britain.

—— —— NOTTINGHAM

930 **Clarke, W. J.** Early Nottingham printers and printing. 2d ed. Nottingham, T. Forman, 1953. (First ed. 1942) ix,71p. 22cm.

'Local collections of early Nottinghamshire newspapers—1710–1775' (p.33–9): publication details and holdings under name of newspaper: 'Books [and pamphlets printed by Nottinghamshire printers up to 1800]' (p.41–53): chronol. checklist under printers' names: 'Chronological list of early Nottinghamshire booksellers, printers, bookbinders and stationers' (p.61–4).

—— —— NEWARK

932 **[Blagg, Thomas Matthews]** [Chronol. checklist, 1778–1836] *in* Newark as a publishing town, by T. M. B. Newark, 1898. p.65–83.

Repr. from the Newark Advertiser.

—— OXFORDSHIRE

933 **Cordeaux, Edward Harold** and **D. H. Merry.** A bibliography of printed works relating to Oxfordshire, excluding the university and city of Oxford. Oxford, O.U.P., 1955. xiv,411p. 19cm.

Classified chronol. checklist of 4,310 entries; 'Newspapers' (1326–80): some locations of copies.

933a —— **[Same]**: Addenda and corrigenda. Bod Lib Rec 6:433–43 F '58; 6:558–71 Ap '60.

934 **Honnold library for the Associated colleges,** CLAREMONT, CALIF. The William W. Clary Oxford collection; a descriptive catalogue edited by Grace M. Briggs. Oxford, Ptd. for the Honnold library of the Associated colleges, Claremont, Calif. by C. Batey at the O.U.P., 1956. xxv,234p. 24cm.

Classified checklist.

Rev: H. H. Davis Arizona Q Ja '56:54–6.

—— —— OXFORD

935 **Gibson, Strickland.** The collation of the Corpus statutorum univ. Oxon.
Bod Q Rec 4n047:271–4 N '25.

Quasifacsim. TP transcr., collation, and bibliogr. notes on 3 ed., 1634–1825.

935a **Madan, Falconer.** Oxford books; a bibliography of printed works relating
to the university and city of Oxford or printed or published there. Oxford,
Clarendon pr., 1895–1931. 3v. facsims. 23cm.

Contents: v.1. The early Oxford press, 1468–1640. (1895).—v.2. Oxford literature, 1450–
1640, and 1641–1650. (1912).—v.3. Oxford literature, 1651–1680. (1931).

Chronol. arrangement, with quasifacsim. TP transcrs., collations, and bibliogr. notes;
'Oxford periodicals, 1651–1680' (v.3, p. 391–4); 'Additions and corrections' and 'General
index' in v.3.

Rev: [A. W. Pollard] Bibliographica 2:127–8 '96; Library 7:9–13 '95; A. W. Pollard
Library ser3 3:237–9 '12; L. S. L[ivingston] Nation 95:9 '12; Athenæum 24 F '12:221;
W. D. J[ohnston] Lib J 37:406 '12; TLS 10 D '31:998; A. W. P[ollard] Library ser4
12:457–9 '32.

936 ——The Oxford press, 1650–75; the struggle for a place in the sun. Library
ser4 6:113–47 S '25.

'Some notable books printed at Oxford, 1650–75' (p.131–7): chronol. checklist with some
bibliogr. notes.

937 —— A chronological list of Oxford books, 1681–1713. [Transcribed from
F. Madan's notebooks by J. S. G. Simmons. Oxford, O.U.P., 1954] iv,72p.
26cm. (Duplicated typescript)

Checklist, with locations of some copies.

—— SOMERSET

938 **Green, Emanuel.** Bibliotheca Somersetiensis; a catalogue of books, pamphlets, single sheets and broadsides in some way connected with the county
of Somerset. Taunton, Barnicott and Pearce, 1902. 3v. 27cm.

Contents: v.1. Bath books.—2–3. County books, Bath excepted.

Author checklist, with extended TP transcrs. of early works.

—— —— BATH

939 **Shum, Frederick.** A catalogue of Bath books . . from the sixteenth century
to the twentieth century, and an alphabetical list of books, pamphlets, and
tracts. Bath, S. W. Simms, 1913. x,243p. 28cm.

Alphabetical list of books, etc. printed or published in, relating to, written by authors
born or resident in, Bath.

—— STAFFORDSHIRE

941 **Stoke-on-Trent. Public libraries.** Staffordshire directories, a union list of
directories relating to . . . Stafford, by N. Emery and D. R. Beard. Stoke-on-
Trent, 1966. vi,46l. 33cm. (Not seen.)

942 **Simms, Rupert.** Bibliotheca Staffordiensis; or, A bibliographical account of
books and other printed matter relating to, printed or published in, or

written by a native, resident . . . of Stafford: giving a full collation and biographical notices of authors and printers. . . . Lichfield, Ptd. for the compiler by A. C. Lomax, 1894. xxv,546p. 29cm.

Author catalogue; no index; the collection was sold in 1897.

—— —— WOLVERHAMPTON

943 **Lawley, George T.** The bibliography of Wolverhampton . . . a record of local books, authors and booksellers. Bilston, Ptd. by Price and Beebee, 1890. xii,72p. 29cm.

Discursive checklist of minimal bibliogr. aid.

944 **Mander, Gerald Poynton.** [A list of their books] *in* Early Wolverhampton books and printers, with a note on some playbills. [Wolverhampton, Whitehead, 1922] p.[17]–31.

Chronol. checklist, of 95 items, 1724–1801, with some TP transcrs. and facsims., collations, and locations of copies.

—— SUSSEX

944a **Piper, A. Cecil.** Note on the introduction of printing into Sussex up to the year 1850, with a chronology of Sussex printers to that date. Library ser3 5:257–65 Jl '14.

Checklist by place, with 'Chronology' (p.262–5)

—— WARWICKSHIRE. BIRMINGHAM

945 **Birmingham. Public libraries.** A catalogue of the Birmingham collection, including printed books and pamphlets, manuscripts, maps, views, portraits, etc.; compiled under the direction of Walter Powell and Herbert Maurice Cashmore. Birmingham, Published for the Public libraries committee by Cornish, 1918. xvi,1132p. 27cm.

946 —— [Same]: Supplement, 1918–1931; compiled under the direction of Herbert Maurice Cashmore. Birmingham, 1931. viii,913p. 27cm.

Author and subject catalogue; 'Books printed in Birmingham, but not otherwise relating to Birmingham' (p.1039–1120; v.2, p.875–902); 'Books published in Birmingham but not otherwise relating to Birmingham' (p.1121–32; v.2, p.903–13).

—— WORCESTERSHIRE

947 **Burton, J. R.** and **F. S. Pearson.** A bibliography of Worcestershire. [Oxford] Worcestershire historical society, 1898–1903. 2v. 28cm.

Contents: V.1. Acts of Parliament relating to the country.—2. Classified catalogue of books and other printed matter relating to the county.

Includes 'Books printed by John Oswen, Ipswich' (v.2, p.5–13): checklist of 29 items, 1548–53, with some bibliogr. notes and locations of copies; 'Works relating to the county generally' (v.2, p.14–107): TP transcrs., locations of copies, 1605–1903, with bibliogr. notes on works by major authors, e.g., Richard Baxter, Boscobel tracts.

—— YORKSHIRE. BARNSLEY

948 **Barnsley. Public library,** Bibliographical list of books, pamphlets, and articles connected with Barnsley and the immediate district compiled by Frank J. Taylor. Barnsley, Public library committee, 1916. 35p. 25cm.

'Barnsley printed books' (p.[28]–35): chronol. checklist by printer.

—— —— BRADFORD

949 **Dickons, J. Norton.** A catalogue of books, pamphlets, &c. published at
Bradford. . . . Bradford, H. Gaskarth, ptr., 1895. viii,241p. 22cm.

Alphabetical checklist, including as appendices 'Hymn books published at Bradford'
(p.189–92); 'A list of magazines and periodical publications printed . . .' (p.193–204);
'Newspapers and occasional papers printed . . . from 1825 to 1894' (p.205–21).

—— —— SHEFFIELD

950 **Freemantle, W. T.** A bibliography of Sheffield and vicinity. Section 1 to
the end of 1700. Sheffield, Ptd. by Pawson and Brailsford; London, Simpkin, Marshall, Hamilton, Kent, 1911. xviii,285p. illus., ports., maps,
facsims. 24cm.

Alphabetical checklist, with biographical and descr. notes, locations of copies, and
numerous TP facsims., etc. 'Appendix: local booksellers and publishers' (p.264–77).

—— —— WHITBY

951 **Keighley, Marion.** Whitby writers; writers of Whitby and district, 1867–
1949. Whitby, Ptd. for the author by Horne, 1957. 245p. 19cm.

Discursive handbook, with checklists in author section.

—— —— YORK

952 **Duff, Edward Gordon.** The printers, stationers, and bookbinders of York
up to 1600. Bib Soc Trans 5pt1:87–107 '99.

'List of books printed at York, or for sale in York, before 1600' (p.107).

953 **Cardiff. Public libraries.** Catalogue of printed literature in the Welsh department; by John Ballinger and James Ifano Jones. Cardiff, Free libraries committee; London, H. Sotheran, 1898. 559p. 26cm.
Short-title dictionary catalogue.

954 **Hughes, William John.** 'A bibliography of some English books about Wales and the Welsh, classified and arranged chronologically' *in* Wales and the Welsh in English literature from Shakespeare to Scott. Wrexham; London, 1924. p.[168]–211.
Checklist; including 'Dictionaries and grammars' (p.208–11).

—— ROADBOOKS AND ITINERARIES

960 **Fordham, sir Herbert George.** The road-books of Wales; with a catalogue, 1775–1850. London, Ptd. by Harrison, 1927. 19p. facsim., 2 fold. pl. 22cm.
Repr. from Archæologia Cambrensis 132pt2:276–91 D '27; chronol. checklist with author index.

—— ANGELSEY

961 **Jones, Thomas Llechid.** Bye-paths in Angelsey bibliography. Welsh Bib Soc J 3:125–65 D '27.

—— CARDIGANSHIRE. ABERYSTWYTH

962 **Evans, George Eyre.** Aberystwyth printed books and pamphlets. Aberystwyth, Welsh gazette, 1902. 17p. 28cm.
Chronol. checklist, 1809–1902.

—— DENBIGHSHIRE

963 **Williams, Owen.** Denbighshire authors and their works. Wrexham, 1937. 209p. 19cm. (Denbighshire. County library. Bibliography of the county. [Ruthin, 1935]–7. V.3.)
Author checklist, with indexes to localities, bardic names and pseudonyms, and authors in chronol. order.

—— PEMBROKESHIRE. HAVERFORDWEST

964 **James, H. E. H.** Haverfordwest printers [The earliest printers of Haverford, 1780–1840] Welsh Bib Soc J 1:114–18 Oc '12; 1:153 Je '13.
Chronol. checklist of 15 items.

REGIONAL BIBLIOGRAPHIES — SCOTLAND

965 **Terry, Charles Sanford.** A catalogue of the publications of Scottish historical and kindred clubs and societies, 1780–1908, and of the volumes relative to Scottish history issued by His majesty's stationery office, 1780–1908, with a subject-index. Glasgow, J. MacLehose, 1909. xiii,253p. 27cm.

966 —— [Same]: 1908–1927, by Cyril Matheson. Aberdeen, Milne and Hutchinson, 1928. viii,232p. 26cm.

967 **New York. Public library.** A list of works relating to Scotland, compiled by George F. Black. [New York] 1916. viii,1233p. 26cm.
Classified checklist, repr. with additions from N.Y. Pub Lib Bull v.18 Ja–D '14.

968 **Mitchell, sir Arthur** and **C. G. Cash.** A contribution to the bibliography of Scottish topography. Edinburgh, Ptd. at the University pr. by T. and A. Constable for the Scottish history society, 1917. 2v.(xii,705p.) 23cm.
Checklist under places in v.1, subjects in v.2, with index; 'Bibliography' (p.483–8); 'Printing' (p.562); 'Maps' (p.563–601).

969 **Aitken, William Russell.** The bibliography of Scottish literature. Lib Assn Rec 59:121–6 Ap '57.
Bibliogr. essay.

970 **Hancock, Philip David.** A bibliography of works relating to Scotland, 1916–50. Edinburgh, Edinburgh U.P. [1959–60] 2v. 23cm.
Supplements Mitchell and Cash, no.968; each volume separately indexed. 'Books and printing' (v.2, p.91–101).
Rev: C. E. Jones Bull Bib 23:126 '61; TLS 30 Je '61:408.

—— ROADBOOKS AND ITINERARIES

975 **Mitchell, sir Arthur.** List of travels and tours in Scotland, 1296 to 1900. Edinburgh [Ptd. by Neill] 1902. 212p. 21cm.
Annotated checklist of 860 items; repr. from Soc Antiqu Scotland Proc 35:431–638 '01.

976 —— [Same]: Supplementary list, with index. Soc Antiqu Scotland Proc 39:500–27 '05.

977 —— [Same]: 2d supplementary list, with index. *ib.* 44:390–405 '10.

—— ABERDEENSHIRE

980 **Robertson, Alexander Webster.** Hand-list of bibliography of the shires of Aberdeen, Banff and Kincardine. Aberdeen, New Spalding club, 1893. 133p. 25cm.
Alphabetical list of 6,000 items; additions by J. F. K. Johnstone in Scottish N&Q, 1895–1904. Superseded by next item.

981 **Johnstone, James Fowler Kellas** and **A. W. Robertson.** Bibliographia Aberdonensis, being an account of books relating to or printed in the shires of Aberdeen, Banff, Kincardine, or written by natives or residents or by

officers, graduates or alumni, of the universities of Aberdeen. Aberdeen, Third Spalding club, 1929–30. 2v. ports., facsims. 26cm.

Supersedes Robertson's Hand-list, 1893, and the Concise bibliography, first pub. in Aberdeen Univ Lib Bull 1:699–738 Ap '12; 2:73–120 Oc '13; 2:301–82 Ap '14.

Contents: 1. 1472–1640.—2. 1641–1700.

Quasifacsim. TP transcrs., collations, etc., with biogr. notes, and locations of copies; 'Index of locations' (v.2, p.597–604), and detailed general index.

Rev: A. W. P[ollard] Library ser4 10:344–8 '29; *ib.* ser4 11:513–14 '31; R. B. McKerrow R Eng Stud 6:246–7 '30.

—— —— ABERDEEN

982 **Ogilvie, James D**. The Aberdeen doctors and the National covenant. Edinburgh Bib Soc Pub 11pt2:73–86 Oc '21.

'Bibliography' (p.83–6): chronol. list of 11 items, fully described, with locations of copies.

983 **[Best, Maud Storr]** Lost local literature. Aberdeen, Aberdeen U.P., 1922. 42p. 23cm.

Author checklist, repr. from Aberdeen Univ Lib Bull 4:575–612 Ja '22; 5:7–8 Jl '22.

—— —— —— UNIVERSITIES

984 **Anderson, Peter John,** *ed.* 'Collections towards a bibliography of the universities of Aberdeen' *in* Studies in the history and development of the University of Aberdeen, 1906. p.[385]–525.

985 —— **[Same]**: [Edinburgh] Ptd. for the Edinburgh bibliographical society, 1907. vii,159p. facsims. 25cm. (Edinburgh Bib Soc Pub 8)

Quasifacsim. TP transcrs., collations, and bibliogr. notes for chronol. entries to 1736; thenceforth, short-title listing.

—— BANFFSHIRE

See Aberdeenshire. Johnstone, James F. K. and A. W. Robertson, 1929–30: no.981.

—— BERWICKSHIRE

986 **Hilson, James Lindsay**. Berwick-upon-Tweed typography. Edinburgh, Ptd. by Neill [1918] 25p. 21cm.

Repr. from Hist Berwickshire Naturalists' Club 23:433–55 '18. Chronol. checklist, 1753–1857, with locations of copies.

987 —— **[Same]**: Supplementary list. [1922] (Not seen)

—— CAITHNESS-SHIRE

989 **Beaton, David**. Bibliography of gaelic books, pamphlets, and magazine articles for the counties of Caithness and Sutherland, with biographical notes. Wick, P. Reid, 1923. 75p. 22cm. (Not seen)

Repr. from John O'Groats J.

990 **Mowat, John.** 'List of books and pamphlets printed or published in Caithness' *in* A new bibliography of the county of Caithness. Wick, 1940. p.113–22.

Chronol. checklist under name of printer or publisher.

—— DUMFRIESSHIRE

992 **Maxwell, sir Herbert Eustace.** 'A classified list of books relating to, or published in, Dumfriesshire and Galloway' *in* A history of Dumfries and Galloway. Edinburgh, 1896. p.363–400.

993 —— [Same]: 2d ed. Edinburgh, 1900. (Not seen)

Classified checklist; 'Fiction' (p.372–3); 'Poetry' (p.384–9); 'Principal maps of Dumfriesshire and Galloway' (p.400).

994 **Shirley, George William.** 'Handlist of books printed at Kirkbride and Dumfries by 18th century printers and their successors' *in* Dumfries printers in the eighteenth century with handlists of their books. Dumfries, 1934. p.35–58.

Repr. from Dumfriesshire & Galloway Nat Hist & Antiqu Soc Trans v.18. Chronol. checklist, 1711–1834, with locations of copies.

—— —— ANNAN

995 **Miller, Frank.** A bibliography of the parish of Annan, with biographical memoranda respecting the authors catalogued. Dumfries, 1925. 91p. 25cm.

Checklist, repr. from Dumfriesshire & Galloway Nat Hist & Antiqu Soc Trans. 'Annan authors and their writings' (p.9–78); 'Various printed books, manuscripts, pictures, etc.' (p.79–91); not indexed.

—— EAST LOTHIAN

996 **Jamieson, James H.** and **E. Hawkins.** Bibliography of East Lothian. Edinburgh, East Lothian antiquarian and field naturalists' society, 1936. xxvii, 107p. 25cm.

Classified annotated checklist.

—— FIFESHIRE. DUNFERMLINE

997 **Beveridge, Erskine.** A bibliography of works relating to Dunfermline and the west of Fife, including publications of writers connected with the district. Dunfermline, Privately ptd. by W. Clark, 1901. xxiv,320p. 25cm. (Also issued as Edinburgh Bib Soc Pub 5)

Alphabetical checklist, with various biogr. and bibliogr. footnotes; 'Chronological list of Dunfermline printers' (p.xvi–xix).

—— —— ST. ANDREWS

998 **Baxter, James Houston.** Collections towards a bibliography of St. Andrews. St. Andrews, W. C. Henderson, 1926. 143p. 23cm.

Classified checklist of 1,208 items; 'Early printed books' (nos.1093–1146); TP transcrs., brief collations, bibliogr. notes, and locations of copies of 46 items from 1552 to 1622.

999 **Bushnell, George Herbert.** Catalogue of the productions of the early presses at St. Andrews. St. Andrews, W. C. Henderson, U.P., 1926. 15p. 25cm.

Rev. version of list in Baxter (no.998); chronol. checklist with bibliogr. descrs., of 46 items, including 6 not in Aldis.

—— —— —— UNIVERSITY

1000 **Cant, Ronald Gordon.** The St. Andrews university theses, 1579–1747; a bibliographical introduction. Edinburgh Bib Soc Trans 2pt2:105–50 '41; Supplement *ib.* 2pt4:263–72 '46.

Classified bibliogr. of 51 items fully descr. with TP facsims. and locations of copies.

—— INVERNESS-SHIRE

1001 **Anderson, Peter John.** A concise bibliography of the printed & manuscript material on the history, topology & institutions of the burgh, parish and shire of Inverness. Aberdeen, Aberdeen U.P., 1917. x,264p. facsim. 23cm.

Rev. from Aberdeen Univ Lib Bull 2no10:415–47 Oc '14; 3no13:88–132 N '15; 3no14: 222–69 Ap '16; 3no15:372–407 Oc '16.

Classified subject and place checklist; excludes items written by local authors or printed locally when not germane to subject.

—— KINCARDINESHIRE

See Aberdeenshire. Johnstone, James F. K. and A. W. Robertson, 1929–30: no.991.

—— LANARKSHIRE. GLASGOW

1002 **Glasgow bibliographical society.** A century of books printed in Glasgow, 1638–1686, shown in the Kelvingrove galleries. . . . Glasgow, Ptd. for the Society by J. Maclehose, 1918. 59p. illus., port., facsims. 23cm. (Also issued as Glasgow Bib Soc Rec 5:1–102 '20)

Chronol. checklist of 100 items, with TP facsims., collations, and bibliogr. notes; numerical index of lenders, and 'A list of books printed in Glasgow from 1638 to 1686 not included . . .' (p.91–5).

1003 **Glasgow. University. Library.** Catalogue of the Wylie collection of books, mainly relating to Glasgow. Glasgow, Jackson, Wylie, 1929. 26l. 44cm.

Alphabetical catalogue prepared by Wilson Steel for inclusion in the General Catalogue of the University library.

—— —— —— ASSEMBLY

1004 **Ogilvie, James D.** A bibliography of Glasgow assembly, 1638. Glasgow Bib Soc Rec 7:1–12 '23.

Checklist of 18 items with TP transcrs., and discussion.

—— ORKNEY ISLANDS

1005 **Cursiter, James Walls.** List of books and pamphlets relating to Orkney and Shetland, with notes of those by local authors. Kirkwall, W. Peace, 1894. 73p. 24cm.

Alphabetical checklist.

—— PEEBLESSHIRE

See Roxburghshire. Sinton, James, 1899: no.1007.

—— PERTHSHIRE. PERTH

1006 **Carnie, Robert Hay.** Publishing in Perth before 1807. [Dundee] Abertay historical society, 1960. 39p. facsims. 23cm.

Chronol. checklist, with locations of copies; 'Appendix A: A list of Perth publications from 1770 to 1807' (p.23–37); 'B: A list of the stationers, booksellers, bookbinders, and printers in Perth from 1591 to 1807' (p.38).
Rev: W. S. Mitchell N&Q 206:40, 33 '61.

—— ROXBURGHSHIRE

1007 **Sinton, James,** *comp.* 'List of books relating to or published in the counties of Roxburgh, Selkirk, and Peebles' *in* Douglas, sir George. A history of the border counties, Roxburgh, Selkirk, Peebles. Edinburgh, 1899. p.433–72.

Classified checklist; 'Fiction' (p.439–40, 460, 467); 'Poetry' (p.449–52, 462–4, 468–9); 'List of maps' (p.471–2).

—— —— HAWICK

1008 **Sinton, James.** Bibliography of works relating to or published in Hawick; with an appendix containing a list of Hawick newspapers, local maps, and music. Hawick, Vair & McNairn, 1908. 16p. 24cm.

Checklist, repr. from Hawick Archæol Soc Trans 49–64 '08.

—— —— JEDBURGH

1009 **Hilson, James Lindsay.** Further yesterdays in a royal burgh. . . . Bibliography and typographia. [Jedburgh, Gazette office, 1912] 13p. 27cm.

Annotated author checklist.

—— SELKIRKSHIRE

See Roxburghshire. Sinton, James, 1899: no.1007.

—— SUTHERLAND

See Caithness-shire. Beaton, David, 1923: no.989.

1010 **Irish book lover.**
See its Notes and queries for occasional notes on local printing and publishing, and corrigenda and addenda to the published lists.

1011 **Dix, Ernest Reginald McClintock.** A list of Irish towns . . . 1903. *See* no.1013.

1012 **New York. Public library.** List of works . . . relating to Ireland, the Irish language and literature. N.Y. Pub Lib Bull 9:90–104, 124–44, 159–84, 201–29, 249–80 Mr–Jl '05.

1013 **Dix, Ernest Reginald McClintock.** A list of Irish towns and the dates of earliest printing in each. . . . 2d ed. Dublin, Corrigan & Wilson, ptrs., 1909. 15p. 19cm.
First pub. London, 1903. (Irish bibliogr. pamphlets, no.6).
See also Cassedy, J., 1923: no.1018.

1014 **Cassedy, James.** Bibliography of local printing. Irish Bk Lover 2:4–6 Ag '10.
Checklist of publications by Dix, John Anderson, James Coleman, James Tuite, and R. S. Maffet, in local archæol. journals.

1015 **Peddie, Robert Alexander.** Bibliography of Irish printing. Irish Bk Lover 3:51–3 N '11.
Classified list of material in the St. Bride Foundation institute library.

1016 **Ireland. National library,** Dublin. Bibliography of Irish philology and of printed Irish literature. Dublin, H.M.S.O., 1913. xii,307p. 26cm.
Comp. by Richard I. Best.

1017 **Best, Richard Irvine.** Bibliography of Irish philology and manuscript literature; publications 1913–1941. Dublin, Dublin institute for advanced studies, 1942. x,253p. 25cm.

1018 **Cassedy, James.** A typographical gazetteer of Ireland, or the beginning of printing in Irish towns. Dublin, M. H. Gill, 1923. 51p. 22cm.
Bibliogr. notes arranged by place; index of printers, but no title index.

1019 **Carberry, Eugene,** *comp.* 'Chronological list of E. R. McC. Dix's contributions to Irish bibliography' *in* Dix, Ernest R. McC. Printing in Dublin prior to 1601. . . . 2d ed. Dublin, 1932. p.34–41.
Dix's own books, usually so recorded in his checklists, are now in the National library, Dublin.

1020 **Eager, Alan Robert.** A guide to Irish bibliographical material, being a bibliography of Irish bibliographies and some sources of information. London, Library association. 1964. xiii,392p. 21cm.
'Printing' (p.159–78), items 1757–2001, including 'Local printing'.
Rev: TLS 9 Jl '64:618; P. J. Quigg Lib Assn Rec 66:371 '65; H. J. Heaney Nature 208:1139 '65.

—— ROADBOOKS AND ITINERARIES

1025 **Fordham, sir Herbert George.** The roadbooks & itineraries of Ireland, 1647–1850; a catalogue. Dublin, J. Falconer, 1923. 14p. 22cm.

Repr. from Bib Soc Ireland Pub 2n04:63–76 '23; chronol. checklist, with some bibliogr. notes.

—— ANTRIM. BELFAST

1026 **Anderson, John.** Catalogue of early Belfast printed books, 1694 to 1830. New enl. ed. Belfast, Belfast library, 1890. (First pub. 1886–7) 85,xip. 28cm.

1027 —— [Same]: Supplement to 3d ed. 1894. 23p. 28cm.

1028 —— [Same]: Supplement. 1902. vi,30p. 27cm.

Chronol. checklist, with locations of copies, and lists of Belfast printers; 'List of Belfast newspapers and periodicals, 1700 to 1830' (p.x–xi). An appendix includes discussion and bibliogr. descr. of Blow's bible of 1751, with locations of 13 copies.
Rev: J. S. Crone Bk Worm 3:289–93 '90; Library 2:475 '90; J. S. Crone Irish Bk Lover 11:13 '19; 12:137 '21.

1029 **Dix, Ernest Reginald McClintock.** List of books and tracts printed in Belfast in the seventeenth century. Roy Acad Ireland Proc Section C 33:73–80 '16.

Chronol. checklist of 18 items, 1694–1700, with some bibliogr. notes, and locations of copies; TP facsim.

1030 **Early** Belfast printed books in Museum library. Belfast Municipal Mus Q 52:8 Je '34.

Chronol. checklist, 1762–1830.

—— ARMAGH

1031 **Dix, Ernest Reginald McClintock.** Ulster bibliography: Armagh. [Books and pamphlets printed . . . in the eighteenth century] Ulster J Archæol 6:245–6 Oc '00; Addenda: Dix [and others] 7:53–7 Ja '01.

1032 —— List of books and pamphlets printed in Armagh in the 18th century. Dublin, W. Tempest, 1901. 12p. 19cm.

Supersedes previous list.

1033 —— [Same]: 2d ed. Dundrum, Cuala pr., 1910. 27p. 19cm. (Irish bibliogr. pamphlets, no.11)

Chronol. checklist, 1740–99, with some bibliogr. notes, and locations of copies.

1034 —— Printing in Armagh, 1801–24. Irish Bk Lover 4:83–4 D '12.

Chronol. checklist, with some bibliogr. notes, and locations of copies.

1035 —— Printing in Armagh since 1825. Irish Bk Lover 14:7–10, 55–6 Ja, Ap '24.

Chronol. checklist, with locations of copies.

—— —— LURGAN

1036 **Dix, Ernest Reginald McClintock.** Printing in Lurgan in 19th century. Irish Bk Lover 13:54–6 N '21.
Chronol. checklist, 1804–98, with some bibliogr. notes, and locations of copies.

1037 **Biblio,** *pseud.* Printing in Lurgan. Irish Bk Lover 13:176 Ap/My '22.

—— —— PORTADOWN

1038 **Dix, Ernest Reginald McClintock.** Printing in Portadown. Irish Bk Lover 7:123–4, 164–5 Ja, Ap/My '16.
Chronol. checklist, 1851–1900, with some bibliogr. notes and locations of copies.

—— CARLOW

1040 **Dix, Ernest Reginald McClintock.** Printing in Carlow in the eighteenth century. Irish Bk Lover 11:75–6, 94, 109–11, 126–7 Mr–Jl '20; 12:11–13 Ag/S '20.
Chronol. checklist, with some bibliogr. notes, and locations of copies.

—— CAVAN

1041 **Dix, Ernest Reginald McClintock.** Ulster bibliography: Cavan. Ulster J Archæol 8:23–4 Ja '02.

1042 —— Printing in Cavan, 1801–1827. Irish Bk Lover 4:165–7 My '13.
Chronol. checklist, with some bibliogr. notes, and locations of copies.

1043 —— Printing in Cavan, 1828–1900. Irish Bk Lover 11:6–7, 22–3, 40–1 Ag/S, Oc/N, D '19.
Chronol. checklist, with some bibliogr. notes, and locations of copies.

1044 —— Early printing in Cavan. Breifny Antiqu Soc J 1no3:279–86 '22. (Not seen; Eager's no.1872)

1044a **Cullen, Sara.** Books and authors of county Cavan; a bibliography and an essay. [Cavan] Cavan county council, 1965. xvi,132p. 23cm. (Not seen)

—— CLARE. ENNIS

1045 **Dix, Ernest Reginald McClintock.** List of books, newspapers and pamphlets in Ennis, co. Clare, in the eighteenth century. [Dublin, Cuala pr.] 1912. 31p. 20cm. (Irish bibliogr. pamphlets, no.8)
Chronol. checklist, 1776–1800, principally of journals, with locations of copies.

—— —— KILRUSH

1046 **Dix, Ernest Reginald McClintock.** Printing in Kilrush in 19th century. Irish Bk Lover 9:73–4 F/Mr '18.
Chronol. checklist, 1847–79, with some bibliogr. notes, and locations of copies.

—— CORK

1047 **Dix, Ernest Reginald McClintock.** List of books, pamphlets, journals, etc., printed in Cork in the 17th and 18th centuries. Cork, 1904. 13pts. 25cm.
Repr. from Cork Hist & Archæol Soc J '00: chronol. checklists, with locations of copies.
See also A. B., Irish Bk Lover 4:125 F '13; R. S. Maffet *ib.* 7:45 Oc '15.

1048 —— List of all pamphlets, books, &c. printed in Cork during the seventeenth century. Roy Irish Acad Proc Section C 30:71–82 '12.

Chronol. checklist of 40 items, with locations of copies.

1049 —— List of books, etc. printed at Cork prior to 1801. Cork Hist & Archæol Soc J ser2 25:107–8 '19.

Addenda to previous list, with some bibliogr. notes.

1050 —— Printing in Cork in the first quarter of the eighteenth century, 1701–1725. Roy Irish Acad Proc Section C 36:10–15 '21.

'List of books &c. printed in Cork, 1705–1725' (p.12–15): chronol. checklist, with some bibliogr. notes and locations of copies.

—— —— FERMOY

1051 **Dix, Ernest Reginald McClintock.** Printing and printers in Fermoy. Irish Bk Lover 13:76–7 D '21; W. H. G. F[lood] *ib.* 13:175–6 Ap/My '22.

Chronol. checklist, 1814–1886.

—— —— YOUGHAL

1052 **Dix, Ernest Reginald McClintock.** Printing in Youghal. Irish Bk Lover 4:24–5 S '12.

Chronol. checklist, 1770–1826, with some bibliogr. notes and locations of copies.

—— DERRY

1053 **Dix, Ernest Reginald McClintock.** Ulster bibliography: Derry. Ulster J Archæol 7:135–6, 174 Jl, Oc '01; 8:24 Ja '02; 9:71 Ap '03.

Chronol. checklist, 1689?–1797, with locations of copies.

1054 —— List of books, pamphlets, newspapers, &c. printed in Londonderry prior to 1801. Dundalk, Ptd. by W. Tempest, 1911. 35p. 19cm. (Irish bibliogr. pamphlets, no.7)

Rev. and enl. version of previous item; chronol. checklist, 1689?–1798, with locations of copies; no index.

—— —— COLERAINE

1055 **Dix, Ernest Reginald McClintock.** Ulster bibliography: Coleraine. Ulster J Archæol 13:22–3 F '07.

Note of 2 items, 1794, 1797 (with repr. of second), and locations of copies.

—— DONEGAL. BALLYSHANNON

1056 **Dix, Ernest Reginald McClintock.** Printing in Ballyshannon to 1900. Irish Bk Lover 17:101–2 S/Oc '29.

Chronol. checklist from 1831, with locations of copies.

—— DOWN

1057 **Dix, Ernest Reginald McClintock.** Ulster bibliography: Downpatrick, Dungannon, and Hillsborough. Ulster J Archæol 7:172–4 Oc '01.

Checklists of 18th century items, with locations of copies.

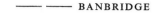 BANBRIDGE

1058 **Dix, Ernest Reginald McClintock.** Printing in Banbridge to 1900. Irish Bk Lover 17:7–8 Ja/F '29.
Chronol. checklist, 1844–94, with locations of copies.

—— —— NEWRY

1062 **Latimer, W. T.** Ulster bibliography: Newry printing. Ulster J Archæol 7:175–6 Oc '01.

1063 **Dix, Ernest Reginald McClintock.** Ulster bibliography: Newry printing. Ulster J Archæol 9:69–71 Ap '03.
Addenda to Latimer.

1064 —— List of books, pamphlets, newspapers, &c. printed in Newry from 1764 to 1810. Ulster J Archæol 13:116–19, 170–3 Ag, N '07; 14:95–6 My/Ag '08; 19:184–5 '09.
Chronol. checklist, with locations of copies.

1065 **Crossle, Philip.** The printers of Newry. Newry Reporter 30 Mr–7 Oc '11. (Not seen; Eager's no.1849)
Includes list of Newry publications, 1764–1909.

1066 **Maffet, R. S.** Printing in Newry. Irish Bk Lover 6:17–18 S '14.
Discursive addenda to Crossle.

—— —— NEWTOWNARDS

1067 **Dix, Ernest Reginald McClintock.** Printing in Newtownards in the nineteenth century. Irish Bk Lover 12:101–2 Mr/Ap '21.
Chronol. checklist, 1845–77, with locations of copies.

—— DUBLIN

1068 **Dix, Ernest Reginald McClintock.** Catalogue of early Dublin-printed books, 1601–1700 . . . compiled by E. R. McC. Dix; historical introduction

and bibliographical notes, by C. Winston Dugan. Dublin [T. G. O'Donoghue; London, B. Dobell, 1898–1912] 5pts. in 3v. (386p.) 27cm.
Checklist, with locations of copies.
Rev: Athenæum 17 S '98:385; J. B. Cork Hist & Archæol Soc J ser2 12:154 '98; Athenæum 17 Ag '12:161.

1069 —— Catalogue of early Dublin-printed books, belonging to mr. E. R. McC. Dix. Dublin, Ptd. by Irish Figaro, 1900. 23p. 19cm. (Not seen)
'This list is confined to the 17th century'. (Eager's no.1913)

1070 —— The earliest Dublin printing, with list of books, proclamations, &c., printed in Dublin prior to 1601. Dublin, O'Donoghue, 1901. 30p. facsim. 18cm.
See no.1072.

1071 **Ryan, Michael J.** A list of Greek and Latin classics printed in Dublin down to 1800. Bib Soc Ireland Pubs 3no2:[1–8] '26.
Checklist from 1692, with locations of copies.

1072 **Dix, Ernest Reginald McClintock.** Printing in Dublin prior to 1601. Dublin, Ptd. for the author by C. O. Lochlainn, 1932. xxiv,41(i.e. 43)p. facsims. (1 fold.) 24cm.
2d ed. of The earliest Dublin printing: no.1070. Chronol. catalogue with bibliogr. descrs. and notes, and locations of copies.
Rev: F. S. I[saac?] Library ser4 13:455 '33.

1073 **O'Hegarty, Patrick Sarsfield.** Dublin printed classics. Irish Bk Lover 27:184 Mr '40.
Addenda to Ryan: no.1071.

———— ———— ROYAL DUBLIN SOCIETY

1074 **Royal Dublin Society.** A bibliography of the publications of the Royal Dublin society from its foundation in . . . 1731, together with a list of bibliographical material relative to the Society. [Dublin, 1951] 39p. 26cm. (Duplicated typescript)

1075 ———— [**Same**]: 2d ed. [Dublin] 1953. 46p. 26cm. (Duplicated typescript)
Chronol. checklist.

———— FERMANAGH. ENNISKILLEN

1080 **Dix, Ernest Reginald McClintock.** Ulster bibliography: Enniskillen. Ulster J Archæol 15:172 '09. (Not seen; Eager's no.1871)

1081 ———— Printing in Enniskillen, 1798–1825. Irish Bk Lover 2:185–6 Jl '11.
Chronol. checklist, with some bibliogr. notes and locations of copies.

1082 ———— Printing in Enniskillen, 1830–1900. Irish Bk Lover 7:3–5 Ag '15.
Chronol. checklist, with locations of copies.

———— GALWAY

1082a **Dix, Ernest Reginald McClintock.** Printing in Galway, 1754–1820. Irish Bk Lover 2:50–4 N '10.
Chronol. checklist, with some bibliogr. notes and locations of copies.

1083 ———— Printing in Galway, 1801–1825. Irish Bk Lover 4:59–61 N '12.
Chronol. checklist, with some bibliogr. notes and locations of copies.

1084 ———— Printing in Galway, 1828–1853. Irish Bk Lover 9:130–1 Je/Jl '18; [1848–1900] 10:9–10 Ag/S '18.
Chronol. checklist, 1828–1900, with some bibliogr. notes and locations of copies.

———— ———— BALLINASLOE

1085 **Dix, Ernest Reginald McClintock.** Printing in Ballinasloe, 1828–1900. Irish Bk Lover 7:147–8 Ap/My '16.
Chronol. checklist, with some bibliogr. notes and locations of copies.

—— —— LOUGHREA

1086 **Dix, Ernest Reginald McClintock.** Printing in Loughrea, 1766–1825. Irish
Bk Lover 2:151–2 My ʼ11.
Chronol. checklist with some bibliogr. notes and locations of copies.

1087 —— Printing in Loughrea. Irish Bk Lover 6:175–6 Je ʼ15.
Chronol. checklist to 1900, with some bibliogr. notes and locations of copies.

—— —— TUAM

1087a **Dix, Ernest Reginald McClintock.** Printing in Tuam. Irish Bk Lover
2:101–2 D ʼ10; 7:40–1 Oc ʼ15.
Chronol. checklist, 1774–1888, with some bibliogr. notes and locations of copies.

—— KERRY. TRALEE

1088 **Dix, Ernest Reginald McClintock.** Printing in Tralee, 1801–30. Irish Bk
Lover 4:149–50 Ap ʼ13.

1089 —— Printing in Tralee, 1828–1900. Irish Bk Lover 10:79–81 Ap/My ʼ19.
Chronol. checklists with some bibliogr. notes and locations of copies.

—— KILDARE. ATHY

1090 **Dix, Ernest Reginald McClintock.** Printing in Athy to 1900. Irish Bk Lover
17:58–9 My/Je ʼ29.
Chronol. checklist from 1802, with locations of copies.

—— KILKENNY

1091 **Dix, Ernest Reginald McClintock.** Printing in the city of Kilkenny in the
seventeenth century. Roy Irish Acad Proc Section C 32:125–37 ʼ14.
Chronol. checklist, with locations of copies

1092 —— Kilkenny printing in the eighteenth century. Irish Bk Lover 16:6–9,
40–1, 55–8 Ja–Je ʼ28.

1093 —— Kilkenny printing in the nineteenth century. Irish Bk Lover. 16:89–
109 Jl/D ʼ28.
Chronol. checklist, 1747–1900, with some bibliogr. notes and locations of copies.

—— LEITRIM

1094 **Dix, Ernest Reginald McClintock.** Early printing in Leitrim. Breifny
Antiqu Soc J 1no3:263–7 ʼ22. (Not seen; Eager's no.1877)

—— LIMERICK

1095 **Coleman, James.** Limerick's early printed books and newspapers. Limerick
Field Club J 1no3:31–5 ʼ99; 1no4:45–7 ʼ00. (Not seen; Eager's no.1972)

1096 —— [**Same**]: A further list, by E. R. McC. Dix [and others]. *ib.* 2no6:136–
7 ʼ02. (Not seen; Eager's no.1973)

1097 **Dix, Ernest Reginald McClintock.** List of books, pamphlets, and news-papers printed in Limerick from the earliest period to 1800. Limerick, Ptd. by Guy, 1907. 32p. 19cm. (Irish bibliogr. pamphlet, no.5)

1098 —— [Same]: 2d ed. Limerick, Ptd. by Guy, 1912. 45p. 19cm. (Irish bibliogr. pamphlet, no.5)

Chronol. checklist, 1690–1800, with some bibliogr. notes and locations of copies.

1099 —— Printing in Limerick in the nineteenth century. Irish Bk Lover 18: 39–42, 75–6, 101–2, 135–6, 163–4 Mr–D '30; 19:117–20, 134–6, 174 Jl–D '31; 20:84–5, 106–8, 124–6 Jl–D '32; 21:7–9, 30–2, 56, 78–80, 109–10 Ja–Oc '33.

Chronol. checklist with collations and locations of copies; 'Limerick eighteenth-century printers who continued to print in nineteenth century' (p.56, 78–80).

1100 **Herbert, Robert.** Limerick printers and printing; part one of a catalogue of the local collection in the city of Limerick public library. Limerick, City of Limerick public library [1942] 61p. 25cm.

Chronol. annotated checklist of some 500 items.

Rev: TLS 14 N '42:564.

—— LONGFORD

1101 **Dix, Ernest Reginald McClintock.** Printing in Longford in 19th century. Irish Bk Lover 12:53–5 D '20.

Chronol. checklist, 1828–97, with some bibliogr. notes and locations of copies.

—— LOUTH. DROGHEDA

1102 **Dix, Ernest Reginald McClintock.** List of books and newspapers printed in Drogheda, co. Louth, in the eighteenth century. Dundalk, Ptd. by W. Tempest, 1904. 14p. 18cm. (Irish bibliogr. pamphlets, no. 3)

Repr. with additions from Drogheda Argus 4 Ja '02; chronol. checklist, 1728–1800, with locations of copies.

1103 —— List of books, pamphlets, newspapers, etc., printed in Drogheda from 1801 to 1825 inclusive. Irish Bk Lover 4:1–3 Ag '12.

Chronol. checklist with some bibliogr. notes and locations of copies; TP facsim.

—— —— DUNDALK

1104 **Dix, Ernest Reginald McClintock.** Printing in Dundalk, 1801–25. Irish Bk Lover 5:46–7, 58–9, 78–80 Oc, N, D '13.

Chronol. checklist, with some bibliogr. notes and locations of copies.

1105 —— Printing in Dundalk, 1825–1900. Irish Bk Lover 8:123–5 Je/Jl '17; 9:4 Ag–S '17.

Chronol. checklist, with some bibliogr. notes and locations of copies.

—— MAYO. ACHILL

1106 **Dix, Ernest Reginald McClintock.** Printing in Achill, 1837–66. Dublin, 1910. (Not seen: Eager's no.1880)

—— —— BALLINROBE

1106a **Dix, Ernest Reginald McClintock.** Printing in Ballinrobe to 1900. Irish Bk Lover 17:9 Ja/F '29.
Chronol. checklist, 1846–1900, with locations of copies.

—— —— CASTLEBAR

1106b **Dix, Ernest Reginald McClintock.** Printing in Castlebar during the nineteenth century. Irish Bk Lover 9:47–9 D/Ja '17/18.
Chronol. checklist, with some bibliogr. notes and locations of copies.

—— MEATH. TRIM

1107 **Dix, Ernest Reginald McClintock.** Printing in Trim. Irish Bk Lover 1:77–8 Ja '10.
Discursive checklist, 1835–60.

—— MONAGHAN

1108 **Dix, Ernest Reginald McClintock.** Ulster bibliography: Monaghan. Ulster J Archæol 7:102–8, 137 Ap, Jl '01; 8:171 Oc '02; 11:48 Ja '05.

1109 —— List of books, pamphlets and newspapers printed in Monaghan in the eighteenth century. Dundalk, Ptd. by W. Tempest, 1906. 16p. 19cm. (Irish bibliogr. pamphlets, no.4)
Rev. and enl. version of previous item; chronol. checklist, with locations of copies; no index.

1110 —— Printing in Monaghan, 1801–25. Irish Bk Lover 4:200–2 Jl '13; 5:2–3, 26–7 Ag, S '13.
Chronol. checklist, with some bibliogr. notes and locations of copies.

1111 —— Printing in Monaghan, 1825–30. Irish Bk Lover 10:34–5 Oc/D '18; 10:55–6 Ja/Mr '19.
Chronol. checklist, with some bibliogr. notes and locations of copies.

—— OFFALY. BIRR

1112 **Dix, Ernest Reginald McClintock.** Printing in Birr, or Parsonstown, 1775–1825. Irish Bk Lover 3:177–9 Je '12.
Chronol. checklist, with locations of copies.

—— ROSCOMMON. BOYLE

1113 **Dix, Ernest Reginald McClintock.** Printing in Boyle. Irish Bk Lover 7:24–6 S '15.
Chronol. checklist, 1822–97, with some bibliogr. notes and locations of copies.

—— SLIGO

1114 **Dix, Ernest Reginald McClintock.** Earliest printing in the town of Sligo. Irish Bk Lover 2:21–4 S '10.

Chronol. checklist, 1752–1800, with some bibliogr. notes and locations of copies.

1115 —— Printing in Sligo during 19th century. Irish Bk Lover 6:52–4, 69–71 N, D '14; 6:89–90 Ja '15; R. S. M[affet] 7:47 Oc '15; J. S. C[rone] 7:139 F/Mr '16; F.J.B. 8:115 Ap/My '17.

Chronol. checklists, with locations of copies.

—— TIPPERARY

1118 **Dix, Ernest Reginald McClintock.** Early printing in the south-east of Ireland. 1906–11. *See* no.1129.

—— —— CASHEL

1119 **Dix, Ernest Reginald McClintock.** Printing in Cashel in the 19th century. Irish Bk Lover 6:194–7 Jl '15.

Chronol. checklist, with some bibliogr. notes and locations of copies.

—— —— CLONMEL

1120 **Dix, Ernest Reginald McClintock.** Printing in Clonmel, 1801–25. Irish Bk Lover 4:42–6 Oc '12.

Chronol. checklist, with some notes and locations of copies; TP facsim.

1121 **Cassedy, James.** Clonmel printing, 1826–1900. Irish Bk Lover 25:90–8 Jl/D '37.

Chronol. checklist, with collations and locations of copies, comp. from ms. of E. R. McC. Dix.

—— TYRONE. COOKSTOWN

1122 **Dix, Ernest Reginald McClintock.** Printing in Cookstown to 1900. Irish Bk Lover 17:137–8 N/D '29.

Chronol. checklist from 1824, with some bibliogr. notes and locations of copies.

—— —— DUNGANNON

1122a **Dix, Ernest Reginald McClintock.** Ulster bibliography: Dungannon. Ulster J Archæol 9:42–3 Ja '03.

Discursive account of 1798 item.

1122b —— Printing in Dungannon, 1801–1827. Irish Bk Lover 4:188–9 Je '13.

Chronol. checklist, with some notes and locations of copies.

1122c **Marshall, John J.** 'Dungannon printing and bibliography' *in* History of Dungannon. Dungannon, 1929. p.129–39.

Chronol. checklist, 1797–1928, with locations of copies, repr. from the Tyrone Courier & Dungannon News; based on lists by J. S. Crone and E. R. McC. Dix in Irish Bk Lover and Ulster J Archæol.

—— —— STRABANE

1123 **Dix, Ernest Reginald McClintock.** List of books . . . printed in Strabane. 1901. *See* no.1125.

1124 —— [Ulster bibliography] Books and pamphlets printed in Strabane in the eighteenth century. Ulster J Archæol 6:3 Ja '00; 8:82, 171 Ap, Oc '02.

1125 —— List of books and pamphlets printed in Strabane, co. Tyrone, in the eighteenth century. 2d ed. Dundrum Dun Emer pr., 1908. (First pub. 1901) 27p. 20cm. (Irish bibliogr. pamphlet, no.1.)
Chronol. checklist, 1779–1800, with some bibliogr. notes and locations of copies.

1126 —— Printing in Strabane, 1801–1825. Irish Bk Lover 4:114–16, 135 F Mr '13.

1127 —— Printing in Strabane [1825–1900] Irish Bk Lover 7:68–9 N '15; A. A. Campbell 7:91 D '15.
Chronol. checklist, with some bibliogr. notes, and locations of copies.

—— WATERFORD

1128 **Coleman, James.** Early printing in Waterford, Kilkenny, &c. Waterford & S.E. Ireland Archæol Soc J 4:186–92 Jl/S '96; [addenda] E. R. McC. Dix 4:258 Oc/D '96; 5:60–4, 172–5 Ja/Mr, Jl/S '99; 6:57–9 Ja/Mr '00 [discursive material on Cashel printing]; 6:171–3, 238–47 Jl/S, Oc/D '00.
Discursive checklists, with various bibliogr. notes.

1129 **Dix, Ernest Reginald McClintock.** Early printing in the south-east of Ireland: Carlow. Waterford & S.E. Ireland Archæol Soc J 9:112–19 Ap/Je '06; Clonmel. 9:217–27 Oc/D '06; Carrick-on-Suir. 10:140–6 ApJ/e '07; Cashel. 10:317–19 Oc/D '07; Roscrea. 11:236–7 Oc/D '08; Wexford. 12:15–19 Ja/Mr '09; Carrick-on-Suir. 13:69–70 Ap/Je '10; Carlow: supplemental list. 14:108–12 Jl/S '11.
Repr. 1910: (not seen: *see* Eager's no.1812). Chronol. checklists, with some bibliogr. notes and locations of copies; TP facsims.

1130 —— Printing in the city of Waterford in the seventeenth century. Roy Irish Acad Proc Section C 32:333–44 '14. (Not seen; Eager's no.1961)

1131 —— Books, newspapers and pamphlets printed in Waterford in the 18th century. Waterford, News printing works, 1916. 19p. 18cm. (Anr. issue: 17p.)
Repr. from the Waterford News; chronol. checklist.
Rev: Irish Bk Lover 7:170–2 '16.

1132 **Cassedy, James.** Waterford printing, 1821–1900. Irish Bk Lover 26:128–33 S '39; 27:149–55 Ja '40.
Chronol. checklist, with locations of copies, comp. from ms. by E. R. McC. Dix.

—— WESTMEATH. ATHLONE

1133 **Dix, Ernest Reginald McClintock.** Earliest printing in Athlone. Irish Bk Lover 2:84–5 Ja '11.

Chronol. checklist of newspapers, 1770–1850.

1134 —— Printing in Athlone in the nineteenth century. Irish Bk Lover 6:106–8 F '15.

Chronol. checklist, with some bibliogr. notes and locations of copies.

—— —— MULLINGAR

1135 **Dix, Ernest Reginald McClintock.** Printing in Mullingar. Irish Bk Lover 2:120–2 Mr '11; 6:127–8, 140–1, 160–1 F, Ap, My '15.

Chronol. checklist, 1773–1900, with some bibliogr. notes and locations of copies.

—— WEXFORD

1136 **Dix, Ernest Reginald McClintock.** Printing in Wexford in the 19th century. Irish Bk Lover 27:250–4 N '40.

Chronol. checklist, 1805–99, with some bibliogr. notes and locations of copies.

—— —— ENNISCORTHY

1137 **Dix, Ernest Reginald McClintock.** Printing in Enniscorthy. Irish Bk Lover 14:83–4 Je '24; 'P.' *ib.* 14:111 Jl/Ag '24.

1138 —— Printing in Enniscorthy to 1900. *ib.* 17:138–9 N/D '29.

Rev. version of preceding item; chronol. checklist, 1841–1900, with locations of copies.

—— —— GOREY

1139 **Dix, Ernest Reginald McClintock.** Printing in Gorey. Irish Bk Lover 14:100–1 Je '24.

Chronol. checklist, 1854–93, with locations of copies.

PRESSES AND PRINTING

BIBLIOGRAPHIES OF PRINTING AND PUBLISHING

1140 **Reed, Talbot Baines.** A list of books and papers on printers and printing under the countries and towns to which they refer. Bib Soc Trans 3pt1:82–152 '95.
Ed. by Alfred W. Pollard; 'England, Wales, Scotland and Ireland' (p.90–5).

1141 **St. Bride foundation institute,** LONDON. Catalogue of the Passmore Edwards library. Compiled by John Southward [and F. W. T. Lange] London, Ptd. for the governors of the Foundation by Bradbury, Agnew, 1897. xv,79p. port., facsim. 21cm.
Short-title dictionary catalogue.

1142 ——— Catalogue of the William Blades library. Compiled by J. Southward [and F. W. T. Lange] London, Ptd. for the governors of the Foundation by Bradbury, Agnew, 1899. xiv,186p. port. 22cm.
Short-title dictionary catalogue of '. . . books mainly on the origin and history of typography and the allied arts'.
Rev: Lib Assn Rec 2:105–6 '99.

1143 ——— **Technical reference library.** Catalogue of works on practical printing, processes of illustration & bookbinding published since the year 1900 and now in the St. Bride foundation technical library. Compiled by R. A. Peddie. London, Ptd. by students of the St. Bride foundation printing school 1911. 32p. 21cm.

1144 **Ross, James.** A select bibliography of the art of printing to 1640. Lib & Bk World 10:28–31, 42–5, 59–64, 78–83, 99–103, 119–26, 142–6, 165–8 Oc '20–My '21.
Chronol. checklist, with indexes.

1146 **St. Bride foundation institute,** LONDON. **Technical reference library.** Catalogue of the Technical reference library of works on printing and the allied arts. London, Ptd. for the governors, 1919. xvi,999p. 22cm.
Short-title author catalogue, comp. by Robert A. Peddie; no index.

1147 ——— Some books on printing; English and American text books published since 1900. Compiled by W. T. Berry. [London] Ptd. by students of St. Bride foundation printing school, 1919–20. 20p. 20cm.
Classified checklist of works on technical aspects of modern printing; no index.

1148 **Norwich. Public libraries.** Books on printing and some related subjects; a select annotated and classified catalogue of books in the . . . library, by George A. Stephen. Norwich, Norwich and district master printers' association, 1921. 31p. 19cm.

1149 **Sheffield. Public libraries.** Catalogue of books in the central libraries on the printing and allied trades. Sheffield, J. W. Northend, 1925. 31p. 19cm.
Classified checklist with subject index.

1150 **Leicester. Public libraries.** Catalogue of works on printing, bookbinding, paper-making and related industries. Leicester, C. H. Gee, 1927. 31p. 19cm.
Classified checklist.

1151 **Bristol. Public libraries.** List of books on printing and the allied trades in the Bristol public libraries, prepared under the direction of James Ross. . . . [Bristol] Ptd. by the Bristol school of printing, Merchant venturers' technical college, 1936. 30p. 21cm.
Classified checklist.

1152 **Ulrich, Carolyn Farquhar** and **K. Küp.** Books and printing; a select list of periodicals, 1800–1942. Woodstock, Vt., W. E. Rudge; N.Y., New York public library, 1943. xi,244p. 25cm.
Classified annotated checklist; 'Bibliography' (p.144–55); 'Collecting' (p.156–64); 'Libraries' (p.165–74); title index.

1153 **Carter, John Waynflete.** A handlist of the writings of Stanley Morison; with some notes by mr. Morison and indexes by Graham Pollard. Cambridge, Ptd. at the C.U.P. for private distribution, 1950. viii,45p. 23cm.

1154 **St. Bride foundation institute,** LONDON. **Technical reference library.** Catalogue of the periodicals relating to printing & allied subjects in the Technical library. . . . London, St. Bride foundation institute, 1951. 35p. 25cm.
Title list with useful annotations.

1155 **Smith, Alan Rae.** A. F. Johnson, historian of printed books. Signat new ser 13:47–56 '51.
'Selected handlist of typographic and calligraphic writings of A. F. Johnson, compiled by Sheila Jones' (p.51–6)

1156 **Berry, William Turner** and **J. Mosley.** Graphic arts book list. Penrose Ann 52:64–9 '58.

1157 —— A graphic arts bibliography. Penrose Ann 53:61–3 '59.

1158 **Handover, Phyllis Margaret.** Stanley Morison, a second handlist, 1950–1959; reprinted from Motif 3. [London] Shenval pr. [1959]. p. [51]–7. port., facsim. 29cm. Covertitle.
'Additions and corrections to the original handlist' [by] John Carter (p.55–7).

1159 **Mosley, James.** A graphic arts booklist, 1959–1961. Penrose Ann 56:155–60 '62.

1160 **Manchester. Public libraries. Reference library.** Subject catalogue, section 655. Printing, pt. 2: Type & typesetting, printing processes, publishing &

bookselling, copyright. Edited by G. E. Haslam. Manchester, Manchester libraries committee, 1963. 87p. 26cm.

1,438 classified entries, with indexes.

Rev: TLS 9 Ap '64:300.

1161 **[Watford. College of technology.]** A catalogue of journals relevant to printing held at Watford college of technology, compiled by Alan Pritchard, April, 1963. Watford [1963]. 16p. 29cm. Covertitle. (Duplicated typescript.)

1162 **Carter, John Waynflete.** Morisonianum. Bk Coll 14no3:365–6 '65.

Addenda to 1950 Handlist.

BOOKLISTS

1165 **Arber, Edward.** Contemporary printed lists of books produced in England. Bibliographica 3:173–91 '97.

Chronol. checklist of 55 items.

1166 **Eames, Wilberforce,** *comp.* 'A list of the catalogues, &c. published for the English booktrade from 1595–1902' *in* Growoll, Adolf. Three centuries of English booktrade bibliography. New York, 1903. p.101–73. (Repr. London, 1964)

Chronol. checklist with notes; 'Periodicals published for the English booktrade, 1797–1903' (p.161–73).

1167 **Clarke, Olive E.** English publishing trade bibiographies. Lib World 13:197–201 Ja '11.

'A chronological list of English publishing trade bibliographies' (p.201).

1168 **Pollard, Graham.** Bibliographical aids to research IV: General lists of books printed in England. Bull Inst Hist Res 12:164–74 F '35.

'Chronological table' (p.172–4).

1169 **Foster, I. J. C.** Publishers' lists. Durham Philobib 1:19–22 My '50.

Checklists of publishers' lists, 1641–1776, not mentioned in the Dictionaries of printers.

1170 **Pollard, Graham** and **A. Ehrman.** 'The Broxbourne material' *in* The distribution of books by catalogue from the invention of printing to A.D. 1800, based on material in the Broxbourne library. Cambridge, 1965. p.283–352.

Checklists, with bibliogr. notes, of British catalogues, retailers' reference books, daybooks, trade cards, and individual catalogues, catalogues in books, proposals, auction catalogues and catalogues of institutional and private libraries.

PRINTING IN ANGLO-SAXON

1172 **Truman, Joan,** 1949: no.224.

1173 **Cambridge. University. Corpus Christi college.** Printing with Anglo-saxon types, 1566–1715; catalogue of a small exhibition. . . . Cambridge, C.U.P., 1952. 13p. 22cm. Covertitle.

Annotated checklist of 16 items, comp. by Bruce Dickins.

PRINTING IN GAELIC

1174 **Dix, Ernest Reginald McClintock.** List of Irish printed books, &c. from
1571 to 1820. An Claidheamh Soluis 5 Ja–Ap '04. (Not seen: Eager's no.
1804)

1175 —— List of books, pamphlets, &c. printed wholly or partly in Irish, from
the earliest period to 1820, compiled by . . . Dix, and Seamus Casaide.
Dublin, 1905. ii,24p. 25cm.
Repr. from preceding item; chronol. checklist of 156 items from 1571, with locations of
copies.

1176 —— [**Same**]: New and enl. ed. Sect. 1. Dublin, Hanna and Neale, 1913.
19p. 16cm.
No more pub.; chronol. checklist, 1571–1700, with locations of copies.

1177 **Cassedy, James.** Some Irish publications in Ulster. Ulster J Archæol
16:97–100 '10. (Not seen: Eager's no.1803)

1178 **MacLean, Donald.** Typographia Scoto-gadelica; or, Books printed in the
Gaelic of Scotland from . . . 1567 to . . . 1914, with bibliographical and
biographical notes. Edinburgh, J. Grant, 1915. x,372p. 27cm.
Author catalogue, with some bibliogr. notes.

1179 **Lynam, Edward W.** The Irish character in print, 1571–1923. Library ser4
4:286–325 Mr '24.

1180 **Aberdeen. University. Library.** Scottish-gaelic holdings: classified list.
Aberdeen, 1966. [9]109p. 27p. (Not seen)

PRINTING IN WELSH

1181 **Swansea. Public library.** . . . Catalogue of Welsh books with English and
other literature relating to Wales & celtic countries . . . Swansea, Ptd. by
C. E. Willing, 1911. v,50p. 24cm.
Comp. by David R. Phillips; author checklist, with a second classified arrangement.
This item complements Rowlands, W. Cambrian bibliography, containing an account of
the books printed in the Welsh language . . . 1546 to the end of the eighteenth century.
. . . Edited and enl. by D. Evans. Llanidloes, J. Pryse, 1869, and Wales. National library,
Aberystwyth. Bibliographica celtica. Aberystwyth, 1910– .

PRINTING ON VELLUM

1182 **Duff, Edward Gordon.** 'List of English books on vellum to 1600' *in* English
printing on vellum to the end of the year 1600. [Aberdeen] 1902. p.[17]–20.
Chronol. checklist, with locations of copies.

PRIVATELY PRINTED BOOKS
See also under *Presses*, and names of individual presses and printers.

1185 **Dobell, Bertram.** Catalogue of books printed for private circulation.
Collected by Bertram Dobell, and now described and annotated by him.
London, 1906. 238p. 22cm.
Issued in 4 pts., 1891–1906, with title: Catalogue of a collection of privately printed
books. . . . 'Second alphabet' (p.202); alphabetical checklist, with descr. notes.

1186 **Barker, Nicolas.** 'Bibliographical table of the publications of the Rox-burghe club' *in* The publications of the Roxburghe club, 1814–1962; an essay. . . . Cambridge, 1964. p.66–99.

TYPOGRAPHY — GENERAL

1187 **Berry, William Turner.** Books on type and type-founding. Bk Coll Q 4:65–75 Oc '31.

1188 **Howe, Ellic.** Bibliotheca typographica. Signat new ser 10:49–64 '50.
Bibliogr. essay.

TYPOGRAPHY — MANUALS

See also Presses — Moxon, Joseph, 1627–1700.

1190 **Wroth, Lawrence Counselman.** Corpus typographicum; a review of English and American printers' manuals. Dolph 2:157–70 '35.
Checklist of 12 items, 1683–1904, with discussion. Repr. in his Typographic heritage. New York, 1949. p.55–90.

1191 **[Hitchings, Sinclair H.** Catalogue of an exhibition of 22 printing manuals of Joseph Moxon and his successors, with location of copies indicated] Print & Graph Arts 5no2:23–36 My '57.
Annotated catalogue of 15 English and 7 American manuals.

1192 **Davis, Herbert John** and **H. G. Carter,** *ed.* 'Later books on printing and their reliance on Moxon' *in* Moxon, Joseph. Mechanick exercises on the whole art of printing. 2d ed. London, 1962. p.442–4. (First pub. 1958)
Annotated checklist of 12 items, 1688–1841.

TYPOGRAPHY — PROPOSALS

1195 **[Carter, Harry Graham]** Proposals in the John Johnson collection; chronological list of proposals for English books up to 1800. Oxford, O.U.P., 1960. 2l. 20 × 25cm. (Duplicated typescript)
Chronol. list of 431 prospectuses at the O.U.P., with bibliogr. notes.

1196 —— **[Same]**: Additions, Jan. 1961 (incorporating and superseding the first addenda). [Oxford, O.U.P., 1961] 5l. 20 × 25cm. (Duplicated typescript)

1197 **Morison, Stanley** and **H. G. Carter.** 'Fell's announcements and proposals' *in* John Fell, the University press and the Fell types. . . . Oxford, 1967. p.[253].

TYPOGRAPHY — SPECIMENS

1200 **Hart, Horace.** Notes on a century of typography at the University press, Oxford, 1693–1794; with annotations and appendices. Oxford, O.U.P., 1900. xvi,172p. illus., facsims. 33cm.
'Summary of the make-up, contents, &c. of the eight University press specimens' (p.1); 'List of founts, etc. mentioned and exemplified in the eight specimens and in the appendixes' (p.3–4).

1201 **Birrell & Garnett, ltd., bksllrs.**, LONDON. Catalogue of I. Typefounders' specimens. II. Books printed in founts of historic importance. III. Works on typefounding, printing & bibliography. London, 1928. vii[viii–xii] 107p. illus., facsims., diagrs. 29cm.

Comp. by Graham Pollard. 'Chronological list of the type specimens listed in Part 1' (p.x–xi); 'Chronological list of types shown by books listed in Part 2' (p. 50–1); classified checklist of 252 items, with notes.

1201a 'Census of copies' *in* [Oxford. University. Clarendon press] A specimen of the several sorts of letter given to the University by dr. John Fell, Oxford, 1693. . . . London, 1928. p.11–13.

'A list of the type specimen books and sheets issued by the Oxford university press' (p.4–15).

1202 **Morison, Stanley.** 'John Bell's type specimens' *in* John Bell, 1745–1831, bookseller, printer, publisher, typefounder, journalist, &c. . . . Cambridge, 1930. p.136.

Chronol. checklist of 4 items, 1788–9, with locations of copies, and facsims.

1203 **St. Bride foundation institute,** LONDON. **Technical reference library.** Catalogue of an exhibition of type specimens, 1918–1930. London, Saint Bride foundation institute [1930] 21p. 18cm.

List of 701 exhibits.

1204 **Berry, William Turner** and **A. F. Johnson.** Catalogue of specimens of printing types by English and Scottish printers and founders, 1665–1830. . . . London, H. Milford, O.U.P., 1935. liii,98p. illus., facsims. (part fold.) 29cm.

Full descrs., extensive facsims., and locations of copies; chronol. index. *See* no.1208.

1205 **Johnson, Alfred Forbes.** An unrecorded specimen sheet of a Scottish printing house. Edinburgh Bib Soc Trans 1pt1:61–4 '36.

Addendum to preceding item, with facsim.

1206 **Gray, Nicolette Mary.** 'List of type specimen books, arranged by foundries' *in* XIXth century ornamented types and title pages. London, 1938. p.107–94.

'Chart of ornamental types' (p.197–207).

1207 **Carter, Harry Graham [and others]** A list of type specimens. Library ser4 22:185–204 Mr '42.

Alphabetical list by printer under country headings, with locations of copies.

1207a **McLean, Ruari.** Printers' type-specimen books in England, 1920–40. Signat new ser 5:33–49 '48.

'The type books' (p.48–9).

1208 **Berry, William Turner** and **A. F. Johnson.** A note on the literature of British type specimens, with a supplement to the Catalogue of specimens of printing types by English and Scottish printers and founders, 1665–1830. Signat new ser 16:29–40 '52.

'The Supplement' (p.31–7); 'Printers' specimens' (p.37–40); full descrs., notes, and locations of copies; 2 facsims.

1209 **Fern, Alan M.** Typographical specimen books; a check-list of the Brox-bourne collection, with an introduction by W. Turner Berry. Bk Coll 5no3:256–72 '56.

'Check-list I. Type specimens issued by founders, publishers and booksellers, 1550–1850' (p.258–69); from the library of A. Ehrman.

1210 **Simmons, John Simon Gabriel.** Specimens of printing types before 1850 in the typographical library at the University press, Oxford. Bk Coll 8no4:397–410 '59.

'Catalogue of specimens' (p.403–9); list of 68 items, with bibliogr. notes and locations of copies.

1211 **Morison, Stanley** and **H. G. Carter.** 'The Fell type specimens' *in* John Fell, the University press and the Fell types. . . . Oxford, 1967. p.[229]–32.

PRESSES — BIBLIOGRAPHIES

1220 **Haas, Irvin.** A bibliography of private presses. Am Bk Coll 5:85–8, 107–10, 140–3, 207–8 Mr–Jl '34.

Classified checklist of 160 items; further parts concern American presses only.

1221 —— A bibliography of material relating to private presses. Chicago, Black cat pr., 1937. xvi,57p. 22cm.

1222 **Rae, Thomas** and **G. Handley-Taylor.** The book of the private press; a check-list. Greenock, Signet pr., 1958. xvi,48p. 20cm.

'. . . every endeavour has been made to list all existing private presses in the English speaking world'. Checklist of presses' names by country, with short bibliogr. notes.

PRESSES — GENERAL

1225 **Steele, Robert Reynolds,** *ed.* The revival of printing; a bibliographical catalogue of works issued by the chief modern English presses. London, Riccardi pr. [1912] xxxiii,89p. facsims. 24cm.

Chronol. checklists under names of 13 private presses.
Rev: Athenæum 20 Ap '12:433; Nation 95:32–3 '12.

1226 **Liverpool. University. Library.** In memoriam William Noble . . . a catalogue of the books . . . bequeathed. . . . Liverpool, Liverpool U.P., 1913. 182p. 26cm.

General author short-title catalogue of English books, with strong private press holdings.

1227 **Tompkinson, G. S.** A select bibliography of the principal modern presses, public and private, in Great Britain and Ireland. London, Published by the [First edition] club, 1928. xxiv,238p. facsims. (part.col.) 26cm.

Complete 'bibliographies' of presses in pt.1, 'brief accounts and selected bibliographies of the less "collectable" presses' in pt.2; chronol. checklists under name of press, with bibliogr. notes; no index.
Rev: TLS 12 Ap '28:273.

1228 **Ransom, Will.** Private presses and their books. New York, R. R. Bowker, 1929. 493p. illus. 22cm.

'Check-lists' (p.191–451); chronol. lists under names of English and American presses; with some bibliogr. notes, but comp. from secondary sources.

1229 **First edition club,** LIVERPOOL. Catalogue of the first exhibition by members, of finely printed books from modern presses. . . . Liverpool, Basnett gallery [1930] 31p. 21cm.

1230 **Ransom, Will.** Selective checklists of press books; a compilation of all important & significant private presses, or press books which are collected. New York, P. C. Duschnes, 1945–50. 12 pts. in 11v. (420p.) 23cm.

Checklists with bibliogr. notes.

1231 **Binns, Norman Evan,** *ed.* Union list of private press material in the East Midlands. [Nottingham] East Midland division of the Association of assistant librarians, 1955. 27p. 19cm. (Duplicated typescript)

1232 **Johannesburg. Public library.** Modern private presses; a catalogue of books in the Johannesburg public library from some modern private and other similar presses. Johannesburg, 1955. iii,55p. 24cm. (Duplicated typescript)

Annotated checklist in rough chronol. order, with some bibliogr. notes.

1233 **Manchester. Public libraries. Reference library.** Subject catalogue: section 094: Private press books. Edited by Sidney Horrocks. Manchester, Libraries committee, 1959– . [2]v. 24cm.

Contents: Pt.1 A–G.—2. H–W. (1960).—

Alphabetical by press, with typographical and bibliogr. notes; indexes.

1234 —— [Same]: Appendix. Manchester R 9:89–90 '60.

1235 **Private** press books, 1959– . Edited by Roderick Cave & Thomas Rae. North Harrow, Private libraries association, 1960– . v. illus. 22cm.

Arranged alphabetically under presses, with descr. notes; indexed. Each annual issue contains a survey of the literature of the private press.

1236 **Times bookshop,** LONDON. English private presses, 1757–1961 [an exhibition, April 12–22, 1961] London, 1961. 62p. 26cm.

Class. chronol. catalogue of 95 items, with bibliogr. notes and refs.
Rev: N. B. [arker?] Bk Coll 11:113 '62.

PRESSES — ACHILL PRESS

1240 **Maffett, R. S.** The Achill press. Irish Bk Lover 2:65–8 D '10.

Chronol. checklist, 1837–66, of works pub. by Edward Nangle, with some bibliogr. notes and locations of copies.

PRESSES — ASHENDENE PRESS

1241 **Ashendene press.** A list of the books printed at the Ashendene press, mdcccxcv–mcmxiii. [Chelsea, 1913]. [8]p. 19cm. Covertitle.

1242 **Newdigate, Bernard Henry.** Mr. C. H. St. John Hornby's Ashendene press. Fleuron 2:77–85 '24.

Annotated chronol. checklist.

1243 **Ashendene press.** A hand-list of the books printed at the Ashendene press, MDCCCXCV–MCMXXV. Chelsea, 1925. 16p. 23cm. Covertitle.

1244 —— A descriptive bibliography of the books printed at the Ashendene press, MDCCCXCV–MCMXXXV. Chelsea, 1935. 172p. illus. (part.col.) facsims. 35cm.

Comp. by Charles H. St. J. Hornby, with collations by Arundell Esdaile, and reset specimen pages; chronol. catalogue of 40 books, with bibliogr. notes and 13 'Minor pieces', 10 'Ephemera'. 'A chronological list of books printed at the press together with the number of copies printed and the issue price of such of them as were offered for subscription' (p.168–71).

Rev: TLS 2 N '35:683; B.'H. Newdigate Lond Merc 33:64 '35; E. Adler N.Y. Times Bk R 19 Jl '36:2.

1245 —— A chronological list with prices of the forty books printed at the Ashendene press, MDCCCXCV–MCMXXXV. Chelsea, 1935. [8]p. 33cm. Covertitle.

'This final list . . . was printed for private circulation only . . .'.

1245a **Balston, Thomas.** 'Summary of the type material in the Cambridge collection' *in* The Cambridge university press collection of private press types. Kelmscott, Ashendene, Eragny, Cranach. Cambridge, 1951. p.44–5.

PRESSES — BAKER, THOMAS, fl.1774–1805

1246 **Marshallsay, D. M.,** 1955: no.167.

PRESSES — BALE PRESS

1247 **Steele, Robert Reynolds.** Hans Luft of Marburg; a contribution to the study of William Tyndale. Library ser3 2:113–131 Ap '11.

'Bibliography' (p.127–31): checklist of 10 items ptd. by Luft, with some bibliogr. notes; 'Bale Press' (p.130–1): checklist of 8 items ptd. by John Bale with Luft's types.

PRESSES — BALLANTYNE, JAMES, 1772–1833

1248 **Johnston, George P.** The first book printed by James Ballantyne, being An apology of Tales of terror, with notes on Tales of wonder and Tales of terror. Edinburgh Bib Soc Pub 1:1–13 [i.e. 21–34] Oc '94.

'Appendix' (p.[11]–13): checklist with bibliogr. descr. of 10 items, with TP facsims.

PRESSES — BASKERVILLE, JOHN, 1706–1775

1249 **Baskerville club,** CAMBRIDGE. Handlist [of Baskerville's books] Cambridge, C.U.P., 1904. 45p. 22cm.

This list of 102 items, like Straus, is not superseded by Gaskell, as it lists books printed in Baskerville's types after his death.

1250 **St. Bride foundation institute,** LONDON. **Technical library.** A catalogue of books [exhibited on the occasion of the visit of the Bibliographical society . . . 1906] on the practical side of the art of printing, 1566–1750. [London, 1906?] 8p. 22cm. (Not seen)

'Catalogue of exhibition of books, letters, specimens, etc. of John Baskerville' (p.5–8).

1251 **Straus, Ralph** and **R. K. Dent.** John Baskerville, a memoir. Cambridge, Ptd. at the C.U.P. for Chatto & Windus, 1907. xi,144p. illus., port., facsims. 30cm.

'Bibliography' (p.66–93): 111 items fully described, with locations of copies; pt. 2 (nos. 112–96) is a handlist of books printed with Baskerville's types, 1763–1891.

1252 **Jay, Leonard,** *comp.* 'Bibliography of works printed by John Baskerville' *in* Baskerville, John. Preface to Milton's Paradise lost. Worcester, 1935. p.10–23.

1253 **Check** list of the John Baskerville collection of Perry Williams Harvey. . . . Yale Univ Lib Gaz 11:63–76 Ja '37.

Chronol. checklist, 1757–1914, with some bibliogr. notes, and Straus and Dent nos.

1254 **Townsend, Rebecca Dutton** and **M. Currier,** *comp.* 'A selection of Baskerville imprints in the Yale university library' in Papers in honor of Andrew Keogh. New Haven, 1938. p.[285]–97.

31 items, with distinction of states and detailed descrs., supplementing Straus and Dent.

1255 **Birmingham. University. Library.** John Baskerville, printer; an exhibition on the occasion of the 74th annual meeting of the Society of chemical industry. . . . Birmingham, 1955. 26p. illus., port. 19cm.

Annotated checklist, comp. by Paul Morgan from the Hely-Hutchinson bequest.

1256 **Gaskell, Philip.** John Baskerville, a bibliography. Cambridge, C.U.P., 1959. xxiii, 71[1]p. facsims. 29cm.

Quasifacsim. TP transcrs. and facsims., and full bibliogr. descrs. of 56 books and 16 specimens and other ephemera; 'Appendix: A list of books printed in Baskerville type at the Oxford university press and by Robert Martin before 1775' (p.71–[2]): 7 items. No index.

Rev: W. B. Todd Pa Bib Soc Am 53:344–5 '59; J. Dreyfus Bk Coll 8:185–9 '59; L. W. Hanson Roy Soc Arts J 107:672–3 '59; C. E. Jones Bull Bib 22:199 '59; R. McL[ean?] Connoisseur 144:48–9 '59; W. White Am Bk Coll 10:8 '59; TLS 29 My '59:328; L. W. Hanson Library ser5 15:135–43 '60; G. J. Kolb Lib Q 30:230 '60.

1257 **Hanson, Laurence William.** John Baskerville, a bibliography. Additional notes. Library ser5 15:201–6 S '60.

Supplements Gaskell: no.1256.

PRESSES — BASSON, THOMAS, 1555–1613

1260 **Dorsten, Jan Adrianus van,** 1961: no.761.

PRESSES — BEAUMONT PRESS

1261 **Beaumont, Cyril William.** 'List of the first twenty books published by the Beaumont press' *in* The first score; an account of the foundation and development of the Beaumont press. . . . London, 1927. p.90–[7].

Chronol. checklist, with bibliogr. notes.

1262 **Loveday, A. J.,** 1951: no.160.

PRESSES — BELL, JOHN, 1745–1831

1263 **First edition club,** LONDON. A catalogue of the books, newspapers, &c. printed by John Bell and by John Browne Bell . . . exhibited at the First edition club, London. London, 1931. 35p. facsim. 24cm.

Annotated checklist of 80 items.

PRESSES — BENSLEY, THOMAS, d.1833

1264 **Croft, sir William.** The achievement of Bulmer and Bensley. Signat new ser 16:3–28 '52; 17:31–54 '53; 18:56–61 '54.

'Handlist of books printed by Bulmer' (p.[11]–28); 'Handlist of books printed by Thomas Bensley' (p.[31]–51); 'Note on the work of Bulmer and Bensley for the Roxburghe club' (p.[52]–4); 'Supplement to list of books printed by William Bulmer' (p.[56]–9); 'Supplement to list of books printed by Thomas Bensley' (p.59–61): alphabetical checklists, with notes and TP facsims. A substantial part of the collection is now in the Bodleian library.

PRESSES — BERTHELET, THOMAS, fl.1550

1265 **Proctor, Robert George Collier.** A short view of Berthelet's editions of the statutes of Henry VIII. Bib Soc Trans 5pt[2]:255–62 '01.

Six pages of tables, based on BM holdings, distinguishing various ed. by ornaments (p.257–62)

PRESSES — BEWICK, THOMAS, 1753–1828
See under Authors.

PRESSES — BIRCHLEY HALL PRESS
See also St. Omers' press.

1266 **Hawkes, Arthur John.** The Birchley hall secret press. Library ser4 7:137–83 S '26.
'Bibliography' (p.160–83); short-title list, with collations, bibliogr. notes, and facsims. of ornaments, etc.

PRESSES — BONMAHON PRESS

1267 **Dix, Ernest Reginald McClintock.** The Bonmahon press. Irish Bk Lover 1:97–100 Mr '10.
Chronol. checklist, 1852–8, with some bibliogr. notes and locations of copies.

PRESSES — BOWYER, WILLIAM, 1699–1777

1268 **Maslen, Keith Ian Desmond,** 1959: no.818.

1269 ——— 1962: no.635.

PRESSES — BRADBURY, HENRY, 1831–1860

1270 **Wakeman, Geoffrey.** Henry Bradbury's nature printed books. Library ser5 21:63–7 Mr '66.
Discussion, with discursive checklist, 1854–9.

PRESSES — BROWNE, SAMUEL, 1611?–1665

1271 **Weil, Ernst.** Samuel Browne, printer to the university of Heidelberg, 1655–1662. Library ser5 5:14–25 Je '50.
'Samuel Browne's publications at Heidelberg' (p.22–4); chronol. checklist of 22 items 1655–62, with locations of copies.

PRESSES — BUCHAN, PETER, 1790–1854

1272 **Cameron, James.** A bibliography of Peter Buchan's publications. Edinburgh Bib Soc Proc 4pt1:105–16 Oc '00.
Chronol. checklist, 1814–91, with some bibliogr. notes, and list of 20 rare chapbooks owned by George Gray, Glasgow (p.114–16).

PRESSES — BULMER, WILLIAM, 1757–1830

1273 **Croft, sir William,** 1952–4: no.1264.

1274 **Isaac, Peter Charles Gerald.** Checklist of books & periodicals printed by William Bulmer. Wylam, Allenholme pr., 1961. 46p. 26cm. (Not seen)

1275 ——— [Same]: First supplement [January, 1962. Wylam] 1962. 4p. 26cm. (Duplicated typescript)

1276 ——— Books printed by William Bulmer. Manchester R 9:344–51 '62/3.
Alphabetical checklist of Bulmer-printed books in the Manchester reference libraries.

PRESSES — CAMBRIDGE UNIVERSITY PRESS

1277 **Roberts, sir Sydney Castle.** 'Cambridge books, 1521–1750' *in* A history of the Cambridge university press, 1521–1921. Cambridge, 1921. p.153–87.

1278 **Cambridge university press.** A list of books printed in Cambridge at the university press, 1521–1800. Cambridge, C.U.P., 1935. 57p. 22cm.
Chronol. checklist; continuation by George R. Barnes of list by Francis Jenkinson (no.877) which was rev. in the preceding item; this now being rev. by J. M. Morris; no index.
Rev: R. B. McKerrow Library ser4 16:353 '35.

1279 **McKenzie, Donald Francis.** The Cambridge university press, 1696–1712, a bibliographical study. Cambridge, C.U.P., 1966. 2v. illus., facsims., fold. tables. 28cm.

'Bibliography' (v.1, p.174–356): descr. bibliogr. of 274 items, 1698–1712, with locations of copies. 'List of types and ornaments' (v.1, p.357–411).

Rev: TLS 25 Ag '66:772; Pa Bib Soc Am 60:409 '66. J. D. Fleeman Library ser5 23:75–9 '68.

PRESSES — CARTER, ISAAC, fl.1718–1730

1280 **Phillips, David Rhys.** Isaac Carter, the pioneer of Welsh printing. Welsh Bib Soc J 1:129–32 Oc '12.

Chronol. checklist of 7 items printed at Trefhedyn and Carmarthen, 1718–30.

PRESSES — CAXTON, WILLIAM, 1422?–1491

1281 **De Ricci, Seymour Montefiore Roberto Rosso.** A census of Caxtons. [Oxford] Ptd. for the Bibliographical society at the O.U.P., 1909. xv,196p. facsims. 29cm.

Chronol. checklist, with some bibliogr. notes and extensive refs. and provenances of copies. 'Summary showing the number of copies existing, untraced, or fragmentary' (p.119–22); 'A list of Caxton's books classified by types and in the chronological order for each type' (p.123–6); 'A list of Caxton's books in chronological order showing the types used in each year' (p.127–9); 'Index to libraries which contain or have contained Caxtons' (p.133–96).

1282 **Aurner, Nellie Slayton.** 'Caxton's books in chronological sequence' and 'Editions and reprints' *in* Caxton, mirror of fifteenth-century letters. London, 1926. p.212–22.

1283 **British museum. Dept. of printed books.** William Caxton, an excerpt from the General catalogue. . . . London, Ptd. by W. Clowes, 1926. 8p. 37cm.

1284 **Munby, Alan Noel Latimer.** Jacob Bryant's Caxtons; some additions to De Ricci's Census. Library ser5 3:218–22 D '48.

1285 **Butterworth, M.,** 1951: no.93.

PRESSES — CHEYNEY, JOHN, 1732–1808

1286 **Cheyney, Christopher Robert.** Early Banbury chap-books and broadsides. Library ser4 17:98–108 Je '36.

'List of chap-books and broadsides printed and sold by the firm of Cheyney. . . .' (p. 107–8).

PRESSES — CHRISTIAANS, WILLEM, fl.1631–1643

1287 **Johnson, Alfred Forbes,** 1955: no.757.

PRESSES — CLOPPENBURG, JAN EVERTZ., 1581–1647

1288 **Johnson, Alfred Forbes,** 1958: no.758.

PRESSES — CORVINUS PRESS

1289 **[Damer, George Lionel S. Dawson-, viscount Carlow]** A list of books printed at the Corvinus press. [n.p., n.d., 1939?] [39] l. (loose-leaf binder) 21cm.

Checklist.

PRESSES — CUALA PRESS
See also Dun Emer press

1290 **Marriner, Ernest C.** Fifty years of the Cuala press. Colby Lib Q ser3 11: 171–83 Ag '53.

Additions (items 73 to 78) to Cuala press publisher's checklist (p.182).

1291 **Wade, Allan.** 'The Cuala press, first called the Dun Emer press' *in* A bibliography of the writings of W. B. Yeats. [2d ed., rev.] London, 1958. p.399–405.

PRESSES — CUNDALL, JOSEPH, 1818–1895

1292 **McLean, Ruari.** Joseph Cundall, a victorian editor, designer, publisher. Penrose Ann 56:82–9 '62.

'Appendices' (p. 87–9): chronol. checklists, 1853–67, of books published and/or supervised by Cundall, and attributed to him.

PRESSES — CURLL, EDMUND, 1675–1747

1292a **Roberts, William.** Curlliana. N&Q ser6 11:381–2 My '85.

1293 **Straus, Ralph.** '[The books] a handlist, 1706–1746' *in* The unspeakable Curll, being some account of Edmund Curll, bookseller. London, 1927. p.201–313.

Annotated chronol. checklist, with some bibliogr. notes and locations of copies; no index.

PRESSES — CURWEN PRESS

1294 **Curwen press.** Catalogue raisonné of books printed at the Curwen press, 1920–23. London, Medici society, 1924. 27p.+illus. 24cm.

Annotated chronol. checklist with some bibliogr. notes.

1295 —— 'Catalogue raisonné of books printed at the Curwen press, 1926–27' *in* A specimen book of types & ornaments in use at the Curwen press. London, 1928. [5]l. at end.

1296 **Simon, Oliver,** *ed.* 'Catalogue raisonné of books printed at the Curwen press, 1928–1930' *in* The Curwen press miscellany. London, 1931. p.125–36.

1297 **Jackson, Holbrook.** 'A list of Curwen press publications' *in* A cross-section of English printing; the Curwen press, 1918–34. London, 1935. p.24.

Checklist, with various other bibliogr. lists relating to the press.

1298 **Phillips, R.,** 1964: no.182.

PRESSES — DANIEL PRESS

1299 **[Madan, Falconer]** The Daniel press. TLS 20 F '03:55–6.

'List of the Daniel press' (p.56): chronol. checklist of 53 items, with some bibliogr. notes.

1300 —— *comp.* 'Bibliography of the press' *in* The Daniel press; memorials of C. H. O. Daniel, with a bibliography of the Daniel press, 1845–1919. Oxford, 1921. p. [37]–183.

1301 ——[Same]: Addenda & corrigenda. Oxford, 1922.

1302 —— [Same]: Corrections of the Addenda, 1923. [Oxford] 1923.

Chronol. catalogue of 203 items, with quasifacsim. TP transcrs., collations, and bibliogr. notes. Appendices: 'A. The Fell type, and Frome and Oxford ornaments and paper.—B. Memoranda: 1. Former lists of the Daniel press. 2. Other private presses at Oxford. 3. The presses and printers at Frome and Oxford.—C. Tables of details.'

Rev: TLS 12 Ja '22:23; I. A. Williams Lond Merc 5:524–5 '22; A. W. Pollard Library ser4 2:275–7 '22; W. G. P[artington] Bkmns J 5:166–7 '22.

PRESSES — DARTON, WILLIAM, 1755–1819

1303 **Milligan, Edward H.**, 1950: no.172.

PRESSES — DAVISON, WILLIAM, 1781–1858

1304 **[Isaac, Peter Charles Gerald]** A tentative checklist of books printed by William Davison. [Wylam, Allenholme pr., 1963] 16l. illus. 25cm. (Duplicated typescript)

Multicoloured author checklist, with some bibliogr. notes; no index.

Rev: J. M. M. Black Art 2:29 '63.

PRESSES — DAY, JOHN, 1522–1584

1305 **Clarke, D. A.**, 1950: no.98.

PRESSES — DIXEY, HAROLD GILES, fl.1919–

1306 **Isaac, Peter Charles Gerald.** H. G. Dixey press. Priv Lib 6:36–9 Ap '65.

'Checklist of books printed by H. G. Dixey' (p.38–9).

PRESSES — DODSLEY, ROBERT, 1703–1764

1307 **Courtney, William Prideaux.** Dodsley's collection of poetry; its contents and contributors. . . . London, A. L. Humphreys, 1910. viii,156p. 16cm.

'Bibliography' (p.71–4) by Edwin J. Byard; the principal work provides details of the contribs. of authors.

1308 **Straus, Ralph.** 'Bibliography' *in* Robert Dodsley, poet, publisher & playwright. London; New York, 1910. p.311–83.

'A list of Dodsley's own works, published during his lifetime, arranged in order of their first editions' (p.311–16); checklist, 1729–64, with some bibliogr. notes and locations of copies; 'A chronological list of all the books published by Robert Dodsley, or bearing his name on the title-page, 1735–1764, with dates of publication, notices of authors, agreements, extracts from advertizements and unpublished letters' (p.316–83).

1309 **Chapman, Robert William.** Dodsley's Collection of poems by several hands. Oxford Bib Soc Proc 3pt3:269–316 '33.

1310 —— [Same]: Additions and corrections. Oxford Bib Soc Pub new ser 1pt1:43–4, 46 '47.

Quasifacsim. TP transcrs., full collations, and bibliogr. notes, with separate list of contents of all volumes described; indexes to authors and first lines.

1311 **Eddy, Donald D.** Dodsley's Collection of poems by several hands (six volumes) 1758: index of authors. Pa Bib Soc Am 60:9–30 '66.

PRESSES — DOVES PRESS

1312 **Doves press.** Catalogue raisonné of books printed & published at the Doves press. . . . [Hammersmith, Doves pr.] 1908. 7p. 24cm.

Further checklists, with similar titles, were issued in 1911 (2d ed., 1911), 1912, 1913, 1914.

1313 —— Catalogue raisonné of the books printed & published at the Doves press, 1900–1916. [Hammersmith, Doves pr.] 1916. 96p. port. 24cm.

'Final ed.' Classified annotated checklist, with 'Chronological table' (p.89–92).

1314 **Clark, William Andrews,** 1921: no.1349.

1315 **Millard, Alice (Parsons)** (mrs George M. Millard). Doves books from the press & bindery of T. J. Cobden-Sanderson . . . assembled by mrs. George M. Millard at the little museum of La miniatura in Pasadena. [South Pasadena, Calif., Ptd. by W. Ritchie] 1933. 60p. 25cm. (Not seen)

PRESSES — DUBLIN UNIVERSITY PRESS

1316 **MacPhail, Ian Shaw.** The Dublin university press in the 18th century. Trinity Coll Dublin Ann Bull 10–14 '56.

Quasifacsim. TP transcrs., collations, and bibliogr. notes, 1738–84.

PRESSES — DUN EMER PRESS

After 1907 known as the Cuala press (q.v.).

1317 **[Maxwell, William]** The Dun Emer press . . . the Cuala press; a complete list of the books, pamphlets, leaflets and broadsides printed by miss Yeats. [Edinburgh] Privately ptd., 1932. 65p. 21cm.

Classified chronol. list with bibliogr. notes; no index.

PRESSES — EAST, THOMAS, 1540?–1608?

1318 **Sopher, A.,** 1959: no.203.

PRESSES — ERAGNY PRESS

1319 **Moore, Thomas Sturge.** 'A bibliographical list of the Eragny books printed in the Vale type by Esther & Lucien Pissarro on their press at Epping, Bedford Park, and the Brook, Chiswick, in the order in which they were issued' *in* A brief account of the origin of the Eragny press. . . . [Hammersmith, 1903] p.15–22.

Checklist of 16 items, with bibliogr. notes.

PRESSES — ERVE, EGIDIUS VAN DER, fl.1555

1320 **Isaac, Frank Swinton,** 1931: no.749.

PRESSES — ESSEX HOUSE PRESS

1321 **[Ashbee, Charles Robert]** A bibliography of the Essex House press, with notes on the designs, blocks, cuts, bindings, etc. from the year 1898. . . . [Campden, Glost., 1904] 23p. illus. 22cm. Headtitle. (Not seen)

1322 **Ashbee, Charles Robert.** 'The bibliography of the Essex House press' *in* The private press, a study in idealism. . . . [Broad Campden, Glost., 1909] p.65–84.

Chronol. checklist, with descr. notes.

PRESSES — FINLASON, THOMAS, fl.1604–1627

1323 **Aldis, Harry Gidney.** Thomas Finlason and his press; with a handlist of books. Edinburgh Bib Soc Pub 1:[14p.] Oc '94.

'Handlist . . . works printed by Thomas Finlason and his successors' (p.12–14): chronol. checklist, 1604–29, with some facsims. of ornaments.

PRESSES — FOULIS, ROBERT, 1707–1776

1324 **Glasgow. Foulis exhibition.** . . . Book of the Foulis exhibition, comprising catalogue. . . . Glasgow, Ptd. for the [Glasgow bibliographical] society by J. MacLehose, 1913. 3pts. in 1v. illus., ports., facsims. 25cm. (Glasgow Bib Soc Rec 2)

Includes the Catalogue, a checklist of 206 ptd. works, with index of lenders.

1325 **Gaskell, Philip.** The early work of the Foulis press and the Wilson foundry. Library ser5 7:77–110, 149–77 Je, S '52.

'Bibliography of books printed for Roubert Foulis' and 'for Robert and Andrew Foulis' (p. 153–77); superseded by no.1327.

1326 **Glasgow. University. Hunterian museum.** Robert and Andrew Foulis; an exhibition in the Hunterian museum to commemorate the silver jubilee of the British records association. [Glasgow] 1958. [106]l. 25cm. Cover-title. (Duplicated typescript)

1327 **Gaskell, Philip.** A bibliography of the Foulis press. London, R. Hart-Davis, 1964. 420p. facsims. 22cm. (Soho bibliographies, XIV)

Descr. bibliogr. of 706 items 'printed for Robert Foulis, 1740–2, . . . by Robert Foulis, and by Robert and Andrew Foulis, 1742–76' and 'by Andrew Foulis the younger, 1776–1806'.

Rev: J. Mosley Bk Coll 13:521–2, 525 '64; Pa Bib Soc Am 59:79–80 '65; D. F. Foxon Library ser5 20:251–2 '65.

PRESSES — FRANCKTON, JOHN, fl.1600–1618

1328 **Dix, Ernest Reginald McClintock.** The ornaments used by John Franckton, printer at Dublin. Bib Soc Trans 8:221–7 '07.

Checklist of 9 works, 1602–17, with locations of copies and facsims.

PRESSES — GED, WILLIAM, 1690–1749

1329 **Gibb, John S.** Notes on William Ged & the invention of stereotyping. . . . Edinburgh Bib Soc Proc 1:1–6 [i.e. 9–14] Oc '92; Supplement *ib.* 1:1–2 [i.e. 15–16] F '96.

Discussion, and short descrs. of 4 items, 1739–44.

PRESSES — GOLDEN COCKEREL PRESS

See also Authors—Gibbings, Robert John, 1889–1958.

1330 **[Gibbings, Robert John]** A bibliography of the Golden cockerel press, April 1921 to July, 1931. Berkshire, Golden cockerel pr., 1931. 10p. (Not seen)

1331 **Churchill, George.** A check list of the prospectuses of the Golden cockerel press. Bk Coll Pkt 3:13–14 My '32.
See Kirkus's item 331 for corrigendum.

1332 **Golden cockerel press.** Chanticleer; a bibliography of the Golden cockerel press, April 1921–1936 August. [London, 1936] 47p. illus. 26cm.
Chronol. catalogue of 112 items.

1333 —— Pertelote, a sequel to Chanticleer, being a bibliography of the Golden cockerel press, October 1936–1943 April. [London, 1943] 51p. illus. 25cm.
Items 113–55.

1334 —— Cockalorum, a sequel to Chanticleer and Pertelote; being a bibliography of the Golden cockerel press, June 1943–December 1948. [London, 1950] 112p. illus. 25cm.
Items 156–81.

PRESSES — GOLDEN HEAD PRESS

1335 **Lister, Raymond.** The Golden head press. Priv Lib 5:62–9 Oc '64.
'Checklist of Golden head press books with some notes concerning their production' (p.65–8).

PRESSES — GREAT TOTHAM PRESS

1336 **Marris, W.** Great Totham press. Manchester R 10:51–5 '63.
'Great Totham press' (p.55): checklist.

PRESSES — GREGYNOG PRESS

1337 **Jones, Thomas.** The Gregynog press; a paper read to the Double crown club on 7 April, 1954. London, O.U.P., 1954. [5]40p. illus. 26cm. (Not seen)
Checklist of the 42 books issued, at end.

1338 **Thomas, M. M. A. A.,** 1956: no.220.

1339 **Haberly, Loyd.** A listing of Loyd Haberly books. Manchester R 9:314–20 '62.
Classified chronol. checklist, 1925–60, with some bibliogr. notes. including works ptd. at Seven acres and Gregynog presses.

PRESSES — HART, ANDREW, d.1621

1340 **Cowan, William.** Andro Hart and his press, with hand list of books. Edinburgh Bib Soc Pub 1pt3:1–14 [i.e. 4–18] Oc '93.
Chronol. checklists of books ptd. for, ptd. by, and ptd. by the heirs of, Hart, 1601–39.

1341 **Johnston, George P.** The life and acts of . . . syr William Wallace. By Henry the minstrel. Edinburgh, Andro Hart, 1620. Edinburgh Bib Soc Pub 12:97 Oc '25.
Bibliogr. descr. and TP facsim.

PRESSES — HERRINGMAN, HENRY, 1627/8–1704

1342 **Miller, Clarence William.** Henry Herringman imprints; a preliminary checklist. Charlottesville, Bibliographical society of the University of Virginia, 1949. 50l. 28cm. (Duplicated typescript)

Section 1: chronological short-title list of publications bearing Herringman's name or initials.—Section 2: author list of books connected with Herringman but without his imprints.—Section 3: short-title index.—Various bibliogr. notes.

PRESSES — HOLYROOD PRESS

1343 **Cowan, William.** The Holyrood press, 1686–1688. Edinburgh Bib Soc Pub 6pt1:83–100 Je '04.

Chronol. list of 39 items, with short collations and locations of copies.

PRESSES — HOURS PRESS

1344 **Cunard, Nancy.** The Hours press: retrospect, catalogue, commentary. Bk Coll 13n04:488–96 '64.

'A catalogue of the productions of the Hours press and commentary' (p.492–6): chronol. list of 24 items, 1928–31, with brief descrs., and notes.

PRESSES — HUTTON, GEORGE, fl.1636–1648

1345 **Oates, John Claud Trewhard.** A bookseller's donation-label. Bk Coll 9n02:192–5 '60.

Includes list of imprints of George Hutton, 1636–48.

PRESSES — JAGGARD PRESS

1345a **Jaggard, William.** The Jaggard press. Athenæum 18 Ja '02:83; B. H. Cowper; A. H. H. *ib.* 1 F '02:145–6; W. R. B. Prideaux 15 F '02:210; W. Jaggard 24 Ja '03:114–15.

Checklist of works ptd. by John, William, and Isaac Jaggard, 1594–1627.

PRESSES — JAY, LEONARD, 1888–

1345b **Wallis, Lawrence W.** 'Bibliography' *in* Leonard Jay, master printer-craftsman . . . London [1963] p.54–106.

Chronol. checklist, 1926–53, with bibliogr. notes.

PRESSES — JAYE, HENRY, 15?–1643

1346 **Rogers, David Morrison.** Henry Jaye, 15?–1643. Biog Stud 1n02:86–111; 1n04:251–2 '52.

'A list of the books printed by Henry Jaye' (p.94–106): checklist of 34 items, with locations of copies.

PRESSES — JOHNSON, RICHARD, 1734–1793
See under Authors.

PRESSES — JONES, THOMAS, b.1648

1347 **[Davies, John H.]** Thomas Jones the almanacer. Welsh Bib Soc J 1:239–45 Jl '15; 2:97–110 D '18.

Discursive checklist, with discussion. 'A list of books printed by Thomas Jones' (p.104–110): 20 items, mainly in Welsh.

PRESSES — KELMSCOTT PRESS
See also Authors—Morris, William, 1834–1896.

1348 **Rinder, Frank.** The Kelmscott press. Connoisseur 1:258–67 '01.
Table of publications in chronol. order, giving size, type, year, number of copies, price, and various auction prices, 1892–1901.

1349 **Clark, William Andrews.** The library of William Andrews Clark, jr. The Kelmscott and Doves press. In two parts: part I. The Kelmscott press; part II. The Doves press. Collated and compiled by Robert Ernest Cowan [and others] with an introduction by Alfred W. Pollard. San Francisco, Ptd. by J. H. Nash, 1921. xxxviii,123p. 27cm.
Detailed chronol. catalogue.

1350 **Cockerell, sir Sydney Carlyle,** *comp.* 'An annotated list of all the books printed at the Kelmscott press in the order in which they were issued' *in* Sparling, Henry H. The Kelmscott press and William Morris, master-craftsman. London, 1924. p.148–74.

1351 **Perry, Marsden Jasiel.** A chronological list of the books printed at the Kelmscott press. . . . [Boston, Merrymount pr., 1928] vii,42p. 21cm.
Checklist with some bibliogr. notes, comp. by George P. Winship.
Rev: Lond Merc 18:301–2 '28.

1352 **Books** from the Kelmscott press. Colby Lib Q ser1 16:249–56 Oc '46.
Locations of copies in 18 New England libraries.

1353 **Cockerell, sir Sydney Carlyle.** The Kelmscott press and William Morris, with Ashendene, Doves, and other private press books . . . sold . . . by Sotheby & co. [London, 1956] 63p. facsims. 25cm. (Not seen)

1354 **William Morris society,** LONDON. The typographical adventure of William Morris; an exhibition arranged by the William Morris society. [London, 1958] 55p. illus., ports., facsims. 22×28cm.
Annotated catalogue of 169 items, with extensive bibliogr. notes; comp. by Ronald C. H. Briggs.

1355 **Brown university,** PROVIDENCE, R.I. **Library.** William Morris and the Kelmscott press; an exhibition. . . . Providence, 1960. iv,49p. illus., facsims. 27cm.
Rev: E. Mason Bull Bib 23:54 '60.

PRESSES — KIRKMAN, FRANCIS, 1652–1680
See under Authors.

PRESSES — LEDELH, JACOBUS, fl.1481–1495

1356 **Beattie, William.** Two notes on fifteenth-century printing. I. Jacobus Ledelh. Edinburgh Bib Soc Trans 3pt1:75–7 '52.
Descr. of 3 items, with locations of copies and bibliogr. refs.

PRESSES — LEDESTON PRESS

1357 **Tuite, James.** J. C. Lyons and the Ledeston press. Irish Bk Lover 1:69–71 Ja '10; J. S. C[rone] *ib.* 4:98–9 Ja '13.
Discursive checklist, with locations of copies.

PRESSES — LILAC TREE PRESS

1358 **Jackson, Bert W.** The Lilac tree press. Priv Lib 6:19–20 Ja '65.
List of 3 items (p.20) with some bibliogr. notes.

PRESSES — LIMITED EDITIONS CLUB

1359 **Warde, Beatrice.** George Macy and the Limited editions club. Penrose Ann 48:35–9 '54.
'A short list of Limited editions club books illustrated and designed, and mostly printed in Great Britain, from the British museum catalogue' (p.38–9).

PRESSES — LINTOTT, BARNABY BERNARD, 1675–1736

1360 **Burdess, James N.,** 1938: no.90.

PRESSES — LLOYD, EDWARD, 1815–1890

1361 **Medcraft, John.** Bibliography of the penny bloods of Edward Lloyd. Dundee, Privately ptd., 1945. [26]p. illus. 16cm.
Chronol. checklist of 200 items, 1836–56.

PRESSES — LUFT, HANS (i.e. Johannes Hoochstraten), fl.1523–1572
See Bale press.

PRESSES — M'CREERY, JOHN, 1768–1832?

1362 **Barker, J. R.,** 1951: no.76.

PRESSES — MACMILLAN & COMPANY, LONDON

1363 **Macmillan & company,** LONDON. A bibliographical catalogue of Macmillan & co.'s publications from 1843 to 1889. London, 1891. vi,715p. ports. 23cm.
Chronol. catalogue, comp. by James Foster.
Rev: Library 3:424–5 '91.

PRESSES — MARBURG PRESS
See Bale press.

PRESSES — MARSHALL, WILLIAM, fl.1533–1537

1364 **Rhodes, Dennis Everard.** William Marshall and his books, 1533–1537. Pa Bib Soc Am 58:219–31 '64.
Discursive checklist of 10 items, with bibliogr. notes and refs.

PRESSES — MENNONS, JOHN, 1747–1818

1365 **Gourlay, James.** John Mennons, an early Glasgow journalist. Glasgow Bib Soc Rec 9:58–72 '31.
'Publications by John Mennons, so far as yet traced' (p.72): checklist.

PRESSES — METAXAS, NICODEMAS, c.1585–1646

1365a **Roberts, R. Julian.** The greek press at Constantinople in 1627 and its antecedents. Library ser5 22:13–43 Mr '67.

'Summary bibliographical descriptions of the extant books printed by or for Nicodemas Metaxas' (p.40–3): bibliogr. descrs. of 9 items, with locations of copies and some TP facsims.

PRESSES — MIERDMAN, STEVEN, b.1510

1366 **Clair, Colin.** On the printing of certain reformation books. Library ser5 18:275–87 D '63.

Discussion and descrs. of 7 items formerly assigned to Richard Jugge but printed in Antwerp by Mierdman, with lists of other reformation tracts printed by Mierdman.

PRESSES — MILLER FAMILY, BOOKSELLERS, 1771–1865

1367 **Couper, William James.** The Millers of Haddington, Dunbar and Dunfermline, a record of Scottish bookselling. London, T. F. Unwin [1914] 318p. illus., ports., facsims. 22cm.

'Bibliography: I. Books, etc. written or edited by the Millers of Dunbar and Haddington. II. The East Lothian press. III. The Dunfermline press' (p.264–312): chronol. checklists, with some bibliogr. notes.

PRESSES — MINERVA PRESS

1368 **Blakey, Dorothy.** The Minerva press, 1790–1820. London, Ptd. for the Bibliographical society at the O.U.P., 1939. 339p. illus., facsims. 23cm.

'Appendix I: Chronological list of publications, 1773–1820' (p.127–271); 'Appendix II: Chronological list of novels showing number of volumes, and price per volume' (p.272–92); 'Supplementary list of publications' (p.293–307): author and title indexes. *Rev*: TLS 23 D '39:748.

PRESSES — MOSELEY, HUMPHREY, d.1661

1369 **Reed, John Curtis.** Humphrey Moseley, publisher. Oxford Bib Soc Proc 2pt2:57–142 '28.

1370 —— [**Same**]: Additions and corrections. Oxford Bib Soc Pub new ser 1:39 '47.

'Chronological list of books published by Humphrey Moseley' (p.[104]–14); indexed.

PRESSES — MOXON, JOSEPH, 1627–1700

1371 **Bliss, Carey S.** Joseph Moxon's Mechanick exercises; a census. Printing & Graphic Arts 5:5–8 F '57.

1372 —— Revised census. Printing & Graphic Arts 6:35–9 Je '58.

Locations of 50 copies in English and American libraries.

1373 —— Further notes for the Moxon census. Printing & Graphic Arts 7:110–11 D '59.

Locations of 9 further items.

1374 **Davis, Herbert John** and **H. G. Carter,** *ed.* 'Moxon's printing and publishing' *in* Moxon, Joseph. Mechanick exercises on the whole art of printing. 2d ed. London, 1962. p.409–41. (First pub. 1958)

Checklist with TP facsims. and bibliogr. notes and refs. of 86 items printed or written by Moxon, and his father James, 1647–86, with locations of copies; *see also* in Addenda (p.486–7). The census of Mechanick exercises (p.[393]–4) lists 37 European copies, nos. 38–61 in America.

PRESSES — NEWBERY, JOHN, 1713–1767

1374a **Thwaite, Mary Florence,** *ed.* 'Bibliography' *in* Newbery, John. A little pretty pocket-book, a facsimile. Oxford, 1966. p.148–77.
Classified chronol. checklist with some bibliogr. notes.

PRESSES — NONESUCH PRESS

1375 **[Johnston, Paul]** The Nonesuch prospectuses. Bk Coll Pkt 2:9–10 Ap '32.
'A check list of the prospectuses of the Nonesuch press' (p.9–10).

1376 **[Flower, Desmond and A. J. A. Symons]** A bibliography of the first ten years of the Nonesuch press . . . in chronological order, notes by the editors of B.C.Q. and a commentary by Francis Meynell. Bk Coll Q 13:45–69 Ja/Mr '34; 14:54–9 Ap/Je '34.
Checklist of 91 items with bibliogr. notes.

1377 **Flower, Desmond,** *comp.* 'Bibliography' [of the first hundred books of the Nonesuch press] *in* Symons, Alphonse J. A., D. Flower [and] F. Meynell. The Nonesuch century. London, 1936. p.[49]–80.
Also issued New York, 1937. Annotated checklist, with bibliogr. notes, followed by TP and text facsims.

PRESSES — PANDORA PRESS

1378 **Graham, Rigby.** The Pandora press. Priv Lib 7no1:5–12 '66.
'A checklist of Pandora publications' (p.11–12): undated items, illus. by Rigby Graham.

PRESSES — PARKER, HENRY, fl.1717–1721

1379 **Maslen, Keith Ian Desmond.** The printers of Robinson Crusoe. Library ser5 7:124–31 Je '52.
'. . . Short list of works printed by [Henry Parker, 1717–21]' (p.131); checklist of 7 items.

PRESSES — PEAR TREE PRESS

1380 **Guthrie, James Joshua.** An account of the aims and intentions of his press, with a list of books. Harting [Petersfield, Hamps., Pear tree pr., 1905]. 34p. illus., facsims. 18cm.
Discursive checklist, with some bibliogr. notes.

PRESSES — PERRY, WILLIAM, fl.1774–1808
See under Authors.

PRESSES — PICKERING, WILLIAM, fl.1556–1571

1381 **Gray, George John.** William Pickering, the earliest bookseller on London bridge, 1556–1571. Bib Soc Trans 4:57–102 '98.
'List A: works issued by Pickering known to exist' (p.66–91): 16 items, with facsims., bibliogr. notes and refs., and locations of copies; 'List B: Ballads and other works licensed to William Pickering not yet found' (p.92–102): 65 items.

PRESSES — PICKERING, WILLIAM, 1796–1854

1382 **Keynes, sir Geoffrey Langdon.** 'Hand-list of publications, 1820–1854' *in* William Pickering, publisher; a memoir & a hand-list of his editions. London, 1924, p.37–83.
Author list, with some bibliogr. notes.

PRESSES — PIENNE, PETER DE, fl.1647-1655

1383 **MacManus, Michael Joseph.** A rare Waterford printed book, 1647 and its printer, Peter de Pienne. Irish Bk Lover 24:75-7 Jl/Ag '36.

TP transcr., collation, and bibliogr. discussion of John Colgan's Lives of the glorious st. David, with checklist of 6 items printed by de Pienne, 1647-55.

PRESSES — PILGRIM PRESS

1384 **Harris, James Kendel** and **S. K. Jones**, 1922: no.745.

PRESSES — PITSLIGO PRESS

1385 **Primrose, James Bartholomew.** The Pitsligo press of George Hay Forbes. Edinburgh Bib Soc Trans 4pt2:53-89 '62.

'Bibliography of the press' (p. 63-89): descrs. with TP facsims. of major and minor works, arranged chronol.; index of titles.

PRESSES — PONDER, NATHANIEL, 1640-1699

1385a **Harrison, Frank Mott.** Nathaniel Ponder, the publisher of The pilgrim's progress. Library ser4 15:257-94 D '34.

'List of works published by Nathaniel Ponder' (p.288-94): chronol. checklist, 1668-96.

PRESSES — PYNSON, RICHARD, d.1530

1385b **Rhodes, Dennis Everard.** Some documents printed by Pynson for st. Botolph's, Boston, Lincs. Library ser5 15:53-7 Mr '60.

Checklist of 8 items, c.1504-22, with TP transcrs., bibliogr. notes and refs., and locations of copies.

PRESSES — RABAN, EDWARD, d.1658

1386 **Axon, William Edward Armytage.** On an unrecorded issue of the Aberdeen press of Edward Raban in 1627, with a handlist of the productions of his presses at Edinburgh, Saint Andrews and Aberdeen. Soc Antiqu Scot Proc 43:24-33 '09.

Chronol. checklist, 1620-40, with TP facsim.

PRESSES — RAE, PETER, 1671-1748

1387 **Stewart, William.** The Rae press at Kirkbride and Dumfries. Edinburgh Bib Soc Pub 6pt2:107-15 Oc '06.

'Hand list' (p.115).

1388 **Shirley, George William.** Mr. Peter Rae, V.D.M., printer. Glasgow Bib Soc Rec 1:216-35 '13.

'Bibliography of issues from the Rae press at Kirkbride and Dumfries' (p.230-35): quasifacsim. TP transcrs., bibliogr. notes, and locations of copies.

PRESSES — RICHARDSON, SAMUEL, 1689-1761
See also under Authors.

1389 **Sale, William Merritt.** 'A list of books printed by Samuel Richardson' *in* Samuel Richardson, master printer. Ithaca, N.Y., 1950. p.145-250.

Author, and chronol., checklists, with some bibliogr. notes.

PRESSES — RUDDIMAN PRESS

1390 **Duncan, Douglas.** 'Publications of the Ruddiman press; short titles of books published during Ruddiman's lifetime' *in* Thomas Ruddiman; a study in Scottish scholarship in the early eighteenth century. Edinburgh, 1965. p.170–3.

Chronol. checklist, 1721–55.

PRESSES — ST. DOMINIC'S PRESS

1391 **St. Dominic's press.** Catalogue of books. [Ditchling, 1929?] 8p. 15cm. Headtitle.

Checklist of 71 items, comp. by Hilary D. C. Pepler.

PRESSES — ST. OMERS' PRESS

See also Birchley Hall press.

1392 **Newdigate, Charles Alfred.** Notes on the seventeenth century printing press of the English college at saint Omers. VII. Characteristics. Library ser3 10:223–42 Oc '19.

Preceding sections contain historical and bibliogr. discussion. 'Group I: Books printed at st. Omers college press, 1608–42' (p.230–41); 'Group II. Books printed probably by Francis Bellet, 1603–09' (p.241–2): chronol. checklists.

1393 —— Birchley—or st. Omers? Library ser4 7:301–20 D '26.

Queries ascription of some works noted by Hawkes (no.1266) and adds bibliogr. details.

PRESSES — SANDERS, ROBERT, 1630?–1694

1394 **Couper, William James.** Robert Sanders the elder. Glasgow Bib Soc Rec 3pt1:26–88 '14.

Chronol. list of 202 items, 1661–94, with TP transcrs., collations, bibliogr. notes and locations of copies.

PRESSES — SCHILDERS, RICHARD, d.1634

1395 **Wilson, John Dover,** 1911: no.743.

PRESSES — SCHOLARTIS PRESS

1396 **Partridge, Eric Honeywood.** The first three years; an account and a bibliography of the Scholartis press. London, Scholartis pr., 1930. ix,54p. 23cm.

'A discursive bibliography' (p.9–45): chronol. checklist with bibliogr. notes.
Rev: TLS 23 Oc '30:869.

PRESSES — SEVEN ACRES PRESS

1397 **Haberly, Loyd,** 1962: no.1339.

PRESSES — SHAKESPEARE HEAD PRESS

1397a **Thorp, Joseph Peter.** 'A selected list from the books produced by B.H.N. at the Shakespeare head press, 1921–1941' *in* B. H. Newdigate, scholar-printer, 1869–1944. Oxford, 1951. p.[44]–7.

Classified checklist, with some bibliogr. notes.

PRESSES — SIBERCH, JOHN, fl.1521–1522

1398 **Gray, George John,** *comp.* 'John Siberch: bibliography' *in* John Siberch; bibliographical notes, 1886–1905. Cambridge, 1906. p.12–29.

Chronol. checklist of 9 items in various states of issue, with bibliogr. notes supplementing list by Henry Bradshaw, 1886; extensive facsims.

1399 **Butterworth, M.,** 1951: no.93.

PRESSES — SIGNET PRESS

1400 **Rae, Thomas.** The Signet press. Black Art 1no3:86–90 '62.
'Checklist of the publications of the Signet press' (p.90).

PRESSES — SIMMES, VALENTINE, fl.1597–1611

1401 **Plomer, Henry Robert.** Shakespeare printers. II. Valentine Simmes. Bibliographer 2no5:299–319 My '03.
TP facsims. and collations of works ptd. by him.

PRESSES — SOULBY, JOHN, 1771 ?–1817

1401a **Tyman, Michael.** 'Appendix: a list of items in the Reading university collection which bear MS notes' *in* John Soulby, printer, a study of the work printed by John Soulby, father and son, between 1796 and 1827. . . . University of Reading [1966] p.49–53.

PRESSES — STANBROOK ABBEY PRESS

1401b **Times bookshop,** LONDON. Books from Stanbrook abbey press and the Vine press, introduced by J. G. Dreyfus. London [1965] 12p. 21cm Cover-title.

PRESSES — STRAWBERRY HILL PRESS
See also Authors—Walpole, Horace, earl of Orford, 1717–1797.

1402 **Dobson, Austin.** Horace Walpole, a memoir, with an appendix of books printed at the Strawberry hill press. New York, Dodd, Mead, 1890. 370p. illus. 25cm.
Rev. ed. pub. in 1893 and 1910; *see* no.1405.

1403 **Wheatley, Henry B.** The Strawberry-hill press. Bibliographica 3:83–98 '97.
'Short list of books and pamphlets printed at Strawberry hill' (p.95–8).

1404 **Merritt, Edward Percival,** 1915: no.1449.

1405 **Dobson, Austin.** 'Appendix. Books printed at the Strawberry hill press' *in* Horace Walpole, a memoir. 4th ed. rev. and enl. by Paget Toynbee. Oxford, 1927. p. [343]–66.

1406 **Hazen, Allen Tracy** and **J. P. Kirby.** A bibliography of the Strawberry hill press, with a record of the prices at which copies have been sold; together with a bibliography and census of the detached pieces. New

Haven, Yale U.P.; London, H. Milford, O.U.P., 1942. 300p. facsims. 26cm.

TP facsims., but no TP transcrs.; two chronol. series: books (42 items) and detached pieces (95 items), with distinction of states and variants, bibliogr. notes and refs.

Rev: J. T. Winterich Sat R Lit 25:11 '42; R. Baughman Philol Q 22:127–30 '43; G. L. McKay Pa Bib Soc Am 37:236–8 '43; G. P. Winship Mod Lang N 58:636–8 '43; TLS 11 S '43:444; D. N. Smith R Eng Stud 20:244–6 '44; P. H. Muir Library ser4 25:95–8 '44.

PRESSES — THOMAS TEGG, 1776–1845

1406a **Plomer, Henry Robert.** On the value of publishers' lists. Library ser2 3:427–33 Oc '02.

'. . . the issues of Thomas Tegg of Cheapside, during the years 1808–9 . . .' (p.429–30): checklist of some 32 items, compiled from publisher's lists.

PRESSES — TOTTEL, RICHARD, d.1594.

1407 **Greg, sir Walter Wilson.** Tottel's Miscellany. Library ser2 5:113–33 Ap '04.

Bibliogr. discussion, with TP transcrs., collations, and facsims. of checkpoints.

PRESSES — TOURNEISEN, JEAN JACQUES, 1754–1803

1408 **Barber, Giles,** 1960: no.759.

PRESSES — TULLIS PRESS

1408a **Doughty, Dennis William.** The Tullis press, Cupar, 1803–1849. Dundee, Abertay historical society, 1967. vi,74p. illus., facsims. 22cm.

'Lists and indexes' (p.23–74): classified checklist of 127 items, with quasifacsim. TP transcrs., and some bibliogr. notes.

PRESSES — TWYN BARLWM PRESS

1409 **Armstrong, Terence Ian Fytton.** The Twyn barlwm press, 1931–1932; a record of the venture and a list of publications by John Gawsworth. . . . London, Privately ptd., 1933. [6]p. 22cm.

Chronol. checklist of 20 items, with some bibliogr. notes.

PRESSES — URIE, ROBERT, 1711?–1771

1410 **M'Lean, Hugh A.** Robert Urie, printer in Glasgow. Glasgow Bib Soc Rec 3pt1:89–108 '14.

'Hand-list of books printed by or for Robert Urie' (p. 98–[108]): chronol. checklist of 314 items, with locations of copies.

PRESSES — VALE PRESS

1411 **[Ricketts, Charles Shannon]** A bibliography of books issued by Hacon & Ricketts. [London, Ballantyne pr., 1904] 41p. illus. 20cm.

Cover-title: Bibliography of the Vale press.

Discursive annotated checklist.

1412 **Humphrey, James.** Books from the Vale press. Colby Lib Q ser3 4:58–67 N '51.

Annotated checklist of 46 items, with New England locations.

PRESSES — VINE PRESS

1412a **Times bookshop,** LONDON, [1965]: no.1401b.

1413 **Dreyfus, John.** The Vine press. Priv Lib 7n02:40–4 '66.
'Notes on the production of Vine press books', by John Peters (p.42–4): 8 items, 1957–63.

PRESSES — WALSH, JOHN, d.1736

1414 **Smith, William Charles.** A bibliography of musical works published by John Walsh during the years 1695–1720. London, Ptd. for the Bibliographical society at the O.U.P., 1949. xxxiv,215p. facsims. 23cm.
Checklist of 622 items, with notes of contents, copy examined, and some bibliogr. notes. The author is preparing a supplement, 1721–1766, to be pub. by the Bibliographical society.
Rev: TLS 10 Je '50:388.

PRESSES — WATER LANE PRESS

1415 **Gaskell, Philip.** The first two years of the Water lane press. Cambridge Bib Soc Trans 2pt2:170–84 '55.
'A check-list of the more substantial pamphlets, etc. printed at the Water lane press' (p.184).

PRESSES — WATSON, JAMES, d.1722

1416 **Gibb, John S.** James Watson, printer; notes of his life and work, with a handlist of books and pamphlets printed by him, 1697–1722. Edinburgh Bib Soc Proc 1:1–8 D '91.
'Handlist' (p.7–8).

PRESSES — WEST, WILLIAM, fl.1811–1831

1417 **Ashton, John.** 'Childhood's drama' *in* Varia. London, 1894. p.[1]–23.
Chronol. checklist, 1811–31, of juvenile dramas pub. by William West.

1418 **Stone, M. W.** Unrecorded plays published by William West. Theat Notebk 1:33–4 Ap '46.
Additions to Ashton.

PRESSES — WHITTINTON, ROBERT, fl.1519

1419 **Bennett, Henry Stanley.** A check-list of Robert Whittinton's grammars. Library ser5 7:1–14 Mr '52.
Complementary to Pafort, Eloise, 1946: no.2279. Checklists under titles of ed. with printers, bibliogr. refs. and some collations and locations of copies.

PRESSES — WIDNALL, SAMUEL PAGE, 1825–1894
See under Authors.

PRESSES — WORDE, WYNKYN DE (JAN VAN WYNKYN) d.1534?

1420 **Bennett, Henry Stanley.** 'Handlist of publications by Wynkyn de Worde, 1492–1535' *in* English books and readers, 1475 to 1557. Cambridge, 1952. p.239–76.
Author checklist, with STC nos. and locations of copies, adding some 250 'titles' to STC.

1420a **Rhodes, Dennis Everard.** The remorse of conscience. Library ser5 13:199–200 S '58.

Redating and reordering of 3 ed., c.1510–15, with bibliogr. notes and refs. and locations of copies.

PRESSES — WREITTOUN, JOHN, fl.1624–1639

1421 **Johnston, George P.** Three unrecorded books printed by John Wreittoun, Edinburgh, 1629–34. Edinburgh Bib Soc Pub 12:31–4 Mr '24.

Descrs. and TP facsims.

1422 **Beattie, William.** A hand-list of works from the press of John Wreittoun at Edinburgh, 1624–c.1639. Edinburgh Bib Soc Trans 2pt2:89–104 '41.

Chronol. checklist of 93 items, with STC and Aldis nos., followed by bibliogr. notes and index.

Rev: TLS 5 S '42:444.

FORMS AND GENRES

ALMANACS AND PROGNOSTICATIONS

1425 **Bosanquet, Eustace Fulcrand.** English printed almanacks and prognostications; a bibliographical history to the year 1600. London, Ptd. for the Bibliographical society at the Chiswick pr., 1917. xi,204p.+xxv facsims. 29cm.

1426 —— [Same]: Corrigenda and addenda. Library ser4 8:456–77 Mr '28.

1427 —— [Same]: Notes on further addenda. . . . Library ser4 18:39–66 Je '37.
Chronol. catalogue of 200 items with quasifacsim. TP transcrs., and indexes.

1428 **Dix, Ernest Reginald McClintock.** Early Dublin printed almanacks, seventeenth century. Bib Soc Ireland Pub 1n02:1–10 '18.
'List . . .' (p.8–10): chronol. checklist.

1429 **London. Guildhall library.** A handlist of almanacs in the Guildhall library. Guildh Misc 1n07:40–6 Ag '56.

1430 **McDonald, William R.** Scottish seventeenth-century almanacs. Biblioth 4n07–8:257–322 '66.
'Catalogue of almanacs' (p.295–322): chronol. checklist of 100 items, 1623–1700, with bibliogr. notes and refs. and locations of copies.

ANONYMA AND PSEUDONYMA

1435 **Cushing, William.** Anonyms; a dictionary of revealed authorship. London, S. Low, Marston, Searle & Rivington, 1890. (First issued Cambridge, Mass., 1889) 2v.(829p.) 25cm.
Arranged by title, with index of names.

1436 **Abbatt, William.** The colloquial who's who; an attempt to identify the many authors, writers and contributors who have used pen-names, initials, etc., 1600–1924. . . . Tarrytown, N.Y., 1924–5. 2v. 22cm.
V.2 Great Britain and colonies.

1437 **Halkett, Samuel** and **John Laing.** Dictionary of anonymous and pseudonymous literature. New and enl. ed. by James Kennedy, W. A. Smith and A. F. Johnson. Edinburgh, Oliver and Boyd, 1926–34. (First pub. 1882–6) 7v. 27cm.
V.6 contains Supplement; v.7 Index and Second supplement.

1438 —— [Same]: Volume eight, 1900–1950, by Dennis E. Rhodes and Anna E. C. Simoni. . . . Edinburgh, Oliver and Boyd [1956] viii,397p. 27cm.

1439 —— [Same]: Volume nine, by Dennis E. Rhodes and Anna E. C. Simoni. . . . Edinburgh, Oliver and Boyd [1962] viii,477p. 27cm.
Additions and corrections up to 1950.

1442 **Stonehill, Charles Archibald [and others].** Anonyma and pseudonyma, by Charles A. Stonehill, Andrew Block, and H. Winthrop Stonehill. London, Ptd. for the subscribers by C. A. Stonehill, 1926–7. 4v.(3448 col.) 20cm.

ANTHOLOGIES

(For Miscellanies *see* Index.)

1443 **Bradner, Leicester.** A finding list of Anglo-Latin anthologies. Mod Philol 27:97–102 Ag '29.

Annotated checklist of 20 items.

AUCTION CATALOGUES

1443a **Norgate, Fred.** Book sales, 1744–1828. Library 3:12–13 Ja '91.

Alphabetical list of Sotheby's catalogues to 1828.

1443b —— Book sales by R. H. Evans, 1812–1845. Library 3:324–30 S '91.

Alphabetical checklist, 1812–45.

1444 **Pollard, Alfred William.** English book-sales, 1676–1680. Bibliographica 1pt3:373–84 '95.

Checklist of 17 items, with extensive discussion.

1445 —— English book-sales, 1681–86. Bibliographica 2pt5:112–26 '96.

Checklist of 74 items.

1446 **Lawler, John.** 'Chronological list of book auctions in England in the seventeenth century' *in* Book auctions in England in the seventeenth century, 1676–1700. London, 1898. p.215–24.

1447 **Madan, Falconer.** List of Thomas Rawlinson sale catalogues in the Bodleian library. Bib Soc Trans 5pt1:85–6 '99.

17 items, 4 D 1721–4 Ap '34.

1447a **Roberts, William.** Catalogues of English book sales. . . . London, Privately ptd., 1900. 10p. 22cm.

Repr. from N&Q ser9 5:429–31, 490–2 Je '00; 6:22–4, 83–5, 142–4 Jl–Ag '00.

1448 **British museum. Dept. of printed books.** List of catalogues of English book sales, 1676–1900, now in the British museum. London, Ptd. by order of the trustees, 1915. xv,523p. 23cm.

Chronol. checklist of 8,000 items, with index of names.

1449 **Merritt, Edward Percival.** An account of descriptive catalogues of Strawberry hill and of Strawberry hill sale catalogues, together with a bibliography. Boston, Privately ptd. by B. Rogers, 1915. x,72p. ports., facsims. 22cm.

List of 15 items (p.61–72) with some bibliogr. notes.

1449a **De Ricci, Seymour Montefiore Roberto Rosso.**[Lists of sale and auction catalogues, *passim*.] *in* English collectors of books & manuscripts, 1530–1930, and their marks of ownership. Cambridge, 1930.

1450 **New York. Public library.** American book auction catalogues, 1713–1934; a union list, compiled by George L. McKay. New York, 1937. xxxii,540p. facsims. 25cm.

'Anglo-American book auctions' (p.492). Repr. from N.Y. Pub. Lib Bull '35–6.

1451 —— **[Same]**: Additions. [New York, 1946] 8p. 25cm.

Repr. from N.Y. Pub Lib Bull 50:177–84 Mr '46.

1452 —— **[Same]**: Supplement no.2. [New York, 1948] 12p. 25cm.

Repr. from N.Y. Pub Lib Bull 52:401–12 Ag '48.
Chronol. union list.

1453 **Doyle, Anthony Ian H.** Sale catalogues. Durham Philobib 1:30–9 My/N '51; 1:58–62 Ja/Mr '53.

TP transcrs. of 42 catalogues, 1706–1876, not in BM.

1454 **O'Kelley, Francis.** Irish book-sale catalogues before 1801. Bib Soc Ireland Pub 6no3:35–55 '53.

Chronol. checklist of 63 items, with locations of copies.

1455 **Doyle, Anthony Ian H.** More sale catalogues. Durham Philobib 2:9–14 Ap '58; 2:52–4 Je '62.

Checklist of 35 catalogues, 1828–72, in the Robert White collection, King's college library, and 9 in the Durham university library, not in the BM list (no.1448).

1456 **Pollard, Graham** and **A. Ehrman.** 'The Broxbourne material' *in* The distribution of books. . . . Cambridge, 1965. p.283–352.

See no.1170.

BALLADS

1460 **[Lindsay, James Ludovic, 26th earl of Crawford]** Bibliotheca Lindesiana. Catalogue of a collection of English ballads of the XVIIth and XVIIIth centuries, printed for the most part in black letter. [Aberdeen] Privately ptd., 1890. (Repr. New York, B. Franklin [1963]) xiii,686p. 26cm.

1,466 entries arranged alphabetically by first line, with bibliogr. descrs.; indexes of printers, publishers and booksellers; 'First lines and titles of the ballads in the Huth and Euing collections'.—The Euing collection is now in the Glasgow university library. *See also* no.1462.

Rev: Library 2:471–2 '90; 3:1–5 '91.

1461 **Davies, John H.** A bibliography of Welsh ballads printed in the 18th century. London, Honourable society of Cymmrodorion in conjunction with the Welsh bibliographical society, 1908–11. 4pts. 20cm.

Checklist of 759 items arranged by place of printing, with indexes of authors, and printers.

1462 **[Esdaile, Arundell James Kennedy]** *comp.* 'Elizabethan ballads' *in* British museum. Catalogue of the fifty manuscripts & printed books bequeathed to the British museum by Alfred H. Huth. London, 1912. p.83–113.

Chronol. catalogue of some 69 items, 1559–1615/16, with bibliogr. notes; 'Later ballads' (p.114–16): 6 items, 1640–1710; 'Index to ballads' (p.127–9).

1463 **London. Stationers' company.** An analytical index to the ballad-entries (1557–1709) in the registers of the Company of stationers of London; compiled by Hyder E. Rollins. Chapel Hill, N.C., University of North Carolina pr.; London, H. Milford, O.U.P., 1924. 324p. 25cm.

Reissue of Stud Philol 21:1–324 Ja '24.

Alphabetical index of titles, 3,081 items, with index of first lines, and of names and subjects.

Rev: TLS 4 S '24:544; C. R. Baskervill Mod Philol 23:119–25 '25; M. F. Mann Anglia Beibl 36:167–8 '25.

1464 **Hamer, Douglas.** Editions of Chevy chase. N&Q 164:381–5, 398–40 Je '33; 165:418–20 Je '33.

Chronol. checklist of 90 entries, with locations of copies.

1465 **Brooks, Harold Fletcher.** Rump songs; an index with notes. Oxford Bib Soc Proc 5pt4:281–304 '40.

1466 **Philbrick, Thomas L.** British authorship of ballads in the Isaiah Thomas collection. Stud Bib 9:255–8 '57.

1467 **Goldstein, Leba M.** An account of the Faustus ballad. Library ser5 16:176–89 S '61.

'A list of extant copies of the Faustus ballad, with some corrections to Wing' (p.188–9)

BIBLE

1469 **Smith, Walter E.** The great 'she' bible. Library 2:1–11, 96–102, 141–53 Ja,Mr,Ap '90.

[Table to facilitate collation] (p.144–52)

1470 **[Arden, George Baillie-Hamilton-, 11th earl of Haddington]** Descriptive catalogue of the collection of bibles at Tyninghame. [n.p., Tyninghame?] 1902. vii,93p. 22cm.

Discursive descrs. of 91 items, 1537–1786.

1471 **British and foreign bible society. Library.** Historical catalogue of the printed editions of holy scripture in the library . . . compiled by T. H. Darlow and H. F. Moule. London, Bible house, 1903–11. 2v. in 4. 26cm.

Contents: v.1. English. (1903).—2. Polyglots and languages other than English. (1911). Chronol. arrangement with TP transcrs., collations, bibliogr. notes, and indexes. A revision is being prepared.

1472 **John Rylands library,** MANCHESTER. . . . Catalogue of an exhibition of bibles illustrating the history of the English versions from Wyclif to the present time. . . . Manchester, 1904. 32p. 24cm.

See no.1482.

1473 —— **[Same]:** Manchester, Ptd. by order of the governors, 1907. vii,55p. illus. 23cm.

See no.1482.

1474 **British museum.** Guide to the manuscripts and printed books exhibited in celebration of the tercentenary of the authorized version. [London] Ptd. by order of the trustees, 1911. (Repr. 1927) 64p. facsims. 21cm.

Checklist, with extensive annotations, those on the printed books being by Alfred W. Pollard.

1475 **Cardiff. Public libraries.** . . . Catalogue of the bibles exhibited in the reference library in celebration of the tercentenary of the authorised version. [Cardiff] Ptd. by order of the Libraries committee, 1911. iii,62p. facsims. 22cm.

Annotated classified checklist.

1476 **Glasgow. University. Library.** Catalogue of an exhibition of bibles in commemoration of the tercentenary of the authorised version, 1611–1911, with . . . notes by George Milligan. . . . [Provisional issue] Glasgow, J. MacLehose, 1911. 39p. port. 22cm.

1477 —— **[Same]:** [1st ed.] Glasgow, Jackson, Wylie, 1925. 54p. illus., port. 23cm.

Annotated checklist of 107 items drawn from bequeathed collection of William Euing.

1478 **Yale. University. Library.** Catalogue of an exhibition of books . . . illustrating the history of the English translation of the bible . . . arranged by Anna M. Monrad. [New Haven] 1911. 14p. 20cm.

Repr. from Report of the librarian, 1911. Checklist.

1479 **Brighton. Public library, museums and fine art galleries.** Catalogue of a collection of rare & valuable bibles, &c. exhibited. . . . Brighton, Dolphin pr. [1918] 12p. 19cm. (Not seen)

1480 **New York. Public library.** An exhibition of bibles of ancient and modern times, selected, arranged, and described by Victor Hugo Paltsits. [New York] 1923. 18p. 24cm.
Classified annotated checklist.

1481 **John Rylands library,** MANCHESTER. Catalogue of an exhibition illustrating the history of the transmission of the bible, with an introductory sketch by the librarian. . . . Manchester, Manchester U.P.; Longmans, Green, 1925. xii,133p. port., facsims. 23cm.
See no.1482.

1482 —— Catalogue of an exhibition illustrating the history of the transmission of the bible, with an introductory sketch by the librarian, and twenty-two facsimiles. . . . Manchester, Manchester U.P., 1935. xiii,112, 13p. ports., facsims. 27cm.
'Catalogue of the exhibition' (p.59–112): classified bibliogr. catalogue. Earlier exhibition catalogues were issued in 1904, 1907, 1908, 1911, and 1925.

1483 **Newberry library,** CHICAGO. The history of the transmission of the English bible; an exhibition. . . . Chicago, 1935. [12]p. 22cm.
Annotated catalogue of 46 items, comp. by Gertrude L. Woodward.

1484 **Bristol. Public libraries.** The fourth centenary of the English bible, 1538–1938; catalogue of bibles on exhibition. . . . Bristol, 1938. 29p. facsims. 25cm.

1485 **Cardiff. Public libraries.** . . . Handlist of bibles exhibited. . . . Cardiff, 1938. 27p. 22cm. Covertitle.

1486 **Petre, Edwin Alfred Robert Rumball-.** Rare bibles, an introduction for collectors and a descriptive checklist. New York, P. C. Duschnes, 1938. 63p. port., facsims. 25cm.
See no.1493.

1487 **Sheffield. Public libraries.** Exhibition of the English bible. Sheffield, City libraries, 1938. 20p. 24cm.

1488 **Norlie, Olaf Morgan.** The Norlie collection of English bibles. Northfield, Minn., St. Olaf college, 1944. 129l. 27cm. (Duplicated typescript)
Checklist.

1489 **Harmsworth, sir Robert Leicester.** Catalogue of the . . . collection of English and foreign bibles and new testaments . . . forming part of the . . . library of the late sir R. Leicester Harmsworth . . . sold by auction by messrs. Sotheby. . . . [London, 1946] 32p. facsims. 26cm.

1490 **Pennsylvania. University. Library.** A catalogue of the T. Edward Ross collection of bibles. Philadelphia, 1947. 95p. ports. 22cm.
Classified catalogue, mainly of English and American items, with bibliogr. notes and refs., comp. by Clifford B. Clapp.

1491 **Pierpont Morgan library,** NEW YORK. The bible; manuscript and printed bibles from the fourth to the nineteenth century; illustrated catalogue of an exhibition. . . . New York, 1947. 47p. illus., facsims. 30cm.

1492 **Hull. University college. Religious activities committee.** An exhibition of bibles . . . catalogue. Hull, Brown, 1954. 24p. 22cm.

1493 **Petre, Edwin Alfred Robert Rumball-.** Rare bibles, an introduction for collectors and a descriptive checklist. [2d ed., rev.] New York, P. C. Duschnes, 1954. (First ed., 1938) 54p. 25cm.

Classified annotated checklist of 'significant' ed.; 'English bibles and testaments' (p.14–24).

1494 **Bristol. Public Libraries.** A select catalogue of bibles in the Central public library, Bristol. To commemorate the three hundred and fiftieth anniversary of the authorized version. Bristol, 1961. 28p. facsims. 22cm.

Annotated checklist, rev. from no.1484.

1495 **Hills, Margaret Thorndike.** The English bible in America; a bibliography of editions of the bible & the New testament published in America, 1777–1957. New York, American bible society and the New York public library, 1961. xxxv,477p. facsims. 27cm.

Chronol. bibliogr., with indexes of publishers and printers arranged both alphabetically and by place; translations, translators and revisers; editors and commentators; edition titles; and general.

Rev: E. Wolf Lib Q 32:107–8 '62.

1496 **London. University. King's college.** Exhibition of bibles from the collection in the college library to mark the 350th anniversary of the first printing of the Authorized version. . . . London, King's college, Private circulation, 1961. 55p. facsim. 22cm. (Duplicated typescript)

1497 **Oxford university press** and **Cambridge university press.** The bible in Britain; an introduction and list of exhibits. . . . [Cambridge, C.U.P., 1961] 34p. facsims. 22cm. Covertitle.

Checklist of 106 items, with locations of copies.

1498 **Washington, D.C. Cathedral of st. Peter and st. Paul. Rare book library.** In the beginning was the word. Washington, 1965. 71p. illus., facsims., ports. 28cm.

Rev: TLS 24 Je '65:548; Pa Bib Soc Am 60:135 '66.

BIBLE. O.T. PSALMS

1505 **Aberdeen. University. Library.** Catalogue of the Taylor collection of psalm versions. Aberdeen, Aberdeen U.P., 1921. v,307p. port. 23cm.

Rev. from Aberdeen Univ Lib Bull 1:267–83, 491–527 Ap, Oc '12; 1:828–31 Ap '13; 2:448–72 Oc '14; 3:60–87 N '15; 3:492–532 Ap '17; 3:621–36 N '17.

Chronol. bibliogr. catalogue, with full descrs. of items to 1800, checklist thereafter; author and title index only.

1506 **Cowan, William.** Early Scottish psalm-tune books. Edinburgh Bib Soc Pub 12pt1:25–30 Mr '24.

'Bibliography' (p.28–30): descrs. and notes of 10 ed., 1666–1753.

BIBLE, WELSH

1507 **[Jones, James Ifano]** *comp.* 'Bibliography' *in* [Ballinger, John] *ed.* The bible in Wales, a study in the history of the Welsh people . . . and a bibliography. London, 1906. p.1–91 at end.

Chronol. catalogue of 382 items, 1546–1900, with bibliogr. notes.

BIOGRAPHIES AND AUTOBIOGRAPHIES

1508 **Stauffer, Donald Alfred.** 'An index of early biographies' *in* English biography before 1700. Cambridge, Mass., 1930. p.[287]–366.

Subject and author checklist.

1509 **Jones, Claude Edward.** Collected biographies to 1825. Bull Bib 17:90–2, 113–16 My/Ag, S/D '41.

Author checklist of 464 items; no index.

1510 **Stauffer, Donald Alfred.** Bibliographical supplement [to The art of biography in eighteenth century England.] Princeton, Princeton U.P.; London, H. Milford, O.U.P., 1941. viii,293p. 23cm.

Author and subject checklist, with chronol. index.

1511 **Matthews, William.** British autobiographies; an annotated bibliography of British autobiographies published or written before 1951. Berkeley, University of California pr., 1955. (Repr. Gloucester, Mass., P. Smith, 1967) xiv,376p. 25cm.

Alphabetical checklist with biogr. annotations and subject index.

Rev: TLS 3 F '56:74; W. White Bull Bib 21:171 '55.

BOOK OF COMMON ORDER

1512 **Cowan, William.** The bibliography of the Book of common order of the Church of Scotland. Edinburgh Bib Soc Proc 1pt1:1–7 [i.e. 9–15] D '91.

'List of editions' (p.4–7).

1513 —— A bibliography of the Book of common order and psalm book of the Church of Scotland, 1556–1644. Edinburgh, Privately ptd., 1913. 48p. facsim. 25cm.

Repr. from Edinburgh Bib Soc Pub 10:53–100 '13. Chronol. list of 70 items with full descrs., and locations of copies.

Rev: J. C. Ewing Scot Hist R 11:297–8 '13.

BOOK OF COMMON PRAYER

1514 **Dowden, bp. John.** Archbishop Laud's prayer-book; notes on the bibliography of the Booke of common prayer and administration of the sacraments, and other parts of divine service for the use of the Church of Scotland, Edinburgh, 1637. Edinburgh Bib Soc Proc 1:1–8 [i.e. 53–61] Oc '94.

Discussion and descr. of the different impressions and issues of the Psalter, and the Book of common prayer.

1515 **Boston. Public library.** Catalogue of selected editions of the Book of common prayer, both English and American . . . on exhibition at the Boston public library. . . . Boston, The trustees, 1907. 52p. 22cm.

Large number of the Books of common prayer lent by Josiah H. Benton.

1516 **Benton, Josiah Henry.** The Book of common prayer and books connected with its origin and growth; catalogue of the collection of Josiah Henry Benton. 2d ed. prepared by William Muss-Arnolt. Boston, Privately ptd., 1914. (First ed., 1910) viii,142p. 26cm.

Classified descr. catalogue.

1517 **Harmsworth, sir Robert Leicester.** The Harmsworth trust library; the seventh portion: catalogue of . . . English prayer books and of psalters . . . which will be sold by auction by messrs. Sotheby. . . . [London, 1946] 36p. facsims. 26cm.

1518 **White, Newport Benjamin.** The Watson collection: prayer books . . . given by Edward John Macartney Watson. Dublin, Representative church body, 1948. 52p. (Not seen: Eager's no.486)

1519 **Adams, H. M.** Tables for identifying the edition of imperfect copies of the Book of common prayer, 1600–1640. Cambridge Bib Soc Trans 1pt1:61–3 '49.

1520 **British museum.** Catalogue of an exhibition commemorating the four hundredth anniversary of the introduction of the Book of common prayer. London, Ptd. by order of the trustees, 1949. 37p. illus., facsims. 20cm.

Chronol. short-title catalogue of 52 items, with extensive descr. notes.

1521 **Gerrard, John Frederick.** Notable editions of the prayer book [. . . on exhibition at the Wigan public library. . . .] Wigan, J. Starr, 1949. 30p. facsims. 20cm.

Annotated short-title catalogue of 30 items, 1549–1821.

1522 **Page, James Rathwell.** A descriptive catalogue of the Book of common prayer and related material in the collection of James R. Page. Los Angeles [Plantin pr.] 1955. 67p. facsims. 30cm.

Short-title catalogue with discursive bibliogr. notes, comp. by Dorothy Bowen.

1523 **Adams, H. M.** Tables for the identification of octavo Books of common prayer. Library ser5 13: facing 284 D '58.

BOOKS IN PARTS

1529 **Gjelsness, Rudolph.** The first edition of the Encyclopædia britannica. Coloph 4pt16:41–8 '34.

1530 **Peckham, Morse.** Dr. Lardner's Cabinet cyclopaedia. Pa Bib Soc Am 45:37–58 '51.
'A check-list of Lardner's Cabinet cyclopaedia' (p.52–8): chronol. by author.

1531 **New York. Public library. Arents collection.** The Arents collection of books in parts and associated literature; a complete checklist with an introductory survey by Sarah Augusta Dickson. New York, 1957. 88p. illus., facsims. 26cm.
Classified checklist with bibliogr. notes, and indexes of authors and anonymous works, and of artists. *See also* no.1533.
Rev: T. Bolton Pa Bib Soc Am 52:224–6 '58; A. D. Wainwright Bk Coll 7:435–6 '58; TLS 20 Je '58:352 '58.

1532 **Wiles, Roy McKeen.** 'Appendix B: Short-title catalogue of books published in fascicules before 1750' *in* Serial publication in England before 1750. Cambridge, 1957. p.[267]–356.
Chronol. checklist with bibliogr. notes. 'Appendix C: Names and addresses of booksellers, printers, and others who had some share in the production and distribution of number books before 1750' (p.357–66).

1533 **New York. Public library. Arents collection.** The Arents collection of books in parts and associated literature; a supplement to the Checklist, 1957–1963. New York, 1964. 38p. 26cm.
Repr. from N.Y. Pub Lib Bull 68:141–52, 259–69 Mr, Ap '64; adds 125 items, with 36 items of associated literature; comp. by Perry O'Neil.

BROADSIDES
See also Pamphlets.

1534 **[Lindsay, James Ludovic, 26th earl of Crawford]** Bibliotheca Lindesiana. Catalogue of English broadsides, 1505–1897. [Aberdeen] Privately ptd., 1898. xi,526p. 26cm.
Chronol. short-title catalogue of 1814 items, ?1505–1897, comp. by John P. Edmond, with index and 'List of printers, publishers, and booksellers'.

1535 **London. University. Goldsmiths' company's library of economic literature.** Catalogue of the collection of broadsides in the University library. . . . London, Published for the University of London by the University of London pr., 1930. 201p. 34cm.
Classified chronol. catalogue of 679 items, including additions from the library of the earl of Sheffield, 1908, with preces, and indexes of printers and publishers, and of subjects; ed. by Reginald A. Rye.

1536 —— **[Same]: Supplement.** . . . London [1930] 4p. 31cm.
Rev: sir F. C. Francis Library ser4 12:467–9 '32.

CHAPBOOKS

1537 **Neuberg, Victor Edward Reuben Parvincio.** Chapbooks; a bibliography of references to English and American chapbook literature of the eigtheenth and nineteenth centuries. London, Vine pr., 1964. 88p. facsims. 23cm.
161 entries, curiously annotated.
Rev: P. Morgan Library ser5 21:167–8 '66; Pa Bib Soc Am 60:130–1 '66.

1538 **Cropper, Percy J.** The Nottinghamshire printed chap-books, with notices of their printers and vendors. Nottingham, F. Murray, 1892. x,32p. illus., facsims. 26cm.

Checklist of 36 items, with discursive descr. notes.

1539 **Ferguson, Richard Saul.** Chapbooks in the library of the Society of anti-quaries. Soc Antiqu Proc ser2 15:338–45 '94.

Discursive checklist of 23 items from the Ashpitel bequest.

1540 —— On the collection of chap-books in the bibliotheca Jacksoniana. . . . Cumberland & Westmorland Antiqu & Archæol Soc Trans 14:1–120 '97; 16:57–79 '99.

Annotated checklist of 180 Cumberland chapbooks.

1540a **Harvey, William.** 'List of chapbooks referred to in the preceding pages' *in* Scottish chapbook literature. Paisley, 1903. p.[145]–7.

1541 **Harvard university. Library.** Catalogue of English and American chap-books and broadside ballads in Harvard college library. Cambridge, Mass., 1905. xi,171p. 25cm.

Short-title catalogue of 2,461 titles, comp. by Charles Welsh and W. H. Tillinghast; indexes of subjects and titles, and of printers, publishers and booksellers.

1542 **New York. Public library.** A catalogue of the chapbooks in the New York public library, compiled by Harry B. Weiss. New York, 1936. 90p. facsims. 26cm.

Repr. with revs. and corr. from N.Y. Pub Lib Bull v.39, '35. Checklist of 1,171 items, with bibliogr. notes and index of printers, etc.

1543 **Kentucky. University. Margaret I. King library,** LEXINGTON. University of Kentucky collection of English chap books. [Lexington, 1952] 21p. 28cm. (Duplicated typescript)

Checklist.

1544 **Durham. University. King's college,** NEWCASTLE-UPON-TYNE. **Library.** Chap-books and garlands in the Robert White collection . . . by Desmond Sparling Bland. Newcastle upon Tyne, 1956. 32p. facsims. 24cm.

'Select bibliography' (p.25–31): classified checklist of 26 items, with quasifacsim. TP transcrs.

Rev: E. M. Wilson Library ser5 12:140–1 '57.

1545 **Ratcliffe, F. W.** Chapbooks with Scottish imprints in the Robert White collection in Newcastle university library. Biblioth 4no3/4:87–174 '64.

Alphabetical title list of 671 items, with indexes.

Rev: TLS 29 Ap '65:340.

1546 **Scotland. National library,** EDINBURGH. Catalogue of the Lauriston castle chapbooks. Boston, Mass., G. K. Hall, 1964. 273p. 36cm.

Dictionary catalogue.

CHARACTERS

1550 **Murphy, Gwendolen.** A bibliography of English character-books, 1608–1700. [Oxford] Ptd. at the O.U.P. for the Bibliographical society, 1925. 179p. 22cm.

Contents: I. Regular character-books.—II. Controversial characters.—III. Appendix: Index of characters.—Index of titles.—Index of authors.

Chronological list of unnumbered entries, with quasifacsim. TP transcrs., collations, and locations of copies.

1551 **Greenough, Chester Noyes.** A bibliography of the Theophrastan character in English, with several portrait characters. . . . Prepared for publication by J. Milton French. Cambridge, Mass., Harvard U.P., 1947. xii,347p. 27cm.

Chronol. list, 1495–1941, with indexes.

Rev: TLS 12 Jl '47:351; D. C. Allen Mod Lang N 63:211–12 '48; J. Robertson Mod Lang R 43:11–12 '48; V. B. Heltzel Philol Q 27:285–8 '48; B. Boyce J Eng Germ Philol 47:92–4 '48; H. Macdonald R Eng Stud 24:255–6 '48.

CHILDREN'S LITERATURE

1552 **Barry, Florence Valentine.** 'Chronological list of children's books from 1700 to 1825' *in* A century of children's books. London [1922] p.224–57. (Anr. issue, New York [1923]).

1553 **Smith, Elva S.** Books of amusement and instruction for good little readers; a list of children's books published in England and America between 1755 and 1835, in the collection of the Carnegie library school. Lib J 48:811–15, 961–5, 1007–10 Oc–D '23.

Classified annotated checklists.

1554 **James, Philip.** Children's books of yesterday. Edited by C. Geoffrey Holme. London, The studio, 1933. 128p. illus., facsims. 28cm. (Studio special autumn no.)

Consists largely of illus. and TP facsims.

Rev: Lond Merc 28:486 '33.

1555 **Smith, Elva S.** 'A chronological list illustrating the development of children's literature' *in* The history of children's literature, a syllabus with selected bibliographies. Chicago, 1937. p.205–14.

1556 **St. Bride foundation institute,** LONDON. An exhibition of a small collection of early children's books. London [1938] 16p. (Not seen)

1557 **Weiss, Harry Bischoff.** 'A preliminary check list of English and American editions of Little red riding hood' *in* Little red riding hood, a terror tale of the nursery. . . . Trenton, 1939. p.15–60.

Alphabetical checklist of 60 items, with locations of copies.

1558 **Fletcher, Ifan Kyrle.** Harlequinades. Theat Notebk 1:46–8 Jl '46.

Harlequinades published by Robert Sayer (p.46–7) and other publishers.

1558a **Green, Roger Lancelyn.** 'Bibliographical notes' *in* Tellers of tales. . . . London, 1946. p. [246]–64.

See no.1571.

1559 **National book league,** LONDON. Children's books of yesterday; a cata-
logue of an exhibition . . . compiled by Percy H. Muir. . . . [London]
Published for the National book league by the C.U.P. [1946] 192p. 17cm.
Classified annotated short-title catalogue of 1,001 items.

1560 **Egoff, Sheila A.** Children's periodicals of the nineteenth century; a survey
and bibliography. London, Library association, 1951. 55p. 23cm. (Library
association pamphlet, no.8)
Chronol. checklist, 1752?–1900 (p.27–43) based on no.118.
Rev: M. J. P. Weedon Library ser5 7:221–2 '52.

1561 **Muir, Percival Horace.** English children's books, 1600–1900. London,
Batsford; New York, Praeger [1954] 255p. illus., facsims. 26cm.
Checklists at ends of chapters.
Rev: P. Opie Library ser5 10:60–1 '55.

1562 **Pierpont Morgan library,** NEW YORK. Children's literature; books and
manuscripts, an exhibition. . . . New York, 1954. iv.(unpaged) illus. 24cm.
(Not seen)
See no.1565c.

1563 **Stone, M. W.** Shakespeare and the juvenile drama. Theat Notebk 8:65–6
Ap/Je '54.
List of juvenile dramas adapted from Shakespeare, with note of publishers.

1564 **Roscoe, Sydney.** Some uncollected authors VI: John Marshall and The
infant's library. Bk Coll 4no2:148–55 '55.
'Provisional bibliography of The infant's library' (p.154–5). *See* nos.1565a–b.

1565 **Sloane, William.** Children's books in England & America in the seventeenth century; a history and checklist, together with The young christian's library, the first printed catalogue of books for children. New York,
King's crown pr., Columbia university, 1955. ix,251p. 24cm.
'The checklist' (p.[113]–231): chronol. annotated list of 261 items, 1557–1710, with
locations of copies.

1565a **Roscoe, Sydney.** The Infant's library. Bk Coll 5no3:279–80 '56.
Addendum to no.1564.

1565b —— Children's books in boxes. Bk Coll 5no1:76 '56.
Contains checklist complementing his no.1564.

1565c 'Milestones of the nursery, a selection from the catalogue of the Pierpont
Morgan library exhibit of children's literature . . .' *in* Targ, William, *ed.*
Bibliophile in the nursery. . . . Cleveland, 1957. p.113–66.
See no.1562.

1566 **Muir, Percival Horace.** Harlequinades. Bk Coll 6no2:182–3 '57.
Supplement to the list in his English children's books (no.1561), p.228–9.

1567 **Toronto. Public libraries. Osborne collection.** The Osborne collection of early children's books, 1566–1910; a catalogue prepared at Boys and girls house, by Judith St. John. Toronto, Toronto public library, 1958. xxiv,561p. illus. (part.col.) facsims. 26cm.

Classified annotated catalogue of some 3,000v. with extensive illus., and bibliogr. notes. Appendices (p.425–502) include a chronological list of editions, 1566–1799, and list of illustrators and engravers. *See also* no.1570.

Rev: E. F. Walbridge Pa Bib Soc Am 53:351–4 '59; TLS 10 Ap '59:216; H. Campbell *ib*. 1 My '59:257; A.M.M. Library ser5 14:302–4 '59.

1568 —— The Osborne collection of early children's books, 1566–1910, an exhibit. . . . [Toronto] Toronto public libraries, 1959. iv.(unpaged) 26cm. (Not seen)

1569 **National book league,** LONDON. Queen Mary collection of children's books. London [1963] 12p. 25cm. (Duplicated typescript)

1570 **Toronto. Public libraries. Osborne collection.** A chronicle of Boys and girls house, and A selected list of recent additions to the Osborne collection of early children's books, 1542–1910, and the Lillian H. Smith collection, 1911–1963. Toronto, 1964. 29cm. illus. 24cm.

Rev: TLS 9 Jl '64:620.

1571 **Green, Roger Lancelyn.** 'Bibliographical notes' *in* Tellers of tales: children's books and their authors from 1800 to 1964. Rev. ed. London [1965] p.[280]–311. (First pub. 1946)

Checklists of children's books by various authors. 'Chronological list of famous children's books, 1800–1964' (p.[302]–10).

1572 **Hammersmith. Public libraries.** Early children's books, a catalogue of the collection in the London borough of Hammersmith public libraries. [London] 1965. 121p. 30cm. (Duplicated typescript)

Author checklist.

1573 **Roscoe, Sydney.** Newbery — Carnan — Power: a provisional check-list of books for the entertainment, instruction and education of children and young people, issued under the imprints of John Newbery and his family, in the period 1742–1802. [London, Dawsons] 1966. viii,81p. facsims. 33cm. (Duplicated typescript)

1573a —— [**Same**]: Addenda & corrigenda . . . 6 Sept., 1966. [Harrow, 1966] il. 33cm. (Duplicated typescript)

Title checklist of 397 titles, with some bibliogr. notes and locations of copies; not indexed.

Rev: TLS 4 My '67:388; Pa Bib Soc Am 61:73 '67; P. H. Muir Bk Coll 16:237–8 '67.

CHURCH OF ENGLAND — BOOK OF COMMON PRAYER
See Book of common prayer.

CHURCH OF SCOTLAND — BOOK OF COMMON ORDER
See Book of common order.

COPYBOOKS

1575 **Heal, sir Ambrose.** 'Bibliography of the copy-books & other works of the English writing-masters, 1570–1800' *in* The English writing-masters and their copy-books, 1570–1800; a biographical dictionary. . . . Cambridge, 1931. p.121–97.
Chronol. list with TP transcrs., bibliogr. notes and locations of copies.

CORANTOS
See Newspapers and periodicals.

DIARIES
See also Biographies.

1576 **MacPike, Eugene Fairfield.** English, Scottish and Irish diaries, journals, commonplace-books, etc., 1550–1900; a bibliographical guide to selected material. Bull Bib 17:183–5, 213–15 S/D, Ja/Ap '42/3.
Chronol. checklist of 243 items.

DICTIONARIES

1577 **Laughton, L. G. Carr.** A bibliography of nautical dictionaries. Mar Mirr 1:84–9, 212–15 Mr, Ag '11.
Classified checklist with locations of copies.

1578 **Starnes, DeWitt Talmage** and **G. E. Noyes.** 'A chronological list of dictionaries with their editions and locations in American libraries' *in* The English dictionary from Cawdrey to Johnson, 1640–1755. Chapel Hill, 1946. p.231–41.

1579 **Starnes, DeWitt Talmage.** A short-title list of Latin–English and English–Latin dictionaries, 1500–circa 1700, in American libraries. Austin, Tex., Dept. of English, University of Texas, 1953. 8p. (Duplicated typescript) (Not seen)

1580 —— 'Short-title list of Latin–English and English–Latin dictionaries, 1500–ca. 1800 in American libraries' *in* Renaissance dictionaries, English–Latin and Latin–English. Austin; Edinburgh, 1954. p.394–9.

1581 **Durham. University. King's college,** NEWCASTLE-UPON-TYNE. **Library.** Catalogue of the Heslop collection of dictionaries in the library . . . [by] William S. Mitchell. Newcastle upon Tyne, 1955. 24p. 24cm.
Alphabetical checklist, with STC nos.
Rev: TLS 16 S '55:547.

1582 **Alston, Robin Carfrae** [1965–]: no.2203.

DRAMA — 1475–
See also Playbills.

1585 **Cameron, James.** A bibliography of Scottish theatrical literature. Edinburgh Bib Soc Proc 1:1–8 [i.e. 27–35] Oc '92.

1586 —— [**Same**]: Supplement. *ib.* 1:1–2 [i.e. 12–13] F '96.
Alphabetical checklist of theatrical magazines and controversial and historical publications.

1587 **Stratman, Carl Joseph.** Dramatic play lists, 1591–1963. [New York] New York public library, 1966. 44p. 26cm.
Repr. from N.Y. Pub Lib Bull 70[:71–85, 169–88 F, Mr '66. Annotated chronol. checklist of 99 works or bibliogrs. containing lists of plays.

1588 **Clarence, Reginald,** *pseud.* The stage cyclopædia; a bibliography of plays. An alphabetical list of plays and other stage pieces of which any record can be found since the commencement of the English stage, together with descriptions, author's names, dates, and places of production and other useful information comprising in all nearly 50,000 plays and extending over a period of upwards of 500 years. London, The stage, 1909. 503p. 23cm.
Concise alphabetical checklist of titles; no author index.

1589 **O'Neill, James J.** A bibliographical account of Irish theatrical literature. Bib Soc Ireland Pub 1no1:63–88 '20.
Classified checklist; first part only published.

1590 **Fletcher, Ifan Kyrle.** British theatre, 1530–1900; an exhibition of books, prints. . . . [London] Published for the National book league by the C.U.P., 1950. 72p. 22cm.

1591 **Nicoll, Allardyce.** A short-title alphabetical catalogue of plays, produced or printed in England from 1660 to 1900. Cambridge, C.U.P., 1959. xii,565p. 23cm. (History of English drama, 1660–1900. 1952–9. V.6)
Supersedes the handlists in the earlier volumes of his History.
Rev: C. E. Jones Bull Bib 22:200 '59; TLS 26 Je '59:380; G. Bullough Eng 13:24 '60; M. Matlaw Educ Theat J 12:149–50 '60; T. B. Stroup Pa Bib Soc Am 54:139–40 '60.

1592 **Bergquist, G. William.** Three centuries of English and American plays; a checklist. England: 1500–1800; United States: 1714–1830. New York, Hafner, 1963. xii,281p. facsims. 28cm.
Alphabetical checklist originally comp. as index to microfilm ed. with same title. 5,500 items with bibliogr. refs.; no title index.
Rev: I. K. Fletcher Theat Notebk 13:34 '64.

1593 **Stratman, Carl Joseph.** A survey of the Bodleian library's holdings in the field of English printed tragedy. Bod Lib Rec 7:133–43 Ja '64.
Statistical survey, with list of 'Authors for whom the Bodleian has the first edition of all tragedies' (p.141–3). (Note also his Survey of the Huntington library's holdings in the field of English printed drama. Huntington Lib Q 24:171–4 F '61. 'Statistical survey' (p.174)).

1594 **Bland, Desmond Sparling.** A checklist of drama at the inns of court. Res Opportunities Renaiss Drama 9:47–61 '66.

Classified checklist of 190 items.

1595 **Stratman, Carl Joseph.** Bibliography of English printed tragedy, 1565–1900. Carbondale, Southern Illinois U.P.; London, Feffer and Simons, 1967. xx,843p. 22cm.

Author checklist of 6,852 entries, with some bibliogr. notes, and locations of copies. 'Anthologies and collections' (p.711–63): 285 items.

Rev: TLS 30 Mr '67:276.

DRAMA — 1475–1640

1599 **Ribner, Irving.** Tudor and Stuart drama. New York, Appleton-Century-Crofts [1966] viii,72p. 23cm. (Goldentree bibliographies)

1600 **Fleay, Frederick Gard.** A biographical chronicle of the English drama, 1559–1642. London, Reeves and Turner, 1891. (Repr. New York, 1962) 2v. 24cm.

Checklists of plays, etc. now superseded by Greg: no.1608.

1601 **Schelling, Felix Emmanuel.** 'A list of plays and like productions written, acted, or published in England between the years 1558–1642' *in* Elizabethan drama, 1558–1642; a history of the drama. . . . Boston, 1908. V.2, p.[538]–624.

DRAMA — 1475–1700

1602 **Greg, sir Walter Wilson.** List of English plays written before 1643 and printed before 1700. London, Ptd. for the Bibliographical society by Blades, East & Blades, 1900. 158p. 22cm.

See no.1608.

1603 —— A list of masques, pageants, &c. supplementary to A list of English plays. London, Ptd. for the Bibliographical society by Blades, East & Blades, 1902. 1v.(various pagings) 23cm.

1604 **Collijn, Isak Gustaf Alfred.** The Hamilton collection of English plays in the Royal library, Stockholm. Uppsala, Almqvist & Wiksells, 1927. 23p. facsims. 26cm.

Checklist of 102 titles, 1616–48, with STC nos.

1605 **Oxford. University. Worcester college. Library.** A handlist of English plays and masques printed before 1750. Oxford, Ptd. for the . . . College at the O.U.P., 1929. 27p. facsim. 19cm.

1606 —— [Same]: Plays added up to March, 1948. [Oxford, O.U.P. 1948] 7p. 19cm.

1607 **Harbage, Alfred Bennett.** A census of Anglo-Latin plays. Pub Mod Lang Assn 53:624–9 Je '38.

Alphabetical checklist, mainly of mss., with locations of copies.

1608 **Greg, sir Walter Wilson.** A bibliography of the English printed drama to the restoration. London, Ptd. for the Bibliographical society by the O.U.P., 1939–59. 4v. facsims. 29cm.

Contents: 1. Stationers' records; plays to 1616: nos. 1–349. (1939).—2. Plays, 1617–1689: nos. 350–836; Latin plays; lost plays. (1951).—3. Collections; appendix; reference lists. (1957).—4. Introduction; additions; corrections; index of titles. (1959).

Chronol. bibliogr. with bibliogr. notes and locations of copies.

Rev: TLS 20 Jl '40:356; E. E. Willoughby Pa Bib Soc Am 36:166–8 '42; K. J. Holzknecht Pa Bib Soc Am 45:363–5 '51; [F. P. Wilson] TLS 7 S '51:572; A. K. McIlwraith R Eng Stud new ser 4:180–2 '53; J. Crow Bk Coll 8:191–6 '59; TLS 15 Ja '60:40; J. Carter Bk Coll 9:367 '60; D. F. Foxon Pa Bib Soc Am 55:254–6 '61; H. Jenkins R Eng Stud new ser 12:201–4 '61.

1609 **Harbage, Alfred Bennett.** Annals of English drama, 975–1700; an analytical record of all plays, extant or lost, chronologically arranged and indexed by authors, titles, dramatic companies, etc. Philadelphia, University of Pennsylvania pr., Published in co-operation with the Modern language association of America, 1940. 264p. 26cm.

See no.1614.

1610 **Carter, Albert Howard.** Harbage's Annals of English drama, 975–1700; bibliographical article. Mod Philol 40:201–12 N '42.

Extensive addenda and corrigenda.

1611 **Chicago. University. Library.** A rough check-list of the University of Chicago libraries' holdings in seventeenth century editions of plays in English. [Chicago, University of Chicago, 1941] 26l. 28cm. (Duplicated typescript)

Comp. by Gerald E. Bentley.

1612 **Linton, Marion P.** National library of Scotland and Edinburgh university library copies of plays in Greg's Bibliography of the English printed drama. Stud Bib 15:91–104 '62.

1613 **Birley, Robert.** Additions from Eton college library to the record of copies in sir W. W. Greg's A bibliography of the English printed drama to the restoration. Library ser5 18:228–9 S '63.

1614 **Harbage, Alfred Bennett.** Annals of English drama, 975–1700; an analytical record of all plays, extant or lost, chronologically arranged and indexed by authors, titles, dramatic companies, &c. Revised by S. Schoenbaum. London, Methuen [1964] (First pub. 1940) xvii, 321p. 25cm.

Rev: TLS 20 Ag '64:748; G. E. Dawson Sh Stud 1:327–8 '65.

1615 **Schoenbaum, Samuel.** Plays, masques, etc., 1552–1659: a rough checklist for prospective editors. Res Opp Renaiss Drama 8:20–45 '65.

Classified title list, with bibliogr. refs. and locations of mss.

DRAMA — 1641–1700

1620 **Paine, Clarence Sibley.** The comedy of manners, 1660–1700; a reference guide to the comedy of the restoration. Boston, F. W. Faxon, 1942. 51p. 21cm.

Repr. from Bull Bib 17:25–7, 51–3 My/Ag, S/D '40; 17:70–2 Ja/Ap '41. Classified checklist of works *about*.

1621 **Grolier club,** NEW YORK. Dramatic folios of the seventeenth century, exhibited . . . . New York [1903] 27p. 18cm.

Chronol. short-title catalogue of 36 items, with some bibliogr. notes.

1622 **Summers, Alphonse Montague Joseph-Mary Augustus.** A bibliography of the restoration drama. London, Fortune pr. [1935] 143p. 17cm.

Author checklist; no title index.

1623 **Harbage, Alfred Bennett.** 'A list, chronologically arranged, of all plays of the caroline, commonwealth, and early restoration periods' *in* Cavalier drama; an historical and critical supplement to the study of the Elizabethan and restoration stage. New York; London, 1936. p.259–84.

1624 **Kirschbaum, Leo.** A census of bad quartos. R Eng Stud 14:20–43 Ja '38.

Annotated checklist.

1625 **Woodward, Gertrude (Loop)** and **J. G. McManaway.** A check list of English plays, 1641–1700. Chicago, Newberry library, 1945. ix,155p. 22cm.

Short-title catalogue of 1,340 items, with locations of copies.

Rev: T. W. Baldwin J Eng Germ Philol 45:457–8 '46; TLS 4 Mr '46:215; D. F. Bond Mod Lang Q 7:504–5 '46; A. H. Carter Lib Q 16:361–2 '46; W. W. Greg Library ser5 1:81–5 '46; H. Macdonald R Eng Stud 22:328–9 '46; K. J. Holtzknecht Pa Bib Soc Am 41:65–7 '47; A. B. Harbage Mod Lang N 62:60–1 '47; I. A. Shapiro Mod Lang R 43:112–13 '47.

1626 **Bowers, Fredson Thayer.** A supplement to the Woodward and McManaway Checklist of English plays, 1641–1700. Charlottesville, Va., Bibliographical society of the University of Virginia, 1949. 22p. 27cm.

Corrigenda and addenda, with expanded list of holdings.

DRAMA — 1701–1800

1631 **Marks, Jeannette Augustus.** 'English pastoral plays, 1584–1660, 1660–1798' *in* English pastoral drama from the restoration to the date of the publication of the Lyrical ballads, 1660–1798. London, 1908. p.[149]–212.

Checklist, with some bibliogr. notes.

1632 **Wood, Frederick Thomas.** Unrecorded XVIII century plays. N&Q 170:56–8 Ja '36; *cf.* Dougald MacMillan *ib.* 170:193–4 Mr '36; F. T. Wood *ib.* 170:319 My '36.

Addenda to Nicoll: no.1591.

1633 **Miller, Frances Schouler.** Notes on some eighteenth century dramas. Mod Lang N 52:203–6 Mr '37.

1634 **Troubridge, sir St.Vincent.** Late xvıııth century plays. Theat Notebk
1:62 Oc '46; 1:96 Ap '47.
Addenda to Nicoll: no.1591.

1635 **Grieder, Theodore.** Annotated checklist of the British drama, 1789–99.
Restor & Eight Cent Theat Res 4:21–47 My '65.
Annotated author checklist by year, comp. largely from Bergquist.

DRAMA — 1801–1900

1638 **Cant, Monica.** A bibliography of English drama from 1890 to 1920. Lib Assn Rec 24:41–57 F '22.
Annotated checklist with title index.

1639 **Rhodes, Raymond Crompton.** The early nineteenth-century drama. Library ser4 16:91–112, 210–31 Je, S '35.
Nicoll addenda.

1640 **Biella, Arnold.** Additions and corrections to the bibliography of the 19th century drama. Philol Q 21:299–322 Jl '42.
Corrects Nicoll's Handlist for 1800–1850; *see* no.1591.

1641 **Ewing, Majl.** Authorship of some nineteenth century plays. Mod Lang N 57:466–8 Je '42.
Addenda to no.1591 for 1800–1850.

1642 —— Notes on Nicoll's Hand list for 1800–1850. Mod Lang N 58:460–4 Je '43.

1643 **Tobin, James Edward.** More English plays, 1800–1850. Philol Q 23:320–32 Oc '44.

1644 —— Early 19th century drama. N&Q 188:156–8,184–5 Ap, My '45.

1645 **Wade, Allan.** Early xixth century plays. Theat Notebk 1:27–32,42–3 Ap, Jl '46.

1646 **Troubridge, sir St. Vincent.** Early xixth century plays. Theat Notebk 1:62–7 Oc '46.

1647 —— and **A. Wade.** Early xixth Century plays. Theat Notebk 3:13–17 Oc–D '48; 3:31–3, 56–9, 76–80 Ja–Mr, Ap–Je, Jl–S '49; 4:24 Oc–D '49; 4:40–3, 68–71 Ja–Mr, Ap–Je '50.
More Nicoll addenda; *see* no.1591.

1648 **Trewin, J. C.** Verse drama since 1800. London, Published for the National book league by the C.U.P., 1956. 27p. 19cm.
Annotated checklist.

1649 **Stratman, Carl Joseph.** Additions to Allardyce Nicoll's Hand-list of plays, 1800–1818. N&Q 206:214–17 Je '61.
38 addenda and corrigenda.

1650 —— English tragedy, 1819–1823. Philol Q 41:465–74 Ap '62.
35 addenda and corrigenda to Nicoll: no.1591

EMBLEM BOOKS

1655 **Hoe, Robert.** Catalogue of books of emblems in the library of Robert Hoe, New York, Privately ptd., 1908. 133p. 23cm.
Short-title author catalogue of 463 titles with some bibliogr. notes, comp. by Carolyn Shipman; no index.

1656 **Freeman, Rosemary.** 'Bibliography of English emblem books to 1700' *in* English emblem books. London, 1948. (Reissued, 1967) p.229–40.

Alphabetical checklist.

ENCOMIA

1656a **Miller, Henry Knight.** The paradoxical encomium, with special reference to its vogue in England, 1600–1800. Mod Philol 53:145–78 F '56.

'List of paradoxical encomia' (p.173–8): chronol. checklist, 1602–1794.

ESSAYS

1657 **Watson, Melvin R.** 'Register of essay serials' *in* Magazine serials and the essay tradition, 1746–1820. Baton Rouge, 1956. p.107–51.

Annotated checklist of 280 items, with 'Check list of magazines containing essay serials' (p.152–5).

FICTION — 1475–

1660 **Grolier club,** NEW YORK. A catalogue of books in first editions selected to illustrate the history of English prose fiction from 1485 to 1870. New York, 1917. ix,149p. 19cm.

1661 —— [Same]: [2d ed., rev. & enl.] New York, 1917. xix,149p.+32l. of facsims. 24cm.

Chronol. short-title catalogue of 161 items, with bibliogr. notes.

1662 **Aldred, Thomas.** A list of English & American sequel stories. [London] Library assistants' association, 1922. 74p. 21cm.

See no.1670.

1663 **Henry E. Huntington library and art gallery,** SAN MARINO, CALIF. The English novel; an exhibition of manuscripts and first editions, Chaucer to Conrad. San Marino, Calif., 1934. 26p. illus., facsims. 22cm.

Annotated short-title catalogue of 68 items.

1664 **Singh, Bhupal.** 'Bibliography. A. Anglo-Indian novels' in A survey of Anglo-Indian fiction. London, 1934. p.[311]–34.

Author checklist.

1665 **Pennsylvania. University. Library.** English fiction to 1820 in the University of Pennsylvania library, based on the collections of Godfrey F. Singer and John C. Mendenhall; compiled by Sidney Gecker [and others] Philadelphia, 1954. xvi,116p. 28cm.

Alphabetical short-title catalogue of 1,112 items, with bibliogr. refs.; no index.

Rev: A. D. McKillop Philol Q 34:228–9 '55.

1666 **Aldred, Thomas.** Sequels; incorporating Aldred & Parker's Sequel stories, compiled by Frank M. Gardner. [4th ed. London] Association of assistant librarians, 1955. 189p. 21cm.

First ed., 1922 rev. from Aldred's list in Lib World, 1900–1; 2d. ed. rev. by Walter H. Parker, 1928; 3d ed. 1947; alphabetical checklist; no title index. *See* no.1670.

1667 **Proctor, Mortimer Robinson.** 'Bibliography of English university fiction' *in* The English university novel. Berkeley, 1957. p.217–22.

Chronol. checklist, 1749–1956.

1668 **California. University. University at Los Angeles. Library.** College life; an exhibit of the English university novel, 1749–1954. . . . [Los Angeles? 1959] 13p. illus. 22cm.

Comp. by Mortimer R. Proctor.

1669 **Clarke, Ignatius Frederick.** The tale of the future from the beginning to the present day; a checklist of those satires, ideal states, imaginary wars and invasions, political warnings and forecasts, interplanetary voyages and scientific romances . . . that have been published in the United Kingdom between 1644 and 1960. London, Library association, 1961. 165p. facsim. 22cm.

Contents: Pt.1. Chronological list with annotations.—2. Short-title index.—3. Author index.

1670 **Gardner, Frank Matthias.** Sequels, incorporating Aldred & Parker's Sequel stories. [5th ed.] [London] Association of assistant librarians, 1967. 214,vii–x,215–91p. 24cm.

Author checklist in 2 pts., adult and junior books; *see* no.1666.

FICTION — 1475–1700

1685 **Esdaile, Arundell James Kennedy.** A list of English tales and prose romances printed before 1740. London, Ptd. for the Bibliographical society by Blades, East & Blades, 1912. xxxv,329p. 23cm.

Alphabetical checklist; no title index.

1685a **O'Dell, Sterg.** A chronological list of prose fiction in English printed in England and other countries, 1475–1640. Cambridge, Mass., Technology pr. of M.I.T., 1954. v,147p. 28cm.

With STC nos. and locations of copies.

1686 **Blum, Irving D.** English Utopias from 1551 to 1699; a bibliography. Bull Bib 21:143–4 Ja/Ap '55.

Annotated chronol. checklist.

FICTION — 1601–1700

1687 **Morgan, Charlotte Elizabeth.** 'Chronological list of the prose fiction first printed in England between 1600 and 1700' *in* The rise of the novel of manners; a study of English prose fiction. . . . New York, 1911. p.154–233.

List of 653 items comp. from secondary sources.

1688 **Mish, Charles Carroll.** English prose fiction, 1600–1700; a chronological checklist. Charlottesville, Va., Bibliographical society of the University of Virginia, 1952. 3pts. in IV. 28cm.

Rev: sir F. C. F[rancis] Library ser5 8:136–9 '53; J. Gerritsen Eng Stud 37:173–4 '56.

FICTION — 1701–1800

1690 **Cordasco, Francesco G. M.** The 18th century novel, a handlist of general histories and articles of the last twenty-five years, with a notice of bibliographical guides. New York, Long Island U.P., 1950. 20p. 24cm. (Eighteenth century bibliographical pamphlets, no.8)

1691 **Conant, Martha Pike.** 'Chronological table: a list of the more important oriental tales published in English. . . .' *in* The oriental tale in England in the eighteenth century. New York, 1908. p.267–93.

1692 **Block, Andrew.** The English novel, 1740–1850; a catalogue including prose romances, short stories, and translations of foreign fiction. London, Grafton, 1939. xi,367p. 25cm.

See no.1697.

1693 **Black, Frank Gees.** The epistolary novel in the late eighteenth century; a descriptive and bibliographical study. Eugene, University of Oregon, 1940. iv,184p. diagrs. 26cm.

Appendices: 'Alphabetical list of epistolary fiction, 1740–1840' (p.112–53); 'Chronological list of epistolary fiction, 1740–1840' (p.154–68); 'Epistolary fiction in verse, 1766–1835' (p.169–70); 'Illustrative list of epistolary fiction in periodicals' (p.171–2).

Rev: E. H. Weatherby Mod Lang Q 1:555–7 '40; R. B. Heilmann Sth Atlan Q 39:354–5 '40; J. T. Hillhouse J Eng Germ Philol 40:588–9 '41; H. Brown Am Lit 13:182–3 '41.

1694 **Gove, Philip Babcock.** The imaginary voyage in prose fiction; a history of its criticism and a guide to its study, with an annotated check list of 215 imaginary voyages from 1700 to 1800. New York, Columbia U.P., 1941. (Repr. [London] 1961) xi,445p. 23cm.

1695 **Day, Robert Adams,** *ed.* 'Bibliography of epistolary fiction, 1660–1740' *in* Davys, Mary. Familiar letters betwixt a gentleman and a lady, 1725. Los Angeles, 1955. p.[1]–10.

Chronol. checklist of 186 items, with locations of copies.

1696 **McBurney, William Harlin.** A check list of English prose fiction, 1700–1739. Cambridge, Mass., Harvard U.P., 1960. x,154p. 22cm.

Chronol. list of 337 titles, with 54 'dubious or unauthenticated titles', including translations.

Rev: W. H. Bonner Mod Lang J 45:282 '61; W. B. Coley Coll Eng 23:166 '61; J. Hayward Bk Coll 10:216,219 '61; B. Boyce Philol Q 40:358–9 '61; D. F. Bond Mod Philol 59:231–4 '62 (extensive corrigenda); A. Wright Library ser5 17:273 '62; J. D. Fleeman Library ser5 21:347–8 '66.

1697 **Block, Andrew.** The English novel, 1740–1850; a catalogue including prose romances, short stories, and translations of foreign fiction. [New and rev., i.e. 2d ed.] London, Dawsons, 1961. xv,349p. 25cm.

Checklist with title index.

Rev: TLS 21 Ap '61:256; J. Hayward Bk Coll 10:216,219 '61.

1698 **Mayo, Robert D.** The English novel in the magazines, 1740–1815; with a catalogue of 1375 magazine novels and novelettes. Evanston, Northwestern U.P.; London, O.U.P., 1962. x,695p. illus., facsims. 21cm.

'A catalogue of magazine novels and novelettes, 1740–1815' (p.431–620): annotated checklist with indexes; 'A register of periodicals containing long prose fiction' (p.653–77).

1699 **Illinois. University. Library.** English prose fiction, 1700–1800, in the University of Illinois library, compiled by William H. McBurney with the assistance of Charlene M. Taylor. Urbana, University of Illinois pr., 1965. [6]162p. 23cm. (Duplicated typescript)

Author checklist of 996 items, with bibliogr. refs.; no index.

Rev: Pa Bib Soc Am 60:273 '66; TLS 25 My '67:476.

1700 **Day, Robert Adams.** 'A chronological list of English letter fiction, 1660–1740' *in* Told in letters; epistolary fiction before Richardson. Ann Arbor [1966] p.237–58.

'Notes on epistolary miscellanies' (p.259–66); 'A list of letter fiction in periodicals' (p.267–70).

FICTION — 1801–1900

1705 **Stevenson, Lionel,** *ed.* Victorian fiction; a guide to research, by Robert Ashley [and others] Cambridge, Mass., Harvard U.P., 1964; Oxford, O.U.P., 1965. vi,440p. 21cm.

Bibliogr. essays on Disraeli, Bulwer-Lytton, Dickens, Thackeray, Trollope, the Brontës, mrs. Gaskell, Kingsley, Collins, Reade, George Eliot, Meredith, Hardy, Moore, and Gissing.

1706 **Sadleir, Michael Thomas Hervey.** Excursions in victorian bibliography. London, Chaundy & Cox, 1922. vii,240p. 23cm.

Contents: Anthony Trollope.—Frederick Marryat.—Benjamin Disraeli.—Wilkie Collins.—Charles Reade.—G. J. Whyte-Melville.—Elizabeth Cleghorn Gaskell.—Herman Melville.—Index of book titles.

Chronol. lists with TP transcrs. and bibliogr. notes. *See* no.1715.

Rev: Lit R 7 Oc '22:92; E. Murphy New Republic 32:105 '22; N&Q ser 12 10:419 '22; I. A. Williams Lond Merc 6:77 '22; TLS 18 My '22:316; New Statesman 19:273–5 '22; Spectator 128:791 '22; Nation Athenæum 31:380–2 '22; H. I. Bkmns J 6:91–2 '22.

1707 **Parrish, Morris Longstreth.** Victorian lady novelists: George Eliot, mrs. Gaskell, the Brontë sisters; first editions in the library at Dormy house, Pine valley, New Jersey. London, Constable, 1933. xii,160p. illus.(1 fold.) ports., facsims.(1 fold.) 26cm.

Bibliogr. catalogue; the collection is now in the Princeton university library; see [The Morris L. Parrish collection of victorian literature] Princeton Univ Lib Chron 8:1–52 N '46; and [Same]: A summary report [with assessments of author collections and details of additions] *ib.* 17n02:50–9 '56.

Rev: TLS 5 Oc '33:676; viscount Esher Bk Coll Q 13:86–9 '34; I. A. Williams Lond Merc 29:254 '34.

1708 **Flower, Desmond John N.** A century of best sellers, 1830–1930. London, National book council, 1934. 24p. 21cm. Covertitle.

1709 **Hogan, Francis Joseph.** Fifty famous novels by English and American authors, 1719–1922; an exhibition of first editions in the collection of. . . . [Washington, 1935] 34[2]p. illus. 24cm. Covertitle. (Not seen)

1710 **Shepperson, Archibald Bolling.** 'A descriptive list of burlesque and parody-burlesque novels from 1830 to 1900' *in* The novel in motley; a history of the burlesque novel in English. Cambridge [Mass.] 1936. p.[249]–80.

Annotated author list.

1711 **Mayer, Douglas W. F.** British science-fiction bibliography. Leeds, Science fiction association, 1937. 18p. 25cm. (Duplicated typescript)

Author checklist.

1712 **Hatton, Thomas.** A complete set of Annals of sporting, first editions of English authors, Dickens, including Pickwick papers, Surtees, Ainsworth, Lever, Thackeray and others . . . sold by . . . order . . . April 20. . . . New York, Parke-Bernet galleries, 1938. 78p. illus., facsims. 25cm.

237 titles; *see also* no.3078.

1713 **Summers, Alphonse Montague Joseph-Mary Augustus.** A gothic bibliography. London, Fortune pr. [1941] 621p. illus., facsims. 23cm.

Annotated checklist arranged by authors and titles of works, from 1728.

Rev: TLS 8 Mr '41:120; cf. M. Summers *ib.* 5 Ap '41:165, 24 My '41:251; A. Craig *ib.* 19 Ap '41:191; E. Bernbaum Mod Lang Q 3:486–8 '42; F. G. Roe Connois 160:168–70 '42.

1714 **National book league,** LONDON. Victorian fiction; an exhibition of original editions arranged by John Carter with the collaboration of Michael Sadleir. London, Published for the National book league by the C.U.P.; New York, Macmillan, 1947. 50p. illus. 19cm.

1715 **Sadleir, Michael Thomas Hervey.** XIX century fiction; a bibliographical record based on his own collection. London, Constable; Berkeley, California U.P. [1951] 2v. illus., facsims. 29cm.

'An author-alphabet of first editions' (v.1, p.1–372): checklist of 3,370 items, with bibliogr. notes; 'Comparative scarcities' (v.1, p.373–84); 'Yellow-back collection' (v.2, p.1–83); 'Novelists libraries, standard novels, the Parlour library, etc.' (v.2, (p.85–176). The collection of 3,761 items is now in the University of California library.

Rev: TLS 13 Ap '51:234; M. J. MacManus Dub Mag 26:52–5 '51; R. D. Altick Philol Q 31:101 '51; P. H. Muir Spect 20 Ap '51:530; H. G. Dick Ninet Cent Fict 6:209–17 '51; viscount Esher Observer 15 Ap '51:7; J. Hayward Sunday Times 20 My '51:3; H. Richardson Sat R 19 Ja '52:26; G. N. Ray Pa Bib Soc Am 47:77–81 '53.

1716 **Leclaire, Lucien.** A general analytical bibliography of the regional novelists of the British Isles, 1800–1950. Paris, Clermont-Ferrand [1954] 399p. fold. maps. 23cm.

Classified checklist.

Rev: M. Sadleir Library ser5 9:275–6 '54; L. Leclaire *ib.* 10:210–11 '55; G. Jones R Eng Stud new ser 8:102–4 '57.

1717 **Henderson, James.** The gothic novel in Wales, 1790–1820. Nat Lib Wales J 11:244–54 '60.

'A check-list of novels connected with Wales, 1790–1820' (p.250–4) with locations of copies.

1718 **Samuels, Jack H.** Nineteenth century fiction, principally 'three deckers'; a selection from the library of Jack H. Samuels exhibited at the Grolier club. . . . [New York, Grolier club, 1963] 17p. illus. 22cm.

Alphabetical short-title catalogue, with some bibliogr. notes.

1719 **Wolff, Robert Lee.** Contemporary collectors XLII: nineteenth-century fiction. Bk Coll 14n04:511–22 '65.

Includes list of '30-odd additional Anglo-Irish novels' not in Sadleir (p.513–14).

1720 **Osborne, Eric Allen,** *comp.* Victorian detective fiction, a catalogue of the collection made by Dorothy Glover & Graham Greene, bibliographically arranged by Eric Osborne and introduced by John Carter. London, Bodley head [1966]. xviii,149p. 26cm.

Alphabetical short-title catalogue of 471 items with some bibliog. notes.

Rev: TLS 8 D '66:1145; D. A. Randall Bk Coll 16:233–6, 237 '67; P. H. Muir Library ser5 23:85 '68.

FORGERIES
See also under names of individual forgers (in Index).

1725 **Peabody institute,** BALTIMORE. **Library.** Crime and the literati; fraud and forgery in literature; exhibition . . . 1962. [Baltimore, 1962] IV.(unpaged) 28cm. Covertitle.

Annotated classified short-title catalogue comp. by P. W. Filby.

GIFT BOOKS
See Presentation books.

GLOSSARIES
See Dictionaries.

GRAMMARS

1726 **Murray, David.** Some early grammars and other school books in use in Scotland, more particularly those printed at or relating to Glasgow. [Glasgow] Royal philosophical society of Glasgow, 1905–6. 2v. 22cm.

Repr. from Roy Philos Soc Glasgow Proc v.36–7, 1904/5, '5/6. Discursive checklists with full discussion and some bibliogr. notes.

1727 **Cordasco, Francesco G. M.** Latin scholarship in 18th century England; a checklist of Latin grammars published in England, 1700–1800. Bull Bib 20:186–7 My/Ag '52.

Annotated chronol. checklist of 25 items.

1728 **Illinois. University. Library.** An exhibition of some Latin grammars used or printed in England, 1471–1687. The first printed Greek grammar. The first printed Hebrew grammar. . . . Introductions and descriptions by Harris Fletcher. Urbana, 1955. 42p. facsims. 23cm.

Annotated chronol. short-title catalogue of 82 items, with collations, and bibliogr. notes and refs.

1729 **Scheurweghs, Grace.** English grammars in Dutch and Dutch grammars in English in the Netherlands before 1800. Eng Stud 41:129–67 Je '60.

Chronol. checklist of 12 grammars by date of first pub. with TP transcrs., bibliogr. notes and locations of copies.

1730 **Alston, Robin Carfrae.** English grammars in Dutch . . . 1960. A supplement. Eng Stud 45:389–94 Oc '64.

1731 **Alston, Robin Carfrae** [1965–]: no.2203.

HYMNS

1732 **Dorricott, I.** and **T. Collins.** Lyric studies, a hymnal guide. . . . London, J. Toulson and T. Danks [1891] viii,328p. 18cm.
Discursive annotated classified checklist.

1733 **Scotland. Church of Scotland. General assembly. Committee on public worship and aids to devotion.** Draft of a catalogue of books on psalters, hymns and hymnology in the National library of Scotland, New college library, Edinburgh, Trinity college library, Glasgow . . . Edinburgh, 1939. 352l. 32cm. (Duplicated typescript)

ILLUSTRATED BOOKS

See also Copybooks; *Emblem books*; *Art*; and under names of individual illustrators (see Index).

ILLUSTRATED BOOKS — GENERAL

1735 **Bland, David Farrant.** A bibliography of book illustration. Cambridge, Published for the National book league by the C.U.P., 1955. 15p. 21cm.
Rev: N&Q new ser 2:321 '55; A. N. L. M[unby] Library ser5 10:141 '55.

1736 **Lewine, J.** Bibliography of eighteenth century art and illustrated books; being a guide to collectors of illustrated works in English and French of the period. London, S. Low, Marston, 1898. xv,615p. plates(incl. facsims.) 25cm.
Alphabetical checklist.

1737 **Sketchley, R. E. D.** English book-illustration of today; appreciations of the work of living English illustrators with lists of their books. London, K. Paul, Trench, Trübner, 1903. xxix,175p. illus. 25cm.
'Bibliographies. I. Some decorative illustrators.—II. Some open-air illustrators.—III. Some character illustrators.—IV. Some children's book illustrations' (p.[121]-73): checklists by illustrator's name, with bibliogr. notes, repr. from Library ser2 3:59-91, 176-213, 271-320, 358-97 Ja-Oc '02.

1738 **Hardie, Martin.** English coloured books. London, Methuen [1906] xxiv, 339p. facsims. 25cm.
Appendix: 1. Coloured books with plates printed by Baxter.—2. Coloured books published by R. Ackermann.—3. Coloured books with plates by Rowlandson.—4. Coloured books with plates by Alken' (p.307-21): checklists.

1739 **Prideaux, Sarah Treverbian.** Aquatint engravings; a chapter in the history of book illustration. London, Duckworth [1909] xv,434p. illus., port. 25cm.
'Books published before 1830 with aquatint plates' (p.325-57); 'Publications by Ackermann with aquatint plates' (p.374-8); 'List of books containing illustrations by T. Rowlandson . . .' (p.379-87); 'Engravers and the books they illustrated' (p.388-405).

1740 **Dulles, William Crothers.** Sporting and coloured plate books; the library of the late William C. Dulles . . . to be sold . . . Anderson auction company . . . New York. [New York, 1912] vi,81p. port. 24cm. (Not seen)
579 titles; *see also* no.1743.

1741 **Levis, Howard Coppuck**. A descriptive bibliography of the most important books in the English language relating to the art & history of engraving and the collecting of prints. London, Ellis, 1912. xix,571p. illus., facsims. 30cm.

1742 —— [Same]: Supplement and index. London, Ellis, 1913. 141p. illus. 30cm.

Discursive checklist, with some TP facsims.

1743 **Harper, Francis Perego**. Coloured plate books and their values. . . . Selected from recent English and American catalogues. . . . To which is added the . . . colored plate books collected by the late William C. Dulles . . . a guide for librarians, collectors, and booksellers. Princeton, 1913. viii,215p. 18cm. (Not seen)

1744 **Woodbury, John P.** Illustrated catalogue of library sets and first editions, art and colored plate books including the . . . collection of Cruikshankiana . . . to be sold . . . American art association. . . . New York, 1922. iv. illus. 22cm.

959 items.

1745 **Salomons, sir David Lionel Goldsmid-Stern**. Rare & valuable coloured plate books & an extensive Cruikshank collection. . . . New York, American art association, 1930. 2v. illus., facsims. 26cm.

Auction catalogue of 1,388 items; the Cruikshanks: nos.336–414.

1746 **Balston, Thomas**. Illustrated series of the 'nineties. Bk Coll Q 11:34–56 Jl/S '33; 14:35–53 Ap/Je '34.

Discussion and checklists of (i) the Cranford series (ii) derivatives (iii) Macmillans' illustrated standard novels (iv) Service & Paton's illustrated English library (v) Dent's illustrated essays, and (vi) Bell's Endymion series.

1746a —— 'English book illustrations, 1880–1900' *in* Carter, John W., *ed*. New paths in book collecting. London [1934] p.[163]–90.

'Check-lists' (p.186–90) rev. from previous entry.

1747 **Tooley, Ronald Vere**. Some English books with coloured plates; their prints, collations & values . . . first half of the nineteenth century. London, Ingpen & Grant, 1935. viii,288p. 26cm.

See no.1752.

1748 **Dunthorne, Robert Gordon**. 'Catalogue raisonné of the works of the 18th and early 19th centuries in which flower and fruit prints are to be found, with complete descriptions of the characteristics of each print, artist, engraver, publisher and other details necessary for their identification' *in* Flower and fruit prints of the 18th and early 19th centuries. . . . London, 1938. p.169–261.

Author list of 335 items, with bibliogr. notes and locations of copies.

1749 **Latimer, Louise Payson**, *comp*. 'A bibliography of illustrators and their works' [and] 'A bibliography of authors' *in* Mahony, Bertha [and others] Illustrators of children's books. Boston, 1946. (Repr. 1961) p.383–508.

Alphabetical checklists.

1750 **Abbey, John Roland.** Scenery of Great Britain and Ireland in aquatint and lithography, 1770–1860, from the library of J. R. Abbey; a bibliographical catalogue. London, Privately ptd. at the Curwen pr., 1952. xx,399p. illus., facsims. 32cm.

Bibliogr. catalogue of 556 entries arranged by place, now in Yale university library; indexes of artists and engravers, authors, printers, publishers and booksellers, and titles.

Rev: K. J. Holzknecht Pa Bib Soc Am 46:280–2 '52; TLS 11 Ap '52:256; J. W. Goodison Bk Coll 1:133–6 '32; J. Piper Signat new ser 16:50–1 '52; I. A. Williams Library ser5 12:276–9 '57.

1751 —— Life in England in aquatint and lithography, 1770–1860; architecture, drawing books, art collections, magazines, navy and army, panoramas, etc., from the library of J. R. Abbey; a bibliographical catalogue, London, Privately ptd. at the Curwen pr., 1953. xxi,427p. illus., facsims. 32cm.

Classified bibliogr. catalogue, with indexes of artists and engravers; authors; printers, publishers, and booksellers; and titles.

Rev: P. Bicknell Bk Coll 2:227–8 '53; TLS 19 Je '53: 404; I. A. Williams Library ser5 12:276–9 '57.

1752 **Tooley, Ronald Vere.** English books with coloured plates, 1790–1860; a bibliographical account of the most important books illustrated by English artists in colour aquatint and colour lithography. London, Batsford [1954] vii,424p. 24cm.

2d enl. ed. of no.1747 (1935). Bibliogr. notes on 517 entries.

Rev: P. H. M[uir] Library ser5 10:134–7 '55.

1753 **Abbey, John Roland.** Travel in aquatint and lithography, 1770–1860, from the library of J. R. Abbey; a bibliographical catalogue. London, Privately ptd. at the Curwen pr., 1956–7. 2v.(xiii,675p.) plates, facsims. 32cm.

Contents: v.1. World, Europe, Africa (1956).—2. Asia, Oceania, Antarctica, America. (1957).

Rev: J. Hayward Bk Coll 6:409–10 '57; A. H. Major Pa Bib Soc Am 51:177–8 '57; I. A. Williams Library ser5 12:276–9 '57; TLS 28 Je '57:404.

1754 **National book league,** LONDON. Victorian book illustration, with original photographs and by early photomechanical processes; catalogue of an exhibition . . . compiled by R. S. Schultze. London [1962] 14p. 30cm. Covertitle.

1755 **Graham, Rigby.** 'The handlist' *in* Romantic book illustration in England, 1943–55. [Pinner, Middlesex, 1965] p.13–[35]

LETTER-WRITERS

1760 **Robertson, Jean.** 'A bibliography of complete letter-writers, 1568–1700'
in The art of letter writing; an essay on the handbooks published in
England during the sixteenth and seventeenth centuries. [Liverpool] 1942.
p.67–80.

Author checklist.

LITURGIES

See Book of common prayer; Book of common order; Primers.

MAPS — GENERAL

For references to individual map-makers *see* Index.

1761 **Fordham, sir Herbert George.** Hand-list of catalogues and works of reference relating to carto-bibliography and kindred subjects for Great Britain
and Ireland, 1720 to 1927. Cambridge, C.U.P., 1928. 25p. 23cm.

An earlier list appeared in his Studies in carto-bibliography. Oxford, 1914. p.[169]–74.

1762 **Chubb, Thomas.** The printed maps in the atlases of Great Britain and
Ireland; a bibliography, 1579–1870. With an introduction by F. P. Sprent,
and biographical notes on the map makers, engravers, and publishers by
T. Chubb [and others] London, Homeland association [1927] xvii,479p.
maps, facsims. 29cm.

The most extensive bibliogr., in chronol. order, with extensive descr. notes and facsims.
All items descr. are in the BM. Succeeds the author's catalogues of Wiltshire (1912),
Gloucestershire (1913), Norfolk (1928), and Somersetshire (1915). *See* no.1770.

Rev: TLS 29 S '27:659.

1762a **Heawood, Edward.** 'Notes' *in* English county maps in the collection of
the Royal geographical society. London, 1932. p.8–[14]

Discursive bibliogr. comments on the Society's series of map reproductions.

1763 **Whitaker, Harold.** The later editions of Saxton's county maps. Imago
Mundi 3:72–86 '39.

Checklist with various bibliogr. notes, supplementing Chubb.

1764 **Leeds. University. Brotherton library.** The Harold Whitaker collection of
county atlases, road-books & maps presented to the University of Leeds;
a catalogue, by Harold Whitaker. Leeds, Brotherton library, 1947. 143p.
illus., maps. 26cm.

'. . . Atlases of English counties in chronological order from 1579 to 1901': items 1–239;
'Roadbooks': items 240–65; 'Yorkshire maps issued separately and books about
Yorkshire containing maps': items 270–433, with refs. to his earlier bibliogrs. (q.v.)

1765 **Rodger, Elizabeth M.** The large scale county maps of the British Isles,
1596–1850; a union list compiled in the Map section of the Bodleian
library. Oxford, Bodleian library, 1960. xiii,52p. 26cm.

Numbered chronol. checklist arranged by county, with locations of copies.

1766 **Tooley, Ronald Vere.** 'The county maps of England and Wales' *in* Maps
and map-makers. [2d ed. rev.] London, 1952. (First pub. 1949.) p.65–85.

'Scotland and Ireland' (p.86–95): checklists.

1767 **National book league,** LONDON. Mirror of Britain; or, The history of British topography: catalogue of an exhibition . . . 1957; introduction and notes by W. G. Hoskins. London, 1957. 91p. 23cm. (Not seen)

1767a **Verner, Coolie.** A carto-bibliographical study of The English pilot, the fourth book. . . . Charlottesville, Va., University of Virginia pr., 1960. viii,87p. maps. 16cm. (Duplicated typescript)

TP transcrs., bibliogr. discussion and refs., locations of copies for The English pilot from 1689, and related works.

1768 **The British Isles**; maps and road books first published before 1800, available in the Manchester reference library. Manchester R 9:120–3 '60/1.

1769 **Crone, Gerald Rae,** *ed.* Early maps of the British Isles, A.D. 1000–A.D. 1579. London, Royal geographical society, 1961. 31p. 30cm. (R.G.S. reproductions of early maps, VII)

Annotated checklist of 20 items, with bibliogr. refs.

Rev: TLS 26 Ja '62:62.

1770 **Skelton, Raleigh Ashlin.** County atlases of the British Isles, 1579–1850, a bibliography compiled by R. A. Skelton in collaboration with members of the staff of the Map room, British museum. London, Map collectors' circle, 1964– . pts. facsims. 25cm.

In progress; supersedes Chubb (no.1762).

MAPS — BUCKINGHAMSHIRE

1775 **Price, Ursula E.** The maps of Buckinghamshire. Rec Buckinghamshire 15:107–33, 182–207, 250–69 '47/52.

Chronol. list, with full descrs. and locations of copies.

MAPS — CAMBRIDGESHIRE

1776 **Fordham, sir Herbert George.** Cambridgeshire maps, a descriptive catalogue of the maps of the county and of the Great level of the Fens, 1579–1900. Cambridge, 1908. 2v.(various pagings) maps. 29cm.

Enl. from Cambridge Antiqu Soc Communications 11:101–73 '05; 6:316–19 '07; 12:152–231 '08.

Chronol. list with full descrs.; 'Cambridgeshire maps, 1179–1800: index list' (v.1, p.153–4); '. . . , 1801–1900' (v.2, p.214–16); 'Maps of the Great level of the Fens' (v.1, p.168); '. . . 1801–1900' (v.2, p.221).

MAPS — CHESHIRE

1777 **Harrison, Harold.** Early maps of Cheshire. Lancashire & Cheshire Antiqu Soc Trans 26:1–26 '08.

'Chronological list of maps of Cheshire down to A.D. 1801' (p.21–6).

1778 **Whitaker, Harold.** A descriptive list of the printed maps of Cheshire, 1577–1900. [London] Ptd. for the Chetham society, 1942. xv,220p. facsims. 22cm.

Chronol. list with full descrs.; 'Tabular index' (p.[187]–214).

MAPS — CUMBERLAND

1779 **Curwen, John Flavel.** The chorography, or a descriptive catalogue of the printed maps of Cumberland and Westmorland. Cumberland & Westmorland Antiqu & Archæol Soc Trans new ser 18:1–92, 261–4 '18.
Discursive chronol. checklist, with tabular index, p.90–2.

MAPS — DURHAM

1780 **Turner, Ruth M.** Maps of Durham, 1576–1872, in the University library, Durham, including some other maps of local interest; a catalogue. Durham, University library. 1954. 40p. 22cm.
Chronol. checklist of 153 items with some bibliogr. notes.

1781 **Doyle, Anthony Ian H.** Maps of Durham, 1607–1872 . . . a supplementary catalogue. [Durham, University library, 1960] 16p. 22cm.

MAPS — ESSEX

1782 **Emmison, Frederick George,** *ed.* County maps of Essex, 1576–1852, a handlist . . . published by the Essex education committee. London, Ptd. by E. T. Heron, 1955. 20p. 29cm.
Chronol. list with short descrs., superseding 'Selected county maps' (p.83–6) in his Catalogue of maps in the Essex record office, 1566–1855. 1947.

MAPS — FENLANDS

1783 **Fordham, sir Herbert George.** 'Descriptive list of the maps of the Great level of the Fens, 1604–1900' *in* Studies in carto-bibliography. Oxford, 1914. p.61–83.
Annotated chronol. checklist, with 'Index list' (p.83).

1784 **Lynam, Edward W.** 'Maps of the Fenland' *in* Page, W., *ed.* Victoria history of the county of Huntingdon. London, 1926–36. V.3, p.291–306.
Chronol. list of 101 items from 1576, with descr. and bibliogr. notes and locations of copies.

1785 **Wisbech society.** Old maps of Wisbech and the Fenland; an exhibition. . . . [Wisbech, 1954?] 8p. 21cm. Covertitle.
Annotated list of 64 items.

MAPS — GLOUCESTERSHIRE

1786 **Chubb, Thomas.** A descriptive catalogue of the printed maps of Gloucestershire, 1577–1911, with biographical notes. [Bristol, 1913] 238p. facsims. 23cm. (Bristol & Gloucestershire Archæol Soc Trans, v.35)
Chronol. list with descr. notes and 'Tabular index' (p.199–238); *see* no.1762.

1787 **Austin, Roland.** Additions [to Chubb]. Bristol & Gloucestershire Archæol Soc Trans 39:233–64 '16.

MAPS — HERTFORDSHIRE

1788 **Fordham, sir Herbert George.** Hertfordshire maps, a descriptive catalogue of the maps of the county, 1579–1900. Hertford, S. Austin, 1907. xii,182p. facsims. 30cm.

1789 —— [**Same**]: Supplement. Hertford, S. Austin, 1914. vii,42p. 30cm.
Enl. from Hertfordshire Nat Hist Soc Trans v.11–13 1901–7; 15:73–104 '14.
Chronol. list with full descrs.; 'Index list' (p.ix–xii).

1790 —— 'Hertfordshire maps, 1579–1900; index list' *in* Studies in carto-
bibliography. Oxford, 1914. p.18–22.
Chronol. table giving date, name, dimensions, and dates of reprs.

MAPS — LANCASHIRE

1791 **Harrison, William.** Early maps of Lancashire and their makers. Lancashire
& Cheshire Antiqu Soc Trans 25:1–31 '07.
'Chronological list of maps of Lancashire down to A.D. 1800' (p.25–31).

1792 **Whitaker, Harold.** A descriptive list of the printed maps of Lancashire,
1577–1900. [London] Ptd. for the Chetham society, 1938. xvi,247p.
facsims. 23cm. (Chetham society. Remains, historical and literary, new
ser 101)
Chronological list with descrs. and bibliogr. notes; 'Tabular index' (p.[213]–40).

MAPS — LANCASHIRE — MANCHESTER

1793 **Lee, J.** Maps and plans of Manchester and Salford, 1650 to 1843, a hand-
list. Altrincham, J. Sherratt [1957] 43p. facsims. 23cm.
Chronol. checklist of 65 items with descr. notes; no index.

MAPS — LEICESTERSHIRE

1794 **Gimson, Basil L.** and **P. Russell.** Leicestershire maps, a brief survey.
Leicester, E. Backus, 1947. viii,40p. facsims. 23cm.
Discursive chronol. list, 1576–1897.

MAPS — LONDON

1795 **Darlington, Ida** and **J. H. Darlington.** Printed maps of London circa 1553–
1850. London, G. Philip, 1964. ix,257p. facsims. 25cm.
Chronol. list of 421 items, with descr. notes and locations of copies.
Rev: TLS 19 N '64:1048; Pa Bib Soc Am 60:133 '66.

MAPS — MAN, ISLE OF

1796 **Cubbon, A. M.** Early maps of the Isle of Man; a guide to the collection
in the Manx museum. Douglas, Manx museum and national trust, 1954.
44p. facsims. 23cm.
Chronol. catalogue, c.1250–1873, with descr. notes.

MAPS — NORFOLK

1798 **Chubb, Thomas.** A descriptive list of the printed maps of Norfolk, 1574–
1916, with biographical notes and a tabular index; and a descriptive list of
Norwich plans by G. A. Stephen. Norwich, Jarrold, 1928. xvi,289p.
facsims.(part fold.) 23cm.
Chronol. list with full descrs.; 'Tabular index' (p.[255]–81). *See* no.1762.

MAPS — NORTHAMPTONSHIRE

1799 **Whitaker, Harold.** A descriptive list of the printed maps of Northamptonshire, A.D. 1576–1900. Northampton, Northamptonshire record society,
1948. xvi,216p. facsims.(part fold.) 26cm.

Chronol. list with full descrs.; 'Tabular index' (p.187–210); 'Addenda' (p.[211]–12).

MAPS — NORTHUMBERLAND

1800 **Whitaker, Harold.** A descriptive list of the maps of Northumberland,
1576–1900. [Newcastle-upon-Tyne] Society of antiquaries of Newcastle
upon Tyne and the Public libraries committee of Newcastle upon Tyne,
1949. xvi,219p. facsims.(part fold.) 26cm.

Chronol. list of 707 items with full descr. notes and 'Tabular index' (p.193–214).

MAPS — SHROPSHIRE

1801 **Cowling, Geoffrey Charles.** A descriptive list of the printed maps of Shropshire, A.D. 1577–1900. Shrewsbury, Salop county council, 1959. viii,234
[2]p. 25cm.

Chronol. list of 751 items with descr. notes and 'Tabular index' (p.207–34); 'Addenda'
([2]p. at end).

MAPS — SOMERSET

1802 **Chubb, Thomas.** A descriptive list of the printed maps of Somersetshire,
1575–1914. Taunton, Somersetshire archæological and natural history
society, 1914. xii,231p. facsims. 23cm.

Chronol. list with descr. notes and 'Tabular index' (p.[177]–231). *See* no.1762.

MAPS — STAFFORDSHIRE

1803 **Burne, Sambrooke Arthur Higgins.** Early Staffordshire maps. Nth Staffordshire Field Club Trans 54:54–87 '20.

'Chronological list of Staffordshire maps down to 1800' (p.85–6).

1804 —— [Same]: Addenda. *ib.* 60:77–81 '25/6.

MAPS — SURREY

1805 **Sharp, Henry Alexander.** An historical catalogue of Surrey maps. Croydon, Public libraries committee, 1929. 56p. 23cm.

Repr. from Croydon Pub Libs Reader's Index, 1927–8; chronol. list, 1599–1927, with
descr. notes.

1806 **Royal institution of chartered surveyors. Surrey branch.** The story of
Surrey in maps; catalogue of an exhibition. [Kingston-upon-Thames,
1956?] 63p. 24cm.

Annotated classified catalogue of 376 exhibits, including 'Printed maps of the county':
items 75–83, 133–9.

MAPS — WARWICKSHIRE

1807 **Harvey, Paul Dean A.** and **H. Thorpe.** The printed maps of Warwickshire,
1576–1900. Warwick, Records and museum committee of the Warwickshire county council, 1959. x,279p. facsims. 25cm.

Chronol. list of 135 items with full descr. notes.

MAPS — WESTMORLAND

1808 **Curwen, John Flavel,** 1918:no.1779.

MAPS — WILTSHIRE

1809 **Chubb, Thomas.** A descriptive catalogue of the printed maps of Wiltshire
from 1576 to the publication of the 25-inch Ordnance survey, 1885.
[Devizes, C. H. Woodward, ptr., 1912] 116p. 22cm. Covertitle.

Repr. from Wiltshire Archæol & Nat Hist Mag v.37 '11. Chronol. list with descr. notes
and 'Tabular index' (p.91–116). *See* no.1762.

MAPS — YORKSHIRE

1810 **Whitaker, Harold.** A descriptive list of the printed maps of Yorkshire and
its ridings, 1577–1900. [Leeds] Ptd. for the [Yorkshire archæological]
society, 1933. xiii,261p. facsims. 23cm.

Chronol. list with full descr. notes, and 'Tabular index' (p.[225]–56).

MAPS — YORKSHIRE — LEEDS

1812 **Bonser, Kenneth John** and **H. Nichols.** Printed maps and plans of Leeds,
1711–1900. Leeds, Thoresby society, 1960. xxiv,147p. fold.facsims. 21cm.

Annotated chronol. list of 374 items, with descr. notes.

MAPS — WALES

1813 **Evans, Olwen Caradoc.** Maps of Wales and Welsh cartographers. London,
Map collectors' circle, 1964. 22p. maps. 25cm. (Not seen)

MAPS — WALES — CARDIGANSHIRE

1813a **Lewis, M. Gwyneth.** The printed maps of Cardiganshire, 1578–1900, in
the National library of Wales; a descriptive list with a tabular index.
Ceredigion: Cardigan Antiqu Soc Trans 2no4:244–7 '55.

Chronol. under place, with descrs.; 'A tabular index . . .' (p.270–6)

MAPS — WALES — MERIONETHSHIRE

1813b **Lewis, M. Gwyneth.** The printed maps of Merioneth, 1578–1900, in the
National library of Wales; a descriptive list with a tabular index. J
Merioneth Hist & Rec Soc 1pt3:162–79 '51.

Checklist of 57 items.

MAPS — SCOTLAND

1814 **Shearer, John E.** Old maps and map makers of Scotland. Stirling, R. S.
Shearer, 1905. vi,86p. illus., facsims.(part fold.) 26cm.

Discursive chronol. checklist.

1815 **Royal Scottish geographical society.** The early maps of Scotland, with an
account of the Ordnance survey. 2d ed., rev. Edinburgh, 1936. (First
pub. 1934) 171p. facsims.(part fold.) 26cm.

Classified chronol. short-title lists with descr. notes and locations of copies; ed. by
H. R. G. Inglis.

1816 **Taylor, Alexander B.** Some additional early maps of Scotland. Scottish Geographical Mag 77no1:37–43 '61.

Addenda to previous item.

MAPS — SCOTLAND — EDINBURGH

1817 **Cowan, William.** The maps of Edinburgh, 1544–1851. 2d ed., rev. with census of copies in Edinburgh libraries by Charles B. Boog Watson. Edinburgh, Edinburgh public libraries, 1937. (First pub. 1932) 136p. port. 24cm.

Discursive lists in various sequences with bibliogr. and descr. notes, and locations of copies.

MAPS — IRELAND

See also 'Cartography: Maps' in Eager (no.1020), items 1181–1222.

1818 **Andrews, John Harwood.** 'Catalogue' *in* Ireland in maps; an introduction, with a catalogue of an exhibition . . . by the Geographical society of Ireland. . . . Dublin, 1961. p.20–33.

Classified short-title catalogue of 120 items.

MINIATURE BOOKS

1819 **Spielmann, Percy Edwin.** Catalogue of the library of miniature books. London, Arnold; New York, St. Martin's pr., 1961. xv,289p. 22cm.

Title checklist with full discursive bibliogr. notes; various indexes.

Rev: TLS 29 D '61:936; Pa Bib Soc Am 56:278 '62; H. M. Nixon Bk Coll 11:249–50 '62; P. H. Muir Library ser5 17:331–2 '62; P. Long N&Q 207:436–7 '62.

MISCELLANIES

See Poetry.

MUSIC

See also under names of individual musicians (in Index): *Hymns*; *Songbooks*.

MUSIC — GENERAL

1825 **Walker, Arthur D.** Music printing and publishing; a bibliography. Lib Assn Rec 65:192–5 My '63.

1826 **Duckles, Vincent Harris.** Music reference and research materials; an annotated bibliography. [New York] Free pr. of Glencoe; London, Collier, 1964. x,331p. 21cm.

1827 **Stainer, sir John.** Catalogue of English song books, forming a portion of the library. . . . London, Ptd. for private circulation by Novello, Ewer, 1891. 107p. 25cm.
Title checklist with some bibliogr. notes; no index.

1828 **O'Donoghue, David James.** Feis Ceoil, 1899; catalogue of the musical loan exhibition held in the National library. . . . Dublin, 1899. (Not seen: Eager's no.2166)
'. . . nearly complete bibliography of collections of Irish music': Eager.

1829 **Deakin, Andrew.** Musical bibliography, a catalogue of the musical works . . . published in England during the fifteenth, sixteenth, seventeenth, and eighteenth centuries, chronologically arranged, with notes and observations. . . . Birmingham, Stockley and Sabin, 1892. 66p. 25cm.

1830 —— Outlines of musical bibliography; a catalogue of early music and musical works printed or otherwise produced in the British Isles. Part I. Birmingham, 1899. 112p. 25cm.
No more pub.; annotated chronol. checklist, c.700–c.1650.

1831 **Kidson, Frank.** British music publishers, printers and engravers: London, provincial, Scottish and Irish . . . With select bibliographical lists of musical works printed and published. . . . London, W. E. Hill [1900] xii,231p. 23cm.
Principally biographical, with occasional checklists; no index; the biogr. portion superseded by Charles Humphries and W. C. Smith. Music publishing in the British Isles . . . a dictionary of engravers, printers, publishers, and music sellers. . . . London [1954].

1832 **Steele, Robert Reynolds.** The earliest English music printing; a description and bibliography of English printed music to the close of the sixteenth century. London, Ptd. for the Bibliographical society at the Chiswick pr., 1903. (Repr. 1965) xi,108p. facsims., music. 28cm.
'A short bibliography of music printing' (p.ix–xi); chronol. list of 197 items, with brief collations and bibliogr. notes.

1833 **Kidson, Frank.** English magazines containing music before the early part of the nineteenth century. Musical Antiqu 3:99–102 Ja '12.
Checklist with some bibliogr. notes.

1834 **Flood, William Henry Grattan.** Dublin music printing from 1685 to [1790]. Bib Soc Ireland Pub 2no1:7–12 '21; 2no5:101–6 '23.
Discursive checklist with TP transcrs., and facsim. of one work.

1835 **Henry E. Huntington library and art gallery,** SAN MARINO, CALIF. Catalogue of music in the Huntington library printed before 1801, by Edythe N. Backus. San Marino, Calif., 1949. ix,773p. 24cm.

Short-title catalogue, mostly of English vocal music, classified under composers' names, with TP transcrs., and some bibliogr. notes. 'Index to first lines of songs' (p.380–773).

Rev: O. E. Deutsch Library ser5 5:69–71 '49.

1836 **Oxford. University. Bodleian library.** English music; guide to an exhibition. Oxford, 1955. 40p.+8 plates. 21cm.

1837 **British union-catalogue** of early music printed before the year 1801; a record of the holdings of over one hundred libraries throughout the British Isles. Editor: Edith B. Schnapper. London, Butterworths, 1957. 2v. 28cm.

Alphabetical by composer, with index to each vol. Sixty percent of the material is contrib. by the BM whose Catalogue of printed music, comp. by William B. Squire (1912) this complements. Includes music printed in or issued as a supplement to books and periodicals.

1838 **King, Alexander Hyatt.** 'Classified lists of past collectors' *in* Some British collectors of music, c.1600–1960. Cambridge, 1963. p.130–48.

Tables of auction or sale catalogues, 1711–1961.

1839 **Tyson, Alan Walker.** The authentic English editions of Beethoven. London, Faber and Faber, 1963. 152p. illus., facsims. 21cm.

'The bibliography' (p.37–130): chronol. arrangement, 1799–1827, with TP transcrs., collations, locations of copies, and bibliogr. notes.

Rev: C. B. Oldman Bk Coll 13:95–9 '64; A. R[osentha]l Music & Letters 45:256–8 '64; TLS 6 F '64:100.

1840 **Neighbour, Oliver Wray** and **A. W. Tyson.** English music publishers' plate numbers in the first half of the nineteenth century. London, Faber and Faber [1965] 48p. facsims. 22cm.

List of plate nos. by publisher.

Rev: A. H. King Lib Assn Rec 67:379 '65; TLS 3 Mr '66:158; Pa Bib Soc Am 60:142–3 '66; H. E. Poole Library ser5 21:350–2 '66.

NEWSBOOKS
See Newspapers and periodicals.

NEWSPAPERS AND PERIODICALS
See also Books in parts.

NEWSPAPERS AND PERIODICALS — 1600–

1845 **Edwards, F. A.,** *comp.* 'A list of Hampshire newspapers' *in* Gilbert, Henry M. and G. N. Godwin. Bibliotheca Hantoniensis; a list of books relating to Hampshire. . . . Southampton [1891] p.[xxxvii]–xliii.

Alphabetical checklist; repr. from Hampshire Antiquary 1:94–7 '91; *cf.* H. L. 2:77–8 '92.

1846 **Marillier, Harry Currie.** 'Synopsis of university magazines and periodicals' *in* University magazines and their makers. London, 1899. p.[75]–99.

1847 —— [Same]: [Anr. ed.] London, 1902. p.71–93.

Annotated chronol. checklist, including Oxford, and Cambridge, magazines.

1848 **British museum. Dept. of printed books.** Catalogue of printed books in the library of the British museum. Supplement: Newspapers published in Great Britain and Ireland, 1801–1900. London, Ptd. by W. Clowes, 1905. 532 col. 35cm.

About 75,000 titles arranged by place, with title index.

1849 **Sheppard, Thomas.** Yorkshire's contribution to science, with a bibliography of natural history publications. London, A. Brown, 1916. 233p. 23cm.

Discursive classified checklist of Yorkshire scientific journals.

1850 **The Times,** LONDON. Tercentenary handlist of English & Welsh newspapers, magazines & reviews. London, 1920. 212l.,216–324,xxxvp. 21cm.

Comp. by Joseph G. Muddiman; chronol. list in 2 sections: London and suburban, and provincial, each with title index.

Additions and corrections: Austin, Roland. N&Q ser12 8:91–3, 118 '21; 10:191–4' 213–14 '22; Sparke, Archibald. *ib.* 8:173–5 '21; Richardson, N. *ib.* 8:252–3, 476 '21.

1851 **Birrell and Garnett, bksllrs.,** LONDON. Early newspapers from 1625 to 1850. [London, 1929] 32p. facsims. 25cm.

Bookseller's catalogue of 168 items; collection acquired by Duke university. Other catalogues were issued in 1931, 1933.

Rev: TLS 6 F '30:108.

1852 **Press club,** LONDON. **Library.** Catalogue of an exhibition illustrating the history of the English newspaper through three centuries. . . . [Cambridge, C.U.P.] 1932. vi,57p. illus., facsims. 24cm.

Annotated checklist of 318 items from 1606, with title index.

Rev: TLS 9 Je '32:428.

1853 **Fletcher, John R.** Early Catholic periodicals in England. Dublin R 198: 284–310 Ap/Je '36.

Annotated chronol. checklist, 1661–1876, with some bibliogr. notes.

1854 **Barnes, Fred** and **J. L. Hobbes.** Handlist of newspapers published in Cumberland, Westmorland and north Lancashire. Kendal, T. Wilson, 1951. 14p. 22cm. (Cumberland & Westmorland Antiqu & Archæol Soc Tract ser XIV)

Checklist of 152 items under place, with title index.

1855 **Bristol. Public libraries.** Early Bristol newspapers; a detailed catalogue of British newspapers published up to and including the year 1800 in the Bristol reference library. [Bristol] Corporation of Bristol, 1956. 32p. 25cm.

Full descrs. of 27 items from 1704.

Rev: TLS 28 S '56:574; G. A. Cranfield Bk Coll 6:85–6 '57.

1856 **Thwaite, Mary Florence.** Hertfordshire newspapers, 1772–1955; a list compiled for the county bibliography. [Welwyn, Herts.?] Hertfordshire local history council, 1956. 42l. 26cm. Covertitle. (Duplicated typescript)

Alphabetical and chronol. checklists of 99 items, with locations of copies and some bibliogr. notes; index of places of pub.

1857 **Brooke, Leslie Ernest John.** Somerset newspapers, 1725–1960. [Yeovil?] 1960. 103p. 26cm. (Duplicated typescript)

Checklist of 181 items, with some locations and bibliogr. notes; index of publishers, editors, printers, etc., and 'Chronological list' (p.89–97) and list of 'Papers published at Bath for children' (p.100).

1858 **Laughton, George Ebenezer** and **L. R. Stephen.** Yorkshire newspapers; a bibliography with locations. [Harrogate] Library association, 1960. 71p. 25cm. (Duplicated typescript)

Alphabetical findinglist; no index.

1859 **Myson, William.** Surrey newspapers, a handlist and tentative bibliography. London, Ptd. for the Surrey libraries group by the Wimbledon borough council, 1961. v,36p. 25cm. (Duplicated typescript)

Classified checklist of 215 items, with locations of copies.

1860 **Stratman, Carl Joseph.** A bibliography of British dramatic periodicals, 1720–1960. New York, New York public library, 1962. 58p. 25cm.

Chronol. short-title list, with locations of copies; title index.

1861 **Fraenkel, Josef.** Exhibition of the Jewish press in Great Britain, 1823–1963, under the auspices of the British section of the World Jewish congress, London, June–July, 1963. London, Ptd. by Narod pr., 1963. 63p. 22cm.

Classified short-title catalogue of English, Hebrew, and Yiddish pubs. in London and the provinces, with locations of copies; 483 items.

1862 **Library association. Reference, special, and information section. North-western group.** Newspapers first published before 1900 in Lancashire, Cheshire and the Isle of Man; a union list of holdings in libraries and newspaper offices within that area. Edited by R. E. G. Smith. London, 1964. 42p. 21cm.

Alphabetical list of 396 items.

Rev: TLS 11 Mr '65:204; Pa Bib Soc Am 60:130 '66.

NEWSPAPERS AND PERIODICALS — 1601–1700

1870 **[Lindsay, James Ludovic, 26th earl of Crawford]** Bibliotheca Lindesiana. Catalogue of English newspapers 1641–1666, together with notes of a few papers of earlier date. [Aberdeen] Privately ptd., 1901. vi,78p. 34cm.

Alphabetical catalogue of 142 entries, comp. by John P. Edmond, with a chronol. checklist.

1871 **Madan, Falconer.** The Oxford press during the civil war. Bib Soc News-sh 1–4 N '07.

'A description of a complete set of Mercurius aulicus' (p.3–4).

1872 —— **[Same]**: Bib Soc Trans 9:111–12 '08.

1873 **Williams, J. B.,** *pseud.* A history of English journalism to the foundation of the Gazette. London, Longmans, Green, 1908. xi,293p. port., facsims. 24cm.

'Catalogue of the periodicals from 1641 to 1666 inclusive' (p.218–65): chronol. checklist of items in the BM Thomason and Burney collections, with 'Some titles of corantos in the Burney collection' (p.215–17).

1873a **Axon, William Edward Armytage.** Newspapers in 1680. N&Q ser10 12:243 S '09; *cf.* R. Welford *ib.* ser10 12:314–15 Oc '09; W. Roberts; W. E. A. Axon 12:358–9 Oc '09.

Chronol. checklist of 19 items, 1665–80.

1874 **Dahl, Folke.** Short-title catalogue of English corantos and newsbooks, 1620–1642. Library ser4 19:44–98 Je '38.

See no.1876.

1875 **Burnett, Virginia S.** Seventeenth-century English newspapers and periodicals. Rutgers Univ Lib J 7:9–27 D '43.

Title catalogue of Rutgers holdings, with some bibliogr. notes.

1876 **Dahl, Folke.** A bibliography of English corantos and periodical newsbooks, 1620–1642. London, Bibliographical society, 1952. 283p. facsims. 23m.

1877 —— **[Same]**: Stockholm, Almqvist & Wiksell, 1953.

Chronol. list with TP transcrs., collations, and bibliogr. notes; no index of titles or printers. Expanded from no.1814.

Rev: TLS 17 Ap '53:255; F. Dahl *ib.* 22 My '53:339; J. C. T. Oates Bk Coll 2:162–3 '53; J. R. Brown Mod Lang R 49:228–9 '53.

1878 **London. Guildhall library.** Handlist of seventeenth century newspapers in the Guildhall library. [London] Reprinted from the Guildhall miscellany, 1954. 11p. 28cm.

Alphabetical short-title catalogue; repr. from Guildh Misc 1no3:46–56 F '54.

Rev: TLS 28 My '54:352.

1879 —— A complete list of the seventeenth-century newspapers in the Guildhall library. Guildh Misc 1no8:33–9 Jl '57.

Short-title catalogue with some bibliogr. notes.

NEWSPAPERS AND PERIODICALS — 1601–1800

1885 **Crane, Ronald Salmon [and others].** A census of British newspapers and periodicals, 1620–1800. Chapel Hill, N.C., University of North Carolina pr.; London, C.U.P., 1927. (Repr. London, Holland pr. [1966]) 205p. 25cm.

Contents: British periodicals, 1620–1800, accessible in American libraries.—British periodicals, 1620–1800, not found in American libraries.—Chronological index.— Geographical index of periodicals published outside London. 2,426 items, with American holdings.

Rev: TLS 20 Oc '27:739; *ib.* 15 D '27:961; 22 D '27:977; G. Binz Angl Beibl 38:349–54 '27; I. A. Williams Lond Merc 16:532–4 '27; W. T. Laprade Sth Atlan Q 27:96–7 '28; E. A. Baker Mod Lang R 23:357–8 '28; R. D. Havens Mod Lang N 43:212–13 '28; J. Hoops Eng Studien 43:326 '28; L. C. Wroth Library ser4 9:75–6 '28; L. F. Powell R Eng Stud 5:241–3 '29; W. Graham J Eng Germ Philol 28:303–7 '29.

1886 **Gabler, Anthony Jacob.** Check list of English newspapers and periodicals before 1801 in the Huntington library. Huntington Lib Bull 2:1–66 N '31.

Short-title title catalogue, with chronol. index.

1887 **Muddiman, Joseph George.** The history and bibliography of English newspapers [review article on Crane, no.1885, with extensive corrigenda] N&Q 160:3–6, 21–4, 40–2, 57–9 Ja '31; *rf.* R. T. Milford and J. C. Burch *ib.* 160:174–5 Mr '31; J. G. Muddiman *ib.* 160:207–9 Mr '31; J. G. Muddiman and E. E. Newton *ib.* 160:227–30, 299–300 Mr, Ap '31.

1888 **Press club,** LONDON. **Library.** An exhibition from the London press club's collection of English newspapers of the seventeenth and eighteenth centuries. [London, Ptd. by G. W. Jones, 1931] [12]p. 24cm.

109 items.

1889 **Oxford. University. Bodleian library.** A catalogue of English newspapers and periodicals in the Bodleian library, 1622–1800, by R. T. Milford and D. M. Sutherland. Oxford, Oxford bibliographical society, 1936. 184p. 24cm.

Repr. from Oxford Bib Soc Proc 4pt2:163–346 '35. Short-title title catalogue, with name index.

Rev: J. R. Sutherland R Eng Stud 13:359–61 '37; K. C. King Angl Beibl 48:300 '37; TLS 9 Ja '37:32; W. Graham J Eng Germ Philol 36:446–7 '37.

1890 **Weed, Katherine Kirtley** and **R. P. Bond.** Studies of British newspapers and periodicals from their beginning to 1800; a bibliography. Chapel Hill, University of North Carolina pr., 1946 [i.e. 1947] vi,233p. 24cm.

Notes general bibliogr. studies and bibliogr. lists of newspapers, then under titles, studies on individual newspapers and periodicals.

Rev: A. Friedman Philol Q 26:99–100 '47; D. F. Bond Mod Philol 45:65–6 '47; C. K. Skipton William & Mary Q 4:376–7 '47; J. R. Moore Mod Lang Q 9:110 '48; A. W. Secord J Eng Germ Philol 48:293–4 '49.

1891 **Berg, Virginia.** Holdings of 17th and 18th century English newspapers in the University of Illinois library. Coranto 2:4–7 Oc '50.

1892 **Stewart, Powell.** British newspapers and periodicals, 1632–1800; a descriptive catalogue of a collection at the University of Texas. Austin, University of Texas, 1950. 172p. 24cm.

Bibliogr. catalogue of 308 items; chronol. index.

Rev: N&Q 196:308 '51; A. T. Hazen Philol Q 30:229–30 '51.

1893 **Brigham, Clarence Saunders.** Check list of newspapers of the British Isles, 1665–1800, in the American antiquarian society. Am Antiqu Soc Proc 65:237–51 '55.
112 items arranged by place, with index.

1894 **Bond, Richmond Pugh** and **M. N. Bond.** The Tatler and the Spectator and the development of the early periodic press in England; a checklist of the collection of . . . . Chapel Hill, N.C. [1965] 137p. 24cm. (Not seen)

NEWSPAPERS AND PERIODICALS — 1701–1800

1900 **Barwick, George Frederick.** Some magazines of the eighteenth century. Bib Soc Trans 10:109–40 '10.
'List of magazines of the eighteenth century' (p.131–40): excerpted from the BM catalogue, classified by subject and place.

1901 **Nangle, Benjamin Christie.** The Monthly review, first series, 1749–1789: indexes of contributors and articles. Oxford, Clarendon pr., 1934. xi,255p. 22cm.

1902 —— [Same]: Second series, 1790–1850. . . . Oxford, Clarendon pr., 1955. xiii,267p. port. 22cm.

1902a **Carlson, Carl Lennart.** 'Contributors to the poetry section' *in* The first magazine; a history of the Gentleman's magazine. Providence, R.I., 1938. p.[243]–65.
Author checklist.

1903 **Coates, Willson Havelock,** *ed.* 'Lists of diurnals' in D'Ewes, sir Simond. The journal. New Haven, 1942. p.[403]–6.
Annotated checklist with locations of copies; 'Printed diurnals' (p.404–6).

1903a **Potter, W. A.** [On early Nottingham printers and printing] Library ser4 25:80–1 Je/S '44.
'List of numbers of Ayscough's Weekly courant' (p.81)

1903b **Curry, Kenneth.** The contributors to The annual anthology. Pa Bib Soc Am 42:50–65 '48.
'Annual anthology . . .' [table of contributors] (p.54–65).

1904 **Cranfield, Geoffrey Alan.** A hand-list of English provincial newspapers and periodicals, 1700–1760. Cambridge, Bowes & Bowes, 1952. vii,30p. 26cm.

1905 —— [Same]: Additions and corrections. Cambridge Bib Soc Trans 2pt3: 269–74 '56.
146 entries by place, with bibliogr. notes, and English holdings; indexes of printers and titles. *See* no.1907.
Rev: TLS 13 Mr '53:176; Bk Coll 2:88–9 '53.

1906 **Ward, William Smith.** Index and finding list of serials published in the British Isles, 1789–1832. Lexington, University of Kentucky pr.[1953] xv, 180p. 27cm.
Rev: N&Q 199:322 '54; J. H. Pafford Mod Lang R 50:108–9 '54; D. B. Green Keats-Sh J 4:108 '55.

1907 **Wiles, Roy McKeen.** Further additions and corrections to G. A. Cranfield's Handlist of English provincial newspapers and periodicals, 1700–1760. Cambridge Bib Soc Trans 2pt5:385–9 '58.

1908 **Todd, William Burton.** A bibliographical account of The annual register, 1758–1825. Library ser5 16:104–20 Je '61.

Schedules of ed. by Dodsley, 1759–93, Rivington, 1795–1826, Olridge, 1795–1814, and Baldwin, Cradock and Joy, 1815–26.

1909 **Riffe, Nancy Lee.** Contributions to a finding list of eighteenth century periodicals. N.Y. Pub Lib Bull 67:431–4 S '63.

Alphabetical checklist of 25 addenda to Crane & Kaye, with locations of copies.

1910 **Todd, William Burton.** A bibliographical account of The gentleman's magazine, 1731–1754. Stud Bib 18:81–109 '65.

'Table I: Register of copies' (p.88–90); 'Table II: Order of woodcuts' (p.90); 'Table III: Order of imprints' (p.91–2); 'Tables IV–V: Analysis of numbers, 1731–1733' (p. 92–9); 'Table VI: Analysis of numbers, 1734–1754' (p.99–102); 'Table VI: First editions. . . .' (p.103–9).

1911 **Wiles, Roy McKeen.** 'Register of English provincial newspapers, 1701–1760' *in* Freshest advices, early provincial newspapers in England. [Columbus, Ohio, 1965] p.374–519.

Chronol. checklist by place; 150 entries, with some bibliogr. notes and locations of copies.

1912 **O'Rourke, D. T.** Early provincial newspapers in Reading university library. Cambridge Bib Soc Trans 4pt3:256 '66.

NEWSPAPERS AND PERIODICALS — 1801-1900

1915 **Houghton, Walter Edwards.** British periodicals of the victorian age, bibliographies and indexes. Lib Trends 7:554-65 Ap '59.
Bibliogr. essay.

1916 **[Knowles, James]** The Nineteenth century and after: catalogue of contributors and contributions to the first 50 volumes, from March, 1877 to December, 1901. London, S. Low, Marston [1903?] 163p. 24cm. Covertitle.

1917 **Jones, James Ifano.** 'Monmouthshire periodicals, 1827-1923' *in* A history of printing and printers in Wales to 1810 and of successive and related printers to 1923. Cardiff, 1925. p.304-6.

1918 **Thrall, Miriam Mulford H.** 'General bibliography of Fraser's magazine' *in* Rebellious Fraser's, Nol Yorke's magazine in the days of Maginn, Thackeray, and Carlyle. New York, 1934. p.266-94.
Author checklist.

1920 **Speer, Felix.** The periodical press of London, theatrical and literary, excluding the daily newspaper, 1800-1830. Boston, F. W. Faxon, 1937. 58p. 26cm. (Useful reference series, no.60) (Not seen)

1921 **Brightfield, Myron Franklin.** Lockhart's Quarterly contributors. Pub Mod Lang Assn 59:491-512 Je '44.
Chronol. checklist, Mr 1826-Je '53.

1922 **Kern, John D., E. Schneider,** and **I. Griggs.** Lockhart to Croker on the Quarterly. Pub Mod Lang R 60:175-98 Mr '45.
Annotated checklist.

1923 **Briggs, Asa.** 'List of Birmingham newspapers and periodicals 1800-35' *in* Press and public in early nineteenth century Birmingham. Oxford, 1949. p.[25]-9.
Annotated checklist.

1924 **Shine, Wesley Hill P.** and **H. C. Shine.** The Quarterly review under Gifford; identification of contributors, 1809-1824. Chapel Hill, University of North Carolina pr., 1949. xx,108p. 24cm.
Annotated chronol. checklist of 733 articles, 1no1 F 1809-31no61 Ap '24, with 'Articles with authors totally unidentified' (p.91-2), and index of contributors.

1925 **Strout, Alan Lang.** The first twenty-three numbers of the Noctes ambrosianae; excerpts from the Blackwood papers in the National library of Scotland. Library ser5 12:108-18 Je '57.
'Authorship of the Noctes ambrosianae, I-XXIII' (p.118)

1925a **Houghton, Esther Rhoads.** The British critic and the Oxford movement. Stud Bib 16:119-37 '63.
'Articles contributed by the tractarians . . . January, 1836-January, 1838' (p.125-7); 'Authorship of articles . . . under Newman, April, 1838-April, 1841' (p.127-34); '. . . under Thomas Mozley, July, 1841-October, 1843' (p.134-7): chronol. checklists.

1926 **Thomas, Alfred.** The month—attribution of articles. N&Q 209:235 Je '64.

1927 **Houghton, Walter Edwards,** *ed.* The Wellesley index to victorian periodicals 1824–1900; tables of contents and identification of contributors, with bibliographies of their articles and stories. [Toronto] University of Toronto pr.; [London] Routledge & K. Paul [1966–   ]. v. 24cm.

> Contents: 1. Blackwood's Edinburgh magazine. The contemporary review. The Cornhill magazine. The Edinburgh review (including . . . 1802–1823). The home and foreign review. Macmillan's magazine. The North British review. The quarterly review. ([1966]).

1927b **Boyle, Andrew.** An index to the annuals. Worcester, A. Boyle, 1967– . v. 21cm.

> Contents: 1. The authors, 1820–1850.
>
> Authors, named or identified.—Contributions 'by the author(s) of'.—Anonyma.
>
> *Rev*: TLS 5 Oc '67:948.

NEWSPAPERS AND PERIODICALS — WALES — 1601–

1928 **Jones, James Ifano.** 'Periodicals, 1713–1923, mentioned in this work' *in* A history of printing and printers in Wales to 1810 and of successive and related printers to 1923. Cardiff, 1925. p.299–303.

> Checklist.

NEWSPAPERS AND PERIODICALS — WALES — 1801–1900

1929 **Jenkins, David Clay.** An index to the Welsh review. Welsh Bib Soc J 9no4:188–210 Ap '65.

NEWSPAPERS AND PERIODICALS — SCOTLAND — 1601–

1930 **Lamb, Alexander C.** Bibliography of Dundee periodical literature. Scott N&Q 3:97–100 D '89; 3:115–18, 135–9, 149–52, 167–71, 183–6 Ja–My '90; 4:10–14, 28–31, 49–51, 70–2, 88–90, 109–12, 134–6, 171–3, 191–3, 214–15, 230–4 Je–My '90–1.

> Discursive chronol. checklist, with some bibliogr. notes.

1931 **Noble, John,** *comp.* 'Bibliography of Inverness newspapers and periodicals' *in* Whyte, John, *ed.* Miscellanea Invernessiana. Stirling, 1902. p.185–220.

> Rev. version of checklist in Scott N&Q, 1888.

1932 **Couper, William James.** The Edinburgh periodical press; being a bibliographical account of the newspapers, journals, and magazines issued in Edinburgh from the earliest times to 1800. Stirling, E. Mackay, 1908. 2v. facsims. 24cm.

> Contents: 1. Introduction, and bibliography, 1642–1711.—2. Bibliography, 1711–1811.
>
> Checklist, with discursive descr. notes, and indexes of supplementary titles, and of persons.

1933 —— A bibliography of Edinburgh periodical literature. Scott N&Q ser3 8:190–3, 207–9, 229–32 Oc–D '30; 9:3–7, 30–2, 47–50, 112–14, 129–32, 143–6, 176–8, 193–6, 211–13, 223–6 Ja–D '31.

> Additional notes on the periodicals discussed in his item 1932, and in Scott N&Q ser2 1 '99/1900–8 '06/7.

1934 **Scotland. Central library,** EDINBURGH. Scottish newspapers held in Scottish libraries, compiled by miss J. P. S. Ferguson. Edinburgh. 1956. 57p. 26cm. (Duplicated typescript)
Title list, with notes of holdings.

NEWSPAPERS AND PERIODICALS — SCOTLAND — 1701–1800

1935 **Craig, Mary Elizabeth.** 'Bibliography: Scottish periodicals, 1750–1789' *in* The Scottish periodical press, 1750–1789. Edinburgh, 1931. p.95–104.
Alphabetical checklist, with locations of copies; the text contains much bibliogr. information.

1935a **Anderson, Peter John.** Scotch academic periodicals. N&Q ser8 6:85 Jl '94; 9:453 Je '96.

NEWSPAPERS AND PERIODICALS — SCOTLAND — 1801–1900

1936 **Copinger, Walter Arthur.** On the authorship of the first hundred numbers of the Edinburgh review. [Manchester, Priory pr., 1895] xxx,58p. 18cm.
Chronol. checklist, Oc 1802–Ja '30.

1937 **Griggs, Irwin, J. D. Kern,** and **E. Schneider.** Early Edinburgh reviewers: a new list. Mod Philol 43:192–210 F '46.

1938 **Sadleir, Michael Thomas Hervey.** 'Tales from Blackwood'. Edinburgh Bib Soc Trans 2pt4:443–5 '46.

1939 **Johnson, L. G.** On some authors of Edinburgh review articles, 1830–1849. Library ser5 7:38–50 Mr '52.
Annotated checklist.

1939a **Fetter, Frank Whitson.** The authorship of economic articles in the Edinburgh review, 1802–47. J Political Econ 61:232–59 Je '53.
'Appendix: articles, authors, and sources' (p.243–59)

1939b **Strout, Alan Lang.** Writers on German literature in Blackwood's magazine, with a note on Thomas Carlyle. Library ser5 9:35–44 Mr '54.
Chronol. checklist supplementing Morgan and Hohlfeld, no.821.

1940 —— The authorship of articles in Blackwood's magazine, numbers xvii–xxiv (August 1818–March 1819). Library ser5 11:187–201 S '56.
Chronol. checklist.

1941 —— A bibliography of articles in Blackwood's magazine, volumes I through XVIII, 1817–1825. Lubbock, Tex., Library, Texas technological college, 1959. vii,201p. 26cm.
Checklist in pub. order, with author index; additional attributions, 1826–70.
Rev: D. Roper N&Q 205:116–17 '60.

1942 **Hudson, Randolph.** Henry Mackenzie, James Beattie, et al. and the Edinburgh mirror. Eng Lang N 1no2:104–8 D '63.
Table of contribs., Ja 1819–My '80.

1943 **Guthrie, Douglas.** Some Edinburgh students' magazines of the nineteenth century. Univ Edinburgh J 22no2:159–63 '65.

Checklist, 1823–32 (p.163).

1944 **Murray, Brian M.** The authorship of some unidentified or disputed articles in Blackwood's magazine. Stud Scott Lit 4:144–54 Ja/Ap '67.

NEWSPAPERS AND PERIODICALS — IRELAND — 1601–

1946 **Campbell, A. Albert.** Irish Presbyterian magazines, past and present: a bibliography. Belfast, H. Greer, 1919. 15p. 19cm.
Repr. from Irish Presbyterian (not seen); discursive checklist.
Rev: Irish Bk Lover 11:20 '19.

1947 **Kirkpatrick, Thomas Percy C.** The periodical publications of science in Ireland. Bib Soc Ireland Pubs 2no3:33–58 '21.
'List of periodicals' (p.44–55): checklist from 1793, with some bibliogr. notes.

NEWSPAPERS AND PERIODICALS — IRELAND — 1601–1700

1948 **Dix, Ernest Reginald McClintock.** Bibliography of Irish newspapers, 1660–1700. Irish Independent 18–20 Ja '05. (Not seen: Eager's no.267)

1949 —— List of newspapers, pamphlets, etc. printed in the town of Tralee from earliest date to 1820. Kerry Archæol Mag 5:280–4 '10. (Not seen: Eager's no.1999)

1950 —— First Irish papers. Irish Bk Lover 4:97–8 Ja '13.
Checklist of 7 journals pub. in Dublin before 1700.

1951 **Munter, Robert LaVerne.** A hand-list of Irish newspapers, 1685–1750. London, Bowes & Bowes [for the Cambridge bibliographical society] 1960. xii,35p. 26cm.
Bibliogr. notes on and locations of 172 items.
Rev: TLS 3 Mr '61:144; F. K[ossman] Het Boek 35:242 '62.

NEWSPAPERS AND PERIODICALS — IRELAND — 1701–1800

1952 **Dix, Ernest Reginald McClintock.** Irish bibliography; tables relating to Dublin newspapers of the 18th century, shewing what volumes, &c. of each are extant and where access to them can be had in Dublin. Dublin, Hanna & Neale, 1910. 12p. 28cm.

NEWSPAPERS AND PERIODICALS — IRELAND — 1801–1900

1953 **The Dublin review,** 1836–1936, complete list of articles published between May, 1836 and April, 1936. London, Burns Oates & Washbourne [1936] 96p. 21cm.
Now entitled Wiseman Review.

1954 **Bowen, B. P.** Dublin humourous periodicals of the nineteenth century. Dublin Hist Rec 13:2–11 Mr/My '52.
'List of periodicals' (p.11): checklist with preceding bibliogr. discussion.

NOVELS
See Fiction.

PAMPHLETS
See also Broadsides; Proclamations; Sermons.

PAMPHLETS — 1475-

1960 **McGill university,** MONTREAL. **Library.** Catalogue of a collection of historical tracts, 1651–1800 . . . collected and annotated by Stuart J. Reid . . . the gift of mrs. Peter Redpath to the Redpath library. . . . London, Ptd. by the donor for private circulation, 1901. 657p. 19cm.

Based on collection of 40v. of pamphlets gathered by sir John Bramston (1611–1700); checklist in order of 582 bound volumes, with author but no title index.

1961 **Aberdeen. University. Library.** Catalogue of pamphlets in the King, the Thomson, and the Herald collection. Aberdeen, Rosemount pr., 1927. ix,691p. 23cm.

Alphabetical checklist comp. by Peter J. Anderson; no title index.

PAMPHLETS — 1475–1640

1965 **California. State library,** SACRAMENTO. **Sutro branch,** SAN FRANCISCO. Catalogue of English pamphlets in the Sutro library. . . . Prepared by the personnel of the Work projects administration. . . . San Francisco, 1941. 2v. 27cm. (Duplicated typescript)

Checklist with TP transcrs., and bibliogr. refs. of items from 1562–1642. Pt.2 is an alphabetical title catalogue of 17th century periodicals, with bibliogr. notes and record of holdings; title index.

1966 **Collins, Douglas Cecil.** A handlist of newspamphlets, 1590–1610. London, South-west Essex technical college, 1943. xix,129p. 23cm.

Annotated chronol. checklist, with indexes.

Rev: L. W. Hanson Library ser4 26:203–4 '45.

PAMPHLETS — 1475–1700

1970 **Lincoln's inn,** LONDON. **Library.** A catalogue of pamphlets, tracts, proclamations, speeches, trials, petitions from 1506 to 1700. . . . London, Ptd. at the Chiswick pr. for the honourable society of Lincoln's inn, 1908. xii,481p. 27cm.

Chronol. short-title catalogue of 2,185 items, comp. by William P. Baildon, with indexes of persons and places, and of subjects.

1971 **Bloom, James Harvey.** English tracts, pamphlets and printed sheets; a bibliography. London, W. Gandy, 1922–3. 2v. facsims. 23cm.

Contents: 1. Early period, 1473–1650. Suffolk. (1922).—2. Early period, 1473–1650. Leicestershire, Staffordshire, Warwickshire, Worcestershire. (1923).

Chronol. by author, with quasifacsim. TP transcrs, locations of copies, but no collations; title index in each volume. The Warwickshire section includes bibliogr. of Shakespeare.

Rev: N&Q 144:438–9 '22; 146:55–6 '24; G.P.M. Lib Assn Rec 2:166–9 '24.

PAMPHLETS — 1641–1700

1972 **British museum. Dept. of printed books. Thomason collection.** Catalogue of the pamphlets, books, newspapers, and manuscripts relating to the civil

war, the commonwealth, and restoration, collected by George Thomason, 1640–1661. . . . London, Ptd. by order of the trustees, 1908. 2v. 26cm.
Chronol. short-title catalogue, with index.

1973 **Wallace, John M.** The engagement controversy, 1649–1652; an annotated list of pamphlets. N.Y. Pub Lib Bull 68:384–405 Je '64.
Annotated chronol. checklist of 72 items, with some bibliogr. notes.

1975 **O'Neill, James J.** The volunteers of 1782. Irish Bk Lover 6:123–4, 144–5 Mr, Ap '15.

Checklist of contemporary pamphlets in the Halliday collection, Royal Irish academy.

1978 **Spinney, Gordon Harold.** Cheap repository tracts: Hazard and Marshall edition. Library ser4 20:295–340 D '39.

'Bibliography' (p.312–40): chronol. checklist of 187 items, with locations of copies and some bibliogr. notes; title index.

PAMPHLETS — 1801–1900

1979 **Jackson, Holbrook.** Business booklets and men-of-letters. Penrose Ann 42:55–62 '40.

Classified checklists of I. Publishers' proposals, catalogues of exhibitions, etc.; II. Printers, papermakers, etc.; III. Tourism, hotels, catering, etc.; IV. Commercial ephemeral publications, with contributions by well-known authors.

PERIODICALS
See Newspapers and periodicals.

PLAYBILLS

1980 **Fletcher, Ifan Kyrle.** British playbills before 1718. Theat Notebk 17no2:48–50 '62.

Annotated checklist of 17 items, with some facsims.

POETRY
See also Ballads; Songbooks.

POETRY — 1475–

1981 **Bush, Douglas.** 'Appendix' [chronological checklist of mythological poems, 1681–1935] *in* Mythology and the romantic tradition in English poetry. Cambridge, Mass., 1937. p.[539]–77.

1982 **Richards, Edward Ames.** 'Hudibrastic verse' *in* Hudibras in the burlesque tradition. New York, 1937. p.[171]–8.

Author checklist, 1662–1830.

1983 **Bradner, Leicester.** 'Chronological list of publications of Anglo-Latin poetry' *in* Musae anglicanae; a history of Anglo-Latin poetry, 1500–1925. New York; London, 1940. p.346–73.

Locations of rarer items. *See* no.1986a.

1984 **National book league,** LONDON. English poetry; a catalogue of first & early editions of works of the English poets from Chaucer to the present day . . . Compiled by John Hayward. [London] Published for the National book league by the C.U.P., 1947. x,140p. 25cm.

1985 —— [Same]: Compiled & rev. by John Hayward. [London] C.U.P., 1950. x,147p.+356 facsims. 26cm.

Short-title catalogue, with bibliogr. notes and locations of copies; indexes of titles and of authors; extensive TP facsims.
Rev: TLS 19 Ap '47:188; F. S. Ferguson *ib*. 3 My '47:211; Library ser5 6:220–2 '51.

1986 **Osborne, Mary Tom.** Advice-to-a-painter poems, 1633–1856; an annotated finding list. [Austin] University of Texas, 1949. 92p. 24cm.

1986a **Bradner, Leicester.** Musae anglicanae, a supplemental list. Library ser5 22:93–103 Je '67.

'Supplemental list' (p.94–100): chronol. checklist with locations of copies. *See* no.1983.

POETRY — 1475–1500

1987 **Ringler, William.** A bibliography and first line index of English verse printed through 1500; a supplement to Brown and Robbins' Index of middle English verse. Pa Bib Soc Am 49:153–80 '55.

Checklist with STC nos., locations of copies. and total number and Index numbers of poems in each volume; the first part is a bibliography of all books printed to 1500 containing English verse.

POETRY — 1475–1700

1988 **Spencer, Theodore,** *comp.* 'A bibliography of studies in metaphysical poetry, 1912–1938' *in* Spencer, Theodore and M. van Doren. Studies in metaphysical poetry; two essays. . . . New York, 1939. p.[31]–83.

1989 **Berry, Lloyd Eason.** A bibliography of studies in metaphysical poetry, 1939–1960. Madison, University of Wisconsin pr., 1964. xi,99p. 23cm.

Continuation of Spencer.

1990 **Wellesley college. Library.** A catalogue of early and rare editions of English poetry, collected and presented to Wellesley college by George Herbert Palmer, with additions from other sources. Boston, Houghton, Miflin, 1923. xii,613p. 23cm.

Author catalogue with TP transcrs. and bibliogr. notes.

1991 **Ault, Norman,** *ed.* 'A short-title list of books containing poetical collections, mainly anonymous and of the XVIIth century . . .' *in* Seventeenth century lyrics from the original texts. London, 1928. p.493–8.

1992 —— [Same]: 2d ed. London, 1950. p.519–27.

1993 **Bush, Douglas.** 'Appendix [chronological conspectus of mythological poems . . . up to 1680]' *in* Mythology and the renaissance tradition in English poetry. Minneapolis, 1932. p.301–23.

1994 **Case, Arthur Ellicott.** A bibliography of English poetical miscellanies, 1521–1750. Oxford, Ptd. for the Bibliographical society at the O.U.P., 1935. xi,386p. 23cm.

Chronol. bibliogr. of 481 titles, with quasifacsim. TP transcrs., collations, and locations of copy; indexes of titles, persons, and books without London imprints.

Rev: TLS 10 Oc '35:626; I. A. Williams Lond Merc 32:479–80 '35.

1995 **Henry E. Huntington library and art gallery,** SAN MARINO, CALIF. Early English poetry. . . . [San Marino, 1940–1] 2v. 28cm. (Duplicated typescript) (Not seen)

1996 **Smith, Courtney Craig.** The seventeenth-century drolleries. Harvard Lib Bull 6no1:40–51 '52.

Case corrigenda and addenda.

1997 **Cameron, William James.** A bibliography of English poetical miscellanies, 1660–1720, in the Alexander Turnbull library. Wellington, Alexander Turnbull library and the Department of English, Victoria university college, 1953. 33p. 26cm. (Duplicated typescript)

Rev: Library ser5 8:212 '53.

1998 **Leach, Elsie.** English religious poetry, 1600–1699, a partial bibliography. Bull Bib 23:132–5 S/D '61.

Checklist based on Huntington, and William A. Clark, UCLA, libraries' holdings.

POETRY — 1701–1800

1999 **Omond, Thomas Stewart.** 'Addenda to and corrigenda in my previous list of works dealing with English verse structure, by native writers' *in* English metrists in the eighteenth and nineteenth centuries. . . . London, 1907. p.255–67.

2000 **Bleackley, Horace W.** A bibliography of forgotten magazines. N&Q ser12 8:143–5 Ag '16.
Checklist with notes of 7 'ribald miscellanies' pub. 1769–1827.

2001 **Beatty, Joseph M.** Churchill's influence on minor eighteenth century satirists. Pub Mod Lang Assn 42:162–76 '27.
Annotated checklist of pubs. 'occasioned by Churchill's works or influenced by them', 1761–83.

2002 **Williams, Iolo Aneurin.** Some poetical miscellanies of the early eighteenth century. Library ser4 10:233–51 D '29.
Bibliogr. discussion, with quasifacsim. TP transcrs., collations, and bibliogr. notes interspersed; expanded in his Points, p. 82–90 (*see* no.2004).

2003 **Bond, Richmond Pugh.** 'Register of burlesque poems' *in* English burlesque poetry, 1700–1750. Cambridge, Mass., 1932. p.[233]–453. (Repr. New York, Russell & Russell, 1964)
Chronol. annotated checklist.

2004 **Williams, Iolo Aneurin.** Points in eighteenth-century verse; a bibliographer's and collector's scrapbook. London, Constable; New York, R. R. Bowker, 1934. ix,144p. facsims. 23cm.
Author catalogue with quasifacsim. TP transcrs., collations, and bibliogr. notes.
Rev: TLS 25 Ja '34:64; J. Carter Pub Wkly 125:790–1 '34; H. Williams Bk Coll Q 15:79 '34; M. J. MacManus Dub Mag 9:53 '34; R. B. McKerrow R Eng Stud 11:118–20 '35.

2005 **Aubin, Robert Arnold.** 'Bibliographies [of (a) Hill-poems, (b) Mine- and Cave-poems, (c) Sea-poems, (d) Estate-poems, (e) Town-poems, (f) Building-poems, (g) Region-poems, (h) River-poems, (i) Journey-poems]' *in* Topographical poetry in XVIIIth century England. New York, 1936. p.[297]–391.
Chronol. checklists, with locations of copies.

2006 **Boys, Richard Charles.** A finding-list of English poetical miscellanies, 1700–48 in selected American libraries. Eng Lit Hist 7:144–62 Je '40.
Chronol checklist of 523 items with Case nos., with American locations and title index.

2007 **Randolph, Mary Claire.** 'Hide-and-seek' satires of the restoration and the XVIII-century. N&Q 183:213–16 Oc '42.
Title checklist of 53 items.

2008 **Smith, David Nichol.** A note on Mum, an eighteenth-century political ballad. Edinburgh Bib Soc Trans 3pt4:249 '57.
TP transcrs. and bibliogr. discussion of 2 ed.

2009 **Otago university,** DUNEDIN, N.Z. **Library.** A checklist of the DeBeer collection of the University of Otago library, consisting mainly of volumes of eighteenth century English verse and prose presented by Esmond S. de Beer. Dunedin, 1963. 62p. 32cm. (Duplicated typescript)

Short-title author catalogue of former Iolo A. Williams collection.

POETRY — 1801–1900

2015 **Raysor, Thomas Middleton,** *ed.* The English romantic poets; a review of research, by Ernest Bernbaum [and others]. Rev. ed. New York, Modern Language association, 1956. (First pub. 1950) 307p. 21cm.

Bibliogr. guide to the romantic movement, Wordsworth, Coleridge, Byron, Shelley, and Keats; no index.

2016 **Faverty, Frederic Everett,** *ed.* The victorian poets; a guide to research, by Paull Franklin Baum [and others] Cambridge, Harvard U.P., 1956. x,292p. 22cm.

Discursive bibliogr. guide to Tennyson, the Brownings, Fitzgerald, Clough, Arnold, Swinburne, the pre-Raphaelites, Hopkins, and the later victorian poets.

2017 **Houtchens, Carolyn Washburn** and **L. H. Houtchens,** *ed.* The English romantic poets & essayists, a review of research and criticism. Rev. ed. [New York] Published for Modern language association of America by New York U.P.; London, University of London pr., 1966. (First ed., 1957) 395p. 23cm.

Bibliogr. essays on Blake, Lamb, Hazlitt, Scott, Southey, Thomas Campbell, Thomas Moore, Landor, Hunt, De Quincey, and Carlyle.

2018 **Guild, Edward C.** Greek mythology in English poetry of the nineteenth century. Brunswick, Me., Bowdoin college library, 1891. 19p. 20cm. Covertitle.

Classified checklist.

2019 **Harvard university. Library.** A list of Newdigate prize poems, the gift of Thornton K. Lothrop. . . . [Harvard, Mass., 1899] 8p. 21cm. Headtitle.

Chronol. checklist.

2020 **Keats-Shelly memorial,** ROME. Titles of the first thousand works acquired by the Keats, Shelley, Byron, Hunt library of the Memorial. Bull **Keats-Sh** Memorial 1:75–187 '10.

2021 —— Titles of the second thousand. . . . *ib.* 2:103–99 '13.

Classified author short-title catalogue, with some bibliogr notes.

2022 **Ewing, James Cameron.** Brash and Reid, booksellers in Glasgow and their collections of Poetry original and collected. Glasgow Bib Soc Rec 12:1–20 '36.

Discursive collations and contents

2023 **Hogan, Francis Joseph.** The romantics, 1801–1820; an exhibition of books and autograph letters from the collection of Frank J. Hogan. . . . Los Angeles, 1938. 16p. front., facsim. 27cm. (Not seen)

Comp. by Ward Ritchie.

2024 **Sanderlin, George William.** A bibliography of English sonnets, 1800–1850. Eng Lit Hist 8:226–40 Je '41.

Author checklist.

2025 **Carron, R. J. F.** The Infant minstrel, 1816. Bk Coll 13no3:354–5 '64.

Quasifacsim. TP transcr., collation, and discussion of copy in Edinburgh university library.

POETRY — 1901–

2030 **Bloomfield, Barry Cambray.** New verse in the '30s. London, Library association, 1960. 22p. 22cm. (Special subject list, no.33)

Checklist of poets and criticism.

2031 **Recorder,** *pseud.* A bibliography of modern poetry, with notes on some contemporary poets. Chapbook 2no12:1–46 Je '20.

Author checklist, 'a complete record of books of poetry published from January, 1912 to the end of May, 1920'.

2032 **Birmingham. Public libraries. Reference dept.** Catalogue of the war poetry collection presented by an anonymous donor. Birmingham, Ptd. for the donor by the Birmingham printers, 1921. vii,60p. 25cm.

Classified short-title catalogue; no index.

2033 **Bloomfield, Barry Cambray.** English poetry in the '30s; a short title list. [London] The library, College of s. Mark & s. John, 1958. i,41p. 25cm. (Duplicated typescript)

Author checklist of 1,295 items; no index.

POETRY — SCOTLAND — 1475–1640

2034 **Geddie, William.** A bibliography of middle Scots poets. . . . Edinburgh, Ptd. for the [Scottish text] society by W. Blackwood, 1912. cix,364p. 23cm.

Simple TP transcrs., collations, bibliogr. refs. and locations of copies for the earlier ed. Includes Collections of poetry, Huchown, sir Hew of Eglintoun, Clerk of Tranent, John Barbour, Andrew of Wyntoun, James I, Blind Harry, sir Richard Holland, Robert Henryson (with Patrick Johnistoun), William Dunbar and Walter Kennedy, Gawin Douglas, John Bellenden, sir David Lyndsay, Alexander Scott, Alexander Montgomerie (with sir Patrick Hume), and Alexander Hume.

POETRY — IRELAND — 1475–

2035 **O'Donoghue, David James.** The poets of Ireland; a biographical and bibliographical directory of Irish writers of English verse. [2d ed.] Dublin, H. Figgis; London, H. Frowde, O.U.P., 1912. (First pub. 1892–3) iv,504p. 25cm.

Bibliographies; 'Collections and anthologies of Irish verse, 1724–1912' (p.502–4).

PRESENTATION BOOKS

2035a **Wilson, Elkin Calhoun.** 'A short-title list of books and manuscripts dedicated, inscribed, or presented to queen Elizabeth' *in* England's Eliza. Cambridge, Mass., 1939. p.[413]–56.

2035b **Rosenberg, Eleanor.** 'A chronological list of works dedicated to the earl of Leicester' *in* Leicester, patron of letters. New York, 1955. p.[355]–362.

Checklist of 94 items, 1559–88.

2036 **Williams, Franklin Burleigh.** Special presentation epistles before 1641; a preliminary checklist. Library ser5 7:15–20 Mr '52.

'Check-list' (p.18–20): 'this list gives brief identification of each book, the normal dedication . . . the present location of each presentation copy, the addresses and any remarkable features' in STC order. *See* no.551.

2037 **Miller, Edwin Haviland.** New year's day gift books in the sixteenth century. Stud Bib 15:233–41 '62.

Annotated checklist of 37 books and 12 mss., 1511–1603.

PRIMERS

2038 **Carruthers, William.** 'Bibliography' *in* The shorter catechism of the Westminster assembly of divines, being a facsimile . . . with historical account and bibliography. London, 1897. p.38–78.

See no.2042.

2038a **Hoskins, Edgar.** Horæ beatæ Mariæ virginis, or Sarum and York primers, with kindred books. . . . London, Longmans, Green, 1901. lvi,577p. 24cm.

'A hand-list of Horæ or primers' (p.1–104); 'Indices' (p.[381]–570); chronol. checklist, with locations of copies.

2039 **Merritt, Edward Percival.** The Royal primer, with checklist of royal primers. Cambridge [Ptd. at the Harvard U.P.] 1925. 31p. facsims. 24cm.

Repr. with added illus. from Bibliographical essays; a tribute to Wilberforce Eames. [Cambridge, Mass.] 1924.

Chronol. checklist (p.30–1) with locations of copies.

2039a **Anders, H.** The Elizabethan ABC with the catechism. Library ser4 16:32–48 Je '35.

'Appendix . . . titles of ABC-books . . . 1534–1603' (p.46–8): annotated checklist.

2040 **Butterworth, Charles C.** The English primers, 1529–1545; their publication and connection with the English bible and the reformation in England. Philadelphia, University of Pennsylvania pr., 1953. xiii,340p. facsims. 24cm.

'Bibliography: A. Primers, books of hours, etc. listed chronologically' (p.305–10).— B. 'Kindred books belonging to the period' (p.310–19): checklists, with STC nos.

2041 **McRoberts, David.** Catalogue of Scottish mediaeval liturgical books and fragments. Glasgow, J. S. Burns, 1953. 28p. facsims. 25cm.

Repr. from Innes R 3no1:49–63 '52. Checklist of 156 items, including mss., with some notes and locations of copy.

2042 **Carruthers, Samuel William.** Three centuries of the Westminster shorter catechism. Fredericton, N.B., Published for the Beaverbrook foundations by the University of New Brunswick, 1957. 128p. facsims. 38cm.

Extended from no.2038. 'Bibliography' (p.17–128): classified checklist with some quasifacsim. TP transcrs., bibliogr. notes, and locations of copies.

Rev: H. Chadwick Library ser5 13:151 '58.

PROCLAMATIONS

2045 **[Lindsay, James Ludovic, 26th earl of Crawford]** . . . A bibliography of royal proclamations of the Tudor and Stuart sovereigns and of others published under authority, 1485–1714, with an historical essay on their origins and use, by Robert Steele. Oxford, Ptd. by the Clarendon pr., 1910. 2v. illus., fold. map. 33cm. (Bibliotheca Lindesiana, v.5+6)

Contents: 1. England and Wales.—2. Ireland. Scotland.

Pub. also with title: Tudor and Stuart proclamations . . . Oxford, 1910.

Chronol. checklist, with preces, and locations of copies; 'Pre-Tudor proclamations, a preliminary hand-list' (p.[clvii]–clxxvi).

2046 —— . . . Handlist of proclamations issued by royal and other constitutional authorities, 1714–1910, George I to Edward VII, together with an index of names and places. Wigan, Roger and Rennick, 1913. xxp., 836[i.e. 870] col., 182p. 36cm. (Bibliotheca Lindesiana, v.8)

Rev. and enl. repr. of previously pub. vols. based on work by John P. Edmond, with index by Arthur G. E. Phillips; chronol. checklist with locations of copies.

2047 **London. University. Goldsmiths' company's library of economic literature.** Catalogue of the collection of English, Scottish and Irish proclamations in the University library. . . . London, University of London pr., 1928. 99p. 34cm.

Chronol. catalogue of 429 items, with bibliogr. refs., preces of contents, and indexes to printers, publishers, and subjects.

2048 **Parsons, Edward John S.** Some proclamations of Charles I, being addenda to Bibliotheca Lindesiana. A bibliography of royal proclamations of the Tudor and Stuart sovereigns by Robert Steele. Bod Q Rec Suppl 8no90:1–28 '36.

Ptd. in full, with Steele nos.

PROHIBITED BOOKS

2050 [**Steele, Robert Reynolds**] Lists of prohibited books I. Bib Soc News–sh 4 F '11; II. [III] *ib*. 3–4 Mr '11.

PROVERBS

2055 **Wilson, Frank Percy.** English proverbs and dictionaries of proverbs. Library ser4 26:51–71 Je '45.
Short-title list (p.64–7) with bibliogr. notes.

PSALTERS
See Bible. O.T. Psalms.

PSEUDONYMA
See Anonyma and pseudonyma

SALE CATALOGUES
See Auction catalogues.

SERIAL PUBLICATIONS
See Books in parts; Newspapers and periodicals.

SERMONS

2060 **Brassey institute,** HASTINGS. **Library.** An alphabetical index to the printed sermons in the reference library. . . . Hastings, Ptd. by F. J. Parsons, 1894. viii,98p. 21cm.
'List of the names of authors and books' (p.[vi]–viii) followed by 'Alphabetical index of sermons'; comp. by Edward H. Marshall.

2061 **Mitchell, William Fraser.** 'Selected bibliography' *in* English pulpit oratory from Andrewes to Tillotson; a study of its literary aspects. London; New York [1932] p.[403]–52.
Classified checklists of 17th century sermons and associated literature.

2062 **Herr, Alan Fager.** 'Bibliography' *in* The Elizabethan sermon; a survey and a bibliography. Philadelphia, 1940. p.[119]–69. (Not seen)

SONGBOOKS

2065 **McCance, Stouppe.** Some old Ulster song books. Irish Bk Lover 7:108–10 Ja '16.
Checklist of 35 items arranged by place.

2066 **Murrie, Eleanore Boswell.** Notes on the printers and publishers of English songbooks, 1651–1702. Edinburgh Bib Soc Trans 1pt3:241–304 '38.
'Hand-list' (p.259–304): alphabetical checklist of booksellers and printers and their songbooks, with title index.

2067 **Day, Cyrus Lawrence** and E. B. Murrie. English song-books, 1651–1702; a bibliography with a first-line index of songs. London, Ptd. for the

Bibliographical society at the O.U.P., Oxford, 1940. xxi,439p. illus., plates, facsims., music. 23cm.

Chronol. bibliogr. of 252 items, with indexes of first lines, composers, authors, singers, and actors, tunes and airs, sources, song-books, and printers, publishers and book-sellers.

Rev: J. G. McManaway Mod Lang N 56:630–1 '41; TLS 22 F '41:96; N. Ault R Eng Stud 17:352–8 '41; E. N. Backus Pa Bib Soc Am 36:234–8 '42.

2068 **Hopkinson, Cecil** and **C. B. Oldman.** Thomson's collections of national song, with special reference to the contributions of Haydn and Beethoven. Edinburgh Bib Soc Trans 2ptl:1–64 '40; addenda and corrigenda 3pt2:121–4 '54.

Full descrs., TP facsims., and thematic catalogues.

2069 —— Haydn's settings of Scottish songs in the collections of Napier and Whyte. Edinburgh Bib Soc Trans 3pt2:85–120 '54.

Supplements Haydn section of previous item.

UNFINISHED BOOKS

2075 **Corns, Albert Reginald** and **A. Sparke.** A bibliography of unfinished books in the English language, with annotations. London, B. Quaritch, 1915. xvi,255p. 24cm.

Alphabetical checklist with notes.

Rev: J. S. C[rone] Irish Bk Lover 7:175–7 '16 (with Irish addenda).

2076 **Wallbridge, E. F.** Bibliography of unfinished English books. Authors' Ann 83–112 '30. (Not seen)

SUBJECTS

ACCOUNTING

2080 **Gordon, Cosmo Alexander.** 'The bibliography of book-keeping': Institute of chartered accountants in England and Wales. Library catalogue. London, 1937. V.2.

2081 —— [**Same**]: First supplement. London, 1939. p.31–6.
Chronol. short-title catalogue with author index and collations of pre-1800 items.

2082 **Thomson, Hugh W.** and **B. S. Yamey.** Bibliography of book-keeping and accounts, 1494 to 1650. Accounting Res 9:239–57 Oc '58.

2083 **Institute of chartered accountants in England and Wales.** The earliest books on book-keeping, 1494–1683; some notes on the origins of double-entry book-keeping. London, 1963. 16p. col. port. 22cm. (Not seen)

2084 **Institute of chartered accountants of Scotland,** EDINBURGH. **Library.** Catalogue of printed books and pamphlets on accounting and allied subjects dated 1494 to 1896 forming a collection of antiquarian interest in the Institute's Edinburgh library. Edinburgh, 1963. 38,vip. 25cm. (Duplicated typescript)
Chronol. checklist.
Rev: [L. S. Thompson] Pa Bib Soc Am 59:81 '65.

2085 **Yamey, Basil Selig, H. C. Edey,** and **H. W. Thomson.** 'Bibliography: books on accounting in English, 1543–1800' *in* Accounting in England in Scotland, 1543–1800. London, 1963. p.202–24.
Chronol. checklist, with locations of copies.

AGRICULTURE
See also Gardening.

2090 **McDonald, Donald.** 'The literature and bibliography of British agriculture' *in* Agricultural writers from sir Walter of Henley to Arthur Young, 1200–1800. . . . London, 1908. p.[199]–224.
Chronol. checklist useful for the numerous TP facsims. and notes in the text.

2091 **Rothamsted experimental station,** HARPENDEN. **Library.** Catalogue of the printed books on agriculture published between 1471 and 1840, with notes on the authors. By Mary S. Aslin. [Aberdeen, Aberdeen U.P., 1926] 331p. facsims. 25cm.
See no.2095.

2092 **Fussell, George Edwin.** Eighteenth century agricultural dictionaries. Bull Inst Hist Res 7no21:144–8 F '30.
Brief survey with checklist of 7 items.

2093 **Great Britain. Ministry of agriculture and fisheries. Library.** Chronological list of early agricultural works in the library . . . by George Edwin Fussell. London, H.M.S.O., 1930. 43p. 24cm.

Short-title catalogue of 359 entries from 1533 to 1860.

2094 **Perkins, Walter Frank.** British and Irish writers on agriculture. 3d ed. Lymington, C. T. King, 1939. (First pub. 1929) ix,226p. 22cm.

Author checklist to 1900, with separate sequences of anonyma and serials.

2095 **Rothamsted experimental station, HARPENDEN. Library.** Library catalogue of printed books and pamphlets. . . . 2d ed. London, 1940. 293p. front. 25cm.

'Alphabetical list of English authors and translations' (p.9–164); 'Incunabula' (p.285).

2096 **Cambridge. University. School of agriculture.** Agricultural periodicals of the British Isles, 1681–1900, and their location. Cambridge, 1950. 15p. 21cm.

Title checklist, comp. by Frederick A. Buttress.

2097 **Fussell, George Edwin.** More old English farming books from Tull to the Board of Agriculture, 1731–1793. London, C. Lockwood [1950] vii,186p. illus. 23cm.

Chronol. checklist with locations of copies.

2098 **Southampton. University. Library.** Catalogue of the Walter Frank Perkins agricultural library. Southampton, 1961. xii,291p. port. 24cm.

Short-title catalogue of 2,009 entries, comp. by A. Anderson from the preliminary work of E. H. Milligan; 'Books printed in England and Scotland up to 1700' (p.281): 36 entries with STC nos.

ALCHEMY

2100 **Ferguson, John.** Bibliographical notes on histories of inventions and books of secrets. Glasgow, Glasgow U.P., 1894–1915. 8pts. in IV. (various pagings) 22cm.

General discussion, with TP transcrs., bibliogr. notes, and checklists interspersed; repr. from Glasgow Archæol Soc Trans. 1882–1915. The collection is now in the Glasgow university library, which issued a catalogue of the whole Ferguson collection (most of which is foreign) in 1943.

2100a **Peddie, Robert Alexander.** English books on alchemy. N&Q ser8 11:363–4, 464–5 My,Je '97.

Author checklist, with BM pressmarks.

ANGLING

2101 **Grolier club,** NEW YORK. A catalogue of an exhibition of angling books ... from the collection of a member of the Grolier club. New York, 1912. viii,59p. 19cm.

Foreword signed D.B.F.; classified checklist of 191 items.

2102 **Robb, James.** 'Notable books' *in* Notable angling literature. London [1946] p.207–23.

Author checklist.

APICULTURE

See Bees.

ARCHERY

2103 **Walrond, H.,** *comp.* 'Bibliography, pictures and prints' *in* Longman, Charles J. and H. Walrond. Archery. London, 1894. p.472–503.

Classified chronol. checklist, repr. in part from Angler's Register, 1892–3.

ART

See also Forms and genres — Illustrated books.

2105 **Ogden, Henry V. and M. S. Ogden.** A bibliography of seventeenth-century writings on the pictorial arts in English. Art Bull 29:196–201 S '47.

Alphabetical checklist, with some bibliogr. notes.

2106 **Rostenberg, Leona.** 'Bibliography of art & architectural books published in England, 1598–1700' *in* English publishers in the graphic arts, 1598–1700. New York, 1963. p.96–9.

Classified checklist of 59 items.

ARTHUR, LEGENDARY KING OF BRITAIN, fl.c.520

For works about, *see under Authors.*

ASTRONOMY

2110 **Johnson, Francis Rarick.** 'A chronological list of books dealing with astronomy printed in England to 1640' *in* Astronomical thought in renaissance England, a study of the English scientific writings from 1500 to 1645. Baltimore, 1937. p.301–35.

Checklist with STC nos.

BEES

2111 **Walker, Herbert John Ouchterlony.** Descriptive catalogue of a library of bee-books collected and offered for sale. . . . [Exeter, J. Townsend, ptrs., 1929] 144p. 20cm.
'Books in English' (p. [3]–81): short-title author catalogue.

2112 **Frost, Maurice.** More bee books. Bk Coll 1n03:193–4 '52.
Annotated checklist, with some collations, of six items supplementing Mace's discursive account in Bk Hndbk 2n04:206–10 '51/2.

BIRDS

2114 **Mullens, William Herbert.** A list of books relating to British birds published before 1815. Hastings & St. Leonard's Natural Hist Soc Pub 3 '03. (Not seen)

2115 [——] *comp.* 'Bibliography: a list of books relating to British birds . . . to . . . 1900' *in* Stonham, Charles. The birds of the British islands. London, 1906–11. V.5, p.943–64.
Chronol. checklist, 1187–1900.

2116 **Mullens, William Herbert** and **H. K. Swann.** A bibliography of British ornithology from the earliest times to the end of 1912. London, Macmillan, 1917 [i.e. 1916–17] 6pts in 1v.(xx,691p.) 23cm.
Author biobibliography, with TP transcrs. and some bibliogr. notes.

2117 **Zimmer, John Todd.** Catalogue of the Edward E. Ayer ornithological library. Chicago, 1926. 2v.(x,706p.) col.port., facsims. 24cm. (Field museum of natural history. Publication 240. Zoological series, v.16)
Annotated author catalogue, with TP transcrs. and some bibliogr. notes.

2118 **National book league,** LONDON. British birds and their books; catalogue of an exhibition . . . arranged by Raymond Irwin. London, Published for the National book league by the C.U.P. [1952] 38p. illus. 19cm. (Not seen)

2119 **Buchanan, Handasyde** and **J. Fisher,** *comps.* 'The bibliography' *in* Sitwell, Sacheverell. Fine bird books, 1700–1900. London, 1953. p.47–116.
Alphabetical checklist with extensive notes on the illustrations.

2120 **Yale university. Library.** Ornithological books in the Yale university library, including the library of William Robertson Coe, compiled by S. Dillon Ripley and Lynnette L. Scribner. New Haven, Yale U.P., 1961. 338p. port. 27cm. (Duplicated typescript)
Short-title author catalogue; 'Falconry' (p.321–38).

BOOK-KEEPING
See Accounting.

BOTANY
See also Agriculture; Flower books; Gardening; Herbals.

2125 **Cardiff. Public libraries.** Catalogue of early works on botany, agriculture and horticulture, exhibited. . . . Cardiff, 1918. 23p. 18cm.
Classified catalogue with bibliogr. notes.

2126 **Bartlett, Harley Harris.** Fifty-five rare books from the botanical library of mrs. Roy Arthur Hunt. Ann Arbor, Clements library, 1949. 55p. 30cm.
Annotated exhibition catalogue.

2127 **Hunt, Rachel McMasters (Miller).** Botanical books, prints & drawings from the collection of mrs. Roy Arthur Hunt. Pittsburgh, Dept. of fine arts, Carnegie institute [1951] xvi,63[15]p.+48pl.(part col.) 23cm.
Annotated exhibition catalogue of 86 items, comp. by Jane Quinby.

2128 **Virginia. University. Bibliographical society.** Exhibition catalogue: books, drawings, prints from the botanical collection of mrs. Roy Arthur Hunt. Annotations by Ruth Evelyn Byrd. [Charlottesville, 1952] IV.(unpaged) 21cm. Covertitle.

2129 **Hunt, Rachel McMasters (Miller).** Catalogue of botanical books in the collection of Rachel McMasters Miller Hunt. Pittsburgh, Hunt botanical library, 1958– . v. plates, port. 26cm.
Contents: v.1. Printed books, 1477–1700, with several manuscripts of the 12th, 15th, 16th and 17th centuries, comp. by Jane Quinby.—2pt1. Introduction to printed books, 1701–1800, comp. by Allan Stevenson.—2pt2. Printed books, 1701–1800, comp. by Allan Stevenson.—
Bibliogr. catalogue, with quasifacsim. TP transcrs., collations, and extensive bibliogr. notes, and refs.
Rev: S. A. Dickson Pa Bib Soc Am 53:85–7 '59; *ib.* 56:275–6 '62; *ib.* 58:332 '64.

2130 **Scotland. National library,** EDINBURGH. Botanical illustration, a loan exhibition. Edinburgh, 1964. 40p. illus., facsim. 24cm. (Not seen)
Rev: D. S. Kalk Pa Bib Soc Am 60:107–8 '66.

BOXING
2135 **Magriel, Paul David.** Bibliography of boxing, a chronological check list of books in English published before 1900. New York, New York public library, 1948. 28p. facsims. 26cm.
Repr. from N.Y. Pub Lib Bull 52:263–88 Je '48; 120 items.

BUTTERFLIES AND MOTHS
2136 **Lisney, Arthur Adrian.** A bibliography of British lepidoptera, 1608–1799. London, Chiswick pr., 1960. xviii,315p. illus., ports., facsims. 24cm.
Chronol. under author, with collations and bibliogr. notes; index of booksellers, printers and publishers, 1608–1899.

CANNING, ELIZABETH, 1734–1773
For works about, *see under Authors.*

CHARLES I, 1600–1649
For works about, *see under Authors.*

CHARLES II, 1630–1685
For works about, *see under Authors.*

CIRCUS

2137 **Stott, Raymond Toole.** Circus and allied arts; a world bibliography, 1500–1957, based mainly on circus literature in the British museum. . . . Derby, Harpur, 1958–62. 3v. facsims. 25cm.
Classified checklist of 9,675 items, with some bibliogr. notes and locations of copies.
Rev: I. K. Fletcher Bk Coll 10:102, 105–6 '61; TLS 9 Je '61:364.

COCKFIGHTING

2138 **Kiddell, A. J. B.** Books on cockfighting. Bk Hndbk 1n07:405–12 '48.
'Bibliography' (p.409–12): chronol. checklist, 1607–1938.

CONJURING

2139 **Findlay, James B.** [Scottish conjuring bibliography] Bibliography of books, pamphlets, magazines, etc. bearing a Scottish imprint, or known to have been published in Scotland. Shanklin, 1951. xvi,43p. 20cm.
Annotated classified author checklist.

2140 **Hall, Trevor Henry.** A bibliography of books on conjuring in English from 1580 to 1850. Lepton, Patmyra pr., 1957. 96p. illus., facsims. 24cm.
Alphabetical checklist, with some bibliogr. notes and TP facsims.

2141 **Heyl, Edgar.** A contribution to conjuring bibliography, English language, 1580 to 1850. Baltimore, 1963. 62p. facsim. 26cm.
Adds 360 items to Hall; author list with some bibliogr. notes, and locations of copies.
Rev: Pa Bib Soc Am 58:74 '64.

2141a **Winder, Roland.** Check list of the older books on conjuring in the library of Roland Winder as at December, 1966. [Leeds, 1966] 32p. illus. 24cm.
'Books in English' (p.7–22)
Rev: I. K. Fletcher Bk Coll 16:238, 241 '67.

COOKERY

2142 **Oxford, Arnold Whitaker.** 'English books on cookery and carving up to . . . 1699' *in* . . . Notes from a collector's catalogue. London, 1909. p.40–96.
'Cookery books from 1700' (p.97–107); chronol. list, with TP transcrs, bibliogr. notes, and locations of copies.

2143 —— English cookery books to the year 1850. London, H. Froude, O.U.P., 1913. 192p. 19cm.
Chronol. arrangement, with TP transcrs. and some bibliogr. notes; indexes to titles and authors.

2144 —— [**Same**]: Supplement. N&Q 147:367 N '24.

2145 **London. Guildhall library.** A handlist of cookery books and books about food in Guildhall library. Guildh Misc 1n09:52–9 Jl '58.

Author checklist.

COURTESY

2146 **Kelso, Ruth.** 'A tentative bibliographical list of treatises on the gentleman and his training published in Europe to 1625' *in* The doctrine of the English gentleman in the sixteenth century. . . . [Urbana, 1929] (Repr. Gloucester, Mass., P. Smith, 1964) p.165–277.

Checklist of 945 items.

2147 **Noyes, Gertrude Elizabeth.** Bibliography of courtesy and conduct books in seventeenth-century England. New Haven [Tuttle, Morehouse & Taylor] 1937. 111p. 23cm.

Checklist of 477 items, with classified index.

Rev: W. Ebisch Angl Beibl 50:12–13 '39; G. Murphy Library ser 419:495–6 '39; W. L. Ustick Mod Lang N 54:476 '39; R. Kelso J Eng Germ Philol 37:601 '38.

2148 **Newberry library,** CHICAGO. A check list of courtesy books in the Newberry library, compiled by Virgil B. Heltzel. Chicago, 1942. ix,161p. 26cm.

Alphabetical list of 1,539 items composed or published before 1775.

2149 **Williams college,** WILLIAMSTOWN, MASS. **Chapin library.** The renaissance gentleman in England; exhibition, March, 1949. [Williamstown, Mass., 1949] 30p. facsim. 23cm. Covertitle.

Classified annotated checklist, comp. by Charles D. Cremeans.

CRICKET

2155 **Weston, George Neville.** My cricket collection. [Kidderminster, G. T. Cheshire, ptrs., 1929] 2pts.(46p.) 22cm.

2156 **Goldman, J. W.** Bibliography of cricket. London, Published privately, 1937. 210p. 24cm.

Alphabetical checklist.

2157 **National book league,** LONDON. Cricket; a catalogue of an exhibition . . . of books, manuscripts and pictorial records presented by the National book league with the co-operation of the Marylebone cricket club. Arranged by Diana Rait Kerr. Cambridge, C.U.P., 1950. 120p. illus. 22cm. (Not seen)

CROMWELL, OLIVER, 1599–1658

For works about, *see under Authors*.

DARIEN COMPANY

2158 **Scott, John.** A bibliography of printed documents and books relating to the Scottish company, commonly called the Darien company. Edinburgh Bib Soc Trans 6pt1:19–70 Je '04.

2159 —— [Same]: Rev. by George P. Johnston. Edinburgh, Privately ptd., 1905. 54p. 39cm.

2160 —— [Same]: With additions and corrections by George P. Johnston. Edinburgh, Privately ptd., 1906. [55]–75p. 30cm.

Classified chronol. list, with TP transcrs., collations, bibliogr. notes, and some locations of copies; repr. from Edinburgh Bib Soc Trans 6pt2:159–79 Oc '06.

2161 **Glasgow. University. Library.** Catalogue of a collection of books and manuscripts relating to the Darien scheme, presented to the University of Glasgow by mr. J. J. Spencer. Glasgow, Jackson, Wylie, 1932. 15 mounted l. 27cm.

Alphabetical checklist.

ECONOMICS

See also Darien company; Poor laws; South sea company.

2162 **Stephens, Thomas Arthur.** A contribution to the bibliography of the Bank of England. London, E. Wilson, 1897. xiii,200p. 22cm.

Classified checklist.

2163 **Wagner, Henry Raup.** Irish economics, 1700–1783; a bibliography with notes. London, J. Davy, The Dryden pr., 1907. 94p. 23cm.

Chronol. checklist of 369 items, with some bibliogr. notes, and location of copy seen.

2164 **Williams, Judith Blow.** Guide to the printed materials for English social and economic history, 1750–1850. New York, Columbia U.P., 1926. (Repr. New York, Octagon books, 1966) 2v. 22cm.

2165 **Higgs, Henry.** A bibliography of economics, 1751–1775. Cambridge, C.U.P.; New York, Macmillan, 1935. xxii,742p. 24cm.

Classified short-title list of 6,741 items, with some bibliogr. notes. *See* no.2169.
Rev: J. Boner Econ J 45:720–3 '35.

2166 **Harvard university. Graduate school of business administration. Baker library. Kress library of business and economics.** Catalogue, covering material published through 1776. . . . Boston, Mass., Baker library, Harvard graduate school of business administration [1940] x,414p. 30cm.

2167 —— [Same]: Supplement. Boston, 1956. vi,175p. 30cm.

Chronol. checklist, with indexes of authors and anonyma.

2168 —— Catalogue, 1777–1817, giving data also upon cognate items in other Harvard libraries. London, Bailey & Swinfen, 1957. vii,397p. 30cm.

Short-title catalogue, arranged alphabetically by year of publication, with full index; ed· by Evelyn Draper. *See also* no.2170.

2169 **Hanson, Laurence William.** Contemporary printed sources for British and Irish economic history, 1701–1750. Cambridge, C.U.P., 1963. xxiii,978p. 20cm.

Classified checklist of 6,497 entries, with some bibliogr. notes, and locations of copies; title index. Supplements Higgs, no.2165.

Rev: M. Canney Bk Coll 13:230, 233–4 '64; L. S. Thompson Pa Bib Soc Am 58:205–6 '64; TLS 1 Ap '65:264; L. S. Sutherland Library ser5 20:66–8 '65.

2170 **Harvard university. Graduate school of business administration. Baker library. Kress library of business and economics.** . . . Catalogue, 1818–1848. . . . Boston, Mass., Baker library, Harvard graduate school, 1964. vi,397p. 30cm.

Continuation of no.2166.

EDUCATION
See also Children's literature; Schoolbooks.

2175 **Muirhead, Arthur Meadcroft.** The English at school; an exhibition of books, documents, and illustrative materials arranged for the National book league. [London] C.U.P., 1949. 80p. 22cm.
Classified checklist.

2175a **Wallis, Peter John.** Histories of old schools, a revised list for England and Wales. Newcastle-upon-Tyne, Dept. of Education, University of Newcastle-upon-Tyne, 1967. 98p. 25cm.

EXPLORATION
See Regional bibliographies—Topography.

FALCONRY
See Hawking.

FARMING
See Agriculture.

FENCING

2176 **Thimm, Carl Albert.** A complete bibliography of the art of the fence. London, F. Thimm, 1891. xii,261p. 18cm.

2177 —— [Same]: Enl. ed. [with title]: A complete bibliography of fencing and duelling. London, J. Lane, 1896. xvi,537p. facsims. 23cm.
Author checklist, with 'Index of subjects . . . in chronological order, according to languages, alphabetically arranged' (p.339–431).

2178 **London. Guildhall library.** A handlist of books in the Guildhall library on the art of fencing. Guildh Misc 2:227–9 Oc '63.

FISHING
See Angling.

FLOWER BOOKS

2179 **Blunt, Wilfrid Scawen.** Flower books and their illustrators; an exhibition arranged for the National book league. [London] C.U.P. [1950] 58,xiip. col.front. 22cm.
Annotated chronol. checklist.

2180 **Society of herbalists,** LONDON. **Library.** An exhibition of flower books from the library of the Society of herbalists. London, Arts council, 1953. 47p. 16cm.
Comp. by Wilfred Blunt and W. T. Stearn.

2181 **Synge, Patrick Millington,** *ed.* 'The bibliography' *in* Sitwell, Sacheverell. Great flower books, 1700–1900; a bibliographical record. . . . London, 1956. p.35–88.
Author checklist with bibliogr. notes; comp. by W. T. Stearn and others.

FOXHUNTING

2182 **Smith, Sydney R.,** *comp.* 'Bibliography' [of books on foxhunting] *in* Higginson, Alexander H. British and American sporting authors, their writings and biographies. London, 1951. p.399–437.
Author checklist; no index.

FREEMASONRY

2183 **Vibert, Arthur Lionel.** The rare books of freemasonry. London, The bookman's journal office, 1923. 40p. 23cm.
Repr. from Bkmns J 8nos19–24:10–11, 62–3, 128, 167–8, 195–6 '23. Classified checklist, with bibliogr. notes; no index.

2183a **Thorp, John T.** Bibliography of masonic catechisms and exposures. Leicester, Ptd. by Johnson, Wykes and Payne, 1929. 45p. 22cm.
Classified chronol. checklist; no index. 'British' (p.[9]–30).

2184 **Cannon, Arthur James S.** The Lodge of research . . . Leicester. A list of the old & rare books in the library of the Freemason's hall, Leicester . . . an appendix to a paper. . . . Leicester, Ptd. by Johnson, Wykes & Paine, 1938. 46p. 22cm.
Classified checklist, with TP transcrs. and some bibliogr. notes.

2185 **Card, Robert A.** and **W. E. Heaton.** Catalogue of rare and early books on freemasonry from the Wallace Heaton collection presented to the United grand lodge of England. [Brighton, Privately ptd. by J. S. North] 1939. 4ll. facsims. 25cm.

GARDENING
See also Herbals.

2186 **Rockley, Alicia Margaret (Amherst), lady.** 'Bibliography of printed books on English gardening' *in* A history of gardening, by the hon. mrs. Evelyn Cecil. 3d and enl. ed. London, 1910. p.332–77. (First pub. 1895)

2187 **Rohde, Eleanor Sinclair.** 'Bibliography . . . the gardening manuals of the sixteenth and seventeenth centuries' *in* The old English gardening books. London, 1924. p.115–39.
Chronol. checklist.

GEOGRAPHY

2188 **Taylor, Eva Germaine Rimington.** 'Catalogue of English geographical or kindred works . . . to 1583' *in* Tudor geography, 1485–1583. London [1930] p.163–90.
Chronol. checklist.

2189 —— 'Bibliography of English geographical literature, 1583–1650' *in* Late Tudor and early Stuart geography, 1583–1650, a sequel to Tudor geography, 1485–1583. London [1934] p.177–298.
Chronol. checklist of 1,933 items.

GOLF

2190 **Hopkinson, Cecil.** Collecting golf-books, 1743–1938. London, Constable [1938] vii,56p. 20cm.

Discursive checklist, with note of earlier bibliogr. lists on p.13–14.

Rev: H.M.N. Library ser4 20:500–2 '39.

GYPSIES

2191 **Leeds. University. Brotherton library.** Catalogue of the Romany collection formed by D. U. McGrigor Phillips. Edinburgh, Published for the Brotherton collection by T. Nelson, 1962. xii,226p. port. 24cm.

Classified short-title catalogue, comp. by David I. Masson; 'Literature: works of imagination with gypsy references or by gypsy authors' (p.119–51).

GLENDOWER, OWEN (OWAIN AB GRUFFYDD) 1359?–1416?

For works about, *see under Authors.*

HAWKING

2192 **Harting, James Edmund.** 'Catalogue of books relating to falconry: English' *in* Bibliotheca accipitraria; a catalogue of books ancient and modern relating to falconry. London, 1891. p.1–44.

Chronol. checklist of 82 items, with some collations and bibliogr. notes.

2193 **Barber, Robert Heberden.** A supplementary bibliography of hawking, being a catalogue of books published in England between 1891 and 1943. . . . Westminster, Privately ptd. by W. H. Fielding, 1943. [13]p. 21cm. Covertitle.

'A synopsis of the books on hawking published between 1575 and 1891' (p.[12–13]).

HENRY FREDERICK, PRINCE OF WALES, 1594–1612

For works about, *see under Authors.*

HERBALS

2194 **Rohde, Eleanor Sinclair.** 'English herbals: printed books' *in* The old English herbals. London, 1922. p.203–24.

Annotated classified list, with TP transcrs.

2195 **Fisch, Ruth B.** and **M. H. Fisch.** The Marshall collection of herbals in the Cleveland medical library. Bull Hist Med 21:224–61 Mr/Ap '47.

Author, short-title catalogue of 298 items, with some bibliogr. refs.

2196 **Shipman, Joseph C.** One hundred herbals, 1472–1671; a chapter in the history of botany; selections from printed works in the University of Kansas libraries and the Linda hall library. Bks & Libs at Univ Kansas 2:9–13 N '65.

Alphabetical checklist with locations of copies.

HOOD, ROBIN

For works about, *see under Authors.*

HORTICULTURE

See Gardening.

HUNTING

2197 **Schwerdt, Charles Francis George Richard.** Hunting, hawking, shooting, illustrated in a catalogue of books, manuscripts, prints and drawings. . . . London, Privately ptd. for the author by Waterlow, 1928–37. 4v. illus., ports., plans, facsims., music. 34cm.

General author catalogue valuable for bibliogr. notes and simple collations, extensively illustrated, with separate indexes of titles, subjects, printers and publishers of books before 1700, artists and engravers (v.4).

JEWS

2198 **Calisch, Edward Nathaniel.** The Jew in English literature, as author and as subject. Richmond, Va., Bell book and stationery, 1909. 277p. 21cm.

'A list of non-Jewish authors who have written on or about the Jews' (p.[199]–221); 'A list of Jewish authors' (p.[222]–65).

2199 **Coleman, Edward D.** The Jew in English drama; an annotated bibliography. New York, New York public library, 1943. xx,237p. 25cm.

Repr. with rev. and additions from N.Y. Pub Lib Bull 42:827–50, 919–32 N–D '38; 43:45–52, 374–8, 443–58 Ja, Ap–My '39; 44:361–72, 429–44, 543–68, 630–34, 675–98, 777–88, 843–66 Ap–N '40.

Annotated classified checklist.

2199a **Roth, Cecil.** The Marrano typography in England. Library ser5 15:118–28 Je '60.

'Bibliography of Spanish and Portuguese works printed in London for Jewish use, etc.' (p.124–8): chronol. checklist, 1649–1820, with bibliogr. refs.

JUVENILE LITERATURE

See Children's literature.

KNITTING

2200 **Potter, Esther.** English knitting and crochet books of the nineteenth century. [Part 2] Library ser5 10:103–19 Je '55.

Classified author checklist of 269 items.

LANGUAGE

See also Forms and genres—Dictionaries; Grammars; and Rhetoric; Shorthand; Spelling-books.

2201 **Kennedy, Arthur Garfield.** A bibliography of writings on the English language from the beginning of printing to the end of 1922. Cambridge & New Haven, Harvard U.P.; Yale U.P., 1927. (Repr. New York, 1961) xvii,517p. 26cm.

2202 —— **[Same]:** Gabrielson, Arvid. A review with a list of additions and corrections. Stud Neophilol (Uppsala) 2no3:117–68 '29.

2203 **Alston, Robin Carfrae.** A bibliography of the English language from the invention of printing to the year 1800. Leeds, Ptd. for the author by E. J. Arnold [1965–   ].   v. 27cm.

Contents: 1. English grammars written in English and English grammars written in Latin by native speakers. [1965].—4. Spelling-books. ([1967]).—5. The English dictionary ([1966]).—7. Logic, philosophy, epistemology, universal language. ([1967]).—8. Treaties on shorthand. ([1966]).

Annotated checklists, with locations of copies, bibliogr. refs., and some bibliogr. notes.

2204 —— A catalogue of books relating to the English language in Swedish libraries. Leeds, Privately ptd., 1965. vi,29p. 22cm. (Duplicated typescript)

LAW

2210 **Beale, Joseph Henry.** A bibliography of early English law books, compiled for the Ames foundation. Cambridge, Harvard U.P.; London, H. Milford, O.U.P., 1926. viii,304p. illus., facsims. 26cm.

Chronol. classified checklist, with collations and some bibliogr. notes.

2211 —— [Same]: A supplement . . . compiled for the Ames foundation by Robert Bowie Anderson. Cambridge, Mass., Harvard U.P., 1943. xii,50p. 26cm.

Rev: TLS 17 F '27:107; A. W. P[ollard] Library ser4 8:135–8 '27.

2212 **Cowley, John Duncan.** The abridgements of the statutes, 1481?–1551. Library ser4 12:125–73 S '31.

TP facsims.

2213 —— A bibliography of abridgments, digests, dictionaries and indexes of English law to the year 1800. London, Quaritch, 1932. xcv,196p. facsims., tables. 23cm.

Classified bibliogr. of 330 items, arranged chronol., with full descrs., TP facsims., and locations of copies and bibliogr. refs.

2214 **A legal bibliography** of the British commonwealth of nations. 2d ed. compiled by W. Harold Maxwell and Leslie F. Maxwell. London, Sweet & Maxwell, 1955– . v. 23cm.

Previously pub. with title: Sweet & Maxwell's Complete law book catalogue.

Partial contents: v.1. English law to 1800, including Wales, the Channel islands, and the Isle of Man. (1955).—v.2. English law from 1801 to 1954. . . . (1957).—v.4. Irish law to 1956. (1957).—v.5. Scottish law to 1956. (1957).

Alphabetical checklists, with some bibliogr. notes.

LEPIDOPTERA
See Butterflies and moths.

MAGIC
See Occult sciences.

MARY STUART, QUEEN OF SCOTS, 1542–1587
For works about, *see under Authors.*

MEDICINE

2215 **Osler, sir William.** Bibliotheca Osleriana; a catalogue of books illustrating the history of medicine and science, collected, arranged and annotated . . . and bequeathed to McGill university. Oxford, Clarendon pr., 1929. xxxv, 785p. 30cm.

Ed. by W. W. Francis, R. H. Hill, and A. Mallock; classified and annotated short-title catalogue particularly useful for lists of English scientists' works.

2216 **Henry E. Huntington library and art gallery,** SAN MARINO, CALIF. Medical knowledge in Tudor England as displayed in an exhibition of books and manuscripts. [San Marino, Calif., 1932] 31p. 22cm.

Annotated checklist of 61 items.

2217 **Exeter. Cathedral. Library.** A catalogue of the medical books and manuscripts including a selection of the scientific works in Exeter cathedral library, compiled by M. P. Crighton. [Birmingham, 1934] 38[6]p. 23cm.
Alphabetical checklist of 202 items.

2218 **LeFanu, William Richard.** British periodicals of medicine, a chronological list. Baltimore, Johns Hopkins pr., 1938. 93p. 26cm.
Repr. from Bull Inst Hist Med 5:735–61, 827–46 Oc,N '37; 6:614–48 Je '38.
Checklist of 1,362 items from 1684, with some locations of copies.

2219 **Poynter, Frederick Noel Lawrence.** Notes on a late-sixteenth-century ophthalmic work in English. Library ser5 2:173–9 S/D '47.
'Bibliography' (p.177–9) of Jacques Gillemeau's A worthy treatise of the eyes, c.1587 with quasifacsim. TP transcrs., collations, bibliogr. notes and locations of copies.

2220 **Russell, Kenneth Fitzpatrick.** A checklist of medical books published in English before 1600. Bull Hist Med 21:922–58 N/D '47.
Rev: W. J. Bishop Library ser5 5:280–1 '51.

2221 —— A bibliography of anatomical books published in English before 1800. Bull Hist Med 23:268–306 My/Je '49.
See no.2228.

2221a **Cowen, David L.** The Edinburgh dispensatories. Pa Bib Soc Am 45:85–96 '51.
'A check-list of the Edinburgh dispensatories' (p.92–6); classified, with some bibliogr. notes.

2222 **Royal college of veterinary surgeons,** LONDON. **Library.** Catalogue of the historical collection: books published before 1850. London, 1953. 36p. 22cm.
Short-title author catalogue.

2223 —— [**Same**]: First supplement.... [London] 1959. 6p. 33cm. (Duplicated typescript)

2224 **Devon and Exeter medico-chirugical society** and **Exeter memorial library.** Medical art and history in Exeter; an exhibition of books, documents and pictures. Exeter, Royal Albert memorial museum, 1955. 37p. illus., ports., facsim. 23cm.

2225 **Royal college of obstetricians and gynaecologists. Library.** Catalogue of the library up to 1850. Manchester, 1956. 73p. 22cm.
Short-title author catalogue, comp. by W. J. Bishop; no index.

2226 **Durham. University. King's college,** NEWCASTLE-UPON-TYNE. **Library.** One hundred medical works exhibited in the library of King's college ... during the meeting of the British medical association. Newcastle upon Tyne, 1957. 26p. facsim. 24cm.
Alphabetical checklist.

2227 **Wellcome historical medical library,** LONDON. A catalogue of printed books in the Wellcome historical medical library. London, 1962– . v. 31cm.

Comp. by Frederick N. L. Poynter.

Contents: v.1. Books printed before 1641. (1962).—2. Books printed from 1641 to 1850; A–E (1966).—

Dictionary short-title catalogue, with some bibliogr. notes and refs.

Rev: W. R. LeFanu Lib Assn Rec 65:182 '63; R. Hunter Library ser5 18:315–16 '63; J Crow Bk Coll 13:375–6 '64; Pa Bib Soc Am 60:275 '66; L. M. Payne Bk Coll 15:492–4 '66. R. Hunter Library ser5 22:270–2 '67.

2228 **Russell, Kenneth Fitzpatrick.** British anatomy, 1525–1800, a bibliography. [Melbourne] Melbourne U.P. [1963] xvii,254p. facsims. 25cm.

Author checklist of 901 items, with some bibliogr. notes and refs. and locations of copies used.

Rev: TLS 31 D '64:1188; F. N. L. Poynter Library ser5 21:74–6 '66.

2229 **Emmerson, Joan Stuart.** Translations of medical classics before 1900: a list. Newcastle upon Tyne [University library] 1965. 82p. 25cm.

Checklist by name of original author; no index of translators or subjects; bibliogr. refs.

Rev: TLS 22 Ap '65:315; E. Gaskell Library ser5 22:85–6 '67.

2230 **Wisconsin. University. Library.** Chemical, medical, and pharmaceutical books printed before 1800 in the collections of the University of Wisconsin libraries. Edited by John Neu; compiled by Samuel Ives, Reese Jenkins, and John Neu. Madison, University of Wisconsin, 1965. viii,280p. 25cm.

Wisconsin acquired most of the Denis I. Duveen collection.

MILITARY

2231 **Cockle, Maurice James Draffen.** A bibliography of English military books up to 1642 and of contemporary foreign works. Edited by H. D. Cockle. London, Simpkin, Marshall, Hamilton, Kent, 1900. (Repr. London, Holland pr. [1957]) xl,267p. ports., facsims., maps. 26cm.

Chronol. bibliogr., 1489–1657 (English: items 1–166), with quasifacsim. TP transcrs., collations, bibliogr. notes and refs. and locations of copies. *See* no.2235–6.

2232 **Leslie, John Henry** and **D. Smith.** A bibliography of works by officers, non-commissioned officers, and men, who have ever served in the Royal Madras, or Bombay artillery. Leicester, 1909–20. 9pts. 25cm.

2233 —— [Same]: A–Leslie. 2d ed., rev. Dartford, 1919. pt.3 only. 25cm. (No more pub.)

Author checklist, with locations of copies.

2234 **Great Britain. Admiralty. Library.** Subject catalogue of printed books. Pt.1. Historical section. London, H.M.S.O., 1912. 374p. 28cm.

Ed. by W. G. Perrin; classified short-title catalogue; no index.

2235 **Spaulding, Thomas M.** Additions and corrections [to Cockle] Pa Bib Soc Am 34:186 '40.

2236 **Skarshaug, mrs. Emory C.** [Addition to Cockle's Military books] Pa Bib Soc Am 35:157 '41.

2237 **Webb, Henry J.** Military newsbooks during the age of Elizabeth. Eng Stud 33:241–51 D '52.

'Bibliography' (p.249–51); chronol. checklist of 31 items concerning the wars in the Netherlands, 1574–1602.

2238 **Waters, David W.,** *ed.* 'English military books to 1587' *in* Greepe, Thomas. The true and perfecte nevves, 1587. Hartford, 1955. p.[73]–86.

Annotated chronol. checklist of 36 items from 1489, with TP transcrs.

2239 **Craig, Hardin.** A bibliography of encyclopedias and dictionaries dealing with military, naval, and maritime affairs, 1626–1959. Houston, Tex., Fondren library, Rice university [1960] ii,40[8]l. 28cm.

2240 —— [Same]: 2d ed. 1577–1961. [1962] 70,vil. 28cm.

Chronol. checklist, with author index.

NELSON, HORATIO, 1ST VISCOUNT NELSON, 1758–1805

For works about, *see under Authors*.

OCCULT SCIENCES

See also Witchcraft.

2241 **Evans, Henry Ridgely.** 'Bibliography of natural magic and prestidigitation . . . English' *in* Hopkins, Albert A. Magic, stage illusions and scientific diversions . . . London, 1897. p.[539]–45.

Author checklist.

2241a **Gardner, Frederick Leigh.** A catalogue raisonné of works on the occult sciences. London, Privately ptd., 1903–12. 3v. illus. 23cm.

> Contents: v.1. Rosicrucian books. (1903).—v.2. Astrological books. (1911).—v.3. Freemasonry; a catalogue of lodge histories (England). (1912).
>
> Annotated checklist.

2242 **London. University. Council for psychical investigation. Research library.** Short-title catalogue of works on psychical research, spiritualism, magic, psychology, legerdemain, and other methods of deception . . . from circa 1450 A.D. to 1929 A.D., compiled by Harry Price. [London, 1929] 67–422p. illus.(1 col.) facsims. 24cm. (National laboratory of psychical research, v.1, pt.2)

2243 —— [Same]: Supplement. London, 1935. 112p. illus., facsims. 25cm. (London. University. Council for psychical investigation. Bulletin, no.1)

2244 —— Exhibition of rare works from the Research library . . . 1490 A.D. to the present day; foreword by Harry Price. London, 1934. 48p. facsims. 23cm.

ORNITHOLOGY
See Birds.

OSSIANIC CONTROVERSY
See Authors. MacPherson, James, 1736–1796.

PARLIAMENT
2245 **Great Britain. Parliament. House of commons. Library.** A bibliography of parliamentary debates of Great Britain. London, H.M.S.O., 1956. 62p. 2 col.diagrs. 25cm. Covertitle. (Not seen)

> Classified annotated checklist, with index.

POOR LAWS
2246 **California. State library,** SACRAMENTO. **Sutro branch,** SAN FRANCISCO. Bibliography of books and pamphlets on the English poor laws, 1639–1890. With an introduction by Hasseltine Byrd Taylor. San Francisco, 1940. iii,53p. 27cm. (Duplicated typescript)

> Chronol. checklist.

POPISH PLOT
2247 **King, C. M. K.,** 1958: no.152.

2248 **Evans, John R.** The popish plot. Nat Lib Wales J 6no1:43–50 '50.

> Chronol. checklist of 72 pamphlets, 1678–86.

RELIGION
See also Formes and genres—Bible; Book of common order; Book of common prayer; Hymns; Primers; Psalters; Sermons.

2250 **Smith, Wilbur Mooreheade.** List of bibliographies of theological and biblical literature published in Great Britain and America, 1595–1931;

with critical, biographical and bibliographical notes. Coalesville, Pa., 1931. viii,62p. 24cm.

Annotated chronol. author list.

2251 **New York. Union theological seminary. Library.** Catalogue of the McAlpin collection of British history and theology, compiled and edited by Charles Ripley Gillett. New York, 1927–30. 5v. 25cm.

Chronol. catalogue with TP transcrs.; index: v.5.

2252 **White, Helen Constance.** 'A short-title list of books consulted: primary' *in* English devotional literature, prose, 1600–1640. Madison, 1931. p.271–91.

RELIGION — ANTIMETHODIST BOOKS

2253 **Green, Richard.** Anti-Methodist publications issued during the eighteenth century; a chronologically arranged and annotated bibliography of all known books and pamphlets written in opposition to the Methodist revival during the life of Wesley, together with an account of replies to them, and of some other publications. . . . London, Published for the author by C. H. Kelly, 1902. vii,175p. 22cm.

Annotated chronol. checklist of 606 titles, 1732–1809.

RELIGION — BAPTIST BOOKS

2254 **Whitley, William Thomas.** A Baptist bibliography; being a register of the chief materials for Baptist history. . . . London, Kingsgate pr., 1916–22. 2v. 29cm.

Contents: v.1. 1526–1776.—2. 1777–1837, and addenda from 1613.

Chronol. short-title catalogue, with locations of copies; index to anonymous works, to 'Baptists and their opponents, Baptist societies, pseudonyms and initials', i.e. to authors, places, and subjects, in each volume.

RELIGION — CATHOLIC BOOKS

2255 **Gillow, Joseph.** A literary and biographical history, or bibliographical dictionary of the English Catholics. . . . London, Burns & Oates; New York, Catholic publishing co. [1885–1902] (Repr. New York, 1961) 5v. 23cm.

Biographies followed by annotated checklists; no indexes.

2255a **Jenkins, Gladys.** The archpriest controversy and the printers, 1601–1603. Library ser5 2:180–6 S/D '47.

[Checklist of secular pamphlets, with bibliogr. refs.] p.181.

2256 **Southern, Alfred Collingwood.** 'Bibliography' *in* Elizabethan recusant prose, 1559–1582; a historical and critical account of the books of Catholic refugees printed and published abroad and at secret presses in England, together with an annotated bibliography of the same. London, Sands [1950] p.367–516.

Full TP transcrs., collations, bibliogr. notes and refs. to 159 items arranged by author; 'Hand-list of printers or publishers' (p.539–41); 'Chronological list' (p.542–4).

Rev: A. F. Allison and D. M. Rogers Library ser5 6:48–57 '51 (important addenda); TLS 3 N '50:691.

2257 **Allison, Antony Francis** and **D. M. Rogers.** A catalogue of Catholic books in English printed abroad or secretly in England, 1558–1640. Bognor Regis, Arundel pr., 1956. 2v.(xiii,187p.) 20cm.

Alphabetical short-title catalogue, with STC nos. and up to 12 locations; chronological index, and list of 'Secret presses operating in England'.

Rev: A. I. Doyle Library ser5 12:127–30 '57; E. P. Willing Catholic Hist R 43:370 '57.

2258 **Byrns, Lois.** Recusant books in America, 1559–1640. New York, P. Kavanagh hand pr. [1959] 64p. 23cm.

2259 —— [Same]: Supplement. [1959] 46p. 23cm.

2260 —— [Same]: 1640–1700. [1961] 70p. 23cm.

2261 —— [Same]: 1700–1829. [1964] 71p. 22cm.

Alphabetical checklists, with locations of copies; no title index.

2262 **Clancy, Thomas H.** 'Chronological list of political writings of the Allen-Persons party: 1572–1613' *in* Papist pamphleteers. . . . Chicago, 1964. p.235–43.

2263 **Oscott. St. Mary's seminary.** Recusant books at st. Mary's, Oscott. New Oscott, 1964– . v. 24cm.

Contents: pt.1. 1518–1687.

Classified checklist, with some bibliogr. notes and refs., of 1,002 items; comp. by G. F. Pullen.

RELIGION — CATHOLIC BOOKS — FRANCISCAN

2264 **Allison, Antony Francis.** Franciscan books in English, 1559–1640. Biog Stud 3no1:16–65 Ap '55.

'Catalogue of Franciscan books' (p.25–35): annotated chronol. checklist of 42 items.

RELIGION — CATHOLIC BOOKS — JESUIT

2265 **Law, Thomas Graves.** 'Bibliographical notes' *in* A historical sketch of the conflicts between Jesuits and seculars in the reign of queen Elizabeth. London, 1889. p.cxxviii–cliii.

Annotated chronol. list of 21 items, with TP transcrs., and some bibliogr. notes.

2266 **Sutcliffe, Edmund Felix.** Bibliography of the English province of the Society of Jesus, 1773–1953. London, Manresa pr., 1957. xii,247p. 28cm.

Author list, with TP transcrs.

RELIGION — FRIENDS BOOKS

2267 **Smith, Joseph.** A descriptive catalogue of Friends' books, or books written by members of the Society of friends, commonly called Quakers. . . . London, 1867. 2v. 22cm.

2268 —— [Same]: Supplement. London, E. Hicks, 1893. 364p. 23cm.

Author checklist, with bio-bibliogr. notes; no index.

2269 [Davies, John H.] Bibliography of Quaker literature in the English language relating to Wales. Welsh Bib Soc J 1:203–22 Ag '14.

Alphabetical checklist, with notes, comp. largely from Smith, and Bibliotheca anti-quakeriana (1873).

2270 **Roberts, Charles.** Illustrated catalogue of the private library of the late Charles Roberts of Philadelphia, comprising an extensive collection of noteworthy Quakeriana. To be sold. . . . [New York, 1918] [138]p. illus., facsims.(1 fold.) 25cm. (Not seen)

556 entries; Fox, nos.143–218; Keith, nos.269–360.

RELIGION — NONCONFORMIST BOOKS

2271 **Crippen, Thomas George.** Early Nonconformist bibliography. Congreg Hist Soc Trans 1:44–57, 99–112, 171–84, 252–65, 410–20; 2:61–71, 219–29; 432–44 Ap '01–Oc '06.

Chronol. checklist, with locations of copies.

2272 **Nuttall, Geoffrey Fillingham.** The beginnings of nonconformity, 1660–1665; a checklist. London, Dr. Williams's library, 1960. lv.(unpaged) 33cm. (Duplicated typescript)

Chronol. checklist, with some locations of copies and bibliogr. refs.; no index.

RELIGION — QUAKERS
See Religion—Friends books.

RELIGION — RECUSANT BOOKS
See Religion—Catholic books.

RHETORIC

2275 **McGrew, J. Fred.** A bibliography of the works on speech composition in England during the 16th and 17th centuries. Q J Speech 15:381–412 Je '29. (Not seen)

2276 **Wallace, Karl Richards.** 'Books on rhetorical theory, 1500–1700' *in* Francis Bacon on communication & rhetoric. Chapel Hill, 1943. p.231–55. Author checklist.

ROBIN HOOD
For works about, *see under Authors.*

SCHOOLBOOKS

2277 **Watson, Foster.** The curriculum and text-books of English schools in the first half of the seventeenth century. Bib Soc Trans 6pt2:159–267 '03. Intermittent checklists of school books.

2278 **Dix, Ernest Reginald McClintock.** School books printed in Dublin from the earliest period to 1715. Bib Soc Ireland Pub 3no1:[5] '26. Checklist from 1634 with some locations of copies.

2279 **Pafort, Eloise.** A group of early tudor school-books. Library ser4 26:227–61 Mr '46. List of ed. with bibliogr. notes.

SHORTHAND

2280 **Carlton, William J.** 'Catalogue of the shorthand books in the library of Samuel Pepys' *in* [Tanner, Joseph R. and others] Bibliotheca Pepysiana, a descriptive catalogue. London, 1914–40. Pt. IV (1940), p.1–124. Chronol. catalogue, with quasifacsim. TP transcrs., collations, and bibliogr. notes and refs.; no full index.

2281 **London. Guildhall library.** A handlist of works on shorthand in the Guildhall library. Guildh Misc 2:39–42 S '60.

2282 **Alston, Robin Carfrae** [1965–   ]: no.2203.

SOUTH SEA COMPANY

2283 **Sperling, John G.** 'A bibliographical finding list for the South sea company' *in* The South sea company; an historical essay and bibliographical finding list. Boston, Mass., 1962. p.50.

Chronol. checklist of 625 18th century items, with pressmarks of 5 British and American libraries.

SPELLING-BOOKS

2283a **Alston, Robin Carfrae** [1965–   ]: no.2203.

SPIRITUALISM
See Occult sciences.

SPORT

See also Angling; *Archery*; *Boxing*; *Cricket*; *Fencing*; *Foxhunting*; *Golf*; *Hawking*; *Hunting*; *Tennis*.

2284 **Slater, John Herbert.** Illustrated sporting books; a descriptive survey of a collection of English illustrated works of a sporting and racy character. . . . London, L. U. Gill, 1899. viii,203p. 19cm.

Title checklist.

2285 **Nevill, Ralph Henry.** 'A bibliography of first and rare editions of some of the principal sporting books' *in* Old English sporting books; edited by Geoffrey Holme. London, 1924. p.23–34.

Discursive author checklist.

2286 **Henry E. Huntington library and art gallery,** SAN MARINO, CALIF. Sporting books in the Huntington library; compiled by Lyle H. Wright. San Marino, Calif., 1937. vii,132p. 23cm.

Classified checklist, with author and title index, of 1,344 items, including many ed. of The compleat angler.

Rev: V. B. Heltzel J Eng Germ Philol 37:123–4 '38.

STATUTES

See Law.

TENNIS

2287 **Henderson, Robert William,** *comp.* 'A bibliography of court tennis and lawn tennis; a chronological list of references to the games' *in* Whitman, Malcolm D. Tennis, origins and mysteries. New York, 1932. p.[161]–244. (Not seen)

THEOLOGY

See Religion.

TOBACCO

2288 **Arents, George.** Tobacco, its history illustrated by the books, manuscripts and engravings in the library of George Arents jr. together with an introductory essay, a glossary and bibliographic notes by Jerome E. Brooks. New York, Rosenbach, 1937–52. 5v. illus., ports., maps, facsims. (all part. col.) 35cm.

Partial contents: v.1, p.189. From the discovery of tobacco in America 1507 to the year 1615.—2. 1615–1698.—3. 1698–1783.—4. 1784–1800; Books, manuscripts, autograph letters, XIX–XX centuries; Addenda, etc.—5. Index of names. Index of subjects.

Chronol. catalogue of 3,956 items, mainly English, with full discussion, digressive descrs. and numerous TP facsims.

Two catalogues drawn from this collection, which is now in the New York public library, of exhibitions at the Library of Congress and at Duke university, appeared in 1938 and 1941.

2289 **New York. Public library. Arents tobacco collection.** Tobacco; a catalogue of the books, manuscripts and engravings acquired since 1942 in the Arents tobacco collection . . . from 1507 to the present. Compiled by Sarah

Augusta Dickson. New York, New York public library, 1958– .   v. illus., facsims. 34cm.

Contents: 1. 1507–1571. 2. 1571–1589.

TRAVEL

See Regional bibliographies—Topography.

VOYAGES

See Regional bibliographies—Topography.

WITCHCRAFT

2290 **Ferguson, John.** Bibliographical notes on the witchcraft literature of Scotland. Edinburgh Bib Soc Pub 3pt2:37–119, 123–4 D '97.

Chronol. checklist of 174 items, with varying bibliogr. but extensive descr. notes.

2291 **Glasgow. University. Hunterian library.** 'Witchcraft and demonology in England' *in* An exhibition of books on witchcraft & demonology. [Glasgow] 1966. p.11–24.

Annotated checklist, with bibliogr. refs.

AUTHORS

ABBOT, ARCHBP. GEORGE, 1562–1633

2300 **Christophers, Richard A.** George Abbot, archbishop of Canterbury, 1562–1633, a bibliography. Charlottesville, Va., Published for the Bibliographical society of the University of Virginia [by] University pr. of Virginia [1966] xxiv,211p. 24cm. (Not seen)

Based on University of London School of librarianship and archives bibliogr.: *see* no.97.

Rev: TLS 3 N '66:1009.

ABBOT, JOHN, 1588–1650?

2301 **Rogers, David Morrison.** John Abbot, 1588–?1650. Biog Stud 1no1:22–33 '51; Further notes, with addenda. 1no4:245–50 '52.

Discussion, and checklist of 4 items.

ABERCROMBIE, LASCELLES, 1881–1938

2302 **Gawsworth, John,** *pseud.*, 1932: no.686.

2303 **Elton, Oliver.** Lascelles Abercrombie, 1881–1938. Proc Brit Acad 25:394–421 '39.

'List of works' (p.418–21): chronol. checklist, 1908–37.

ACTON, JOHN EMERICH EDWARD DALBERG, 1ST BARON ACTON, 1834–1902

2304 **Shaw, William Arthur,** 1903: no.2918.

ADAMS, SARAH FULLER (FLOWER), 1805–1848

2305 **Stephenson, H. W.** 'Writings' *in* The author of Nearer my God to thee. ... London, 1922. p.69–70.

Chronol. checklist of periodical contribs.

ADDISON, JOSEPH, 1672–1719

2306 **Greenough, Chester Noyes,** *comp.* 'Bibliography' *in* Addison, Joseph. Selections from the writings; edited by B. Wendell and C. N. Greenough. Boston [1905] p.xlvii–lxi.

Classified chronol. list, with TP transcrs., bibliogr. notes, and locations of copies.

2307 **Horn, Robert D.** The early editions of Addison's Campaign. Stud Bib 3:256–61 '50.

Corrects CBEL and A. C. Guthkelch's ed. (1914), with descr. of 4 early ed.

Æ., *pseud. of* GEORGE WILLIAM RUSSELL, 1867–1935

2308 **[MacManus, Michael Joseph]** Bibliographies of Irish authors, no.1. Æ. (George W. Russell) Dublin Mag new ser 5:44–52 Ja/Mr '30; 10:74–6 Oc/D '35.

TP transcrs., collations, and bibliogr. notes of first ed., 1894–1928.

2309 **Kindilien, Carlin T.** The George Russell collection at Colby college, a check list. Colby Lib Q ser4 2:31–55 My '55.

2310 **Black, Hester Mary,** 1956: no.4867.

2311 **Denson, Alan.** Printed writings of George W. Russell (Æ): a bibliography with notes on his pictures and portraits. London, Northwestern U.P., 1961. 255p. port. 23cm.

2312 —— [Same]: Evanston, Ill., Northwestern U.P., 1962.

Classified, part chronol., part alphabetical arrangement of works, mss., ephemera, ana, etc., with discursive collations, locations of copies, and bibliogr. notes.

Rev: TLS 9 N '62:864; Pa Bib Soc Am 56:513 '62.

AIKIN, ANNA LÆTITIA (MRS. BARBAULD), 1743–1825

2313 **Clarke, Stella Marjorie,** 1949: no.99.

AINSWORTH, WILLIAM HARRISON, 1805–1882

2314 **Ellis, Stewart Marsh.** 'Bibliography: I. Contributions to magazines, etc. II. Contributions to books. III. Published works' *in* William Harrison Ainsworth and his friends. London, 1911. V.2, p.345–83.

2315 **Locke, Harold.** A bibliographical catalogue of the published novels and ballads of William Harrison Ainsworth. London, E. Mathews, 1925. 68p. 23cm.

Chronol. checklist, with some bibliogr. notes.

Rev: TLS 24 D '25:900; S. M. Ellis *ib.* 31 D '25:909.

AKENSIDE, MARK, 1721–1770

2316 **Williams, Iolo Aneurin,** 1924: no.633.

ALCOCK, DEBORAH, fl.1866–1910

2317 **Byard, Edwin John.** Deborah Alcock, a bibliography. Irish Bk Lover 4:150–1 Ap '13.

Chronol. checklist.

ALDINGTON, RICHARD, 1892–1962

2318 **Kershaw, Alister.** A bibliography of the works of Richard Aldington from 1915 to 1948. Burlinghame, Calif., W. P. Wreden; London, Quadrant pr., 1950. xi,57p. 22cm.

An 'extended checklist' of 231 items arranged chronol. by genre, with some bibliogr. notes but no collations.

Rev: TLS 25 Je '50:396.

2319 **Schlueter, Paul,** *comp.* 'A chronological check list of the books by Richard Aldington' *in* Kershaw, Alister and F-J. Temple, *ed.* Richard Aldington, an intimate portrait. Carbondale [1965] p.175–86.

ALDISS, BRIAN WILSON, 1925–

2320 **Manson, Margaret.** Item forty-three: Brian W. Aldiss, a bibliography, 1954–1962, with annotations by Brian Aldiss. [Wisbech, 1963?] [28]p. 23cm.

Classified checklist of prose, poetry, and translations; miscellaneous writings, and volumes edited.

ALLEN, CARD. WILLIAM, 1532–1594

2321 **Gillow, Joseph,** *comp.* 'Bibliography' *in* Haile, Martin. An Elizabethan cardinal, William Allen. London, 1914. p.375–9.

Checklist, with some bibliogr. notes.

ALLINGHAM, WILLIAM, 1824–1889

2322 **Allingham, Helen** and **D. Radford,** *ed.* 'List of works' *in* William Allingham, a diary. London, 1907. p.[390]–1.

Chronol. checklist, 1850–93, with some bibliogr. notes.

2322a **Gawsworth, John,** *pseud.* [1933]: no.687.

2323 **O'Hegarty, Patrick Sarsfield.** A bibliography of William Allingham. Dublin, Privately ptd. by A. Thom, 1945. 12p. 25cm.

Repr. from Dublin Mag new ser 20:42–52 Ja/Mr '45. TP transcrs., collations, and bibliogr. notes.

ANSELM, ST., 1033–1109

2324 **Cook, D. F.,** 1955: no.102.

ANSTEY, CHRISTOPHER, 1724–1805

2325 **Williams, Iolo Aneurin.** [Bibliography of the first editions of Anstey] London Merc 11:300–2, 414–17, 526–8, 643–4 Ja–Ap '25; 12:194, 300–1 Je–Jl '25.

Quasifacsim. TP transcrs., collations, and bibliogr. notes.

2326 **Munby, Alan Noel Latimer.** Anstey's Election ball and The epistle to Bampfylde. Bk Coll Q 16:19–23 Oc/D '34.

Full descr. of the second title.

ANSTEY, F., *pseud. of* THOMAS ANSTEY GUTHRIE, 1856–1934

2327 **Lucas, E. V.** F. Anstey (Thomas Anstey Guthrie). Eng Illus Mag new ser 29:544–5 Ag '03.

'Bibliography' (p.545).

2328 **Turner, Martin John.** A bibliography of the works of F. Anstey (Thomas Anstey Guthrie). London, Privately ptd., 1931. vii,44p. port. 22cm.

Quasifacsim. TP transcrs. of 33 items, with collations and bibliogr. notes.

ARBUTHNOT, FORSTER FITZGERALD, 1833–1901

2329 **Wright, Thomas.** 'Bibliography of Forster Fitzgerald Arbuthnot' *in* The life of sir Richard Burton. London, 1906. V.2, p.x at end.

Chronol. checklist of 7 items, 1881–1902.

ARBUTHNOT, JOHN, 1667–1735

2330 **Aitken, George Atherton.** 'Bibliography' *in* The life and works of John Arbuthnot. Oxford, 1892. p.[176]–88.

Collected works, single works, and attributed works in three alphabetical checklists, with 'Works relating to Arbuthnot and his writings' (p.186–7) and 'Some imitations of the History of John Bull' (p.187–8).

2331 **Miller, Charles William Kerby-   , ed.** 'A bibliography of the principal editions of The memoirs of Martinus Scriblerus' *in* Memoirs of the . . . life . . . of Martinus Scriblerus. New Haven, 1950. p.[78]–84.

Chronol. list of ed. from 1741 to 1751, and of major ed. since 1751, with bibliogr. notes and refs.

ARGYLE, ARCHIBALD CAMPBELL, 9TH EARL OF, d.1685
See Campbell, Archibald, 9th earl of Argyle.

ARMSTRONG, JOHN, 1709–1779

2332 **Williams, Iolo Aneurin,** 1924: no.633.

ARMSTRONG, MARTIN DONISTHORPE, 1882–

2333 **Bristol. Public libraries.** Martin Armstrong, poet and novelist; a bibliography. Bristol [1937] [4]p. 17cm. Covertitle.

Classified checklist of works and ana.

ARNOLD, MATTHEW, 1822–1888

2334 **Bonnerot, Louis.** 'Bibliographie' *in* Matthew Arnold, poète; essai de biographie psychologique. Paris, 1947. p.[541]-66.

2335 **Faverty, Frederic Everett,** *ed.,* 1956: no.2016.

2336 **Smart, Thomas Burnett.** The bibliography of Matthew Arnold. London, J. Davy, 1892. x,90p. 23cm.

Rev. shorter version pub. in the compiler's ed. of The works [London, 1903–4] v.15, p.341–99.

Bibliogr. catalogue of prose and verse, and ana. 'Syntoptical table' (p.[81]–90) indexes every poem in each of the collected volumes.

Rev: Library 4:258–9 '92; Nation 55:449–50 '92.

2337 **Mainwaring, Marion.** Notes toward a Matthew Arnold bibliography. Mod Philol 49:189–94 F '52.

Annotated checklist of essays, letters, Oxford orations, and lectures, addresses and occasional speeches, supplementing Smart.

2338 **Neiman, Fraser.** Some newly attributed contributions of Matthew Arnold to the Pall Mall gazette. Mod Philol 55:84–92 N '57.

Checklist with discussion.

2339 **Brooks, Roger L.** A census of Matthew Arnold's Poems, 1853. Pa Bib Soc Am 54:184–6 '60.

Lists 46 copies, and notes inscriptions.

2340 —— A septuagenarian poet: an addition to the Matthew Arnold bibliography. Mod Philol 57:262–3 My '60.
Addendum to Neiman.

2341 —— An unrecorded American edition of the Selected poems of Matthew Arnold. Library ser5 16:213–14 S '61.
Discursive descr. of 1878 Harper ed.

ARTHUR, LEGENDARY KING OF BRITAIN, fl.520

2345 **Modern language association of America.** A bibliography of critical Arthurian literature, 1922–35. New York, 1931–6. 2v. 25cm.

Contents: 1. 1922–1929, ed. by John J. Parry. (1931).—2. 1930–1935. By J. J. Parry and Margaret Schlauch. (1936).

2346 **A bibliography** of critical Arthurian literature for the years 1936–1939– [1962] in Modern language quarterly 1no2 Je '40–'63. Annually.

2347 **Newberry library, Chicago.** The Arthurian legend; a checklist of books in the Newberry library, compiled by Jane D. Harding. Chicago, 1933. 120p. 23cm.

2348 —— **[Same]:** Supplement. 1938. iv,90p. 23cm. (Duplicated typescript) (Not seen)

Classified short-title catalogue of texts and critical works.

2349 **Harries, E. R.** The legend of king Arthur, a list of books in the Flintshire county library. Hawarden, Flintshire county library, 1963. 1v.(unpaged) 26cm. (Duplicated typescript)

Classified checklist of 1,156 items, including 'Novels, poetry and plays' (nos.1019–156).
Rev: Pa Bib Soc Am 59:349 '65.

ASCHAM, ROGER, 1515–1568.

2350 **Tannenbaum, Samuel Aaron** and **D. R. Tannenbaum.** Roger Ascham, a concise bibliography. New York, 1946. 27l. 28cm. (Elizabethan bibliographies, no.37) (Duplicated typescript)

Classified checklist of works and ana.

2351 **Thomas, B. E.,** 1949: no.219.

ASHWOOD, BARTHOLOMEW, fl.1638–1678

2352 **Dredge, John Ingle,** 1889–99: no.886.

ASTELL, MARY, 1666?–1731

2353 **Norton, Jane Elizabeth.** Some uncollected authors XXVII: Mary Astell, 1666–1731. Bk Coll 10no1:58–65 '61.

'Check-list of Mary Astell's works' (p.61–5): chronol. list of early ed. of 8 items, with quasifacsim. TP transcrs., collations, bibliogr. notes and refs.

AUDEN, WYSTAN HUGH, 1907–

2354 **Writings** by W. H. Auden. New Verse 26/7:32–46 N '37.

2355 **Clancy, Joseph P.** A W. H. Auden bibliography, 1924–1955. Thought 30:260–70 '55.

2356 **Beach, Joseph Warren.** 'Volumes by Auden including poetry' in The making of the Auden canon. [Minneapolis, 1957] p.301–2.

2357 **Callan, Edward Thomas O'Dwyer.** An annotated check list of the works of W. H. Auden. London, A. Swallow [1958] 26p. 23cm.

Repr. from Twent Cent Lit 4:30–50 Ap/Jl '58.

2358 **Bloomfield, Barry Cambray.** Notes and corrections on The making of the Auden canon, by J. W. Beach. N&Q 204:227–8 Je '59.

See no.2356.

2359 —— W. H. Auden, a bibliography: the early years through 1955. Charlottesville, Published for the Bibliographical society of the University of Virginia [by] the University pr. of Virginia, 1964. xix,171p. 25cm.

Classified bibliogr. of books and pamphlets, principally first ed.; works ed. or having contribs. by Auden; and contribs. to periodicals and miscellaneous items, with various appendices, including 'Bibliography and criticism of Auden's work' (p.136–42); *see* no.88.
Rev: R. J. Roberts Bk Coll 14:389–90, 393 '65; TLS 1 Jl '65:568; L. Ash Pa Bib Soc Am 59:331–2 '65; L. E. D. Priv Lib 6:61 '65.

AUNGERVILLE, RICHARD (RICHARD DE BURY), 1287–1342?

2360 **Hogan, Charles Beecher.** The Bement collection of the Philobiblon. Yale Univ Lib Gaz 6:25–30 Oc '31.

Detailed descrs. of first eight ed., except for fifth and sixth not in Yale, and checklist of later ed.

2361 **Zeitgeist,** *pseud.* The first English bibliophile. Am Bk Coll 4:233–6 N '33.

'Short bibliography of Bury's Philobiblon' (p.235–6): checklist, with some bibliogr. notes.

2362 **Maclagan, Michael,** *ed.* 'Bibliography of printed editions and manuscripts' *in* Aungerville, Richard. Philobiblon. Oxford, 1960. p.xxxvii–lxxiii.
Discursive checklist.

AUSTEN, JANE, 1775–1817

2363 **Edmonds, Jean Lowrie.** Jane Austen, biography and criticism; a bibliography. Bull Bib 12:129–34 My/Ag '25.

Complements list of ana in G. Smith's Life: no.2365.

2364 **Chapman, Robert William,** 1955: no.2368.

2365 **Anderson, John Parker,** *comp.* 'Bibliography' *in* Smith, Godwin. Life of Jane Austen. London, 1890. p.i–v.

2366 **Keynes, sir Geoffrey Langdon.** Jane Austen, a bibliography. London, Ptd. for the Nonesuch pr., 1929. xxv,289p. illus., port., facsims. 20cm.

Full descrs., locations of copies, and extensive facsims. of labels. half-titles, and TPs.
Rev: TLS 3 Oc '29:762; G. M. Troxell Sat R Lit 6:432–3 '29.

2367 **Chapman, Robert William.** Jane Austen, a critical bibliography. Oxford, Clarendon pr., 1953. viii,62p. 19cm.

2368 —— [Same]: 2d ed. Oxford, Clarendon pr., 1955. viii,62p. 19cm.

Annotated and classified checklist of works by and about, with Keynes numbers, and additions to Keynes' list of translations.
Rev: W. Husbands R Eng Stud new ser 6:331:2 '55.

AUSTIN, ALFRED, 1835–1913

2369 **Crowell, Norton B.** 'Works by Austin' *in* Alfred Austin, victorian. London [1955] p.[268]–73. (First pub. 1953)

Checklist of books and periodical contribs.

AVEBURY, SIR JOHN LUBBOCK, BARON, 1834–1913
See Lubbock, sir John, baron Avebury.

AYRES, PHILIP, 1638–1712

2370 **Saintsbury, George Edward Bateman.** Philip Ayres. Bibliographer 2n04: 215–24 Ap '03.

'Collations' (p.223–4) of Emblems and Lyric poems.

BACON, FRANCIS, BARON VERULAM AND VISCOUNT ST. ALBAN,
1561–1626

2371 **Livingston, Dorothy F.** and **M. M. Patton.** 'Contribution to a bibliography of Francis Bacon; editions before 1700 in Yale libraries' *in* Papers in honor of Andrew Keogh. New Haven, 1938. p.[95]–143.
Quasifacsim. TP transcrs. of 67 items, with brief descrs.

2372 **Gibson, Reginald Walter.** Francis Bacon; a bibliography of his works and of Baconiana to the year 1750. Oxford, Scrivener pr., 1950. xvii,369p. ports., facsims. 29cm.

2373 —— [**Same**]: Supplement. [Oxford] Privately issued [under auspices of the Francis Bacon foundation, inc., Pasadena, Calif.] 1959. iii,20l. 29cm. (Duplicated typescript)
Full, somewhat peculiar descrs. of 680 items, extensive TP facsims; 'List of the portraits of Francis Bacon' (p.328–30); 'Index to printers, publishers, &c.' (p.333–9). The Supplement lists corrigenda and addenda, and is indexed.
Rev: J. H. Pafford Library ser5 6:222–7 '51; TLS 24 N '50:756; H. Macdonald R Eng Stud new ser 3:175–7 '52; J. H. Pafford Library ser5 14:307 '59.

2374 **Spurrell, J.,** 1955: no.206.

BAGE, ROBERT, 1728–1801

2375 **Osborne, Eric Allen.** A preliminary survey for a bibliography of the novels of Robert Bage. Bk Hndbk 1:30–6 '47.
Checklist, with bibliogr. notes and TP facsims.

BAGEHOT, WALTER, 1826–1877
2376 **Muizz, M. A.,** 1939: no.175.

BAILEY, PHILIP JAMES, 1816–1902

2377 **Peckham, Morse.** American editions of Festus, a preliminary survey. Princeton Univ Lib Chron 8:177–84 Je '47.
'A checklist of American editions' (p.180–4): 41 items descr. in varying fullness, with discrimination of issues, etc., complemented by bibliogr. discussion in his English editions of Philip James Bailey's Festus. Pa Bib Soc Am 44:55–8 '50.

BAILLIE, JOANNA, 1762–1851

2378 **Carhart, Margaret Sprague.** 'Bibliography' *in* The life and work of Joanna Baillie. New Haven; London, 1923. p.[207]–10.
Checklist of books and periodical contribs.

BAIN, ALEXANDER, 1810–1877
2379 **Nairn, A.,** 1960: no.177.

BAINES, SIR EDWARD, 1800–1890

2380 **Little, G. F.** Select bibliographies, no. 22. Bibliography of sir Edward Baines, 1800–1890. Bull Brit Lib Pol Sci 21:18–22 F '23.
Chronol. checklist of works, 1826–93, and ana.

BAKER, JAMES FRANKLIN BETHUNE-, 1861–1951

2381 **Wynn, bp. Harold Edward.** James Franklin Bethune-Baker, 1861–1951.
Proc Brit Acad 39:355–62 '53.
'Bibliography' (p.361–2): checklist, 1888–1934.

BAKER, THOMAS, fl.1622–1660

2382 **Dredge, John Ingle,** 1889–99: no.886.

BALE, JOHN, 1495–1563

See also Presses and printing—Bale press.

2383 **Davies, William Twiston.** A bibliography of John Bale. Oxford Bib Soc
Proc 5pt4:201–79 '39.

2384 —— **[Same]:** [Addendum, item 10] Oxford Bib Soc Pub new ser 1:44–5
'49.
'Bibliography' (p.[247]–79): quasifacsim. TP transcrs., full descrs. and extensive discussion; no index.
Rev: A. F. Johnson Library ser4 23:143–4 '42.

BALFOUR, ARTHUR JAMES, 1ST EARL OF BALFOUR, 1848–1930

2385 **Robertson, John M.** The right hon. Arthur James Balfour. . . . Eng Illus
Mag new ser 29:435–6, 442 Jl '03.
'Bibliography' (p.436, 442): checklist of works and ana.

BAMFIELD, SAMUEL, fl.1750–1764

2386 **Dredge, John Ingle,** 1889–99: no.886.

BARBAULD, MRS. ANN LÆTITIA, 1743–1825

See Aikin, Ann Lætitia (mrs. Barbauld)

BARBOUR, JOHN, 1316?–1395

2387 **Geddie, William,** 1912: no.2034.

2388 **M'Kinlay, R.** Barbour's Bruce. Glasgow Bib Soc Rec 6:20–38 '20.
Checklist of ed. from 1571 with some bibliogr. notes.

BARING, MAURICE, 1874–1945

2389 **Bibliographies** of modern authors. The hon. Maurice Baring. Lond Merc
2n09:346–7 Jl '20.

2390 **Chaundy, Leslie.** A bibliography of the first editions of the works of
Maurice Baring. London, Dulau, 1925. 48p. 19cm.
Quasifacsim. TP transcrs., brief collations, and bibliogr. notes.

BARKER, WILLIAM, fl.1500

2391 **Parks, George B.** William Barker, tudor translator. Pa Bib Soc Am 51:
126–40 '57.
Checklist of 7 items, with discussion.

BARLOW, GEORGE, 1847–1913

2392 **W., C.,** *ed.* 'Bibliography' *in* Selected poems . . . by George Barlow. London [1921] p.163–4.
Checklist.

BARLOW, JOHN, d.1629

2393 **Dredge, John Ingle,** 1889–99: no.886.

BARNES, WILLIAM, 1801–1886

2394 **Flanagin, Isobel E.,** 1939: no.123.

BARRIE, SIR JAMES MATTHEW, 1860–1937

2395 **Shields, Katharine Gheen.** Sir James Matthew Barrie, bart., being a partial bibliography. . . . Bull Bib 16:44–6, 68–9 My–D '37; 16:97, 119, 140–1 Ja–D '38; 16:162 Ja/Ap '39.
Classified annotated checklist of first ed., and extensive ana.

2396 **Barron, J. H.** J. M. Barrie. Eng Illus Mag new ser 29:207–9 My '03.
'Bibliography' (p.208).

2397 **Garland, Herbert.** A bibliography of the writings of sir James Matthew Barrie. London, Bookman's journal, 1928. 146p. facsims. 23cm.
TP transcrs. and some TP facsims., collations and bibliogr. notes of editiones principes; contribs. to books, etc.; and contribs. to periodicals.

2398 **Cutler, Bradley Dwyane.** Sir James M. Barrie; a bibliography, with full collations of the American unauthorized editions. New York, Greenberg [1931] 242p. facsims. 20cm.
Chronol. bibliogr. with collations and bibliogr. notes.
Rev: Sat R Lit 7:935 '31.

2399 **Block, Andrew.** Sir J. M. Barrie, his first editions: points and values. London, W. & G. Foyle [1933] xiv,48p. 19cm.
Checklist, with some bibliogr. notes and chronol. index.

BARTLETT, WILLIAM, 1679–1720

2400 **Dredge, John Ingle,** 1889–99: no.886.

BATE, GEORGE, 1608–1669

2401 **Madan, Francis Falconer.** A bibliography of George Bate's Elenchus motuum nuperorum in Anglia. Library ser5 6:189–99 D '51.
Supersedes summary in his Milton, Salmasius and Dugard (no.4230); 21 items with TP transcrs., collations, locations of copies, and some bibliogr. notes and refs.

BATES, HERBERT ERNEST, 1905–

2402 **Gawsworth, John,** *pseud.* [1933]: no.687.

2403 **Jones, J. M.,** 1964: no.148.

BAXTER, GEORGE, 1804–1867

2403a **Lewis, C. T. Courtney.** 'Illustrations for books and music' *in* George Baxter, colour printer, his life and work: a manual for collectors. London, 1908. p.236–54.

Alphabetical checklist with some bibliogr. notes.

2404 **Clarke, Harold George** and **J. H. Rylatt.** 'A catalogue résumé of his works: pocketbook prints, royal portraits, general portraits, decorative prints, historical subjects, religious and missionary subjects, book illustrations, needle-box prints, pocket books' *in* The centenary Baxter book. . . . Leamington Spa, 1936. p.57–170.

Full descrs.; title index.

BAXTER, RICHARD, 1615–1691

2405 **Matthews, Arnold Gwynne.** The works of Richard Baxter; an annotated list. [Farmcote, Oxted, Surrey, Privately ptd., 1933] 52p. 22cm.

Annotated checklist of 141 items.

BAYLEY, WALTER, 1529–1593

2406 **Power, sir D'Arcy.** Dr. Walter Bayley and his works, 1529–1592. Library ser2 8:370–92 Oc '07.

Discursive checklist; TP facsim.

BEARDSLEY, AUBREY VINCENT, 1872–1898

2407 **Gallatin, Albert Eugene.** Aubrey Beardsley; catalogue of drawings and bibliography. New York, Grolier club, 1945. 141p. illus., ports. 24cm.

Classified bibliogr. catalogue.

Rev: K. Küp Pa Bib Soc Am 40:176–8 '45; L. C. Wroth N.Y. Herald Trib Bk R 4 Ag '46:17.

2408 **Princeton university. Library.** The Gallatin Beardsley collection in the Princeton university library, a catalogue compiled by A. E. Gallatin and Alexander D. Wainwright. Princeton, N.J., Princeton U.P., 1952. 43p. illus., port. 24cm.

Repr. with add. from Princeton Univ Lib Chron 10:81–4 '49; 12:67–82, 126–47 '51.

BEAUMONT, CYRIL WILLIAM, 1891–

See Presses and printing—Beaumont press.

BEAUMONT, FRANCIS, 1584–1616, AND JOHN FLETCHER, 1579–1625

2410 **Potter, Alfred Cleghorn.** A bibliography of Beaumont and Fletcher. Cambridge, Mass., Library of Harvard university, 1890. 20p. 25cm.

Repr. from Harvard Univ Bull 6:46–67, 95–104, 151–8 My–Oc '90.

Checklist.

2411 **Leonhardt, Benno.** Nachtrag. Angl 19:542–8 Ag '97.

Corrigenda and addenda to Potter.

2412 **Tannenbaum, Samuel Aaron.** Beaumont & Fletcher, a concise bibliography. New York, 1938. x,94p. 23cm. (Elizabethan bibliographies, no.3)

2413 —— [Same]: Supplement, by S. A. Tannenbaum and Dorothy R. Tannenbaum. New York, 1946–50. 23l. 28cm. (Duplicated typescript)
Checklist of works by and about.

BECKETT, SAMUEL, 1906–

2414 **Davis, Robin John,** 1966: no.106a.

BECKFORD, WILLIAM, 1759–1844

2415 **Chapman, Guy** and **J. Hodgkin.** A bibliography of William Beckford of Fonthill. London, Constable, 1930. (New York, Bowker, 1931) xxii,127p. illus., port., facsims. 23cm. (Bibliographia; studies in book history and book structure, 1750–1900. [No.2])
Quasifacsim. TP transcrs. and TP facsims, full descrs.; no index.
Rev: TLS 4 D '30:1034; A. W. P[ollard] Library ser4 11:386–7 '30; W. King New Criterion 10:369–71 '31; Dublin Mag 6:47 '31; R. E. Gathorne-Hardy Bk Coll Q 1:59–63 '30/1; G. Buck Anglia Beibl 44:373–8 '33.

2416 **Parreaux, André.** 'Select bibliography' *in* The publication of The monk, a literary event, 1796–1798. Paris, 1960. p.[167]–90.
Full titles and imprints, with bibliogr. notes, of The monk and related works, valuable mainly for addenda and corrigenda to earlier lists.

2417 **Yale university. Library.** William Beckford of Fonthill, writer, traveller, collector, caliph, 1760–1844; a brief narrative and catalogue of an exhibition . . . by Howard B. Gotleib. . . . New Haven, Conn., 1960. 100p. illus., ports., facsims. 22cm.
Discursive, unreliable (see reviews) catalogue of 257 exhibits.
Rev: TLS 28 Oc '60:699; J. H[ayward] Bk Coll 10:109–10 '61; R. F. M[etzdorf] and L. S. T[hompson] Pa Bib Soc Am 56:131–5 '62.

2418 **Summers, Peter.** William Beckford: some notes on his life in Bath . . . and, A catalogue of the exhibition in the Holburne of Menstrie museum . . . compiled and written by Philippa Bishop. [Bath, Holburne museum, 1966] 31p. illus. 22cm. (Not seen)

2418a **Gemmett, Robert J.** An annotated checklist of the works of William Beckford. Pa Bib Soc Am 61:243–58 '67.
Classified annotated checklist, complementing Chapman.

BEDDOES, THOMAS LOVELL, 1803–1849

2419 **Donner, Henry Wolfgang,** *ed.* 'Printed works' *in* The works of Thomas Lovell Beddoes. London, 1935. p.791–8.
Quasifacsim. TP transcrs., collations, and bibliogr. notes.

BEDE, THE VENERABLE, 673–735

2420 **Kemp, J. A.,** 1953: no.149.

BEDE, CUTHBERT, *pseud. of* EDWARD BRADLEY, 1827–1889

2421 **Ellis, Stuart Marsh.** 'List of works by Edward Bradley "Cuthbert Bede"' *in* Wilkie Collins, LeFanu and others. London. 1931. p.203–8. (Reissued 1951)

Chronol. checklists of 28 items, 1853–87, with some bibliogr. notes.

BEECHING, HENRY CHARLES, 1859–1919

2422 **Stephen, George Arthur.** An annotated bibliography of the writings of dean Beeching and the works edited by him. Norwich Pub Lib Readers' Guide 7no6:82–90 Ap '19.

Chronol. checklist.

BEERBOHM, SIR HENRY MAXIMILIAN, 1872–1956

2425 **Lane, John,** *comp.* 'The works of Max Beerbohm, a bibliography' *in* The works of Max Beerbohm. London; New York, 1896. p.[161–79]

2426 **Bibliographies** of modern authors. Max Beerbohm. Lond Merc 1no5:625–6 Mr '20.

2427 **Danielson, Henry.** Bibliographies of modern authors, no.7. Max Beerbohm. Bkmns J 1no10–11:202, 225 '20.

2428 —— 1921: no.680.

2429 **Lynch, John Gilbert.** 'Bibliography' *in* Max Beerbohm in perspective. London, 1921. p.171–81.

2430 **Gallatin, Albert Eugene.** Sir Max Beerbohm; bibliographical notes. Cambridge, Mass., Harvard U.P., 1944. xiii,121p. illus., facsims. 24cm.

2431 **Grolier club,** NEW YORK. Max Beerbohm [notes on an exhibition of books, caricatures, manuscripts, portraits and other memorabilia. . . .] Grolier Club Gaz 2no3:65–71 Oc '44.

2432 **Gallatin, Albert Eugene.** A bibliography of the works of Max Beerbohm. Cambridge [Mass.] Harvard U.P.; London, R. Hart-Davis, 1952. x,60p. 27cm.

Repr. with revs. and additions from Harvard Lib Bull 5:77–93, 221–41, 338–61 '51 which succeeded no.2430; these lists describe different categories of material in varying fullness, this item listing only the collected and separately-ptd. works. Descrs. of ideal copy based on that in Harvard university library's Gallatin collection; 37 items fully described, with distinction of states and impressions.

Rev: H. Cahoon Lib J 1 Oc '52:1659; New Statesman 20 S '52:327–8; TLS 26 S '52:636; I. R. Willison Library ser5 8:130–5 '53; W. B. Bond *ib.* 9:56–8 '54; R. H. Taylor Bk Coll 1:276–7 '52.

2433 **Riewald, Jacobus Gerhardus.** 'Bibliography' *in* Sir Max Beerbohm, man and writer. 's-Gravenhage, 1953. p.[213]–343. (Anr. issue, The Hague, 1953, with illus.)

Quasifacsim. TP transcrs., collations, bibliogr. notes and locations of copies for first ed., slighter information about later ed.

BEGGS, THOMAS, 1789–1821

2434 **Bigger, Francis Joseph.** Thomas Beggs, an Antrim poet, and the Four towns book club. Ulster J Archæol 8:119–27 Jl '02.
Chronol. checklist, with some bibliogr. notes, p.126–7.

BELL, GERTRUDE MARGARET LOWTHIAN, 1868–1926

2435 **Wingate, H. E.,** 1956: no.237.

BELLENDEN, JOHN, fl.1533–1587

2436 **Geddie, William,** 1912: no.2034.

BELLOC, HILAIRE, 1870–1953

2437 **Bibliographies** of modern authors. Hilaire Belloc. Lond Merc 1no3:366–7 Ja '20.

2438 **Nicholls, Norah.** The first editions of Hilaire Belloc. Bkmn 81:62, 126–7 Oc,N '31.

2439 **Cahill, Patrick Cornelius.** The English first editions of Hilaire Belloc; a chronological catalogue of 153 works attributed to that author, including transcripts of the title-pages and a collector's description of the pagination, covers, variants, etcetera. . . . London, 1953. 51p. 22cm.
Rev: TLS 23 Ja '53:64; N&Q 198:365 '53; P. Cahill *ib*. 198:452 '53; P. Gaskell Bk Coll 2:165–7 '53.

BENLOWES, EDWARD, 1603?–1676

2440 **Saintsbury, George Edward Bateman.** Edward Benlowes's Theophila. Bibliographer 2no1:3–13 Ja '03.
Discussion with collation (p.12–13).

BENNETT, ENOCH ARNOLD, 1867–1931

2441 **Lafourcade, Georges,** 'Bibliography' *in* Arnold Bennett, a study. London [1939] p.281–[93]
Classified chronol. checklist of works and ana.

2442 **Hepburn, James G.** Arnold Bennett manuscripts and rare books; a list of holdings. Eng Fict Transit 1no2:23–9 '58.
List of libraries, with notes of holdings, principally mss.

2443 **Perkin, M. J.,** 1964: no.180.

2444 **White, B. E. Grove-,** 1964: no.229.

BENSON, EDWARD FREDERICK, 1867–1940

2445 **Moore, F. Frankfort.** Edward Frederick Benson. Eng Illus Mag new ser 31:416–18, 422 Jl '04.
'Bibliography' (p.422): checklist of works; dramatic work; works edited; and articles about.

BENSON, STELLA (MRS. J. C. O'G. ANDERSON), 1892–1933

2446 **Gawsworth, John,** *pseud.* [1933]: no.687.

BENTHAM, JEREMY, 1748–1832

2447 **Everett, Charles Warren,** *comp.* 'Bibliography' *in* Halévy, Élie. The growth of philosophic radicalism. London, 1928. p.522–46.

2448 —— [Same]: London, 1952 [i.e. 1953] Corr. repr. of 1934 ed.
Classified checklist, with chronol. list of Bentham's works (p.545–6).

BENTLEY, RICHARD, 1662–1742

2449 **Bartholomew, Augustus Theodore.** Richard Bentley, D.D., a bibliography of his works and of all the literature called forth by his acts or his writings. Cambridge, Bowes and Bowes, 1908. xix,115p. illus., ports., facsim. 22cm.
Classified annotated checklist of 310 items, with full descrs. in the old style.

BERESFORD, JOHN DAVYS, 1873–1947

2450 **Gerber, Helmut E.** J. D. Beresford; a bibliography. Bull Bib 21:201–4 Ja/Ap '56.
Classified checklist, noting both American and English first ed.

BERKELEY, BP. GEORGE, 1685–1753

2451 **Mead, Herman Ralph.** A bibliography of George Berkeley, bishop of Cloyne. Berkeley, University of California pr., 1910. 46p. 24cm.

2452 **Jessop, Thomas Edmund.** A bibliography of George Berkeley . . . with an inventory of Berkeley's manuscript remains, by A. A. Luce. London, H. Milford, O.U.P., 1934. xi,99p. 23cm.
Classified annotated checklist of works by, on, and translations of, Berkeley, with indexes.
Rev: R. Metz Anglia Beibl 45:277–8 '34; M. J. MacManus Dublin Mag 10:61–2 '35; J.S.B.S. Eng Hist R 50:554 '35; R. J. Aaron Mind 44:105–7 '35.

2453 **Lameere, Jean [and others]** [Supplement to Jessop, 1933–53] R Internat Philos 7:152–6 '53.

2454 **Dublin. University. Trinity college. Library.** Catalogue of the manuscripts, books and Berkeleiana exhibited in the library of Trinity college, Dublin, on the occasion of the commemoration of the bicentenary of the death. . . . [Dublin] Dublin U.P. [1953] 35[2]p. 22cm.
Annotated list of 137 exhibits, with Jessop nos.

BERNARD, RICHARD, 1568–1642

2455 **Dredge, John Ingle.** The writings of Richard Bernard; a bibliography. Horncastle, W. K. Morton, 1890. 25l. port. 21cm.

2456 —— [Same]: [Anr. issue, with, at head of title] Lincolnshire bibliographies, no.1. 1890. 25p. 21cm.
24 items fully descr. in the old style.

BESANT, ANNIE (WOOD), 1847–1933

2457 **Besterman, Theodore Deodatus Nathaniel.** A bibliography of Annie Besant. London, Theosophical society in England, 1924. 114p. 20cm.
Chronol. checklist of 448 books and pamphlets, 1873–1921.

BETHUNE-BAKER, JAMES FRANKLIN, 1861–1951
See Baker, James Franklin Bethune.

BEWICK, THOMAS, 1753–1828

2458 **Newcastle-upon-Tyne. Public libraries. Bewick collection.** . . . Catalogue of the Bewick collection (Pease bequest). By Basil Anderton and W. H. Gibson. [Newcastle-upon-Tyne, R. Ward, 1904] iv,110p. illus., ports. 25cm.

2459 **Roscoe, Sydney.** Thomas Bewick; a bibliography raisonné of editions of the General history of quadrupeds, the History of British birds and the Fables of Aesop issued in his lifetime. London, G. Cumberlege, O.U.P., 1953. xxx,198p. facsims. 26cm.

Full bibliogr. descrs., with TP facsims. replacing TP transcrs.; locations of copies.

Rev: N. Lewis Observer 6 Jl '53:9; TLS 29 Ja '54:76; M. Weekley Bk Coll 2:290–2 '53; D. F. Foxon Library ser5 8:206–9 '53; cf. S. Roscoe and D. F. Foxon *ib.* 9:208–9 '54.

BINYON, ROBERT LAURENCE, 1869–1943

2460 **Bibliographies** of modern authors. Robert Laurence Binyon. Lond Merc 2no1:114–15 My '20.

Chronol. checklist of poetry and prose, 1890–1919.

BIRD, CUTHBERT HILTON GOLDING-, 1848–1939

2461 **Winston, George A. R.** . . . Bibliography of the published writings, 1876–1924, of Cuthbert Hilton Golding-Bird. . . . [London] 1924. 11p. port. 22cm. (Bibliographies of Guy's men, no.10) (Not seen)

BIRMINGHAM, GEORGE A., *pseud. of* JAMES OWEN HANNAY, 1865–1950

2462 **Mackey, W. E.** The novels of George A. Birmingham, a list of first editions. Trinity Coll Dublin Ann Bull 14–16 '55.

Chronol. checklist of 60 items, 1905–50.

BIRRELL, AUGUSTINE, 1850–1933

2463 **Bibliographies** of modern authors. The rt. hon. Augustine Birrell, K.C. Lond Merc 3no16:435–6 F '21.

Chronol. checklist of prose, 1884–1911.

BLACKMORE, RICHARD DODDRIDGE, 1825–1900

2464 **Keogh, Andrew,** 1910: no.662.

2465 **Ellis, Stuart Marsh.** 'List of works by R. D. Blackmore' *in* Wilkie Collins, LeFanu and others. London, 1931. p.134–9. (Reissued 1951)

Chronol. checklist of 21 items, 1854–97, with some bibliogr. notes.

BLACKSTONE, SIR WILLIAM, 1723–1780

2466 **Yale university. School of law. Library. William Blackstone collection.** The William Blackstone collection in the Yale law library; a bibliographical catalogue, by Catherine Spicer Eller. [New Haven] Published for the Yale law library by the Yale university pr., 1938. xvii,113p. 23cm. (Not seen)

BLADES, WILLIAM, 1824–1890

2467 **St. Bride foundation institute,** LONDON. Catalogue of an exhibition in commemoration of the centenary of William Blades . . . compiled by William Turner Berry. [London, Ptd. by Blades and Blades, 1924] 39p. 22cm.

Annotated checklist, with quasifacsim. TP transcrs.

BLAIR, ERIC, 1903–1950
See Orwell, George, pseud.

BLAIR, HUGH, 1718–1800
2468 **Adams, R. E.,** 1962: no.711.

BLAKE, MARTIN, c.1596–1673
2469 **Dredge, John Ingle,** 1889–99: no.886.

BLAKE, WILLIAM, 1757–1827
2470 **Houtchens, Carolyn Washburn,** and **L. H. Houtchens,** *ed.* [1966]: no.2017.

2471 **Grolier club,** NEW YORK. Catalogue of books, engravings, water-colours & sketches by William Blake. Exhibited at the Grolier club. . . . [New York, DeVinne pr., 1905] xvii,147p. 18cm.

2472 **Keynes, sir Geoffrey Langdon.** A bibliography of William Blake. New York, Grolier club of New York, 1921. xvi,516p. illus., ports., facsims. 29cm.

Classified bibliogr. of works and ana, with full bibliogr. descrs. and notes.
Rev: Library ser4 3:58–61 '22.

2473 **MacKay, mrs. Alexander.** Catalogue of rare books by William Blake . . . sold by auction by Christie, Manson, & Woods, April 26, 1921. [London, 1921] (Not seen; Bentley's no.486)

2474 **Jugaku, Bunsho.** William Blake shōshi. Tokyo, Grolier society, 1929. xxxii,724p. facsims. 30cm.

Principally in Japanese; 'reprints and extends Keynes' (Bentley, no.497).

2475 **Lowery, Margaret Ruth.** A census of copies of William Blake's Poetical sketches, 1783. Library ser4 17:354–60 S '36.

2476 **Millard, Alice (Parsons) (mrs. George M. Millard).** A descriptive hand-list of a loan exhibition of books and works of art by William Blake, 1757–1827, chiefly from the collection of mr. Lessing J. Rosenwald, assembled by mrs. George M. Millard at the Little museum of La miniatura . . . Pasadena. [Pasadena, Calif., 1936] 32p. 22cm.

2477 **Moss, William Edward.** Catalogue of the . . . library . . . comprising a most important and extensive collection of the works of William Blake and of books and Mss. relating to him . . . sold by . . . Sotheby & co. . . . on March, 2–5, 8 & 9, 1937. [London, 1937] 206p. illus. (part.col.) 22cm.

Blake: nos. 138–284F.

2478 **Smith, George C.** William Blake; the renowned collection of first editions, of original drawings . . . collected by . . . public sale. . . . New York, Parke-Bernet galleries, 1938. 2pts. illus., ports. 27cm.

2479 **Philadelphia. Museum of art.** William Blake, 1757–1827; a descriptive catalogue of an exhibition of the works of William Blake selected from collections in the United States. Philadelphia, 1939. xix,175p. illus., facsims. 26cm.

Comp. by Edwin Wolf and E. Mongan.

2480 **Keynes, sir Geoffrey Langdon.** Blake's Poetical sketches. TLS 17 Mr '45:132.

Census of 21 copies.

2481 ——, and **E. Wolf.** William Blake's illuminated books; a census. New York, Grolier club of New York, 1953. xviii,124p. plates. 29cm.

Extends Section E of Keynes's Bibliography (no.2472); bibliogr. notes on 211 copies.

Rev: TLS 19 Mr '54:192; J. Harthan Library ser5 9:137–9 '54; D. G. Williams Lib Q 25:130–1 '55; H. Lehmann-Haupt Coll Res Lib 16:122–4 '55.

2482 —— Engravings by William Blake; the separate plates, a catalogue raisonné. Dublin, E. Walker, 1956. xiii,86p.+45 plates (part. col.) 32cm.

Descrs. of the states of 45 separate engravings, with census of existing impressions and bibliogr. notes.

2483 **Preston, Kerrison.** William Blake, 1757–1827; notes for a catalogue of the Blake library at the Georgian house, Merstham. Cambridge, Golden head pr., 1960 [i.e. 1961] 47p. 25cm.

Rev: TLS 28 Jl '61:472; sir G. L. Keynes Library ser5 17:172–3 '62.

2484 —— [Same]: [2d ed., rev.] Cambridge, Golden head pr., 1962. 48p. 24cm.

2485 **Bentley, Gerald Eades, jr.** and **M. K. Nurmi.** A Blake bibliography; annotated lists of works, studies and Blakeana. Minneapolis, University of Minnesota, 1964. xx,393p. 25cm.

Classified annotated checklist; the section 'Editions of Blake's writings' (p.41–74) supplements Keynes (no.2472). Since no note has been made in the present bibliography of sections on Blake's books in catalogues principally of his engravings, drawings, etc., Bentley and Nurmi's 'Catalogues and bibliographies' (p.173–92) should be consulted.

Rev: sir G. L. Keynes Bk Coll 14:250, 253 '65; TLS 2 S '65:756.

2486 **Caro, A. E.,** 1964: no.951.

2487 **White, William.** A Blake bibliography; review with additions. Bull Bib 24:155–6 My/Ag '65.

Addenda to Bentley and Nurmi.

BLESSINGTON, MARGUERITE (POWER), COUNTESS, 1789–1849
See Gardiner, Marguerite (Power), countess Blessington.

BLISS, PHILIP, 1787–1857

2490 **Gibson, Strickland** and **C. J. Hindle.** Philip Bliss, 1787–1857, editor and bibliographer. Oxford Bib Soc Proc 3pt2:173–260 '32.

2491 —— [Same]: Additions and corrections. *ib.* 3pt3:367–8 '33.
'Works edited by Bliss and his contributions to periodicals, etc.' (p.244–55): annotated list of 17 books, and periodical contribs., with some bibliogr. notes.

BLOMEFIELD, FRANCIS, 1705–1752

2492 **Norwich. Public libraries.** . . . Francis Blomefield, 1705–1752, historian and topographer; exhibition . . . in the Central public library . . . [Norwich, 1952] 12p. 23cm.
Introduction by C. L. S. Linnell.

BLOMEFIELD, MILES, 1525–1574?

2493 **D., K. W.** Miles Blomefield. TLS 10 S '25:584; *rf.* N. B. White *ib.* 20 Oc '25:719; R. N. Green-Armytage 5 N '25:739.
Checklist of 7 items.

BLOOMFIELD, ROBERT, 1766–1823

2494 **Whitmore, P.,** 1937: no.231.

2495 **Hardy, John David Gathorne-, earl of Cranbrook,** and **J. Hadfield.** Some uncollected authors xx: Robert Bloomfield, 1766–1823. Bk Coll 8no2:170–9 '59.
'Handlist of Robert Bloomfield's printed works' (p. 173–9): quasifacsim. TP transcrs., collations, and bibliogr. notes on 12 works and their early ed.

2496 **Clements, Jeff.** Early editions of Bloomfield's poems. Bk Coll 11no2:216–17 '62.
Addenda to preceding item.

2497 **Bloomfield, Barry Cambray.** Bloomfield's Rural tales, 1802. Bk Coll 11no4:482 '62.
Addenda to Hardy's no.2c.

BLOUNT, CHARLES, 1654–1693

2498 **Gilmour, John Scott Lennox.** Some uncollected authors XVII: Charles Blount, 1654–1693. Bk Coll 7no2:182–7 '58.
'Check-list of Charles Blount's works' (p.184–7): quasifacsim. TP transcrs., collations, and bibliogr. notes on 15 works and their early ed.

BLUNDEN, EDMUND CHARLES, 1896–

2499 **Fung, S-K. S.,** 1961: no.125.

BLUNT, WILFRID SCAWEN, 1840–1922

2500 [**Looker, Samuel J.**] The poetry of Wilfrid Scawen Blunt, with bibliography. Poetry R 12no4:193–204 Jl/Ag '21.
'A bibliographical note' (p.203–4): checklist.

BODKIN, THOMAS PATRICK, 1887–1961

2500a **Denson, Alan.** Thomas Bodkin, a bio-bibliographical survey with a bibliographical survey of his family. Dublin, Bodkin trustees, 1966. 236p. 34cm. (Duplicated typescript)

Classified chronol. checklist, with some bibliogr. notes.

BOLINGBROKE, HENRY SAINT JOHN, 1ST VISCOUNT, 1678–1751
See Saint John, Henry, 1st viscount Bolingbroke.

BONE, SIR DAVID WILLIAM, 1874–1959

2501 **Skallerup, Harry R.** Sir David Bone, 1874–1959, a selected bibliography. Bull Bib 23:234–6 Ja/Ap '63.

Classified checklist of books; stories in collections; miscellaneous writings; reviews of his works; and ana.

BOOTH, CONSTANCE GEORGINE (GORE-), 1868–1927
See Markievicz, Constance Georgine Gore-Booth.

BORROW, GEORGE HENRY, 1803–1881

2502 **Knapp, William Ireland.** 'Chronological bibliography, 1823–1874' *in* The life, writings and correspondence of George Borrow. . . . New York; London, 1899. V.2, p.341–75.

2503 **Thomas, Philip Edward.** 'Bibliography' *in* George Borrow, the man and his books. London, 1912. p.[323]–3.

2504 **Stephen, George Arthur.** George Borrow: bibliography. Norwich Pub Lib Readers' Guide 2:81–5 Jl '13.

2505 **Wise, Thomas James.** A bibliography of the writings in prose and verse of George Henry Borrow. London, Ptd. for private circulation only by R. Clay, 1914. xxii,316p. facsims. 23cm.

Chronol. catalogue of editiones principes, and 'Contributions to periodical literature, etc.' and 'Borroviana' (p.311–16) with TP transcrs., and facsims., collations, and bibliogr. notes; no index.

2506 **Stephen, George Arthur.** 'Bibliography of Borrow' *in* Borrow house museum; a brief account of the life of George Borrow and his Norwich home. Norwich, Norwich public libraries committee, 1927. p.17–32.

BOSWELL, JAMES, 1740–1795

2507 **Fitzgerald, Percy Hetherington.** 'Catalogue raisonné of Boswell's works' *in* The life of James Boswell. . . . London, 1891. V.2, p.275–84.

2508 **Pottle, Frederick Albert.** The literary career of James Boswell, esq.; being the bibliographical materials for a life of Boswell. Oxford, Clarendon pr., 1929. (Repr. Oxford, O.U.P., 1966) xliv,335p. facsims. 23cm.

TP transcrs., and facsims., collations, and bibliogr. notes in classified sequences.

Rev: R. S. Crane Yale R 19:616–19 '30; D. M. Stuart Nation & Athenæum 15 Je '29:374; E. N. S. Thompson Philol Q 9:87–8 '30; I. A. Williams Lond Merc 20:618 '29; New Statesman 8 Je '29:278, 280; TLS 16 My '29:408; L. Cazamian R Anglo-Am 8:157–9 '30; T. B. Simpson J Eng Germ Philol 29:289–90 '30; J. Wilks Mod Lang R 25:488–90 '30; G. P. Winship Mod Lang N 45:254–6 '30; N&Q 158:179 '30.

BOURGUIGNON, HUBERT-FRANÇOIS, 1699–1773
See Gravelot, Hubert François.

BOWBER, THOMAS, fl.1663–1695.
2509 **Dredge, John Ingle,** 1889–99: no.886.

BOWEN, ELIZABETH DOROTHEA COLE (MRS. A. C. CAMERON), fl.1927–
2510 **Heath, William Webster.** [Checklist of 'those works by miss Bowen that can be considered literature or relevant to literature'] *in* Elizabeth Bowen, an introduction to her novels. Madison, Wisc., 1961. p.170–3.

BOWEN, MARJORIE, *pseud. of* GABRIELLE MARGARET VERE (CAMPBELL) LONG, 1888–1952
2511 **Wagenknecht, Edward.** Bowen, Preedy, Shearing & co.; a note in memory and a checklist. Boston Univ Stud Eng 3no3:181–9 '57.
Title checklist.

BOWLES, WILLIAM LISLE, 1762–1850
2512 **Woolf, Cecil.** Some uncollected authors XVIII: William Lisle Bowles, 1762–1850. Bk Coll 7no3:286–94; 7no4:407–16 '58.
'Checklist of first editions: Part I: Verse' (p.289–94); 'Part II: Prose' (p.407–16): quasifacsim. TP transcrs., collations, and some bibliogr. notes on 27 works in verse and 32 in prose.

BOYD, ZACHARY, 1585?–1653
2513 **Brown, William.** Zachary Boyd's Forme of catechising, 1639. Edinburgh Bib Soc Pub 3pt3:153–4 Mr '99.
Discussion and descr. with TP facsim.

BOYLE, ROBERT, 1627–1691
2514 **Fulton, John Farquhar.** A bibliography of the honourable Robert Boyle, fellow of the Royal society. Oxford, O.U.P.; New Haven, Privately ptd. 1932. 171p. port., facsims. 26cm.
Repr. from Oxford Bib Soc Proc 3pt1:1–172 '31; *see* no.2518.

2515 —— [Same]: Addenda. . . . Oxford Bib Soc Proc 3pt3:339–65 '33.

2516 —— [Same]: Second addenda. . . . Oxford Bib Soc Pub new ser 1:33–8 '47.

2517 **[Keynes, sir Geoffrey Langdon]** The honourable Robert Boyle, a handlist of his works. G.L.K. . . . London, 1932. [12]l. 15cm.

2518 **Fulton, John Farquhar.** A bibliography of the honourable Robert Boyle, fellow of the Royal society. 2d ed. Oxford, Clarendon pr., 1961. xxvi, 218p. port., facsims. 26cm.
Classified bibliogr. with quasifacsim. TP transcrs., and facsims., collations, bibliogr. notes, and locations of copies, of 541 items.
Rev: sir G. L. Keynes Bk Coll 10:344–8 '61; W. R. LeFanu Library ser5 17:164–6 '62; E. F. Horine Pa Bib Soc Am 56:268–70 '62.

BOYLE, ROGER, 1ST EARL OF ORRERY, 1621–1679

2519 **Clark, William Smith,** *ed.* 'Bibliography of Orrery's dramatic works' *in* The dramatic works of Roger Boyle, earl of Orrery. Cambridge, Mass., 1937. V.2, p.[954]–62.

Quasifacsim. TP transcrs. of 7 separate works (17 items) and 3 collected ed., with discursive collations and some bibliogr. notes.

2519a **Miller, Clarence William.** A bibliographical study of Parthenissa by Roger Boyle, earl of Orrery. Stud Bib 2:115–37 '49.

'. . . revised listing of the various editions, states . . . and variant title-page imprints' [with locations of copies] (p.135–7).

BRADDON, MARY ELIZABETH (MRS. MAXWELL), 1837–1915

2519b **Bolt, Fred E.** Mary Elizabeth Braddon: bibliography. N&Q ser11 11:227 Mr '15; A. Sparke; G. L. Apperson; A.N.Q.; T.R.; W. A. Frost *ib.* ser11 11:282–4 Ap '15; Mac.; T. Ratcliffe; B.B. 11:366 My '15.

Chronol. checklist, 1861–1911 (p.282).

BRADLEY, EDWARD, 1827–1889
See Bede, Cuthbert, pseud.

BRADLEY, FRANCIS HERBERT, 1846–1924

2520 **Taylor, A. E.** Francis Herbert Bradley, 1846–1924. Proc Brit Acad 11:458–68 '24/5.

'Bibliography' (p.466–8): checklist of books and periodical contribs.

BRADLEY, HENRY, 1845–1923

2520a 'Bibliography' *in* The collected papers of Henry Bradley . . . Oxford, 1928. p.[259]–79.

Chronol. checklist, 1877–1923.

BRAMAH, ERNEST, *pseud. of* ERNEST BRAMAH SMITH, 1868–1942

2521 **White, William.** Ernest Bramah, a first checklist. Bull Bib 22:127–31 My/Ag '58.

Classified checklist of books; appearances in periodical and anthologies; reviews of his books; and biography and criticism.

2522 —— Some uncollected authors XXXVII: Ernest Bramah, 1869?–1942. Bk Coll 13no1:54–63 '64.

'Check-list of Ernest Bramah's works' (p.60–3): quasifacsim. TP transcrs., collations, and some bibliogr. notes on 16 first ed., 1894–1940, with notes of later ed.

BRADSHAW-ISHERWOOD, CHRISTOPHER WILLIAM, 1904–
See Isherwood, Christopher William Bradshaw-.

BRANDE, WILLIAM THOMAS, 1788–1886

2523 **Horne, Alan John.** A bibliography of William Thomas Brande, 1788–1886. [London] Royal institution library [1955] 17l. 33cm. (Duplicated typescript)

Classified checklist of works and ana.

BRETON, NICHOLAS, 1545?–1626?

2524 **Tannenbaum, Samuel Aaron** and **D. R. Tannenbaum**. Nicholas Breton, a concise bibliography. New York, 1947. i,34l. 28cm. (Elizabethan bibliographies, no.39) (Duplicated typescript)
Classified checklist of works and ana.

BRIDGES, ROBERT SEYMOUR, 1844–1930

2525 [**Daniel, Charles Henry Olive**] Notes on a bibliography of Bridges. Oxford Mag 13n024:446–7 Je '95.

2526 [**Chaundy, Leslie** and **E. H. M. Cox**] Bibliographies of modern authors, no.1. Robert Bridges. London, L. Chaundy, 1921. 8p. 18cm.
Expanded from Lond Merc 1n06:753–4 Ap '20.

2527 **Boutell, Henry Sherman.** English first editions, Robert (Seymour) Bridges . . . a bibliographical check list of the first editions of his books. Pub Wkly 117:2650–4 My '30.

2528 **McKay, George Leslie.** A bibliography of Robert Bridges. New York, Columbia U.P.; London, O.U.P., 1933. xii,215p. port. 22cm.
Quasifacsim. TP transcrs., collations and bibliogr. notes on 146 items, with index of first lines; based on the collection of Frederick Coykendall.
Rev: TLS 7 D '33:884; cf. C. H. Wilkinson *ib*. 28 D '33:924; D. A. Randall Pub Wkly 124:1758–9 '33; N&Q 166:467–8 '34; P. F. Baum Sth Atlan Q 33:205 '34; 'R' Sat R Lit 10:463 '34; viscount Esher Bk Coll Q 13:89–90 '34.

2529 **Smith, Simon Nowell-.** Check list of the works of Robert Bridges. Bk Coll Q 16:30–40 Oc/D '34.

BRIGHT, MARY CHAVELITA (DUNNE), 1859–1945
See Egerton, George, pseud.

BRIGHT, TIMOTHY, 1550–1615

2530 **Keynes, sir Geoffrey Langdon.** Dr. Timothie Bright, 1550–1615, a survey of his life with a bibliography of his writings. London, Wellcome historical medical library, 1962. 47p. facsims. 25cm.
Quasifacsim. TP transcrs., collations, locations of copies, and bibliogr. notes and refs. on 23 early ed. from 1580.
Rev: TLS 14 S '62:696; J. L. Thornton Lib Assn Rec 64:401 '62; W. LeFanu Bk Coll 11:514, 517 '62; C. E. Kellett N&Q 208:318 '63.

BROCK, ARTHUR CLUTTON-, 1868–1924

2531 **Bibliographies** of modern authors. Arthur Clutton-Brock. Lond Merc 1n03:366–7 Ja '20.
Chronol. checklist, 1900–19.

BROME, RICHARD, d.1652

2532 **Andrews, Charles Edward.** 'Bibliography of Brome's works' *in* Richard Brome; a study of his life and works. New York, 1913. p.[37]–45.
Checklist with some bibliogr. notes.

BRONTË FAMILY

2533 **Stevenson, Lionel,** *ed.,* 1964: no.1705.

2534 **Wood, Butler.** A bibliography of the works of the Brontë family, including a list of books and magazine articles on the Brontës. . . . Bradford, For the [Brontë] society by C. Greening, 1895. 34p. 21cm.

2535 —— [Same]: A supplement. Bradford, For the [Brontë] society by M. Field, 1897. 19p. 22cm.

2536 **Manchester. Public libraries. Moss side branch.** Catalogue of the Cleave Brontë collection in the Moss side free library, Manchester. By John Albert Green. Moss Side, 1907. 32p. front. 24cm.

2537 **Wise, Thomas James.** A bibliography of the writings in prose and verse of the members of the Brontë family. London, Ptd. for private circulation only by R. Clay, 1917. xv,255p. front., facsims. 23cm. (Repr. London, Dawsons, 1965)
See no.2539.

2538 **Brontë society. Museum and library,** HAWORTH. Catalogue of the museum & library, the Brontë society. Compiled by J. Alex. Symington. Haworth, 1927. 199p. illus., ports., maps, facsims. 22cm.
Note also catalogues of the objects in the Museum, 1896, 1908.

2539 **Wise, Thomas James.** A Brontë library; a catalogue of printed books, manuscripts, and autograph letters by the members of the Brontë family, collected by Thomas James Wise. London, Ptd. for private circulation only, 1929. xxiii,82p. illus., facsims. 27cm.
Chronol. catalogue under name of each member of the family, with TP transcrs. and facsims., and bibliogr. notes. The collection is now in the BM.
Rev: TLS 31 Oc '29:876.

2540 **Brontë society. Museum and library,** HAWORTH. **Bonnell collection.** Catalogue of the Bonnell collection in the Brontë parsonage museum. Haworth, 1932. 90p. illus., port., facsims. 22cm.
'Books' (p.77–89).

2541 **Parrish, Morris Longstreth,** 1933: no. 1707.

2542 **Randall, David Anton** and S. Adelman. The first American edition of the Brontës' Poems. Bk Coll 9no2:199–202 '60.
List of 8 ed. with bibliogr. notes and some locations of copies.

BROOKE, RUPERT, 1887–1915

2545 **Bibliographies** of modern authors. Rupert Brooke. Lond Merc 1n01: 122–3 N '19.

2546 **Danielson, Henry.** Bibliographies of modern authors, no.8. Rupert Brooke. Bkmns J 1n012–13:243, 262 '20.

2547 —— 1921: no.680.

2548 **Potter, Richard Montgomery Gilchrist.** Rupert Brooke, a bibliographical note on his works published in book form, 1911–1919. Hartford, 1923. 28cm. 26cm.

2549 **Keynes, sir Geoffrey Langdon.** A bibliography of Rupert Brooke. London, R. Hart-Davis, 1954. 147p. illus., port., facsims. 23cm.

2550 —— [Same]: [2d ed., rev.] London, R. Hart-Davis, 1959. 158p. illus., port., facsims. 23cm.

Quasifacsim. TP transcrs. and facsims.; collations, and bibliogr. notes of 47 books; periodical contribs.; poems in ms.; and ana; index of first lines.

BROOKE, STOPFORD AUGUSTUS, 1832–1916

2551 **Standley, Fred L.** Stopford Augustus Brooke, 1832–1916; a primary bibliography. Bull Bib 24:79–82 My/Ag '64.

Classified chronol. checklist of books; articles, pamphlets, printed sermons, etc.; and ana.

BROUGHAM, HENRY PETER, BARON BROUGHAM AND VAUX, 1778–1868

2552 **Schneider, Elisabeth, I. Griggs,** and **J. D. Kern.** Brougham's early contributions to the Edinburgh review; a new list. Mod Philol 42:152–73 F '45.

Annotated chronol. checklist.

BROUGHTON, RICHARD, d.1634

2553 **Webster, Raymund.** Richard Broughton, a priest in persecution. Downside R new ser 54:495–514 Oc '36.

'Note on Broughton's writings' (p.510–12): checklist of 17 items with STC nos. and bibliogr. notes.

BROWN, JOHN, 1715–1776

2554 **Roberts, sir Sydney Castle.** Some uncollected authors xxiv: 'Estimate' Brown, 1715–1776. Bk Coll no2:180–87 '60.

2555 —— [Same]: [Additions: no.15a] *ib.* 10no2:198 '61.

'Bibliography of "Estimate" Brown' (p.183–7): quasifacsim. TP transcrs., collations and bibliogr. notes on 25 works.

BROWN, JOHN ALEXANDER HARVIE-, 1844–1916

2556 **[Brown, John Alexander Harvie-]** Bibliography of the writings of J. A. Harvie-Brown . . . arranged . . . in chronological order. [Dunipace] Privately ptd. [1896] 32p. 28cm.

Chronol. checklist of 199 items, 1864–96, with some bibliogr. notes.

BROWN, THOMAS, 1663–1704

2557 **Boyce, Benjamin.** 'Bibliography' *in* Tom Brown of facetious memory;
Grub street in the age of Dryden. Cambridge, Mass., 1939. p.[187]–207.
Checklist of 84 items.

BROWN, THOMAS EDWARD, 1830–1897

2558 **[Parrott, Thomas Mabbott]** A note on Thomas Edward Brown, the Manx-
man poet, with a bibliographical list of his writings. Bkmns J ser3 17no11:
165–9 '29.
'The bibliography of Thomas Edward Brown' (p.169).

2559 **Radcliffe, William.** 'A bibliography' in Thomas Edward Brown, a
memorial volume, 1830–1930. Cambridge, 1930. p.[213]–29.
Tables of poems' titles, dates of composition, and place of previous publication for
poems in Collected works, with addenda (p.223) and ana (p.227-9).

2560 **Cubbon, William.** Thomas Edward Brown, the Manx poet, 1830–1897; a
bibliography . . . compiled and edited by William Cubbon. Douglas, Ptd.
by the Victoria pr. and published by the Manx museum and ancient monu-
ments trustees, 1934. 64p. port., facsims. 21cm.
Section taken from v.2 of A bibliographical account of works relating to the Isle of
Man: *see* no.923.

2561 **Smith, Simon Nowell-.** Some uncollected authors XXXIII: Thomas Edward
Brown, 1830–1897. Bk Coll 11no3:338–44 '62.
'Check-list of first editions of T. E. Brown's works' (p.341-4): quasifacsim. TP transcrs.,
collations, and bibliogr. notes on 13 'literary books and pamphlets, issued in Brown's
lifetime . . .'.

BROWNE, EDWARD, 1644–1708

2562 **Keynes, sir Geoffrey Langdon.** 'Appendix III: dr. Edward Browne' *in*
A bibliography of sir Thomas Browne. Cambridge, 1924. p.[221]–9.
TP transcrs., collations, bibliogr. notes and locations of copies, items 507–21, 1669–
1923.

BROWNE, SIR THOMAS, 1605–1682

2653 **Williams, Charles.** The bibliography of the Religio medici. Norwich, 1905.
15p. 26cm.

2653a—— **[Same]:** 2d ed. Norwich, For private circulation, 1907. 20p. 26cm.
Chronol. checklist, 1642–1906, with bibliogr. notes and locations of copies.

2563b **Monroe, Thomas Kirkpatrick.** The early editions of sir Thomas Browne.
Glasgow Bib Soc Rec 7:44–61 '23.

2564 **Keynes, sir Geoffrey Langdon.** A bibliography of sir Thomas Browne, kt.,
M.D. Cambridge, C.U.P., 1924. xii,255p. illus., ports., facsims. 26cm.
Classified bibliogr. with TP transcrs. and facsims., collations, bibliogr. notes and loca-
tions of copies, of 506 works and ana, with 'List of libraries containing copies of books
recorded' (p.[244]).
Rev: F. Birrell Nation Athenæum 35:21,650 '24; TLS 21 Ag '24:512; A. W. P[ollard]
Library ser4 5:184–9 '24; A. E. Lib. Assn Rec 2:165–6 '24; 'Biblio' Bkmns J 11:17–18
'24; N&Q 147:181–2 '24; I. A. Williams Lond Merc 10:522–3 '24; G. C. M. Smith
Mod Lang R 20:91–2 '25.

2565 [Alexander, Mary] Sir Thomas Browne; a catalogue of works by and about sir Thomas Browne in the Norwich public libraries. Norwich Public libraries committee, 1925. 4p. port. 22cm.

Repr. from Norwich Pub Lib Readers' Guide v.8 '25.

2566 **Leroy, Olivier.** A French bibliography of sir Thomas Browne. London, G. G. Harrap, 1931. 97p. 26cm.

Classified checklist, with locations of Browne's works in Paris libraries, lists of imitations, translations, and ana.

Rev: TLS 25 F '32:132; Oxford Mag 16 Je '32:846.

BROWNING, ELIZABETH (BARRETT), 1806–1861
See also Browning, Robert, 1812–1889.

2567 **Forman, Harry Buxton.** E. B. Browning and her scarcer books, a bio-bibliographical note. London, Privately ptd., 1896. 29p. facsims. 21cm.

Repr. from no.659.

2568 **Wise, Thomas James.** A bibliography of the writings in prose and verse of Elizabeth Barrett Browning. London, Ptd. for private circulation only by R. Clay, 1918. xv,249p. illus., ports., facsims. 23cm.

See no.2586.

2569 **Carter, John Waynflete** and **G. Pollard.** 'Census of copies of the Reading Sonnets' *in* An enquiry into the nature of certain nineteenth century pamphlets. London; New York, 1934. p.[361]–8.

Checklist of 36 copies with locations.

2570 **Taplin, Gardner B.** Mrs. Browning's contributions to periodicals; addenda. Pa Bib Soc Am 44:275–6 '50.

Checklist of 12 Wise addenda.

2571 **St. Marylebone. Public libraries.** Elizabeth Barrett Browning, 1806–1861; catalogue of the centenary exhibition. . . . London [1961] 21p. 22cm.

Ed. by Lauchlan P. Kelley.

BROWNING, ROBERT, 1812–1889

2576 **Brooklyn. Public library.** Robert Browning, 1812–1889; a list of books and of references to periodicals in the Boston public library, Brooklyn, N.Y., 1912. 43p. 16cm.

2577 **Baylor university,** WACO, TEXAS. **Library.** Browningiana in Baylor university, compiled by Aurelia E. Brooks. [Waco, Tex., Baylor U.P., 1921] viii, 405p. ports., facsims. 23cm.

Author and title catalogue of one of the largest collections in America.

2578 **Förster, Meta** and **W. M. Zappe.** Robert Browning bibliographie. Halle, M. Niemayer, 1939. 35p. 24cm.

2579 **Armstrong, A. Joseph.** 'A bibliography of foreign Browningiana' *in* Browning the world over; being Baylor university Browning interests, series six: Browning's international influence; and series seven: A bibliography of foreign Browningiana. Waco, Texas, Baylor university, 1933. p.[97]–187.

2580 **Raymond, William Odber.** 'Browning studies in England and America, 1910–1949' *in* The infinite moment and other essays. Toronto, 1950. p.153–231.
Bibliogr. essay.

2581 **De Vane, William Clyde.** A Browning handbook. New York, Appleton-Century-Crofts [1955] viii,594p. 21cm.
'Selected bibliography' (p.581–8). Earlier ed. in 1935, 1937, and 1955.

2582 **Litzinger, Boyd** and **K. L. Knickerbocker,** *ed.* 'Bibliography' *in* The Browning critics. [Nashville, Tenn., 1965] p.[391]–417.
Supplements Broughton, Northup, and Pearsall, for 1950–65.

2582a **Faverty, Frederic Everett,** *ed.,* 1956: no.2016.

2583 **Wise, Thomas James.** A bibliography of the writings of Robert Browning. Athenæum 193–4, 256–7, 422, 569–70 11 Ag–27 Oc '94; 354, 418–20, 564–6, 758–9, 905–6 12 S–26 D '96; 17–18 2 Ja '97.

2584 —— Materials for a bibliography of Robert Browning *in* Nicoll, sir William Robertson and T. J. Wise. Literary anecdotes of the nineteenth century. London, 1895–6. V.1, p.361–627.

2585 —— A complete bibliography of the writings in prose and verse of Robert Browning. London, Ptd. only for private subscribers, 1897. 8,243[3]p. facsims. 21cm.

2586 —— A Browning library; a catalogue of printed books, manuscripts, and autograph letters by Robert Browning and Elizabeth Barrett Browning, collected by Thomas James Wise. London, Ptd. for private circulation only, 1929. xxxii,126p. illus., ports., facsims. 27cm.
'The writings of Robert Browning' (p.3–69); 'The writings of Elizabeth Barrett Browning' (p.73–106); 'Browningiana' (p.109–29); unindexed chronol. catalogue with TP transcrs. and facsims., discursive collations, and bibliogr. notes.
Rev: TLS 25 Ap '29:333.

2587 **Sone, Tamotsu,** *comp.* 'A bibliography of Robert Browning' *in* Griffin, William H. and H. C. Minchin. The life of Robert Browning . . . translated by T. Sone. [Tokyo] 1931. p.356–558 (Not seen)
'. . . by far the most painstaking and detailed general bibliography to date': Broughton's no. B17.

2588 **Greer, Louise.** 'American editions of Browning's works and other publications indicating the growth of his popularity in America' *in* Browning and America. Chapel Hill [1952] p.231–49.

Chronol. checklist, with locations of copies. See also 'The number and size of impressions and editions of Browning's works printed by his authorized American publishers' (p.250–64).

2589 **Broughton, Leslie Nathan [and others]** Robert Browning; a bibliography, 1830–1950; compiled by Leslie Nathan Broughton, Clark Sutherland Northup and Robert Pearsall. Ithaca, N.Y., Cornell U.P., 1953. xiv,446p. 25cm.

Classified list of works and ana, with TP transcrs., collations, and bibliogr. notes, with list of early bibliographies (p.75) and sales catalogues (p.78).

Rev: R. D. Altick Pa Bib Soc Am 48:212–14 '54; TLS 27 Ag '54:548; D. F. Foxon Bk Coll 3:315–17 '54; D. Bush Mod Lang N 70:219–20 '55; M. M. Bevington Sth Atlan Q 55:126–7 '55.

BRYANT, THOMAS, 1828–1914

2595 **Winston, J. H. E.** . . . . Bibliography of the published writings, 1856–1902, of Thomas Bryant. [London] 1915. 24p. port. 21cm. (Bibliographies of Guy's men, no.6)
Chronol. checklist.

BRYCE, JAMES, VISCOUNT BRYCE, 1838–1922

2596 **Garnett, Richard.** The right hon. James Bryce, D.C.L. Eng Illus Mag new ser 29:210–12 My '03.
'Bibliography' (p.212): classified checklist.

BRYDGES, SIR SAMUEL EGERTON, 1762–1837

2597 **Woodworth, Mary Katherine.** 'Bibliography' *in* The literary career of sir Samuel Egerton Brydges. Oxford, 1935. p.167–88.

2598 —— [**Same**]: Addenda. TLS 16 N '35:744.
Chronol. checklist of 137 books and 21 periodicals containing contribs. by him, and ana.

BUCHAN, JOHN, BARON TWEEDSMUIR, 1875–1940

2598a **Cox, J. Randolph.** John Buchan, lord Tweedsmuir: an annotated bibliography of writings about him. Eng Lit Transit 9no5–6:241–91,292–325 '66.

2599 **Hanna, Archibald.** John Buchan, 1875–1940; a bibliography. Hamden, Conn., Shoe string pr., 1953. xi,135p. 23cm.
Classified chronol. checklist.

2600 **Kingston, Ont. Queen's university. Douglas library.** Checklist of works by and about John Buchan in the John Buchan collection. Boston, Mass., 1961. 38[26]p. ports. 25cm.
Classified short-title catalogue comp. by B. C. Wilmot.

BUCHAN, PETER, 1790–1854
See under Presses and printing.

BUCHANAN, GEORGE, 1506–1582

2605 **Murray, David.** 'Catalogue of printed books, manuscripts, and other documents relating to George Buchanan or illustrative of his life' *in* George Buchanan, Glasgow quatercentenary studies, 1906. Glasgow, 1907. p.[393]–505.
Annotated chronol. short-title catalogue. of early ed., with some bibliogr. notes, and ana (p.496–505); 'Books presented to the library . . . by George Buchanan' (p.506–16).

BUCHANAN, ROBERT WILLIAMS, 1841–1901

2606 **Jay, Harriett.** 'Chronological list of the poetical and prose writings of Robert Buchanan' *in* Robert Buchanan; some account of his life, his life's work and his literary friendships. London, 1903. p.316–19.

2607 **Smith, Simon Nowell-.** An early work of R. W. Buchanan. Biblioth 4n06: 249 '65.

Quasifacsim. TP transcr., collation and some bibliogr. notes on Poems and love lyrics [1858].

BUCKLER, EDWARD, 1610–1706

2608 **Mead, Herman Ralph.** Three issues of A buckler against the fear of death. Library ser4 21:199–206 S '40.

Quasifacsim. TP transcrs., collations, bibliogr. notes, and locations of copies.

BULL, JOHN, 1562–1628

2609 **Henry, Leigh.** 'Appendix D: Works by Bull: major collections, printed editions, etc.' *in* Dr. John Bull, 1562–1628. [London, 1937] p.298–9.
Checklist.

BULWER-LYTTON, EDWARD ROBERT, 1ST EARL OF LYTTON, 1831–1891
See Lytton, Edward Robert Bulwer, 1st earl of Lytton.

BUNYAN, JOHN, 1628–1688

2610 **Tibbutt, H. G.** Bunyan libraries. Assn Brit Theol Philos Libs Bull 16:3–8 Mr '62.

Survey of principal collections and catalogues.

2611 **First** editions of John Bunyan's Pilgrim's progress. Pub Wkly 114:2063–5 N '28.

Locations and discursive descrs. of 11 known copies.

2612 **Harrison, Frank Mott.** A bibliography of the works of John Bunyan. [Oxford] Ptd. at the O.U.P. for the Bibliographical society, 1932. xxviii, 83p. port. 22cm. (Bibliographical society supplement, no.6)

Chronol. arrangement of 57 items, with quasifacsim. TP transcrs., collations, locations of copies, and bibliogr. notes; no index.

Rev: Dub Mag 8:56 '33; TLS 29 S '32:696.

2613 **Bedford. Public library.** Catalogue of the John Bunyon library (Frank Mott Harrison collection). Bedford [Ptd. by Diener & Reynolds] 1938. 42p. facsims. 23cm.

Rev: R. B. McK[errow] Library ser4 19:496–7 '39.

2614 **Morrison, Frank Mott.** A handlist of the first part of the Pilgrim's progress. . . . [Brighton, Sussex, Duplicated by Stesco, 1941] 115l. 26cm. (Duplicated typescript)

Checklist of English ed., 1678–1939; no index.

2615 **Silver, Louis H.** Bunyan's Barren fig tree, 1670. Library ser5 5:61 Je '50.

TP transcr., collations, and bibliogr. discussion amending Harrison and CBEL.

2616 **Bunyan meeting library and museum,** BEDFORD. Catalogue . . . by Cyril Hargreaves and M. Greenshields. Bedford, Published by the trustees, 1955. 42p. illus. 22cm.

2617 **Wharey, James Blanton,** *ed.* 'Introduction' *in* The pilgrim's progress. 2d ed., rev. by Roger Sharrock. Oxford, 1960. p.xix–cxviii.

TP facsim., collations, and bibliogr. notes; locations and descrs. of individual copies.

2618 **Smith, David E.** Publication of John Bunyan's works in America. N.Y. Pub Lib Bull 66:630–52 D '62.

'Checklist of American editions of the works of John Bunyan, 1681–1830' (p.644–52): 143 items, with some locations of copies and bibliogr. notes.

BURKE, EDMUND, 1729–1797

2620 **Cordasco, Francesco G. M.** Edmund Burke, a handlist of critical notices &
studies. New York, B. Franklin for Long Island U.P., 1950. 12p. 22cm.
(Eighteenth century bibliographical pamphlets, no.12)

2621 **Todd, William Burton.** The bibliographical history of Burke's Reflections
on the revolution in France. Library ser5 6:100–8 S '51.
Differentiation of 6 impressions of first 3 ed.

2622 —— A bibliography of Edmund Burke. London, R. Hart-Davis, 1964.
312p. facsims. 23cm. (Soho bibliographies, XVII)
Classified bibliogr. of separate ed. and selections; collected works; false attributions;
and imitations, parodies, and fictitious works; with quasifacsim. TP transcrs., collations,
locations of copies, and bibliogr. notes.
Rev: W. Rees-Mogg Bk Coll 14:241–2 '65; C. B. Cone Pa Bib Soc Am 59:338–9 '65;
TLS 7 Jl '66:604.

BURKE, THOMAS, 1886–1945

2623 **Gawsworth, John,** *pseud.* [1933]: no.687.

BURNE-JONES, SIR EDWARD COLEY, 1833–1898
See Jones, Sir Edward Coley Burne-.

BURNET, BP. GILBERT, 1643–1715

2624 **Foxcroft, Helen Charlotte,** *comp.* 'Appendix II. Chronological table of
Burnet's published works' *in* Clarke, Thomas E. S. and H. C. Foxcroft.
A life of Gilbert Burnet, bishop of Salisbury. Cambridge, 1907. p.[522]–56.
Chronol. checklist, 1665–1717, with some bibliogr. notes.

2625 **Mogg, William Rees.** Some reflections on the bibliography of Gilbert
Burnet. Library ser5 4:100–13 S '49.
Quasifacsim. TP transcrs. and discursive bibliogr. discussion and collations.

2626 **Dobell, R. J.** The bibliography of Gilbert Burnet. Library ser5 5:61–3
Je '50.
Addenda to Mogg; ed. and states of Some passages of . . . Rochester, 1680, with quasi-
facsim. TP transcrs., collations, and variant readings.

BURNEY, CHARLES, 1726–1814

2627 **Scholes, Percy Alfred.** 'Burney's published books' *in* The great dr. Burney,
his travels, his works, his family and his friends. London, 1948. V.2,
p.[331]–92.
Chronol. checklist, 1769–1897, with some bibliogr. notes and locations of copies. Also
contains checklist of works by other members of the Burney family.

BURNEY, FRANCES (MRS. D'ARBLAY), 1752–1840

2628 **Scholes, Percy Alfred.** 'Works of Fanny Burney (later D'Arblay) published
and unpublished' *in* The great dr. Burney, his travels, his works, his family
and his friends. London, 1948. V.2, p.353–6.
Checklist, 1778–1890, with some bibliogr. notes.

BURNS, ROBERT, 1759–1796

2629 **T., H.** A contribution to Burns bibliography. N&Q ser8 10:41–2 Jl '96.
Chronol. checklist of Burnsiana in N&Q.

2629a **Muir, John.** Bibliography of Burns. Burns Chron 1:104–23 '92; 2:153–82 '93.

2630 **Barrett, F. T.,** *comp.* 'Editions of the writings of Burns' *in* Burns exhibition, Glasgow, 1896. Memorial catalogue of the Burns exhibition held in the galleries of the Glasgow institute of the fine arts. . . . Glasgow, 1898. p.201–348.

2631 **Angus, William Craibe.** The printed works of Robert Burns; a bibliography in outline. Glasgow, Privately ptd., 1899. xl,134p. 24cm.

2632 —— Catalogue of the valuable & interesting collection of Burnsiana formed by the late W. Craibe Angus. . . . To be sold by auction by mr. Dowell. . . . [Edinburgh, A. & D. Padon, 1902] 89p. 24cm.

2633 **Ewing, James Cameron.** A bibliography of Robert Burns, 1759–1796. Edinburgh Bib Soc Pub 9pt1:57–72 F '09.

2634 **MacKie Burnsiana library,** KILMARNOCK. Catalogue . . . compiled by David Sneddon. Kilmarnock, Standard print., 1909. vi,170p. 23cm.

2635 **McNaught, Duncan.** 'Some reviews, press notices, etc. which appeared during the lifetime of the poet' *in* The truth about Burns. Glasgow, 1921. p.222–40.
Also lists appearances of poems in contemporary periodicals.

2636 **British museum. Dept. of printed books.** Robert Burns, an excerpt from the General catalogue of printed books. . . . London, Ptd. by W. Clowes, 1939. 40 col. 34cm.

2637 **Dunfermline. Public libraries.** The Murison Burns collection; a catalogue of the books and pamphlets presented by sir Alexander Gibb to the city and royal burgh of Dunfermline; compiled by Nancie Campbell. [Dunfermline] 1953. 140p. illus. 22cm.

2638 **Edinburgh. Public libraries.** Robert Burns exhibition; manuscripts, letters, books and relics of the poet, his family and associates, arranged by the Edinburgh district Burns clubs association and the Edinburgh public libraries committee. . . . [Edinburgh] 1953. 17p. illus., ports.(1 col.) 18cm.

2639 **Mitchell library,** GLASGOW. Catalogue of the Robert Burns collection in the Mitchell library, Glasgow. [Glasgow] Glasgow corporation public libraries, 1959. vii,217p. port. 25cm.
Based on the original work of James C. Ewing; the collection is believed to be the largest in the world; ed. by Anthony G. Hepburn.

2640 **Texas. University. Humanities research center.** A splore in honor of the two-hundredth anniversary of the birth of Robert Burns, 1759–1959. . . . [Austin, 1959] 15p. illus. 25cm.

2641 **Nevada. University. Library.** Robert Burns, an exhibition in the Noble H. Getchell library. . . . Catalogue by G. Ross Roy. [Reno] University of Nevada pr., 1962. 27p. 23cm.

2642 **Egerer, Joel Warren.** A bibliography of Robert Burns. Edinburgh, Oliver & Boyd, 1964. 396p. 23cm.

Quasifacsim. TP transcrs., collations, and bibliogr. notes; chronol. with undated ed., items 985–1176. 'Translations arranged alphabetically by languages' (p.324–32); 'Original material first published in periodicals' (p.333–56).

Rev: R. J. Roberts Bk Coll 14:242, 245–6 '65; TLS 4 F '65:96; J. Roberts Priv Lib 6:61–2 '65; J. Kinsley Library ser5 21:76–9 '66.

2643 **Roy, George Ross.** Some notes on the facsimiles of the Kilmarnock Burns. Biblioth 4n06:241–5 '65.

Checklist, 1867–1913, with some bibliogr. notes.

2644 —— Robert Burns. University of South Carolina, Dept. of English, 1966. 24p. facsims. 21cm.

Catalogue of exhibition at McKissick memorial library, from Roy's collection.

BURTHOGGE, RICHARD, fl.1637–1705

2645 **Dredge, John Ingle,** 1889–99: no.886.

BURTON, EDWARD, 1794–1836

2645a **Whitfield, A. Stanton.** Edward Burton bibliography. N&Q ser11 11:169 F '15.

Chronol. checklist, 1821–1857.

BURTON, SIR RICHARD FRANCIS, 1821–1890

2646 **Burton, Isabel, lady.** 'List of captain sir Richard F. Burton's works' *in* The life of captain sir Richard F. Burton. London, 1893. V.2, p.[453]–5.

2647 **Stisted, Georgiana M.** 'List of sir Richard Burton's works' *in* The true life of capt. sir Richard F. Burton. London, 1896. p.417–19.

2648 **Jones, Herbert,** *comp.* 'List of Burton's works, original and translated' *in* Quaritch, Bernard. Contributions towards a dictionary of English book-collectors. London, 1898. Pt.11, p.7–8.

2649 **Wright, Thomas.** 'Bibliography of Richard Burton' *in* The life of sir Richard Burton. London, 1906. V.2, p.[iii]–x at end.

2650 **Penzer, Norman Mosley.** An annotated bibliography of sir Richard Francis Burton. London, A. M. Philpot, 1923. xvi,351p. port., facsims. 27cm.

TP transcrs., with some TP facsims., and bibliogr. notes with distinction of issues.

Rev: I. A. Williams Lond Merc 8:190 '23; TLS 3 My '23:308; cf. N. M. Penzer *ib.* 10 My '23:323; A. R. Butterworth *ib.* 14 Je '23:404.

BURTON, ROBERT, 1557–1640

2652 **Potter, Alfred Claghorn.** Robert Burton. N&Q ser9 1:42–3 Ja '98.

Checklist of ed. of Anatomy, 1800–96 (p.43).

2653 **Duff, Edward Gordon** and **F. Madan.** 'Notes on the bibliography of the Oxford editions of the Anatomy' *in* Robert Burton and the Anatomy of melancholy. Oxford, 1926. p.[191]–7.

Repr. from Oxford Bib Soc Proc 1pt3:159–246 '25.

2654 **Doane, Gilbert Harry.** A checklist of the editions of the Anatomy of melancholy. Am Coll 5:247–9 Mr '28. (Not seen)

2655 **Smith, Paul Jordan-.** 'A bibliography of Robert Burton' *in* Bibliographia Burtoniana; a study of Robert Burton's The anatomy of melancholy. . . . Stanford, Calif., 1931. p.79–98.

Quasifacsim. TP transcrs., discursive collations, and bibliogr. notes; 'A list of books greatly indebted to Burton's The anatomy of melancholy' (p.106–9).

Rev: P. Haines Am Bkmn 74:332 '31; Am Merc 24:30, 32 '31; G. M. Troxell Sat R Lit 8:127 '31; TLS 17 Mr '32:203; A. W. Witherspoon Univ Calif Chron 34:99–103 '32; H. Jackson Bk Coll Q 8:35–8 '32; sir G. L. Keynes R Eng Stud 9:337–9 '33.

2656 **Honnold library for the associated colleges,** CLAREMONT, CALIF. Burton's Anatomy of melancholy and Burtoniana; a checklist of a part of the collection in memory of Sarah Bixby Smith, 1871–1935, compiled by Paul Jordan-Smith, assisted by Margaret Mulhauser. Oxford, O.U.P., 1959. xiii,37p. 24cm.

BUTLER, SAMUEL, 1612–1680

2660 **Johnson, Reginald Brimley,** *ed.* 'Bibliographical and other notes' *in* The poetical works; a revised edition. London, 1893. V.1, p.[xxiii]–ci.

Includes 'Early editions of Hudibras' (p.xxiii–xxix); 'Illustrated editions of Hudibras' (p.xxix–xli); 'Some translations of Hudibras' (p.xli–xlvii); 'Other works by Butler' (p.li–lvii); 'Imitations of Hudibras' (p.lxiv–lxxvi); 'Early writers of Hudibrastic verse' (p.lxxix–lxxxii).

2661 **Chew, Beverly C.** Some notes on the three parts of Hudibras. Bibliographer 1no4:123–38 Ap '02.

2662 —— [**Same**]: *in* Essays and verses about books. New York, 1926. p.65–97.
TP facsims., collations, and bibliogr. notes.

2663 **Thorson, James L.** The publication of Hudibras. Pa Bib Soc Am 60:418–38 '66.

'A bibliography of editions of Hudibras published during the lifetime of Samuel Butler' (p.426–38): 'complete descriptions of all of the editions . . .', with TP facsims.

2664 **Wilders, John,** *ed.* 'Early editions' *in* Samuel Butler: Hudibras. Oxford, 1967. p.xlviii–liv.
Bibliogr. descrs., and locations of copies, 1663–80.

BUTLER, SAMUEL, 1835–1902

2665 **Jones, Henry Festing.** 'A short bibliography of the writings of Samuel Butler and of the books and articles concerning him' *in* Samuel Butler, author of Erewhon, 1835–1902, a memoir. London, 1919. V.1, p.xxi–xxx.

2666 —— and **A. T. Bartholomew.** 'Books and music written by Butler' *in* Cambridge. University. St. John's college. Samuel Butler collection. The Samuel Butler collection at saint John's college, Cambridge; a catalogue and a commentary. Cambridge, 1921. p.15–25.

2667 **Hoppé, Alfred John.** A bibliography of the writings of Samuel Butler, author of Erewhon, and of writings about him. . . . London, Office of The bookman's journal [1925] xv,184p. facsims.(part fold.) 23cm.

'Editiones principes, etc.' (p.3–100): TP transcrs., collations, and bibliogr. notes on 50 items; 'Contributions to periodical literature' (p.103–26).
Rev: Bkmns J 12:147 '25; TLS 16 Jl '25:476; Library ser4 6:202–3 '25.

2668 **Bartholomew, Augustus Theodore.** Catalogue . . . of manuscripts and books by and about Samuel Butler . . . sold by auction by messrs. Sotheby . . . London, Ptd. by J. Davy, 1930. 28p. facsims. 25cm.

2669 **Williams college,** WILLIAMSTOWN, MASS. **Chapin library.** Catalogue of the collection of Samuel Butler. . . . Portland, Me., Southworth-Anthoensen pr., 1945. vii,35p. port. 22cm.

Comp. by Carroll A. Wilson; no index.

2670 **Harkness, Stanley Bates.** The career of Samuel Butler, 1835–1902; a bibliography. London, Bodley head [1955] 154p. 23cm.

Classified, sometimes annotated, checklists on various aspects of Butler's writings and reputation; ana (p.93–150).

Rev: TLS 29 Ap '55:228.

BUTT, ISAAC, 1813–1879

2671 **MacD[onagh], F[rank]** Bibliography of Isaac Butt. Irish Bk Lover 5:54–6 N '13.

Classified checklist.

BUXTON FAMILY

2672 **Downward, M. E.,** 1957: no.111.

BYRON, GEORGE GORDON, BARON BYRON, 1788–1824

2675 **Chew, Samuel Cleggett.** 'Bibliography' *in* Byron in England, his fame and after-fame. London; New York, 1924. p.353–407.

'The fullest list of Byroniana'—CBEL.

2676 **Raysor, Thomas Middleton,** *ed.*, 1956: no.2015.

2677 **Anderson, John Parker,** *comp.* 'Bibliography' *in* Noel, Roden B. W. Life of lord Byron. London, 1890. xxxviiip. at end.

2678 **Coleridge, Ernest Hartley,** *ed.* 'A bibliography of the successive editions and translations of lord Byron's poetical works' *in* The works. . . . New rev. & enl. ed. London, 1898–1905. V.7, p.[89]–348.

2679 **British museum. Dept. of printed books.** Catalogue of printed books. Byron. London, Ptd. by W. Clowes, 1906. 54 col. 35cm. Covertitle.

2680 **English association,** 1912: no.650.

2681 **Intze, Ottakar.** Byroniana, consisting of I. A list of catalogues of various Byron collections. II. Catalogue of his separate works. . . . [Birmingham] New meeting pr. [1914] 23p. 22cm.

2682 **Nottingham. Mechanics institute.** Catalogue of the Byron exhibition. . . . [Nottingham, 1915] 40p. illus., port. 22cm.

2682a **Chew, Samuel Cleggett.** The Byron apocrypha. N&Q ser12 5:113–15, 143–5 My,Je '19.

Annotated checklist of 33 items at some time attrib. to Byron.

2683 **Texas. University. Library.** A descriptive catalogue of an exhibition of manuscripts and first editions of lord Byron . . . compiled and annotated by R. H. Griffith and H. M. Jones. Austin, Tex., University of Texas pr., 1924. xiii,106p. port., facsims. 27cm.

Rebuked by First edition club for 'inclusion of needlessly detailed descriptions of some of the later editions' for which it may still be useful.

2684 **First edition club,** LONDON. Bibliographical catalogue of first editions, proof copies & manuscripts of books by lord Byron exhibited at the fourth exhibition held by the First edition club, January 1925. [London] 1925. xvii,97p. facsims. 26cm.

Exhibits supplied by John Murray and T. J. Wise on whose 'researches' the catalogue is based; TP transcrs. and some facsims., Wise-style collations and bibliogr. notes; not indexed.

2685 **Ryan, Michael J.** The adventures of lord Byron's Prefaces; additional notes to the bibliography of the poet. Bkmns J 16n08:419–30 '28.

TP transcrs., discursive collations, and bibliogr. notes on The liberal, no.1, Manfred, and Werner.

2686 **Wise, Thomas James.** A Byron library; a catalogue of printed books, manuscript and autograph letters by George Gordon Noel, baron Byron, collected by Thomas James Wise. London, Ptd. for private circulation only, 1928. xxvii,144p. port., facsims. 26cm.

2687 **Mathews, Elkin, ltd., bkslrs.,** LONDON. Byron and Byroniana; a catalogue of books. London [1930] ix,125p. facsims. 23cm.

2688 **Wise, Thomas James.** A bibliography of the writings in verse and prose of George Gordon Noel, baron Byron. . . . London, Ptd. for private circulation only, 1932–3. (Repr. London, Dawsons, 1964) 2v. illus., ports., facsims. 23cm.

Chronol. bibliogr. of works, and Byroniana (V.2, p.63–131), with TP transcrs. and facsims., discursive collations and bibliogr. notes; no index.

Rev: TLS 15 S '32:642; cf. J. Carter *ib.* 29 S '32:696; *ib.* 19 Mr '64:244.

2689 **Newstead abbey. Roe-Byron collection.** The Roe-Byron collection, Newstead abbey. [Nottingham] Corporation of Nottingham, 1937. 188p. ports., facsims. 25cm.

2690 **Henry E. Huntington library and art gallery,** SAN MARINO, CALIF. Byron, 1788–1938; an exhibition at the Huntington library. [San Marino, Calif., 1938] 15p. facsims. 22cm.

Comp. by Ricardo Quintana.

2691 **Eaves, Thomas Cary Duncan.** A note on lord Byron's Select works, 1823. Library ser5 1:70–2 Je '46.

Reissue of various early ed. of individual publications; TP transcrs. and bibliogr. refs. for 5 items, supplementing Coleridge.

CAINE, SIR THOMAS HENRY HALL, 1853–1931

2695 **Melville, Lewis,** *pseud.* Thomas Henry Hall Caine. Eng Illus Mag new ser 31:212–15 My '04.
'Bibliography' (p.214–15): checklist of works; dramatic works; introductions; articles and books about.

CAIRNES, JOHN ELLIOTT, 1823–1875

2696 **Select** bibliographies, no.3. Bibliography of John Elliott Cairnes, 1823–1875. Bull Brit Lib Pol Sci 3:11–12 Jl '13.
Chronol. checklist of works, 1854–75, and ana, with locations of copies.

CALVERLEY, CHARLES STUART, 1831–1883

2697 **Sendall, sir Walter J.,** *ed.* 'Bibliographical note' *in* The complete works of Charles Stuart Calverley. London, 1901. p.[xi]
Checklist.

CAMBRENSIS, GIRALDUS DE BARRI, 1146?–1220?
See Giraldus de Barri, Cambrensis.

CAMPBELL, ARCHIBALD, 9TH EARL OF ARGYLE, d.1685

2698 **Brown, William.** Notes on Argyll's Declaration printed at Campbeltown 1685. Edinburgh Bib Soc Proc 3pt3:149–51 Mr '99.
Discussion and descr.

CAMPBELL, GEORGE, 1761–1817

2699 **Goy, J. R.,** 1964: no.130.

CAMPBELL, JOSEPH, 1879–1944

2700 **O'Hegarty, Patrick Sarsfield.** A bibliography of Joseph Campbell. . . . Dublin, Privately ptd. by A. Thom, 1940. 6p. 24cm.
Repr. from Dublin Mag new ser 15:58–61 Oc/D '40; TP transcrs. collations and bibliogr. notes on 10 items.

CAMPBELL, THOMAS, 1763–1854

2701 **Houtchens, Carolyn Washburn** and **L. H. Houtchens,** *ed.* [1966]: no.2017.

CAMPION, EDMUND, 1540–1581

2702 **Hodges, John,** *comp.* 'Bibliography' *in* Simpson, Richard. Edmund Campion, a biography. New ed. London, 1896. p.[491]–506.
Checklists of works and ana, with some bibliogr. notes.

CANNING, ELIZABETH, 1734–1773

2703 **McCue, Lillian Bueno.** 'Elizabeth Canning in print' *in* Elizabethan studies and other essays in honor of George F. Reynolds. Boulder, Col., 1945. p.223–32.
Chronol. checklist of 65 items relating to her, 1753–1945, with locations of copies.

CANNING, GEORGE, 1770–1827

2704 **Little, G. F.** Selected bibliographies, no.31. George Canning. Bull Brit Lib Pol Sci 30:26–33 My '25.

Chronol. checklist of works, 1787–1889, and ana.

CAREY, WILLIAM, 1761–1834

2704a **Khan, M. Siddiq.** William Carey and the Serampore books, 1800–1834. Libri 11no3:197–280 '61.

'A selective and annotated bibliography of Serampore books' (p.258–77): chronol. checklist of 222 items, 1800–34, including works by Carey.

CARLETON, WILLIAM, 1794–1869

2705 **O'Donoghue, David James.** 'Bibliography of William Carleton's writings' *in* The life of William Carleton. . . . London, 1896. V.1, p.lvii–lxiv.

Chronol. checklist, 1828–95.

CARLYLE, THOMAS, 1795–1881

2706 **Houtchens, Carolyn Washburn** and **L. H. Houtchens,** *ed.* [1966]: no.2017.

2707 **Michigan. University. Library.** A catalogue of the dr. Samuel A. Jones Carlyle collection, with additions from the general library, compiled by Mary Eunice Weed. Ann Arbor, University of Michigan, 1919. xi,119p. port. 23cm.

2708 **Dyer, Isaac Watson.** A bibliography of Thomas Carlyle's writings and ana. Portland, Me., Southworth pr., 1928. xii,587p. port. 25cm.

Classified list with TP transcrs., collations, bibliogr. notes, and some locations of copies.

Rev: C. F. Harrold J Eng Germ Philol 28:307–9 '29; C. F. Harrold Sewanee R 37:240–2 '29; C. F. Harrold Sth Atlan Q 28:320–2 '29; C. F. H[arrold] Mod Lang N 44:545–7 '29; C. F. Harrold Philol Q 9:89–90 '30; B. H. Lehman Univ Calif Chron 32:124–5 '30; W. Leopold Eng Studien 66:287–90 '31.

2709 **Coffin, Edward Francis.** American first editions of Carlyle. Am Bk Coll 4:236–8 N '33.

Chronol. checklist, 1828–81.

2710 **Thrall, Miriam Mulford H.** 'Bibliography of Carlyle' *in* Rebellious Fraser's, Nol Yorke's magazine in the days of Maginn, Thackeray, and Carlyle. New York, 1934. p.299.

Checklist of contribs. to Fraser's magazine.

2711 **Clitheroe, B. M.,** 1937: no.100.

2712 **Tennyson, G. B.** Carlyle's poetry to 1840: a check-list and discussion. . . . Vict Poet 1no3:161–81 '63.

'A checklist of Carlyle's poetry to 1840': (p.163–4).

CARPENTER, EDWARD, 1844–1929

2715 **Sheffield. Public libraries.** A bibliography of Edward Carpenter; a catalogue of books, manuscripts, letters etc. by and about . . . in the Carpenter

collection . . with some entries from other sources. [Sheffield] Sheffield city libraries, 1949.
Short-title classified catalogue.

CARPENTER, JOHN, 1570–1620
2716 **Dredge, John Ingle,** 1889–99: no.886.

CARPENTER, NATHANAEL, fl.1605–1635
2717 **Dredge, John Ingle,** 1889–99: no.886.

CARPENTER, RICHARD, 1577?–1627
2718 **Dredge, John Ingle,** 1889–99: no.886.

CARROLL, LEWIS, *pseud. of* CHARLES LUTWIDGE DODGSON, 1832–1898
2720 **Collingwood, Stuart Dodgson.** 'Bibliography' *in* The life and letters of Lewis Carroll. London, 1898. p.431–43.

2721 **Williams, Sidney Herbert.** A bibliography of the writings of Lewis Carroll (Charles Lutwidge Dodgson). New York, R. R. Bowker; London, Bookman's journal, 1924. xiii,142p. facsims. 26cm.
Still useful for its list of minor works; *see* no.2734.
Rev: Library ser4 5:381–2 '25; TLS 10 Ap '24:228.

2722 **Parrish, Morris Longstreth.** A list of the writings of Lewis Carroll (Charles L. Dodgson) in the library at Dormy house. . . . [New York] Privately ptd., 1928. viii,148[i.e. 152]p. illus., port., facsims. 26cm.

2723 —— [Same]: A supplementary list. . . . [Philadelphia] Privately ptd., 1933. ix,115p. facsims. 25cm.

2724 **Williams, Sidney Herbert** and **F. Madan.** A handbook of the literature of the rev. C. L. Dodgson (Lewis Carroll). London, H. Milford, O.U.P., 1931. xviii[6]336p. port., facsims. 23cm.

2725 —— [Same]: Supplement. Corrigenda and addenda, the latter covering 1932–1934 and including the centenary year, 1932, by F. Madan. Oxford, H. Milford, O.U.P., 1935. 24p. 22cm.
See no.2734.

2726 **Columbia university.** Catalogue of an exhibition at Columbia university to commemorate the one hundredth anniversary of the birth of Lewis Carroll (Charles Lutwidge Dodgson) 1832–1898. New York, Columbia U.P., 1932. 153p. ports. 21cm.
Rev: J. T. Winterich Sat R Lit 9:278 '32.

2727 **Harvard university. Library.** The Harcourt Amory collection of Lewis Carroll in the Harvard college library, compiled by Flora V. Livingston. Cambridge, Mass., Privately ptd., 1932. ix,190p. plates, port., facsims. 24cm.
Rev: J. T. Winterich Sat R Lit 9:278 '32.

2728 **Lewis Carroll centenary exhibition,** LONDON, **1932.** . . . Catalogue, by Falconer Madan. . . . London, The old court house, J. & E. Bumpus, 1932. xv,116p. port. 19cm.

2729 —— [Same, with title]: The Lewis Carroll centenary in London, 1932, including a catalogue. . . . London, J. & E. Bumpus, 1932. xvi,138p.+6 plates. port. 20cm.

2730 **Archibald, R. C.** Bibliography of Lewis Carroll; additions. N&Q 179:134–5 Ag '40.

2731 **Green, Roger Lancelyn.** Lewis Carroll's periodical publications. N&Q 199:118–21 Mr '54.
Chronol. checklist, 1854–97.

2732 **Nathanson, H.** The first edition of Carroll's Phantasmagoria, 1869. Bk Coll 8no2:184 '59; rf. Roger L. Green ib. 8no3:309 '59; John M. Shaw ib. 8no3:309 '59.

2733 **Shaw, John Mackay.** The parodies of Lewis Carroll and their originals; catalogue of an exhibition, with notes. . . . [Tallahassee] Florida state university library, 1960. 14p. 27cm. (Duplicated typescript)

2734 **Williams, Sidney Herbert** and **F. Madan.** The Lewis Carroll handbook, being a new version of A handbook of the literature of the rev. C. L. Dodgson. . . . Rev., aug. and brought up to 1960, by Roger Lancelyn Green. London, O.U.P., 1962. xv,307p. illus., port., facsims. 21cm.
Quasifacsim. TP transcrs., collations, and bibliogr. notes.
Rev: J. Hayward Bk Coll 11:372–6 '62; P.W. Priv Lib 4:49 '62; TLS 13 Jl '62:516; S. Godman N&Q 208:476–8 '63; C. J. Hindle Library ser5 18:314–15 '63.

2735 **Weaver, Warren.** 'Appendix: checklist of editions of translations' *in* Alice in many tongues: the translations of Alice in wonderland. Madison, 1964. p.[110]–39.

CARTER, FREDERICK, fl.1926–1932

2740 **Gawsworth, John,** *pseud.* [1933]: no.687.

CARY, ARTHUR JOYCE LUNEL, 1888–1957

2741 **Beebe, Maurice, J. Lee,** and **S. Henderson.** Criticism of Joyce Cary, a selected checklist. Mod Fict Stud 9:284–8 '63.

CARY, JOHN, c.1754–1835

2745 **Fordham, sir Herbert George.** John Cary, engraver, map, chart and print-seller and globe-maker, 1754 to 1835; a bibliography, with an introduction and biographical notes. Cambridge, C.U.P., 1925. xxxiv,135p. facsim. 23cm.

'Catalogue of the atlases, maps, plans, itineraries and other engravings and publications of John Cary and his successors' (p.1–122); 'Classified index-list with dates of all known re-impressions' (p. 123–34): chronol. descriptive list, with bibliogr. notes.

CASEMENT, ROGER DAVID, 1864–1916

2746 **O'Hegarty, Patrick Sarsfield.** A bibliography of Roger Casement. Dublin, Privately ptd., 1949. 6p. 25cm.

Repr. from Dublin Mag new ser 24:31–4 Ap/Je '49. TP transcrs., collations, and some bibliogr. notes on 13 items, 1909–22.

CAVENDISH, MARGARET, DUCHESS OF NEWCASTLE, 1624?–1724

2747 **Colquhoun, J.,** 1950: no.101.

CAXTON, WILLIAM, 1422?–1491
See under Presses and printing.

CECIL, EDGAR ALGERNON ROBERT GASCOYNE, VISCOUNT CECIL OF CHELWOOD, 1864–1958

2748 **Stirling, M. V.,** 1959: no.212.

CENTLIVRE, SUSANNA, 1667?–1723

2749 **Bowyer, John Wilson.** Susanna Freeman Centlivre. Mod Lang N 43:78–80 F '28.

Additions to CBEL.

2750 **Norton, Jane Elizabeth.** Some uncollected authors XIV: Susanna Centlivre. Bk Coll 6no2,3:172–8, 280–5 '57.

Quasifacsim. TP transcrs., collations, [and bibliogr. notes on 19 plays, 19 poems, and 4 prose items.

CHALMERS, THOMAS, 1780–1847

2751 **Watt, Hugh.** The published writings of dr. Thomas Chalmers, 1780–1847; a descriptive list. [Edinburgh] Privately ptd., 1943. 86p. 18cm.

Chronol. checklist of 208 items, 1805–1912, with TP transcrs.; no index.

CHAMBERLEN, HUGH, fl.1630–1720

2752 **Select** bibliographies, no.6. Hugh Chamberlain, the elder, physician and economist. Bull Brit Lib Pol Sci 6:12–13 Ap '14.

Chronol. checklist of works, 1685–1702, and ana.

CHAMBERS, RAYMOND WILSON, 1874–1942

2753 **Husbands, H. Winifred.** A bibliography of the works of R. W. Chambers. Proc Brit Acad 30:440-5 '44.

Chronol. checklist, 1900–42.

CHAMBERS, ROBERT, 1802–1871

2754 **Chambers, Charles Edward Steuart.** A catalogue of some of the rarer books . . . in the collection . . . with a bibliography of the works of William and Robert Chambers. Edinburgh, Privately ptd., 1891. (First pub. 1886) 45p. 17cm.

2755 —— A catalogue of some of the rarer books, also manuscripts, in the collection of C. E. S. Chambers. . . . Edinburgh, Ptd. for private circulation, 1929. 64p. 18cm.

'Chambers, Robert, 1802–1871' (p.54-9); 'Chambers, William, 1800–1883' (p. 59–62); chronol. checklists.

2755a **Millhauser, Milton.** 'The principal writings of Robert Chambers' *in* Just before Darwin; Robert Chambers and Vestiges. Middletown, Conn. [1959] p.212-17.

Classified checklist of works and ana.

CHAMBERS, WILLIAM, 1800–1883

2756 **Chambers, Charles Edward Steuart,** 1929: no.2755.

CHAPMAN, GEORGE, 1559?–1634

2757 **Brettle, Robert Edward.** Eastward hoe, 1605, by Chapman, Jonson and Marston; bibliography and circumstances of production. Library ser4 9:287-302 D 28; *rf.* W. W. Greg *ib.* ser4 9:303-4 D '28.

TP transcrs., collations, and bibliogr. discussion on first 3 ed., 4 issues.

2758 **Tannenbaum, Samuel Aaron.** George Chapman, a concise bibliography. New York, 1938. viii,40p. 23cm. (Elizabethan bibliographies, no.5)

Classified checklist of 668 items of works and ana. *See* no.2761

2759 —— and **D. R. Tannenbaum.** Supplement. New York, 1946. 17l. 28cm. (Duplicated typescript)

2760 **Fay, H. C.** Chapman's text corrections in his Iliads. Library ser5 7:275–81 D '52.

TP transcrs., collations, and bibliogr. notes and discussion of 3 ed. of parts of the Iliad, 1598–1611.

2761 **Yamada, Akihiro.** George Chapman, a checklist of editions, biography, and criticism, 1946–1965. Res Opp Renaiss Drama 10:75–86 '67.

Continuation of Tannenbaum.

CHARLES I, KING OF GREAT BRITAIN AND IRELAND, 1600–1649

2762 **Almack, Edward.** A bibliography of The king's book, or Eikon basilike. London, Blades, East & Blades, 1896. 143[79]xxip. illus., col.facsims. 30cm.

2763 **Sutton, E.**, 1948: no.215.

2764 **Madan, Francis Falconer.** A new bibliography of the Eikon basilike of king Charles the first; with a note on the authorship. [Oxford, O.U.P., 1950] vii,199p. facsims. 26cm.

TP facsims. but no transcrs.; collations and extensive bibliogr. notes, with locations of copies; table of Almack nos.
Rev: TLS 9 F '51:88.

CHARLES II, KING OF GREAT BRITAIN AND IRELAND, 1630–1685

2770 **Horrox, William Arthur.** A bibliography of the literature relating to the escape and preservation of king Charles II after the battle of Worcester, 3 September, 1651, exclusive of Mss., plays, novels. . . . Aberdeen, Aberdeen U.P., 1924. 64p. 21cm.

Chronol. checklist, with location of copy examined.

2771 **Alden, John Eliot.** The muses mourn; a checklist of verse occasioned by the death of Charles II. Charlottesville, Va., Bibliographical society, University of Virginia, 1958. 61p. 17cm.

Annotated alphabetical checklist of 68 items, with locations of copies, and index of first lines.

2772 . . . **Charles II** and the restoration; an exhibition to commemorate the tercentenary of the restoration of the monarchy, held in the Chapter house, Exeter. [Exeter, Devon record office, 1960] 54p. 25cm. (Duplicated typescript)

CHATTERTON, THOMAS, 1752–1770

2775 **Hyett, Francis Adams** and **W. Bazeley.** Chattertoniana; being a classified catalogue of books, pamphlets, magazine articles & other printed matter relating to the life or works of Chatterton, or to the Rowley controversy. . . . Gloucester, J. Bellows, 1914. 43p. 24cm.

Checklist, with locations of copies, repr. from the Bibliographer's manual of Gloucestershire literature 3:318–37 '97.

2776 **Bristol. Public libraries.** [Chattertoniana] *in* Bristol bibliography. . . . Bristol, 1916. p.[55]–82.

2777 **Drake, S.**, 1947: no.112.

CHAUCER, GEOFFREY, 1340?–1400

2778 **Hammond, Eleanor Prescott.** Chaucer, a bibliographical manual. New York, P. Smith, 1933. (First pub. London, Macmillan, 1908) x,579p. 23cm.
'Editions of the works, from Pynson to Skeat, etc.' (p.114–49).

2779 **Martin, Willard Edgar.** A Chaucer bibliography, 1925–1933. Durham, N.C., Duke U.P., 1935. xii,97p. 24cm.

2780 **Griffith, Dudley David.** Bibliography of Chaucer, 1908–1953. Seattle, University of Washington pr., 1955. xviii,398p. 23cm. (Duplicated typescript)

First pub. 1926 with title: A bibliography of Chaucer, 1908–1924.

2780a **Crawford, William R.** Bibliography of Chaucer, 1954–1963. Seattle, University of Washington pr. [1967] xliv,144p. 23cm.

2781 **Grolier club,** NEW YORK. An exhibition of original and other editions, portraits, and prints, commemorative of the five hundredth anniversary of the death of Geoffrey Chaucer, the father of English poetry. [New York, DeVinne pr., 1900] 45p. 18cm.

2782 **Hetherington, John R.** Chaucer, 1532–1602; notes and facsimile texts designed to facilitate the identification of defective copies of the black-letter folio editions of 1532, 1542, c.1550, 1561, 1598 and 1602. Birmingham, 1964. 21p. facsims. 23cm. (Duplicated typescript)

Bibliogr. notes and facsims. with type specimens, locations of copies and STC nos.
Rev: D.J.C. Priv Lib 6:63 '65.

CHESTERFIELD, PHILIP DORMER STANHOPE, 4TH EARL OF, 1694–1773
See Stanhope, Philip Dormer, 4th earl of Chesterfield.

CHESTERTON, GILBERT KEITH, 1874–1936

2784 **Bibliographies** of modern authors. G. K. Chesterton. Lond Merc 1no4:496–7 F '20.

2785 **Alexander, Mary.** G. K. Chesterton. Norwich Pub Lib Readers' Guide 8no15:197–200 Jl/S '25.

2786 **Sutherland, F. M.,** 1949: no.214.

2787 **Sullivan, John.** G. K. Chesterton, a bibliography. . . . London, University of London pr.[1958] 208p. port., facsims. 23cm.

Classified list, with quasifacsim. TP transcrs., collations, and bibliogr. notes.
Rev: TLS 8 Ag '58:452; M. White Dublin R 383–4 '58/9; I. R. Willison Bk Coll 7:440, 443 '58.

CHILCOTT, WILLIAM, 1664–1711
2788 **Dredge, John Ingle,** 1899–99: no.886.

CHILD, SIR JOSIAH, 1630–1699

2789 **Scroggs, E. S.** Select bibliographies, no.15. Bibliography of sir Josiah Child, bart., 1630–1699. Bull Brit Lib Pol Sci 14:15–17 My '21.

Chronol. checklist of works, 1668–1775, and ana.

2790 **Bowyer, Tony Harold.** The published forms of sir Josiah Child's A new discourse of trade. Library ser5 11:95–102 Je '56.

'The predecessors and complete editions of A new discourse of trade' (p.97–101): quasifacsim. TP transcrs., collations, and bibliogr. notes on 17 items, 1668–1804.

CHILDERS, ROBERT ERSKINE, 1870–1922

2791 **O'Hegarty, Patrick Sarsfield.** Bibliographies of 1916 and the Irish revolution, no.XVI. Erskine Childers. Dublin Mag new ser 23:40–3 Ap/Je '48.

TP transcrs., collations and some bibliogr. notes on 13 items, 1900–22.

CHISHULL, JOHN, d.1674?

2792 **Dredge, John Ingle,** 1889–99: no.886.

CHURCHILL, CHARLES, 1731–1764

2793 **Williams, Iolo Aneurin,** 1924: no.633.

2794 **Whitford, Robert Calvin.** Gleanings of Churchill bibliography. Mod Lang N 43:30–4 Ja '28.

Addenda to Joseph M. Beatty 'Churchill's influence on minor eighteenth century satirists'. Pub Mod Lang Assn 42:162–76 '27.

2795 **Grant, Douglas.** Some uncollected authors VIII: Charles Churchill. Bk Coll 4n04:316–23 '55.

'Check-list of first editions' (p.317–23): quasifacsim. TP transcrs., collations, and bibliogr. notes.

CHURCHILL, SIR WINSTON LEONARD SPENCER, 1874–1965

2796 **Pennsylvania. University. Library.** Benjamin Franklin, Winston Churchill: an exhibition. . . . [Philadelphia, 1951] 55p. 23cm.

Comp. by Edwin Wolf.

2797 **Farmer, Bernard J.** Bibliography of the works of sir Winston S. Churchill. London, 1958. 62p. 27cm. Covertitle. (Duplicated typescript)

2798 **Eaton, Peter.** Churchilliana. Bk Coll 13n03:352–3 '62.

2799 **Woods, Frederick W.** A bibliography of the works of sir Winston Churchill. London, N. Vane [1963] 340p. port. 23cm.

Classified arrangement of 142 items entirely by Churchill with quasifacsim. TP transcrs., collations, and bibliogr. notes, with list of miscellanea and ana.

Rev: R. J. Roberts Bk Coll 12:248, 250 '63; M. Ashley Bks 347:97–8 '63; H. A. Cahn Priv Lib 4:115 '63; TLS 10 My '63:348; D. Flower Library ser5 20:161–2 '65; J. B. Meriwether Pa Bib Soc Am 60:114–22 '66 (important).

CIBBER, COLLEY, 1671–1757

2805 **Barker, Richard Hindry.** 'Bibliography' *in* Mr. Cibber of Drury lane. New York, 1939. p.[261]-7.

Chronol. checklist, with some bibliogr. notes, of works, 1695–1777, and attributions, 1711–45.

2806 **Peavy, Charles Druery,** 1964: no.4445.

CLARE, JOHN, 1793–1864

2807 **Peterborough natural history, scientific, and archaeological society.** Catalogue of the centenary exhibition of portraits, books, manuscripts . . . belonging to or connected with John Clare. . . . Peterborough, 1893. viii,28p. illus. 21cm.

Ed. by Charles Dack.

2808 **Smith, C. Ernest,** *comp.* 'Bibliography of John Clare' *in* Gale, Norman, *ed.* Poems by John Clare. Rugby, 1901. p.[158–60]

Checklist.

2809 **Powell, D.,** 1953: no.188.

CLARK, JOHN WILLIS, 1833–1910

2810 **[Bartholomew, Augustus Theodore** and **C. Gordon]** *comp.* 'A short bibliography of J. W. Clark' *in* Fasciculus Ioanni Willis Clark dicatus. Cambridge, 1909. p.570.

Chronol. checklist, 1857–1909, signed A. T. B. and C. G.

CLARKE, AUSTIN, 1896–

2811 **MacManus, Michael Joseph.** Bibliographies of Irish writers, no.8. Austin Clarke. Dublin Mag new ser 10:41–3 Ap/Je '35.

TP transcrs., discursive collations, and notes on 8 first ed., 1917–32.

2812 **Miller, Liam,** *comp.* 'The books of Austin Clarke, a checklist' *in* Montague, John and L. Miller, *ed.* A tribute to Austin Clarke on his seventieth birthday. . . . [Dublin, 1966] p.23–7.

Chronol. checklist of 31 items, 1917–66, with some bibliogr. notes; rev. from Dubliner v.6 '63.

CLARKE, THOMAS JAMES, fl.1916

2813 **O'Hegarty, Patrick Sarsfield.** Bibliographies of 1916 and the Irish revolution. [VI. The O'Rahilly. VII. Thomas J. Clarke. VIII. Constance Gore-Booth, countess de Markevicz. IX. Michael O'Hanrahan] Dublin Mag new ser 11:57–9 Jl/S '36.

TP transcrs., collations, and bibliogr. notes on first ed.

CLERK OF TRANENT, c.1450?

2814 **Geddie, William,** 1912: no.2034.

CLEVELAND, JOHN, 1613–1658

2815 **Withington, Eleanor.** The canon of John Cleveland's poetry. N.Y. Pub Lib Bull 67:307–27, 377–94 My, Je '63.

2816 **Woodward, Daniel H.** Notes on the canon of John Cleveland's poetry. N.Y. Pub Lib Bull 68:517–24 Oc '64.

Bibliogr. notes and descrs. *passim.*

2816a **Morris, Brian R.** John Cleveland, 1613–1658, a bibliography of his poems, London, Bibliographical society, 1967. vi,54[55–61]p. port., diagrs. 25cm.

Bibliogr. of early ed. of 4 works, with TP transcrs., collations, bibliogr. notes and refs., and locations of copies; no index. 'Contents of the editions' (p.[55–61]).

CLOUGH, ARTHUR HUGH, 1819–1861

2817 **Faverty, Frederic Everett,** *ed.* 1956: no.2016.

2818 **Houghton, Walter Edwards.** The prose works of Arthur Hugh Clough: a checklist and calendar. . . . N.Y. Pub Lib Bull 64:377–94 Jl '60.

'The checklist' (p.378–92): 68 items, 1835–60, with descr. and bibliogr. notes; and appendix (p.392–4) of 'essays or speeches which Clough *may* have written'.

2819 **Gollin, Richard M., W. E. Houghton,** and **M. Timko.** Arthur Hugh Clough, a descriptive catalogue: poetry, prose, biography and criticism. N.Y. Pub Lib Bull 70:554–85 N '66; 71:55–8, 173–99 Ja, Mr '67.

CLUTTON-BROCK, ARTHUR, 1868–1924

See Brock, Arthur Clutton-.

COBBETT, WILLIAM, 1762–1835

2820 **Melville, Lewis,** *pseud.* 'Bibliography of first editions of William Cobbett' *in* The life and letters of William Cobbett in England & America. . . . London, 1913. V.2, p.[265]–309.

First pub. as 'Cobbett bibliography' N&Q serII 6:1–3, 22–5, 62–4, 84–6, 122–5, 142–4, 183–5 Jl–S '12; cf. L.L.K. *ib.* 6:217 S '12; F. L. Tavare 6:398 N '12.

2820a **Cole, George Douglas Howard.** 'A brief bibliography of Cobbett's writings' *in* The life of William Cobbett . . . 3d ed., rev. London, 1947. p.438–45.

Based on and supplementing Melville.

2821 **Pearl, Morris Leonard.** William Cobbett, a bibliographical account of his life and times. London, G. Cumberlege, O.U.P., 1953. vii,266p. 23cm.

Chronol. list of early ed., 1792–1835, with short TP transcrs., some bibliogr. notes, and locations of copies.

Rev: TLS 26 Je '53:419; G. D. H. Cole, M. L. Pearl *ib.* 17 Jl '53:468; Listener 50:699 '53; R.S.L. Étude Angl 8:77 '53.

2821a **Manks, Dorothy S.** Some early American horticultural writers and their works I. John Adlum and William Cobbett. Huntia 2:59–110 '65.

Cobbett (p.65–110): TP facsims., collations, and bibliogr. notes and refs. for early ed. of 10 agricultural works.

COBDEN, RICHARD, 1804–1865

2822 **Axon, William Edward Armytage.** 'Cobden bibliography' *in* Cobden as citizen, a chapter in Manchester history. . . . London, 1907. p.[155]–99.

Classified chronol. checklist of works and ana; no index. Repr. from N&Q serIo 1:481–2 Je '04; 2:3–5, 62–3, 103–5, 142–3 Jl,Ag '04.

COCKER, EDWARD, 1631–1675

2823 **Heal, Ambrose.** 'Cocker's Arithmetick'. N&Q 156:82–4,100–3 F '29; cf.
E. E. Newton *ib.* 156:214–5 Mr '29.

'A list of the editions of Cocker's Arithmetick and the publishers' (p.83–4, 100–3):
checklist with some bibliogr. notes.

COLERIDGE, SAMUEL TAYLOR, 1772–1834

2825 **Kennedy, Virginia Wadlow** and **M. N. Barton.** Samuel Taylor Coleridge;
a selected bibliography of the best available editions of his writings, of
biographies and criticisms of him, and of references showing his relations
with contemporaries, for student and teachers. Baltimore, Enoch Pratt
free library, 1935. vii,151p. 24cm.

2826 **Raysor, Thomas Middleton,** *ed.*, 1956: no.2015.

2827 **Shepherd, Richard Herne.** The bibliography of Coleridge; a bibliographical
list, arranged in chronological order, of the published and privately-
printed writings in verse and prose of Samuel Taylor Coleridge . . . by the
late Richard Herne Shepherd; revised, corrected and enlarged by W. F.
Prideaux. London, F. Hollings, 1900. x,95p. 20cm.

Repr. from N&Q ser 8 7:361–3, 401–3, 443–5, 482–3, 502–3 My–Je '95.

2828 **Haney, John Louis.** A bibliography of Samuel Taylor Coleridge. Philadelphia, Ptd. for private circulation, 1903. xv,144p. port. 25cm.

Classified chronol. checklist of 'All editions (English, continental, and American) of
Coleridge's works . . .' with ana and marginalia, and 'Table of editions' (p.144).

2829 **English association,** 1912: no.650.

2830 **Catalogue** of a unique Coleridge collection. [London, C. Whittingham,
1913] 127p. facsims. 29cm.

2831 **Wise, Thomas James.** A bibliography of the writings in prose and verse of
Samuel Taylor Coleridge. London, Ptd. for the Bibliographical society by
R. Clay, 1913. x,316p. illus., facsims. 23cm.

2832 —— Coleridgeiana, being a supplement. . . . 1919. 38p. 23cm.

Quasifacsim. TP transcrs. and facsims., collations, and bibliogr. notes on editiones principes, contribs. to periodical literature, and collected editions; the Supplement consists
chiefly of criticism and biography; no index.

2833 —— 1927: no.5171.

2834 **Exeter. University college of the south west of England.** S. T. Coleridge.
. . . centenary exhibition. . . . [Exeter, 1934] 19p. illus., facsims. 18cm.

2835 **British museum. Dept. of printed books.** Coleridge; an excerpt from the
General catalogue of printed books. . . . London, Ptd. by W. Clowes,
1947. 36 col. 34cm.

COLLIER, JOHN, 1901–

2840 **Gawsworth, John,** *pseud.* [1933]: no.687.

COLLINS, CHARLES ALLSTON, 1828–1873

2841 **Ellis, Stuart Marsh.** 'List of works by Charles Allston Collins' *in* Wilkie Collins, LeFanu and others. London, 1931. p.73. (Reissued 1951)
Chronol. checklist of 6 items, 1859–66.

COLLINS, MICHAEL, 1890–1922

2842 **O'Hegarty, Patrick Sarsfield,** 1937: no.3533.

COLLINS, MORTIMER, 1827–1876

2843 **Ellis, Stuart Marsh.** 'List of works by Mortimer Collins' *in* Wilkie Collins, LeFanu and others. London, 1931. p.110–16. (Reissued 1951)
Chronol. checklist of 29 items, 1855–91.

COLLINS, WILLIAM, 1721–1759

2844 **Bronson, Walter Cochrane,** *ed.* 'Bibliography' *in* The poems of William Collins. Boston, 1898. p.lxxix–lxxxv.
Chronol. checklist, with some bibliogr. notes and locations of copies.

2845 **Winchester college. Library.** William Collins . . . [exhibition catalogue. Winchester, Wykeham pr., 1959] 14p. 25cm. Covertitle.
Comp. by Jack Blakiston.

COLLINS, WILLIAM WILKIE, 1824–1889

2846 **Cordasco, Francesco G. M.** and **K. W. Scott.** Wilkie Collins and Charles Reade, a bibliography of critical notices and studies. New York, Long island U.P., 1949. vi,7p. 24cm.

2847 **Stevenson, Lionel,** *ed.,* 1964: no.1705.

2848 **Sadleir, Michael Thomas Hervey,** 1922: no.1706.

2849 **Williams, Iolo Aneurin,** 1924: no.633.

2849a **Ellis, Stuart Marsh.** 'Note' *in* Wilkie Collins, LeFanu and others. London, 1931. p.53. (Reissued 1951)
Addenda to Sadleir: no.1706.

2850 **Parrish, Morris Longstreth** and **E. V. Miller.** Wilkie Collins and Charles Reade; first editions (with a few exceptions) in the library at Dormy house. . . . London, Constable, 1940. x,354p. illus., ports., facsims. 26cm.
'Bibliography, Wilkie Collins' (p.6–161); 'Bibliography of Charles Reade' (p.165–310); 'Contributions by Wilkie Collins' (p.323–5); 'Addenda' (p.331–40): quasifacsim. TP transcrs., collations, and bibliogr. notes.
Rev: D. A. Randall Pa Bib Soc Am 35:168–71 '41.

2851 **Andrew, R. V.** A Wilkie Collins check-list. Eng Stud Africa 3:79–98 Mr '60.
Alphabetical checklist (p.82–94) with chronol. list (p.94–8) of Collins' works in early ed.

COLMAN, GEORGE, 1732–1794

2855 **Page, Eugene Richard.** 'A chronological list of all acted plays written or altered by George Colman' *in* George Colman the elder, essayist, dramatist and theatrical manager, 1732–1794. New York, 1935. p.[303]–5.
Checklist of 45 items; a checklist of all his works is in 'Bibliography' (p.[309]–23).

CONRAD, JOSEPH, *pseud. of* JOSEF TÈODOR KONRAD KORZENIOWSKI, 1857–1924

2856 **Beebe, Maurice.** Criticism of Joseph Conrad; a selected checklist with an index to studies of separate works. Mod Fict Stud 1:30–45 F '55.

2857 **Lohf, Kenneth A.** and **E. P. Sheehy.** Joseph Conrad at mid-century; editions and studies, 1895–1955. Minneapolis, University of Minnesota pr.; [London, O.U.P.] 1957. xiii,114p. 24cm.
Classified checklist with some bibliogr. notes, chiefly useful for ana.
Rev: W. White Bull Bib 22:78 '57; TLS 29 N '57; J. H. Miller Mod Lang N 73:131–2 '57; L. Gurko Am Schol 27:128–30 '57.

2858 **Bojarski, Edmund A.** and **H. T. Bojarski.** Joseph Conrad, a bibliography of masters' theses and doctoral dissertations, 1917–1963. Lexington, University of Kentucky libraries, 1964. 33p. 28cm. (Kentucky university libraries. Occasional contributions, no.157) (Not seen)

2859 **Sanger, Vincent.** Bibliographies of younger reputations. Bkmn 35:70 Mr '12.

2860 **Walpole, sir Hugh Seymour.** 'A short bibliography of Joseph Conrad's principal writings' *in* Joseph Conrad. London, 1916. p.121–2.
'American bibliography' (p.123–4): checklist of American ed.

2861 **Eno, Sara W.** Joseph Conrad, a contribution toward a bibliography. Bull Bib 9:137–9 Ap '17.

2862 **Bibliographies** of modern authors. Joseph Conrad. Lond Merc 2no10:476–7 Ag '20.

2863 **Wise, Thomas James.** A bibliography of the writings of Joseph Conrad, 1895–1920. London, Ptd. for private circulation only by R. Clay, 1920. xv,107p. port., facsims. 23cm.

2864 —— [**Same**]: 2d ed., rev. and enl. London, 1921. (Repr. London, Dawsons, 1964) xv,125p. port., facsims. 23cm.
Catalogue of editiones principes, uncollected contribs. to periodical literature, and Conradiana, with TP transcrs. and facsims., collations, and bibliogr. notes; no index. *See* no.2867.

2865 **Stauffer, Ruth M.** 'Conrad's works' *in* Joseph Conrad, his romantic-realism. Boston, 1922. p.92–101.

2866 'A short bibliography of Joseph Conrad's works' *in* Joseph Conrad, a sketch. . . . New York [1924] p.[39]–45.

2867 **Wise, Thomas James.** A Conrad library; a catalogue of printed books, manuscripts, and autograph letters by Joseph Conrad . . . collected by Thomas James Wise. London, Ptd. for private circulation only, 1928. xvii,66[2]p. port., facsims. 27cm.

2868 **Keating, George T.** A Conrad memorial library; the collection of George T. Keating. Garden City, N.Y., Doubleday, Doran, 1929. xvi,448p. illus., ports., facsims. 27cm.

2869 **Babb, James T.** A check list of additions to a Conrad memorial library, 1929–38. Yale Univ Lib Gaz 13:30–40 Jl '38.

2870 **Polish library,** LONDON. Joseph Conrad, 1857–1924. [Catalogue of an exhibition organised by the Polish library . . . compiled by Janina Zabielska. London, 1956] 24p. 26cm. (Duplicated typescript)

Short-title catalogue of 202 items, including many Polish ed.

2871 **Maser, F. E.** A collection of the books of Joseph Conrad presented to Temple university. Temple Univ Lib Bull 2n02: 21p. '57. (Not seen)

2872 **Krzyżanowski, Ludwik.** 'Joseph Conrad, a bibliographical note' *in* Joseph Conrad; centennial essays. New York, 1960. p.163–74.

Addenda, chiefly of Polish material, to Lohf and Sheehy (no.2857).

CONYBEARE, JOHN, 1691–1755

2875 **Dredge, John Ingle,** 1889–99: no.886.

COOK, JAMES, 1728–1779

2876 **New South Wales. Public library,** SYDNEY. Bibliography of captain James Cook . . . comprising the collections in the Mitchell library and general reference library, the private collections of William Dixon, . . . and J. A. Ferguson, . . . and items of special interest in the National library, Canberra, the Australasian pioneer club, Sydney, and in the collection of the Kurnell trust. Sydney, Govt. print., 1928. 172p. 25cm.

2877 **Holmes, sir Maurice Gerald.** An introduction to the bibliography of captain James Cook, R.N. London, F. Edwards, 1936. 59p. 23cm.

2878 —— Captain James Cook . . . a bibliographical excursion. London, F. Edwards, 1952. 103p. facsims. 25cm.

Rev. and enl. ed. of previous item; TP transcrs., collations, and bibliogr. notes on early ed. and ana.

Rev: TLS 4 Ap '52:244; P. M. Hill Bk Coll 1:132–3 '52; R. A. Skelton Library ser5 7:220–1 '52.

2879 **Spence, Sydney Alfred.** Captain James Cook . . . a bibliography of his voyages, to which is added other works relating to his life, conduct & nautical achievements, Mitcham, 1960. 50p. ports. 28cm.

COOPER, ANTHONY ASHLEY, 3D EARL OF SHAFTESBURY, 1671–1713

2880 **Elson, Charles.** [Checklist] *in* Wieland and Shaftesbury. New York, 1913. p.129–31.

2880a **Alderman, William E.** English editions of Shaftesbury's Characteristics. Pa Bib Soc Am 61:315–34 '67.

'Authenticated English editions' (p.332–4): chronol. checklist, 1711–1964.

COPLAND, ROBERT, fl.1508–1547

2880b **Heseltine, George Coulehan,** *ed.* 'English editions of the Kalendar of shepherds' *in* The kalendar & compost of shepherds. London, 1931. p.176.

Chronol. checklist of 19 items, 1503–1892.

COPPARD, ALFRED EDGAR, 1878–1957

2881 **Schwartz, Jacob.** The writings of Alfred Edgar Coppard; a bibliography. London, Ulysses bookshop, 1931. 73p. facsims. 23cm.

Not superseded by Fabes; bibliogr. descrs. and notes, followed by further notes by Coppard; no index.

Rev: TLS 7 My '31:368; Lond Merc 24:163 '31; viscount Esher Bk Coll Q 3:78–9 '31.

2882 **Fabes, Gilbert Henry.** The first editions of A. E. Coppard, A. P. Herbert and Charles Morgan, with values and bibliographical points. London, Myers [1933] 154p. 23cm.

Coppard (p.3–52) Herbert (p.55–125) Morgan (p.129–45): TP transcrs., and bibliogr. notes.

Rev: TLS 21 S '33:634.

CORVO, BARON, *pseud. of* FREDERICK ROLFE, 1860–1913
See Rolfe, Frederick William Serafino Austin Lewis Mary (baron Corvo).

CORY, WILLIAM JOHNSON, 1823–1892

2883 **Carter, John Waynflete.** A hand-list of the printed works of William Johnson, afterwards Cory. Cambridge Bib Soc Trans 1pt1:69–87 '49.

Chronol. checklist, 1842–98, of 23 items, with discursive bibliogr. notes, and 'Some contributions to books and periodicals' (p.85–6).

2883a —— [**Same**]: Addenda and corrigenda. Cambridge Bib Soc Trans 4pt4:318–20 '67.

2884 ——, *comp.* 'A list of William Cory's printed works' *in* MacKenzie, Faith C., lady. William Cory, a biography. . . . London, 1950. p.189–92.

Checklist of 21 items, with notes based on previous item.

COSIN, BP. JOHN, 1594–1672

2885 **Hanson, Laurence William.** John Cosin's Collection of private devotions 1627. Library ser5 13:282–7 D '58.

Full descr. and discussion of 3 ed., with locations of copies.

COTTON, CHARLES, 1630–1687
See under Walton, Izaak, 1593–1683.

COTTON, JOHN, 1802–1849

2886 **Casey, Maie.** John Cotton, 1802–1849. J Soc Bib Nat Hist 4:85–91 Ja '63.

'John Cotton's publications' (p.91): checklist of 4 items.

COUCH, SIR ARTHUR THOMAS QUILLER-, 1863–1944
See Q, pseud.

COURTHOPE, WILLIAM JOHN, 1842–1917

2887 **Herford, Charles Harold.** William John Courthope. Eng Illus Mag new ser 31:419–22 Jl '04.
'Bibliography' (p.422): checklist of works; works edited; and ana.

COWELL, JOHN, C.1554–1611

2888 **Dredge, John Ingle,** 1889–99: no.886.

COWLEY, ABRAHAM, 1618–1667

2889 **Loiseau, Jean.** 'Bibliographie . . . L'œuvre de Cowley' in Abraham Cowley, sa vie, son œuvre. Paris, 1931. p.[655]–73.
Classified chronol. checklists, with checklist of ana, p.674–87.

2890 **Mead, Herman Ralph.** Two issues of Cowley's Vision. Pa Bib Soc Am 45:77–81 '51.
Quasifacsim. TP transcrs., and facsims., collations, and bibliogr. notes.

2891 **Perkin, M. R.,** 1964: no.180.

COWLEY, HANNAH, 1743–1809

2892 **Norton, Jane Elizabeth.** Some uncollected authors xvi: Hannah Cowley, 1743–1809. Bk Coll 7no1:68–76 '58.
Quasifacsim. TP transcrs., collations, and bibliogr. notes on 13 plays and 5 poems.

2893 **Todd, William Burton.** Hannah Cowley: re-impressions, not reissues. *ib.* 7no3:301 '58.

COWPER, WILLIAM, 1731–1800

2894 **Hartley, Lodwick Charles.** William Cowper, a list of critical and bibliographical studies published from 1895 to 1949. North Carolina State Coll Rec 49:1–24 F '50.

2895 —— William Cowper, the continuing revaluation; an essay and a bibliography of Cowperian studies from 1895 to 1960. Chapel Hill, University of North Carolina pr., 1960. x,159p. 25cm.

2895a **Ryskamp, Charles.** 'Memoir of William Cowper . . .' by Maurice J. Quinlan. . . . [review] Mod Philol 53:67–70 Ag '55.
'. . . a tentative bibliography of the first ∩ editions . . .' (p.68–70).

2896 **Russell, Norma Hull (Hodgson).** A bibliography of William Cowper. Oxford, Oxford bibliographical society, 1963. xii,339p. ports., facsims. 24cm.
'Concerned with everything written by and about Cowper and published during his lifetime and the thirty-seven years following his death in 1800.' Classified bibliogr. with Cowper's original works and translations arranged chronol.; quasifacsim. TP transcrs., collations, locations of copies, and bibliogr. notes.
Rev: S. Baker Pa Bib Soc Am 58:318–20 '64; TLS 14 My '64:421; E. A. Bloom Mod Lang R 59:463–4 '64.

COX, WALTER, C.1770–1837

2897 **Cassedy, James.** Watty Cox and his publications. Bib Soc Ireland Pubs 5no2:19–38 '35.

'Works published or projected' (p.25–38): TP transcrs., with some bibliogr. notes.

COXE, HENRY OCTAVIUS, 1811–1881

2898 **R., J. N. B.** A large-hearted librarian; portrait of a victorian bibliophile. Desiderata 2no41:1–3 '49.

'A list of Coxe's own works' (p.3): chronol. checklist, 1841–73, of 12 items.

CRABBE, GEORGE, 1754–1832

2898a **[Anderson, John Parker]** *comp.* 'Bibliography' *in* Kebbel, Thomas E. Life of George Crabbe. London, 1888. p.[i]–v at end.

2899 **[Ganz, Charles]** *ed.* Souvenir of the Crabbe celebration and catalogue of the exhibits at Aldeburgh, Suffolk. [Lowestoft, Powell, print. 1905] iv. (unpaged) illus., facsims. 23cm.

Superficial checklist of works exhibited, and some TP facsims.

2900 **Bartholomew, Augustus Theodore,** *comp.* 'Bibliography of Crabbe's poems' *in* Ward, Adolphus W., *ed.* Poems. Cambridge, 1905–7. V.3, p.554–67[1]

Chronol. checklist, 1772–1906, of 77 items, with some bibliogr. notes.

2901 **Huchon, René Louis.** 'Bibliography' *in* George Crabbe and his times, 1754–1832, a critical and biographical study. Translated . . . by Frederick Clarke. London, 1907. p.518–30. (Repr. 1968)

English trans. of Un poète réaliste anglais, George Crabbe. Paris, 1906.

Chronol. checklist of ed., and principal ana.

2902 **Batdorf, Franklin P.** Notes on three editions of George Crabbe's Tales. Pa Bib Soc Am 44:276–9 '50.

Quasifacsim. TP transcrs., collations, and bibliogr. notes on 3 ed. not previously listed.

2903 **Aldeburgh festival of music and the arts, 7th, 1954.** George Crabbe, 1754–1832; bicentenary celebrations: exhibition of works and manuscripts held at Moot hall, Aldeburgh. Aldeburgh, Festival committee and Suffolk institute of archæology, 1954. 43p. facsims. 22cm.

Repr. in Suffolk Inst Archæol Proc 26pt2:98–136 '53.

TP facsims. and collations of first ed.; some bibliogr. notes.

2904 **Matthews, D. A.,** 1954: no.168.

CRACKANTHORPE, HUBERT, 1870–1896

2910 **Harris, Wendell V.** A bibliography of writings about Hubert Crackanthorpe. Eng Lit Transit 6no2:85–91 '63.

2911 **Danielson, Henry.** Bibliographies of modern authors, no.1. Hubert Crackanthorpe. Bkmns J 1no1:8 '19.
TP transcrs., collations, and bibliogr. notes on 5 first ed.

2912 ——, 1921: no.680.

CRAIGIE, PEARL MARY TERESA (RICHARDS), 1867–1906
See Hobbes, John Oliver, pseud.

CRAIGIE, SIR WILLIAM ALEXANDER, 1867–1957

2913 **A memoir** and a list of the published writings of sir William A. Craigie. Oxford, Clarendon pr., 1952. 38p. port. 23cm.
'Published writings' (p.21–31): classified checklist.

CRAIK, MRS. DINAH MARIA, 1826–1887

2914 **Skerl, M.,** 1949: no.199.

CRANE, WALTER, 1845–1915

2915 **Massé, Gertrude C. E.** A bibliography of first editions of books illustrated by Walter Crane. London, Chelsea pub. co., 1923. 59p. port. 23cm.
Chronol. checklist, 1862–1915, with some bibliogr. notes.

CRASHAWE, WILLIAM, 1572–1626

2916 **Wallis, Peter John.** William Crashawe, the Sheffield puritan; pt.IV: about books. Hunter Archæol Soc Sheffield Trans 8pt5:245–62 '63.
'William Crashawe's writings' (p.247–57): checklist of early ed. of 39 items, including ms. letters, with some bibliogr. notes, and STC nos.

CRAWFORD, FRANCIS MARION, 1854–1909

2917 **Bennett, Edward.** Francis Marion Crawford. Eng Illus Mag new ser 31: 504–6, 510 Ag '04.
'Bibliography' (p.506, 510): checklist of works, 1882–1903; plays; and ana.

CREIGHTON, BP. MANDELL, 1843–1901

2918 **Shaw, William Arthur.** A bibliography of the historical writings of dr. Creighton . . . dr. Stubbs . . . dr. S. R. Gardiner, and the late lord Acton. Edited for the Historical society. London, Offices of the society, 1903. 63p. 22cm.
Classified chronol. checklists.

CROCKETT, SAMUEL RUTHERFORD, 1860–1914

2919 **Bizet, George.** S. R. Crockett. Eng Illus Mag new ser 29:644–6 S '03.
'Bibliography' (p.646): checklist of works; works edited or introduced by; and ana.

CROKER, JOHN WILSON, 1780–1857

2920 **Brightfield, Myron Franklin.** 'A bibliography of Croker's writings' *in* John Wilson Croker. Berkeley, Calif., 1940. p.451–9.

Chronol. checklist of separate pubs., 1803–71, and articles in the Quarterly review, 1809–54.

CROMWELL, OLIVER, 1599–1658

2921 **Abbott, Wilbur Cortez.** A bibliography of Oliver Cromwell; a list of printed materials relating to Oliver Cromwell. . . . Cambridge, Harvard U.P.; [London, H. Milford, O.U.P.] 1929. xxviii,540p. ports. 25cm.

Annotated chronol. checklist of works mentioning Cromwell, including Cromwell's official pubs.

Rev: TLS 14 N '29:921; A. W. P[ollard] Library ser4 11:238–40 '30; C. L. Grose J Mod Hist 2:305–7 '30.

2922 **Hardacre, Paul H.** Writings on Oliver Cromwell since 1940. J Mod Hist 33:1–14 Mr '61.

CROSSE, HENRY, fl.1603

2923 **Hummel, Ray Orvin.** Henry Crosse's Vertue's commonwealth. Pa Bib Soc Am 43:196–9 '49.

Descr. and discussion of STC 6070–1, and anr. issue.

CROWNE, JOHN, 1640?–1703?

2924 **Winship, George Parker.** The first Harvard playwright; a bibliography of the restoration dramatist John Crowne. . . . Cambridge, Ptd. at the Harvard U.P. for E. H. Wells, New York, 1922. 21p. 23cm.

Repr. from Harvard Lib N 2:46–52 Oc '20. Alphabetical title catalogue with TP transcrs. and some bibliogr. notes; no index.

CRUDEN, ALEXANDER, 1701–1770

2925 **Abrahams, Aleck.** Alexander Cruden's bibliography. N&Q ser12 11:208 S '22.

Chronol. checklist of 10 items, 1740–55.

CRUIKSHANK, GEORGE, 1792–1878

2926 **Stephens, Frederic G.** 'Chronological list of the principal books illustrated by George Cruikshank' *in* A memoir of George Cruikshank. London, 1891. p.[132]–42.

2927 **Marchmont, Frederick,** *pseud.* The three Cruikshanks, a bibliographical catalogue, describing more than 500 works . . . illustrated by Isaac, George, & Robert Cruikshank. London, W. T. Spencer, 1897. ii,128,xviip. illus., facsims. 23cm.

2928 **Douglas, Richard John Hardy.** The works of George Cruikshank classified and arranged with references to Reid's catalogue and their approximate values. London, Ptd. by J. Davy, 1903. vi,301p. front. 27cm.

2929 **Harvard university. Library. Widener collection.** A catalogue of the works illustrated by George Cruikshank and Isaac and Robert Cruikshank in the library of Harry Elkins Widener, by A. S. W. Rosenbach. Philadelphia, Privately ptd., 1918. 279p. illus. 29cm.

2930 **Cohn, Albert Mayer.** A bibliographical catalogue of the printed works illustrated by George Cruikshank. London, Longmans, Green, 1914. 226p. 26cm.
See no.2934.

2931 —— Catalogue of . . . collection of the works of George Cruikshank . . . with a representative selection of works illustrated by Isaac and Isaac Robert Cruikshank; works illustrated by Thomas Rowlandson . . . sold by auction by messrs. Sotheby, Wilkinson & Hodge. . . . London, Riddle, Smith & Duffus, 1920. 155p. 26cm.

2932 **Clark, William Andrews,** 1921–3: no.3069.

2933 **Woodbury, John P.,** 1922: no.1744.

2934 **Cohn, Albert Mayer.** George Cruikshank; a catalogue raisonné of the work executed during the years 1806–1877, with collations, notes, approximate values, facsimiles and illustrations. London, Office of The bookman's journal, 1924. (First pub. 1914) xvi,375p. port., plates (1 col.) facsims. 30cm.
'Printed books' (p.3–244): items 1–863; author list, with bibliogr. notes.
Rev: H.M.H. Library ser4 5:282–4 '24.

2935 **Holbrook, John Pinckney.** A Cruikshank catalogue raisonné; notes and corrections to Albert Cohn's George Cruikshank . . . 1924. Pa Bib Soc Am 41:144–7 '47.

CUDWORTH, RALPH, 1617–1688
2940 **Passmore, John A.** 'A Cudworth bibliography' *in* Ralph Cudworth, an interpretation. Cambridge, 1951. p.[114]–18.
Chronol. checklist of works and ana.

CUMBERLAND, RICHARD, 1732–1811
2941 **Williams, Stanley Thomas.** 'Cumberland's work' *in* Richard Cumberland, his life and dramatic works. New Haven, 1917. p.331–6.
Chronol. checklist of dramatic and non-dramatic first ed.

CURLING, HENRY, 1803–1864
2942 **Tillotson, A.** List of books by Henry Curling. Bk Hndbk 1no8/9:454 '50.

CURLL, EDMUND, 1675–1747
See under Presses and Printing.

CUSACK, MARY FRANCES, 1830–1899
2943 **Byard, Edwin John.** [Checklist of works of Mary Frances Cusack, the nun of Kenmare] Irish Bk Lover 6:134 Mr '15.

DALRYMPLE, SIR DAVID, LD. HAILES, 1726–1792

2944 **Carnie, Robert Hay.** Lord Hailes's contributions to contemporary magazines. Stud Bib 9:233–44 '57.
Annotated checklist: (p.238–44).

DALTON, JOHN, 1766–1844

2945 **Smyth, Albert Leslie.** John Dalton, 1766–1844; a bibliography of works by and about him. [Manchester] Manchester U.P. [1966] xvi,114p. illus., ports., facsims. 25cm.

Classified checklist of 771 items, with some bibliogr. notes and locations of copies.

DANIEL, SAMUEL, 1562–1619

2946 **Sellers, Harry.** A bibliography of the works of Samuel Daniel, 1585–1623, with an appendix of Daniel's letters. Oxford Bib Soc Proc 2pt1:29–54 '27.

2947 —— [**Same**]: Supplementary note. *ib.* 2pt2:341–2 '28.

Chronol. bibliogr. of ptd. works and commendatory poems, with TP transcrs., collations, locations of copies, and bibliogr. notes; 'Index' (p.48).

2948 **Tannenbaum, Samuel Aaron.** Samuel Daniel, a concise bibliography. New York, 1942. viii,37p. 23cm. (Elizabethan bibliographies, no.25)

Classified checklist of works, and 'Biography and commentary' (p.20–32).

D'ARBLAY, FRANCES (BURNEY), 1752–1840
See Burney, Frances (mrs. D'Arblay).

DARLEY, GEORGE, 1795–1846

2949 **Abbott, Claude Colleer.** 'Bibliography of the works of George Darley' *in* The life and letters of George Darley, poet and critic. London, 1928. p.[271]–4. (Repr. Oxford [1967])

Checklist of poetry and drama; prose; and introductions, with some bibliogr. notes.

2950 **Woolf, Cecil.** Some uncollected authors XXVIII: George Darley, 1795–1846. Bk Coll 10no2:186–92 '61.

'Check-list of first editions of Darley's works' (p.189–92): quasifacsim. TP transcrs., collations and bibliogr. notes on 16 items.

DARWIN, CHARLES ROBERT, 1809–1882

2951 **Cambridge. University. Christ's college.** Darwin centenary; the portraits, prints and writings of Charles Robert Darwin, exhibited at Christ's college, Cambridge. [Cambridge, C.U.P., 1909] 47p. 21cm.

2952 **Lehigh university,** BETHLEHEM, PA. On the origin of species . . . a centennial exhibition. . . . [Bethlehem, Pa., 1959] 17p. 24cm. Covertitle.

2953 **Peckham, Morse,** *ed.* 'Bibliographical description' *in* The origin of species, by Charles Darwin; a variorum text. Philadelphia, 1959. p.787–[92]

Bibliogr. descr. and notes on early ed., followed by 'Illustrations of the principal binding variants'.

2954 **Todd, William Burton.** Variant issues of On the origin of species, 1859. Bk Coll 9no1:78 '60.

Distinction of binding variants.

2955 **Burton, M. E.,** 1964: no.91.

2956 **Freeman, Richard Broke.** Issues of the fifth edition of On the origin of species. Bk Coll 13no3:350 '64.

Distinction of 3 binding variants, supplementing Peckham.

2957 —— The works of Charles Darwin, an annotated bibliographical handlist. London, Dawsons, 1965. x,81p. illus., facsims. 22cm.

Chronol. checklist of English, and foreign, ed., with some bibliogr. notes.

Rev: TLS 15 Jl '65:604; W. LeFanu Bk Coll 14:389 '65; Pa Bib Soc Am 59:343 '65.

DASHWOOD, EDMÉE ELIZABETH MONICA (DE LA PASTURE), 1890–1943
See Delafield, E. M., pseud.

DAVENANT, CHARLES, 1656–1714

2960 **Waddell, David.** The writings of Charles Davenant, 1656–1714. Library ser5 11:206–12 S '56.

Checklists of pub., unpub., and attributed writings, with some bibliogr. notes.

D'AVENANT, SIR WILLIAM, 1606–1668

2961 **Harbage, Alfred Bennett.** 'Davenant's works' *in* Sir William Davenant, poet, venturer, 1606–1668. Philadelphia; London, 1935. p.288–94.
Checklist.

DAVIDSON, JOHN, 1857–1909

2962 **Moncrieff, Charles Kenneth Scott.** John Davidson. Lond Merc 4:299–300 Jl '21.

Checklist of 35 items, 1886–1909.

2963 **Stonehill, Charles Archibald** [1925]: no.682.

2964 **Lester, John Ashby.** John Davidson, a Grub street bibliography. Charlottesville, Va., University of Virginia pr. [1958] 30p. 18cm. (Virginia university bibliographical society. Secretary's news sheet, 40) (Not seen)

DAVIES, SIR JOHN, 1569–1626

2965 **Sparrow, John.** Some later editions of sir John Davies's Nosceteipsum. Library ser5 1:136–42 S '46.

Quasifacsim. TP transcrs., and discussion of 1688, 1689, 1697 ed.

DAVIES, JOHN, 1627?–1693

2966 **Tucker, Joseph Eagon.** John Davies of Kidwelly, 1627?–1693, translator from the French; with an annotated bibliography of his translations. Pa Bib Soc Am 44:119–52 '50.

'Bibliography of Davies' translations from the French' (p.141–52): chronol. checklist of 25 items, 1653–1736, with some bibliogr. notes.

DAVIES, RHYS, 1903–

2967 **Gawsworth, John,** *pseud.* [1932]: no.686.

DAVIES, WILLIAM HENRY, 1871–1940

2968 **Bibliographies** of modern authors. W. H. Davies. Lond Merc 1:122–3 N '19.

2969 **Murphy, Gwendolen.** Bibliographies of modern authors, no.3. W. H. Davies. Lond Merc 17:76–80 N '27; 17:301–4, 684–8 Ja, Ap '28.
Chronol. checklist of early ed., 1905–27, with TP transcrs., collations, and some bibliogr. notes, with a list of periodical contribs. (p.687).

2970 **Wilson, George Francis.** A bibliography of William Henry Davies. Bkmns J 5no6:202 '22; 6no7–8:29,59 '22.

2971 **Looker, Samuel J.** W. H. Davies, his later bibliography, 1922–1928. Bkmns J 17no10:123–7 '29.
Supplements Wilson.

DAVIS, THOMAS OSBORNE, 1814–1845

2972 **Schiller, Johannes Friedrich.** 'Bibliographie: A. Ausgaben' *in* Thomas Osborne Davis; ein irischer Freiheitssänger. Wien, 1915. p.[ix]–x.

2973 **Moody, Theodore Williams.** 'Writings of Davis' *in* Thomas Davis, 1814–45; a centenary address. . . . Dublin, 1945. p.61–3.
Discursive checklist of books and periodical contribs.

DEFOE, DANIEL, 1661?–1731

2976 **Wright, Thomas.** 'Mr. Lee's list of Daniel Defoe's works, with a few alterations by the author' *in* The life of Daniel Defoe. London, 1894. p.[405]–27.
The rev. & enl. ed., 1931, contains only a 'List of Defoe's principal works' (p.412–23).

2977 **Trent, W. P.** Bibliographical notes on Defoe. Nation 84:515–18 '07; 85:29–32, 180–3 '08. (Not seen)

2978 **Lloyd, William Supplee.** Catalogue of various editions of Robinson Crusoe and other books by and referring to Daniel Defoe. [Philadelphia, Shaw printing co., 1915] 43p. facsim. 23cm.

2979 **Dottin, Paul.** 'Liste des œuvres de De Foe' *in* Daniel De Foe et ses romans. . . . Paris; London, 1924. V.3, p.[799]–849. *See* no.2982

2980 **Hutchins, Henry Clinton.** Robinson Crusoe and its printing, 1719–1731; a bibliographical study. New York, Columbia U.P., 1925. xix,201p. 25cm.
Quasifacsim. TP transcrs., and facsims., collations, and bibliogr. notes, with distinction of issues. The collection is now in the University of Illinois library.
Rev: TLS 22 Oc '25:695; T. Scott Sat R Lit 2:339 '25; N&Q 149:467–8 '25; H. Williams Lib Assn Rec 4:24–5 '26.

2981 —— Two hitherto unrecorded editions of Robinson Crusoe. Library ser4 8:58–72 Je '27.

2982 **Dottin, Paul.** 'List of Daniel De Foe's works' *in* The life and surprising adventures of Daniel De Foe . . . translated from the French by Louise Ragan. New York [1929] p.267–304.

Trans. from v.1 of no.2979.

2983 **Fletcher, Edward Garland.** Some University of Texas copies of Robinson Crusoe, part 1. N&Q 164:4–5 Ja '33.

Collation and discussion of bibliogr. points.

2984 **Deneke, Otto.** Robinson Crusoe in Deutschland; die frühdrucke, 1720–1780. Göttingen, 1934. 38p. 25cm. (Not seen)

2985 **British museum. Dept. of printed books.** Daniel Defoe; an excerpt from the General catalogue of printed books. . . . London, Trustees of the British museum, 1953. 122 col. 35cm. Covertitle.

Rev: TLS 1 Ja '54:14.

2986 **Brigham, Clarence Saunders.** Bibliography of American editions of Robinson Crusoe to 1830. Am Antiqu Soc Proc 67:137–83 '58.

Checklist of 125 items, 1774–1830, with short collations, bibliogr. notes, and locations of copies.

2987 **Moore, John Robert.** A checklist of the writings of Daniel Defoe. Bloomington, Indiana U.P., 1960. xviii,254p. 24cm.

Checklist, with locations of copies and some bibliogr. notes, of 'Books, pamphlets, poems, and manuscripts', 'Undated works published posthumously', and 'Periodicals', with indexes.

Rev: D. Whitten Pa Bib Soc Am 55:164–7 '61 (with corrigenda and addenda); E. L. McAdam Sevent Cent Newsl 19:12–13 '61; G. H. Healey Philol Q 40:383–4 '61; W. B. Todd Bk Coll 10:493–4, 497–8 '61 (important); B. Fabian Archiv 201:460–1 '64.

2988 **Stoke Newington. Public libraries.** Daniel Defoe, 1660–1731; commemoration in Stoke Newington of the tercentenary of his birth: an exhibition of books, pamphlets, views, portraits and other items. . . . [Stoke Newington, 1960] 40p. 23cm.

Classified catalogue of 397 items (with duplicated addenda sheet of 8 items) with some bibliogr. notes.

Rev: J. Hayward. Commentary. Bk Coll 9:268–9 '60.

2989 **Foxon, David Fairweather.** Defoe, a specimen of a catalogue of English verse, 1701–1750. Library ser5 20:277–97 D '65.

Alphabetical checklist of Defoe's verse given as example of projected catalogue; collations, bibliogr. refs. and some notes; locations of copies for 142 items.

DEKKER, THOMAS, 1570?–1641?

2995 **Taylor, N. E.,** 1936: no.218.

2996 **Tannenbaum, Samuel Aaron.** Thomas Dekker, a concise bibliography. New York, 1939. 46p. 23cm. (Elizabethan bibliographies, no.7)
Classified checklist of 728 items of plays; masks; and entertainments; nondramatic works; selections; songs and music; and biography and commentary.

DELAFIELD, E. M., *pseud. of* EDMÉE ELIZABETH MONICA (DE LA PASTURE) DASHWOOD, 1890–1943

2997 **Gawsworth, John,** *pseud.* [1933]: no.687.

DE LA MARE, WALTER JOHN, 1873–1956

2998 **Bibliographies** of modern authors. Walter de la Mare. Lond Merc 1:122–3 N '19.

2999 **Danielson, Henry.** Bibliographies of modern authors, no.14. Walter de la Mare. Bkmns J 2no39–43:197, 214, 230, 248, 268 '20.

3000 ——, 1921: no.680.

3001 **Murphy, Gwendolen.** Bibliographies of modern authors, no.1. Walter de la Mare. Lond Merc 15:526–31, 635–9 Mr, Ap '27; 16:70–3 My '27.

3002 **Parsons, K. O.,** 1949: no.179.

3003 **Clark, Leonard.** A handlist of the writings in book form, 1902–1953, of Walter de la Mare. Stud Bib 6:197–218 '54.

3004 —— [Same]: Addendum: a checklist of Walter de la Mare. *ib.* 8:269–70 '56.
Chronol. checklist, 1902–53.

3005 **A list** of Walter de la Mare's contributions to the London Times literary supplement. Boston Univ Stud Eng 1no4:243–55 '55.
Chronol. checklist of 214 items, 1908–38.

3006 **National book league,** LONDON. Walter de la Mare; a checklist prepared on the occasion of an exhibition of his books and Mss. at the National book league. . . . [London] Published for the National book league at the C.U.P., 1956. xvi,55p. illus., port. 23cm.
Comp. by Leonard Clark.

DE MORGAN, WILLIAM FREND, 1839–1917

3010 **Keogh, Andrew,** 1910: no.622.

DENHAM, SIR JOHN, 1615–1669

3011 **Banks, Theodore Howard,** *ed.* [Bibliography] *in* The poetical works of sir John Denham. New Haven, 1928. p.[351]–6.
Chronol. checklists of collected ed., Cooper's hill, and Poems, with TP transcrs., and some bibliogr. notes.

DENNIS, JOHN, 1657–1734

3012 **Paul, Harry Gilbert.** 'List of Dennis's writings' *in* John Dennis, his life and criticism. New York, 1911. p.213–18.
Chronol. checklist, 1682–1817.

DENT, EDWARD JOSEPH, 1876–1957

3013 **Haward, Lawrence.** Edward J. Dent, a bibliography. Cambridge, Privately ptd. at the University pr. for King's college, 1956. 36p. 24cm.
Supersedes a list in Music R 7:242–62 N '46; classified checklist of 347 items.

DE QUINCEY, THOMAS, 1785–1859

3014 **Jordan, John E.** 'Loci critici' *in* Thomas de Quincey, literary critic. Berkeley, 1952. p.273–7.

3015 **Moreux, Françoise.** 'Appendice bibliographique' *in* Thomas de Quincey; la vie, l'homme, l'œuvre. Paris, 1964. p.[583]–610.
'L'œuvre' (p.[583]–90) and ana.

3016 **Houtchens, Carolyn Washburn** and **L. H. Houtchens,** *ed.* [1966]: no.2017.

3017 **Masson, David,** *ed.* 'Appendix, chronological and bibliographical' *in* The collected writings of Thomas De Quincey. Edinburgh, 1889–90. V.14 (1890), p.[375]–90. (Reissued London, 1897)

3018 **Manchester. Public libraries. Moss side branch.** Thomas De Quincey, a bibliography based upon the De Quincey collection in the Moss side library; compiled by J. A. Green. Manchester, 1908. vii,110p. 20cm.
Classified short-title catalogue of 796 items, including ana.

3019 **Axon, William Edward Armytage.** The canon of De Quincey's writings, with some references to his unidentified articles. Essay by Divers Hands; Roy Lit Soc Trans ser2 32:1–46 '14.
Checklist of contribs. to Blackwood's magazine (p.40–2).

DEVERE, AUBREY THOMAS, 1814–1902

3025 **Reilly, Mary Paraclita.** 'Bibliography' *in* Aubrey de Vere, victorian observer. [Lincoln, Neb., 1953] p.198–207.

3026 —— **[Same]:** Dublin; London [1956] p.167–74.
Classified checklist of works and ana.

DIBDIN, CHARLES, 1745–1814

3027 **Dibdin, Edward Rimbault.** A bibliographical account of the works of Charles Dibdin. N&Q ser9 8:39–40, 77–8, 197–9, 279–81 Jl–S '01; 9:421–3 My '02; 10:122–4, 243–5 Ag–S '02; 11:443–4 Je '03; 12:183–4, 283–5, 423–5, 462–3 S–D '03.
Checklist, 1760–1805, with some bibliogr. notes.

3027a **Kidson, Frank.** Bibliography of Charles Dibdin the elder. N&Q ser10 11:402–4 My '09; E. R. Dibdin *ib.* ser10 11:483–5 Je '09.
'Additions to the Dibdin bibliography' (p.403–4).

3028 **Dibdin, Edward Rimbault.** A Charles Dibdin bibliography. Liverpool, Privately ptd., 1937. 146p. 22cm.
Rev. version of N&Q checklist; discursive checklist, 1754–1905.

DIBDIN, THOMAS FROGNALL, 1776–1847

3029 **Cordasco, Francesco G. M.** A bibliography of Thomas Frognall Dibdin, author of the Bibliomania. Brooklyn, Long Island U.P., 1950. 12p. 23cm. (Eighteenth century bibliographical pamphlets, no.6)

3030 **Jackson, William Alexander.** An annotated list of the publications of the reverend Thomas Frognall Dibdin, D.D., based mainly on those in the Harvard college library, with notes of others. Cambridge, Mass., Ptd. for the Houghton library, 1965. 63p. port., facsims. 30cm.
Checklist of 106 items with some bibliogr. notes.
Rev: TLS 14 Ap '66:336; J. W. Carter Library ser5 21:352–4 '66.

3031 **Bond, W. H.** Jackson's Dibdin: a revised entry. Bk Coll 15no3:352–3 '66.
Jackson's no.98.

DICKENS, CHARLES JOHN HUFFAM, 1812–1870

3032 **Kitton, Frederick George.** Dickensiana, a bibliography of the literature relating to Charles Dickens and his writings. London, G. Redway, 1886. 56p. port. 19cm.

3032a **Carty, Charles F.** Some addenda to Kitton's Dickensiana. Lit Coll 12/14:43–6 '02/3.

3033 **Brooklyn. Public library.** Charles Dickens, 1812–1870; a list of books and of references to periodicals in the Brooklyn public library. Brooklyn, N.Y., 1912. 68p. 16cm.

3034 **Gummer, Ellis Norman.** 'List of German critical works on Dickens, 1870–1937' *in* Dickens' works in Germany, 1837–1937. Oxford, 1940. p.[175]–9.
'List of articles on Dickens in German periodicals, 1837–1870' (p.[180]–4).

3035 **Miller, William.** The Dickens student and collector; a list of writings relating to Charles Dickens and his works, 1836–1945. Cambridge, Mass., Harvard U.P.; London, Chapman & Hall, 1946. xii,351p. 22cm.

3036 —— **[Same]**: A second supplement to The Dickens student. . . . Hove, Sussex, Privately ptd., 1953. 15p. 22cm.

3037 **Stevenson, Lionel,** *ed.,* 1964: no.1705.

3050 **Fitzgerald, Percy Hetherington.** 'Bibliography of Pickwick' *in* The history of Pickwick . . . with a bibliography. London, 1891. p.[357]–75.

3051 **Kitton, Frederick George.** The novels of Charles Dickens, a bibliography and sketch. London, E. Stock, 1897. ix,245p. port. 18cm.
See no.3053.

3052 **Grego, Joseph.** Pictorial Pickwickiana; Charles Dickens and his illustrators. . . . London, Chapman and Hall, 1899. 2v. illus., facsims. 19cm.
Checklist, and bibliogr. notes throughout; no index.

3053 **Kitton, Frederick George.** The minor writings of Charles Dickens; a bibliography and sketch. London, E. Stock, 1900. xi,260p. 18cm.
The collection was presented to the London Guildhall library in 1908.

3054 —— The Dickens exhibition held at the Memorial hall, London. . . . Catalogue of exhibits. . . . London, Dickens fellowship [1903] 66p. 22cm.

3055 **Dickens' birthplace museum,** PORTSMOUTH. List of books, prints . . . memorials exhibited at Dickens' birthplace museum . . . by W. H. Saunders. Portsmouth, W. H. Barrell, 1904. 61p. illus., ports. 17cm.
See no.3065.

3056 **Thomson, Joseph Charles.** Bibliography of the writings of Charles Dickens. Warwick, J. Thomson, 1904. 108p. 22cm.

3057 **Wilkins, William Glyde.** First and early American editions of the works of Charles Dickens. Cedar Rapids, Ia., Privately ptd., 1910. 51p. facsims. 25cm.

3058 **Franklin club of St. Louis.** An exhibition of books, prints, drawings, manuscripts & letters commemorative of the centenary of Charles Dickens. . . . [St. Louis, 1912] vi,48[2]p. 18cm.

3059 **Victoria and Albert museum,** SOUTH KENSINGTON, LONDON. Dickens exhibition, March to October, 1912. [Rev. ed.] London, H.M.S.O., 1912. (First pub. with illus., 1912) 63p. 25cm.

3060 **Eckel, John C.** The first editions of the writings of Charles Dickens and their values; a bibliography. London, Chapman & Hall, 1913. xviii,296p. illus., port., facsims. 23cm.
See no.3079.

3061 **Fitzgerald, Percy Hetherington.** 'Dickens's own contributions to his two journals' *in* Memories of Dickens, with an account of Household words and All the year round. . . . Bristol; London [1913] p.365–71.

3062 **Grolier club,** NEW YORK. Catalogue of an exhibition of the works of Charles Dickens. . . . New York, 1913. 220p. 18cm.

3063 —— [Same]: with an introduction by Royal Cortissoz. New York, 1913. xxvi,230p. ports., facsims. 24cm.
Chronol. catalogue of 263 works, with bibliogr. notes.

3064 **Pierce, Gilbert Ashville.** 'A condensed bibliography of the writings of Charles Dickens, based upon the full bibliography prepared by Richard Herne Shepherd' *in* Dickens dictionary. . . . Rev. ed. with bibliography. Boston, 1914. p.588–94. (First pub. 1872; repr. New York, Kraus, 1965)

3065 **Dickens' birthplace museum,** PORTSMOUTH. List of books, prints . . . memorials exhibited at Dickens' birthplace museum. . . . [Anr. ed.] Compiled by Alfred A. Searle. Portsmouth, W. H. Barrell, 1914. (First ed. 1904) 71p. illus., ports., facsims. 16cm.

3066 **Geissendoerfer, J. Theodor.** 'Zweiter teil' *in* Dickens' Einfluss auf Ungern-Sternberg Hesslein, Stolle, Raabe und Ebner-Eschenbach. [New York] 1915. p.28–50.
Checklists of German translations, and of English ed. pub. in Germany.

3067 **Harvard university. Library. Widener collection.** A catalogue of the writings of Charles Dickens in the library of Harry Elkins Widener, by A. S. W. Rosenbach. Philadelphia, Privately ptd., 1918. 111p. 29cm.

3068 **Clark, William Andrews.** The library of William Andrews Clark, jr. The posthumous papers of the Pickwick club, by Charles Dickens. The Douglas-Austin copy, a bibliographical description. San Francisco, Ptd. by J. H. Nash, 1920. 12p. 27cm.

3069 —— The library of William Andrews Clark, jr. Cruikshank and Dickens. In two parts: part I. Cruikshank; part II. Dickens. Collated and compiled by Robert Ernest Cowan and William Andrews Clark. San Francisco, Ptd. by J. H. Nash, 1921–3. 2v. 27cm.

3070 **Stonehouse, John Harrison,** *comp.* 'A first bibliography of the reading editions of Charles Dickens's works' *in* Sikes and Nancy, a reading by Charles Dickens. . . . London, 1921. p.[49]–57.

3071 **Suzannet, Alain de.** 'Œuvres de Charles Dickens' *in* Catalogue d'un choix de livres imprimés . . . provenant de ma bibliothèque. . . . Biarritz, 1925. V.1. (83p.)
See no.3092.

3072 **Bath. Public libraries.** Charles Dickens; list of works, criticisms, etc., Dickensiana, biography and illustrations in books and periodicals in the libraries. [Bath] 1926. [4]p. 30cm. Caption title.

3073 **British museum. Dept. of printed books.** Charles Dickens, an excerpt from the General catalogue of printed books . . . . London, Ptd. by W. Clowes, 1926. 29p. 37cm.
See no.3098.

3074 **McCutcheon, George Barr.** The renowned collection of first editions of Charles Dickens and William Makepeace Thackeray, formed by George Barr McCutcheon. New York, American art association [1926] IV. (unpaged) illus., facsims. 24cm.

3075 **Eckel, John C.** Prime Pickwicks in parts; census with complete collation, comparison, and comment. New York, E. H. Wells; London, C. J. Sawyer, 1928. 91p. illus., facsims. 25cm.

3076 **Edgar, Herman LeRoy** and **R. W. G. Vail.** 'Early American editions of the works of Charles Dickens' *in* New York. Public library. Charles Dickens, his life. . . . New York, 1929. p.14–31.
Repr. from N.Y. Pub Lib Bull 33:291–319 My '29.

3077 **Lehmann, Frederick William.** A Charles Dickens collection . . . the library of Frederick W. Lehmann . . . sold . . . . New York, American art association, 1930. 173p. illus., facsims. 26cm.
1,050 items.

3078 **Hatton, Thomas.** Catalogue of the important collections, mainly of the writings of Charles Dickens and of other XIX century authors . . . sold by auction by messrs. Sotheby . . . on . . . the 30th of November, 1931. . . . London, Ptd. by J. Davy [1931] 39p. illus., facsims.(1 fold.) 29cm.
298 titles; *see also* no.1712.

3079 **Eckel, John C.** The first editions of the writings of Charles Dickens and their values; a bibliography. [2d ed.] rev. & enl. New York, M. Inman; London, Maggs, 1932. xvi,272p. illus., port., facsims.(part col.) 25cm.
See also no.3082.

3080 **Sawyer, John E. S.** and **F. J. H. Darton**, *comp.* 'The first editions, a bibliography' *in* Darton, Frederick J. H. Dickens: positively the first appearance, a centenary review, with a bibliography of Sketches of Boz. London, 1933. p.[129]–39.
Bibliogr. notes on the parts.

3081 **Hatton, Thomas** and **A. H. Cleaver.** A bibliography of the periodical works of Charles Dickens; bibliographical, analytical and statistical. London, Chapman & Hall, 1933. xix,383p. illus., facsims.(1 fold.) 26cm.
'. . . every bibliographical detail . . . relating to the first issue of the first editions of the thirteen important books written by . . . Dickens, and published in periodical form'; extensive facsims. of original wrappers.

Rev: TLS 22 Mr '34:220; A. de Suzannet *ib.* 12 Ap '34:268; J. W. Carter Pub Wkly 125:1303–6 '34; M. T. H. Sadleir Dickensian 30:147–50 '34; rf. *ib.* 30:193–6 '34.

3082 **Eckel, John C.** The library of John C. Eckel, Philadelphia . . . to be dispersed at public sale. . . . [New York] American art association, Anderson galleries, 1935. 88p. facsim. 24cm.

See nos.3075, 3079.

3083 **Miller, William** and **E. H. Strange.** The original Pickwick papers; the collation of a perfect first edition. Dickensian 31:35–40, 95–9, 284–6 '35.

3084 **A Dickens** library; exhibition catalogue of the Sawyer collection of the works of Charles Dickens. . . . [Letchworth] Privately ptd., 1936. 108p. illus., port., facsims. 24cm.

Foreword signed J. E. S. S[awyer].

3085 **Dyboski, Roman.** 'Dickens w Polsce' *in* Charles Dickens, życie i twórczość. Lwów [1936] p.[103]–7.

Checklist of Polish translations of Dickens' works.

3086 **Miller, William** and **E. H. Strange.** A centenary bibliography of the Pickwick papers. [London] Argonaut pr. [1936] 223p. illus., port., facsims. 22cm.

Rev: TLS 28 Mr '36:249–50.

3087 **Read, Newbury Frost.** The American editions of Pickwick. Dickensian 33:21–6 D '36.

Chronol. checklist, 1836–1935, of 127 items, with some bibliogr. notes.

3088 **Southwark. Public libraries and Cuming museum.** Catalogue of books . . . an exhibition arranged to commemorate publication of Pickwick papers by Charles Dickens in 1836. London, 1936. 27p. 18cm.

3089 **Victoria. Public library, museum, and national gallery,** MELBOURNE. . . . Dickens exhibition, 1936; guide to the books, autographs . . . exhibited in celebration of the centenary of the publication of the Pickwick papers. . . . Melbourne, Ptd. for the trustees by Fraser & Jenkinson, 1936. 18p. 22cm.

Comp. by Albert B. Foxcroft.

3090 **Pierce, Dorothy.** The stage versions of Dickens' novels. Bull Bib 16n01:10 S/D '36; 16n02–3:30–2, 52–4 Ja/Ap, My/Ag '37.

3091 **Hatton, Thomas,** *comp.* 'A bibliographical list of the original illustrations to the works of Charles Dickens, being those made under his supervision' *in* Nonesuch press. Retrospectus and prospectus; the Nonesuch Dickens. Bloomsbury, 1937. p.55–78.

3092 **Suzannet, Alain de.** Catalogue of a further portion of the well-known library . . . the celebrated collection of materials concerning Charles Dickens . . . Sotheby & co. . . . 11th of July, 1938. London, 1938. (Not seen)

3093 **Rand, Frank Hugh.** 'Adaptations' *in* Les adaptations théâtrales des romans de Dickens en Angleterre, 1837–1870. Paris, 1939. p.[185]–94.

3094 **Elkins, William McIntire.** The life and works of Charles Dickens, 1812–1870; an exhibition from the collection of William M. Elkins . . . held at the Free library. [Philadelphia] Free library of Philadelphia, 1940. xiii, 58p. illus., facsims. 26cm.

3095 **[Dexter, Walter]** A new Dickens bibliography. Dickensian 39:99–101, 149–53,173–5 Mr, Je, S '43; 40:36–8, 76–8, 143–5 D '43–Mr, Je '44.

3095a **Calhoun, Philo** and **H. J. Heaney.** Dickens' Christmas carol after a hundred years; a study in bibliographical evidence. Pa Bib Soc Am 39:271–317 '45.

'The known presentation copies . . . and a few dated copies of bibliographical interest' (p.310–15).

3096 **Collins, Philip Arthur William.** Dickens's periodicals; articles on education; an annotated bibliography. Leicester, Vaughan college, 1957. iii,36p. 20cm. Covertitle. (Duplicated typescript)

Classified checklist of articles in Household words, and All the year round; no index.

3097 **New York. Public library. Berg collection.** Reading for profit; the other career of Charles Dickens; an exhibition from the Berg collection, by John Gordan. New York, New York public library, 1958. 28p. port. 26cm.

Repr. from N.Y. Pub Lib Bull 62:425–42, 515–22 S, Oc '58.

Annotated catalogue illustrating Dickens as a reader in public.

3098 **British museum. Dept. of printed books.** Dickens; an excerpt from the General catalogue of printed books in the British museum. London, Ptd. by order of the trustees, 1960. [72]p. 35cm. Covertitle.

3099 **Texas. University. Humanities research center.** Catalogue of the Dickens collection at the University of Texas, compiled by Mary Callista Carr. Austin, Tex., 1961. ix,195p. illus., port., facsims. 26cm.

Classified short-title catalogue, with bibliogr. notes.

Rev: E. A. Osborne Bk Coll 10:231–5 '61 (unfavourable); S. Nowell-Smith Library ser5 17:173–5 '62.

3100 **Gimpel, Richard.** An exhibition of 150 manuscripts, illustrations, and first editions of Charles Dickens . . . selected from his collection and described by Richard Gimpel. Yale Univ Lib Gaz 37:47–93 Oc '62.

3101 **McPherson, Brian,** *comp.* 'Charles Dickens, 1812–1870; catalogue, Alfred and Isobel Reed Dickens collection, Dunedin public library, New Zealand' *in* Ryan, John S., *ed.* Charles Dickens and New Zealand, a colonial image. Wellington, 1965. vii,64p. at end.

DIGBY, SIR KENELM, 1603–1665

3145 **Watson, B.,** 1938: no.227.

DISRAELI, BENJAMIN, IST EARL OF BEACONSFIELD, 1804–1881

3146 **Stevenson, Lionel,** *ed.,* 1964: no.1705.

3147 **Contributions** to a bibliography of Benjamin Disraeli, earl of Beaconsfield.
N&Q ser8 3:321–3, 361–3, 401–3, 443–5, 482–3 Ap–Je '93; 4:22–4 Jl '93.
Checklist, 1820–92, with some bibliogr. notes and locations of copies.

3148 **Sadleir, Michael Thomas Hervey,** 1922: no.1706.

3149 **Stewart, R. W.** 'Writings of Benjamin Disraeli' *in* Blake, Robert N. W.
Disraeli. London, 1966. p.772–8.
Classified checklist of coll. ed., books and pamphlets, letters, articles, and speeches.

DIXEY, HAROLD GILES, fl.1919
See under Presses and printing.

DIXON, RICHARD WATSON, 1833–1900

3150 **Smith, Simon Nowell-.** Some uncollected authors XXIX: Richard Watson
Dixon, 1833–1900. Bk Coll 10no3:322–8 '61.
'Check-list of first editions of R. W. Dixon's works' (p.326–8): quasifacsim. TP transcrs.,
collations, and some bibliogr. notes on 12 verse and 7 prose items.

DOBSON, HENRY AUSTIN, 1840–1921

3151 **Murray, Francis Edwin.** A bibliography of Austin Dobson. Derby, F.
Murray, 1900. xvii,347p. 13 × 17cm.

3152 **Murdock, W. G. Blaikie.** Henry Austin Dobson. Eng Illus Mag new ser
30:423–5, 559–61 Ja,F '04.
'Bibliography' (p.424, 559–61).

3153 **Dobson, Alban T. A.** A bibliography of the first editions of published and
privately printed books and pamphlets by Austin Dobson. London, First
edition club, 1925. xii,88p. illus., facsims. 21cm.
Chronol. arrangement of 62 items, 1872–1923, with TP transcrs., collations, and bibliogr.
notes; based on the compiler's collection: *see* no.3154.
Rev: TLS 24 D '25:900.

3154 **London. University. Library.** Catalogue of the collection of the works of
Austin Dobson, 1840–1921. London, 1960. 62p. 21cm.
Classified short-title catalogue, comp. by Alban T. A. Dobson.
Rev: M. Canney Bk Coll 9:478, 481 '60.

3155 **Ealing. Public library.** Austin Dobson. [Ealing, 1962] 16p. 16cm. Covertitle. (Duplicated typescript)

DODGSON, CHARLES LUTWIDGE, 1832–1898
See Carroll, Lewis, pseud.

DODSLEY, ROBERT, 1703–1764
See under Presses and printing.

DONNE, JOHN, 1573–1631

3158 **White, William.** John Donne since 1900; a bibliography of periodical articles. Boston, F. W. Faxon, 1942. v,23p. 26cm.

Repr. from Bull Bib 17:86–9, 113 My/Ag, S/D '41; 17:165–71, 192–5 My/Ag, S/N '42.

3159 **Keynes, sir Geoffrey Langdon.** A bibliography of the works of dr. John Donne, dean of saint Paul's. Cambridge, Ptd. for the Baskerville club, 1914. xii,167p. illus., ports., facsims. 26cm.

3160 —— A bibliography of dr. John Donne. . . . 2d ed. Cambridge, C.U.P., 1932. xiv,195p. illus., ports., facsims. 26cm.

3161 **Simpson, Evelyn M. (Spearing).** 'A chronological arrangement of Donne's sermons' *in* A study of the prose works of John Donne. 2d ed. Oxford, 1948. p.340–56. (First pub. 1924)

3162 **Keynes, sir Geoffrey Langdon.** A bibliography of dr. John Donne, dean of st. Paul's. 3d ed. Cambridge, C.U.P., 1958. xviii,285p. illus., ports., facsims. 28cm.

Classified bibliogr. with TP transcrs. and facsims., collations, bibliogr. notes and locations of copies: 151 items. 'Bibliography and criticism, a check-list unnumbered' (p.[223]–58).

Rev: TLS 27 Je '58:368; H. Gardner Bk Coll 7:432 '58; Sevent Cent News 16:37 '58; G. D. McDonald Pa Bib Soc Am 52:322–6 '58; E. M. S. Simpson R Eng Stud new ser 11:118–19 '60.

3163 **White, William.** Sir Geoffrey Keynes's Bibliography of John Donne, a review with addenda. Bull Bib 22:186–9 Ja/Ap '59.

Adds some 200 items to 1900–57 Donneana.

DONNE, JOHN, 1604–1662

3165 **Keynes, sir Geoffrey Langdon.** 'Works by John Donne, D.C.L.' *in* A bibliography of dr. John Donne. . . . 3d ed. Cambridge, 1958. p.[192]–8.

Bibliogr. of items 152–8, 1623–63.

DORSET, CHARLES SACKVILLE, 6TH EARL OF, 1638–1691
See Sackville, Charles, 6th earl of Dorset.

DOUGHTY, CHARLES MONTAGU, 1843–1926

3166 **Bibliographies** of modern authors. Charles Montagu Doughty. Lond Merc 4no19:87 My '21.

Chronol. checklist of verse and drama; and prose, 1884–1920.

DOUGLAS, LADY ELEANOR (TOUCHET), d.1652

3167 **Hindle, Christopher John.** A bibliography of the printed pamphlets and broadsides of lady Eleanor Douglas, the seventeenth-century prophetess.

Rev. ed. Edinburgh, Edinburgh bibliographical society, 1936. 34p. facsims. 27cm.

First ed. 1934 repr. from Edinburgh Bib Soc Pub 15:35–54 '34; this ed. repr. from Edinburgh Bib Soc Trans 1pt1:65–98 '36.

Quasifacsim. TP transcrs. and facsims., collations, and bibliogr. notes on 53 items, 1625–52.

Rev: S.G.W. Bod Q Rec 7:22 '35.

DOUGLAS, BP. GAVIN, 1474?–1522

3168 **Geddie, William,** 1912: no.2034.

DOUGLAS, NORMAN, *pseud. of* GEORGE NORMAN DOUGLASS, 1868–1952

3169 **Stonehill, Charles Archibald.** A bibliography of the writings of Norman Douglas. [London] Supplement to The bookman's journal, 1926. 7p. 28cm.

Issued with Bkmns J 14n059 '26.

3170 **McDonald, Edward David.** A bibliography of the writings of Norman Douglas; with notes by Norman Douglas. Philadelphia, Centaur book shop, 1927. 165p. port., facsim. 20cm.

3171 **[Woolf, Cecil]** Memorial exhibition of works by Norman Douglas . . . on display during July 1952 at Edinburgh central library. . . . Edinburgh [1952] 8p. 22cm.

3172 —— A bibliography of the works of Norman Douglas. London, R. Hart-Davis, 1954. 201p. illus., port., facsim. 23cm. (Soho bibliographies, VI)

Chronol. arrangement of books and pamphlets; contributions; and translations, with quasifacsim. TP transcrs., collations, and bibliogr. notes, with distinction of issues.

Rev: D. M. Low Bk Coll 3:157–8 '54; I. R. Willison Library ser5 9:142–5 '54; C. Woolf *ib.* 10:211 '55.

DOUGLASS, GEORGE NORMAN, 1868–1952
See Douglas, Norman, pseud.

DOWDEN, EDWARD, 1843–1913

3173 **Shorter, Clement.** Edward Dowden. Eng Illus Mag new ser 29:204–6 My '03.

'Bibliography' (p.206): classified checklist.

3174 **Byard, Edwin John.** Bibliography of Edward Dowden. Irish Bk Lover 4:185–7 Je '13.

Chronol. checklist, 1863–1912.

DOWLAND, JOHN, 1563?–1626?

3175 **Sopher, R.,** 1959: no.204.

DOWSON, ERNEST CHRISTOPHER, 1867–1900

3176 **Harrison, H. Guy.** 'Bibliography' *in* Plarr, Victor G. Ernest Dowson, 1888–1897; reminiscences. . . . New York, 1914. p.[131]–42.

3177 **Stonehill, Charles Archibald** [1925]: no.682.

3178 **Longaker, John Mark.** 'Bibliography: a chronology of Dowson's works' *in* Ernest Dowson. Philadelphia; London, 1944. p.273–7.
Chronol. checklist of works, 1886–1934, and ana.

3179 **Whalley, J. I.,** 1950: no.228.

DOYLE, SIR ARTHUR CONAN, 1859–1930

3180 **À Beckett, Arthur William.** Sir Arthur Conan Doyle. Eng Illus Mag new ser 31:209–11, 215 My '04.
'Bibliography' (p.210, 215).

3181 **Locke, Harold.** A bibliographical catalogue of the writings of sir Arthur Conan Doyle. . . . Tunbridge Wells, D. Webster, 1928. 84p. 23cm.
Classified list of first ed., with TP transcrs., brief collations, and bibliogr. notes.

3182 **St. Marylebone. Public libraries.** Sherlock Holmes; catalogue of an exhibition held . . . 1951. [London] Presented for the Festival of Britain by the Public libraries committee of the Borough of st. Marylebone [1951] ii[2]59p. illus. 22cm.
Printed and various Holmesiana.

3183 **LaCour, Tage.** Ex bibliotheca Holmesiana; the first editions of the writings of Sherlock Holmes. Amat Bk Coll 5:3–6 '55. (Not seen)

3184 **Bengis, Nathan L.** The signs of our times, an irregular bibliography. New York, 1956. 29p. 29cm. (Duplicated typescript)
Checklist of ed. of The sign of four, 1890–1952, with bibliogr. notes and discussion

3185 **Christ, Jay Finlay.** The fiction of sir Arthur Conan Doyle, arranged alphabetically and chronologically. [Harbert, Mich.] Privately ptd., 1959. 34p. 23cm. (Not seen)

DRAYTON, MICHAEL, 1563–1631

3186 **Elton, Oliver.** 'Bibliography' *in* An introduction to Michael Drayton. [Manchester] 1895. p.67–86.

3187 —— 'Bibliography' *in* [**Same**]: [enl. & rev. ed., with title] Michael Drayton, a critical study. London, 1905. p.157–205.
The bibliogr. is not the same as that in the earlier ed. Chronol. checklist of principal ed. of 23 works, with TP transcrs., locations of copies, and some bibliogr. notes.

3188 **Tannenbaum, Samuel Aaron.** Michael Drayton, a concise bibliography. New York, 1941. viii,54p. 23cm. (Elizabethan bibliographies, no.22)
Classified checklist of works and ana.

3189 **Tillotson, Geoffrey** and **B. Juel-Jensen,** *comp.* 'Bibliography of the early editions of the writings of Michael Drayton' *in* Hebel, John W., *ed.* The works. Introductions, notes, variant readings ed. by K. Tillotson and B. H. Newdigate. [Corr. ed.] Oxford, 1961. V.5, p.265–306.

First pub. 1931–41 with bibliogr. by G. Tillotson; now substantially rev. by B. Juel-Jensen. Quasifacsim. TP transcrs. *or* facsims., collations, bibliogr. notes, and locations of copies, with distinction of issues.

DRINKWATER, JOHN, 1882–1937

3190 **Danielson, Henry.** Bibliographies of modern authors, no.11. John Drinkwater. Bkmns J 1no21–2:405,421 '20.

TP transcrs., collations, and bibliogr. notes on 21 first ed., 1903–17, brought up to date in next item.

3191 ——, 1921: no.680.

3192 **[Partington, Wilfred George]** Persuasion; the privately printed edition of mr. Drinkwater's sonnets. Bkmns J 5no4:139 '22.

3193 **Times bookshop,** LONDON. John Drinkwater, 1882–1937; catalogue of an exhibition of books . . . to mark the twenty-fifth anniversary of his death. London, 1962. 51p. 25cm.

Classified catalogue with collations and bibliogr. notes and refs., comp. by Timothy d'Arch Smith.

DRUMMOND, WILLIAM HAMILTON, 1778–1865

3194 **Millin, Samuel Shannon.** The poetry of William Hamilton Shannon. Ulster J Archæol 7:37–43 Ja '01.

'List of poetical works . . .' (p.42–3): chronol. checklist.

DRURY, JOHN, 1590–1680

3194a **Turnbull, George Henry.** 'Writings' *in* Hartlib, Drury and Comenius; gleanings from Hartlib's papers. Liverpool, 1948. p.300–22.
Classified checklist of books and mss.

DRYDEN, JOHN, 1631–1700

3195 **Monk, Samuel Holt.** Dryden; a list of critical studies published from 1895 to 1948. Minneapolis, University of Minnesota pr.; London, O.U.P. [1950] v,52p. 24cm.

3196 **Keast, W. R.** Dryden studies, 1895–1948. Mod Philol 48:205–10 F '51.
Additions to Monk.

3197 **Grolier club,** NEW YORK. Catalogue of an exhibition of first and other editions of the works of John Dryden . . . commemorative of the two hundredth anniversary of his death. New York, 1900. 97p. port. 24cm.

3198 **S., C.** A check-list of Dryden's plays. Bibliographer 1no8:374–8 N '02.

3199 **Dobell, Percy John.** John Dryden; bibliographical memoranda. London, 1922. 30p. 23cm.

3200 **Wise, Thomas James.** A Dryden library; a catalogue of printed books, manuscripts, and autograph letters by John Dryden . . . collected by Thomas James Wise. London, Ptd. for private circulation only, 1930. xxiv,89[2]p. port., facsims. 26cm.

3201 **Macdonald, Hugh.** John Dryden, a bibliography of early editions and of Drydeniana. Oxford, Clarendon pr., 1939. x,358p. port. 26cm.

Classified bibliogr. of 334 items, including Drydeniana, with quasifacsim. TP transcrs., collations, and bibliogr. notes.
Rev: N&Q 177:231–2 '39; A.E. Lib Assn Rec 6:527 '39; TLS 10 Je '39:348; H. Williams Library ser4 20:341–3 '39; J. W. Carter Pub Wkly 136:2215–6 '39; W. Kalthoff Ang Beibl 51:192–4 '40; V. de Sola Pinto Mod Lang R 35:238–9 '40; G. R. Potter R Eng Stud 16:221–3 '40; L.I.B. Philol Q 19:196–7 '40; E. N. Hooker and H. T. Swedenberg Mod Lang N 56:74–5 '41.

3202 **Osborn, James Marshall.** Macdonald's bibliography of Dryden; an annotated check list of selected American libraries. Mod Philol 39:69–98,197–212 Ag,N '41.

3203 **Pettit, Henry J.** Dryden's works in Dryden, New York. Bull Bib 18n09:198 Ja/Ap '46.

Checklist of 21 pre-1700 items in the John Willard Fiske collection of the Dryden public library.

3204 **Steck, James S.** Dryden's Indian emperour; the early editions and their relation to the text. Stud Bib 2:139–52 '49.

Supplements Macdonald, and Osborn for the first 13 ed., with a table of the rev. order, and Macdonald nos.

3205 **Hamilton, Marion H.** The early editions of Dryden's State of innocence. Stud Bib 5:163–6 '52.

Table of rev. order of first 9 quartos, with Macdonald nos.

3206 **Browne, Ray B.** Dryden and Milton in nineteenth-century popular song-books. Bull Bib 22:143–4 My/Ag '58.

Title checklist of 12 Dryden and 21 Milton items.

3207 **Cameron, William James.** John Dryden in New Zealand; an account of early editions of the writings of John Dryden, 1631–1700, found in various libraries throughout New Zealand. . . . Wellington, Library school, National library service, 1960. 31p. 22cm.

Checklist supplementing Macdonald and Osborn (p.12–29).

3208 **Stratman, Carl Joseph.** John Dryden's All for love: unrecorded editions. Pa Bib Soc Am 57:77–9 '63.

Checklist of 15 ed., 1710–92, with locations of copies, supplementing Macdonald.

DUCK, STEPHEN, 1705–1756

3211 **Davis, Rose Mary.** 'Bibliography A: Works by Duck' *in* Stephen Duck, the thresher poet. Orono, Me., 1926. p.[179]–80.

Chronol. checklist, 1730–1830.

DUCLAUX, MARY, *pseud. of* AGNES MARY FRANCES ROBINSON, 1856–1944

3211a **Holmes, Ruth Van Zuyle.** Mary Duclaux, 1856–1944: primary and secondary checklists. Eng Lit Transit 10n01:27–46 '67.

Classified checklist of works and ana.

DUFF, EDWARD GORDON, 1863–1924

3212 **Marsh, A. S.,** 1953: no.166.

DUFFY, SIR CHARLES GAVAN, 1816–1903

3213 **Douglas, John M.** Sir Charles Gavan Duffy: bibliography. Irish Bk Lover 7:177–80 Je/Jl '16.

DUGARD, WILLIAM, 1606–1662
See under Presses and printing.

DUGDALE, SIR WILLIAM, 1605–1686

3214 **Maddison, Francis R. [and others]** Sir William Dugdale, 1605–1686; a list of his printed works and of his portraits. . . . Warwick, L. E. Stephens for the Records and museum committee of the Warwickshire county council, 1953. 92p. illus., port., facsims. 19cm.

'The printed works . . .' (p.16–68): checklist of 88 items, with some bibliogr. notes. *See* next item.

3215 —— Exhibition of the life and works of sir William Dugdale, 1605–1686 . . . description of the exhibits produced as a supplement to sir William Dugdale, 1605–1686, a list of his printed works. . . . Warwick [Warwickshire county council, Records and museum committee] 1953. 49p. 26cm. (Duplicated typescript)

'Corrections and additions to Sir William Dugdale . . . a list . . .' (p.47–9).

DUIGNAN, WILLIAM HENRY, 1824–1914

3215a **Whitfield, A. Stanton.** W. H. Duignan: bibliography. N&Q ser11 11:373–4 My '15; H. S. Pearson *ib.* ser11 11:461 Je '15; A. S. Whitfield 12:6 Jl '15.

Chronol. checklist, 1865–1912 (p.373–4).

DU MAURIER, GEORGE LOUIS PALMELLA BUSSON, 1834–1896

3216 **Feipel, Louis Nicholas.** The American issues of Trilby. Coloph new ser 2no4:537–49 '37.

Distinction of states, and bibliogr. discussion

DUNBAR, WILLIAM, 1465?–1530?

3217 **Geddie, William,** 1912: no.2034.

DUNSANY, EDWARD JOHN MORETON DRAX PLUNKETT, BARON, 1878–1957
See Plunkett, Edward John Moreton Drax, baron Dunsany.

DUNTON, WALTER THEODORE WATTS-, 1832–1914

3218 **Middlemast, K.,** 1950: no.169.

3219 **Truss, Tom J.** Theodore Watts-Dunton, a primary bibliography. Bull Bib 23:114–17 My/Ag '61.

Checklist of works in periodicals signed by, or variously attrib. to him, chronol. arranged and contribs. to units other than periodicals.

D'URFEY, THOMAS, 1653–1723

3220 **Day, Cyrus Lawrence.** Dates and performances of D'Urfey's plays. [Charlottesville, Va., Bibliographical society of the University of Virginia, 1950] 24l. 28cm. (Duplicated typescript)

Checklist of 24 items, with some bibliogr. notes.

3221 **Sanville, Donald Walker.** Thomas D'Urfey's Love for money, a bibliographical study. Lib Chron Univ Pennsylvania 17no1:71–7 '50.

Quasifacsim. TP transcrs., collations, and bibliogr. notes on 6 variants of 2 quartos of 1691, and 1696 quarto, with locations of copies.

3222 **Biswanger, Raymond Adam.** Thomas D'Urfey's Richmond heiress, 1693, a bibliographical study. Stud Bib 5:169–78 '52.

Quasifacsim. TP transcrs., locations of copies, and bibliogr. discussion of 2 issues and variants.

DURHAM, JAMES, 1622–1658

3223 **Christie, George.** A bibliography of James Durham, 1622–1658. Edinburgh Bib Soc Pub 11pt1:35–46 S '18.

Chronol. list of 11 works fully descr., with short descrs. of later ed., and locations of copies.

DURRELL, LAWRENCE GEORGE, 1912–

3224 **Thomas, Alan G.** and **L. C. Powell.** Some uncollected authors XXIII: Lawrence Durrell; recollections of a Durrell collector. Bk Coll 9no1:56–63 '60.

'Books of Lawrence Durrell' (p.59–63): checklist of books, translations, prefaces, and some contribs. to books, with some annotations by Durrell; some bibliogr. notes.

3225 **California. University. University at Los Angeles. Library.** Lawrence Durrell; a checklist, compiled by Robert A. Potter and Brooke Whiting. Issued on the occasion of the presentation of Lawrence Clark Powell's Durrell collection to the UCLA library. . . . Los Angeles, 1961. 50p. facsims. 22cm.

Chronol. short-title catalogue of 311 items, 1931–60, with some bibliogr. notes.

3226 **Knerr, Anthony.** Regarding a checklist of Lawrence Durrell. Pa Bib Soc Am 55:142–52 '61.

Addenda and corrigenda to Thomas and Powell.

3227 **Stone, Bernard,** *comp.* 'Bibliography' *in* Perles, Alfred. My friend Lawrence Durrell, an intimate memoir. . . . London, 1961. p.47–62.

DUTTON, ANN (WILLIAMS), 1692–1765

3230 **Whitebrook, John Cudworth.** 'A bibliography of mrs. Ann Dutton' *in* Ann Dutton, a life and bibliography. London [n.d., 1922] p.15–20.

Chronol. checklist of 53 items, 1734–1803, with some locations of copies. Rev. from N&Q ser12 2:471–2 D '16; 3:136 F '17.

EARLE, BP. JOHN, 1601?-1665

3230a **Jensen, Bent Juel-.** The 1628 editions of John Earle's Micro-cosmo-graphie. Library ser5 21:231-4 S '66.

Quasifacsim. TP transcrs., collations, locations of copies and bibliogr. notes and refs., with distinction of issues, on 4 ed.

EASTE, WILLIAM, fl.1591-1625

3231 **Dredge, John Ingle,** 1889-99: no.886.

EASTON, THOMAS, fl.1681-1695

3232 **Dredge, John Ingle,** 1889-99: no.886.

EDDISON, ERIC RÜCKER, 1882-1945

3233 **Hamilton, George Rostrevor.** E. R. Eddison. Bk Hndbk 1no1:53-7 '47.

'Bibliography' (p.55-7): full but peculiar descrs. of 7 items.

EDGEWORTH, MARIA, 1767-1849

3234 **Slade, Bertha (Coolidge).** Maria Edgeworth, 1767-1849, a bibliographical tribute. London, Constable [1937] xxxii,252p. illus., facsims. 23cm.

Quasifacsim. TP transcrs., and some facsims., with collations, locations of copies, and bibliogr. notes with distinction of issues; 'Appendix II: Press numbers' (p. 230-6).

Rev: J. W. Carter Pub Wkly 132:2026-8 '37; M. T. H. Sadleir Observer 7 N '37; J. M. Hone Spectator 22 Oc '37:698; M. T. H. Sadleir Library ser4 19:252-7 '38.

EGERTON, GEORGE, pseud. of MARY CHAVELITA (DUNNE) BRIGHT, 1859-1945

3235 **Gawsworth, John,** pseud. [1932]: no.686.

EGLINTOUN, SIR HEW, c.1450?

3240 **Geddie, William,** 1912: no.2034.

ELIOT, GEORGE, pseud. of MARY ANN (EVANS) CROSS, 1819-1880

3245 **Barry, James D.** The literary reputation of George Eliot's fiction: a supplementary bibliography. Bull Bib 22:176-82 Ja/Ap '59.

3246 **Stevenson, Lionel,** ed., 1964: no.1705.

3247 **Anderson, John Parker,** comp. 'Bibliography' in Browning, Oscar. Life of George Eliot. London, 1890. p.[i]-xiv.

3248 **Waldo, Frank** and **G. A. Turkington,** comp. 'Bibliography' in Blind, Mathilde. George Eliot. New ed. Boston, 1904. p.[331]-48. (First ed. 1883)

3249 **Muir, Percival Horace.** A bibliography of the first editions of books by George Eliot (Mary Ann Evans) 1819-1880. Bkmns J 15no4:42-50 '27; 16no5:51-8 '28.

Issued as Supplement to the Bookman's Journal; and in Bibliographies of modern authors. 3d series. London, 1931. See no.685.

3250 **Parrish, Morris Longstreth,** 1933: no. 1707.

ELIOT, THOMAS STEARNS, 1888–1965

3255 **Gallup, Donald Clifford.** A catalogue of English and American first editions of writings by T. S. Eliot, exhibited in the Yale university library. [Portland, Me., Southworth–Anthoensen pr.] 1937. 42p. 23cm.

3256 —— A bibliographical check-list of the writings of T. S. Eliot, including his contributions to periodicals and translations of his work into foreign languages. New Haven, Yale university library, 1947. 128p. 24cm.

3256a **Rajan, B.,** *ed.* 'A check list of T. S. Eliot's published writings' *in* T. S. Eliot, a study of his writings by several hands. London, 1947. p.139–53. (Repr. 1966)

3257 **Gallup, Donald Clifford.** T. S. Eliot; a bibliography, including contributions to periodicals and foreign translations. London, Faber & Faber [1952] xii,177p. 23cm.

Rev. enl. ed. of no.3256. Classified arrangement of books, contribs. to periodicals, translations into foreign languages, and miscellanea, with quasifacsim. TP transcrs., short collations, and bibliogr. notes.

Rev: TLS 26 D '52:860; J. E. Walsh Bk Coll 1:273–4 '52; F. Meyer Am Merc 77:142–3 '54; R. Daniel Sewanee R 62:354–5 '54; B. L. Études Angl 6:175–6 '54; R. Halsband Sat R 22 Ag '53; 35–6; I. R. Willison Library ser5 8:130–5 '53.

3258 **Texas. University. Humanities research center.** An exhibition of manuscripts and first editions of T. S. Eliot. [Austin] 1961. 45p. port., facsims. 26cm.

Annotated checklist; introduction by Ann Bowden.

Rev: TLS 11 Ag '61:539.

3259 **Bentz, Hans Willi.** Thomas Stearns Eliot in Übersetzungen; Thomas Stearns Eliot translated. . . . Frankfurt am Main [1963] xiii,59p. 32cm. (Duplicated typescript)

ELIZABETH I, QUEEN OF ENGLAND AND IRELAND, 1533–1603

3263 **Jackson, William Alexander.** The funeral procession of queen Elizabeth. Library ser4 26:262–71 Mr '46.

'Appendix [of surviving pamphlets memorializing queen Elizabeth]' (p.270–1).

ELLIOTT, EBENEZER, 1781–1849

3265 **Sheffield. Public libraries** and **Rotherham. Public libraries.** 'A bibliography of Ebenezer Elliott' *in* Ebenezer Elliott, the corn-law rhymer, 1781–1849; a commemorative brochure. . . . Sheffield, 1950. p.21–35.

Chronol. checklist of poetry, prose, and manuscripts, with some bibliogr. notes and locations of copies; ana (p.27–35).

ELLIS, HENRY HAVELOCK, 1859–1939

3266 **Burne, Glenn S.** Havelock Ellis, an annotated selected bibliography of primary and secondary works. Eng Lit Transit 9n02:55–107 '66.

ELYOT, SIR THOMAS, 1490?–1546

3267 **Lemberg, Stanford E.** 'Editions of Elyot's works' *in* Sir Thomas Elyot, tudor humanist. Austin [1960] p.197–8.

Chronol. checklist, 1522–45, with STC nos. and some bibliogr. notes and locations of copies.

3268 **Freeman, E. J.,** 1962: no.124.

EMMET, ROBERT, 1778–1803

3269 **Chicago. Public library.** Robert Emmet. . . list of books and magazine articles in the Chicago public library. [Chicago] 1910. 5p. 16cm. (Not seen)

3270 **Bourke, Francis Stephen.** The rebellion of 1803; an essay in bibliography. Bib Soc Ireland Pubs 5n01:1–16 '33.

'A bibliography of the insurrection of 1803' (p.9–16).

ETHEREGE, SIR GEORGE, 1635?–1691

3271 **Smith, Herbert Francis Brett Brett-,** *ed.* 'Bibliography of the plays' *in* The dramatic works of sir George Etherege. Oxford, 1927. V.1, p.xciii–cviii.

Quasifacsim. TP transcrs., collations, locations of copies, and bibliogr. notes on early ed.

ETHERIDGE, SAMUEL, 1778–c.1840

3272 **Newport. Public libraries, museum and art gallery,** 1939: no.3365.

EVANS, EDMUND, 1826–1905

3272a **McLean, Ruari,** *ed.* 'A selective list of books containing colour printing by Edmund Evans' *in* The reminiscences of Edmund Evans. Oxford, 1967. p.77–[84]

Chronol. checklist, 1852–90, with some bibliogr. notes.

EVANS, SIR JOHN, 1823–1908

3273 **Forrer, L.** Sir John Evans, 1823–1908; biographie et bibliographie. Chalon-sur-Saône, É. Bertrand, 1909. 35p. port. 28cm.

Repr. from Gaz Numismatique Française '09; classified chronol. checklist.

EVELYN, JOHN, 1620–1706

3274 **Wheatley, Henry B.** [Bibliography of John Evelyn] Bib Soc Trans 1pt1/2:77–90 '93.

3275 [**Keynes, sir Geoffrey Langdon** and **A. T. Bartholomew**] A handlist of the works of John Evelyn . . . and of books connected with him. Cambridge, 1916. 19l. 25cm.

3276 **Keynes, sir Geoffrey Langdon.** John Evelyn, a study in bibliophily & a bibliography of his writings. New York, Grolier club; Cambridge, C.U.P., 1937. xvii,308p. illus., ports., facsims. 26cm.

Chronol. arrangement of early ed., 180 items, with TP transcrs., and facsims., collations, bibliogr. notes, and locations of copies.

Rev: TLS 18 S '37:670; J. Hayward Observer 17 Oc '37; I. A. Williams Lond Merc 36:565 '37; H. Macdonald Library ser4 19:250–2 '38; F. E. Budd R Eng Stud 15:220–1 '39.

EVELYN, JOHN, 1655–1699

3277 **Keynes, sir Geoffrey Langdon.** 'Works by John Evelyn junior and his son' *in* John Evelyn, a study in bibliophily. . . . New York; Cambridge, 1937. p.281–5.

Six items, 1672–1700, with TP transcrs., collations, bibliogr. notes and locations of copies.

EVELYN, SIR JOHN, 1682–1763

3278 **Keynes, sir Geoffrey Langdon,** 1937: no.3276.

EVERARD, THOMAS, 1560–1633

3279 **Allison, Antony Francis.** An early seventeenth-century translator, Thomas Everard, S.J.; a study of the bibliographical evidence. Biog Stud 2no3: 188–215 '54.

Locations of copies, and bibliogr. discussion of some 13 items.

FABER, FREDERICK WILLIAM, 1814–1863

3280 **Guibert, J.** 'Bibliographie de Faber' *in* Le réveil du catholicisme en Angleterre au XIXᵉ siècle. Paris, 1907. p.[365]–71.

Classified chronol. checklist of works and ana.

FAIRFIELD, CICILY ISABEL, 1892–
See West, Rebecca, pseud.

FALKNER, JOHN MEADE, 1858–1932

3281 **Pollard, Graham.** Some uncollected authors xxv: John Meade Falkner, 1858–1932. Bk Coll 9no3:318–25 '60.

'Bibliography of Meade Falkner': (p.323–5): quasifacsim. TP transcrs., and bibliogr-notes on 10 items, with note of later ed.

FARADAY, MICHAEL, 1791–1867

3282 **Jeffreys, Alan Edward.** Michael Faraday, a list of his lectures and published writings. London, Published on behalf of the Royal institution of Great Britain by Chapman and Hall [1960] (Also pub. New York, Academic pr. [1961]) xxviii,86p. illus., ports., facsims. 26cm.

Chronol. checklist of 489 separate and periodical pubs. in English and in the U.K., 1816–1956, based on London university School of librarianship and archives bibliography: *see* no.146.

Rev: B. Dibner Pa Bib Soc Am 56:135–7 '62.

FARQUHAR, GEORGE, 1678–1707

3283 **Gibb, I. P.,** 1952: no.126.

FEARN, JOHN RUSSELL, 1908–1960

3283a **Harbottle, Phillip James.** John Russell Fearn, the ultimate analysis; a bibliography. [Wallsend-on-Tyne, 1965] [94]p. illus. 33cm. (Duplicated typescript)

Annotated classified checklist.

FELKIN, MRS. A. L., 1860–1929

See Fowler, Ellen Thorneycroft (mrs. A. L. Felkin).

FELL, BP. JOHN, 1625–1686

3283b **Morison, Stanley** and **H. G. Carter.** John Fell, the University press and the Fell types. . . . Oxford, Clarendon press, 1967. xvi,278p. illus., port., facsims. 39cm.

'List of the published writings of John Fell' (p.[215]–26): chronol., checklist, 1638–1868, with varying descrs., bibliogr. notes and refs. 'The Fell type specimens' (p.[229]–32); 'Fell's announcements and proposals' (p.[251]–2); 'Books in Fell type published by the University of Oxford from 1902 to 1927' (p.[253]).

FERGUSON, JOHN, d.1915

3284 **Alexander, Elizabeth H.** A bibliography of John Ferguson. . . . [Glasgow] Reprinted with alterations from the Transactions of the Glasgow bibliographical society, 1920. 32p. port. 26cm.

Chronol. checklist of 89 items, 1863–1916, with index; repr. from Glasgow Bib Soc Trans 6:40–63 '20.

3285 —— A further bibliography of the late John Ferguson. [Glasgow] Reprinted with alterations from the Records of the Glasgow bibliographical society, 1934. 47p. port., facsims. 26cm.

Discursive checklist; no index; repr. from Glasgow Bib Soc Rec 12:82–127 '36.

FERGUSON, JOHN, fl.1912–1929

3286 **Scottish chapbook,** 1922–3: no.724.

FERGUSON, SIR SAMUEL, 1810–1886

3287 **Ferguson, Mary C., lady.** 'Sir S. Ferguson's works' *in* Sir Samuel Ferguson in the Ireland of his day. Edinburgh, 1896. V.2, p.[369]–74.

Chronol. checklist, 1832–88, of books and papers.

3288 **Graves, Alfred Perceval.** 'Bibliography' *in* Poems of sir Samuel Ferguson. Dublin; London [1918] p.395–400.

Chronol. checklist, 1832–88.

FERGUSSON, ROBERT, 1750–1774

3289 **Fairley, John A.** Bibliography of Robert Fergusson. Glasgow, J. Maclehose, 1915. 49p. ports., facsims. 26cm.

Repr. with extended preface, from Glasgow Bib Soc Rec 3pt2:115–55 '15. TP transcrs., short collations, some bibliogr. notes, and location of copy examined, for 93 items 1769–1914, including ana.

FIELD, GUY CROMWELL, 1887–1955

3295 **Allan, D. J.** Guy Cromwell Field, 1887–1955. Proc Brit Acad 42:311–18 '56.
'Principal writings of G. F. Field' (p.317–18): checklist.

FIELD, JOHN, 1782–1837

3296 **Hopkinson, Cecil.** A bibliographical thematic catalogue of the works of
John Field, 1782–1837. London, 1962. xxiii,175p. illus., port., facsims.
29cm.

Chronol. arrangement, 1795–1852, with TP or headtitle transcrs., collations, and
bibliogr. notes.

Rev : TLS 4 My '62:328; *rf.* C. Hopkinson *ib.* 18 My '62:364.

FIELD, NATHAN, 1587–1620

3297 **Peery, William Wallace,** *ed.* 'Bibliography: 1. Works by Field' *in* The
plays of Nathan Field. Austin, 1950. p.321–3.

Checklists of original, collaborative, and attributed works.

FIELDING, HENRY, 1707–1754

3298 **Cordasco, Francesco G. M.** Henry Fielding, a list of critical studies published from 1895 to 1946. Brooklyn, Long Island U.P., 1948. 17p. 22cm.
(Eighteenth century bibliographical pamphlets, no.5)

3299 **Henley, William Ernest,** *ed.* 'A bibliographical list of the first editions' *in*
The complete works of Henry Fielding. New York [1902–3] V.16, p.xlvii–
lxii.

3300 **Cross, Wilbur Lucius.** 'Bibliography' *in* The history of Henry Fielding.
New Haven; London, 1918. V.3, p.[287]–366.

Quasifacsim. TP transcrs., with some bibliogr. notes, principally of first ed. of separate
works, works of uncertain authorship, works erroneously attrib. to, and plays based
on Fielding or his works.

3301 **Dudden, Frederick Homes.** 'Bibliography' *in* Henry Fielding, his life,
works and times. Oxford, 1952. V.2, p.1126–51. (Repr. Hamden, Conn.,
Archon books, 1966)

3302 **Masengill, Jeanne Addison.** Variant forms of Fielding's Coffee-house
politician. Stud Bib 5:178–83 '52.

Quasifacsim. TP transcrs., collations, and bibliogr. notes and discussion of 3 issues of
first and only 1730 ed. of Rape upon rape.

3303 **Todd, William Burton.** Three notes on Fielding. Pa Bib Soc Am 47:70–5
'53.

Collations and bibliogr. notes on An apology for the life of Mr. T[heophilus] C[ibber]
1740; A dialogue between a gentleman of London . . . and an honest alderman of the
country party, 1747; and Amelia, 1752.

3304 **Jarvis, Rupert C.** Fielding and the 'forty-five. N&Q 202:19–24 Ja '57.

Section of serial article which lists (p.24) corrections to the canon and standard bibliogrs.,
with collations and bibliogr. notes.

3305 **Greason, A. LeRoy.** Fielding's The history of the present rebellion in Scotland. Philol Q 37:119–23 Ja '58.

Quasifacsim. TP transcrs., collations, and discussion of 5 ed., 1745–6.

FIELDING, SIR JOHN, 1721–1780

3310 **Melville, Alexander Ronald Leslie-.** 'Sir John Fielding's works [and] Books attributed to sir John Fielding' *in* The life and work of sir John Fielding. London [1934] p.305–6.
Checklist.

FIELDING, SARAH, 1710–1768

3311 **Johnson, Reginald Brimley,** *ed.* 'List of Sarah Fielding's works' *in* Lives of Cleopatra and Octavia, by Sarah Fielding. [London] 1928. p.[xi]–xiii.
Chronol. checklist, 1757–85, with some bibliogr. notes.

FIGGIS, DARRELL, 1882–1925

3312 **O'Hegarty, Patrick Sarsfield.** A bibliography of the books of Darrell Figgis. Dublin, A. Thom, print., 1937. 10p. 24cm. (Bibliographies of 1916 and the Irish revolution, no.15)
Chronol. catalogue of 27 items. 1909–27, with quasifacsim. TP transcrs., collations, and bibliogr. notes.

FINLAY, GEORGE, 1799–1875

3313 **Miller, William.** The Finlay papers. Eng Hist R 39:386–98 Jl '24.
'Bibliography of Finlay's published minor works' (p.398): discursive checklist of 16 entries.

FIRBANK, ARTHUR ANNESLEY RONALD, 1886–1926

3314 **Muir, Percival Horace.** A bibliography of the first editions of books by Arthur Annesley Ronald Firbank, 1886–1926. [London] Supplement to the Bookman's journal, 1927. 8p. 24cm.
First pub. with Bkmns J 15no1 '27; also issued in Bibliographies of modern authors. 3d series. London, 1931; *see* no.685.

3315 **Benkovitz, Miriam Jeanette.** A bibliography of Ronald Firbank. London, R. Hart-Davis, 1963. 103p. port. 23cm. (Soho bibliographies, xvi)
Chronol. arrangement of books and pamphlets; contribs. to periodicals; and manuscripts and typescripts, with quasifacsim. TP transcrs., collations, and bibliogr. notes.
Rev: TLS 28 Je '63:484; *rf. ib.* 30 Ag '63:660; 25 Oc '63:876; lord Horder Bk Coll 12:380–3 '63; Pa Bib Soc Am 58:322 '64.

FIRTH, SIR CHARLES HARDING, 1857–1936

3316 **[Firth, sir Charles Harding]** A bibliography of the writings of sir Charles Firth. Oxford, Clarendon pr., 1928. iv,45p. 24cm.
Classified checklist, with some bibliogr. notes.

FISHER, BP. JOHN, 1459–1535

3317 **Oxford. University. Bodleian library** [1935]: no.4282.

3318 **Steiner, J. H.,** 1952: no.210.

FITZGERALD, EDWARD, 1809–1883

3319 **Brooklyn. Public library.** Edward Fitzgerald, 1809–1883; a list of books, with references to periodicals in the Brooklyn public library. Brooklyn, 1909. 10p. 16cm.

3320 **Faverty, Frederic Everett,** *ed.*, 1956: no.2016.

3321 **Caxton club,** CHICAGO. A chronological list of the more important issues of Edward Fitzgerald's version of the Rubaiyat of Omar Khayyam, and of other books, written, translated, edited or owned by, him . . . exhibited by the Caxton club. Chicago, 1899. 65p. illus. 18cm.

Annotated classified short-title catalogue of 71 items with some bibliogr. notes; 'Other books . . . by Edward Fitzgerald' (items 21–38); no index.

3322 **Jackson, Holbrook.** 'A bibliography of the English renderings of the Rubaiyat of Omar Khayyam' *in* Edward Fitzgerald and Omar Kháyyám, an essay and a bibliography. London, 1899. p.35–41.

3323 **Prideaux, William Francis.** Notes for a bibliography of Edward Fitzgerald. London, F. Hollings, 1901. x,88p. illus. 19cm.

Repr. from N&Q ser9 5:201,221,241 '00; 6:61 '00; classified list of separate and posthumous works and contribs. to books and periodicals, with TP transcrs., discursive collations, and bibliogr. discussion; no index.

3324 **Potter, Ambrose George.** A bibliography of the Rubáiyát of Omar Khayyám, together with kindred matter in prose and verse pertaining thereto. London, Ingpen and Grant, 1929. xiii,313p. 23cm.

Pt.1 (p.1–129) is concerned with Fitzgerald's and other English versions; TP transcrs., collations, and bibliogr. notes.

3325 **Bentham, George,** *ed.* [Bibliography of Edward Fitzgerald] *in* The variorum and definitive edition of the poetical and prose writings of Edward Fitzgerald. New York, 1902–3. V.7. (Not seen)

3326 **[Humphry, James]** *comp.* 'A check-list of the Rubáiyát collection now in the Colby college library' *in* Weber, Carl J., *ed.* Fitzgerald's Rubáiyát; centennial edition. Waterville, Me., 1959. p.119–52.

Chronol. short-title catalogue, 1859–1959, of 215 items; 'over two-thirds are American editions, almost one-third are London imprints'; with index of illustrators, artists, and designers (p.155–6) and 'A census of extant copies of the 1859 edition now in American libraries' (p.113–18): 18 items.

FITZGERALD, PERCY HETHERINGTON, 1834–1925

3327 **Fitzgerald, Percy Hetherington.** 'List of the author's writings, from the catalogue of the British museum' *in* An output; a list of writings . . . dramas, music, lectures . . . being a record of work done . . . 1850–1912. . . . London [n.d., 1913?] p.[5]–11.

FITZHERBERT, SIR ANTHONY, 1470–1538

3328 **Graham, Howard Jay** and **J. W. Heckel.** The book that made the common law; the first printing of Fitzherbert's Le graunde abridgement, 1514–1516. Law Lib J 51:100–16 My '58.

'Census of copies' (p.103).

FITZMAURICE, GEORGE, fl.1914

3329 **Miller, Liam.** George Fitzmaurice, a bibliographical note. Irish Writing 15:47–8 '51.

Checklist of works and periodical contribs., with some bibliogr. notes.

FLAXMAN, JOHN, 1755–1826

3330 **Bentley, Gerald Eades, jr.** Notes on the early editions of Flaxman's classical designs. N.Y. Pub Lib Bull 68:277–307, 361–80 My,Je '64.

Quasifacsim. TP transcrs., collations, locations of copies, and bibliogr. notes on early ed.

FLETCHER, ANDREW, 1655–1716

3331 **Macfie, Robert Andrew Scott.** A bibliography of Andrew Fletcher of Saltoun, 1653–1716. Edinburgh, Privately printed, 1901. 32p.+34 facsims. 26cm.

Repr. from Edinburgh Bib Soc Proc 4pt2:117–48 '01; classified arrangement of early ed., etc., with short titles and TP facsims., discursive collations, and bibliogr. notes and locations of copies.

FLETCHER, GILES, 1549?–1611

3332 **Berry, Lloyd Eason.** Giles Fletcher, the elder; a bibliography. Cambridge Bib Soc Trans 3pt3:200–15 '61.

Classified bibliogr. of manuscripts, ed., and letters, with quasifacsim. TP transcrs., collations, bibliogr. notes and refs., and locations of copies for 11 ptd. works, 1571–1678; no index.

Rev: J. Horden Library ser5 18:231–4 '63.

FLETCHER, JOHN, 1579–1625
See also Beaumont, Francis, 1584–1616, and John Fletcher, 1579–1625.

3333 **Bowers, Fredson Thayer.** A bibliographical history of the Fletcher-Betterton play, The prophetess, 1690. Library ser5 16:169–75 S '61.

Distinction of first ed., 2 issues, and 2d ed., with collation, bibliogr. notes and discussion and locations of copies.

FLEURE, HERBERT JOHN, 1877–
3334 **Sinnhuber, A. M. W.,** 1954: no.198.

FLOWER, ROBIN ERNEST WILLIAM, 1881–1946

3335 **Bell, H. I.** Robin Ernest William Flower, 1881–1946. Proc Brit Acad 32:353–79 '46.

'Bibliography' (p.[375]–9): chronol. checklist, 1910–45.

FOOTE, SAMUEL, 1720–1777

3336 **Belden, Mary Megie.** 'Bibliography' *in* The dramatic works of Samuel Foote. New Haven; London, 1929. p.[196]–206.

Classified checklist of works and ana.

FORBES, GEORGE HAY, fl.1821–1875
See under Presses and printing—Pitsligo press.

FORBES, JOHN, 1570–1606

3337 **Law, Thomas Graves.** The bibliography of the lives of two Scottish Capuchins, John Forbes and George Leslie, both named in religion Archangel. Edinburgh Bib Soc Pub 1pt1:1–12 [i.e. 17–29] D'91.

'List of editions [for Forbes]' (p.3–4); [for Leslie] (p.7–12).

FORD, FORD MADOX, 1873-1939

3338 **Gerber, Helmut E.** Ford Madox Ford, an annotated checklist of writings about him. Eng Fict Transit 1no2:2-19 '58.

3338a —— [**Same**]: Supplement, by Frank MacShane. *ib.* 4no2:19-29 '61.

3339 **Naumburg, Edward.** A catalogue of a Ford Madox Ford collection. Princeton Univ Lib Chron 9:134-65 Ap '48.

3340 **MacShane, Frank.** Ford Madox Ford: collections of his letters, collections of his manuscripts, periodical publications by him, his introductions, prefaces and miscellaneous contribution to books by others. Eng Fict Transit 4no2:11-18 '61.

Classified checklist.

3341 **Harvey, David Dow.** Ford Madox Ford, 1873-1939: a bibliography of works and criticism. Princeton, N.J., Princeton U.P., 1962; London, O.U.P., 1963. xxiii,633p. port. 24cm.

Classified annotated checklist of books, contribs. to books; manuscripts, letters and miscellanea; contribs. to periodicals; and ana (p. 273-633), with various bibliogr. notes.
Rev: TLS 14 Je '63:447; H. E. Gerber Eng Lit Transit 6:57-8 '63; W. White Bull Bib 24:7 '63; M. Allott Mod Lang R 59:123-4 '64; N. Rougier-Lenoir Études Angl 18: 87-8 '64; J. A. Bryant Sewanee R 72:495-500 '64.

FORD, JOHN, fl.1639

3345 **Tannenbaum, Samuel Aaron.** John Ford, a concise bibliography. New York, 1941. viii,31p. 23cm. (Elizabethan bibliographies, no.20)
Classified checklists of works and ana; 385 items.

FORD, RICHARD, 1796–1858

3346 **Ford, Brinsley.** Richard Ford's articles and reviews. Bk Hndbk 1no8:369–80 '49.
'Articles . . .' (p.374–8); 'Books' (p.378–80): checklist.

FORD, SIMON, c.1619–1699

3347 **Dredge, John Ingle,** 1889–99: no.886.

FORSHAW, CHARLES F., fl.1885–1900

3347a **Forshaw, Charles F.** Bibliography of Charles F. Forshaw, LL.D. N&Q ser8 5:64–5 Ja '94.
Chronol. checklist, 1885–92.

FORSTER, EDWARD MORGAN, 1879–

3348 **Gerber, Helmut E.** E. M. Forster, an annotated checklist of writings about him. Eng Fict Transit 2no1:4–27 '59.

3349 **Stallybrass, O. G. W.,** 1958: no.207.

3350 **Greiff, Louis K.** E. M. Forster, a bibliography. Bull Bib 24:108–12 S/D '64.

3351 **Kirkpatrick, Brownlee Jean.** A bibliography of E. M. Forster. London, R. Hart-Davis, 1965. 200p. port.,facsim. 23cm. (Soho bibliographies, XIX)
Classified bibliogr. of books and pamphlets; contribs. to books and pamphlets; contribs. to periodicals and newspapers; translations into foreign languages; and miscellaneous; quasifacsim. TP transcrs., collations, and bibliogr. notes on first ed.
Rev: TLS 1 Jl '65:568; Pa Bib Soc Am 59:456 '65; R. J. Roberts Bk Coll 15:75–6,79 '66.

3352 **Shipley, John B.** Additions to the E. M. Forster bibliography. Pa Bib Soc Am 60:224–5 '66.

FOSTER, THOMAS, fl.1591–1614

3355 **Dredge, John Ingle,** 1889–99: no.886.

FOWLER, ELLEN THORNEYCROFT (MRS. A. L. FELKIN), 1860–1929

3356 **Chesterton, Gilbert Keith.** Ellen Thorneycroft Fowler. Eng Illus Mag new ser 29:86, 90 Ap '03.
'Bibliography' (p.86, 90): checklist of novels, articles, and poems.

FOX, AUGUSTUS HENRY LANE, afterwards PITT-RIVERS, 1827–1900
See Rivers, Augustus Henry Lane Fox Pitt-.

FOXE, JOHN, 1516–1587

3357 **Mozley, James Frederic.** 'Foxe's minor works' *in* John Foxe and his book. London; York [1940] p.243–5.
Chronol. checklist, c.1547–87, with some bibliogr. notes.

FOXWELL, HERBERT SOMERTON, 1849–1936

3358 **Keynes, John Maynard, 1st baron Keynes.** Herbert Somerton Foxwell,
June 17, 1849–August 3, 1936. Econ J 46:589–614 D '36.
'Publications' (p.611–14): chronol. checklist, 1884–1927.

FRANKLIN, SIR JOHN, 1786–1847

3359 **Osborne, Eric Allen.** Bibliography [of sir John Franklin, arctic explorer] Bk
Hndbk 1no1:46–9 '47.
Short-title checklist, with notes.

FRASER, CLAUD LOVAT, 1890–1921

3360 **[Millard, Christopher Sclater]** The printed work of Claud Lovat Fraser.
London, H. Danielson, 1923. x,106p. illus.(1 col.) port., facsims. 26cm.
Classified checklist of 743 items with some bibliogr. notes; no index.

FRAZER, SIR JAMES GEORGE, 1854–1941

3361 **Besterman, Theodore Deodatus Nathaniel.** A bibliography of sir James
Frazer. . . . London, Macmillan, 1934. xxi,100p. ports., facsim. 21cm.
Chronol. list, 1884–1933, with 'Classified list' (p.85–93). A list of addenda and corrigenda, by lady Lilly Frazer, 1937, listed by Besterman in his World bibliography, has
not been located.

FREEMAN, EDWARD AUGUSTUS, 1823–1892

3362 **Stephens, William Richard Wood.** 'Bibliography' *in* The life and letters of
Edward A. Freeman. London, 1895. V.2, p.[481]–91.
Checklist of books and articles.

FREEMAN, JOHN, 1880–1929

3363 **Bibliographies** of modern authors. John Freeman. Lond Merc 1no4:496–7
F '20.
Chronol. checklist, 1909–19.

FREEMAN, RICHARD AUSTIN, 1862–1943

3364 **Checklist** bibliographies of modern authors. Richard Austin Freeman. Bk
Trade J 64:20–1 Jl '36.
Chronol. checklist, 1898–1933, with notes on bindings.

FROST, JOHN, 1784?–1877

3365 **Newport. Public libraries, museum, and art gallery.** John Frost and the
chartist movement in Monmouthshire; catalogue of chartist literature,
prints, relics, etc., by John Warner and W. A. Gunn. Newport, Chartist
centenary committee, 1939. xii,55p. 25cm.
Annotated classified short-title catalogue; 'Pamphlets by John Frost' (p.2–6); 'Pamphlets by Samuel Etheridge' (p.11–12).
Rev: C. Fay Econ J 50:305–6 '39.

FULLER, THOMAS, 1608–1661

3366 **Axon, William Edward Armytage,** *comp.* 'Bibliotheca Fulleriana' *in* Bailey, John E. and W. E. A. Axon, *ed.* The collected sermons of Thomas Fuller. London, 1891. V.2, p.576–84.

Checklist, superseding that in Bailey's Life, 1874.

3367 **Manchester. Public libraries. Reference library.** The Fuller collection in the Free reference library. Manchester, H. Blacklock, print., 1891. ii,8[2]p. 25cm. (Not seen)

Comp. by John E. Bailey.

3369 **Gibson, Strickland.** A bibliography of the works of Thomas Fuller, D.D. Oxford Bib Soc Proc 4pt1:63–161 '34.

3370 —— **[Same]**: Additions and corrections. Oxford Bib Soc Pub new ser 1:44 '49.

Classified chronol. arrangement of separate works, 1631–1781; selections, works contrib. to, and biographies, etc.; with quasifacsim. TP transcrs., and facsims., locations of copies, with some bibliogr. notes; no index.

Rev: TLS 13 Je '36:504.

FULLWOOD, FRANCIS, d.1693

3371 **Dredge, John Ingle,** 1889–99: no.886.

FURNIVALL, FREDERICK JAMES, 1825–1910

3372 **Littlehales, Henry,** *comp.* 'F. J. Furnivall, a bibliography' *in* An English miscellany presented to dr. Furnivall. . . . Oxford, 1901. p.[481]–9.

Chronol. checklist, 1850–99.

3373 **Sidgwick, Frank.** Frederick James Furnivall. Eng Illus Mag new ser 30: 556–9 F '04.

'Bibliography' (p.558–9): checklist of works; introductions and prefaces; works edited; and miscellaneous.

FUSELI, HENRY (JOHANN HEINRICH FUESSLI), 1741–1825

3374 **Hammelmann, H. A.** Eighteenth-century English illustrators: Henry Fuseli, R.A. Bk Coll 6n04:350–60 '57.

'Handlist of books with illustrations by Fuseli' (p.354–60): chronol. checklist, 1765–1810, with bibliogr. notes.

3375 **Schiff, Gert.** Books with illustrations by Fuseli. Bk Coll 7n03:299–300 '58.

7 additions and corrections to Hammelmann.

GALSWORTHY, JOHN, 1867–1933

3380 **Gerber, Helmut E.** John Galsworthy, an annotated checklist of writings about him. Eng Fict Transit 1n03:7–29 '58.

—— **[Same]**: Supplement 1, by Earl E. Stevens. *ib.* 7n02:93–110 '64.

3382 **'A bibliography** of the works of John Galsworthy' *in* John Galsworthy, an appreciation together with a bibliography. London, 1926. p.15–[22]

3383 **Marrot, Harold Vincent.** A bibliography of the works of John Galsworthy. London, E. Mathews & Marrot; New York, C. Scribner's, 1928. xii,252p. port., facsims. 23cm.

Classified arrangement of first ed. (p.3–134) and shorter contribs. and translations (p.139–92) and ana.; TP transcrs., collations, and bibliogr. notes, with distinction of issues.

Rev: TLS 18 Oc '28:760; I. A. Williams Lond Merc 19:81–2 '28; N&Q 155:306 '28; Life & Letters 1:631–2 '28; A. W. P[ollard] Library ser4 9:418–21 '29.

3384 **Fabes, Gilbert Henry.** John Galsworthy, his first editions: points and values. London, W. & G. Foyle, 1932. xxiv,64p. 18cm.

Rev: TLS 4 Ag '32:558.

GALT, JOHN, 1779–1839

3390 **Lumsden, Harry.** The bibliography of John Galt. Glasgow Bib Soc Rec 9:1–41 '31.

'Bibliography' (p.23–41): chronol. checklist, 1802–1925.

3391 **Gordon, Robert Kay.** 'List of Galt's writings' *in* John Galt. Toronto, 1920. p.118–21.

3392 **Booth, Bradford Allen.** A bibliography of John Galt. Bull Bib 16:7–9 S/D '36.

Checklist of periodical contribs., American ed., and biographical material and criticism, complimenting Lumsden.

GARDINER, MARGUERITE (POWER), COUNTESS BLESSINGTON, 1789–1849

3293 **Sadleir, Michael Thomas Hervey.** 'Hand-list of lady Blessington's books' in Blessington-D'Orsay, a masquerade. London [1933] p.373–5.

3394 —— [Same, rev.] *in* [Same]: New ed., rev. and enl. London [1947] p.366–7.

Chronol. checklist, 1822–56.

GARDINER, SAMUEL RAWSON, 1829–1902

3395 **Shaw, William Arthur,** 1903: no.2918.

GARNET, HENRY, 1555–1606

3396 **Allison, Antony Francis.** The writings of fr. Henry Garnet, S.J., 1555–1606. Biog Stud 1no1:7–21 '51.

Annotated checklist of 5 items, with locations of copies.

GARNETT, RICHARD, 1835–1906

See also Garnett family.

3397 **Pollard, Alfred William.** Richard Garnett. Eng Illus Mag new ser 30:553–5, 559 F '04.

'Bibliography' (p.555, 559): checklist of works; prefaces and works ed.; and articles about.

GARNETT FAMILY

3398 **Texas. University. Humanities research center.** The Garnetts, a literary family: an exhibition. [Austin] 1959. 15p. illus. 25cm. Covertitle.

Checklist, with some bibliogr. notes, of works by Richard, Edward, Constance, David, Richard Duncan, and William Garnett.

GARRICK, DAVID, 1717–1779

3399 **Knapp, Mary Etta.** A checklist of verse by David Garrick. Charlottesville, University of Virginia pr. for the Bibliographical society of the University of Virginia, 1955. 69p. 23cm.

Alphabetical title checklists of occasional verse; prologues and epilogues; theatrical skits; and songs, printed and manuscript; 479 items.

Rev: M. O'Nan Bks Abroad 31:81 '57.

GASCOIGNE, GEORGE, 1525?–1577

3400 **Schelling, Felix Emmanuel.** 'Bibliography' *in* The life and writings of George Gascoigne. . . . Boston; Halle a. S. [1893] p.117–23.

Checklists of manuscripts; collected ed.; separate works; and works attrib. to.

3401 **Tannenbaum, Samuel Aaron.** George Gascoigne, a concise bibliography. New York, 1942. viii,22p. 23cm. (Elizabethan bibliographies, no.26)

Classified checklist of works and ana; 387 items.

GASCOYNE, DAVID, 1916–

3402 **Atkinson, Ann (Curnow).** David Gascoyne, a check-list. Twent Cent Lit 6:180–92 Ja '61.

Classified chronol. checklist of 200 items from 1932, based on University of London School of librarianship and archives bibliography: *see* no.104.

GASKELL, ELIZABETH CLEGHORN, 1810–1865

3403 **Stevenson, Lionel,** *ed.*, 1964: no.1705.

3404 **Axon, William Edward Armytage** and **E. Axon.** Gaskell bibliography; a list of the writings of mrs. E. C. Gaskell . . . and of her husband, the rev. William Gaskell. Manchester, J. Heywood, 1895. 22p. 21cm. Covertitle.

Repr. from Manchester Lit Club Pa v.21 1894/5. 'List of the writings of the rev. William Gaskell' by Ernest Axon (p.16–22): chronol. checklist, 1831–94.

3405 **Chadwick, Esther Alice.** 'Bibliography' *in* Mrs. Gaskell; haunts, homes, and stories, by mrs. Ellis H. Chadwick. London, 1910. p.454–64.

3406 —— [Same]: New and rev. ed. London, 1913. p.321–30.

3407 **Manchester. Public libraries. Moss side branch.** A bibliographical guide to the Gaskell collection in the Moss side library, by John Albert Green. Manchester, Reference library, 1911. 68p. ports., facsims. 19cm.

Supersedes a Handlist by Green, 1903, not seen but prob. unpublished.

3408 **Sadleir, Michael Thomas Hervey,** 1922: no.1706.

3409 **Whitfield, A. Stanton.** 'A bibliography of the works of Elizabeth Cleghorn Gaskell' *in* Mrs. Gaskell, her life and work. London, 1929. p.221–36.

3410 **Northup, Clark Sutherland,** *comp.* 'Bibliography' *in* Sanders, G. DeW. Elizabeth Gaskell . . . . New Haven; London, 1929. p.[163]–267.

Classified checklist of collective; single, and undated ed.; and ana, with some bibliogr. notes.

3411 **Parrish, Morris Longstreth,** 1933: no.1707.

3412 **Hopkins, Annette B.** Mrs. Gaskell in France, 1849–1890. Pub Mod Lang Assn 53:545–74 Je '38.

'Table 1: mrs. Gaskell's publications in France' (p.550–4): checklist of 18 items, with bibliogr. notes, and addenda to Northup.

3413 **Halls, C. M. E.,** 1957: no.135.

GASKELL, WILLIAM, 1805–1884

3414 **Axon, William Edward Armytage** and **E. Axon**, 1895: no.3404.

GAUDEN, JOHN, 1605–1662

3415 **Dredge, John Ingle,** 1889–99: no.886.

GAY, JOHN, 1685–1732

3416 **Wright, William Henry Kearly,** *ed.* 'Chronological list of the various editions of Gay's Fables' *in* The fables of John Gay. New ed. London, 1889. p.299–313.

3416a **Faber, Geoffrey C.,** *ed.* 'Bibliographical summary' *in* The poetical works of John Gay. . . . London, 1926. p.[xxxv]–xlvii.
Checklists of early and modern ed.

GAYLARD, DOCTOR, fl.1721–1736

3416b **Limouze, A. Sanford.** Doctor Gaylard's Loyal observator reviv'd. Mod Philol 48:97–103 N '50.
'. . . contents of the surviving numbers of The loyal observatory reviv'd' (p.101–3).

GERARD, ALEXANDER, 1728–1795

3417 **Goy, J. R.,** 1964: no.130.

GIBBINGS, ROBERT JOHN, 1889–1958
See also Presses and printing—Golden cockerel press.

3418 **Balston, Thomas.** 'Books illustrated by Robert Gibbings' *in* The wood engravings of Robert Gibbings. London, 1949. p.9–11.

3419 **Kirkus, Agnes Mary.** Robert Gibbings, a bibliography; edited by Patience Empson and John Harris. . . . London, J. M. Dent [1962] xiii,170p. illus., port., facsims. 21cm.
'Part one: a descriptive bibliography of books written and illustrated by Robert Gibbings, compiled by A. Mary Kirkus' (p.3–77): classified chronol. arrangement of 67 first ed., with quasifacsim. TP transcrs., collations, bibliogr. notes, but no locations of copies. 'Part two: a chronological check list of books, articles and ephemera, written, illustrated, printed or published by Robert Gibbings, compiled by Patience Empson and John Harris' (p.81–121): items 68–305; ana (p.125–44).
Rev: TLS 1 Je '62:420; P. H. Muir Bk Coll 12:109–10 '63.

GIBBON, EDWARD, 1737–1794

3420 **Cordasco, Francesco G. M.** Edward Gibbon, a handlist of critical notices & studies. New York, Long Island U.P., 1950. 8p. 24cm. (Eighteenth century bibliographical pamphlets, no.10)

3421 **Royal historical society.** 'Catalogue of the exhibition of manuscripts, books . . . at the British museum, November, 1894' *in* Proceedings of the Gibbon commemoration, 1794–1894. London, 1895. p.36–52.
'Printed works': items 57–63.

3422 **Beatty, H. M.,** *comp.* 'Bibliography of Gibbon's History, minor and miscellaneous works, and letters; and of the controversial replies to History' *in* The history of the decline and fall; ed. by J. B. Bury. London [1914] V.7, p.348–64.

3423 **Norton, Jane Elizabeth.** A bibliography of the works of Edward Gibbon. [Oxford] O.U.P., 1940. xvi,256p. illus., facsims. 23cm.

Chronol. arrangement of 160 items, mostly pre-1838; quasifacsim. TP transcrs., collations, bibliogr. notes and locations of copies. 'List of attacks on Gibbon' (p.[233]–47): chronol. checklist, 1776–1874.

Rev: J. W. Carter Pub Wkly 138:2041–2 '40; TLS 16 N '40:584; N&Q 179:431–2 '40; D. M. Low R Eng Stud 17:361–3 '41; sir G. L. Keynes Spectator 13 D '41:650–2; G. Jones Mod Lang R 37:381–2 '42.

GIBBON, LEWIS GRASSIC, *pseud. of* JAMES LESLIE MITCHELL, 1901–1935

3424 **Wagner, Geoffrey.** James Leslie Mitchell / Lewis Grassic Gibbon. Biblioth 1n01:3–21 '56.

'James Leslie Mitchell / Lewis Grassic Gibbon: a chronological checklist of his writings' (p.7–21): checklist of works, 1928–50, and ana.

3425 **Aitken, William Russell.** Further notes on the bibliography of James Leslie Mitchell / Lewis Grassic Gibbon. Biblioth 1n02:34–5 '57.

GIBBON, SKEFFINGTON, fl.1796–1831

3426 **Cassedy, James.** Skeffington Gibbon in the Goldsmith country. Irish Bk Lover 22:58–62 Ja/F '34.

'Bibliography' (p.61–2): chronol. checklist, 1829–64, with locations of copies.

GIBSON, WILFRID WILSON, b.1878

3427 **Gawsworth, John,** *pseud.* [1932]: no.686.

Collection is now in the University of Kansas library.

GIFFORD, GEORGE, d.1620

3428 **Carlson, Leland H.,** *ed.* 'George Gifford's writings' *in* The writings of Henry Barrow, 1590–1591. London [1966] p.378–80.

Chronol. checklist, 1573–1612.

GILBERT, SIR JOHN, 1817–1897

3428a **Thomas, Ralph.** Sir John Gilbert, J. F. Smith and the London journal. N&Q ser11 10:102–3,114,183–5,223–5,262–3,301–3 Ag–Oc '14.

'A complete list of the tales sir John Gilbert illustrated in The London journal' (p.183–5).

GILBERT, SIR JOHN THOMAS, 1829–1898

3429 **Gilbert, Rose Mulholland, lady.** 'Bibliography of the works of sir John T. Gilbert' *in* Life of sir John T. Gilbert. . . . London, 1905. p.445–8.

Chronol. checklist, 1851–99.

GILBERT, SIR WILLIAM SCHWENCK, 1836–1911

3430 **Searle, R. Townley.** A bibliography of sir William Schwenck Gilbert. . . . London, Privately pr., 1931. (Not seen)

3431 —— [Same, with title]: Sir William Schwenck Gilbert, a topsy-turvy adventure. London, Alexander-Ouseley, 1931. 105p. illus., facsims. 26cm.

Discursive classified checklist, with some TP transcrs. and bibliogr. notes on works and ana.

Rev: G. M. Troxell Sat R Lit 8:127 '31; Lond Merc 24:362 '31; J. W. Carter Bk Coll Q 4: 61–4 '31.

3432 **Dubois, Arthur Edwin.** Additions to the bibliography of W. S. Gilbert's contributions to magazines. Mod Lang N 47:308–14 My '32.

Addenda and corrigenda to Searle.

3433 **Allen, Reginald.** W. S. Gilbert, an anniversary survey and exhibition checklist. . . . Charlottesville, Va., Bibliographical society of the University of Virginia, 1964. 82p. illus., facsims. 24cm.

'The Grolier Club W. S. Gilbert exhibition checklist' (p.17–82).

Rev: TLS 19 Mr '64:244; P. H. Muir Theat Notebk 18:137–9 '64.

GILL, ARTHUR ERIC ROWTON, 1882–1940

3435 **Gill, Evan Robertson.** Bibliography of Eric Gill. London, Cassell [1953] xv,223p. illus., port., facsims. 26cm.

Classified arrangement of works and ana, with TP transcrs. or facsims., collations, bibliogr. notes, including account of illus.; 679 items.

Rev: P. H. Muir Bk Coll 2:229–31 '53.

3436 **Stanford university. Library.** Catalogue of an exhibition of Eric Gill from the collections of Albert Sperisen & others. . . . Stanford university, 1954. ix,23p. illus. 25cm.

Comp. by J. Terry Bender.

3437 **[Smith, Roger]** Eric Gill; a catalogue of manuscripts, books, engravings . . . in the collection of mr. and mrs. S. Samuels. Liverpool, 1963. 50p. illus. 23cm.

Works written or illustrated by Eric Gill (p.1–22): checklist of 658 items, with some bibliogr. notes; 'Books and miscellanea not listed in the Bibliography [i.e. no.3435]' (p.23–4).

GILPIN, WILLIAM, 1724–1804

3438 **Templeman, William Darby.** [Title checklist] *in* The life and work of William Gilpin, 1724–1804. . . . Urbana, 1939. p.311–15.

GIRALDUS DE BARRI, CAMBRENSIS, 1146?–1220?

3439 **Williams, Eileen A.** A bibliography of Giraldus Cambrensis, *c*.1147–*c*. 1223. Nat Lib Wales J 12no2:97–140 '61.

Based on London university School of librarianship and archives bibliography: *see* no.232. 'Author bibliography [a classified checklist]' (p.127–34); 'Subject bibliography' (p.134–40).

GISSING, GEORGE ROBERT, 1857–1903

3440 **Korg, Jacob.** George Gissing [an annotated bibliography of writings about him] Eng Fict Transit 1no1:24–8 '57.

3441 ——[Same]: Supplement, by Joseph J. Wolff. *ib.* 3no2:3–33 '60.

3442 ——[Same]: Foreign journals: supplement II, by Pierre Coustillas and P. Goetsch. *ib.* 7no1:14–26 '64.

3443 ——[Same]: Supplement III, by Joseph J. Wolff. *ib.* 7no2:73–92 '64.

3444 **Stevenson, Lionel,** *ed.,* 1964: no.1705.

3445 **Courtney, W. L.** George Gissing. Eng Illus Mag new ser 30:188–92 N '03. 'Bibliography' (p.192).

3446 **Danielson, Henry.** Bibliographies [of modern authors] no.13. George Gissing. Bkmns J 2no30–7:52, 69, 86, 101, 116, 134, 150, 166 '20.

3447 ——, 1921: no.680.

3448 **Scott, Temple,** *pseud.,* *ed.* 'Bibliography of George Gissing' *in* Critica studies of the works of Charles Dickens. . . . New York, 1924. p.161–5.

3449 **Polak, R-L.,** 1950: no.187.

3450 **New York. Public library. Berg collection.** George Gissing, 1857–1903; an exhibition from the Berg collection, by John D. Gordan. New York, New York public library, 1954. 45p. port. 26cm.
     Repr. in N.Y. Pub Lib Bull 58:489–96, 551–66, 611–18 '54; 59:35–46 '55.

3451 **Coustillas, Pierre.** Gissing's short stories, a bibliography. Eng Lit Transit 7no2:57–72 '64.
     Annotated chronol. checklist, 1877–1923, with lists of collections and translations.

GLADSTONE, WILLIAM EWART, 1809–1898

3455 **Contributions** to a bibliography of the right hon. W. E. Gladstone. N&Q ser8 2:461–3, 501–3 D '92; 3:1–3 41–3 Ja '93.
Checklist, 1827–92, with some bibliogr. notes and locations of copies.

3456 **Ward, James.** Collection of relics . . . letters, books, etc. relating to W. E. Gladstone . . . in the possession of . . . . [Nottingham] 1901. 5p. 17cm.

3457 **Brooklyn. Public library.** William Ewart Gladstone, 1809–1898, a list of books and of references to periodicals in the Brooklyn public library. Brooklyn, 1909. 30p. 16cm.

GLANVILL, JOSEPH, 1636–1680

3458 **Dredge, John Ingle,** 1889–99: no.886.

GLENDOWER, OWEN (OWAIN AB GRUFFYDD), 1359?–1416?

3459 **Phillips, David Rhys.** . . . A select bibliography of Owen Glyndwr. Swansea, B. Glas, 1915. 48p. 21cm.
Annotated classified list of refs. to him in literature.

GODWIN, BP. FRANCIS, 1562–1633

3459a **Lawton, H. W.** Bishop Godwin's Man in the moone. R Eng Stud 7:23–55 Ja '31.
'Bibliographical note' (p.52–5): checklist of early ed., with bibliogr. notes and locations of copies.

GODWIN, MARY WOLLSTONECRAFT (MRS. SHELLEY), 1797–1851

3460 **Wise, Thomas James,** 1924: no.4652.

GODWIN, WILLIAM, 1756–1836

3461 **Cordasco, Francesco G. M.** William Godwin, a handlist of critical notices & studies. New York, Long Island U.P., 1950. 8p. 24cm. (Eighteenth century bibliographical pamphlets, no.9)

3462 **Brown, Ford K.** 'The works . . .' in The life of William Godwin. London, 1926. p.xi–xii.
Chronol. checklist, 1783–1873.

GOFF, THOMAS, 1591–1629

3463 **Saintsbury, George Edward Bateman.** Thomas Goff. Bibliographer 2no5: 291–8 My '03.
'Collations' (p.297–8) now superseded by Greg, no.1608.

GOLDSMITH, OLIVER, 1728–1774

3464 **Williams, Iolo Aneurin,** 1924: no.633.

3465 **Bonner, Willard Hallam.** Poems for young ladies, a bibliographical note. N&Q 155:129–32 Ag '28.
TP transcrs., collations, and bibliogr. notes on ed. of 1767, 1770, and 1785.

3466 **Dix, Ernest Reginald McClintock.** The works of Oliver Goldsmith; hand-list of Dublin editions before 1801. Bib Soc Ireland Pubs 3n09:93–101 '28.

Classified chronol. checklist, 1762–1800, with locations of copies and some bibliogr. notes.

3467 **Scott, Temple,** *pseud.* Oliver Goldsmith bibliographically and bio-graphically considered; based on the collection of material in the library of W. M. Elkins. New York, Bowling Green pr., 1928. xix,368p. col.front., illus., ports., facsims. 27cm.

Discursive bibliogr. catalogue of early ed., with numerous TP facsims.

Rev: TLS 28 F '29:161; H. J. Smith Univ California Chron 31:429–36 '29; H. J. Smith Sat R Lit 5:788 '29; E. Clark N.Y. Times Bk R 3 Mr '29:2; L. L. Mackall Bks 2 Je '29:23; Dublin Mag 5:87–8 '30.

3468 **Yale university. Library.** An exhibition in the Yale university library of the works of Oliver Goldsmith. . . . New Haven, 1928. 7p. 27cm.

3469 **Stone, Wilbur Macey.** The history of Little goody two-shoes. Am Antiqu Soc Proc new ser 49:333–70 '39.

'Bibliography' (p.357–70): chronol. checklist of British ed., 1765–1850, and American ed., 1774–1850, with TP facsims., discursive bibliogr. notes and locations of copies.

3469a **Friedman, Arthur.** Goldsmith's contributions to the Critical review. Mod Philol 44:23–52 Ag '46.

'I. Reviews contributed by Goldsmith.—II. Possible contributions. . . .—III. Reviews to be dropped from the canon' (p.52).

3470 **Todd, William Burton.** The private issues of The deserted village. Stud Bib 6:25–44 '54.

'Textual collation' (p.37–9); 'Check-list of separate unauthorized editions of the Deserted village, with notes on other piracies' (p.39–44): TP transcrs., collations, and locations of copies.

3471 —— The first editions of The good natur'd man and She stoops to con-quer. Stud Bib 11:133–42 '58.

Distinguishes 5 impressions of the first play, and 6 of the second, with locations of copies.

3472 **Friedman, Arthur.** Two notes on Goldsmith: 1. The first edition of Gold-smith's Life of Bolingbroke. 2. The 1772 edition of Goldsmith's Traveller. Stud Bib 13:232–5 '60.

Quasifacsim. TP transcr., collation, bibliogr. notes and locations of copies for item 1; distinction of 2 unnumbered 1770 ed., with locations of copies, for item 2.

3473 **Roberts, R. Julian.** The 1765 edition of Goody two-shoes. Brit Mus Q 29n03/4:67–70 '65.

TP facsim., bibliogr. notes and discussion of first [1765] ed.

GOODMAN, BP. GODFREY, 1583–1656

3475 **Soden, Geoffrey Ingle.** 'The works of Godfrey Goodman' *in* Godfrey Goodman, bishop of Gloucester, 1583–1656. London, 1953. p.480–2.
Discursive checklist of 10 items.

GORDON, ALEXANDER, 1841–1931

3476 **McLachlan, Herbert.** 'A list of the published writings of Alexander Gordon' *in* Alexander Gordon. . . . [Manchester] 1932. p.125–86.
Chronol. checklist, 1869–1930.

GORDON, THOMAS, d.1750

3477 **Bulloch, John Malcolm.** Thomas Gordon, the independent whig. Aberdeen, Aberdeen U.P., 1918. 33p. 22cm.
Repr. from Aberdeen Univ Lib Bull 3:598–612 N '17; 3:733–49 My '18; bio-bibliogr. checklist.

GOSSE, SIR EDMUND WILLIAM, 1849–1928

3478 **Garnett, Richard.** Edmund Gosse, LL.D. Eng Illus Mag new ser 29:641–3, 648, 650 S '03.
'Bibliography' (p.642, 648, 650): classified checklist of works, translations, works ed. or introduced by, and ana.

3479 **Bibliographies** of modern authors. Edmund [William] Gosse. Lond Merc 3no14:212–13 D '20.
Select chronol. checklist of verse and drama; and prose, 1870–1919.

GOSSE, PHILIP HENRY, 1810–1888

3480 **Lister, Raymond George.** A bibliographical check-list of works by Philip Gosse. Cambridge, J. P. Gray, 1952. 20p. port. 21cm.

3481 **Stageman, Peter.** A bibliography of the first editions of Philip Henry Gosse, F.R.S. Cambridge, Golden head pr., 1955. xi,87p. illus. 22cm.
Chronol. arrangement of 46 first ed., with 'Contributions to periodicals' (p.77–83): quasifacsim. TP transcrs., collations, and bibliogr. notes; no index.
Rev: W. R. LeFanu Bk Coll 4:334–6 '55; sir G. L. K[eynes] Library ser5 11:64–5 '56.

GOSSON, STEPHEN, 1554–1624

3482 **Ringler, William.** 'Bibliography' *in* Stephen Gosson, a biographical and critical study. Princeton, 1942. p.[139]–51.
TP transcrs., collations, bibliogr. notes and locations of copies for ms. and printed, genuine, and doubtful or spurious works.

GOSTWYKE, ROGER, 1597–1645

3483 **Dredge, John Ingle,** 1889–99: no.886.

GOTHER, JAMES, d.1704

3484 **Brockway, Duncan.** Some new editions from the reign of James II. Pa Bib Soc Am 55:118–30 '61.
Distinction of ed. of works by Gother, with quasifacsim. TP transcrs., collations, locations of copies, and bibliogr. notes.

3485 **Doig, Ronald P.** A bibliographical study of Gough's British topography. Edinburgh Bib Soc Trans 4pt3:103–36 '63.

Minute descr. of 1780 ed., with locations of copies.

GRAHAM, DOUGAL, 1724–1779

3486 **Fairley, John A.** Bibliography of the chap-books attributed to Dougal Graham. Glasgow Bib Soc Rec 1:125–215 '13.

TP transcrs., discursive collations, and locations of copies for 290 items from 1746.

GRAHAM, ROBERT BONTINE CUNNINGHAME, 1852–1936

3490 **Chaundy, Leslie.** A bibliography of the first editions of the works of Robert Bontine Cunninghame Graham. London, Dulau, 1924. 16p. 18cm.

Quasifacsim. TP transcrs., with short collations and bibliogr. notes; no index.

3491 **West, Herbert Faulkner.** The Herbert Faulkner West collection of R. B. Cunninghame Graham presented . . . to the Dartmouth college library. . . . [Dartmouth] Privately ptd., 1938. 20p. 24cm.

3492 **Watts, C. T.** R. B. Cunninghame Graham, 1852–1936; a list of his contributions to periodicals. Biblioth 4no5:186–99 '65.

GRAHAME, KENNETH, 1859–1932

3492a **Green, Roger Lancelyn.** Kenneth Grahame. TLS 9 Je '45:276.

3492b **Green, Peter.** 'Bibliography 1' *in* Kenneth Grahame, 1859–1932: a study of his life, work, and times. London [1959] p.377–80.

Chronol. checklist of 85 items, 1873–1933, based on previous item.

GRAND, SARAH, d.1943

3493 **Sarah** Grand. Eng Illus Mag new ser 29:283–5 Je '03.

'Bibliography' (p.284–5): chronol. checklist of works, 1888–1901, with ana.

GRANT, JAMES, 1822–1887

3494 **Playfair, J. K. H.,** 1957: no.185.

GRAUNT, JOHN, 1620–1674

3494a **Hull, Charles Henry,** 1899: no.4416a.

GRAVELOT, HUBERT FRANÇOIS, 1699–1773

3495 **Hammelmann, H. A.** English eighteenth-century book illustrators. Bk Hndbk 2no3:127–46 '51.

'English books illustrated by Gravelot' (p.129–34): chronol. checklist.

3496 —— [Same]: Supplement. *ib.* 2no4:189–90 '51/2.

GRAVES, ALFRED PERCEVAL, 1846–1931

3497 **Graves, Alfred Perceval.** 'Bibliography' *in* To return to all that; an auto-biography. London, 1930. p.347–50.

Classified checklist of prose, poetry, anthologies, musical pubs., and plays.

GRAVES, RICHARD, 1715–1804

3498 **Hill, Charles Jarvis.** 'A bibliography of the first editions of the works of Richard Graves' *in* The literary career of Richard Graves, the author of The spiritual Quixote. Northampton, Mass. [1935] p.131–44.

TP transcrs., discursive collations, and some bibliogr. notes.

GRAVES, ROBERT RANKE, 1895–

3499 **Higginson, Fred Hall.** A bibliography of the works of Robert Graves. London, N. Vane, 1966. 328p. port., facsims. 21cm.

Classified bibliogr. of books and pamphlets; contribs. to books; contribs. to the press and periodicals; miscellanea; ana.; and 'Appendix II: European editions in English'.

Rev: TLS 10 N '66:1032; Pa Bib Soc Am 61:158 '67; R. J. Roberts Library ser5 23:85–7 '68.

GRAY, JOHN HENRY, 1866–1934

3501 **Anderson, Alan,** *comp.* 'Bibliography of John Gray' *in* Sewell, Brocard, *ed.* Two friends, John Gray and André Raffalovich: essays biographical and critical. [Aylesford] 1963. p.178–87.

TP transcrs., and bibliogr. notes on 20 items, with 'Check-list of contributions to books' (p.185–7): items 21–33.

GRAY, THOMAS, 1716–1771

3501a **Northup, Clark Sutherland.** Gray's Elegy: translations and parodies. N&Q ser11 3:62–4, 144–5, 204–5 Ja–Mr '11; E. Bensly *ib.* ser11 4:90–2 Jl '11; C. W. Brodribb 4:135 Ag '11; L.R.M. Strachan 6:157–8 Ag '12; W.B.H. 6:517 D '12.

Classified checklist incorporated in next item.

3502 —— A bibliography of Thomas Gray. New Haven, Yale U.P.; London, H. Milford, O.U.P., 1917. xiii,296p. 22cm.

Classified title arrangement of works and ana, with some TP transcrs., and bibliogr. notes; locations of copies. *See* no.3505.

Rev: Nation 106:214–15 '18; TLS 20 D '17:635; R. S. Crane Pa Bib Soc Am 12:58–62 '18; M. A. Buchanan Nation 106:404 '18.

3503 **Fukuhara, Rintaro.** A bibliographical study of Thomas Gray. . . . [Tokyo] 1933. 68p. facsims. 27cm.

3504 **Rothkrug, Michael.** 'An apparently unrecorded appearance of Gray's Elegy, 1751; an appendix to Stokes' *in* Papers in honor of Andrew Keogh. New Haven, 1938. p.[343]–53.

TP facsim. and list of variants.

3505 **Starr, Herbert Wilmarth.** A bibliography of Thomas Gray, 1917–1951; with material supplementary to C. S. Northup's Bibliography of Thomas Gray. Philadelphia, University of Pennsylvania pr., for Temple university publications, 1953. xii,152p. 24cm.

3506 **Jones, William Powell.** Imitations of Gray's Elegy, 1751–1800. Bull Bib 23no10:230–2 Ja/Ap '63.

Chronol. checklist, supplementing Northup, and Starr.

GREENAWAY, CATHERINE ('KATE'), 1846–1901

3510 **Spielmann, Marion Harry** and **G. S. Layard.** 'List of books, etc., illustrated wholly or part by Kate Greenaway' *in* Kate Greenaway. London, 1905. p.285–9.
Chronol. list, 1871–1900, with TP transcrs.

GREENE, HENRY GRAHAM, 1904–

3511 **Birmingham, William.** Graham Greene criticism, a bibliographical study. Thought 27:72–100 '52.

3512 **A bibliography** of Graham Greene. Marginalia 2:16–19 Ap '51.

3513 **Beebe, Maurice.** Criticism of Graham Greene: a selected checklist, with an index to studies of separate works. Mod Fict Stud 3no3:281–8 '57.

3514 **Hargreaves, Phylis.** Graham Greene, a selected bibliography. Bull Bib 22:45–8 Ja/Ap '57.

3515 —— [Same]: Mod Fict Stud 3no3:269–80 '57.
Expansion of previous item.

3516 **Brennan, Neil,** *comp.* 'Bibliography' *in* Evans, Robert O., *ed.* Graham Greene, some critical considerations. [Lexington, 1963] p.[245]-76.
Chronol. checklist of first ed., 39 items, 1925–63; contributions to books, 29 items; a note on Greene's periodical contribs.; and ana.

GREENE, ROBERT, 1560?–1592

3520 **Tannenbaum, Samuel Aaron.** Robert Greene, a concise bibliography. New York, 1939. [viii]58p. 25cm. (Elizabethan bibliographies, no.8)
Classified checklist of works and ana.

3521 —— [Same]: Supplement. New York, 1950 [i.e., '1945 and 1950'] 23l. 28cm. (Duplicated typescript)

3522 **Miller, Edwin Haviland.** The editions of Robert Greene's A quip for an upstart courtier. Stud Bib 6:107–16 '53.
Quasifacsim. TP transcrs., collations, bibliogr. notes, and locations of copies of 6 1592 ed.

3523 **Parr, Johnstone [and others]** List of editions, copies, and locations of the works of Robert Greene, compiled . . . by J. Parr and I. A. Shapiro and N. J. Sanders. Birmingham, Shakespeare institute, 1958. 13p. 25cm. (Duplicated typescript)
Comp. from STC and various supplements and catalogues.

3524 **Johnson, Francis Rarick.** The editions of Robert Greene's three parts of Conny-catching, a bibliographical analysis. Library ser5 9:17–24 Mr '54.
Quasifacsim. TP transcrs., collations, STC nos., and locations of copies for 8 ed.

GREENWOOD, CHRISTOPHER, 1786–1855

3527 **Harley, John Brian.** 'A chronological list of maps and other works by Christopher Greenwood and partners' *in* Christopher Greenwood, county map-maker. . . . Worcester, 1962. p.59–68.

GREGORY, ISABELLA AUGUSTA (PERSSE), LADY, 1852–1932

3528 **Coxhead, Eileen Elizabeth,** 'Lady Gregory's principal publications, *in* Lady Gregory, a literary portrait. 2d ed., rev. and enl. London, 1966. p.[219]–20. (First pub. 1961)
Chronol. checklist, 1894–1946.

GREY, EDWARD, 1ST VISCOUNT GREY OF FALLODON, 1862–1933

3530 **Dawson, N. F.,** 1953: no.107.

GREY, SIR GEORGE, 1812–1898

3531 **Kilgour, A. D.** Sir George Grey, 1812–1898; a bibliography. [Cape Town] University of Cape Town, School of librarianship, 1950. iv,30l. 37cm. (Duplicated typescript)
Classified checklist of works and ana based on material in 3 South African libraries.

GREY, HENRY GEORGE, 3D EARL GREY, 1802–1894

3532 **Doig, Ronald P.** 3rd Earl Grey pamphlets. Durham Philobib 2:28–32 Mr '59; 2:33–4 Ja '60; 2:54–5 Je '62.
Chronol. checklist of 33 items.

GRIEVE, CHRISTOPHER MURRAY, 1892–
See MacDiarmid, Hugh, pseud.

GRIFFITH, ARTHUR, 1872–1922

3533 **O'Hegarty, Patrick Sarsfield.** Bibliographies of 1916 and the Irish revolution, XII. Arthur Griffith. [XIII. Michael Collins. XIV. Kevin O'Higgins] Dublin Mag new ser 12:61–7 Ja/Mr '37.
Checklists of first ed., with TP transcrs., collations, and bibliogr. notes.

GRIFFITH, ELIZABETH, 1720?–1793

3534 **Norton, Jane Elizabeth.** Some uncollected authors XXII: Elizabeth Griffith, 1727–1793. Bk Coll 8no4:418–24 '59.
'Handlist of Elizabeth Griffith's printed works' (p.420–4): chronol. arrangement of 18 works, with quasifacsim. TP transcrs., collations, and bibliogr. notes on first ed.

GROSSE, ALEXANDER, d.1654

3535 **Dredge, John Ingle,** 1889–99: no.886.

GROTE, GEORGE, 1794–1871

3536 **Ziman, E. R.,** 1954: no.240.

GRUFFYDD, OWAIN AB, 1359?–1416?
See Glendower, Owen.

GUINEY, LOUISE IMOGEN, 1861–1920

3537 **Tenison, E. M.** A bibliography of Louise Imogen Guiney, 1861–1920. Bkmns J 7no15–16,18:86–7, 123–4, 181–2 '23.

TP transcrs., collations and bibliogr. notes on original works; works trans., ed., or prefaced by; and unpublished mss.

GUNN, NEIL MILLER, 1891–

3538 **Aitken, William Russell.** Neil Miller Gunn. Biblioth 3no3:89–95 '61.

'A first check list of his books' (p.90–5): chronol. checklist of 47 items, with ana.

3539 **Duval, K. D., bksllr.** [1961]: no.726.

GUNNING, SUSANNAH (MINIFIE), 1740?–1800

3540 **Heley, J.,** 1938: no.139.

GUTHRIE, JAMES JOSHUA, fl.1895–1951

3541 **Scottish chapbook,** 1922–3: no.724.

GUTHRIE, THOMAS ANSTEY, 1856–1934

See Anstey, F., pseud.

GWYNNETH, JOHN, fl.1557

3542 **Jones, J. J.** A Welsh catholic controversialist. Welsh Bib Soc J 5:90–2 Jl '38.

'Short-title list of Gwynneth's works' (p.92); TP facsim.

HADDON, WALTER, 1516–1572

3543 **Ryan, Lawrence V.** Walter Haddon, Elizabethan latinist. Huntington Lib Q 17:99–124 F '54.

'A list of the works of Walter Haddon' (p.118–24): checklists of ed.; fugitive and uncertain works; contemporary transcriptions, translations, and reprints; with STC nos. and some bibliogr. notes.

HAGGARD, SIR HENRY RIDER, 1856–1925

3544 **Barron, J. H.** H. Rider Haggard. Eng Illus Mag new ser 31:296–9 Je '04.

'Bibliography' (p.298–9).

3545 **McKay, George Leslie.** A bibliography of the writings of sir Rider Haggard. London, Bookman's journal, 1930. 110p. 25cm.

First part first pub. as Supplement to Bkmns J 18no14:1–67 '30.

3546 —— and **J. E. Scott.** Additions and corrections to the Haggard bibliography. London, Mitre pr., 1939. ii,28p. 25cm.

3547 **Scott, James Edward.** A bibliography of the works of sir Henry Rider Haggard, 1856–1925. Takeley, E. Mathews, 1947. 258p. port., facsims. 23cm.

Classified arrangement of first ed.; articles, pub. letters, etc., with TP transcrs., collations and bibliogr. notes.

Rev: E. F. Walbridge Pa Bib Soc Am 41:358–61 '47; TLS 23 Ag '47:432.

HAILES, SIR DAVID DALRYMPLE, LD., 1726–1792
See Dalrymple, sir David, ld. Hailes.

HAKEWILL, GEORGE, 1579–1649
3548 **Dredge, John Ingle,** 1889–99: no.886.

HAKLUYT, RICHARD, 1552?–1616
3548a **Kerr, William Holmes.** The treatment of Drake's circumnavigation in Hakluyt's Voyages, 1589. Pa Bib Soc Am 34:281–302 '40.
'Census of the 1589 Hakluyt's Voyages' (p.300–2).

3549 **Skelton, Raleigh Ashlin,** *comp.* 'Bibliographical description' *in* Quinn, David B. and R. A. Skelton, *ed.* The principall navigations, voyages and discoveries of the English nation, by Richard Hakluyt. . . . Cambridge, 1965. V.1, p.liii.
'Provisional check-list of surviving copies' (p.liv–lx): 114 copies.

HALIFAX, GEORGE SAVILE, 1ST MARQUIS OF, 1633–1695
See Savile, George, 1st marquis of Halifax.

HALL, JOHN, 1529?–1566?
3550 **Fraser, Russell A.,** *ed.* 'The surviving copies' *in* The court of virtue, 1565. London, 1961. p.366–70.
Discursive descrs. of 4 surviving copies; 'Table of misprints' (p.371–2).

HALLAM, ARTHUR HENRY, 1811–1833
3551 **Motter, Thomas Hubbard Vail.** Arthur Hallam's centenary, a bibliographical note. Yale Univ Lib Gaz 8:104–9 Ja '34.
Quasifacsim. TP transcrs., with locations of copies and some bibliogr. notes, of 20 early ed. principally at Yale.

3552 —— Hallam's Poems of 1830, a census of copies. Pa Bib Soc Am 35:277–80 '41.
Locations of 15 copies.

HALLEY, EDMOND, 1656–1742
3553 **McPike, Eugene Fairfield.** Dr. Edmond Halley. N&Q ser10 4:526 D '05.

3554 **Rudolph, Alexander Joseph.** Material for a bibliography of dr. Edmond Halley, 1656–1742 . . . with some notes and addenda by E. Fairfield McPike. Boston, F. W. Faxon, 1905. 13p. 27cm. (Not seen)
Repr. from Bull Bib 4:53–7 Jl '05. Chronol. checklist.

3555 **McPike, Eugene Fairfield.** Doctor Edmond Halley. [Chicago, 1909] 4p. (Not seen)
Repr. from Popular Astronomy 17:408–12 '09.

3556 —— Dr. Edmond Halley, 1656–1742; a bibliographical guide to his life and work, arranged chronologically. . . . London, Taylor and Francis, 1939. 54p. 25cm. (Not seen)

3557 —— Dr. Edmond Halley, 1656?–1741/2; bibliographical addenda. N&Q 184:298–302 My '43; 186:42–4, 268 Ja, Je '44.

3558 **Royal society,** LONDON. Celebration of the tercentenary of the birth of Edmond Halley . . . conversazione. . . . [London, 1956] 17p. col.port. 25cm. Covertitle.

3559 —— [Same]: [Anr. issue, with title]: Edmond Halley, 1656–1742; a conversazione to celebrate the tercentenary of his birth held by the British astronomical association. [London, 1956] 17p. col.port. 25cm. Covertitle.

HAMILTON, ANTHONY, 1646?–1720

3560 **Clark, Ruth.** 'Bibliography' *in* Anthony Hamilton . . . his life and works and his family. London, 1921. p.313–26.
Classified checklist of works and translations.

HAMILTON, EUGENE LEE-, 1845–1907

3560a **Lyon, Harvey T.** A publishing history of the writings of Eugene Lee-Hamilton. Pa Bib Soc Am 51:141–59 '57.
Classified checklist of works and ana.

3560b **Pantazzi, Sybille.** Eugene Lee-Hamilton. Pa Bib Soc Am 55:231–2 '61.
Additions to Lyon.

HAMILTON, WILLIAM, 1704–1754

3561 **Bushnell, Nelson Sherwin.** 'A bibliography of the published writings of William Hamilton' *in* William Hamilton of Bangour, poet and jacobite. Aberdeen, 1957. p.150–3.
Chronol. checklists of pubs. containing first known printings, and reprints of Hamilton's poems.

HAMILTON, SIR WILLIAM, 1730–1803

3562 **Limentani, Uberto.** 'Bibliografia hamiltoniana' *in* Campi Phlegræi. Milano, 1962. p.39–42.
Classified checklist of 20 items of works, items about Hamilton's collection and other ana.

HAMMOND, JOHN LAWRENCE LEBRETON, 1872–1949

3563 **Tawney, Richard Henry.** J. L. Hammond, 1872–1949. Proc Brit Acad 46:267–94 '60.
'List of works' (p.293–4): classified checklist.

HANDEL, GEORGE FRIDERIC, 1685–1759

3564 **Sasse, Konrad.** Händel Bibliographie . . . under Verwendung des im Händel-Jahrbuch 1933 von Kurt Taut . . . Abgeschlessen im Jahre 1961. Leipzig, Deutscher verlag für Musik [1963] 352p. 28cm.

3565 **Flower, sir Walter Newman.** Catalogue of a Handel collection formed by Newman Flower. Sevenoaks, Kent [1921] 32p. ports., facsims. 25cm.

3566 [**Smith, William Charles**] *comp.* 'Bibliography' *in* Flower, sir Walter N. George Frideric Handel. London, 1923. p.341–58.

See no.3571.

3567 **Scotland. National library,** EDINBURGH. George Frideric Handel, 1685–1759: catalogue of an exhibition. Edinburgh, 1948. 20p. 21cm.

Comp. by William C. Smith.

3568 **British museum.** Henry Purcell, 1659?–1695; George Frideric Handel, 1685–1759: catalogue of a commemorative exhibition, London, Published by the trustees, 1959. 47p. port., facsims. 25cm.

Annotated catalogue of 246 entries, comp. by Alexander H. King.

3569 **Music association of Ireland.** George Frideric Handel, 1685–1759. Dublin, 1959. (Not seen)

Catalogue of the Handel exhibition at the Civic museum, Dublin, with note of the works ptd. in Dublin: Eager's no.2161.

3570 [**Smith, William Charles**] *comp.* 'Bibliography' in Flower, sir Walter N. George Frideric Handel. New and rev. ed. London, 1959. p.[363]–82.

3571 —— and **C. Humphries.** Handel, a descriptive catalogue of the early editions. London, Cassell [1960] xxiii,366p. facsim. 25cm.

Classified short-title list with bibliogr. notes and locations of copies, of 'all the early editions issued by John Walsh and other publishers up to the time of the composer's death, the first and other important editions up to the end of the eighteenth century, and a few works first published in the early part of the nineteenth century'.

HARDY, THOMAS, 1840–1928

3575 **Weber, Carl Jefferson.** The first hundred years of Thomas Hardy: 1840–1940; a centenary bibliography of Hardiana. Waterville, Me., Colby college library, 1942. 276p. 23cm.

3576 **Stevenson, Lionel,** *ed.*, 1964: no.1705.

3577 **Lane, John,** *comp.* 'Thomas Hardy, a bibliography, 1865–1894' *in* Johnson, Lionel P. The art of Thomas Hardy. London; New York, 1894. p.i–[lxiv] at end.

See no.3585.

3578 **Sherren, Wilkinson.** 'Bibliography of Thomas Hardy' *in* The Wessex of romance. London, 1902. p.305–12.

Also pub. in New and rev. ed. London, 1908, p.286–[96].

3579 **Nevinson, Henry Woodd.** Thomas Hardy. Eng Illus Mag new ser 29:280–2, 285 Je '03.

'Bibliography' (p.282, 285).

3580 **Keogh, Andrew,** 1910: no.662.

3581 **Danielson, Henry.** The first editions of Thomas Hardy and their values; a bibliographical handbook for collectors, booksellers, librarians and others. London, Allen & Unwin [1916] 38p. 19cm.

3582 **Webb, A. P.** A bibliography of the works of Thomas Hardy, 1865–1915. London, F. Hollings, 1916. xiii,127p. port., facsims. 21cm.

3583 **Bibliographies** of modern authors. Thomas Hardy. Lond Merc 1n01:122–3 N '19.

3584 **Danielson, Henry.** Bibliographies of modern authors, no.12. Thomas Hardy. Bkmns J 1n024–6:454, 469, 489 '20; 2n027–8:7, 24 '20. Incomplete.

3585 **Lane, John,** *comp.* 'Thomas Hardy, a bibliography of first editions, 1865–1922' *in* Johnson, Lionel P. The art of Thomas Hardy. 2d ed. New York, 1923. p.297–346.
Rev. version of checklist first pub. 1894: *see* no.3577

3586 **McCutcheon, George Barr.** The renowned collection of first editions of Thomas Hardy, Rudyard Kipling, Robert Louis Stevenson, formed by George Barr McCutcheon. New York, American art association [1925] IV. (unpaged) illus., facsims. 25cm.

3587 **Yale university. Library.** Thomas Hardy, O.M., 1840–1928; catalogue of a memorial exhibition of first editions, autograph letters, and manuscripts, prepared by Richard L. Purdy. New Haven, 1928. 41p. 22cm.

3588 **Colby college,** WATERVILLE, ME. **Library.** Hardy at Colby; a check list of the writings by and about Thomas Hardy now in the library . . . compiled by Carl J. Weber. Waterville, Me., 1936. 152p. 23cm.

3589 **[Rush, N. Orwin]** *comp.* 'Bibliography' *in* Weber, Carl J. Rebekah Owen and Thomas Hardy. . . . Waterville, Me., 1939. p.94–5.

3590 **Colby college,** WATERVILLE, ME. **Library.** A century of Thomas Hardy; catalogue of a centennial exhibition, Colby college library. [Fairfield, Me., Ptd. by the Galahad pr., 1940] 14p. illus., ports., facsims. 23cm.

3591 **Grolier club,** NEW YORK. A descriptive catalogue of the Grolier club centenary exhibition, 1940, of the works of Thomas Hardy. Waterville, Me., Colby college library, 1940. 4l., 80p. illus., ports., facsims. 24cm.
Comp. by Carroll A. Wilson.

3592 **Colby college,** WATERVILLE, ME. **Library.** The jubilee of Tess, 1841–1941; catalogue of an exhibition in commemoration of the fiftieth anniversary of the publication of Tess of the D'Urbervilles, by Thomas Hardy. Waterville, Me., 1941. 62p. illus., ports. 24cm.
Comp. by Carl J. Weber? *See* no.3599.

3592a **Weber, Carl Jefferson.** Hardy's grim note in The return of the native. Pa Bib Soc Am 36:37–45 '42.
Contains checklist of 55 ed., 1878–1942.

3593 **Weber, Carl Jefferson.** 'American publishers of Hardy' *in* Hardy in America, a study of Thomas Hardy and his American readers. Waterville, Me., 1946. p.273–88.
Checklist of American ed. arranged by name of American publisher.

3594 —— Jude from obscurity via notoriety to fame. Colby Lib Q ser1 13:209–15 Ja '46.
Discursive checklist of Jude the obscure.

3595 [Weber, Carl Jefferson] Hardy additions. Colby Lib Q ser2 3:46–9 Ag '47.
Addenda to Hardy in America, no.3593.

3596 Hatch, Benton L. Notes towards the definitive bibliography of Thomas Hardy's Poems of the past and present. Colby Lib Q ser2 12:195–8 N '49.

3597 Wilson, Carroll Atwood. 'Thomas Hardy' in Thirteen author collections of the nineteenth century . . . Edited by Jean C. S. Wilson and David Randall. New York, 1950. p.39–117.
Chronol. short-title catalogue with bibliogr. notes.

3598 Purdy, Richard Little. Thomas Hardy, a bibliographical study. London, G. Cumberlege, O.U.P., 1954. ix,387p. facsims. 23cm.
Quasifacsim. TP transcrs., collations, and extensive bibliogr. notes on editiones principes; collected ed.; and uncollected contribs. to books, periodicals and newspapers.
Rev: H. Reed Listener 52:975 '55; F. B. Adams Bk Coll 4:82–4 '55; C. J. Weber Pa Bib Soc Am 49:85–9 '55; cf. F. B. Adams ib. 49:285–7 '55; F. B. Adams Nineteenth Cent Fict 10:75–9 '55; TLS 11 Mr '55:156; C. J. Weber Mod Philol 52:282–4 '55; M. T. H. Sadleir Library ser5 10:137–9 '55.

3599 [Weber, Carl Jefferson] Tess since 'forty-one. Colby Lib Q ser3 14:232–4 My '54.
Chronol. checklist of additions to no.3592 on p.234.

3600 —— Russian translations of Hardy. Colby Lib Q ser3 15:253–6 Ag '54.
Chronol. checklist, 1898–1937: p.256.

3601 Yarmolinsky, Avrahm. Hardy behind the iron curtain. Colby Lib Q ser4 2:64–6 My '55.
Addenda to previous item.

3602 Yamamoto, Bunnosuke. Thomas Hardy bibliography in Japan, with reference books in England and America; outlines of his principal works. Tokyo, Shinozaki Shorin [1957] ix,294p. port. 22cm. (Not seen)
Text chiefly in Japanese.

HARINGTON, SIR JOHN, 1561–1612

3610 **Kirwood, Albert Ernest Maldon.** The metamorphosis of Aiax and its sequels. Library ser4 12:208–34 S '31.

'Bibliographical appendix. I. Early editions' (p.231–4): quasifacsim. TP transcrs., collations, bibliogr. notes and refs., and location of copy collated, for 8 items.

HARRINGTON, JAMES, 1611–1677

3611 **Lust, J.,** 1950: no.161.

HARRISON, FREDERIC, 1831–1923

3612 **Farquarson, Spenser.** Frederic Harrison. Eng Illus Mag new ser 30:81–5 Oc '03.

'Bibliography' (p.82, 84–5): checklist of works; introductions; translations; and works ed. by; and ana.

3613 **Harrison, Frederic.** Bibliography of Fred Harrison. Hawkhurst, Ptd. by F. Williams, 1908. 22l. 20cm.

Classified checklist.

HARTING, JAMES EDMUND, 1841–1928

3614 **[Harting, James Edmund]** Titles of works by J. E. Harting, 1866–1913. Weybridge, Rawlings & Walsh, 1925. 8p. 23cm. Covertitle.

Chronol. checklist.

HARTLIB, SAMUEL, d.1662

3614a **Turnbull, George Henry.** 'Publications' in Hartlib, Drury and Comenius; gleanings from Hartlib's papers. Liverpool, 1948. p.88–109.

Annotated chronol. checklist of 65 items, 1634–53.

HARVEY FAMILY

3615 **McKerrow, Ronald Brunlees,** *ed.* 'The works of the Harveys' in The works of Thomas Nashe. Oxford, 1910. V.5, p.[163]–75.

3616 —— **[Same]**: Reprinted . . . with corrs. . . . Ed. by F. P. Wilson. Oxford, 1958. V.5, p.[163]–75.

Chronol. checklist, with quasifacsim. TP transcrs., collations, and some bibliogr. notes.

HARVEY, GABRIEL, 1550?–1631
See Harvey family.

HARVEY, JOHN, 1564–1592
See Harvey family.

HARVEY, RICHARD, 1560?–1623?
See Harvey family.

HARVEY, WILLIAM, 1578–1657

3617 **Keynes, sir Geoffrey Langdon.** A bibliography of the writings of William Harvey, M.D., discoverer of the circulation of the blood. . . . Cambridge, C.U.P., 1928. xii,67p. plates, ports., facsims. 27cm.

3617a **Weil, Ernst.** William Fitzer, the publisher of Harvey's De motu cordis, 1628. Library ser4 24:142–64 D/Mr '43/4.

'Copies of William Harvey's De motu cordis, Frankfurt, 1628' (p.160–4): census, with some bibliogr. notes.

3618 **Keynes, sir Geoffrey Langdon.** A bibliography of . . . William Harvey. . . . 2d ed., rev. Cambridge, C.U.P., 1953. xii,79p. illus., ports., facsims. 26cm.

Chronol. bibliogr. of 54 items, with TP transcrs., and facsims., collations, bibliogr· notes, and locations of copies.

Rev: W. White Bull Bib 21:56–7 '54; W. LeFanu Bk Coll 2:293–6 '53.

3619 **Royal college of physicians,** LONDON. William Harvey, 1578–1657; an exhibition of books and manuscripts illustrating his life and work. London, 1957. 25p. port. 25cm.

Comp. by L. M. Payne.

HAWKER, ROBERT STEPHEN, 1803–1875

3620 **Wallis, Alfred,** *ed.* 'Bibliography of the poetical works of the rev. R. S. Hawker' *in* The poetical works of Robert Stephen Hawker. London, 1899. p.[xxiii]–xxxi.

3621 **Woolf, Cecil.** Some uncollected authors XXXIX: Hawker of Morwenstow, 1803–1875. Bk Coll 14no1:62–71 '65; 14no2:202–11 '65.

'Short-title list of Hawker's works in verse & prose' (p.67–8); 'Check-list of first editions' (p.68–71, 202–11): quasifacsim. TP transcrs., collations, and bibliogr. notes on 53 items.

HAWKINS, SIR JOHN, 1719–1789

3621a **Scholes, Percy Alfred.** 'Books and articles by Hawkins and his family' *in* The life and activities of sir John Hawkins, musician, magistrate and friend of Johnson. London, 1953. p.[231]–7.

Classified checklist of books, pamphlets and other writings, with some bibliogr. notes.

HAYLEY, WILLIAM, 1745–1820

3622 **Barker, N. J.** Some notes on the bibliography of William Hayley. Cambridge Bib Soc Trans 3pt1:103–12 '59; 3pt2:167–76 '60.

'Annotated list' of all ed. pub. during Hayley's lifetime: 46 items, with some TP facsims., collations, and bibliogr. notes.

HAYMAN, FRANCIS, 1708–1776

3623 **Hammelmann, H. A.** Eighteenth-century English illustrators: Francis Hayman, R.A. Bk Coll 2no2:116–32 '53.

'Books illustrated by Francis Hayman' (p.125–32): chronol. checklist, 1742–74, with some bibliogr. notes.

HAYWARD, SIR JOHN, 1564?–1627

3624 **Plomer, Henry Robert.** Examination of some existing copies of Hayward's Life and raigne of Henrie IV. Library ser2 3:13–23 Ja '02.

Discussion with TP transcr., collation, bibliogr. notes, and locations of copies, with distinction of ed. and issues.

HAYWOOD, MRS. ELIZA, 1693–1756

3625 **Whicher, George Frisbie.** 'A list of mrs. Haywood's writings' *in* The life and romances of mrs. Eliza Haywood. New York, 1915. p.176–204.

Title checklist of 67 single works, with locations of copies; collected works; and attribs.

HAZLITT, WILLIAM, 1778–1830

3626 **Houtchens, Carolyn Washburn** and **L. H. Houtchens,** *ed.* [1966]: no.2017.

3627 **Douady, Jules.** Liste chronologique des œuvres de William Hazlitt. Paris, Librairie Hachette, 1906. ix,53p. 24cm.

3628 **Keynes, sir Geoffrey Langdon.** Bibliography of William Hazlitt. London, Ptd. for the Nonesuch pr., 1931. xix,135p. port., facsims. (1 fold.) 23cm.

TP transcrs. and facsims., collations, locations of rare copies and bibliogr. notes on 138 separately pub. items, 1805–1930.
Rev: TLS 8 Oc '31:772; A. W. P[ollard] Library ser4 12:362–3 '31; viscount Esher **Bk** Coll Q 5:31–2 '32.

HEARNE, THOMAS, d.1722

3629 **Guyatt, E. J.,** 1952: no.134.

HENLEY, WILLIAM ERNEST, 1849–1903

3630 **Chesterton, Gilbert Keith.** W. E. Henley. Eng Illus Mag new ser 29:546–8 Ag '03.

'Bibliography' (p.548).

3631 **Sadleir, Michael Thomas Hervey.** Some uncollected authors X: William Ernest Henley. Bk Coll 5no2:162–8 '56.

'Check-list of Henley publications' (p.164–8): chronol. list of 22 items, 1880–1908, with some bibliogr. notes.

HENRY FREDERICK, PRINCE OF WALES, 1594–1612

3632 **Edmond, John Philip.** Elegies and other tracts issued on the death of Henry, prince of Wales, 1612. Edinburgh Bib Soc Proc 6pt2:141–58 Oc '06.

Title list of 44 items with simple TP transcrs., some facsims., collations, and locations of copies.

HENRY THE MINSTREL (BLIND HARRY), fl.1470–1492

3633 **Geddie, William,** 1912: no.2034.

3634 **Miller, J. F.** Blind Harry's Wallace. Glasgow Bib Soc Rec 3:1–25 '14.

'Bibliography' (p.15–25): chronol. list, 1488–1910, with TP transcrs., collations, locations of copies, and some bibliogr. notes.

3635 —— Some additions to the bibliography of Blind Harry's Wallace. *ib.* 6:14–19 '20.

HENRYSON, ROBERT, 1430?–1506

3636 **Geddie, William,** 1912: no.2034.

HENTY, GEORGE ALFRED, 1832–1902

3637 **Coffin, Louis.** George Alfred Henty, a bibliographical study of Henty and his writings for boys. Bull Bib 19:241–3 My/Ag '49.
Works grouped by type and period of subject.

3638 **Kennedy, Roderick Stuart** and **B. J. Farmer.** Bibliography of G. A. Henty and Hentyana. London, B. J. Farmer [1956] 93l. 27cm. Covertitle. (Duplicated typescript)
Alphabetical title list, with TP transcrs., collations and bibliogr. notes; no index.
Rev: TLS 3 F '56:76.

HERBERT, SIR ALAN PATRICK, 1890–

3639 **Fabes, Gilbert Henry** [1933]: no.2882.

HERBERT, EDWARD, 1ST BARON HERBERT OF CHERBURY, 1583–1648

3640 **Palmer, George Herbert,** 1911: no.3641.

HERBERT, GEORGE, 1593–1633

3641 **Palmer, George Herbert.** A Herbert bibliography, being a catalogue of a collection of books relating to George Herbert. . . . Cambridge, Mass., Privately ptd., 1911. iv,61l. 26cm.

3642 —— [Same]: Cambridge, Mass., Library of Harvard university, 1911. iv,19p. 26cm.
TP transcrs., collations, and some bibliogr. notes on biographies, mss., writings other than The temple; writings of George Herbert's brothers; books relating to Nicholas Ferrar; ana; and desiderata.

3643 **Tannenbaum, Samuel Aaron** and **D. R. Tannenbaum.** George Herbert, a concise bibliography. New York, 1946. 52l. 29cm. (Elizabethan bibliographies, no.35) (Duplicated typescript)
Classified checklist of poems; prose; collected ed.; selections; songs and hymns (357 items); and ana.

HERBERT FAMILY

3644 **Palmer, George Herbert,** 1911: no.3641.

HERON, ROBERT, 1764–1807

3645 **Sinton, James.** Robert Heron and his writings, with a bibliography. Edinburgh Bib Soc Pub 15:17–33 Oc '32.
'Bibliography' (p.24–33): chronol. checklist of 49 items.

HERRICK, ROBERT, 1591–1674

3646 **Warre, C. F.** Robert Herrick bibliography. Edinburgh R 199:109–207 Ja '04.

3647 **Cox, Edwin Marion.** Notes on the bibliography of Herrick. Library ser3 8:105–19 Ap '17.
Discursive account of early and more recent ed. with some TP transcrs., collations, and locations of copies.

3648 **Kerr, M. M.,** 1936: no.151.

3649 **Some** editions of Herrick. Bk Hndbk 1no5:281 '48.
Checklist with bibliogr. notes.

3650 **Tannenbaum, Samuel Aaron** and **D. R. Tannenbaum.** Robert Herrick, a
concise bibliography. New York, 1949. iii,58p. 27cm. (Elizabethan bibliographies, no.40) (Duplicated typescript)
Classified checklist of works and ana.

HEWLETT, MAURICE HENRY, 1861–1923

3651 **Thompson, Francis.** Maurice Hewlett. Eng Illus Mag new ser 30:426–9
Ja '04
'Bibliography' (p.429).

3652 **Bibliographies** of modern authors. Maurice Hewlett. Lond Merc 1no5:
625–6 Mr '20.

3653 **Muir, Percival Horace.** A bibliography of the first editions of books by
Maurice Henry Hewlett, 1861–1923. [London] Supplement to the Book-
man's journal, 1927. 10–36p. 24cm.
First pub. with Bkmns J 15no2–3 '27; also issued in Bibliographies of modern authors;
3d series. London, 1931. (*See* no.685.)
TP transcrs., collations, and bibliogr. notes on 58 items.

3654 —— [**Same**]: Addenda & corrigenda. [London, 1931?] 4p. 22cm.

3655 **Sutherland, Bruce.** Maurice Henry Hewlett, a bibliography. Boston, F. W.
Faxon, 1935. 15p. 21cm. (Not seen)
Repr. from Bull Bib 15:126–9 My/Ag '35. Classified checklist of works; translations;
reviews and prefaces; and ana, with some bibliogr. notes.

HEYWOOD, JOHN, 1497?–1580?

3656 **Cameron, Kenneth Walter.** 'A specialized bibliography of scholarship on
John Heywood' *in* The background of John Heywood's Witty and wit-
less. . . . Raleigh, N.C., 1941. p.[35]–41.

3657 **Tannebaum, Samuel Aaron** and **D. R. Tannenbaum.** John Heywood, a concise bibliography. New York, 1946. 31l. 29cm. (Elizabethan bibliographies, no.36) (Duplicated typescript)
Classified checklist of works and ana; 426 items.

HEYWOOD, THOMAS, 1514?–1641

3658 **Clark, Arthur Melville.** A bibliography of Thomas Heywood. Oxford Bib
Soc Proc 1pt2:97–153 '24.
TP transcrs., collations, bibliogr. notes and location of copies for works; works ed. by;
works for which Heywood wrote commendatory verses; and lost works, arranged
chronol.

3659 **Tannenbaum, Samuel Aaron.** Thomas Heywood, a concise bibliography.
New York, 1939. [viii]43p. 23cm. (Elizabethan bibliographies, no.6)
Classified checklist of works and ana.

HIBBERT, JULIAN, 1800–1834

3660 **Gilmour, John Scott Lennox.** Some uncollected authors XXVI: Julian Hibbert, 1800–1834. Bk Coll 9no4:446–51 '60.

'Check-list of Julian Hibbert's works' (p.449–51): quasifacsim. TP transcrs., collations, and bibliogr. notes on 4 first ed.

HICKES, WILLIAM, fl.1669–1682

3661 **Shelley, Philip Allison.** William Hickes, native of Oxford. Harvard Stud & N Philol & Lit 20:81–98 '38.

'A bibliography of the publications in prose and verse of William Hickes of Oxford' (p.92–8): chronol. checklist of 35 ed., with bibliogr. refs. and locations of copies.

HIERON, SAMUEL, c.1572–1617

3662 **Dredge, John Ingle,** 1889–99: no.886.

HIGGINS, FREDERICK ROBERT, 1896–1941

3663 **MacManus, Michael Joseph.** Bibliography of F. R. Higgins. Dublin Mag new ser 21:43–5 Jl/S '46.

TP transcrs., collations, and bibliogr. notes on 7 first ed.

HIGLETT, G. A., fl.1920–1929

3664 **Melville, Frederick John.** The Higlett booklets, a bijou bibliography. [Perth, 1925] 9p. port. 22cm.

Annotated chronol. checklist, 1913–25.

HILTON, JAMES, 1900–1954

3665 **Checklist** bibliographies of modern authors. James Hilton. Bk Trade J 62:20 Jl '36.

Chronol. checklist, 1920–34, with notes on bindings.

HOBBES, JOHN OLIVER, *pseud. of* PEARL MARY TERESA (RICHARDS) CRAIGIE, 1867–1906

3666 **Murray, David Christie.** John Oliver Hobbes. Eng Illus Mag new ser 30: 185–7 N '03.

'Bibliography' (p.186): checklist of works, plays, and ana.

HOBBES, THOMAS, 1588–1679

3667 **Hargreaves, Joan M.,** 1949: no.137.

3668 **Macdonald, Hugh** and **J. M. Hargreaves.** Thomas Hobbes, a bibliography. London, Bibliographical society, 1952. xvii,83p. port., facsims. 22cm.

Quasifacsim. TP transcrs., and facsims., collations, locations of copies and bibliogr. notes on all ed. of works to 1725, translations to 1700, and collected ed. to date; 108 entries.

Rev: TLS 24 Ap '53:276; L. W. Hanson, H. Macdonald *ib.* 8 My '53:307; F. C. Francis *ib.* 5 Je '53:365; J. Kinsley R Eng Stud new ser 5:83–5 '54; A. Muirhead Bk Coll 2:83–5 '53.

3669 **Mizuta, Hiroshi.** List of works of, and relating to, Thomas Hobbes appended to The formation of the modern concept of human nature. [Tokyo] 1954. 35p. 18cm.

Partly in Japanese.

HODGKIN, THOMAS, 1831–1913

3670 **Creighton, Louise (von Glehn).** 'Bibliography' *in* Life and letters of Thomas Hodgkin. London, 1917. p.419–27.

Chronol. checklists of separate historical and antiquarian pubs., historical and archaeo-logical addresses and articles; miscellaneous books, articles, etc.

HODGSON, RALPH, 1871–1962

3671 **Westlake, Neda M.** Ralph Hodgson exhibition. Lib Chron Univ Pennsylvania 30no2:85–7 '64.

Annotated short-title catalogue of 15 exhibits.

HOFLAND, BARBARA, 1770–1844

3672 **Russell, J.,** 1950: no.193.

HOGAN, MICHAEL, fl.1852–1924

3673 **Herbert, Robert.** A bibliography of Michael Hogan, bard of Thomond. Irish Bk Lover 27:276–9 F '41.

Chronol. checklist of 24 items, 1852–1924.

HOGARTH, WILLIAM, 1697–1764

3674 **Dobson, Austin.** 'A bibliography of books, pamphlets, etc., relating to Hogarth and his works' *in* William Hogarth. London, 1891. p.[199]–237. (Also pub. in 1898, 1902, 1907)

3675 **Weitenkampf, Frank.** A bibliography of William Hogarth. Cambridge, Library of Harvard university, 1890. 14p. 25cm. Covertitle.

Checklist, with bibliogr. notes.

3676 **J., C.** Hogarth as illustrator, a checklist. N&Q 202:544–5 D '57.

Checklist of 38 items.

HOGG, JAMES, 1770–1835

3680 **Hogg, William Dods.** The first editions of the writings of James Hogg, the Ettrick shepherd. Edinburgh Bib Soc Pub 12pt1:53–68 Mr '24.

'Bibliography' (p.58–68): chronol. checklist of 33 early ed., 1801–88, with TP transcrs., collations, and some bibliogr. notes.

3681 **Batho, Edith Clara.** 'Bibliography' *in* The Ettrick shepherd. Cambridge, 1927. p.183–221.

Chronol. checklist, 1794–1912.

3682 —— Note on the bibliography of James Hogg, the Ettrick shepherd. Library ser4 16:309–26 D '35.

'A. Additions to the 1927 Bibliography' (p.311–17); 'B. A note on the publication of Hogg's songs' (p.317–18); 'C. Corrections to the 1927 Bibliography' (p.318–25); 'D. Doubtful works' (p.325–6).

HOLCROFT, THOMAS, 1745–1809

3683 **Colby, Elbridge.** A bibliography of Thomas Holcroft. N&Q ser11 10:1–3, 43–6, 83–5, 122–5, 163–5, 205–7, 244–7, 284–6, 323–5, 362–5, 403–5, 442–4, 484–6 Jl–D '14; 11; 4–5, 43–4, 84–5, 123–5, 164–5, 203–4, 244–5 Ja–Mr '15.

3683a —— A bibliography of Thomas Holcroft. [New York] New York public library, 1922, 94p. 26cm.

Repr. with additions from N.Y. Pub Lib Bull 26:455–92, 664–86, 765–87 Je–S '22. Chronol. checklist with some bibliogr. notes.

3684 **Todd, William Burton.** Holcroft's Follies of a day, 1785. Bk Coll 14no4:544 '65.

Distinction with points of 2 impressions of the first English ed. of Beaumarchais' La folle journée.

HOLE, RICHARD, 1746–1803

3685 **Dredge, John Ingle,** 1889–99: no.886.

HOLE, WILLIAM, 1709–1791

3686 **Dredge, John Ingle,** 1889–99: no.886.

HOLLAND, PHILEMON, 1552–1637

3687 **[Silvette, Herbert]** A short-title list of the writings of Philemon Holland of Coventry, doctor of physicke. [Charlottesville, Va.] Privately ptd. for H. Silvette at the University of Virginia pr. by J. S. Peters, 1939. x,18p. facsim. 21cm.

Classified checklist of 52 items preliminary to next item.

3688 —— Catalogue of the works of Philemon Holland of Coventry, doctor of physicke, 1600–1940. Charlottesville, Va., Ptd. at the University of Virginia pr., J. S. Peters, 1940. xvi,27p. port. 21cm. (Not seen)

HOLLAND, SIR RICHARD, fl.1450

3689 **Geddie, William,** 1912: no.2034.

HOLME, CONSTANCE, fl.1913–

3690 **[Osborne, Eric Allen]** Checklist bibliographies of modern authors: Constance Holme. Bk Trade J 63:28 Jl '36.

3691 **Rota, Bertram.** Some uncollected authors XI: Constance Holme. Bk Coll 5n03:250–5 '56.

'Check-list of first editions' (p.252–5): list of 14 items, 1913–[37], with some bibliogr. notes; 'Books containing contributions . . .' (p.255).

HOLMES, THOMAS RICE EDWARD, 1855–1933

3692 **Thomas** Rice Edward Holmes, 1855–1933. Proc Brit Acad 22:358–79 '36.

'Materials for a bibliography of the writings published by T. R. E. Holmes' (p.[373]–9): chronol. checklist, 1879–1936, with some bibliogr. notes.

HOLTBY, WINIFRED, 1898–1935

3693 **Taylor, Geoffrey Handley-.** Winifred Holtby, a concise and selected bibliography. London, A. Brown, 1955. xv,76p. illus., ports., facsims. 23cm.

Classified checklist of works and ana with bibliogr. notes.

HOLYOAKE, GEORGE JACOB, 1817–1906

3694 **Goss, Charles William Frederick.** A descriptive bibliography of the writings of George Jacob Holyoake. . . . London, Crowther & Goodman, 1908. lxxxii,118p. 19cm.

Classified and annotated checklist of works and ana.

HOME, JOHN, 1722–1808

3695 **Lefèvre, Jean M. (Simpson).** John Home, a check list of editions. Biblioth 3n04:121–38 '61.

Classified checklist of 152 items based on London university School of librarianship thesis: *see* no.197.

HOOD, ROBIN

See Robin Hood.

HOOD, THOMAS, 1799–1845

3696 **Gilmour, John Scott Lennox.** Some uncollected authors VII: Thomas Hood. Bk Coll 4n03:239–48 '55.

'Check-list' (p.240–[8]); classified list based on author's collection, with collations and bibliogr. notes on early ed.

HOOKE, ROBERT, 1635–1703

3697 **Ayres, F. H.,** 1951: no.75.

3698 **Keynes, sir Geoffrey Langdon.** A bibliography of dr. Robert Hooke. Oxford, Clarendon pr., 1960. xix,155p. illus., port., facsims. 26cm.

TP transcrs., and facsims., collations, locations of copies and bibliogr. notes and refs. on 40 items; with ana.

Rev: W. T. Stearn Bk Coll 10:219–20, 223 '61; TLS 6 Ja '61:16; H. D. Horblit Pa Bib Soc Am 55:264–5 '61; F. N. L. Poynter Library ser5 16:153–4 '61; A. Armitage Nature 188:828–9 '60.

HOOKER, RICHARD, 1554?–1600

3699 **Edmonston, M. E.,** 1939: no.117.

HOPE, SIR WILLIAM HENRY ST.JOHN, 1854–1919

3700 **Thompson, Alexander Hamilton.** 'Bibliography' *in* A bibliography . . . of sir William St.John Hope with a . . . memoir. Leeds, 1929. p.[27]–50.
Chronol. checklist of 255 items, 1872–1925.

HOPKINS, GERARD MANLEY, 1844–1889

3701 **Weyand, Norman T.,** *ed.* 'A chronological Hopkins bibliography' *in* Immortal diamond; studies in Gerard Manley Hopkins. London, 1949. p.393–441.

3702 **Charney, Maurice.** A bibliographical study of Hopkins criticism, 1918–1948. Thought 25:297–326 Je '50.
'Bibliography' (p.320–6).

3703 **Patricia, sr. Mary.** Forty years of criticism; a chronological check list of criticism of the works of Gerard Manley Hopkins from 1909 to 1949. Bull Bib 20:38–44, 63–7 My/Ag, S/D '50.

HORMAN, WILLIAM, d.1535

3706 **James, Montague Rhodes,** *ed.* 'List of Horman's works' *in* Vulgaria, by William Horman . . . now reprinted. Oxford, 1926. p.xxiv–xxvi.

HORNE, RICHARD HENRY ('HENGIST'), 1802–1884

3710 **Shumaker, Eri Jay.** A concise bibliography of the complete works of Richard Henry (Hengist) Horne, 1802–1884. Granville, Ohio [Denison university] 1943. vi,14p. port. 23cm.
Chronol. checklist of works; contribs. to Household words; missing Horne items, etc.; no index.
Rev: E. C. Batho Mod Lang R 39:206 '44.

HORSLEY, SIR VICTOR ALEXANDER HADEN, 1857–1916

3710a **Holder, C. E.,** 1949: no.142.

HOTTEN, JOHN CAMDEN, 1832–1873

3711 **Hytch, F. J.** John Camden Hotten. N&Q ser11 11:357–8 My '15; Robert Pierpont; W.B.H. *ib.* ser11 12:13–14 Jl '15; R.P.B. 12:147 Ag '15; W.B.H. 12:231 S '15; F. J. Fytch 12:270 Oc '15.
'Books written or edited by John Camden Hotten' (p.357–8): checklist.

HOUGHTON, ARTHUR BOYD, 1836–1875

3712 **Housman, Laurence.** A forgotten book illustrator. Bibliographica 1pt3: 275–90 '95.
Annotated checklist of 6 items, p.278–9.

HOUGHTON, CLAUDE, *pseud. of* CLAUDE HOUGHTON OLDFIELD, 1889–

3713 **Walpole, sir Hugh Seymour** and **C. Dane.** 'A bibliography of the works of Claude Houghton' *in* Claude Houghton; appreciations. . . . London, 1935. p.6–8.
Checklist of early ed.

HOUSMAN, ALFRED EDWARD, 1859–1936

3714 **[Gow, Andrew Sydenham Farrar]** A. E. Housman, a list of adversaria, etc. . . . compiled by A.S.F.G., printed for A.S.F.G., E.H., D.S.R., A.F.S. [Cambridge] 1926. 11p. 23cm.
See no.3720.

3715 —— 'List of writings' *in* A. E. Housman, a sketch, together with a list of his writings and indexes to his classical papers. New York; Cambridge, 1936. p.63–80.
Supersedes previous item.

3716 **Carter, John Waynflete** and **J. Sparrow.** A. E. Housman, an annotated check-list. Library ser4 21:160–91 S '40.
See no.3724.

3717 **Ehrsam, Theodore George.** A bibliography of Alfred Edward Housman. Boston, F. W. Faxon, 1941. 44p. 23cm.
See also no.3719.

3718 **White, William.** A. E. Housman; an annotated check-list: additions and corrections. Library ser4 23:31–41 Je '42; J. W. Carter *ib.* 23:42–3 Je '42; R. C. Bald 23:43–4 Je '42; G. B. A. Fletcher 23:133 S/D '42.
Supplements Carter and Sparrow: *see also* no.3725.

3719 **Stallman, Robert Wooster.** Annotated bibliography of A. E. Housman, a critical study. Pub Mod Lang Assn 60:463–502 Je '45.
'IV. Additions to T. G. Ehrsam's Bibliography of Housman: a critical selection' (p.499–502).

3720 **Fletcher, G. B. A.** Supplements to the bibliography of Housman and other Housmaniana. Durham Univ J 38:85–93 Je '46.
Supplement to Gow (no.3715).

3721 **Warner, Gilmore.** The fiftieth anniversary of A Shropshire lad. Colby Lib Q ser1 14:217–32 Mr '46.
Chronol. checklist, 1896–1946, with some bibliogr. notes.

3722 **Weber, Carl Jefferson,** *ed.* 'Fifty years of A Shropshire lad' [a semi-centennial bibliography] *in* A Shropshire lad. Waterville, Me., 1946. p.83–102.

3723 **White, William.** To A. E. Housman; echoes in novels and verses. Bull Bib 19:73–5 My/Ag '47.
Author checklist of 'poems to', 'books using lines from his poetry', parodies, cartoons, and similar miscellanea.

3724 **Carter, John Waynflete** and **J. Sparrow.** A. E. Housman, an annotated hand-list. London, R. Hart-Davis, 1952. 54p. port., facsims. 22cm. (Soho bibliographies, II)
Bibliogr. notes and discussion of 49 'first and other significant editions', and 'the first printings of his poems in periodicals'; no index. Carter's Housman collection is now in the Indiana university library.
Rev: TLS 8 Ag '52:524; W. White Library ser5 7:285 '52; Bull Bib 22:56 '56; Bk Coll 1:272 '52.

3725 **White, William.** A. E. Housman, an annotated checklist: additions and corrections III. Library ser5 7:201–10 S '52.

Addenda to Carter and Sparrow.

3726 —— Published letters of A. E. Housman, a survey. Bull Bib 22:80–2 S/D '57.

Supersedes list in Mark Twain Q v.5 '43.

3727 —— A. E. Housman anthologised; evidence in the growth of a poet's reputation. Bull Bib 21:43–8 S/D '53; 21:68–72 Ja/Ap '54.

Chronol. checklist, 1890–1953.

3728 **London. University. University college.** A. E. Housman; catalogue of an exhibition on the centenary of his birth, assembled by John Carter [and] Joseph W. Scott. London, 1959. 35p. 22cm.

Rev: TLS 4 S '59:512; W. White *ib*. 16 Oc '59:593; S. Nowell-Smith 6 N '59:643; W. White Bull Bib 23:7 '60.

3729 **White, William.** A checklist of A. E. Housman's writings in Latin. Pa Bib Soc Am 54:188–90 '60.

Chronol. checklist of 12 items, with some bibliogr. notes.

HOWARD, HENRY, EARL OF SURREY, 1517?–1547

3735 **Padelford, Frederick Morgan,** *ed.* 'Bibliography' *in* The poems of Henry Howard, earl of Surrey. Seattle [1920] p.219–22.

3736 —— [**Same**]: Rev. ed. Seattle, 1928. p.[257]–63.
Superficial checklist of mss. and books.

HOWARD, JOHN, 1726–1790

3737 **Baumgartner, Leona.** John Howard, 1726–1790, hospital and prison reformer; a bibliography. Baltimore, Johns Hopkins pr., 1939. 79p. illus. 26cm.

Repr. from Bull Hist Medicine 7:486–534, 595–626 My, Je 39. Chronol. bibliogr. by date of first pub. of work; contribs. to journals; biography and criticism; and ana, with TP transcrs. and facsims; collations, location of copies, and bibliogr. notes; no index.

Rev: TLS 26 Ag '39:508; E. L. Tinker N.Y. Times Bk R 29 Oc '39:26.

3738 **Durling, Richard J.** John Howard, a bibliographical note. J Hist Medicine 14:375–8 Jl '59.

HOWARD, ROBERT, b.1597

3739 **Allison, Antony Francis.** Robert Howard, Franciscan. Library ser5 3:288–91 Mr '49.

Quasifacsim. TP transcr., collation, bibliogr. notes and locations of copies for STC 17567, and another not in STC.

HOWELL, JAMES, 1594?–1666

3740 **Jacobs, Joseph,** *ed.* 'Bibliographical list of Howell's works' *in* Epistolæ ho-Elianæ, the familiar letters of James Howell. . . . London, 1892. V.1, p.[lxxxiii]–ciii.

3740a **Vann, William Harvey.** Notes on the writings of James Howell. [Waco, Tex., Baylor U.P., 1924] 71p. 18cm.

TP transcrs., short collations, locations of copies and some bibliogr. notes on authentic works; Epistolæ ho-Elianæ; introductions and commendatory verses; doubtful and incorrect attributions.

3741 **Winship, George Parker.** Notes on certain peculiarities in early editions of James Howell. Grolier Club Gaz 1no8:182–5 Ap '26.

Descr., collation, and discussion of 2d ed. of Epistolæ ho-Elianæ.

HOWITT, MARY (BOTHAM), 1799–1888

3742 **Woodring, Carl Ray,** 1951: no.3743.

HOWITT, WILLIAM, 1792–1879

3743 **Woodring, Carl Ray.** William and Mary Howitt: bibliographical notes. Harvard Lib Bull 5no2:251–5 '51.

Checklists supplementing CBEL, etc.

HOWSE, SIR HENRY GREENWAY, 1841–1914

3744 **Winston, J. H. E.** . . . Bibliography of the published writings, 1869–1904, of sir Henry Greenway Howse. [London] 1915. 6p. port. 21cm. (Bibliographies of Guy's men, no.4)
Chronol. checklist.

HUDSON, STEPHEN, *pseud. of* SYDNEY SCHIFF, 1869?–1944

3745 **Gawsworth, John,** *pseud.* [1932]: no.686.

HUDSON, WILLIAM HENRY, 1841–1922

3746 **Bibliographies** of modern authors. William Henry Hudson. Lond Merc 3no13:100–1 N '20.

3747 **Wilson, George Francis.** A bibliography of the writings of W. H. Hudson. London, Bookman's journal, 1922. (Also pub. New York, R. R. Bowker, 1922) 79p. facsims. 23cm.
TP transcrs., collations, and bibliogr. notes on first ed., pamphlets, leaflets, etc.; contribs. to periodical literature, prefaces to books, etc.; no index.

3748 —— The real first edition of Hudson's Hampshire days, and other notes. Bkmns J 7no18:170–1 '23.

3749 —— A rare Hudson pamphlet. *ib.* 9no29:178 '24.
Addenda to his bibliogr.

HUDSON-WILLIAMS, THOMAS, 1873–1961
See Williams, Thomas Hudson—.

HUGHES, GEORGE, 1603–1667

3750 **Dredge, John Ingle,** 1889–99: no.886.

HUGHES, THOMAS, 1822–1896

3751 **Kirby, H. T.** Thomas Hughes' Scouring of the white horse, with a bibliographical list of his works. Bkmns J ser3 17no11:150–5 '29; 17no12:223 '30.
'A bibliographical list of the writings of Thomas Hughes' (p.152–5).

3752 **Parrish, Morris Longstreth** and **B. K. Mann,** 1936: no.3929.

3753 **Cutler, C. V.,** 1950: no.105.

HUGHES, THOMAS, fl.1853–1875

3755 **Parrish, Morris Longstreth** and **B. K. Mann,** 1936: no.3929.

HUME, ALEXANDER, 1560?–1609

3756 **Geddie, William,** 1912: no.2034.

HUME, DAVID, 1711–1776

3757 **Johnston, George P.** The first edition of Hume of Godscroft's History. Edinburgh Bib Soc Pub 4:149–71 Oc '01.
'List of manuscripts and printed editions of The history' (p.[167]–71): chronol. list of 8 ed., with collations, bibliogr. notes, and locations of copies.

3758 **Jessop, Thomas Edmund.** A bibliography of David Hume and of Scottish philosophy from Francis Hutcheson to lord Balfour. London, A. Brown, 1938. xiv,201p. 26cm.

'David Hume' (p.1–71): chronol. checklists of collected works; works pub. by Hume, and translations of these; posthumously pub. works; spuria; and ana; 'Scottish philosophy' (p.74–189): chronol. checklists by author; some bibliogr. notes.

Rev: J. C. Lib Assn Rec 40:492 '38.

3759 **[Lameere, Jean]** Notes bibliographiques. R Internat de Philos 6no2: 250–3 '52.

Humeiana, supplementing Jessop.

HUME, SIR PATRICK, fl.1580

3760 **Geddie, William,** 1912: no.2034.

HUNNIS, WILLIAM, fl.1549–1597

3760a **Stopes, Charlotte Carmichael.** William Hunnis. Sh Jahrb 27:200–16 '92.

'The works of William Hunnis' (p.208–16): classified annotated checklist.

HUNT, JAMES HENRY LEIGH, 1784–1859

3761 **Houtchens, Carolyn Washburn** and **L. W. Houtchens,** *ed.* [1966]: no.2017.

3762 **Mitchell, Alexander.** A bibliography of the writings of Leigh Hunt, with critical notes. London, Bookman's journal [n.d., 1931] 73p. 24cm.

Preceded by his Notes on the bibliography of Leigh Hunt. Bkmns J 15no1:3–19 '27, and first pub. with Bkmns J 18no15–16 '30–'31. TP transcrs., collations and bibliogr. notes on early ed.

3763 **Brewer, Luther Albertus.** My Leigh Hunt library. Cedar Rapids, Ia., Privately ptd., 1932–8. 2v. ports., facsims. 25cm.

Contents: 1. The first editions.—2. The holograph letters.

3764 **Landré, Louis.** 'Bibliographie' *in* Leigh Hunt, 1784–1859; contribution à l'histoire du romantisme anglais. Paris, 1936. V.2, p.[483]–595.

Chronol. checklists of works and ana.

HUNTER, JOHN, 1728–1793

3770 **Royal college of surgeons of England.** List of books, manuscripts, portraits, &c. relating to John Hunter in the Royal college.... [London] 1891. 8p. 22cm.

Classified checklist.

HUNTER, WILLIAM, 1718–1784

3771 **LeFanu, William Richard.** The writings of William Hunter, F.R.S. Biblioth 1no3:3–14 '58.

Chronol. checklist of 33 works, with some bibliogr. notes.

3772 —— **[Same]:** Goodall, A. L. [Addenda] *ib.* 1no4:46–7 '58.

HUTTON, EDWARD, 1875–

3773 **Rhodes, Dennis Everard.** The writings of Edward Hutton, a bibliographical tribute compiled and presented to Edward Hutton on his eightieth birthday. . . . London, Hollis & Carter, 1955. 64p. illus., port. 22cm.

Chronol. checklist of 225 items, 1898–1954, with quasifacsim. TP transcrs., some bibliogr. notes and locations of copies.

Rev: E. R. Vincent Library ser5 12:76 '57.

HUXLEY, ALDOUS LEONARD, 1894–1963

3774 **Clareson, Thomas D.** and **C. S. Andrews.** Aldous Huxley, a bibliography, 1960–1964. Extrapolation 6:2–21 '64. (Not seen)

3775 **Muir, Percival Horace** and **B. van Thal.** Bibliographies of the first editions of books by Aldous Huxley and T. F. Powys. London, Dulau, 1927. 61p. 20cm.

Contents: Aldous Leonard Huxley, by P. H. Muir, p.[9]–41.—Theodore Francis Powys, by B. van Thal and P. H. Muir, p.47–61.

TP transcrs., collations, and bibliogr. notes.

3776 **Duval, Hanson R.** Aldous Huxley, a bibliography. New York, Arrow editions [1939] 205p. 26cm.

3777 **Eschelbach, Claire John** and **J. L. Shober.** Aldous Huxley, a bibliography, 1916–1959. Berkeley, University of California pr., 1961. x,150p. 24cm.

Classified checklists of works (959 items) and ana.

Rev: N. Barker Bk Coll 11:109–10 '62; Pa Bib Soc Am 56:277 '62; R. J. Roberts Library ser5 18:159–60 '63.

3778 **Zeitlin, Jacob Israel.** Aldous Huxley: the writings of Aldous Huxley, 1916–1943, an exhibition of the collection of Jacob I. Zeitlin at the library of the University of California, Los Angeles. . . . [Los Angeles, 1943] [16]p. 23cm. Covertitle.
Comp. by Lawrence C. Powell.

HYDE, DOUGLAS, 1860–1949

3780 **O'Hegarty, Patrick Sarsfield.** A bibliography of dr. Douglas Hyde. . . . Dublin, Privately ptd., by A. Thom, 1939. 19p. 24cm.

Repr. from Dublin Mag new ser 14:57–66, 72–8 Ja/Mr, Ap/Je '39. Chronol. checklist of 38 items, 1889–1937, with TP transcrs., collations, and bibliogr. notes; no index.

3781 **De Bhaldraithe, Tomas.** Aguisin le clar saothair An Chraoibhin. Galvia 4:18–24 '57. (Not seen)

Supplements O'Hegarty.

INCHBALD, ELIZABETH (SIMPSON), 1753–1821

3782 **Joughin, George Louis.** An Inchbald bibliography. Univ Texas Stud Eng 14:59–74 '34.

Title checklist of early ed., with locations of copies.

INGRAM, JOHN KELLS, 1823–1907

3783 **[Lyster, Thomas William]** Bibliography of the writings of John Kells Ingram, 1823–1907, with a brief chronology. Compiled for Cumann na Leabharlann. Dublin, 1907–8. An Leabharlann 3:3–46 Je '09.

Chronol. checklist, 1840–1909, with some bibliogr. notes.

IRVING, SIR JOHN HENRY BRODRIBB-, 1838–1905

3784 **Lawes, F. T.,** 1949: no.155.

ISHERWOOD, CHRISTOPHER WILLIAM BRADSHAW-, 1904–

3785 **Philpot, V. J.,** 1957: no.183.

JACOBS, WILLIAM WYMARK, 1863–1943

3786 **Rook, Clarence.** W. W. Jacobs. Eng Illus Mag new ser 29:647–9 S '03.

'Bibliography' (p.648).

3787 **Osborne, Eric Allen.** Epitome of a bibliography of W. W. Jacobs. Am Bk Coll 5:201–4, 268–72, 286–8, 331–4, 358–62 '34.

Discursive account.

JACOBSON, WALTER HAMILTON ACLAND, fl.1877–1907

3788 **Winston, George A. R.** . . . Bibliography of the published writings, 1877–1923, of Walter Hamilton Acland Jacobson. . . . [London] 1924. 8p. port. 22cm. (Bibliographies of Guy's men, no.9) (Not seen)

JAMES I, KING OF ENGLAND, 1566–1625

3789 **Geddie, William,** 1912: no.2034.

3790 **Craigie, James,** *ed.* 'Bibliography' *in* The Basilicon doron of king James VI. Edinburgh, 1942–50. V.2, p.136–90.

TP transcrs., discursive collations, locations of copies, and bibliogr. notes and refs. for mss., printed, collected, translated and adapted versions.

3791 —— The Latin folio of king James's prose works. Edinburgh Bib Soc Trans 3pt1:19–30 '52; 3pt2:155 '54.

Discussion, distinction of forms, and locations of copies.

3792 —— Basilicon doron: a late seventeenth edition. Edinburgh Bib Soc Trans 3pt2:155–6 '54.
Short descr. of Harvard university copy of Wing J128A.

3793 **Glasgow. University. Hunterian library.** James VI and I: an exhibition to commemorate the quartercentenary of the birth of James Charles Stuart . . . held in the Hunterian library. . . . [Glasgow, 1966] 20p. 25cm. (Duplicated typescript)

JAMES VI, KING OF SCOTLAND, 1566–1625
See James I, king of England.

JAMES, GEORGE PAYNE RAINSFORD, 1799–1860

3794 **Frost, W. A.** The novels and short stories of G. P. R. James. N&Q ser12 2:167–8 Ag '16.
Chronol. checklist of 56 items, 1829–59.

3795 **Ellis, Stewart Marsh.** 'A chronological list of the works of G. P. R. James, with bibliographical and other notes' *in* The solitary horseman, or, the life and adventures of G. P. R. James. Kensington, 1927. p.272–96.

JAMES, HENRY, 1843–1916

3796 **Richardson, Lyon N.** 'Bibliography' *in* Henry James: representative selections. . . . New York [1941] p.xci–cxi.

3797 —— [**Same**]: repr. *in* Dupee, Frederick W., *ed.* The question of Henry James. . . . New York, 1945. p.281–97.

3798 —— [**Same**]: London, 1947. p.288–303.

3799 **Hamilton, Eunice C.** Biographical and critical studies of Henry James, 1941–1948. Am Lit 20:424–35 Ja '49.
Extends checklist in Richardson: no.3796; includes modern ed.

3800 **Dunbar, Viola R.** Addenda to Biographical and critical studies of Henry James, 1941–1948. Am Lit 22:56–61 Mr '50.

3801 **King, Frederick Allen,** *comp.* 'Bibliography' *in* Cary, Elisabeth L. The novels of Henry James, a study. New York, 1905. p.189–215.

3802 **Phillips, LeRoy.** A bibliography of the writings of Henry James. Boston, Houghton, Miflin, 1906. ix,187p. 22cm.

3803 —— [**Same**]: 2d ed. New York, Coward, McCann, 1930. xviii,285p. 23cm.

3804 [**Shorter, Clement**] *ed.* 'Bibliography of Henry James' *in* Letters to an editor, by Henry James. [London, 1916] p.13–16.

3805 **Kenton, Edna.** Some bibliographical notes on Henry James. Hound & Horn 7:535–40 Ap/My '34.

3806 **McElderry, B. R.** The published letters of Henry James; a survey. Bull Bib 20:165–7, 187 Ja/Ap, My/Ag '52.

3807 **Edel, Leon** and **D. H. Laurence.** A bibliography of Henry James. London, R. Hart-Davis, 1957. 411p. illus., port. 23cm. (Soho bibliographies, VIII)
See no.3809.

3808 **Okita, Hajime.** Henry James bibliography in Japan. Kyoto, Showado, 1958. 62p. (Not seen)

3809 **Edel, Leon** and **D. H. Laurence.** A bibliography of Henry James. [2d ed., rev.] London, R. Hart-Davis, 1961. 427p. illus., facsims. 23cm. (Soho bibliographies, VIII)

Classified bibliogr. of early ed. of original works; contribs. to books; published letters; contribs. to periodicals; translations; and miscellanea; with quasifacsim. TP transcrs., collations, and bibliogr. notes.

JAMES, MONTAGUE RHODES, 1862–1936

3815 **Scholfield, A. F.,** *comp.* 'List of writings' *in* Lubbock, S. G. A memoir of Montague Rhodes James. . . . Cambridge, 1939. p.47–[87].
Chronol. checklist.

3816 **Osborne, Eric Allen.** Bibliographical notes [on M. R. James] Bk Hndbk 1n04:253 '47.
Checklist with some bibliogr. notes.

JAMES, THOMAS, 1573?–1629

3816a **Wheeler, George William.** List of the works of Thomas James, S.T.P. Bod Q Rec 4n042:138–41 Jl '24.
Chronol. checklist, 1598–1627.

JEFFERIES, JOHN RICHARD, 1848–1887

3817 **Salt, Henry Stephens.** 'Bibliographical appendix' *in* Richard Jefferies, a study. London; New York, 1894. p.121–7.
Classified checklist of works and ana.

3818 **Thomas, Philip Edward.** 'Bibliography' *in* Richard Jefferies, his life and work. London, 1909. p.329–35. (*See* no.3819a)

3819 **Masseck, Clinton Joseph.** 'Œuvres de Jefferies' *in* Richard Jefferies, étude d'une personnalité. Paris, 1913. p.[247]–56.

3819a **Thomas, Philip Edward.** 'Books and other writings of John Richard Jefferies' *in* Richard Jefferies, his life and work. [2d ed. London, 1938] p.300–3.
Chronol. checklist, 1866–1937.

3820 **Swindon. Public libraries.** A catalogue of books in the Richard Jefferies collection [compiled by] Harold Joliffe. Swindon, Libraries, museum, arts and music committee, 1948. 16p. port., facsim. 23cm.

JENKS, EDWARD, 1861–1939

3821 **Lee, R. W.** Edward Jenks, 1861–1939. Proc Brit Acad 26:399–423 '40.
'Bibliography' (p.421–3): chronol. checklist of books and periodical articles.

JENNER, EDWARD, 1749–1823

3822 **Wellcome historical medical museum,** LONDON. Catalogue of an exhibition of books, manuscripts and relics commemorating the bicentenary of Edward Jenner. . . . London, Published for the trustees by G. Cumberlege, O.U.P., 1949. 36p. illus., port. 25cm.

3823 **LeFanu, William Richard.** A bio-bibliography of Edward Jenner, 1749–1823. London, Harvey and Blythe, 1951. xx,176p. port., facsims. 25cm.
Classified chronol. arrangement of experiments and observations; principal works; posthumous works; letters; miscellanea; biographies, dedications and portraits, with TP facsims., collations, locations of copies, and some bibliogr. notes.
Rev: TLS 27 Jl '51:571; E. Weil Library ser5 8:205 '53.

JENNINGS, RICHARD, 1881–1953

3824 **Carter, John Waynflete.** Thomas J. Wise and Richard Gullible. Bk Coll 8no2:182–3 '59.
Checklist of 6 leaflets, with some bibliogr. notes.

JEPHSON, ROBERT, 1736–1803

3825 **Peterson, Martin Severin.** [Checklist] *in* Robert Jephson, 1736–1803, a study of his life and works. Lincoln, Neb., 1930. p.44.

JERMIN, MICHAEL, c.1591–1659

3826 **Dredge, John Ingle,** 1889–99: no.886.

JERROLD, DOUGLAS WILLIAM, 1803–1857

3826a **Jerrold, Walter.** Douglas Jerrold's dramatic works. N&Q ser8 11:121–2 F '97.
Chronol. checklist of 68 items, 1821–54.

JEVON, THOMAS, 1652–1688

3827 **Scouten, Arthur H.** and **L. Hughes.** The devil to pay, a preliminary check list. Lib Chron Univ Pennsylvania 15no1:15–24 '48.
TP transcrs., collations, bibliogr. notes, and locations of copies for 18 items, 1731–71, with checklist of later ed.

JOHNISTOUN, PATRICK, fl.1450?

3828 **Geddie, William,** 1912: no. 2034.

JOHNSON, ALFRED FORBES

3828a **Smith, Alan Rae,** 1951: no.1155.

JOHNSON, CHARLES, fl.1724–1736

3829 **Gosse, Philip Henry G.** A bibliography of the works of capt. Charles Johnson. London, Dulau, 1927. 8op. facsim. 22cm.
TP transcrs., collations, and bibliogr. notes on 64 items (2 works), 1724–6; no index.

JOHNSON, LIONEL PIGOT, 1867–1902

3830 **Danielson, Henry.** A bibliography of Lionel Johnson. Bkmns J 5no1–3: 29–30, 68, 103–4 '21.
Bibliographies of modern authors, no.16. TP transcrs., collations, and bibliogr. notes on 12 early ed., 1894–1921.

JOHNSON, RICHARD, 1734–1793

3831 **Weedon, Margaret J. P.** Richard Johnson and the successors of John Newbery. Library ser5 4:25–63 Je '49.
'List of Richard Johnson's writings' (p.39–63): title checklist of 91 items, mainly separate pubs., with locations of copies and some bibliogr. notes.

JOHNSON, SAMUEL, 1709–1784

3832 **Brooklyn. Public library.** Samuel Johnson, 1709–1784; a list of books with references to periodicals in the Brooklyn public library. Brooklyn, N.Y., 1909. 18p. 16cm.

3833 **[Yale university. Library]** List of books and articles relating to Samuel Johnson, 1709–1784, compiled on the occasion of the exhibition. . . . [New Haven, 1909] 24cm. 19cm.

3834 **Clifford, James Lowry.** Johnsonian studies, 1887–1950, a survey and bibliography. Minneapolis, University of Minnesota pr.; London, G. Cumberlege, O.U.P. [1951] ix,140p. 24cm.

Rev: M. C. Hyde Pa Bib Soc Am 45:365–7 '51; H. W. Liebert Philol Q 31:277–8 '52; R. W. Chapman R Eng Stud new ser 3:299–300 '52; E. L. McAdam Mod Lang N 67:498 '52; G. J. Kolb Mod Philol 50:215–16 '53.

3835 —— and **D. J. Greene.** 'Additions and corrections to Johnsonian studies, 1887–1950. . . .' in Wahba, Magdi, ed. Johnsonian studies. Cairo, 1962. p.[263]–350.

3836 **Grolier club,** NEW YORK. Catalogue of an exhibition commemorative of the bicentenary of the birth of Samuel Johnson, 1709–1909; consisting of original editions of his published works, special presentation copies, and several of his original manuscripts. . . . [New York, DeVinne pr., 1909] viii,106p. ports. 18cm.

3837 **Yale university. Library.** Catalogue of an exhibition of manuscripts, first editions, early engravings, and serious literature relating to Samuel Johnson . . . by Chauncey Brewster Tinker. [New Haven] 1909. 12p. 18cm.

See no.3842.

3838 **Courtney, William Prideaux.** A bibliography of Samuel Johnson; revised and seen through the press by David Nicol Smith. Oxford, Clarendon pr. 1915. (Reissued with facsims., 1925) viii,186p. 24cm.

Discursive chronol. checklist with copious notes, some bibliogr. See also no.3843.

Rev: Athen 26 Je '15:567; N&Q ser 11 11:503 '15; T. Scott Sat R Lit 2:339 '25; I. A. Williams Lond Merc 12:298 '25; A. W. Reed R Eng Stud 2:105–7 '26; Library ser4 6:201–2 '25.

3839 **Adam, Robert Borthwick.** Catalogue of the Johnsonian collection of R. B. Adam. . . . Buffalo, N.Y., Privately ptd., 1921. iv.(unpaged) ports., facsims. 22cm.

An earlier catalogue (Johnsoniana in the library . . . Buffalo, 1895. [32]p.) has not been seen. See no.3841.

3840 **Mathews, Elkin, bksllrs.,** LONDON. A catalogue of books by or relating to dr. Johnson & members of his circle, offered for sale. . . . London, 1925. vi,110p. illus. 22cm.

Comp. by Arthur W. Evans.

3841 **Adam, Robert Borthwick.** The R. B. Adam library relating to dr. Samuel Johnson and his era. Buffalo, N.Y., Ptd. for the author; London, O.U.P., 1929–30. 4v. illus., ports., plates, map., facsims. 28cm.

Contents: 1. Letters of Samuel Johnson, James Boswell, Edmund Burke, Joshua Reynolds, and David Garrick. (1929).—2. Catalogue of books. (1929).—3. Miscellaneous autograph letters. (1929).—4. [Miscellany, including collection of works relating to Edmund Burke] (1930).

Extensive facsims.; the collection is now in the University of Rochester library, N.Y.

3842 **Yale university. Library.** A catalogue of an exhibition of first editions of the works of Samuel Johnson in the library of Yale university, 8 November to 30 December, 1935, by Allen T. Hazen and Edward L. McAdam, jr. New Haven, 1935. 32p. 23cm.

3842a **Hazen, Allen Tracy.** Samuel Johnson's prefaces and dedications. New Haven, Yale U.P.; London, H. Milford, O.U.P., 1937. xxiii, 257p. 22cm.

Discursive bibliogr. with collations, locations of copies, and bibliogr. notes. 'Chronological list' (p.[251]–2).

Rev: N&Q 173:215–16 '37; P. Meissner Angl Beibl 49:52–3 '38; R. W. Chapman R Eng Stud 14:359–65 '38; C. Rinaker J Eng Germ Philol 37:316–18 '38.

3843 **Chapman, Robert William** and **A. T. Hazen.** Johnsonian bibliography, a supplement to Courtney. Oxford Bib Soc Proc 5pt3:117–66 '39.

Mainly provides collations and bibliogr. notes to item no.3838. *See* next item.

3844 —— The collection of books by or relating to Samuel Johnson and James Boswell . . . June 1, 1945 . . . Sotheby. . . . London, 1945. (Not seen)

3845 **Liebert, Herman W.** An addition to the bibliography of Samuel Johnson. Pa Bib Soc Am 41:231–8 '47.

TP transcrs. and facsim., collation, and discussion of Poems to her majesty, to which is added a new tragedy . . . The earl of Somerset, by Henry Lucas, 1779; the tragedy rev. by Johnson.

3845a **Greene, D. J.** Johnson's contributions to the Literary magazine. R Eng Stud new ser 7no28:367–92 '56.

Checklists of attributions, 15 Ap–15 S 1756, *passim.*

3846 [**Birmingham. Public libraries**] Catalogue of an exhibition of books in the Birmingham library . . . of dr. Johnson. [Birmingham, 1959] 12p. 17cm.

3847 **Birmingham. Public libraries.** Dr. Samuel Johnson, 1709–1784; celebrations in Birmingham of the 250th anniversary of his birth: an exhibition of books, manuscripts, views and portraits. . . . [Birmingham, Museum and art gallery, 1959] 28p. 21cm.

3848 **Pierpont Morgan library,** NEW YORK. Samuel Johnson, LL.D., 1709–1784; an exhibition of first editions, manuscripts, letters and portraits to commemorate the 250th anniversary of his birth, and the 200th anniversary of the publication of his Rasselas. . . . New York, 1959. [45]p. ports., facsims. 31cm.

3849 **Eddy, Donald D.** Samuel Johnson's edition of Shakespeare, 1765. Pa Bib Soc Am 56:428–44 '62.

Distinction and discussion of 3 1765 ed., with tables of pages and press figures, and locations of copies.

3850 **Hyde, Donald.** Catalogue bibliothecæ Hydeianæ; the Hyde collection of the works of Samuel Johnson, compiled by J. D. Fleeman. Cambridge [Mass.] Harvard college library, 1965. 3v. facsims. 28cm. (Duplicated typescript)

JOHNSTON, ARTHUR, 1587–1641

3855 **Johnston, William.** The bibliography and portraits of Arthur Johnston . . . physician to James VI and Charles I. Aberdeen, Aberdeen U.P., 1896. ii,28p. ports., facsims. 30cm.

Repr. from Scot N&Q 9:50–2 [i.e. 4], 65–7, 82–4 S–N '95, and repr. in Geddes, sir William D., *ed.* Musa latina Aberdonensis. Aberdeen, 1895. V.2, p.xlii–lvi.

Discursive classified checklist of works and ana, with collations and bibliogr. notes.

3856 **Anderson, Peter John.** Arthur Johnson bibliography. N&Q ser11 10:346 Oc '14.

Adds item to previous item.

JONES, SIR EDWARD COLEY BURNE-, 1833–1898

3857 **Griffiths, J. M. I.,** 1937: no.133.

JONES, GRIFFITH, 1683–1761

3858 **Gregory, A. D.,** 1939: no.131.

JONES, HENRY ARTHUR, 1851–1929

3859 **Jones, Doris Arthur.** 'The plays of Henry Arthur Jones'; 'The writings and speeches of . . . Jones' *in* The life and letters of Henry Arthur Jones. London, 1930. p.411–31.

Chronol. checklists, 1869–1928.

JONES, THOMAS, c.1820–1913?

3860 **Alpha——Uriel.** Welsh Bib Soc J 2:174–6 Ja '21.

Checklist of 12 items by Thomas Jones of Rhosllanerchrugog hall, Denbighshire.

JONES, THOMAS GWYNN, 1871–1949

3861 **Denbighshire. County library.** A bibliography of Thomas Gwynn Jones . . . compiled by Owen Williams. Wrexham, Principality pr., 1938. 53p. 22cm.

Chronol. checklist of 496 items, 1891–1937; repr. from The bibliography of Denbighshire, pt.3.

JONES, SIR WILLIAM, 1746–1794

3862 **Cannon, Garland Hampton.** William Jones, orientalist; an annotated bibliography of his works. Honolulu, University of Hawaii pr. [1952] xvi,88p. port. 22cm.

Discursive chronol. survey, with 'Edition-printing index' (p.75–82) with locations of copies; 'Bibliography' (p.83–8): ana from 1800.

JONSON, BENJAMIN, 1573?–1637

3863 **Ford, Herbert Lewis.** Collation of the Ben Jonson folios, 1616–31–1640. Oxford, O.U.P., 1932. 30p. ports. 22cm.

Discursive account with bibliogr. notes.

Rev: TLS 1 S '32:610; A. W. P[ollard] Library ser4 13:111–12 '32.

3864 **Tannenbaum, Samuel Aaron.** Ben Jonson, a concise bibliography. New York, Scholars' facsimiles and reprints, 1938. viii,151p. 23cm. (Elizabethan bibliographies, no.2)

3865 —— [**Same**]: Supplement. . . . New York, 1947. ii,85l., 28cm. (Duplicated typescript)
Classified checklist of works and ana.

3866 **Steensma, Robert C.** Ben Jonson, a checklist of editions, biography, and criticism, 1947–1964. Res Opportunities Renaiss Drama 9:29–46 '66.
Supplements Tannenbaum.

JOYCE, JAMES AUGUSTINE, 1882–1941

3870 **Spoerri, James Fuller.** James Joyce; books and pamphlets relating to the author and his works. Bib Soc Univ Virginia Secretary's Newsh 34:1–12 Oc '55; *ib*. 37:2–3 S '57; 42:[5–8] Ag '59; 48: [5–6] Je '62; 51:5–6 F '64.

3871 **Kain, Richard M.** Supplement to James Joyce bibliography, 1954–1957. James Joyce R 1no4:38–40 '57.

3872 **White, William.** Addenda to James Joyce bibliography, 1950–1953. James Joyce R 1no2:9–25 '57.

3873 —— [**Same**]: 1954–1957. James Joyce R 1no3:3–24 '57.

3874 **Beebe, Maurice** and **W. Litz.** Criticism of James Joyce, a selected checklist with an index to studies of separate works. Mod Fict Stud 4no1:71–99 '58.

3875 **Cohn, Alan Mayer.** Further supplement to James Joyce bibliography, 1950–1957. James Joyce R 2no1/2:40–54 '58.
Checklist of writings by Joyce, including translations; recordings; Joyce material in books; and ana.

3876 —— and **H. K. Croessmann.** Additional supplement to James Joyce bibliography, 1950–1959. James Joyce R 3no1/2:16–39 '59.

3877 —— and **R. M. Kain.** Supplemental JJ checklist. James Joyce Q 1no2:15–22 '64.

3878 **Cohn, Alan Mayer.** Supplemental JJ checklist, 1963. James Joyce Q 2no1: 50–60 '64.

3879 **Deming, Robert H.** A bibliography of James Joyce studies. [Lawrence, Kansas] University of Kansas libraries, 1964. 180p. 27cm.
Annotated classified checklist to 1961.

3880 **O'Hegarty, Patrick Sarsfield.** A bibliography of James Joyce. Dublin, Privately ptd. by A. Thom, 1946. 12p. 25cm.
Repr. from Dublin Mag new ser 21:38–47 Ja/Mr '46.

3881 **Spoerri, James Fuller.** Catalogue of a collection of the works of James Joyce, exhibited at the Newberry library. . . . Chicago, 1948. [69]p. 24cm.
The collection is now in the University of Kansas library.

3882 **Parker, Alan Dean.** James Joyce, a bibliography of his writings, critical material and miscellanea. Boston, F. W. Faxon, 1948. 256p. 24cm.

3883 **Gheerbrant, Bernard.** James Joyce, sa vie, son œuvre, son rayonnement. Paris, La Hune, 1949. iv.(unpaged) illus., ports., facsims. 18cm.

Collection now in Lockwood memorial library, University of Buffalo.

3884 **White, William.** James Joyce; addenda to Alan Parker's bibliography. Pa Bib Soc Am 43:401–11 '49.

Principally ana.

3885 **Slocum, John Jermain** and **H. Cahoon.** A bibliography of James Joyce, 1882–1941. New Haven, Yale U.P.; London, R. Hart-Davis, 1953. ix,195p. facsims. 24cm. (Soho bibliographies, v)

Quasifacsim. TP transcrs., collations, and bibliogr. notes on separate pubs.; contribs. to books, periodicals and newspapers; translations of; mss.; musical settings of; and miscellany. The Slocum collection is now in the Yale university library.

Rev: W. Y. Tindall N.Y. Times Bk R 28 Je '53:13; TLS 30 Oc '53:700; R. M. Kain Sewanee R 61:717–22 '53; W. White Pa Bib Soc Am 47:401–2 '53; M. Craig Bk Coll 2:225–7 '53; I. R. Willison Library ser5 8:130–5 '53.

3886 **Spoerri, James Fuller.** Finnegans wake by James Joyce, a checklist. . . . Evanston, Ill., Northwestern university library, 1953. 18p. 16cm.

3887 **Illinois. Southern Illinois university,** CARBONDALE. **Library.** James Joyce, an exhibition from the collection of dr. H. K. Croessmann. . . . [Carbondale, 1957] iii,13p. 23cm.

Comp. by Alan M. Cohn.

3888 **Walker, Brenda M.** James Joyce, a bibliography. Manchester R 8:151–60 '58.

3889 **Cornell university. Library.** The Cornell Joyce collection, a catalogue compiled by Robert E. Scholes. Ithaca, N.Y., Cornell U.P. [1961] xvii, 225p. 22cm.

3890 **Staley, Thomas F.** James Joyce, a bio-bibliographical note. Bklovers Answ no8/9:22–3 N/F '63/4.

JUNIUS, *pseud.*

3895 **Edmands, John.** A Junius bibliography. Bull Mercantile Lib Philadelphia 2n03–9:48–52, 64–8, 85–8, 105–8, 121–4, 142–4 Jl '90–Ja '92.

3896 **Cordasco, Francesco G. M.** A Junius bibliography, with a preliminary essay on the political background, text, and identity. . . . New York, B. Franklin, 1949. 125p. port. 23cm.

3897 —— A supplement to the Junius bibliography. Bull Bib 21:48 S/D '53.

3898 —— Addendum to the Junius bibliography. *ib.* 22:96 S/D '57.

8399 **Bowyer, Tony Harold.** A bibliographical examination of the earliest editions of the letters of Junius. Charlottesville, Va., University of Virginia pr., 1957. xxxiv,147p. facsims. 18cm.

Full descrs. with quasifacsim. TP transcrs., and facsims., and locations of copies; 31 items arranged chronol. Based on University of London School of librarianship and archives bibliogr., 1952: *see* no.891.

Rev: F. G. M. Cordasco Bull Bib 32:78 '57; D. F. F[oxon] Bk Coll 6:425–6 '57; P. Gaskell Library ser5 13:72–3 '58; W. B. Todd J Eng Germ Philol 57:346–7 '58; TLS 20 Je '58:352.

3900 **Evans, Gwynne Blakemore.** The missing third edition of Wheble's Junius, 1771. Stud Bib 13:235–8 '60.

Addendum to Bowyer.

KEANE, AUGUSTUS HENRY, 1833–1912

3901 **[Keane, Augustus Henry]** Anthropological, philological, geographical, historical and other writings, original and translated, by A. H. Keane. [London, 1898] 18p. 21cm. Covertitle.

3902 —— **[Same]**: Supplement, 1899–1901. [London, 1902] 4p. 21cm.

Annotated classified checklist.

KEATS, JOHN, 1795–1821

3903 **Marsh, George L.** and **N. I. White.** Keats and the periodicals of his time. Mod Philol 32:37–53 Ag '34.

Annotated checklist, 1816–21, of notices of Keats's works.

3903a **Raysor, Thomas Middleton,** *ed.*, 1956: no.2015.

3904 **Forman, Harry Buxton,** *ed.* 'List of principal works consulted' *in* The complete works of John Keats. Glasgow, 1900. V.1, p.[xvii]–xxii.

3905 **English association,** 1912: no.650.

3906 **[Forman, Maurice Buxton]** *comp.* 'List of principal works concerning Keats' *in* Forman, Harry B., *ed.* The poetical works and other writings of John Keats. Rev. with add. by Maurice Buxton Forman. Hampstead ed. New York, 1938. V.1, p.xcix–cxxviii.

3907 **MacGillivray, James Robertson.** Keats, a bibliography and reference guide, with an essay on Keats' reputation. [Toronto] University of Toronto pr., 1949. lxxxii,210p. 24cm.

Classified list of books; collected ed.; periodical contribs.; and ana.

Rev.: N&Q 195:395 '50; G. L. Marsh Mod Philol 48:134–6 '50; C. D. Thorpe Philol Q 29:122 '50; G. H. Ford Mod Lang Q 13:310–11 '50; Dalhousie R 29:464–5 '50; TLS 24 F '50:120; F. Page R Eng Stud new ser 2:404 '51.

3908 **Rice, sr. Pio Maria.** John Keats, a classified bibliography of critical writings on John Keats's poems . . . 1947–1961. Bull Bib 24:167–8, 187–92 My/Ag, S/D '65.

Continues MacGillivray to start of the annual bibliogr. in the Keats-Sh J, 1951– .

3909 **Boston. Public library.** Catalogue of a loan exhibition commemorating the anniversary of the death of John Keats, 1821–1921, held at the Public library of the city of Boston. . . . [Boston, 1921] 63p. 16cm.

From the collection of Fred Holland Day.

3910 **Wise, Thomas James,** *comp.* 'A bibliography of the writings of John Keats' *in* Keats house committee, Hampstead. The John Keats memorial volume [ed. by G. C. Williamson] London, 1921. p.209–15.

Catalogue of 8 editiones principes, and ana, with TP transcrs., collations, and bibliogr. notes.

KEBLE, JOHN, 1792–1866

3915 **Lock, Walter.** 'Published writings' *in* John Keble, a biography. London, 1893. p.242–5.

Chronol. checklist, 1812–85.

KEENE, CHARLES SAMUEL, 1823–1891

3916 **Chesson, Wilfrid Hugh,** *comp.* 'List of books illustrated by Charles Keene' *in* Pennell, Joseph. The work of Charles Keene. London, 1897. p.277–89.

Chronol. checklist, 1842–95, with quasifacsim. TP transcrs., some bibliogr. notes, and notes on the illus.

KELLETT, EDWARD, fl.1608–1641

3917 **Dredge, John Ingle,** 1889–99: no.886.

KEMBLE, JOHN MITCHELL, 1807–1857

3918 **Dickins, Bruce.** 'Writings of John Mitchell Kemble' *in* J. M. Kemble and old English scholarship. London, H. Milford, O.U.P. [1940] p.[31]–6.

Chronol. checklist, 1832–63; repr. from Proc Brit Acad 25:51–84 '39.

KEMPE, WILLIAM, fl.1580–1593

3919 **Dredge, John Ingle,** 1899–99: no.886.

KENDALL, GEORGE, 1610–1663

3920 **Dredge, John Ingle,** 1889–99: no.886.

KENNEDY, JAMES, fl.1920?

3921 **Scottish chapbook,** 1922–3: no.724.

KENNEDY, WALTER, 1460?–1508?

3922 **Geddie, William,** 1912: no.2034.

KENNY, COURTNEY STANHOPE, 1847–1930

3923 **Hazeltine, H. D.** Courtney Stanhope Kenny, 1847–1930. Proc Brit Acad 18:345–406 '32.

'List of some of Courtney Stanhope Kenny's published writings, arranged in chronological order' (p.404–6).

KILLIGREW, THOMAS, 1612–1683

3924 **Harbage, Alfred Bennett.** 'Bibliography' *in* Thomas Killigrew, cavalier dramatist, 1612–83. Philadelphia; London, 1930. p.232–3.

Checklist of early ed.

KING, JOSIAH, fl.1648–1698

3925 **Dredge, John Ingle,** 1889–99: no.886.

KING, WILLIAM, 1685–1763

3926 **Williams, sir Harold.** The old trumpeter of Liberty hall. Bk Coll Q 4:29–56 Oc '31.

'Dr. William King, a bibliographical list' (p.44–56): chronol. checklist, 1730–1819, with TP transcrs., collations, and bibliogr. notes.

KINGSLEY, CHARLES, 1819–1875

3927 **Stevenson, Lionel,** *ed.,* 1964: no.1705.

3928 **Barrett, H. M.,** 1936: no.81.

3929 **Parrish, Morris Longstreth** and **B. K. Mann.** Charles Kingsley and Thomas Hughes; first editions (with a few exceptions) in the library at Dormy house. . . . London, Constable, 1936. xi,165p. plates, port., facsims. 26cm.

'Charles Kingsley' (p.3–102); 'Thomas Hughes' (p.103–48); 'Appendix IV [books by Thomas Hughes of Reading, and Thomas Hughes of Market Rasen]: p.154. Chronol. catalogue with quasifacsim. TP transcrs., collations, and bibliogr. notes.

Rev: TLS 22 Ag '36:684; J. W. Carter Pub Wkly 130:525–6 '36; P. Brooks N.Y. Times Bk R 27 S '36:26; M. F. Thorp Mod Lang N 52:454–5 '37; Sat R Lit 15:21 '37.

3930 **Thorp, Margaret (Farrand).** 'Bibliography of Charles Kingsley's works' *in* Charles Kingsley, 1819–1875. Princeton; London, 1937. p.[191]–204.

Chronol. checklist, 1836–1916, with many new attributions.

KINGSLEY, HENRY, 1830–1876

3931 **Ellis, Stewart Marsh.** 'Bibliography' *in* Henry Kingsley, 1830–1876: towards a vindication. London, 1931. p.269–78.

Chronol. checklist of first ed. and contribs. to magazines, with some bibliogr. notes.

3932 **Wolff, Robert Lee.** Henry Kingsley. Harvard Lib Bull 13:195–226 '59.

'Appendix B: Catalogue of books' (p.222–6): chronol. checklist of 22 items, with Sadleir nos. and some bibliogr. notes.

KIPLING, RUDYARD, 1865–1936

3934 **Gerber, Helmut E.** and **E. Lauterbach.** Rudyard Kipling; an annotated bibliography of writings about him. Eng Fict Transit 3n03/5:1–235 '60.

3935 **Prideaux, William Francis.** Mr. Kipling's Allahabad books, a bibliographical essay. N&Q ser9 1:101–3 F '98.

3936 [**Mansfield, Milburg Francisco**] Some contributions to a bibliography of the works of Rudyard Kipling. Kipling Notebk 11:161–76 D '99; 12:177–88 Ja '00.

3937 **Roberton, William.** 'Bibliography' *in* The Kipling guide book. . . . Birmingham, 1899. p.[43]–51.

3938 **Knowles, Frederic Lawrence.** 'Bibliography of first editions' *in* A Kipling primer. London, 1900. p.200–6.

3939 **Lane, John,** *comp.* 'Rudyard Kipling, a bibliography, 1881–1899' *in* Le Gallienne, Richard. Rudyard Kipling, a criticism. London, 1900. p.i–xlvi at end.

3940 [**Livingston, Luther Samuel**] *comp.* The works of Rudyard Kipling; the description of a set of the first editions of his books in the library of a New York collector [R. F. Pick] New York, Dodd, Mead, 1901. viii,91p. port., facsims. 26cm.

3941 **Powell, F. York.** Rudyard Kipling. Eng Illus Mag new ser 30:295–8 D '03; 30: 429–32 Ja '04.
'Bibliography' (p.298, 429–32).

3942 **Keogh, Andrew,** 1910: no.662.

3943 **Young, W. Arthur.** Uncollected Kipling items. N&Q ser11 8:441–2, 464–5, 485–6 D '13; A. Braund *ib.* 8:515 D '13.

3944 **Martindell, Ernest Walter.** Catalogue of . . . books . . . including a . . . collection of the writings of Rudyard Kipling, the property of capt. E. W. Martindell . . . sold by auction by messrs. Sotheby, Wilkinson & Hodge. . . . London, J. Davy [1921] 32p. facsims. 26cm.

3945 —— A bibliography of the works of Rudyard Kipling, 1881–1921. London, Bookman's journal; New York, J. F. Drake, 1922. xiii,111p. front., facsims. 23cm.

3946 —— [Same]: New ed., much enl. London, J. Lane, 1923. xvi,221p. front., facsims. 23cm.

3947 **Livingston, Flora Virginia (Milner).** Bibliography of the works of Rudyard Kipling. New York, E. H. Wells, 1927. xviii,523p. facsims. 22cm.
Chronol. bibliogr. of 504 early ed., 1879–1926, and collected ed., with collations and bibliogr. notes.

3948 —— [Same]: A footnote to bibliography. Coloph 7:[4p.] '31.

3949 —— [Same]: Supplement. Cambridge [Mass.] Harvard U.P., 1938. xv,333p. port. 22cm.

Classified arrangement of corrigenda and addenda to 1937; pirated pamphlets, 1922–34; translations; and ana.

Rev: TLS 5 My '27:324.

3950 **Chandler, Lloyd Horwitz.** A summary of the works of Rudyard Kipling, including items ascribed to him. New York, Grolier club, 1930. xxvii, 465p. 26cm.

Not a bibliogr. but a useful bibliogr. handbook.

3951 **Grolier club,** NEW YORK. Catalogue of the works of Rudyard Kipling exhibited at the Grolier club. . . . New York, 1930. xi,201p. ports., facsims. 25cm.

3952 **Ballard, Ellis Ames.** Catalogue intimate and descriptive of my Kipling collection; books, manuscripts and letters, with reproductions of rarities. . . . Philadelphia, Privately ptd., 1935. 253p. illus., port., facsims. 25cm.

See no.3954.

3953 **Alexander Turnbull library,** WELLINGTON, N.Z. A selected list of the more important books by Rudyard Kipling . . . compiled by M. Shirley Grin-linton. Wellington, 1941. 6p. 27cm. (Duplicated typescript)

3954 **Ballard, Ellis Ames.** The renowned collection of first editions, autograph letters and manuscripts of Rudyard Kipling . . . sold by order. New York, Parke-Bernet galleries, 1942. 110p. illus., port., facsims. 28cm.

3955 **British museum. [Dept. of printed books]** Catalogue of printed books: accessions: Rudyard Kipling. London, Ptd. by W. Clowes, 1949. 54p. 29cm.

3956 **Stewart, James McGregor.** Rudyard Kipling, a bibliographical catalogue. Edited by A. W. Yeats. Toronto, Dalhousie U.P. and University of Toronto pr., 1959. xv,673p. port., facsims. 25cm.

Classified bibliogr. catalogue of major and other works (763 items); items in sale catalogues; uncollected prose and verse; works in anthologies and readers; collected sets; musical settings; and unauthorized ed. The collection is now in the Dalhousie university library, Halifax.

Rev: S. Millet J Eng Germ Philol 59:741–3 '60; R. J. Roberts Bk Coll 9:482, 485 '60; Univ Toronto Q 29:484–5 '60; Dalhousie R 39:534–8 '60; TLS 2 S '60:568; B. Dobrée Crit Q 2:286 '60; C. T. Naumburg Pa Bib Soc Am 55:64–5 '61: I. Angus Library ser5 16:63–5 '61; R. L. Green R Eng Stud new ser 13:102–3 '62.

3957 **Yeats, Alvice Whitehurst.** Kipling collections in the James McG. Stewart and the University of Texas libraries; an appraisal of resources for literary investigation. Austin, Tex., 1961. 18l. 28cm. (Duplicated typescript)

3958 **Princeton university. Library.** Something of Kipling, 1865–1965; an exhibition in the Princeton university library. . . . [Princeton, N.J., 1965] 8p. 22cm.

3959 **Cornell, Louis L.** 'Kipling's uncollected newspaper writings' *in* Kipling in India. London; New York, 1966. p.192–203.

Annotated checklist of 25 items. 'A chronological list of Kipling's writings from October 1882 to March 1889.' (p.167–84)

3960 **Monteiro, George.** Rudyard Kipling: early printings in American periodicals. Pa Bib Soc Am 61:127–8 '67.

KIRKMAN, FRANCIS, 1652–1680

3965 **Gibson, Strickland.** A bibliography of Francis Kirkman, with his prefaces, dedications and commendations, 1652–80. Oxford Bib Soc Pub new ser 1pt2:47–148 '49.

'Bibliography' (p.109–48): quasifacsim. TP transcrs., collations, locations of copies and some bibliogr. notes on early ed. of 41 titles; 'Publications associated with Francis Kirkman, 1652–80' (p.140–3).

Rev: sir F. C. Francis Library ser4 5:277–8 '51; TLS 14 Ap '50:236; H. Macdonald R Eng Stud new ser 3:77–8 '52.

KNIGHT, CHARLES, 1791–1873

3966 **Clowes, Alice A.** 'Books written by Charles Knight' in Charles Knight, a sketch. London, 1892. p.[254]–7.

'Works edited or conducted by Charles Knight' (p.[258]–65): chronol. checklists.

KNOWLES, JAMES SHERIDAN, 1784–1862

3967 **Meeks, Leslie Howard.** 'The works of James Sheridan Knowles' in Sheridan Knowles and the theatre of his time. Bloomington, Ind., 1933. p.221–6.

Classified checklist.

KNOX, RONALD ARBUTHNOTT, 1888–1957

3968 **Bede, mother M.** Ronald Knox. Bull Assn Brit Theol & Philos Libs 19:22 Jl '64.

KORZENIOWSKI, JÓSEF TEODOR KONRAD, 1857–1924
See Conrad, Joseph, pseud.

KYD, THOMAS, 1557?–1595?

3969 **Tannenbaum, Samuel Aaron.** Thomas Kyd, a concise bibliography. New York, 1941. viii,34p. 23cm. (Elizabethan bibliographies, no.18)

Checklist (576 items) of canonical, apocryphal, and selected works; biography and commentary, and 'Kyd and Hamlet'.

LAING, DAVID, 1793–1878

3970 **Goudie, Gilbert.** 'Literary work' in David Laing, LL.D., a memoir of his life and literary work. Edinburgh, 1913. p.148–237.

Chronol. checklist of 214 items, 1815–80, with some bibliogr. notes.

LAMB, CHARLES, 1775–1834

3971 **Houtchens, Carolyn Washburn** and **L. H. Houtchens,** *ed.* [1966]: no.2017.

3972 **North, Ernest Dressel.** 'Bibliography' in Martin, Benjamin E. In the footprints of Charles Lamb. New York, 1890. p.150–93.

3973 —— [**Same**]: London, 1891. p.[147]–93.

3974 **Dodd, Mead & co., bksllrs.,** NEW YORK. Descriptions of a few books from Charles Lamb's library, and of some presentation copies and first editions of his rarer books, with collations and notes. New York [1899] 22p. facsims. 25cm.

3975 **Livingston, Luther Samuel.** Some notes on three of Lamb's juveniles. Bibliographer 1no6:215–30 Je '02.

Discursive descrs. and discussion with TP facsims. of 7 works written for children, 1805–11.

3976 —— A bibliography of the first editions in book form of Charles and Mary Lamb published prior to . . . 1834. New York, Ptd. for J. A. Spoor at the DeVinne pr., 1903. xv,209p. illus., ports., facsims.(part fold.) 24cm.

Based on the Spoor collection; *see* no.3982.

3977 **Hutchinson, Thomas,** *ed.* 'Bibliographical list, 1794–1834, of the published writings of Charles and Mary Lamb' *in* The works in prose and verse of Charles and Mary Lamb. London [1908] V.1, p.[xvii]–xlvii. (*See* no.3979)

3978 **Thomson, Joseph Charles.** Bibliography of the writings of Charles and Mary Lamb; a literary history. Hull, J. R. Tutin, 1908. xiv,141p. 20cm.

Chronol. checklist of ed. and periodical contribs. pub. to date of Lamb's death, with TP transcrs., collations, and bibliogr. notes.

Rev: N&Q ser10 9:440 '08; Athenæum 19 S '08:331; Lib J 33:301 '08; Nation 86:462 '08.

3979 **Hutchinson, Thomas,** *ed.* 'Bibliographical list, 1794–1834, of the published writings of Charles and Mary Lamb' *in* The works. . . . London, 1924. p.[xvii]–xxxix.

3980 **Tregaskis, James, bksllr.,** LONDON. An important collection of some of the rarer works of Charles Lamb, together with some Lambiana. . . . London, 1927. 20p. facsims. 23cm.

3981 **Texas. University. Library.** Charles Lamb; . . . an exhibition of books and manuscripts in the library . . . commemorative of the centenary of his death. Austin, Tex., 1935. 7p. 23cm. Covertitle.

Comp. by Reginald H. Griffith.

3982 **Spoor, John A.** First editions of English XVIII–XIX century and American XIX century authors . . . the renowned library of the late John A. Spoor. . . . New York, Parke-Bernet galleries, 1939. 2pts. facsims. 26cm.

Important Lamb collection of 1,206 entries, with extensive facsims.

3983 **Finch, Jeremiah S.** The Scribner Lamb collection. Princeton Univ Lib Chron 7:133–48 Je '46.

3984 **Woodring, Carl Ray.** Charles Lamb in the Harvard library. Harvard Lib Bull 10no2:208–39 '56; 10no3:367–402 '56.

Checklist of 42 first ed.; manuscripts and other items, with bibliogr. notes.

3985 **Foxon, David Fairweather.** The chapbook editions of the Lamb's Tales from Shakespear. Bk Coll 6no1:41–53 '57.

Checklist of single tales and collections, with collations, locations of copies, and some bibliogr. notes.

LAMB, MARY ANN, 1764–1847
See under Charles Lamb, 1775–1834.

LAMBOURN, PETER SPENDELOWE, 1722–1774

3990 **Morris, J. M.** A check-list of prints made at Cambridge by Peter Spende-lowe Lambourn, 1722–1774. Cambridge Bib Soc Trans 3pt4:295–312 '62.

Catalogue of book illus. (94 items) with some bibliogr. notes, locations of copies, and 'Loose prints in chronological order' (items 95–120) and 2 'Private plates'.

LAMPSON, FREDERICK LOCKER-, 1821–1895

3991 **Livingston, Flora Virginia (Milner).** Bibliography of the works of F. Locker-Lampson. Bkmns J 10no32,34–6:46–7, 145–6, 175–7, 211 '24; *rf.* A. M. Cohn *ib.* 10:106 '24.

Checklist with collations and bibliogr. notes, 1857–79.

LANDOR, WALTER SAVAGE, 1775–1864

3992 **Houtchens, Carolyn Washburn** and **L. H. Houtchens,** *ed.* [1966]: no.2017.

3993 **Wheeler, Stephen,** *ed.* 'Bibliography' *in* Letters and other unpublished writings of Walter Savage Landor. London, 1897. p.[245]–76.

3993a —— Landor bibliography: poems in The examiner. N&Q ser11 3:364–5 My '11.

3994 **Wise, Thomas James** and **S. Wheeler.** A bibliography of the writings in prose and verse of Walter Savage Landor. London, Ptd. for the Biblio-graphical society by Blades, East & Blades, 1919. xxii,426p. port., facsims. 23cm.

Chronol. bibliogr. of editiones principes; contribs. to periodical literature; collected ed.; and 'Landoriana', with quasifacsim. TP transcrs. and facsims., collations, BM press-marks, and bibliogr. notes; no index.

3995 **Wise, Thomas James.** A Landor library; a catalogue of printed books, manuscripts and autograph letters by Walter Savage Landor, collected by Thomas James Wise. London, Ptd. for private circulation only, 1928. xxi,103p. ports., facsims. 26cm.

Chronol. catalogue of early ed. and ana, with quasifacsim. TP transcrs. and facsims., collations and bibliogr. notes.

Rev: TLS 19 Jl '28:525–6; C. G. Crump *ib.* 2 Ag '28:568.

3996 **Super, Robert Henry.** Landor's unrecorded contributions to periodicals. N&Q 197:497–8 N '52.

Checklist of 26 additions and 3 corrections to Wise and Wheeler.

3997 **Vitoux, Pierre.** 'Bibliographie' *in* L'œuvre de Walter Savage Landor. Paris, 1964. p.[445]–58.

LANE, SIR WILLIAM ARBUTHNOT, 1856–1943

4000 **Wale, William.** Bibliography of the published writings, 1883–1912, of sir William Arbuthnot Lane, bart. . . . [London] 1914. 19p. port. 22cm. (Bibliographies of Guy's men, no.3) (Not seen)

4001 **[Lane, sir William Arbuthnot]** Bibliography of the published writings, 1883–1938, of sir William Arbuthnot Lane. [London, 1938] 24p. port., 22cm.

Chronol. checklist of books and periodical contribs., 1883–1938.

LANG, ANDREW, 1844–1912

4002 **Falconer, Charles MacGregor.** The writings of Andrew Lang . . . arranged in the form of a bibliography with notes. Dundee, Privately ptd., 1894. 24p. 22cm.

4003 **[——]** Catalogue of a library, chiefly of the writings of Andrew Lang. Dundee, Privately ptd., 1898. viii,32p. 17cm.

See no.4006.

4004 **Courtney, W. L.** Andrew Lang. Eng Illus Mag new ser 30:682–5, 688–90 Mr '04.

'Bibliography' (p.684–5, 688–90).

4005 **Green, Roger Lancelyn.** 'An Andrew Lang book list' *in* Andrew Lang. London [1962] p.78–84.

4006 **——** Descriptions from the Darlington collection of Andrew Lang. Indiana Univ Bkmn 7:73–101 Ap '65.

Quasifacsim. TP transcrs., collations and bibliogr. notes on 25 items, preceded by an account of the Falconer-Darlington collection in the Lilly library, with 'A checklist of the works [1863–1962]' (p.91–9); 'Articles contributed to the Encyclopaedia britannica' (p.100–1).

LAUD, ARCHB. WILLIAM, 1573–1645

4007 **Collins, bp. William Edward,** *ed.* 'Laudian bibliography' *in* Archbishop Laud commemoration, 1895; lectures on archbishop Laud. . . . London, 1895. p.[163]–269.

Chronol. checklist of works and ana, with some bibliogr. notes. 'Catalogue of the exhibition of Laudian relics and other objects of interest' (p.[279]–320).

LAUDER, SIR THOMAS DICK, 1784–1848

4008 **Smith, mrs. J. S.** 'Catalogue of sir Thomas Dick Lauder's works' *in* The grange of st. Giles. Edinburgh, 1898. p.337–48. (Not seen: noted by Northup)

LAURENCE, JOHN, 1668–1732

4008a **Gilmour, John Scott Lennox.** The rev. John Laurence, 1668–1732. Huntia 2:117–37 '65.

TP transcrs. and facsims., collations, bibliogr. notes, and locations of copies for early ed. of 14 horticultural and religious works.

LAVIS, HENRY JAMES JOHNSTON-, 1856–1914

4009 **[Lavis, Henry James Johnston-]** List of books, memoirs, articles, letters, etc. of H. J. Johnston-Lavis. London, Doherty, 1912. 24p. 21cm.
Annotated chronol. checklist, 1876–1912.

LAW, WILLIAM, 1686–1761

4009a **Ralph, Brenda Anne,** 1966: no.189a.

LAWES, HENRY, 1596–1662

4010 **Harington, J.,** 1957: no.138.

LAWRENCE, DAVID HERBERT, 1885–1930

4011 **Kreemers, Ralph.** David Herbert Lawrence, 1885–1930. Leuvensche Bijdragen 27:13–25 '35.

4012 **Beebe, Maurice** and **A. Tommasi.** Criticism of D. H. Lawrence; a separate checklist, with an index to studies of separate works. Mod Fict Stud 5no1:83–98 '59.

4013 **Bibliographies** of modern authors. David Herbert Lawrence. Lond Merc 4no30:193 Je '21.

4014 **McDonald, Edward David.** A bibliography of the writings of D. H. Lawrence. Philadelphia, Centaur book shop, 1925. 145p. port., facsim. 20cm.

4015 —— The writings of D. H. Lawrence, 1925–1930; a bibliographical supplement. Philadelphia, Centaur book shop, 1931. 134p. facsim. 20cm.

4016 **Fabes, Gilbert Henry.** D. H. Lawrence, his first editions: points and values. London, W. & G. Foyle [1933] xvi,112p. 19cm.

4017 **Powell, Lawrence Clark.** D. H. Lawrence and his critics: a chronological excursion in bio-bibliography. Coloph new graph ser 4 1:63–74 Ja '40.

4018 **White, William.** D. H. Lawrence, a checklist, 1931–1950. Detroit, Wayne U.P., 1950. 46p. 22cm.
Rev. from Bull Bib 19:174–7 D '48; 19:209–11, 235–8 '49, supplementing McDonald (no.4014).

4019 **Illinois. Southern Illinois university,** CARBONDALE. **Library.** D. H. Lawrence; an exhibition of first editions, manuscripts, paintings, letters, and miscellany at Southern Illinois university library. . . . Edited by Earl Tannenbaum. Carbondale, 1958. xiii,61p. illus., ports., facsim. 23cm.

4020 **Nottingham. University. Library.** D. H. Lawrence after thirty years, 1930–1960; catalogue of an exhibition. . . . Edited by V. de S. Pinto. [Nottingham] 1960. 55p. illus. 25cm.
306 items mainly from G. L. Lazarus collection.

4021 **Roberts, Warren Everett.** A bibliography of D. H. Lawrence. London, R. Hart-Davis, 1963. 399p. illus., port., facsims. 23cm. (Soho bibliographies, XII)

Chronol. bibliogr. of early ed. of books and pamphlets; contribs. to books; contribs. to periodicals; translations; manuscripts; and ana, with quasifacsim. TP transcrs., collations, and bibliogr. notes.

Rev: H. T. Moore Kenyon R 25:555–8 '63; TLS 23 Ag '63:648; cf. G. M. Gliddon and P. R. Fozzard ib. 6 S '63:673; J. M. Newton 13 S '63:689; A. Arnold 21 N '63:956; F. Carter 28 N '63:993; H. T. Moore 12 D '63:1038; R. J. Roberts Bk Coll 12:383–4, 387 '63; Pa Bib Soc Am 58:340 '64; V. de S. Pinto Mod Lang R 59:130–1 '64; B. C. Bloomfield Library ser5 20:69–71 '65; H. T. Moore Pa Bib Soc Am 59:75–7 '65.

4022 **Hepburn, James G.** D. H. Lawrence's plays, an annotated bibliography. Bk Coll 14no1:78–81 '65.

LAWRENCE, GEORGE ALFRED, 1827–1876

4025 **Ellis, Stuart Marsh.** 'List of works by George Lawrence' in Wilkie Collins, LeFanu and others. London, 1931. p.209–10. (Reissued 1951)

Chronol. checklist of 14 items, 1845–74, with some bibliogr. notes.

LAWRENCE, THOMAS EDWARD, afterwards SHAW, 1888–1935

4026 **Reed, T. German-.** Bibliographical notes on T. E. Lawrence's Seven pillars of wisdom and Revolt in the desert. London, W. & G. Foyle, 1928. 16p. 19cm.

4027 **[Armstrong, Terence Ian Fytton]** Annotations on some minor writings of T. E. Lawrence, by G. [*pseud.*] London, E. Partridge, Scholartis pr., 1935. 28p. port. 16cm.

4028 **Duval, Elizabeth W.** T. E. Lawrence, a bibliography. New York, Arrow editions [1938] 95p. 26cm.

Classified chronol. and title arrangement of works; introductions and prefatory letters; periodical and newspaper contribs.; miscellanea; and letters, with TP transcrs., collations, and bibliogr. notes.

LAWSON JOHN, d.1712

4028a **Kirkham, E. Bruce.** The first English editions of John Lawson's Voyage to Carolina: a bibliographical study. Pa Bib Soc Am 61:258–65 '67.

Quasifacsim. TP transcrs., bibliogr. notes, and locations of copies for 5 ed., 1709–18.

LEAR, EDWARD, 1812–1888

4029 **[Field, William B. Osgood]** Edward Lear on my shelves. [Munich] Privately ptd., 1933. 456p. illus., port., facsims. 33cm.

Ed. by Bertha Coolidge.

Discursive catalogue of published works; original drawings, etc.; with TP transcrs., collations, and bibliogr. notes.

LEAVIS, FRANK RAYMOND, 1895–

4030 **McKenzie, Donald Francis** and **M. P. Allum.** F. R. Leavis, a check-list, 1924–1964. London, Chatto & Windus, 1966. 87p. 21cm.

Chronol. checklist of works (334 items) and ana, 1924–64.

Rev: TLS 18 Ag '66:738; Pa Bib Soc Am 61:159 '67.

LEDWIDGE, FRANCIS, 1891–1917

4031 **Danielson, Henry.** Bibliographies of modern authors, no.iv. Francis Let-widge, with introductions by lord Dunsany. Bkmns J 1no4:82 '19.

TP transcrs., collations, and bibliogr. notes on 4 first ed., 1916–19.

4032 ——, 1921: no.680.

LEE, NATHANIEL, 1653?–1692

4033 **Bowers, Fredson Thayer.** Nathaniel Lee; three probable seventeenth piracies. Pa Bib Soc Am 44:62–6 '50.

Quasifacsim. TP transcrs., locations of copies, and bibliogr. notes.

4034 **McLeod, A. L.** A Nathaniel Lee bibliography, 1670–1960. Sevent & Eighteenth Cent Theat Res 1:27–39 N '62.

Classified chronol. checklist of collected works; individual plays; occasional poems (137 items), and ana; with some locations of copies and bibliogr. notes.

LEE, VERNON, *pseud. of* VIOLET PAGET, 1856–1935

4036 **[Weber, Carl Jefferson]** An interim bibliography of Vernon Lee. Colby Lib Q ser3 8:123–7 N '52.

Chronol. checklist of separate works, 1880–1935.

LEECH, JOHN, 1817–1864

4037 **Chambers, Charles Edward Steuart.** A list of works containing illustrations by John Leech. Edinburgh, W. Brown, 1892. 22p.interleaved. 24cm.

4038 **Grolier club,** NEW YORK. Catalogue of an exhibition of works by John Leech, 1817–1864, held at the Grolier club . . . with an introduction by Stanley Kidder Wilson. New York, 1914. xxii,187p. illus.(part col.) port. 23cm.

4039 **[Field, William B. Osgood]** John Leech on my shelves. [Munich] Privately ptd., 1930. 313p. illus. 33cm.

Ed. by Bertha Coolidge.

Discursive catalogue of illus. books; Leechiana; original drawings and sketches, etc.; with TP transcrs., collations, and bibliogr. notes.

LEE-HAMILTON, EUGENE, 1845–1907
See Hamilton, Eugene Lee-.

LEFANU, JOSEPH SHERIDAN, 1814–1873

4040 **Ellis, Stuart Marsh.** 'List of works by Joseph Sheridan LeFanu' in Wilkie Collins, LeFanu and others. London, 1931. p.179–91. (Reissued 1951.)

Classified chronol. checklists of magazine contribs., and books, with some bibliogr. notes.

LEFROY, EDWARD CRACROFT, 1855–1891

4041 **Smith, Timothy D'Arch.** Some uncollected authors xxx: Edward Cracroft Lefroy, 1855–1891. Bk Coll 10no4:442–5 '61.

'Check-list of Lefroy's works' (p.444–5): quasifacsim. TP transcrs., collations, and bibliogr. notes on 10 early ed.

LE GALLIENNE, RICHARD, 1866–1947

4042 **Lingel, Robert J. C.** A bibliographical checklist of the writings of Richard Le Gallienne. Metuchen, N.J., 1926. 95p. port. 25cm. (Not seen)

4043 **Mead, Herman Ralph.** Richard Le Gallienne's Perseus and Andromeda. Pa Bib Soc Am 43:399 '49.
Quasifacsim. TP transcrs., collations and bibliogr. notes on 2 issues of 1902 ed.

LEHMANN, ROSAMOND NINA, fl.1927

4044 **Gustafson, Margaret T.** Rosamond Lehmann, a bibliography. Twent Cent Lit 4:143–7 Ja '59.
Classified chronol. checklist.

LENNOX, CHARLOTTE (RAMSAY), 1720–1804

4045 **Small, Miriam Rossiter.** 'The works of Charlotte Ramsay Lennox' *in* Charlotte Ramsay Lennox, an eighteenth century lady of letters. New Haven; London, 1935. p.248–60.
Chronol. checklist, with locations of copies and some bibliogr. notes; 'List of periodicals containing references to mrs. Lennox or her works' (p.260–4).

LESLIE, GEORGE, c.1590–1637

4046 **Law, Thomas Graves,** 1891: no.3337.

L'ESTRANGE, SIR ROGER, 1616–1704

4047 **Kitchin, George.** 'List of L'Estrange's political works' *in* Sir Roger L'Estrange, a contribution to a history of the press in the seventeenth century. London, 1913. p.411–18.
Chronol. checklist of 58 items, 1647–87; doubtful works (p.416–18).

LEVER, CHARLES JAMES, 1806–1872

4048 **Stevenson, Lionel.** 'Works of Charles Lever' *in* Dr. Quicksilver, the life of Charles Lever. London [1939] p.297–300.
Chronol. checklist, 1837–70.

LEWIS, CLIVE STAPLES, 1898–1963

4049 **Green, Roger Lancelyn.** 'C. S. Lewis book list' *in* C. S. Lewis. London, 1963. p.62–4.
Classified checklist.

4050 **[Hooper, Walter]** *comp.* 'A bibliography of the writings of C. S. Lewis' *in* Gibb, Jocelyn, *ed.* Light on C. S. Lewis, by Owen Barfield [and others] London, 1965. p.117–60.
Classified checklist of books; short stories; books ed. or with prefaces by; essays and pamphlets; poems; reviews by, and published letters.

LEWIS, MATTHEW GREGORY, 1775–1818

4051 **Middleton, J.,** 1948: no.170.

4052 **Todd, William Burton.** The early editions and issues of The monk, with a bibliography. Stud Bib 2:3–24 '49.

'Bibliography' (p.21–4): quasifacsim. TP transcrs., collations, locations of copies examined, and bibliogr. note on ed. and issues, 1796–1800.

LEYDEN, JOHN, 1775–1811

4053 **Sinton, James,** *ed.* 'Bibliography of the life and writings of dr. John Leyden' *in* Journal of a tour in the highlands and western islands of Scotland in 1800, by John Leyden. Edinburgh, 1903. p.[285]–318.

Classified chronol. checklist of poetry; prose and translations; manuscripts; and ana.

LIDDEL, DUNCAN, 1561–1613

4054 **[Anderson, Peter John]** Duncan Liddell . . . professor in the University of Helmstedt, 1591–1607. [Aberdeen, Ptd. at the University pr., 1910] 20p. port., facsim. 26cm.

Repr. in following item.

4055 —— Notes on academic theses, with bibliography of Duncan Liddel. [Aberdeen] Ptd. for the University of Aberdeen, 1912. 52p. illus.(part col.) port., facsims. 27cm.

Repr. as following item.

4056 —— Notes on academic theses [with a bibliography of Duncan Liddel] Edinburgh Bib Soc Pub 10:1–52 '13.

'Liddel's career and writings' (p.27–42): chronol. list of 19 items, 1596–1651, with quasifacsim. TP transcrs., collations, and locations of copies; ana.

LIDDON, HENRY PARRY, 1829–1890.

4057 **Johnston, John Octavius,** *ed.* 'List of dr. Liddon's printed works' *in* Life and letters of Henry Parry Liddon. London, 1904. p.[405]–11.

Chronol. checklist, 1858–91.

LILBURNE, JOHN, 1614?–1657

4058 **Peacock, Edward.** John Lilburne, a bibliography. N&Q ser7 5:122–3, 162–3, 242–3, 342–3, 423–4, 502–3 F–Je '88; Charles L. Lindsay *ib.* ser8 6:61 Jl '94.

Chronol. checklist, 1638–59, with locations of copies.

4058a **Wolfe, Don Marion.** '. . . List of pamphlets by and about Lilburne' *in* Milton in the puritan revolution. New York, 1941. p.469–80. (Repr. London, 1963)

Chronol. checklist, with locations of copies.

LILLO, GEORGE, 1693–1739

4059 **Griffith, Reginald Harvey.** Early editions of Lillo's London merchant. Univ Texas Stud Eng 15:23–7 '35.

Checklist of 3 18th century ed., with collations and location of copy.

LINDLEY, JOHN, 1799–1865

4060 **Allford, J. M.,** 1953: no.73.

LINDSAY, SIR DAVID, fl.1490–1555

4061 **Cowan, William.** An edition of sir David Lyndsay's Squyer Meldrum, 1634. Edinburgh Bib Soc Pub 6pt2:103–4 Oc '06.

Descr. and discussion with TP facsim. of 1634 ed., supplementing Laing, David. Poetical works. Edinburgh, 1879. V.3, p.259–98.

4062 **Geddie, William,** 1912: no.2034.

4063 **Hamer, Douglas,** *ed.* 'Bibliography' *in* The works of sir David Lindsay of the Mount. Edinburgh, 1936. V.4, p.[1]–122.

Chronol. bibliogr. of Works; Ane satyre; and Squyer Meldrum; with quasifacsim. TP transcrs., and some facsims.; collations, locations of copies, and discursive bibliogr. notes.

LINGARD, JOHN, 1771–1851

4064 **Haile, Martin** and **E. Bonney.** 'Lingard's published works' *in* Life and letters of John Lingard, 1771–1851. London [1911] p.383–8.

Classified checklist of books and periodical contribs.

LISTER, JOSEPH, 1ST BARON LISTER, 1827–1912

4065 **Wellcome historical medical museum,** LONDON. 'A bibliography of Lister's writings' *in* Lister centenary exhibition . . . handbook. London, 1927. p.[155]–66.

Chronol. checklist, 1853–1922.

4966 **LeFanu, William Richard.** A list of the original writings of Joseph, lord Lister, O.M. Edinburgh, E. & S. Livingstone, 1965. 20p. 19cm.

Classified checklist of 114 items; no index.

LIVINGSTONE, DAVID, 1813–1873

4067 **Appleyard, Margaret Elizabeth.** Dr. David Livingstone, a bibliography. [Capetown] University of Capetown, School of librarianship, 1949. ix,50p. 25cm. (Duplicated typescript)

Classified checklist of works and ana.

LOCKE, JOHN, 1632–1704

4068 **Marion, Henri.** 'Liste complète des écrits de Locke' *in* John Locke, sa vie et son œuvre d'apres des documents nouveaux. 2e. ed. Paris, 1893. p.145–51.

4069 **Christophersen, Hans Oskar.** A bibliographical introduction to the study of John Locke. Oslo, J. Dybwad, 1930. 134p. 28cm.

Discursive checklist of works and ana.

LOCKE, WILLIAM JOHN, 1863–1930

4070 **Danielson, Henry.** Bibliographies of modern authors, no. XVI. William J. Locke. Bkmns J 3n062:162 '20; 3n063–9:183, 192, 214, 228, 245, 274, 286 '21.

TP transcrs., collations, and bibliogr. notes on 25 first ed., 1895–1921.

LOCKER-LAMPSON, FREDERICK, 1821–1895
See Lampson, Frederick Locker-.

LOCKHART, JOHN GIBSON, 1794–1854

4071 **Hildyard, Margaret Clive,** *ed.* 'Bibliography of Lockhart's critical writings *in* Lockhart's literary criticism. . . . Oxford, 1931. p.153–64.
Classified chronol. checklist of periodical contribs., and other works.

LODGE, SIR OLIVER JOSEPH, 1851–1940

4072 **Besterman, Theodore Deodatus Nathaniel.** A bibliography of sir Oliver Lodge. London, O.U.P., H. Milford, 1935. xiv,218p. port. 23cm.
Chronol. checklist of works and ana, 1875–1935.

LODGE, THOMAS, 1558?–1625

4073 **Paradise, Nathaniel Burton.** 'A chronological list of the writings of Thomas Lodge' *in* Thomas Lodge, the history of an Elizabethan. New Haven; London, 1931. p.[231]–43.

4074 **Tannenbaum, Samuel Aaron.** Thomas Lodge, a concise bibliography. New York, 1940. 30p. 23cm. (Elizabethan bibliographies, no.11)
Checklist of plays; novels and romances; tracts, translations, etc.; poems; selections and ana: 473 items.

LONG, GABRIELLE MARGARET VERE (CAMPBELL), 1888–1952
See Bowen, Marjorie, pseud.

LONG, THOMAS, c.1621–1707

4075 **Dredge, John Ingle,** 1889–99: no.886.

LOVELACE, RICHARD, 1618–1658

4076 **Ker, C. S.,** 1949: no.150.

LOWER, RICHARD, 1631–1691

4077 **Fulton, John Farquhar.** A bibliography of two Oxford physiologists, Richard Lower, 1631–1691, and John Mayow, 1643–1679. Oxford Bib Soc Proc 4pt1:1–62 '34.
Chronol. lists of works and ana, with quasifacsim. TP transcrs. and facsims., collations, locations of copies, and bibliogr. notes.

LUBBOCK, SIR JOHN, BARON AVEBURY, 1834–1913

4078 **Gomme, Laurence.** Lord Avebury. Eng Illus Mag new ser 31:103–6 Ap '04.
'Bibliography' (p.104, 106): checklist of works; introductions, prefaces, or works ed. by; and books and articles on.

LUCK, ROBERT, c.1674–1747

4079 **Dredge, John Ingle,** 1889–99: no.886.

LUPSET, THOMAS, 1495?–1530

4080 **Gee, John Archer.** 'Bibliography and canon of Lupset's works' *in* The life and works of Thomas Lupset. . . . New Haven; London, 1928. p.[157]–74.
Classified checklist with locations of copies and discursive bibliogr. notes.

LYLY, JOHN, 1554?–1606

4081 **Bond, Richard Warwick,** *ed.* 'The text and bibliography' *in* The complete works of John Lyly. Oxford, 1902. V.1, p.83–118; v.2, p.230. (Repr. [1967])

'List of editions' (p.100–5); 'Titles, colophons, and results of collations of the quarto editions' (p.106–18).

4082 **Tannenbaum, Samuel Aaron.** John Lyly, a concise bibliography. New York, 1940. viii,38p. 23cm. (Elizabethan bibliographies, no.12)

Chronol. checklist of plays and entertainments; non-dramatic works; collected works; selections; and ana: 667 items.

LYNCH, PATRICK, 1754–1818

4083 **Cassedy, James.** List of works projected or published by Patrick Lynch. Waterford & S.E. Ireland Archæol Soc J 15:107–18 J/S '12.

Chronol. checklist of 34 items, 1792–1828, with some bibliogr. notes and locations of copies.

LYNDSAY, SIR DAVID, 1490–1555
See Lindsay, sir David.

LYTTLETON, GEORGE, IST BARON LYTTLETON, 1709–1773

4084 **Todd, William Burton.** Multiple editions of Lyttleton's The court-secret, 1741. Pa Bib Soc Am 47:380–1 '53.

Quasifacsim. TP transcrs., collations, locations of copies, and bibliogr. notes.

LYTTON, EDWARD ROBERT BULWER, IST EARL OF LYTTON, 1831–1891

4085 **Stevenson, Lionel,** *ed.*, 1964: no.1705.

4086 **Sadleir, Michael Thomas Hervey.** 'Appendixes' *in* Edward and Rosina, 1803–1836. . . . Boston, 1931. p.379–97. (Also issued with title: Bulwer and his wife. . . . London [1933])

'Knight's Quarterly magazine: Bulwer's contributions' (p.419–21); 'New monthly magazine: Bulwer's contributions during his period of editorship . . .' (p.427–31): checklists.

4087 **Harlan, Aurelia Emma (Brooks).** 'Chronological list of works by Lytton' *in* Owen Meredith, a critical biography of Robert, first earl of Lytton. New York, 1946. p. [267]–8.

Books and periodical contribs.

MACARTNEY, GEORGE, IST EARL MACARTNEY, 1737–1806

4090 **Besterman, Theodore Deodatus Nathaniel.** A bibliography of lord Macartney's embassy to China, 1792–1794. [London, 1928] 7p. 22cm.

Repr. from N&Q 154:201–4, 221–5 Mr '28. Chronol. classified list with TP transcrs., collations, and some bibliogr. notes.

MACDIARMID, HUGH, *pseud. of* CHRISTOPHER MURRAY GRIEVE, 1892–

4091 **Aitken, William Russell.** C. M. Grieve / Hugh MacDiarmid. Biblioth 1n04:3–23 '58.

'Hugh MacDiarmid (Christopher Murray Grieve b.1892) a first check list' (p.5–23): chronol. checklist of books; selections; periodicals ed.; works announced; and ana.

4092 **Duval, K. D., bksllr.** [1961]: no.726.

MACDONALD, GEORGE, 1824-1905

4093 **Johnson, Joseph.** 'The books of George MacDonald' *in* George Mac-Donald, a biographical and critical appreciation. London, 1906. p. 286-9.

4094 **Bulloch, John Malcolm.** A centennial bibliography of George Macdonald. Aberdeen, Aberdeen, U.P., 1925. 72p. facsims. 24cm.

Repr. with corr. from Aberdeen Univ Lib Bull 5:679-747 F '25. Title checklist of ed. and ana. with some bibliogr. notes; no index.

MCGEE, THOMAS D'ARCY, 1825-1868

4095 **Coleman, James.** Bibliography of Thomas D'Arcy McGee. Bib Soc Ireland Pubs 2n07:135-9 '25.

Chronol. checklist.

MACHEN, ARTHUR LLEWELYN JONES, 1863-1947

4096 **Danielson, Henry.** Arthur Machen, a bibliography . . . with notes, bio-graphical and critical, by Arthur Machen. . . . London, 1923. x,59p. port., facsims. 22cm.

4097 **Van Patten, Nathan.** Arthur Machen, a bibliographical note. Kingston [Ont.] 1926. 4p. 25cm. (Not seen)

4098 **Goldstone, Adrian H.** and **W. Sweetser.** A bibliography of Arthur Machen. Austin, Tex., University of Texas [1965] 180p. illus., ports., facsims. 23cm.

Classified bibliogr. of early ed. of books and pamphlets; translations; contribs. to periodicals; criticism and commentary; with quasifacsim. TP transcrs. of first ed., collations, and some bibliogr. notes. The collection is now in the University of Texas library.

Rev: TSL 17 Mr '66:232; S. A. Reynolds Bk Coll 15:229-30 '66; Pa Bib Soc Am 60:395 '66.

MACKENZIE, SIR EDWARD MONTAGUE COMPTON, 1883-

4099 **Danielson, Henry.** Bibliographies of modern authors, no. xv. Compton Mackenzie. Bkmns J 3n058-60:92,109,129 '20.

4100 ——, 1921: no.680.

MACKENZIE, SIR GEORGE, 1636-1691

4101 **Ferguson, Frederic Sutherland.** A bibliography of the works of sir George Mackenzie, lord advocate, founder of the Advocate's library. Edinburgh Bib Soc Trans 1pt1:1-60 '36.

Chronol. arrangement of 26 titles, 1660-1713; with TP transcrs., collations, locations of copies, and bibliogr. notes.
Rev: TLS 13 F '37:116.

MACLACHLAN, EWEN, 1775-1822

4102 **Anderson, Peter John.** Ewen MacLachlan. N&Q ser10 11:150-2 F '09.

4103 —— [Same]: [revised]: Celtic Mthly 17:157-9 My '09.

4104 **[Anderson, Peter John]** Ewen MacLachlan, 1773–1822. . . . Aberdeen Univ Lib Bull 3:643–72 Mr '18.

'Bibliography' (p.651–72): annotated chronol. checklist, 1798–1879.

MACLEAN, MURDOCH, fl.1916–1919

4105 **Scottish chapbook,** 1922–3: no.724.

MCMANUS, L., *pseud. of* CHARLOTTE ELIZABETH MCMANUS, d.1944

4106 **O'Hegarty, Patrick Sarsfield.** L. McManus. Dublin Mag new ser 20:68 Ja/Mr '45.

MACPHERSON, JAMES, 1736–1796

4107 **Tombo, Rudolf.** 'German bibliography' *in* Ossian in Germany. New York, 1901. p.4–65.

Chronol. checklist of German ed., trans., and ana, 1762–1897.

4107a **O'Neill, The.** Ossian. N&Q ser10 6:287 Oc '06; H. A. Strong; H. Krebs; D.J. *ib.* ser10 6:336–7 Oc '06.

Checklist of early ed. and ana.

4108 **Black, George Fraser.** Macpherson's Ossian and the ossianic controversy; a contribution towards a bibliography. New York, New York public library, 1926. 34p. 26cm.

Repr. from N.Y. Pub Lib Bull 30:413–15, 424–39, 508–24 Je–Jl '26.

Classified checklist of works, and the ossianic controversy with some bibliogr. notes; no index.

MACSWINEY, TERENCE JOSEPH, d.1920

4109 **O'Hegarty, Patrick Sarsfield.** Bibliographies of 1916 and the Irish revolution, x. Terence MacSwiney. [xi. F. Sheehy Skeffington] Dublin Mag new ser 11:74–8 Oc–D '36.

Quasifacsim. TP transcrs., collations, and bibliogr. notes on first ed.

MAGINN, WILLIAM, 1794–1842

4110 **Sadleir, Michael Thomas Hervey.** 'William Maginn, 1794–1842: bibliography and epitaph' *in* Bulwer and his wife, a panorama, 1803–1836. London [1933] p.419–21.

Checklist of books and collected periodical contribs.

4111 **Thrall, Miriam Mulford H.** 'Bibliography of Maginn' *in* Rebellious Fraser's, Nol Yorke's magazine in the days of Maginn, Thackeray, and Carlyle. New York, 1934. p.300–6.

Checklist of acknowledged, established, and probable contribs. to Fraser's magazine, with other works.

MAITLAND, FREDERICK WILLIAM, 1850–1906

4112 **Smith, Arthur Lionel.** 'Bibliography' *in* F. W. Maitland; two lectures and a bibliography. Oxford, 1908. p.[59]–71.

Chronol. checklist of works and ana.

MALLOCH, GEORGE RESTON, d.1953

4113 **Scottish chapbook,** 1922–3: no.724.

MALLOCK, WILLIAM HURRELL, 1849–1923

4114 **Nickerson, Charles C.** A bibliography of the novels of W. H. Mallock. Eng Lit Transit 6no4:190–8 '63.

Quasifacsim. TP transcrs., collations with distinction of issues, and bibliogr. notes, on 9 items, 1877–1908.

MANDEVILLE, BERNARD, 1670?–1733

4115 **Kaye, Frederick Benjamin.** The writings of Bernard Mandeville, a bibliographical survey. J Eng Germ Philol 20:419–67 Oc '21.

Discursive chronol. checklists of authentic, doubtful, and erroneously attrib. works, with TP transcrs., collations, and some bibliogr. notes.

4116 —— The Mandeville canon, a supplement. N&Q 146:317–21 My '24.

Corrects attribs. of 21 items in Wrenn library catalogue.

MANGAN, JAMES CLARENCE, 1803–1849

4117 **O'Hegarty, Patrick Sarsfield.** A bibliography of James Clarence Mangan. Dublin, Privately ptd. by A. Thom, 1941. 8p. 24cm.

Repr. from Dublin Mag new ser 16:56–61 Ja/Mr '41.

Chronol. arrangement of 10 items, 1845–1903, with TP transcrs., collations, and bibliogr. notes.

4117a **Holzapfel, R. P.** Mangan's poetry in the Dublin university magazine: a bibliography. Hermathena 105:40–54 '67.

'Bibliography' (p.46–53): chronol. checklist, Ja 1834–My '49.

MANNING, CARD. HENRY EDWARD, 1808–1892

4118 **Guibert, J.** 'Bibliographie de Manning' *in* Le réveil du catholicisme en Angleterre au XIXᵉ siècle. Paris, 1907. p.[372]–88.

Classified chronol. checklist of works and ana.

MANSFIELD, KATHERINE, *pseud. of* KATHLEEN (BEAUCHAMP) MURRY, 1888–1923

4118a **Harrison, Elizabeth M.,** 1958: no.138a.

4118b **Stonehill, Charles Archibald** [1925]: no.682.

4118c **Mantz, Ruth Elvish.** The critical bibliography of Katherine Mansfield. London, Constable, 1931. xx,204p. 25cm.

Classified annotated checklists of works and ana, with some bibliogr. notes; no index.

4118d **Morris, Guy Norman.** Katherine Mansfield in ten languages. New Zealand Mag 23no3:23–5 My/Je '44. (Not seen)

4118e **[Lawlor, Patrick Anthony]** Mansfieldiana, a brief Katherine Mansfield bibliography, with an introduction by G. N. Morris. Wellington, Beltane book bureau, 1948. vi,9p. illus. 21cm.

MARKHAM, GERVASE, 1568?–1637

4119 **Poynter, Frederick Noël Lawrence.** A bibliography of Gervase Markham, 1568?–1637. Oxford, Oxford bibliographical society, 1962. vi,218p. facsims. 26cm.

Bibliogr. arranged by subject and form, with quasifacsim. TP transcrs., collations, locations of copies, bibliogr. notes and refs; 'STC concordance' (p.[194]); 'Wing concordance' (p.195).

Rev: J. W. Y. Higgs Library ser5 18:317–18 '63; K. F. Pantzer Pa Bib Soc Am 58:64–6 '64.

MARKIEVICZ, CONSTANCE GEORGINE (GORE-BOOTH), 1868–1927

4120 **O'Hegarty, Patrick Sarsfield,** 1936: no.2813.

MARLOWE, CHRISTOPHER, 1564–1593

4121 **Bakeless, John Edwin.** 'Checklist of extant early editions' *in* Christopher Marlowe, the man in his time. New York, 1937. p.348–51.

4122 **Tannenbaum, Samuel Aaron.** Christopher Marlowe, a concise bibliography. New York, Scholars' facsimiles and reprints, 1937. 95p. 23cm. (Elizabethan bibliographies, no.1)

4122a —— [Same]: Additions. Sh Assn Bull 12:252: 5 Oc '37.

4123 ——[Same]: Additions . . . Supplement 1. [n.p.] 1937. [5]p. 22cm.

4124 —— [Same]: Supplement . . . by Samuel A. Tannenbaum and Dorothy R. Tannenbaum. New York [1947] ii,99l. 28cm. (Duplicated typescript)
Classified checklist of works and ana.

4125 **Boas, Frederick S.** 'A list of principal documents and early editions' *in* Christopher Marlowe, a biographical and critical study. Oxford [1940] p.315–28. (Repr. 1953, 1960)
Includes checklist, with some locations, of printed works.

4126 **Bakeless, John Edwin.** 'Check list of extant early editions' *in* The tragicall history of Christopher Marlowe. Cambridge, Mass., 1942. V.2, p.304–6.

MARRYAT, FREDERICK, 1792–1848

4130 **Sadleir, Michael Thomas Hervey,** 1922: no.1706.

MARSHALL, ALFRED, 1842–1924

4131 **Keynes, John Maynard, 1st baron Keynes.** Bibliographical list of the writings of Alfred Marshall. Econ J 34:627–37 D '24.
Chronol. checklist of 81 items, 1872–1923.

MARSHALL, ARCHIBALD, 1866–1934

4132 **Bibliographies** of modern authors. Archibald Marshall. Lond Merc 2no12:740–1 Oc '20.
Chronol. checklist, 1899–1920.

MARSTON, JOHN, 1575?–1634

4133 **Greg, sir Walter Wilson.** Notes on old books: John Marston The malcontent. Library ser4 2:49–57 Je '21.
Quasifacsim. TP transcrs., collations, and bibliogr. notes and discussion of 3 impressions of 1604 quarto.

4134 **Brettle, Robert Edward.** Bibliographical notes on some Marston quartos and early collected editions. Library ser4 8:336–48 D '27.
TP transcrs., collations, and distinction of issues and ed., locations of copies, and bibliogr. notes.

4135 —— More bibliographical notes on Marston. Library ser4 12:235–42 S '31.

4136 —— Marston bibliography, a correction. Library ser4 15:241–2 S '34.

4137 **Tannenbaum, Samuel Aaron.** John Marston, a concise bibliography. New York, 1940. viii,34p. 23cm. (Elizabethan bibliographies, no.14)
Classified checklist of works and ana; 538 items.

MARTIN, JOHN, 1789–1854

4138 **Balston, Thomas.** John Martin, 1789–1854; illustrator and pamphleteer. Library ser4 14:383–432 Mr '34.
'Check lists' (p.409–32): works illus. and/or written by John Martin, and ana; William Martin (p.428–30), and Richard and Jonathan Martin (p.430–2).

MARTIN, VIOLET FLORENCE, 1865–1915

For works written under pseud. of Martin Ross in collaboration with E. A. Œ. Somerville, see Somerville, Edith Anna Œnone, 1858–1949.

MARTIN, WILLIAM, 1772–1851

4139 **Balston, Thomas,** 1934: no.4038.

MARTINEAU, HARRIET, 1802–1876

4140 **Rivlin, Joseph Barry.** Harriet Martineau; a bibliography of her separately printed books. New York, New York public library, 1947. 150p. 25cm.
Repr. with rev. and add. from N.Y. Pub Lib Bull 50:387–408, 476–98, 550–72, 789–808, 838–56, 888–908 '47.
Title list with later ed. arranged chronol.; TP transcrs. collations, locations of copies, and bibliogr. notes.

4141 **Webb, Robert Kiefer.** A handlist of contributions to the Daily news by Harriet Martineau, 1852–1866. [New York, 1959] 5l. 35cm. (Duplicated typescript)

MARTYN, JOHN, 1699–1768

4142 **Albu, K. M.,** 1956: no.72.

MARTYN, THOMAS, 1735–1825

4143 **Albu, K. M.,** 1956: no.72.

MARVELL, ANDREW, 1621–1678

4144 **[Hull. Marvell tercentenary celebration committee]** Andrew Marvell tercentenary celebration; descriptive catalogue of exhibits at the Wilberforce museum. . . . Hull, A. Brown, 1921. 35p. 23cm.

4145 **Margoliouth, Herschel Maurice,** *ed.* 'General note on the text' *in* The poems & letters of Andrew Marvell. Oxford, 1927. V.1, p.206–14.
See no.4147.

4146 **Legouis, Pierre.** 'Bibliographie' *in* André Marvell, poète, puritain, patriote, 1621–1678. Paris, 1928. p.[451]–87.

4147 **Margoliouth, Herschel Maurice,** *ed.* 'General note on the text' *in* The poems & letters of Andrew Marvell. 2d ed. Oxford, 1952. V.1, p.206–14.
Classified checklists of early ed., with TP transcrs., collations, locations of copies, and bibliogr. notes.

MARY STUART, QUEEN OF SCOTS, 1543–1587

4148 **Scott, John.** A bibliography of works relating to Mary, queen of Scots, 1544–1700. [Edinburgh] Ptd. for the Edinburgh bibliographical society, 1896. viii,96[6]p.+20l. facsims. 25cm. (Edinburgh bibliographical society. Publications, v.2)
Chronol. list of 289 items, with full TP transcrs., collations, and bibliogr. notes and locations of copies.
Rev: Library 9:190–1 '97; Lib Assn Rec 1:453 '99.

4149 —— Catalogue of the . . . library . . . sold by auction by messrs. Sotheby, Wilkinson & Hodge. . . . [London] Dryden pr., J. Davy [1905] v,311p. 26cm.

4150 **France. Bibliothèque nationale,** PARIS. Collection de manuscrits, livres, estampes et objets d'art relatifs à Marie Stuart. . . . Paris, J. Meynial, 1931. xiii,325p. illus., port., facsims. 28cm.
Classified short-title catalogue based on the donation of mrs. George T. Dwight Bliss, by Gabrielle Odend'hal.

4151 **Tannenbaum, Samuel Aaron** and **D. R. Tannenbaum.** Marie Stuart, queen of Scots, a concise bibliography. New York, 1944–6. 3v. port. 23cm.
'Bibliographic materials' (v.3, p.1–3); includes details of Mary Stuart in literature.

MASEFIELD, JOHN EDWARD, 1878–1967

4152 **Sherman, Clarence E.** John Masefield, a contribution towards a bibliography. Bull Bib 8:158–60 Ap '15.

4153 **Danielson, Henry.** Bibliographies of modern authors, no.9. John Masefield. Bkmns J 1no14–17:284, 303, 318, 334 '20.

4154 ——, 1921: no.680.

4155 **Williams, Iolo Aneurin.** John Masefield [a bibliography] London, L. Chaundy; New Haven, Brick row book shop, 1921. iii,12p. 18cm.
Based on list in Lond Merc 2noll:607–8 S '20, by C. E. Sherman?
Rev: N&Q 167:500 '21; H. Danielson Bkmns J 4:252 '21.

4156 **Hamilton, William Hamilton.** 'Bibliography' *in* John Masefield, a critical study. London; New York [1922] p.153–5. (*See* no.4158)

4157 **Biggane, Cecil.** [A list of books by John Masefield] *in* John Masefield, a study. Cambridge, 1924. p.53.

4158 **Hamilton, William Hamilton.** 'Bibliography' *in* John Masefield, a popular study. London [1925] p.167–70. (2d ed. of item no. 4156)

4159 **Simmons, Charles Herbert.** A bibliography of John Masefield. New York, Columbia U.P., 1930. xi,171p. illus., port. 22cm.
Bibliogr. catalogue of first ed.; pubs. containing contribs. by; and ana, with TP transcrs., collations, and bibliogr. notes.
Rev: TLS 9 Jl '31:545; A. W. P[ollard] Library ser4 11:509–10 '31; viscount Esher Bk Coll Q 3:76–8 '31.

4160 **New York. Public library.** John Masefield Salt-water ballads; an exhibition compiled by John D. Gordan. New York, 1952. 26p. 26cm.

4161 **Drew, Fraser Bragg.** Some contributions to the bibliography of John Masefield: I. Book reviews published in the Manchester guardian. II. Corrections and additions to C. H. Simmon's bibliography. Pa Bib Soc Am 53:188–96, 262–7 '59.

4162 **Taylor, Geoffrey Handley-.** John Masefield, O.M. . . . a bibliography and eighty-first birthday tribute. London, Cranbrook tower pr. [1960] 96p. illus., ports., facsims. 22cm.
Contains notes on major collections of Masefieldiana, and chronol. checklist with some bibliogr. notes.

MASON, ALFRED EDWARD WOODLEY, 1865–1948

4164 **Green, Roger Lancelyn.** 'Short title bibliography' *in* A. E. W. Mason. London [1952] p.[267]–8.

Chronol. checklist of books, plays, uncollected short stories, and miscellaneous.

MASON, WILLIAM, 1724–1797

4165 **Draper, John William.** 'Bibliography: A. Works by Mason' *in* William Mason, a study in eighteenth century culture. New York, 1924. p.[337]–48.

'Works that mention Mason' (p.[349]–65).

4166 **Gaskell, Philip.** The first editions of William Mason. Cambridge, Bowes and Bowes, 1951. xiv,41p. 26cm.

4167 —— [Same]: Addenda and corrigenda. Cambridge Bib Soc Trans 1:360–1 '52.

TP transcrs., collations, locations of copies and bibliogr. notes; includes periodical contribs. and privately-ptd. pamphlets; no index.

Rev: W. B. Todd Pa Bib Soc Am 46:406–8 '52; TLS 7 Mr '52:180; H. Williams Bk Coll 1:131–2 '52.

MASSIE, JOSEPH, d.1784

4168 **Shaw, William Arthur,** *ed.* 'Books, pamphlets and letters written by Joseph Massie' *in* Bibliography of the collection of books and tracts on commerce, currency, and poor law, 1557 to 1763, formed by Joseph Massie. ... London, 1937. p.[xiii]–xxxix.

Annotated chronol. checklist of 24 items, 1750–81.

Rev: TLS 13 N '37:876.

MASSINGER, PHILIP, 1583–1640

4169 **Tannenbaum, Samuel Aaron.** Philip Massinger, a concise bibliography. New York, 1938. viii,39p. 23cm. (Elizabethan bibliographies, no.4)

Classified checklist of works and ana; 676 items.

MASSON, DAVID, 1822–1907

4170 **Plincke, E. M.,** 1952: no.186.

MATURIN, CHARLES ROBERT, 1782–1824

4171 'A list of works by Charles Robert Maturin, with translations and adaptations by other authors' *in* Melmoth the wanderer, by Charles Robert Maturin. New ed. London, 1892. V.1, p.[lx]–lxv.

Checklist of works and ana.

MAUGHAM, WILLIAM SOMERSET, 1874–1965

4172 **Bason, Frederick T.** Bibliography of the writings of William Somerset Maugham. London, Unicorn pr., 1931. 78p. illus., facsim. 23cm.

4173 **Jonas, Klaus W.** A bibliography of the writings of W. Somerset Maugham. [South Hadley, Mass.] 1950. xvii,97p. port., facsims. 23cm.

4174 —— More Maughamiana. Pa Bib Soc Am 44:378–83 '50.

Addenda to Stott and Jonas.

4175 **Stott, Raymond Toole.** Maughamiana, the writings of W. Somerset Maugham and of his contributions to certain selected periodicals. London, Heinemann; Garden city, N.Y., Doubleday, 1950. xiii,73p. 23cm.

4175a **Van Patten, Nathan.** Icelandic translations of Maugham. Pa Bib Soc Am 45:158–9 '51.

4176 **Stott, Raymond Toole.** The writings of William Somerset Maugham, a bibliography. London, B. Rota, 1956. 136p. facsims. 24cm.

Classified chronol. arrangement of first ed. of books and pamphlets; collected ed.; works ed. or with contribs. by; periodical contribs.; plays novelised or books dramatised by others; and some ana, with quasifacsim. TP transcrs., collations, and bibliogr. notes. *Rev*: K. W. Jonas Bk Coll 6:86–8 '57; J. Dobrinsky Étud Angl 10:275–6 '57; TLS 25 Ja '57:56.

4177 **Stanford university. Library.** A comprehensive exhibition of the writings of W. Somerset Maugham, drawn from various private collections and libraries. . . . [Stanford, Calif.] Albert M. Bender room, Stanford university library [1958] lv.(unpaged) port. 20cm.

Comp. by J. Terry Bender.

4178 **Stott, Raymond Toole.** The writings of William Somerset Maugham . . . 1961 supplement. London, B. Rota [1961] 20p. 22cm. (Not seen)

'. . . the original work and supplement now published together by Nicholas Vane, ltd.' —BNB.

Rev: Pa Bib Soc Am 57:391 '63.

MAXWELL, MARY ELIZABETH (BRADDON), 1837–1915
See Braddon, Mary Elizabeth (mrs. Maxwell).

MAYNE, JASPER, 1604–1672
4185 **Dredge, John Ingle,** 1889–99: no.886.

MAYNE, ZACHARY, c.1631–1694
4185a **Dredge, John Ingle,** 1889–99: no.886.

MAYOW, JOHN, 1643–1679
4186 **Fulton, John Farquhar,** 1934: no.4077.

MEAD, RICHARD, 1673–1754
4187 **Ferguson, V. A.,** 1959: no.121.

MEDWIN, THOMAS, 1788–1869
4188 **Forman, Harry Buxton,** *ed.* 'An annotated list of books brought out by Thomas Medwin' *in* The life of Percy Bysshe Shelley, by Thomas Medwin. New ed. London, 1913. p.487–505.

Quasifacsim. TP transcrs., collations, and bibliogr. notes on first ed., 1820–62.

MELVILLE, GEORGE JOHN WHYTE-, 1821–1878
4189 **Sadleir, Michael Thomas Hervey,** 1922: no.1706.

4190 **Freeman, James C.** George John Whyte-Melville, 1821–1878; a bibliography. Bull Bib 19:267–8 S/D '49.
Supplements CBEL.

MENNONS, JOHN, 1747–1818
See under Presses and Printing.

MEREDITH, GEORGE, 1828–1909

4191 **Sawin, H. Lewis.** George Meredith, a bibliography of Meredithiana. Bull Bib 21:186–90 S/D '55; 21:215–16 Ja/Ap '56.
Complements M. B. Forman's Meredithiana; *see* no.4201.

4192 **Stevenson, Lionel,** *ed.,* 1964: no.1705.

4193 **Lane, John,** *comp.* 'George Meredith and his reviewers, a bibliography' *in* Le Gallienne, Richard. George Meredith, some characteristics. London, 1890. p.i–lxxiii at end. (Rev. ed. 1900)

4194 **Chisholm, Hugh.** George Meredith. Eng Illus Mag new ser 30:549–52, 690 F, Mr '04.
'Bibliography' (p.550, 552, 690)

4195 **Esdaile, Arundell James Kennedy.** Bibliography of the writings in prose and verse of George Meredith. London, W. T. Spencer, 1907. 70p. port. 20cm.

4196 **Bailey, Elmer James.** 'George Meredith in America, a comment and a bibliography' *in* Studies in language and literature in celebration of . . . James Morgan Hart. . . . New York, 1910. p.[43]–64.
'II. A bibliography' (p.50–64).

4197 **Esdaile, Arundell James Kennedy.** 'A chronological list of George Meredith's publications, 1849–1911' *in* The works of George Meredith; memorial edition. London, 1911. V.27 ('Bibliography and various readings'), p.[305]–69.
See no.4199.

4198 **[Livingston, Luther Samuel]** First editions of George Meredith; being the description of a collected set of his books, . . . offered for sale. . . . New York, Dodd & Livingston [1912?] 37p. 24cm.

4199 **Esdaile, Arundell James Kennedy.** A chronological list of George Meredith's publications, 1849–1911. London, Constable, 1914. 65p. 24cm.
Slightly rev. from no.4197.

4200 **Forman, Maurice Buxton.** A bibliography of the writings in prose and verse of George Meredith. Edinburgh, Ptd. for the Bibliographical society at the Dunedin pr., 1922. xxxii,324p. facsims. 23cm.

Wise-style bibliogr. of editiones principes; contribs. to periodical literature, etc.; collected ed.; and ana, with TP transcrs., collations, BM pressmarks, and bibliogr. notes; no index.

Rev: I. A. Williams Lond Merc 8no44:190–1 '23 ; TLS 31 My 23:376; *rf*. A. J. A. Symons *ib*. 21 Je '23:422; 12 Jl '23:472; M. Judge 28 Je '23:440; Lib Assn Rec 1:120 '23.

4201 —— Meredithiana, being a supplement to the Bibliography . . . Edinburgh, Ptd. for the Bibliographical society at the Dunedin pr., 1924. vii,315p. 23cm.

Contains lists of selections from the poetical and prose works; reviews; ana; and additions to the bibliography; no index.

4202 **Yale university. Library.** A catalogue of the Altschul collection of George Meredith in the Yale university library, compiled by Bertha Coolidge. [Boston] Privately ptd., 1931. xvii,195p. 28cm.

MERRICK, LEONARD, 1864-1939

4205 **Danielson, Henry.** Bibliographies of modern authors, no.5. Leonard Merrick. Bkmns J 1no5-7:101, 123, 143-4 '19.
TP transcrs., collations, and bibliogr. notes on 17 first ed., 1888-1918.

4206 ——, 1921: no.680.

MEYERSTEIN, EDWARD HARRY WILLIAM, 1889-1952

4207 **Bristol. Public libraries.** Edward H. W. Meyerstein, poet and novelist; a bibliography. Bristol [1938] [4]p. 18cm. Covertitle.
Classified checklist of works and ana.

4207a **West, Charles Barry,** 1966: no.227a.

MEYNELL, ALICE CHRISTIANA GERTRUDE, 1847-1922

4208 **Nevinson, Henry Woodd.** Alice Meynell. Eng Illus Mag new ser 30:78-80 Oc '03.
'Bibliography' (p.80).

4209 **Bibliographies** of modern authors. Alice Meynell. Lond Merc 1no6:753-4 Ap '20.

4210 **Stonehill, Charles Archibald** [1925]: no.682.

4211 **Tuell, Anne Kimball.** 'Bibliographical notes upon the work of mrs. Meynell' *in* Mrs. Meynell and her literary generation. New York, 1925. p.259-71.
Classified chronol. checklist of books and essays.

4212 **Connolly, Terence Leo,** *comp.* 'Alice Meynell, a short-title list of poetry, essays, miscellaneous works, anthologies, translations, editings and introductions . . . in the complete collection at Boston college' *in* Alice Meynell centenary tribute, 1847-1947; a symposium opening an exhibition of Alice Meynell manuscripts, letters, first and rare editions . . . edited by Terence L. Connolly. Boston [1948] p.[41]-72.

4213 **National book league,** LONDON. Alice Meynell, 1847-1922: catalogue of the centenary exhibition of books, manuscripts, letters and portraits. Compiled by Francis Meynell. London, 1948. 45p. 19cm.

MIDDLETON, RICHARD BARHAM, 1882-1911

4214 **Danielson, Henry.** Bibliographies of modern authors, no.6. Richard Middleton. Bkmns J 1no8-9:161,183 '19.
TP transcrs., collations, and bibliogr. notes on 5 first ed., 1912-13, and ana.

4215 ——, 1921: no.680.

MIDDLETON, THOMAS, 1570?-1627

4216 **Tannenbaum, Samuel Aaron.** Thomas Middleton, a concise bibliography. New York, 1940. viii,35p. 23cm. (Elizabethan bibliographies, no.13)
Classified checklist of works and ana; 563 items.

MILL, JOHN STUART, 1806–1873

4217 **MacMinn, Ney Lannes,** *ed.* Bibliography of the published writings of John Stuart Mill, edited from his manuscript, with corrections and notes by Ney MacMinn, J. R. Hainds and James McNab McCrimmon. Evanston, Ill., Northwestern university, 1945. xiv,101p. 24cm.

Annotated chronol. checklist, 1822–73; no index.

Rev: J. Viner Mod Philol 43:105–10, 149–50 '45; TLS 26 J '46:48; W. M. Templeman J Eng Germ Philol 45:115–16 '46.

MILLER FAMILY, BKSLLRS., 1771–1865

See under Presses and printing.

MILNER, BP. JOHN, 1752–1826

4218 **Guibert, J.** 'Bibliographie de Milner' *in* Le réveil de catholicisme en Angleterre au XIX⁰ siècle. Paris, 1907. p.[305]–10.

Classified chronol. checklist of works and ana.

MILTON, JOHN, 1608–1674

4218a **Hanford, James Holly** and C. W. Crupi. Milton. New York, Appleton-Century-Crofts [1966] viii,63p. 24cm. (Goldentree bibliographies)

4219 **Thompson, Elbert Nevius Sèbring.** John Milton: topical bibliography. New Haven, Yale U.P.; London, H. Milford, O.U.P., 1916. xi,104p. 17cm.

4220 **Anderson, John Parker,** *comp.* 'Bibliography' *in* Garnett, Richard. The life of John Milton. London, 1890. p. i–xxxix at end.

4221 **Baxter, Wynne Edwin.** Milton's Paradise lost. Bibliographer 2no2:73–91 F '03.

TP transcrs. and facsims. *See* no.4228.

4222 **Grolier club,** NEW YORK. Catalogue of an exhibition commemorative of the tercentenary of the birth of John Milton, 1608–1908, including original editions of his poetical and prose works. . . . [New York, DeVinne pr., 1908] vi,116p. facsims. 18cm.

4223 **John Rylands library,** MANCHESTER. Catalogue of an exhibition of original editions of the principal works of John Milton arranged in celebration of the tercentenary of his birth. [Manchester] Ptd. by order of the governors, 1908. 24p. 22cm.

4224 **[Sayle, Charles Edward]** *comp.* 'On the early editions of Milton's works' *in* Cambridge. University. Christ's college. Milton tercentenary; the portraits, prints, and writings of John Milton exhibited. . . . [Cambridge, 1908] p.123–60. (2d ed., 1908)

4225 **Stoke Newington. Public libraries.** Milton tercentenary; catalogue of exhibits. . . . [London, Ptd. by Willis, 1908] 55p. port., facsims. 22cm.

4226 **Pollard, Alfred William.** The bibliography of Milton. Library ser2 10:1–33 Ja '09.

Discursive account of Milton's works in order of pub.

4227 **Allison, William Talbot,** *ed.* 'Bibliography: editions of The tenure . . .' *in* The tenure of kings and magistrates, by John Milton. New York, 1911. p.[173]–4.

Checklist of 5 items, 1649–1818.

4228 **Baxter, Wynne Edwin.** A catalogue of the . . . Milton collection formed by . . . which will be sold by auction by messrs. Hodgson . . . July 12th, 1921 . . . [London, Athenæum pr., 1921] 50p. 25cm.

4229 **[Grose, Sidney William]** Early editions of Milton's works in Christ's college library. [Cambridge, C.U.P., 1921] 8p. 16cm.

Repr. from Christ's Coll Mag v.33 '21.

4230 **Madan, Francis Falconer.** Milton, Salmasius, and Dugard. Library ser4 4:119–45 S '23.

'List of separate editions of the Defensio printed by William Dugard' (p.125–8); '. . . not printed by William Dugard' (p.128–35); 'Editions of the Elenchus motuum nuperorum in Anglia' (p.138–43); 'Editions of the Defensio regia' (p.143–5); TP transcrs., collations, locations of copies, and bibliogr. notes and refs. *See* no.4242.

4231 **Stevens, David Harrison.** Reference guide to Milton from 1800 to the present day. Chicago, Ill., University of Chicago pr. [1930] x,302p. 24cm.

Classified list of later ed., and ana; supplemented by Fletcher (no.4232) and Huckabay (no.4244).

Rev: E. N. S. Thompson Philol Q 9:317 '30; G. Saintsbury Bkmn 78:161–2 '30; TLS 10 Ap '30:320; N&Q 158:450 '30; E. C. Batho and E. J. Vaughan Mod Lang R 26:203–4 '31; D. Saurat R Eng Stud 7:472–4 '31; R. S. C[rane?] Mod Philol 28:380–1 '31; H. F. Fletcher Mod Lang N 46:539–41 '31; S. B. Liljegren Angl Beibl 43:369–71 '32.

4232 **Fletcher, Harris Francis.** Contributions to a Milton bibliography, 1800–1930, being a list of addenda to Stevens's Reference guide to Milton. [Urbana, Ill.] University of Illinois, 1931. 116p. 26cm. (Repr. N.Y., Russell & Russell [1967])

4233 **Whitney, Henry Austin.** The John Milton collection formed by Henry Austin Whitney. [New York, Alexander pr., 1935?] 21p. 23cm. Covertitle.

4234 **Candy, Hugh C. H.** John Milton, a catalogue of works by or relating to John Milton, largely comprising the library of . . . the late prof. Hugh C. H. Candy . . . Maggs brothers. . . . London [1936] 56p. illus., port., facsims. 24cm.

321 items.

4235 **Parker, William Riley.** Contributions toward a Milton bibliography. Library ser4 16:425–38 Mr '36.

Discursive bibliogr. descrs. and bibliogr. notes on Comus; Of reformation; Of prelatical episcopacy; and Animadversions . . . against Smectymnus.

4236 **Kelley, Maurice.** A note on Milton's Pro populo Anglicano defensio. Library ser4 17:466–7 Mr '37.

Addenda to Madan (no.4230).

4237 **Pershing, James H.** The different states of the first edition of Paradise lost. Library ser4 22:34–66 Je '41.

Quasifacsim. TP transcrs. and facsims., locations of copies, and bibliogr. notes and refs. for 6 TP variants, and other matters.

4238 **Lewis, Clarissa O.** A further note on Milton's Pro populo Anglicano defensio. Library ser4 23:45–7 Je '42.

University of Illinois library additions to Madan (no.4230).

4239 **Baker, C. H. Collins.** Some illustrators of Milton's Paradise lost, 1688–1850. Library ser5 3:1–21, 101–19 Je,S '48.

4240 —— [Same]: Balston, Thomas. [Addenda] *ib.* ser5 4:146–7 S '49.

Chronol. checklist of ed. and designs, with some bibliogr. notes and facsims.

4241 **Illinois. University. Library.** Collection of first editions of Milton's works, University of Illinois library: an exhibition . . . Introduction and notes prepared by Harris F. Fletcher. Urbana, University of Illinois, 1953. 23p. port. 21cm.

4242 **Madan, Francis Falconer.** A revised bibliography of Salmasius' Defensio regia and Milton's Pro populo Anglicano defensio. Library ser5 9:101–21 Je '54.

Replaces item no.4230. Defensio regia, 15 items; Pro populo . . ., 20 items; TP transcrs., collations, locations of copies, and bibliographical notes and refs.; 'Note on George Bate's Elenchus . . .' (p.121).

4242a **Harkness, Bruce.** The precedence of the 1676 editions of Milton's Literæ pseudo-senatus anglicani. Stud Bib 7:181–5 '55.

Bibliogr. descrs. of 2 1676 ed. (p.182).

4243 **Browne, Ray B.,** 1958: no.3206.

4244 **Huckabay, Calvin.** John Milton, a bibliographical supplement, 1929–1957. Pittsburgh, Pa., Duquesne U.P.; Louvain, E. Nauwelaerts, 1960. xii,211p. 26cm.

Continuation of Stevens and Fletcher.

Rev: J. T. Shawcross Sevent Cent N 19:29–34 '61 (with extensive addenda and corrigenda).

4245 **Ayers, Robert W.** A suppressed edition of Milton's Defensio secunda, 1654. Pa Bib Soc Am 55:75–87 '61.

Quasifacsim. TP transcr., collation, locations of copies, and bibliogr. notes on 3 ed. pr. by Adrian Vlacq, 1654.

4246 **British Columbia. University. Library.** Critical studies of John Milton and his works, 1958–1963. [Vancouver] 1964. 14l. 29cm.

Supplements Huckabay (no.4244).

MINSHEU, JOHN, fl.1617

4250 **Williams, Franklin Burleigh.** 'Variant issues of the Catalogue of names (STC 17944a)' *in* 'Scholarly publication in Shakespeare's day, a leading case' *in* Joseph Quincy Adams memorial studies, ed. by James G. McManaway [and others] Washington, 1948. p.766.
Distinction of 10 issues, with locations of copies.

MIRK, JOHN, fl.1403?

4251 **Kenyon, Lloyd Tyrell-, baron Kenyon.** Mirk's Liber festivalis and Quattuor sermones. Library ser5 5:59–60 Je '50.
Descrs. of 2 1499 Pynson items.

MITCHEL, JOHN, 1815–1875

4252 **Douglas, John M.** Bibliography of John Mitchel. Irish Bk Lover 7:86–8 D '15.
Chronol. checklist.

4253 **MacManus, Michael Joseph.** Bibliography of the writings of John Mitchel. Dublin Mag new ser 16:42–50 Ap/Je '41.
TP transcrs., collations, and bibliogr. notes, 1845–1918.

MITCHEL, WILLIAM, 1670?–1739

4254 **Johnston, George P.** William Mitchel, the Tincklarian doctor, a bibliography, 1711–39. Edinburgh Bib Soc Pub 11pt2:113–37 Oc '21.
Chronol. checklist of 81 items, with short collations and locations of copies.

4255 —— [**Same**]: Additions. *ib.* 12pt2:99–104 Oc '25.

4256 —— [**Same**]: Addenda. *ib.* 14pt1:87 Je '28.

MITCHELL, JAMES LESLIE, 1901–1935
See Gibbon, Lewis Grassic, pseud.

MITFORD, MARY RUSSELL, 1787–1855

4257 **Loney, C. E.,** 1948: no.158.

4258 **Mary** Mitford's books. Bk Hndbk 1no5:316 '48.
Checklist, with TP facsim.

4259 **Coles, William A.** Magazine and other contributions by Mary Russell Mitford and Thomas Noon Talfourd. Stud Bib 12:218–26 '58.
Checklists of contribs. to the New monthly magazine; Museum; Lady's magazine; Monthly magazine, and others.

4260 **Ewing, Douglas C.** A note on Mary Russell Mitford's Belford regis. Pa Bib Soc Am 60:473 '66.
Addenda to Sadleir: no.1715.

MOLESWORTH, MARY LOUISA (STEWART), 1839–1921

4260a **Green, Roger Lancelyn.** 'A mrs. Molesworth book list' *in* Mrs. Molesworth. London [1961] p.73–80.

MOLYNEUX, WILLIAM, 1656–1698

4261 **Dix, Ernest Reginald McClintock.** The case of Ireland's being bound by the acts of parliament in England stated, by William Molyneux of Dublin, esq.; list of editions. Irish Bk Lover 5:116–18 F '14.
Checklist with locations, of 12 ed., 1698–1897.

MONTAGUE, CHARLES EDWARD, 1867–1928

4262 **Stapleton, Margaret.** A bibliography of writings by and about C. E. Montague. Bull Bib 16:135–6 S/D '38; 16:157–8 Ja/Ap '39.
Classified checklist.

MONTGOMERIE, ALEXANDER, 1556?–1610?

4263 **Geddie, William,** 1912: no.2034.

MOORE, FRANCIS, fl.1656–1681

4264 **Dredge, John Ingle,** 1889–99: no.886.

MOORE, GEORGE AUGUSTUS, 1852–1933

4265 **Gerber, Helmut, E.** George Moore, an annotated bibliography of writings about him. Eng Fict Transit 2no2:1–91 '59; Supplement I 3no2:34–46 '60; Supplement II 4no2:30–42 '61.

4266 **Stevenson, Lionel,** *ed.,* 1964: no.1705.

4267 **Williams, Iolo Aneurin.** Bibliographies of modern authors, no.3. George Moore. London, L. Chaundy; New Haven, Brick row book shop, 1921. 3l.,13p. 18cm.
Based on list in Lond Merc 3no18:660–1 Ap '21.

4268 **Danielson, Henry.** 'George Moore, a bibliography, 1878–1921' *in* Freeman, John. A portrait of George Moore in a study of his work. London, 1922. p.[231]–78.
Chronol. checklist of first ed., 1878–1919, with TP transcrs., collations, and bibliogr. notes.

4269 **Hone, Joseph Maunsell.** 'The works of George Moore, a short bibliography' *in* The life of George Moore. . . . London, 1936. p.[498]–502.

4270 **Black, Hester Mary,** 1955: no.4782.

MOORE, THOMAS, 1779–1852

4271 **Houtchens, Carolyn Washburn** and **L. H. Houtchens,** *ed.* [1966]: no.2017.

4272 **Gibson, Andrew.** Thomas Moore and his first editions; a lecture. Belfast, Ptd. for private circulation at the office of the Northern whig, 1904. 28p. 18cm.

4273 **MacManus, Michael Joseph.** A bibliographical hand-list of the first editions of Thomas Moore. Dublin, Ptd. for the author by A. Thom, 1934. 24p. 25cm.

Repr. from Dublin Mag new ser 8:55–61, 60–5, 56–63 Ap, Jl, Oc '33.

Chronol. checklist, 1800–78, with quasifacsim. TP transcrs., collations, and bibliogr. notes.

MOORE, THOMAS STURGE, 1870–1944

4274 **Bibliographies** of modern authors. Thomas Sturge Moore. Lond Merc 3no13:100–1 N '20.

Chronol. checklist of verse and drama; and prose, 1899–1920.

MORE, HENRY, 1614–1687

4275 **Landes, Margaret Winifred,** *comp.* 'Bibliography: Henry More, 1614–1687' *in* MacKinnon, Flora I., *ed.* Philosophical writings of Henry More. New York, 1925. p.235–45.

Chronol. checklist, with locations of copies.

MORE, SIR THOMAS, 1478–1535

4276 **Sullivan, Frank** and **M. P. Sullivan.** Moreana, 1478–1945; a preliminary check list of material by and about saint Thomas More. Kansas city, Mo., Rockhurst college, 1946. [175]p. 22cm. (Duplicated typescript)

4277 —— Moreana; materials for the study of saint Thomas More, G–M. Los Angeles, Calif., Loyola university, 1965. 360p. 28cm. (Duplicated typescript)

4278 **Steele, Robert Reynolds,** *ed.* 'List of editions of More's Utopia, 1576–1898' *in* Sir Thomas More's Utopia. . . . London, 1898. p.176–81.

See no.4280.

4279 **London. Guildhall library.** The Alfred Cock memorial; catalogue of books, portraits, etc. of, or relating to sir Thomas More, collected by the late Alfred Cock. . . . London, Ptd. by direction of the library committee, 1903. 28p. illus. 16cm.

4280 **Steele, Robert Reynolds,** *ed.* 'Bibliography' *in* Sir Thomas More's Utopia. . . . London, 1908. p.[241–7]

4281 **Guthkelch, Adolph C. L.,** *comp.* 'Bibliography' *in* Sampson, George, *ed.* The Utopia of sir Thomas More. London, 1910. p.[425]–42.

4282 **Oxford. University. Bodleian library.** An exhibition in commemoration of the canonization of sir Thomas More and bishop John Fisher, including works of Robert Southwell and the Oxford rescusants, 1535–1660. [Oxford, O.U.P., 1935] 7p. 26cm.

Repr. from Bod Q Rec 8no85:66–72 '35.

4283 **Sullivan, Frank.** Syr Thomas More, a first bibliographical notebook. . . . Los Angeles, Loyola university, 1953. 111p. facsims. 28cm,

4284 **Gibson, Reginald Walter.** St. Thomas More, a preliminary bibliography of his works and of Moreana to the year 1750. With a bibliography of utopiana, compiled by R. W. Gibson and J. Max Patrick. New Haven, Yale U.P., 1961. xx,499p. facsims. 25cm.

Quasifacsim. TP transcrs. and facsims., discursive collations, locations of copies, and bibliogr. notes on works (nos.1–159) and Moreana (nos.160–601); 'Section IX. Utopias and dystopias, 1500–1750, nos. 602–859' (p.[291]–412).

Rev: TLS 13 Ap '62:256; R. W. Gibson *ib.* 11 My '62:346; G. Negley Sevent Cent N 20n03:42–3 '62; L. V. R[yan] *ib.* 20n01–2:20 '62; A. Brown Bk Coll 11:359–60 '62; D. E. Rhodes R Eng Stud new ser 14:283–5 '63; R. J. Schoeck J Eng Germ Philol 62:369–72 '63; F. Sullivan Library ser5 18:68–9 '63.

MORES, EDWARD ROWE, 1731–1778

4290 **Carter, Harry Graham** and **C. Ricks,** *ed.* 'List of printed works by Edward Rowe Mores' *in* Mores, Edward R. A dissertation upon English typographical founders and founderies. Oxford, 1961. p.125–6.

Annotated checklist with locations of copies.

MORGAN, CHARLES LANGBRIDGE, 1894–1958

4291 **Fabes, Gilbert Henry** [1933]: no.2882.

MORGAN, WILLIAM FREND DE, 1839–1917
See De Morgan, William Frend.

MORLEY, HENRY, 1822–1894

4292 **Duffy, E. M. T.,** 1952: no.114.

MORLEY, JOHN, VISCOUNT MORLEY OF BLACKBURN, 1838–1923

4293 **Stead, W. T.** Right hon. John Morley. Eng Illus Mag new ser 30:289–91, 294 D '03.

'Bibliography' (p.290, 294): checklist of works; translations, introductions, or works ed.; books and articles on.

MORLEY, THOMAS, 1557–1604?

4294 **Deutsch, Otto Erich.** The editions of Morley's Introduction. Library ser4 23:127–9 S/D '42.

Descr. and collation of 1597 and 1608 ed., with discursive account of variants, and locations of copies.

MORRIS, WILLIAM, 1834–1896
See also Presses and Printing—Kelmscott press.

4295 **Cleveland. Public library.** William Morris; some books and periodicals in the Cleveland public library. [Cleveland] 1910. 15p. 17cm.

4296 **Fredeman, William Evan.** William Morris and his circle, a select bibliography. J William Morris Soc 1no4:23–33 '64.

4297 —— William Morris and his circle: a selective bibliography of publications, 1963–65. J William Morris Soc 2no1:13–26 '66.

4298 **Forman, Harry Buxton.** The books of William Morris described, with some account of his doings in literature and in the allied crafts. London, F. Hollings, 1897. xv,224p. port. 23cm.

Discursive chronol. checklists, with varying bibliogr. notes of contribs. to periodicals; ptd. works; lectures, letters, etc.; and 'The Kelmscott press and the editiones principes issued from it' (p.[155]–92); no index.

4299 **Scott, Temple,** *pseud., comp.* 'A bibliography of the original writings, translations, and publications of William Morris' *in* Vallance, Aymer. The art of William Morris, a record. London, 1897. p.i–xxx at end.

4300 —— A bibliography of the works of William Morris. London, G. Bell, 1897. vii,120p. 20cm.

Classified checklist of works and ana, with some bibliogr. notes; no index.

4301 **Vallance, Aymer.** 'Appendix I. Chronological list of the printed works of William Morris' *in* William Morris, his art, his writings, and his public life: a record. London, 1897. p.[447]–52.

'Appendix II: Publications of the Kelmscott press' (p.[453]–4). The checklist is based on that of Temple Scott (no.4229). Other ed. appeared in 1897, 1898, and 1909.

4302 **Vaughan, Charles Edward,** 1914: no.4850.

4303 **Briggs, Ronald C. H.** A handlist of the public addresses of William Morris to be found in generally accessible publications. [Kew, William Morris society, 1961] 16p. 23cm. Covertitle.

'Public addresses' (p.9–16).

4304 **William Morris society,** LONDON. The work of William Morris, an exhibition. . . . London, Published for the William Morris society by the Times bookshop, 1962. 75p. illus. 17cm.

Comp. by R. C. H. Briggs.

MOSELEY, HUMPHREY, d.1661
See under Presses and Printing.

MOTHERWELL, WILLIAM, 1797–1835
4310 **Hinton, V. H. F. A.,** 1960: no.140.

MOTTEUX, PETER ANTHONY, 1663–1718
4311 **Cunningham, Robert Newton.** 'A chronological list of the writings of Peter Anthony Motteux' *in* Peter Anthony Motteux, 1663–1718, a biographical and critical study. Oxford, 1933. p.200–5.

4312 —— A bibliography of the writings of Peter Anthony Motteux. Oxford Bib Soc Proc 3pt3:317–37, 368 '33.

Chronol. arrangement of major works; minor works; and doubtful works, with TP transcrs., collations, locations of copies, and bibliogr. notes; no index.

MOTTRAM, RALPH HALE, 1883–
4313 **Fabes, Gilbert Henry.** The first editions of Ralph Hale Mottram. London, Myers, 1934. 128p. illus., port., facsim. 22cm.

Chronol. checklist of first and limited ed., books with contribs. by, prefaces, etc., with TP transcrs., collations, and bibliogr. notes.

Rev: I. A. Williams Lond Merc 31:102 '34.

MOXON, JOSEPH, 1627–1700
See under Presses and printers.

MUIR, EDWIN, 1887–1959
4314 **Duval, K. D., bksllr.** [1961]: no.726.

4315 **Mellown, Elgin W.** Bibliography of the writings of Edwin Muir. University, Ala., University of Alabamba pr. [1964] 139p. 22cm.

4316 —— [Same]: [Rev. ed.] London, N. Vane, 1966. 7–43[5]49–137[7]p. 21cm.

Classified bibliogr. of books and pamphlets; contribs. to books; contribs. to periodicals and newspapers; and translations by Edwin and Willa Muir, with selected ana; quasi-facsim. TP transcrs., collations, and some bibliogr. notes.

Rev: TLS 22 S '66:888; R. J. Roberts Bk Coll 16:385–6,389 '67.

MUNDAY, ANTHONY, 1553–1633

4317 **Tannenbaum, Samuel Aaron.** Anthony Mundy, including the play of Sir Thomas Moore, a concise bibliography. New York, 1942. viii,36p. 23cm. (Elizabethan bibliographies, no.27)

Classified checklists of works and ana; 394 items; 'Sir Thomas Moore' (p.[23]–30).

MUNRO, HECTOR HUGH, 1870–1916
See Saki, pseud.

MURRAY, DAVID, 1842–1928

4318 **Murray, Sylvia W.** 'Horae subecivae; recreations in the intervals of a busy life' *in* David Murray, a bibliographical memoir. Dumbarton, 1933. p.27–52.

Chronol. checklist, 1863–1932.

MURRAY, GEORGE GILBERT AIMÉ, 1866–1957

4319 **Bibliographies** of modern authors. George Gilbert Aimé Murray. Lond Merc 3no15:326–7 Ja '21.

Chronol. checklist of verse and drama; and prose, 1886–1920.

MURRY, JOHN MIDDLETON, 1889–1957

4320 **Lilley, G. P.,** 1964: no.157.

MURRY, KATHLEEN (BEAUCHAMP), 1888–1923
See Mansfield, Katherine, pseud.

NAPIER, JOHN, 1550–1617

4321 **Sampson, R. A.** 'Bibliography of books exhibited at the Napier tercentenary celebration, July, 1914' *in* Knott, Cargill G., *ed.* Napier tercentenary memorial volume. London, 1915. p.[177]–242.

Annotated classified short-title catalogue of 82 items, with some bibliog. notes.

NASH, PAUL, 1889–1946

4322 **Graham, Rigby.** 'An annotated list of illustrated books' *in* A note on the book illustrations of Paul Nash. Wymondham [1965] p.[10–25]

NASHE, THOMAS, 1567–1601

4323 **McKerrow, Ronald Brunlees,** *ed.* 'Note on copies of the early editions of Nashe's works' *in* The works of Thomas Nashe. Oxford, 1910. V.5, p. [204]–7.

4324 —— [Same]: Repr. . . . with corrs. . . . Ed. by F. P. Wilson. Oxford, 1958. V.5, p.[204]–7.

Chronol. checklist, with locations of copies.

4325 **Tannenbaum, Samuel Aaron.** Thomas Nashe, a concise bibliography. New York, 1941. viii,31p. 23cm. (Elizabethan bibliographies, no.21)
Classified checklist of works and ana; 511 items.

NELSON, HORATIO, 1ST VISCOUNT NELSON, 1758–1805

4326 **Laughton, sir John Knox.** 'Nelson bibliography' *in* The Nelson memorial; Nelson and his companions in arms. London, 1896. p.335–51. (2d ed. 1899 not seen)

4326a **Hooper, James.** Nelson in fiction. N&Q ser10 3:26 Ja '05; Jonathan Nield *ib.* ser10 3:77,116 Ja,F '05.

4327 **Stephen, George Arthur.** Horatio, viscount Nelson; a catalogue of the books, pamphlets, articles, and engravings relating to Nelson in the Norwich public library. Norwich, Public library committee, 1915. 19p. port. 22cm. Covertitle.
Repr. from Norwich Pub Lib Readers' Guide 4no4:94–110 Jl '15.

4328 **Philadelphia. Free library.** An exhibition of autograph letters, books, and relics of Horatio, lord Nelson, from the collection of Morris Wolf. Philadelphia, 1934. [6]p. 18cm.

NEVILE, HENRY, 1620–1694

4330 **Ford, Worthington Chauncey.** 'Bibliography' *in* The isle of pines, 1668; an essay in bibliography. Boston, Mass., 1920. p.91–109.
List of 39 ed. by country of pub., with TP transcrs. and facsims., BM holdings, and some bibliogr. notes.

NEWBOLT, SIR HENRY JOHN, 1862–1938

4331 **Bibliographies** of modern authors. Sir Henry John Newbolt. Lond Merc 2no1:114–15 My '20.
Chronol. checklist of poetry and prose, 1892–1918.

NEWCASTLE, MARGARET CAVENDISH, DUCHESS OF, 1624?–1724
See Cavendish, Margaret, duchess of Newcastle.

NEWMAN, CARD. JOHN HENRY, 1801–1890

4332 **Guibert, J.** 'Bibliographie de Newman' *in* Le réveil du catholicisme en Angleterre au XIX⁰ siècle. Paris, 1907. p.[311]–35.

4333 **Guitton, Jean Marie P.** 'Les œuvres de Newman' *in* La philosophie de Newman; essai sur l'idée de développement. Paris, 1933. p.195–213.

4334 **Kiener, sr. Mary Aloysi.** 'Bibliography' *in* John Henry Newman, the romantic, the friend, the leader. Boston, Mass., 1933. p.[457]–86.

4335 **Worcester, Mass. College of the holy cross. Dinand library.** John Henry Newman, an illustrated brochure of his first editions, by Clarence E. Sloane. [Worcester, Mass., 1953] 54p. illus., ports., facsims. 26cm.
Annotated catalogue, with TP facsims. and some bibliogr. notes.

NEWTON, SIR ISAAC, 1642–1727

4336 **Gray, George John.** A bibliography of the works of sir Isaac Newton, together with a list of books illustrating his life and works. 2d ed., rev. and enl. Cambridge, Bowes and Bowes, 1907. (First pub. 1888) 80p. 22cm.

Classified chronol. arrangement of early and later ed. of coll. and separated works; miscellaneous works; works ed. by; and ana; with TP transcrs., collations, and some bibliogr. notes on early ed.

4337 **Babson institute,** BABSON PARK, MASS. **Library.** A descriptive catalogue of the Grace K. Babson collection of the works of sir Isaac Newton and the material relating to him in the Babson institute library, Babson park, Mass. New York, H. Reichner, 1950. xiv,228p. illus., ports., facsims. 26cm.

4338 **Macomber, Henry P.** A census of the owners of copies of the 1687 first edition of Newton's Principia. Pa Bib Soc Am 47:269–92 '53.

189 copies arranged by place of location, with some bibliogr. notes.

4339 —— A census of the owners of copies of the 1726 presentation issue of Newton's Principia. Pa Bib Soc Am 47:292–300 '53.

34 items arranged by place of location, with some bibliogr. notes. A revised Census is being prepared by mrs. Frederick W. Harrison.

4340 **Mackenzie, A. G.** Newton: Commercium epistolicum. Durham Philobib 2:14–16 Mr '58.

Distinction of 9 states, with bibliogr. discussion and locations of copies, correcting Gray (no.4336).

NICHOLS, JOHN, 1745–1826
4345 **Smith, A. H.,** 1958: no.201.

NICHOLS, ROBERT MALISE BOWYER, 1893–1944
4346 **Gawsworth, John,** *pseud.* [1932]: no.686.

NICHOLSON, VICTORIA MARY, LADY, 1892–1962
See West, Victoria Mary Sackville-.

NIGHTINGALE FLORENCE, 1820–1910

4347 **California. University. University at Los Angeles. Biomedical library.** The Elmer Belt Florence Nightingale collection, presented to the University of California Biomedical library. . . . [Los Angeles, 1958] 19p. facsim. 23cm.

Comp. by Kate T. Steinitz.

4348 **Bishop, William John** and **S. Goldie.** A bio-bibliography of Florence Nightingale. London, Dawsons for the International council of nurses, 1962. 160p. ports., facsims. 26cm.

Classified annotated checklist of works and ana, with 'Chronological list of works' (p.147–51).

4349 **Wayne state university,** DETROIT. **Library.** The Florence Nightingale collection at Wayne state university; an annotated bibliography compiled by Howard A. Sullivan. Detroit, 1963. iv,20p. 21cm.

NIVEN, ANNA JANE (VARDILL), 1781–1852

4350 **Axon, William Edward Armytage.** Anna Jane Vardill Niven, the authoress of Christobell . . . With a bibliography. . . . *in* Essays by divers hands: Roy Soc Lit Trans ser2 28:57–88 '08.

'Bibliography' (p.80–5): checklist of separate works, and contribs. to the European magazine.

NORDEN, JOHN, 1548–1625?

4351 **Gerish, William Blyth.** 'Bibliography' *in* John Norden, 1548–1626(?) a biography. Ware, 1903. p.x–xiv.

Chronol. checklist, 1585–1845.

4352 —— 'Bibliography' *in* Speculi Britaniæ pars, a description of Hartford-shire, in 1598, by John Norden. Ware, 1903. p.x–xiv.

NORTH, CHRISTOPHER, *pseud. of* JOHN WILSON, 1785–1854

4353 **Swann, Elsie.** 'Titles of principal editions of John Wilson's works' *in* Christopher North (John Wilson). Edinburgh, 1934. p.248–52.

Checklist, with TP transcrs.

NOYES, ALFRED, 1880–1958

4354 **Tobin, James Edward.** Alfred Noyes, a corrected bibliography. Cathol Lib World 15:181–4 '45. (Not seen)

O'BRIEN, MICHAEL FITZ-JAMES, 1828–1862

4355 **Wolle, Francis.** 'Bibliography' *in* Fitz-James O'Brien, a literary bohemian of the eighteen-fifties. Boulder, Col., 1944. p.252–93.

Classified checklist of coll. ed.; poems; stories, plays, etc.; and ana.

O'CASEY, SEAN, 1880–1964

4356 **Black, Hester Mary.** A check list of first editions of works by lord Dunsany and Sean O'Casey. Trinity Coll Dublin Ann Bull 4–8 '57.

Chronol. checklist, 1919–57: p.8–9.

O'CURRY, EUGENE, 1794–1862

4357 **Royal Irish academy,** 1961: no.4358.

O'DONOVAN, JOHN, 1806–1861

4358 **Royal Irish academy.** John O'Donovan, 1806–1861. Eugene O'Curry, 1794–1862; centenary celebration. . . . Roy Irish Acad Proc (Minutes) v.62 '61. (Not seen: Eager's no.1217)

O'FLAHERTY, LIAM, 1897–

4359 **Gawsworth, John,** *pseud.* [1933]: no.687.

OGILBY, JOHN, 1600–1676

4360 **Fordham, sir Herbert George.** John Ogilby, 1600–1676; his Britannia, and the British itineraries of the eighteenth century. Library ser4 6:157–78 S '25.

Discursive checklist with bibliogr. notes interspersed, and facsims.

O'GRADY, STANDISH, 1846–1928

4361 **Bibliographies** of Irish authors, no.2. Standish O'Grady. Dublin Mag new ser 4[i.e. 5]:49–56 Ap/Je '30.

TP transcrs., collations, and bibliogr. notes on first ed., 1875–1917.

4362 **McKenna, John R.** The Standish O'Grady collection at Colby college, a check list. Colby Lib Q ser4 16:291–303 N '58.

Classified and annotated short-title catalogue of works and ana.

O'HANRAHAN, MICHAEL, fl.1914

4363 **O'Hegarty, Patrick Sarsfield,** 1936: no.2813.

O'HIGGINS, KEVIN CHRISTOPHER, 1892–1927

4364 **O'Hegarty, Patrick Sarsfield,** 1937: no.3533.

O'KELLY, SEUMAS, 1881–1918

4365 **O'Hegarty, Patrick Sarsfield.** Bibliographies of 1916 and the Irish revolution, IV. Seumas O'Kelly. Dublin Mag new ser 9:47–51 Oc/D '34.

Chronol. list of first ed., 1906–22, with quasifacsim. TP transcrs., collations, and bibliogr. notes.

OLDFIELD, CLAUDE HOUGHTON, 1889–
See Houghton, Claude, pseud.

OLDHAM, JOHN, 1653–1683

4366 **Brooks, Harold Fletcher.** A bibliography of John Oldham, the restoration satirist. Oxford Bib Soc Proc 5pt1:1–38 '36.

Classified chronol. arrangement of separate; coll., and contrib. works; with quasifacsim. TP transcrs., collations, locations of copies, and bibliogr. notes; no index.

Rev: TLS 14 N '36:932.

OLIVER, GEORGE, 1873–1961
See Onions, Oliver, pseud.

ONIONS, CHARLES TALBUT, 1873–1965

4367 **A list** of the published writings of Charles Talbut Onions. Oxford, Clarendon pr., 1948. 18p. port. 21cm.

Checklist, 1902–48.

ONIONS, OLIVER, *pseud.* of GEORGE OLIVER, 1873–1961

4368 **Gawsworth, John,** *pseud.* [1933]: no.687.

OPIE, AMELIA (ALDERSON), 1769–1853

4369 **MacGregor, Margaret Eliot.** 'The writings of mrs. Opie' *in* Amelia Alderson Opie, worldling and friend. Northampton, Mass. [1933] p.130–4.

Classified checklists of prose and verse, in books and periodicals.

ORRERY, ROGER BOYLE, 1ST EARL OF, 1621–1679
See Boyle, Roger, 1st earl of Orrery.

ORWELL, GEORGE, *pseud. of* ERIC BLAIR, 1903–1950

4370 **Willison, Ian R.,** 1953: no.234.

4371 **Zeke, Zoltan G.** and **W. White.** George Orwell, a selected bibliography. Boston, Boston linotype print, 1962. 12p. 25cm. Covertitle.
Repr. from Bull Bib 23:110–14, 140–4 My/Ag, S/D '61; 23:166–8 Ja/Ap '62.

4372 **McDowell, Margaret Jennifer.** George Orwell, bibliographical addenda. Bull Bib 23:224–9 Ja/Ap '63; 24:19–24, 36–40 My/Ag, S/D '63.
Classified checklist of works and ana.

4373 **Willison, Ian R.** and **I. Angus.** George Orwell: bibliographical addenda. Bull Bib 24:180–7 S/D '65.

OSBORNE, FRANCIS, 1593–1659

4375 **Madan, Francis Falconer.** Some notes on the bibliography of Francis Osborne. Oxford Bib Soc Pub new ser 4:55–60 '50.
TP transcrs., collations, locations of copies, and bibliogr. notes and refs. on 17 ed. of 3 works.

OSBORNE, JOHN JAMES, 1929–

4376 **Bailey, Shirley Jean.** John Osborne, a bibliography. Twent Cent Lit 7:118–20 Oc '61.
Chiefly ana.

O'SULLIVAN, SEUMAS, *pseud. of* JAMES SULLIVAN STARKEY, 1879–

4377 **MacManus, Michael Joseph.** Bibliographies of Irish authors, no.3. Seumas O'Sullivan. Dublin Mag new ser 4[i.e. 5]:47–50 Jl/S '30.
TP transcrs., collations, and bibliogr. notes on first ed., 1905–29.

O'SULLIVAN, TIMOTHY, fl.1795

4378 **Cassedy, James.** The bibliography of Timothy O'Sullivan's Tadhg Gaidhlach / Pious miscellany. Gaelic J new ser 15no4:49–51 '05.
Discursive checklist, with locations of copies.

4379 —— Some editions of O'Sullivan's Miscellany. Waterford & S.E. Ireland Archæol Soc J 14:113–22 Jl/S '11.
Checklist of 24 ed., 1795–1903, with some bibliogr. notes and locations of copies; TP facsim.

O'SULLIVAN, VINCENT, 1872–1940

4380 **Sims, George.** Some uncollected authors xv: Vincent O'Sullivan. Bk Coll 6no4:395–402 '57.
'A. Books by Vincent O'Sullivan' (p.399–400); 'B. Contributions to books' (p.400–1); chronol. checklists, with some bibliogr. notes.

OUSELEY, SIR FREDERICK ARTHUR GORE, 1825–1889

4381 **Bumpus, John Skelton.** The compositions of the rev. sir Frederick A. Gore Ouseley. . . . London, Ptd. for the author by Bowden, Hudson, 1892. 34p. 22cm.
Classified checklist.

OVERBURY, SIR THOMAS, 1581–1613

4382 **Paylor, Wilfrid James.** The editions of the Overburian characters. Library ser4 17:340–8 D '36.

Supplements Murphy (no.1550), with notes on first 17 ed.

OVERTON, RICHARD, fl.1642–1663

4383 **Wolfe, Don Marion.** [Chronological checklist, with locations of copies] *in* Milton in the puritan revolution. New York, 1941. p.480–1. (Repr. London, 1963)

4384 —— Unsigned pamphlets of Richard Overton, 1641–1649. Huntington Lib Q 21:167–201 F '58.

Chronol. checklist of 17 items, with collations and bibliogr. refs. and discussion.

OWEN, ROBERT, 1771–1858

4385 **Dolléans, Édouard.** 'Bibliographie' *in* Robert Owen, 1771–1858. [2e ed.] Paris, 1907. p.[357]–69.

4386 **Wales. National library,** ABERYSTWYTH. A bibliography of Robert Owen, the socialist, 1771–1858. Aberystwyth [Pr. of the National library of Wales] 1914. 54p. 23cm.

Compared by Arthur J. Hawkes.

4387 —— [Same]: 2d ed., rev. & enl. Aberystwyth, Published by the National library of Wales in association with the Press board of the University of Wales, 1925. viii,90p. 23cm.

Ed. by William Williams. Classified chronol. checklist of works and periodicals, and ana.

4388 **Gotō, Shigeru.** Robert Owen, 1771–1858, a new bibliographical study. [Osaka] Osaka university of commerce, 1934. viii,220,18p. facsims. 23cm.

Chronol. arrangement of works, with quasifacsim. TP transcrs., collations, and locations of copies. with notes in Japanese.

4389 **London. University. Library.** Robert Owen, 1771–1858, catalogue of an exhibition of printed books held in the library of the University of London. London, 1959. 40p. facsims. 21cm.

Comp. by Margaret B. C. Canney.

OWEN, WILFRED, 1893–1918

4390 **White, William.** Wilfred Owen, 1893–1918: a bibliography. Serif Kent State Univ Lib Q 2no4:5–16 '65. (Not seen)

PAGET, SIR JAMES, 1814–1899

4391 **Putnam, Helen Cordelia.** Sir James Paget in his writings: bibliography. [Providence R.I., 1902] 24p. 20cm.

Repr. from Trans Rhode Island Med Soc Je '02; chronol. checklist, 1834–94 (p.19–24).

PAGET, VIOLET, 1856–1935
See Lee, Vernon, pseud.

PALGRAVE, FRANCIS TURNER, 1824–1897

4392 **C., R. N.** and **W. G. P[artington]** The golden treasury, its bibliography and adventure: the varying issues of the first editions. Bkmns J 16no5:268–70 '28.

TP transcrs., collations, and bibliogr. notes.

PALMER, HERBERT EDWARD, b.1880

4393 **Gawsworth, John,** *pseud.* [1932]: no.686.

PARR, SAMUEL, 1747–1825

4394 **Sparrow, John.** Some uncollected authors IX: Samuel Parr, 1747–1825. Bk Coll 5no1:63–72 '56.

'Parr's works' (p.64–72); annotated checklist of 15 items and ana, with some bibliogr. notes.

4395 **Neill, Desmond G.** Samuel Parr's Notes on Rapin's Dissertation on whigs and tories. Bk Coll 10no2:199–200 '61.

PASSFIELD, SIDNEY JAMES WEBB, BARON, 1859–1947
See Webb, Sidney James, baron Passfield.

PATER, WALTER HORATIO, 1839–1894

4396 **Stonehill, Charles Archibald** [1925]: no.682.

PATERSON, DANIEL, 1738–1825

4397 **Fordham, sir Herbert George.** Paterson's Roads; Daniel Paterson, his maps and itineraries, 1738–1825. Library ser4 5:333–56 Mr '25.

Discursive checklist, 1766–[1832], with some bibliogr. notes and TP facsims.

PATMORE, COVENTRY KERSEY DIGHTON, 1823–1896

4398 **Page, Frederick,** *ed.* 'An essay towards a bibliographical list of Coventry Patmore's prose contributions to periodical literature' *in* Courage in politics, and other essays, 1885–1896, by Coventry Patmore. London, 1921. p.203–10.

4399 **Patmore, Derek,** *ed.* 'The principal editions of Coventry Patmore's writings' *in* Selected poems of Coventry Patmore. London [1931] p.157–60.

4400 **Reid, John Cowrie.** 'Select bibliography' *in* The mind and art of Coventry Patmore. London [1957] p.330–46.

Classified checklists of manuscripts; prose; poetry; periodical contribs.; and ana.

PATTISON, MARK, 1813–1884

4401 **Hoare, J.,** 1953: no.141.

PAYNE, JOHN, 1842–1916

4402 **Wright, Thomas.** 'Bibliography of John Payne' *in* The life of sir Richard Burton. London, 1906. V.2, p.xi at end.

Chronol. checklist of 17 items, 1870–1904.

PEAKE, MERVYN LAURENCE, 1911–

4403 **Farmer, G. A. J.** Mervyn Peake, book illustrator, and a check-list of his works. Aust Lib J 8:134–7 Jl '59.

'Mervyn Peake, a preliminary check-list' (p.135–7).

PEARSE, PADRAIC HENRY, 1879–1916

4404 **O'Hegarty, Patrick Sarsfield.** Bibliographies of 1916 and the Irish revolution, no.1. P. H. Pearse. Dublin Mag new ser 6:44–9 Jl/S '31.

TP transcrs., collations, and bibliogr. notes on 18 first ed., 1898–1922.

PECHEY, JOHN, 1655–1716

4404a **Peachey, George C.** The works of John Pechey, physician, 1654–1718. N&Q ser11 7:328 Ap '13; G. Y. Baldock *ib.* ser11 7:376 My '13.

PEELE, GEORGE, 1558?–1597?

4405 **Larsen, Thorleif.** A bibliography of the writings of George Peele. Mod Philol 32:143–56 N '34.

TP transcrs., collations, locations of copies, and bibliogr. notes, 1579?–95, with notes of later ed.

4406 **Tannenbaum, Samuel Aaron.** George Peele, a concise bibliography. New York, 1940. x,36p. 23cm. (Elizabethan bibliographies, no.15)

Classified chronol. checklist of works and ana; 587 items.

PENN, WILLIAM, 1644–1718

4407 **Goodbody, Olive C.** and **M. Pollard.** The first edition of William Penn's Great case of liberty of conscience, 1670. Library ser5 16:146–9 Je '64.

Quasifacsim. TP transcr., collation, locations of copies, and discursive bibliogr. notes.

PENNANT, THOMAS, 1726–1798

4408 **Powell, Lawrence Fitzroy.** The tours of Thomas Pennant. Library ser4 19:134–54 S '38.

'Collations and descriptions of the editions and supplements' (p.136–52).

PENNECUIK, ALEXANDER, 1652–1722

4409 **Brown, William.** Writings of Alexander Pennecuik, M.D., and Alexander Pennecuik, merchant. Edinburgh Bib Soc Pub 6pt2:117–31 Oc '06.

Discursive checklists, with collations, some locations of copies and bibliogr. notes.

PENNECUIK, ALEXANDER, d.1730

4410 **Brown, William,** 1906: no.4409.

PENNY, ANNE BULKELEY (HUGHES), b.1728

4411 **Lloyd, Hugh.** Mrs. Anne Penny. Welsh Bib Soc J 3:38–48 Ja '26.

Discussion and checklist of 5 anonyma.

PEPYS, SAMUEL, 1633–1703

4412 **Chappell, Edwin.** Catalogue of Pepysiana belonging to mr. Edwin Chappell, exhibited at the annual general meeting of the Society for nautical
research . . . [London, 1931] [12]p. 22cm.

4413 —— Bibliographia Pepysiana. [Blackheath, Ptd. by E. Chappell] 1933.
[18]p. 19cm.
Caption title : A short-title Pepys bibliography, compiled for the most part from copies
in my own possession.
Classified checklist of works and ana.

PERCY, THOMAS, 1729–1811

4415 **Powell, Lawrence Fitzroy.** Percy's Reliques. Library ser4 9:113–37 S '28.
Collation of first 3 ed., 1765–75 (p.125–6).

PERRY, WILLIAM, fl.1774–1808

4416 **Law, Alexander.** William Perry, his academy and printing press in Edinburgh, and his publications. Edinburgh Bib Soc Trans 4pt3:91–102 '63.
'List of Perry's works published in the United Kingdom' (p.100–2).

PETTY, SIR WILLIAM, 1623–1687

4417 **Hull, Charles Henry,** *ed.* 'Bibliography of the printed writings of sir
William Petty' *in* The economic writings of sir William Petty. Cambridge,
1899. p.[633]–52.
Chronol. checklist of 34 items, 1648–93, with some bibliogr. notes; 'Supplement'
(p.[653]–7); 'Bibliography of the Natural and political observations [by John Graunt]'
(p.[658]–60. Enl. from N&Q ser8 8:163–5, 202–3 Ag,S '95.

4417a **Smith, R. S.,** 1950: no.202.

PHILIPPS, JOHN HENRY, 1808–1876
See Scourfield, sir John Henry.

PHILIPS, AMBROSE, 1675?–1749

4418 **Segar, M. G.,** *ed.* 'Bibliographical note' *in* The poems of Ambrose Philips.
Oxford, 1937. p.liv–lvi.
Checklist of coll. and single works, with collations.

4419 **Bayley, D. J.,** 1952: no.82.

PHILIPS, JOHN, 1676–1709

4420 **Todd, William Burton.** Philips' Cyder, 1708. Bk Coll 10no1:68 '61.
Distinction of and bibliogr. notes on 3 variants.

PHILLIP, JOHN, fl.1560–1590

4420a **Greg, sir Walter Wilson.** John Phillip, notes for a bibliography. London,
A. Moring, 1911. 54p. facsims. 26cm.
Repr. from Library ser3 1:302–28, 295–423 Jl,Oc '10. Discursive chronol. checklist of
24 items.

PHILLIPPS, SIR THOMAS, 1792–1872

4421 **Munby, Alan Noël Latimer.** 'The catalogue of printed books at Middle hill' *in* The catalogues of manuscripts & printed books of sir Thomas Phillipps; their composition and distribution. Cambridge, 1951. p.35–[40]

Quasifacsim. TP transcrs., with collations and bibliogr. notes.

PHILLIPS, JOHN, 1631–1706

4422 **Ayers, Robert W.** The John Phillips–John Milton Angli responsio: editions and relations. Pa Bib Soc Am 56:66–72 '62.

Quasifacsim. TP transcrs., collations, and bibliogr. notes on 4 ed., 1652.

PHILLIPS, STEPHEN, 1864–1915

4423 **Streatfeild, Richard A.** Stephen Phillips. Eng Illus Mag new ser 29:441–3 Jl '03.

'Bibliography' (p.442): chronol. checklist of works, plays, and ana.

PHILLPOTTS, EDEN, 1862–1960

4424 **Hinton, Percival.** Eden Phillpotts; a bibliography of first editions. Birmingham, G. Worthington, 1931. xvi,164p. port., facsim. 24cm.

Quasifacsim. TP transcrs., collations, and bibliogr. notes on first ed., 1888–1931.
Rev: A. W. P[ollard] Library ser4 12:362–3 '31; Bk Coll Q 5:111 '32.

PIOZZI, HESTER LYNCH (SALUSBURY), 1741–1821

4425 **Roberts, sir Sydney Castle,** *ed.* 'Bibliography' *in* Anecdotes of the late Samuel Johnson . . . by Hester Lynch Piozzi. Cambridge, 1925. p.[ix]–xii.

Chronol. checklist, with some bibliogr. notes.

PITT-RIVERS, AUGUSTUS HENRY LANE FOX, 1827–1900

See Rivers, Augustus Henry Lane Fox Pitt-.

PLAT, SIR HUGH, 1552?–1611?

4426 **Fussell, George Edwin** and **K. R. Fussell,** *ed.* 'Bibliography of sir Hugh Plat's printed works' *in* Delightes for ladies, by sir Hugh Plat. London, 1948. p.xxvi.

4427 **Jensen, Bent Juel-.** Some uncollected authors XIX: sir Hugh Plat, ?1552–?1611. Bk Coll 8no1:60–8 '59.

'Handlist of sir Hugh Plat's printed works' (p.62–8): checklist of 52 early items, with collations, locations of copies, some bibliogr. notes and refs.

4428 —— [Same]: Errata and addenda. *ib.* 8no2:179 '59.

4429 —— [Same]: [Corrigenda] *ib.* 15no2:212–13 '66.

PLAYFORD, JOHN, 1623–1686

4430 **Smith, Margaret Dean-,** *ed.* 'A bibliographical list of all editions of The dancing master from 1651 to 1728' *in* Playford's English dancing master, 1651: a facsimile reprint. . . . London, 1957. p.xxi–xxxi.

Rev. from J Eng Folk Dance & Song Soc 11:43–5 '42.

PLUNKETT, EDWARD JOHN MORETON DRAX, BARON DUNSANY, 1878–1957

4430a **Danielson, Henry.** Bibliographies of modern authors, no.3. Lord Dunsany. Bkmns J 1no3:58 '19.

TP transcrs., collations, and bibliogr. notes on 12 first ed., 1905–19.

4431 ——, 1921: no.680.

4432 **Black, Hester Mary,** 1957: no.4356.

POLLARD, ALFRED WILLIAM, 1859–1944

4433 **Bibliographies** of modern authors. Alfred William Pollard. Lond Merc 3no17:549–50 Mr '21.

Chronol. checklist of prose, 1882–1919.

4434 **[Murphy, Gwendolen]** A select bibliography of the writings of Alfred W. Pollard. Oxford, O.U.P. for the subscribers, 1938. ix,69p. port. 23cm.

Chronol. checklist, with annotations by Pollard.

POPE, ALEXANDER, 1688–1744

4435 **Tobin, James Edward.** Alexander Pope, a list of critical studies published from 1895 to 1944. New York, Cosmopolitan science and art service, 1945. 30p. 23cm.

4436 **Lefferts, Marshall Clifford.** Alexander Pope; notes towards a bibliography of early editions of his writings; a catalogue of Marshall C. Leffert's great collection . . . offered for sale by Dodd, Mead & company. [Cedar Rapids, Ia., Torch pr., 1910] 50p. 25cm. (Also issued with facsims.)

Comp. by Luther S. Livingston; the collection was acquired by Harvard university library.

4437 **Grolier club,** NEW YORK. A catalogue of the first editions of the works of Alexander Pope. . . . New York, 1911. vii,85p. ports., facsim. 24cm.

4438 —— An exhibition of the first editions . . . together with a collection of the engraved portraits of the poet and his friends. [New York, DeVinne pr., 1911?] vii,80p. 18cm.

4439 **Aitken, George Atherton.** Notes on the bibliography of Pope. Bib Soc Trans 12:113–43 Oc/Ap '11/13.

4440 **Griffith, Reginald Harvey.** Alexander Pope, a bibliography. Austin, University of Texas pr., 1922–7. (Repr. 1962) 2v. 23cm.

Contents: pt1. Pope's own writings, 1709–1734.—pt2. Pope's own writings, 1735–1751. Chronol. arrangement of early ed. and issues, with TP transcrs., collations, some locations of copies and bibliogr. notes.

Rev: R. A. Law Alcade 10:1840–1 '23; N&Q ser12 12:240 '23; I. A. Williams Lond Merc 8:191 '23; TLS 12 Ap '23:252; G. Sherburn Mod Philol 22:327–36 '25; TLS 1 Mr '28:147; F. T. Wood Eng Studien 66:428 '32; I. A. Williams Lond Merc 31:584 '35; D. G. Neill Bk Coll 12:244, 247 '63.

4441 **Case, Arthur Ellicott.** Notes on the bibliography of Pope. Mod Philol 24:297–313 F '27.

Supplements Griffith, v.1.

4442 **Wise, Thomas James.** A Pope library; a catalogue of plays, poems, and prose writings by Alexander Pope, collected by Thomas James Wise. London, Ptd. for private circulation only, 1931. xxiv,112p. ports., facsims 26cm.

4443 **Pottle, Frederick Albert.** The Pope collection at Colby. Colby Lib Q ser1 7:106–12 Je '44.
Checklist, with Griffith nos.

4444 **Todd, William Burton.** Concealed Pope editions. Bk Coll 5no1:48–52 '56.
Distinction of early ed. of 4 poems, with TP transcrs., collations, locations of copies, and bibliogr. notes and refs.

4445 **Peavy, Charles Druery.** The Pope–Cibber controversy, a bibliography. Restor 18th Cent Theat Res 3:51–5 N '64.
Annotated chronol. checklist of 34 items, 1717–44.

POTOCKI, GEOFFREY, COUNT POTOCKI OF MONTALK, 1903–

4448 **Graham, Rigby.** A tentative checklist of the work of Geoffrey count Potocki. Priv Libs 8no1:23–6 '67.
Annotated checklist, 1923–66.

POTTER, HELEN BEATRIX, 1866-1943

4450 **Quinby, Jane.** Beatrix Potter, a bibliographical check list. New York, 1954. 121p. illus., facsims. 23cm.

Chronol. list of first ed. in English, 1901–44, with collations, bibliogr. notes, and locations of copies.

Rev: D. A. Randall Pa Bib Soc Am 49:375–6 '54; L. Linder Bk Coll 3:155–7 '54.

POWER, SIR D'ARCY, 1855-1941

4450a 'A short-title bibliography of writings of sir D'Arcy Power' *in* Sir D'Arcy Power: selected writings, 1877–1930. Oxford, 1931. p.330–55.

POWYS, JOHN COWPER, 1872-1963

4451 **Siberell, Lloyd Emerson.** A bibliography of the first editions of John Cowper Powys. Cincinnati, Ailanthus pr., 1934. 53p. facsim. 22cm.

Checklist of early ed., 1896–1930, with TP transcrs., collations, and some bibliogr. notes; and of contribs. to periodicals; no index.

Rev: P. H. Muir Bk Coll Q 17:75–7 '35.

4452 **Langridge, Derek Wilton.** [Chronological checklist of works and ana, 1914–63] *in* John Cowper Powys, a record of achievement. London, 1966. p.74–229.

POWYS, THEODORE FRANCIS, 1875-1953

4455 **Muir, Percival Horace,** 1927: no.3775.

4455a **Riley, Peter.** A bibliography of T. F. Powys. Hastings, R. A. Brimmell, 1967. 72p. 21cm.

Classified bibliogr. of books and pamphlets; periodical contribs.; and ana; no index.

Rev: Pa Bib Soc Am 61:401–2 '67; R. J. Roberts Bk Coll 17:103–5 '68.

PRAED, ROSA CAROLINE MACKWORTH (PRIOR), 1851-1935

4456 **McCarthy, Justin.** Mrs. Campbell Praed. Eng Illus Mag new ser 30:686–8 Mr '04

'Bibliography' (p.688): checklist, 1880–1903.

PREEDY, GEORGE R., *pseud.*

See Long, Gabrielle Margaret Vere (Campbell), 1888–1952.

PRIESTLEY, JOHN BOYNTON, 1894-

4457 **Jones, I. Alun.** The first editions of J. B. Priestley. Bkmn 80:46 Ap '31.

Chronol. checklist, 1922–9, with some bibliogr. notes.

4458 **Day, A. E.,** 1959: no.108.

PRIESTLEY, JOSEPH, 1733-1804

4459 **Fulton, John Farquhar** and **C. H. Peters.** An introduction to a bibliography of the educational and scientific works of Joseph Priestley. Pa Bib Soc Am 30:150–67 '36.

'A short-title list of the writings' (p.164–7).

4460 —— Works of Joseph Priestley, 1733–1804, a preliminary short title list New Haven, Conn., Laboratory of physiology, Yale university school of medicine, 1937. 20p. 28cm. (Duplicated typescript)

4461 —— [**Same**]: Addenda. [New Haven, Conn.] 1938. vip. 28cm.
Title checklist of separately pub. works, with locations of copies.

4462 **Crook, Ronald Eric.** A bibliography of Joseph Priestley, 1733–1804. London, Library association [1966] xiv,201p. 26cm.
Classified checklist, with locations of copies, based on London University School of librarianship and archives thesis: no.103.
Rev: TLS 8 D '66:1160; Pa Bib Soc Am 61:159 '67; J. L. Marks Bk Coll 16:389–90, 393 '67.

PRIMROSE, GEORGE HAY, 1821–1875
See Presses and printing—Pitsligo press.

PRINGLE, THOMAS, 1789–1834

4464 **Robinson, George W.** A bibliography of Thomas Pringle's Afar in the desert. Pa Bib Soc Am 17pt1:21–54 '23.
'Bibliography' (p.31–54): discursive checklist, 1824–1916, with bibliogr. notes.

PRIOR, MATTHEW, 1664–1721

4465 **Wright, H. Bunker** and **M. K. Spears,** *ed.* 'Principal collected editions' *in* The literary works of Matthew Prior. Oxford, 1959. V.1, p.xxxvii–xxxix.

PRYNNE, WILLIAM, 1600–1669

4466 **Kirby, Ethyn Morgan (Williams).** 'Bibliography of William Prynne' *in* William Prynne, a study in puritanism. Cambridge, Mass., 1931. p.[193]–219.

4467 [**Fry, Mary Isobel** and **G. Davies**] William Prynne in the Huntington library. Huntington Lib Q 20:53–93 N '56.
Short-title catalogue, with some bibliogr. notes and refs. and additional locations of copies.

PUCKLE, JAMES, 1667?–1724

4468 [**Kohlmetz, George W.**] Bibliographical notes on a collection of editions known as Puckle's club, from the library of a member of the Rowfant club . . . with an introduction by Austin Dobson. Cleveland, Rowfant club, 1899. 69p. illus., ports., facsims. 27cm.
Chronol. list of 31 items, 1711–1872, with TP transcrs. and facsims., collations, and some bibliogr. notes.

PURCELL, HENRY, 1659?–1695

4469 **British museum.** Henry Purcell, 1659?–1695, George Frideric Handel, 1685–1759; catalogue of a commemorative exhibition. London, Published by the trustees, 1959. 47p. port., illus., facsims. 21cm.
Annotated catalogue of 246 entries, comp. by Alexander H. King.

PURNEY, THOMAS, 1695–c.1727

4470 **White, H. O.,** *ed.* 'Bibliography' *in* The works of Thomas Purney. Oxford, 1933. p.91–3.

Chronol. checklist of 6 items, 1717–23, with locations of copies and some bibliogr. notes.

PUSEY, EDWARD BOUVERIE, 1800–1882

4471 **[Madan, Falconer]** *comp.* 'A bibliographical list of the printed works of dr. Pusey *in* Liddon, Henry P. Life of Edward Bouverie Pusey. London, 1893–7. V.4 (1897), p.[395]–446.

Chronol. checklist, with bibliogr. notes.

PUTTENHAM, GEORGE, d.1590

4472 **Willcock, Gladys Doidge** and **A. Walker,** *ed.* 'Bibliographical note' *in* The arte of English poesie, by George Puttenham. Cambridge, 1936. p.ciii–cx.

'Description of BM G.11548 with notes on bibliographical variations in other copies examined' (p.cviii–cx).

PYE-SMITH, PHILIP HENRY, 1839–1914

See Smith, Philip Henry Pye-.

Q, *pseud. of* SIR ARTHUR THOMAS QUILLER-COUCH, 1863–1944

4473 **Nevinson, Henry Woodd.** A. T. Quiller-Couch. Eng Illus Mag new ser 32:185–8 N '04.

'Bibliography' (p.186,188).

4474 **Bibliographies** of modern authors. Sir Arthur Thomas Quiller-Couch. Lond Merc 4no23:532–3 S '21.

4475 **Brittain, Frederick.** 'Chronological list of Q's publications, including a selection from his contributions to periodical literature' *in* Arthur Quiller-Couch, a biographical study of Q. Cambridge, 1947. (Repr. 1948) p.159–66.

4476 —— Four Q rarities. Bk Hndbk 2no1:27–35 '51.

Short descrs., notes, and TP facsims.

QUICK, JOHN, 1636–1706

4477 **Dredge, John Ingle,** 1889–99: no.886.

QUILLER-COUCH, SIR ARTHUR THOMAS, 1863–1944

See Q, pseud.

RACKHAM, ARTHUR, 1867–1939

4480 **Coykendall, Frederick.** Arthur Rackham, a list of books illustrated by him. . . . [New York] Privately ptd., 1922. 22p. port. 24cm.

4481 **Latimore, Sarah Briggs** and **G. C. Haskell.** Arthur Rackham. a bibliography. Los Angeles, Suttonhouse, 1936. x,111p. illus.(1 col.) port. 25cm.

Chronol. list of books, 1893–1936, with TP transcrs. and bibliogr. notes; magazine illus.; dust wrappers; commercial and theatrical work; books contrib. to; children's books, and other indexes.

4482 **Osborne, Eric Allen.** A checklist bibliography of books illustrated by Arthur Rackham. Bk Trade J 71, 73–6, 78–81:30–1, 26–7, 26–7, 24–5, 24–5, 18–19, 22–3, 20–1, 10–11 S–N '36.

4483 **Rota, Bertram,** *comp.* 'The printed work of Arthur Rackham: a checklist' *in* Hudson, Derek R. Arthur Rackham, his life and work. New York [1960] p.164–81.

Classified chronol. checklist of first printings and important new ed.; of books illus. wholly by; books contrib. to; contribs. to periodicals; and ephemera.

RALEIGH, SIR WALTER, 1552?–1618

4484 **Brushfield, Thomas Nadauld.** The bibliography of sir Walter Raleigh, with notes. 2d ed., with notes, rev. and enl. Exeter, J. G. Commin, 1908. (First pub. 1886) 181p. illus., ports., facsims. 23cm.

Classified checklist of 330 items, with TP transcrs. and facsims., and discursive bibliogr. notes.

Rev: Nation 86:396 '08; Devonshire N&Q 5no2:72 '08.

RALEIGH, SIR WALTER ALEXANDER, 1861–1922

4485 **[Chapman, Robert William]** Sir Walter Raleigh, a bibliography. [Oxford, O.U.P., 1922] 7p. 26cm.

Repr. from Periodical 8:10–15 S '22. Chronol. checklist, 1883–1922, with some bibliogr. notes.

RAMSAY, ALLAN, 1686–1758

4486 **Martin, Burns.** Bibliography of Allan Ramsay. Glasgow, Jackson, Wylie, 1931. 114p. facsims. 27cm.

Repr. from Glasgow Bib Soc Rec 10:1–114 '31.

'Editions arranged chronologically' (p.[21]–110): 411 items, 1713–1899, with TP transcrs., collations, locations of copies, and some bibliogr. notes; 'Major works arranged by title [an index]' (p.111–14); no index.

Rev: TLS 2 Je '32:404.

RANDOLPH, THOMAS, 1605–1635

4487 **Parry, John Jay,** *ed.* 'Bibliography' *in* The poems and Amyntas of Thomas Randolph. New Haven; London, 1917. p.39–45.

4488 **Tannenbaum, Samuel Aaron** and **D. R. Tannenbaum.** Thomas Randolph, a concise bibliography. New York, 1947. 24p. 28cm. (Elizabethan bibliographies, no.38) (Duplicated typescript)

Classified chronol. checklist of works and ana; 347 items.

RANSOME, ARTHUR MITCHELL, 1884–1967

4489 **Rota, Anthony.** Some uncollected authors XXI: Arthur Ransome, b. 1884. Bk Coll 8no3:289–93 '59.

'Check list of first editions of books by Arthur Ransome' (p.291–3): checklist of 34 items, 1904–59, with some bibliogr. notes.

RAY, JOHN, 1627–1705

4490 [Keynes, sir Geoffrey Langdon] John Ray, F.R.S., a handlist of his works. G.L.K. for C.E.R. Cambridge, 1944. 21p. 16cm.

4491 —— John Ray, a bibliography. London, Faber and Faber [1951] xv,163p. ports., facsims. 26cm.

TP transcrs. and facsims., collations, locations of copies, and bibliogr. notes on early ed.; 117 items.

Rev: W. T. Calman Nature 168:352–3 '51; TLS 25 My '51:332; Bk Hndbk 2no3:154–6 '52; I. B. Cohen Isis 43:276–7 '52; W. R. LeFanu Library ser5 8:285–6 '53.

READE, CHARLES, 1814–1884

4492 **Cordasco, Francesco G. M. and K. W. Scott,** 1949: no.2846.

4493 **Stevenson, Lionel,** *ed.,* 1964: no.1705.

4494 **Sadleir, Michael Thomas Hervey,** 1922: no.1706.

4495 **Elwin, Malcolm.** 'Bibliography' *in* Charles Reade, a biography. London, 1931. p.365–72.

Classified checklist of books; plays; contribs. to periodicals and newspapers; and pamphlets.

4496 **Parrish, Morris Longstreth,** 1940: no.2850.

4497 **Rives, Léone.** 'Bibliographie' *in* Charles Reade, sa vie, ses romans. Toulouse, 1940. p.479–511.

Classified checklist of novels; plays; periodical articles; translations; adaptations, and ana.

READE, WILLIAM WINWOOD, d.1875

4500 **Gilmour, John Scott Lennox.** Some uncollected authors XIII: William Winwood Reade. Bk Coll 6no1:62–6 '57.

Checklist of separate pubs. (9 items, 1859–75) with TP transcrs., collations, and some bibliogr. notes; and contribs. to periodicals, etc.

REED, TALBOT BAINES, 1852–1893

4501 **Handover, Phyllis Margaret.** Some uncollected authors XXXV: Talbot Baines Reed, 1852–1893. Bk Coll 12no1:62–7 '63.

'Check-list of the writings of Talbot Baines Reed' (p.65–7): checklist of typographica and books for boys, 24 items, 1877–1905, with some bibliogr. notes.

REEVES, BP. WILLIAM, 1815–1892

4502 **Garstin, John Ribton,** *comp.* 'Bibliography of the works of William Reeves' *in* Ferguson, Mary C., lady. Life of the rt. rev. William Reeves. . . . Dublin; London, 1893. p.[187]–210.

Discursive classified checklist of books and contribs. to periodicals, with some bibliogr. notes.

REID, FORREST, 1875–1947

4503 **Belfast. Public libraries.** . . . Forrest Reid; an exhibition of books and manuscripts in the Museum and art gallery. . . . [Belfast] City and county borough of Belfast libraries, museums and art committee, 1953. iv. (unpaged) 22cm. (Duplicated typescript)

See no.4505.

4504 **Burlingham, Russell.** 'A bibliography of the writings of Forrest Reid' *in* Forrest Reid, a portrait and a study. London, 1953. p.227–50.

Classified list of books, 26 items, 1904–47, with some bibliogr. notes; periodical articles; and ana.

4505 **Belfast. Public libraries.** Forrest Reid, an exhibition of books and manuscripts held in the Museum and art gallery, Belfast. . . . [Belfast] City and county borough of Belfast libraries, museums and art committee, 1954. 35p. port. 23cm.

REID, THOMAS MAYNE, 1818–1883

4506 **Hunter, J. V. B. Stewart.** Captain of romance. Bk Hndbk 1no8/9:455–68 '50.

'Short title list of books by Thomas Mayne Reid, 1818–1883' (p.463).

REPTON, HUMPHRY, 1752–1818

4507 **Holiday, J. P.**, 1953: no.143.

REYNOLDS, JOHN HAMILTON, 1796–1852

4508 **Marsh, George L.** The writings of Keats' friend Reynolds. Stud Philol 25: 491–510 Oc '28.

Annotated chronol. checklist of 132 items, 1814–48.

4509 **Jensen, Bent Juel-.** Some uncollected authors III: John Hamilton Reynolds. Bk Coll 3no3:211–15 '54.

4510 —— [Same]: Gallup, Donald C. Additions & corrections. *ib.* 4n02:156 '55.
TP transcrs., collations, and some bibliogr. notes on 14 items, 1813–38.

4511 —— [Same]: Jensen, Bent Juel-. [Corrigenda.] *ib.* 15n02:210–11 '66.

REYNOLDS, SIR JOSHUA, 1723–1792

4512 **Hilles, Frederick Whiley.** 'A bibliography of sir Joshua's writings' *in* The literary career of sir Joshua Reynolds. New York; Cambridge, 1936. p.[277]–300.
Chronol. list of early ed., 28 items, 1759–98, with TP transcrs., collations, locations of copies, and some bibliogr. notes.

RHODES, CECIL JOHN, 1853–1902

4513 **Thomson, Daphne W.** Cecil John Rhodes, a bibliography. [Cape Town] University of Cape Town School of librarianship, 1947. vi,29l. 23cm. (Duplicated typescript)
Classified checklist of works about Rhodes.

RICHARDSON, DOROTHY MILLER (MRS. ALAN ODLE), 1882–1957

4514 **Gawsworth, John,** *pseud.* [1933]: no.687.

4515 **Prescott, Joseph.** 'A preliminary checklist of the periodical publications of Dorothy M. Richardson' *in* Wallace, A. D. and W. O. Ross, *ed.* Studies in honor of John Wilcox. Detroit, 1958. p.219–25.

4516 **Glikin, Gloria.** A checklist of writings by and about Dorothy M. Richardson. Eng Lit Transit 8no1:1–35 '65.
Classified checklist.

RICHARDSON, SAMUEL, 1689–1761
See also under Presses and printing.

4517 **Cordasco, Francesco G. M.** Samuel Richardson, a list of critical studies published from 1896 to 1946. New York, Long Island U.P., 1948. 12p. 24cm. (Eighteenth century bibliographical pamphlets, no.3)

4518 **Thomson, Clara Linklater.** 'Bibliography' *in* Samuel Richardson, a biographical and critical study. London, 1900. p.292–301.

4519 **Sale, William Merritt.** Samuel Richardson, a bibliographical record of his literary career, with historical notes. New Haven, Yale U.P.; London, H. Milford, O.U.P., 1936. xxiv,141p. facsims. 27cm.
Chronol. arrangement of works, and 'books inspired by the publishing of his novels', 90 items, 1736–1804, with reduced TP facsims., collations, and bibliogr. notes.
Rev: TLS 10 Ap '37:270; J. W. Beach J Eng Germ Philol 36:438–42 '37; E. A. Baker Mod Lang R 32:614–15 '37; D. A. Randall Pub Wkly 131:1347–8 '37; Reading & Coll 1:13 '37; A. D. McKillop Mod Lang N 53:218–20 '38; B. C. Nangle Pa Bib Soc Am 31:77–8 '37.

4520 **Dudley, E.,** 1937: no.113.

RIDDELL, CHARLOTTE ELIZABETH LAWSON (COWAN), 1832–1906

4521 **Ellis, Stuart Marsh.** 'List of works by mrs. Riddell' *in* Wilkie Collins, LeFanu and others. London, 1931. p.323–5. (Reissued 1951)

Chronol. checklist of 56 items, 1855–1902, with some bibliogr. notes.

RITSON, JOSEPH, 1752–1803

4522 **Burd, Henry Alfred.** 'A bibliography of the published works of Joseph Ritson' *in* Joseph Ritson, a critical biography. [Urbana] 1916. p.209–13.

4523 **Bronson, Bertrand Harris.** 'A Ritson bibliography' *in* Joseph Ritson, scholar-at-arms. Berkeley, 1938. p.751–802.

Classified chronol. list of works, manuscripts, and ana, with quasifacsim. TP transcrs. collations, some locations of copies, and bibliogr. notes.

RIVERS, AUGUSTINE, 1588–1650?
See Abbot, John.

RIVERS, AUGUSTUS HENRY LANE FOX PITT-, 1827–1900

4524 **Gray, Harold St.George.** 'Bibliographical list of books, pamphlets, articles and papers read before learned societies by . . . Pitt-Rivers . . .' *in* Index to Excavations in Cranborne chase, and King John's house, Tollard royal. . . . Taunton castle, 1905. (Excavation series, v.5) p.[xxxvi]–xliii.

Chronol. checklist of 95 entries, 1858–1900.

RIVERS, JOHN, 1588–1650?
See Abbot, John.

ROBERTS, MORLEY CHARLES, 1857–1942

4525 **Jameson, Margaret Ethel Storm.** Morley Roberts, the last of the true victorians. Lib Chron Univ Pennsylvania 27no2:93–127 '61.

'A check-list of the works of Morley Roberts' (p.124–5).

ROBERTSON, BARTHOLOMEW, fl.1617–1620

4526 **Crow, John.** A thing called Adagia. Library ser5 4:71–3 Je '49.

Quasifacsim. TP transcrs., collations, and bibliogr. notes on 2 ed. of Adagia, by Bartholomew Robertson (or Robinson).

ROBIN HOOD

4527 **Frost, W. A.** Robin Hood romances. N&Q ser11 8:203–4 S '13; H. G. Emery *ib.* ser11 8:297 Oc '13; J. B. McGovern 8:313–14 Oc '13; J. Ardagh 12:170 Jl '15; ser12 1:427 My '16.

4527a **Gable, J. Harris.** Bibliography of Robin Hood. [Lincoln, Neb., 1939] 163p. facsims. 22cm.

Author checklist with locations of copies, and indexes.

ROBINSON, AGNES MARY FRANCES, 1856–1944
See Duclaux, Mary, pseud.

ROBINSON, BARTHOLOMEW, fl.1617–1620
See Robertson, Bartholomew.

ROCHESTER, JOHN WILMOT, 2D EARL OF, 1647–1680
See Wilmot, John, 2d earl of Rochester.

ROGERS, SAMUEL, 1763–1855

4528 **Rycroft, Harry,** Samuel Rogers, 1763–1855: bibliographical notes. Bk Hndbk 1no3:215–18 '47.
Checklist with bibliogr. notes.

4529 **Gilmour, John Scott Lennox.** The early editions of Rogers's Italy. Library ser5 3:137–40 S '48.
Checklist of 6 items, 1822–8, with TP transcrs., collations, and bibliogr. notes.

4530 **Smith, Simon Nowell-.** Samuel Rogers. Human life, 1819. Bk Coll 14no3: 362–5 '65.
Collations and bibliogr. notes on issues of octavo and quarto ed., with locations of copies.

ROLFE, FREDERICK WILLIAM SERAFINO AUSTIN LEWIS MARY ('BARON CORVO'), 1860–1913

4531 **Woolf, Cecil.** Some uncollected authors v: Frederick Rolfe. Bk Coll 4no1:63–8 '55.

4532 —— A bibliography of Frederick Rolfe, baron Corvo. London, R. Hart-Davis, 1957. 136p. illus., port., facsims. 23cm. (Soho bibliographies, VII)
Classified chronol. bibliogr. of books and pamphlets; contribs. to books and pamphlets; contribs. to periodicals; with quasifacsim. TP transcrs. and facsims., collations, and bibliogr. notes.
Rev: P. H. M[uir] Library ser5 12:135–7 '57; N&Q 202:275–6 '57; G. Sims Bk Coll 6:88, 91–2 '57.

4533 **St. Marylebone. Public libraries.** Frederick William Rolfe, baron Corvo; a catalogue prepared on the occasion of a loan exhibition . . . to mark the centenary of his birth. . . . [London, 1960] 10p. 26cm. (Duplicated typescript)
Comp. by Cecil Woolf and T. d'Arch Smith.

ROS, ANNA MARGARET ('AMANDA') (McKITTRICK), d.1939

4535 **Mercer, T. Stanley,** *comp.* 'Amanda M. Ros, a bibliography' *in* Loudan, Jack. O rare Amanda! the life of Amanda McKittrick Ros. London, 1954. p.195–200.

TP transcrs., and some bibliogr. notes on 14 early ed., 1897–1954.

ROSCOE, WILLIAM, 1753–1831

4536 **Mathews, Godfrey W.** [Chronological checklist] *in* William Roscoe, a memoir. London [1931] p.47–52.

4537 **Chandler, George.** 'Books, pamphlets and manuscripts by William Roscoe' *in* William Roscoe of Liverpool. London [1953] p.153–7.

Chronol. checklist, 1770–1853, and ana.

ROSENBERG, ISAAC, 1890–1918

4538 **Leeds. University. Brotherton library.** Isaac Rosenberg, 1890–1918; a catalogue of an exhibition held at Leeds university, May–June, 1959, together with the text of unpublished material. Leeds, University of Leeds with Partridge pr. [1959] 36p. illus. 26cm.

Comp. by Jon Silkin and M. de Sausmarez. 'Catalogue' (p.21–7): 65 items; manuscripts; letters; ptd. works; books owned by Rosenberg, etc.

ROSS, J. H.

See Lawrence, Thomas Edward, afterwards Shaw, 1888–1935.

ROSS, MARTIN, *pseud. of* VIOLET FLORENCE MARTIN, 1865–1915

For works written in collaboration with E. A. Œ. Somerville, see Somerville, Edith Anna Œnone, 1858–1949.

ROSS, SIR RONALD, 1857–1932

4539 **Gawsworth, John,** *pseud.* [1932]: no.686.

4540 **Mégroz, Rodolphe Louis.** 'Bibliography' *in* Ronald Ross, discoverer and creator. London, 1931. p.263–73.

Checklists of works on malaria; mathematics and pathometry; verse and prose.

ROSSETTI, CHRISTINA GEORGINA, 1830–1894

4541 **[Anderson, John Parker]** *comp.* 'Bibliography' *in* Bell, Mackenzie. Christina Rossetti, a biographical and critical study. London, 1898. p.339–51.

Classified checklist of contribs. to periodicals; musical settings; works; and ana.

ROSSETTI, DANTE GABRIEL, 1828–1882

4542 **[Anderson, John Parker]** *comp.* 'Bibliography and catalogue of pictures' *in* Knight, Joseph. Life of Dante Gabriel Rossetti. London, 1887. p.[i]–xviii at end.

4542a **Vaughan, Charles Edward,** 1914: no.4850.

4543 **Prideaux, William Francis.** Additions to the bibliography of the works of Dante Gabriel Rossetti. Bibliographer 2n04:243–7 Ap '03.

Addenda to W. M. Rossetti: *see* next item.

4544 **Rossetti, William Michael.** Bibliography of the works of Dante Gabriel Rossetti. London, Ellis, 1905. 53p. 20cm.

Rev. and enl. from Bibliographer 1n09:420–30 D '02; 2n01:34–44 Ja '03.

Annotated chronol. checklist of 54 separate and periodical contribs., 1843–1904, and 'Books illustrated by Rossetti' and 'Translations from Rossetti' (p.41–5); with discursive bibliogr. notes.

4545 **Giannantonio, Pompeo.** Bibliografia di Gabriele Rossetti, 1806–1958. Firenze, Sansoni antiquariato, 1959. 250p. illus., ports., facsims. 25cm.

Chronol. checklist of 175 works, 1806–1955, and ana, with quasifacsim. TP transcrs. and some facsims., bibliogr. notes, and locations of copies.

ROWE, JOHN, 1626–1677

4546 **Dredge, John Ingle,** 1889–99: no.886.

ROWE, NICHOLAS, 1674–1718

4550 **Sutherland, James Runcieman,** *ed.* 'Bibliography' *in* Three plays . . . by Nicholas Rowe. London, 1929. p.39–[47]

Classified chronol. checklist of plays; poems and miscellaneous works; and contemporary criticisms and pamphlets.

4551 **Jackson, Alfred.** Rowe's edition of Shakespeare. Library ser4 10:454–73 Mr '30.

Quasifacsim. TP transcrs., collations, and bibliogr. discussion of 1709 and 1714 ed.

ROWLANDSON, THOMAS, 1756–1827

4552 **Grolier club,** NEW YORK. Catalogue of books illustrated by Thomas Rowlandson exhibited at the Grolier club. New York [DeVinne pr.] 1916. xiv,109p. 18cm.

4553 —— A catalogue of books illustrated by Thomas Rowlandson together with a collection of original drawings by him, exhibited at the Grolier club. . . . New York [DeVinne pr.] 1916. xv,124p. col.plates. 24cm.

Classified short-title catalogue with bibliogr. notes, of 70 items by or influenced by Rowlandson.

RUSKIN JOHN, 1819–1900

4554 **Wise, Thomas James** and **J. P. Smart.** A complete bibliography of the writings in prose and verse of John Ruskin, with a list of the more important Ruskiniana. London, Ptd. for subscribers only, 1893. (Repr. London, Dawsons, 1964) 2v. port., facsims. 26cm.

Issued in parts, including 'Illustrations to the Bibliography of John Ruskin', 1889–93

Chronol. arrangement of editiones principes; periodical contribs.; and ana, with TP transcrs., collations, and bibliogr. notes.

4555 **Jameson, Mary Ethel.** A bibliographical contribution to the study of John Ruskin. Cambridge [Mass.] Ptd. at the Riverside pr., 1901. viii,154p. port. 20cm.

4556 **Cook, sir Edward Tyas** and **A. D. O. Wedderburn,** *ed.* 'Bibliography' *in* The works of John Ruskin. London; New York, 1903–12. V.38 (1912)
Classified chronol. checklist of works and ana, largely superseding Wise and Smart.

RUSSELL, BERTRAND ARTHUR WILLIAM, 3D EARL RUSSELL, 1872–

4560 **Jacob, Gertrude.** Bertrand Russell, an essay towards a bibliography. Bull Bib 13:198–9 S/D '29; 14:28–30 My/Ag '30.
Classified checklist of works and ana.

RUSSELL, GEORGE WILLIAM, 1867–1935
See Æ., pseud.

RUTHERFORD, MARK, *pseud. of* WILLIAM HALE WHITE, 1831–1913

4560a **Davis, W. Eugene.** William Hale White (Mark Rutherford): an annotated bibliography of writings about him. Eng Lit Transit 10no2,3:97–117, 150–60 '67.

4561 **Smith, Simon Nowell-.** Mark Rutherford, a short bibliography of the first editions. [London] Supplement to The bookman's journal, 1930. 23p. illus., facsims. 24cm.
First issued with Bkmns J ser3 18 '30. Classified list of first English book issues of original works; works ed.; and trans. by; letters; TP transcrs., collations, and some bibliogr. notes.

4562 **Maclean, Catherine Macdonald.** 'The works of Mark Rutherford' *in* Mark Rutherford, a biography of William Hale White. London [1955] p.407–8.

RUTHERFURD, SAMUEL, c.1600–1661

4563 **Bissett, John.** The bibliography of Samuel Rutherfurd. Glasgow Bib Soc Rec 6:79–83 '20.
Chronol. checklist of early ed., 1636–1802; 27 items.

RYE, WALTER, 1843–1929

4564 **Rye, Walter.** 'Bibliography of the works of Walter Rye. . . .' *in* An autobiography of an ancient athlete & antiquary. Norwich, 1916. p.220–6.

4565 —— . . . Bibliography of the works of Walter Rye, all of which are in the local collection. . . . [n.p.] 1916. 7p. 22cm.
Extracted from previous item.

4566 **Stephen, George Arthur.** Walter Rye: memoir, bibliography and catalogue of his Norfolk manuscripts in the Norwich public libraries. Norwich, Norwich public libraries committee, 1929. 32p. 21cm.
Chronol. checklist of books and pamphlets; principal articles, and ana.

RYLE, BP. JOHN CHARLES, 1816–1900

4567 **Catalogue** of publications written by . . . bishop Ryle. Stirling, Drummond's tract depot [1900] 8p. 18cm.
Bookseller's catalogue.

SACHEVERELL, HENRY, 1674?-1764

4567a **Simpson, W. Sparrow.** The Sacheverell controversy. N&Q ser8 5:3-4, 44-5, 102-3, 181-3, 264-5 Ja-Ap '93.

SACKVILLE, CHARLES, 6TH EARL OF DORSET, 1638-1691

4568 **Bagley, Helen Antoinette.** A checklist of the poems of Charles Sackville, sixth earl of Dorset and Middlesex. Mod Lang N 47:454-61 N '32.
Chronol. checklist of 26 items, 1664-1701.

SACKVILLE-WEST, VICTORIA MARY, 1892-1962
See West, Victoria Mary Sackville-.

ST.ALBAN, FRANCIS BACON, BARON VERULAM AND VISCOUNT, 1561-1626
See Bacon, Francis, baron Verulam and viscount St.Alban.

ST.GERMAN, CHRISTOPHER, 1460?-1540

4568a **Thorne, S. E.** St.Germain's Doctor and student. Library ser4 10:421-6 Mr '30.
Discussion and checklist, with bibliogr. notes and refs., of early ed., 1530-1.

SAINT-JOHN, HENRY, 1ST VISCOUNT BOLINGBROKE, 1678-1751

4569 **Sichel, Walter Sydney.** 'Bibliography' in Bolingbroke and his times. London, 1901-2. V.2, p.[456]-7.

4570 **Petrie, sir Charles Alexander.** 'Bolingbroke's works' *in* Bolingbroke. London, 1937. p.362-4.
Sichel's bibliography.

4571 **Barber, Giles.** Some uncollected authors XLI: Henry Saint John, viscount Bolingbroke, 1678-1751. Bk Coll 14no4:528-37 '65.
'Check-list of works by Bolingbroke' (p.531-7): poems; and separate prose works; quasifacsim. TP transcrs., collations, and some bibliogr. notes on 23 items, 1710-54.

SAINTSBURY, GEORGE EDWARD BATEMAN, 1845-1933

4575 **James, W. P.** George Edward Bateman Saintsbury. Eng Illus Mag new ser 30:75-7, 80 Oc '03.
'Bibliography' (p.76, 80): checklist of works, trans., works ed. or introduced by; and ana.

4576 **Bibliographies** of modern authors. George Saintsbury. Lond Merc 1no2:238-9 D '19.
Chronol. checklist, 1866-1917.

SAKI, *pseud. of* HECTOR HUGH MUNRO, 1870-1916

4577 **Drake, Robert.** Selected annotated bibliography of writings about Saki. Eng Fict Transit 5no1:12-26 '62.

SALA, GEORGE AUGUSTUS, 1828-1896

4578 **Straus, Ralph.** 'Check list of separate publications' *in* Sala, the portrait of an eminent victorian. London [1942] p.284-94.
Works wholly, or partially, by Sala, 1847-97, with some bibliogr. notes.

SALTER, JAMES, c.1648–1718

4579 **Dredge, John Ingle,** 1889–99: no.886.

SALTER, JAMES, c.1695–1767

4580 **Dredge, John Ingle,** 1889–99: no.886.

SANDYS, GEORGE, 1578–1644

4581 **Bowers, Fredson Thayer** and **R. B. Davis.** George Sandys, a bibliographical catalogue of printed editions in England to 1700. New York, New York public library, 1950. 53p. 26cm.

Repr. from N.Y. Pub Lib Bull 54:159–81, 223–44, 280–6 Ap–Je '50.
Rev: L. Leary 5th Atlantic Q 50:267–9 '50.

SASSOON, SIEGFRIED LORRAINE, 1886–1967

4582 **Keynes, sir Geoffrey Langdon.** A bibliography of Siegfried Sassoon. London, R. Hart-Davis, 1962. 199p. ports., facsims. 24cm. (Soho bibliographies, x)

Classified chronol. arrangement of poetry and prose; contribs. to books; contribs. to periodicals; with quasifacsim. TP transcrs., collations, and bibliogr. notes.
Rev: R. J. Roberts Bk Coll 11:518, 521 '62; A. Rota Library ser5 18:243–5 S '63.

SAVAGE, RICHARD, d.1743

4583 **Makower, Stanley Victor.** 'The works of Richard Savage' *in* Richard Savage, a mystery in biography. London, 1909. p.332.

Chronol. checklist, 1717–44.

SAVILE, GEORGE, 1ST MARQUIS OF HALIFAX, 1633–1695

4584 **Canney, Margaret Bérengère Campbell,** 1948: no.94.

4585 **Macdonald, Hugh,** *ed.* 'Bibliography' *in* Observations upon a late libel. ... Cambridge, 1940. p.[39]–51.

Quasifacsim. TP transcrs., collations, and some bibliogr. notes on 33 'separate editions of Halifax's writings to 1700'.

SAYERS, DOROTHY LEIGH (MRS. FLEMING), 1893–1957

4586 **Sandoe, James.** Contribution toward a bibliography of Dorothy L. Sayers. Bull Bib 18:76–81 My/Ag '44.

Classified annotated checklist of tales of detection; novels written in collaboration; short stories; plays; verse; works ed. by; works trans. by; articles, letters and lectures; trans. of.

SAYLE, CHARLES EDWARD

4586a **Gray, George John,** 1925: no.47a.

SCHIFF, SYDNEY, 1869?–1944
See Hudson, Stephen, pseud.

SCLATER, WILLIAM, fl.1626–1660

4587 **Dredge, John Ingle,** 1889–99: no.886.

SCOTT, ALEXANDER, 1525?–1584?

4588 **Cranstoun, James,** *ed.* 'Editions of the poems' *in* The poems of Alexander Scott. Edinburgh, 1896. p.xviii–xxii.
Annotated checklist of 10 items.

4589 **Geddie, William,** 1912: no.2034.

SCOTT, JOHN, 1710–1782

4590 **Russell, Norma Hull (Hodgson).** Some uncollected authors XL: John Scott of Amwell, 1710–1782. Bk Coll 14no3:350–60 '65.
'Check-list of works by John Scott of Amwell' (p.355–60): quasifacsim. TP transcrs., collations, bibliogr. notes, and locations of copies; 20 items.

SCOTT, MICHAEL, 1175?–1234?

4595 **Ferguson, John.** Bibliographical notes on the works of Michael Scott. Glasgow Bib Soc Rec 9:75–100 '31.
Checklist of 56 items, with bibliogr. notes and refs., and locations of copies. Ed. by Elizabeth H. Alexander.

SCOTT, SIR WALTER, 1771–1832

4596 **Corson, James Clarkson.** A bibliography of sir Walter Scott, a classified and annotated list of books and articles relating to his life and works, 1797–1940. Edinburgh, Oliver and Boyd, 1943. xv,428p. 24cm.

4597 **Houtchens, Carolyn Washburn,** and **L. H. Houtchens,** *ed.* [1966]: no.2017.

4598 **[Anderson, John Parker]** *comp.* 'Bibliography' *in* Yonge, Charles D. Life of sir Walter Scott. London, 1888. p.[i]–xlix at end.

4598a **C., W. H.** Scott bibliography. N&Q ser8 4:126 Ag '93.
Addenda to Anderson.

4599 **Thomson, John.** Descriptive catalogue of the writings of sir Walter Scott. Philadelphia [J. B. Lippincott] 1898. 106p. 27cm.

4600 **Ball, Margaret.** 'Bibliography' *in* Sir Walter Scott as a critic of literature. New York, 1907. p.147–73. (Repr. Port Washington, N.Y., Kennikat pr. [1966])

4601 **Churchman, Philip H.** and **E. A. Peers.** A survey of the influence of sir Walter Scott in Spain. R Hispanique 55:227–310 Juin '22.
'Bibliography of translations of Scott into Spanish' (p.266–310): chronol. checklist, 1823–1908, with locations of copies and some bibliogr. notes; indexes.

4602 **Caplan, Albert.** The bibliography of sir Walter Scott. Philadelphia, Head of Scott pr. [1928] 44p. facsims. 33cm.

4603 **Worthington, Greville.** A bibliography of the Waverley novels. . . . London, Constable; New York, R. R. Smith [1931] xv,143p. front., facsims. 23cm. (Bibliographia, no.4)

4604 **Catalogue** of the sir Walter Scott exhibition in the National gallery of Scotland, Edinburgh. . . . Edinburgh, T. & A. Constable, 1932. vii,70p. port. 19cm.

4605 **Van Antwerp, William Clarkson.** A collector's comment on his first editions of the works of sir Walter Scott. San Francisco, Gelber, Lilienthal, 1932. 156p. port., facsims. 25cm.

Major Scott collection, now in Pierpont Morgan library.

4606 **Randall, David Anton.** Waverley in America. Coloph new ser 1no1:39–55 '35.

American ed. of Scott's works, 1822–32, with TP transcrs. and bibliogr. notes.

4607 **Stevenson, E. Elizabeth D.,** 1936: no.211.

4608 **Ruff, William.** A bibliography of the poetical works of sir Walter Scott, 1796–1832. Edinburgh Bib Soc Trans 1pt2:99–239 '37.

4609 —— [**Same**]: Additions and corrections. *ib.* 1pt3:277–81 '38.

TP transcrs., collations, locations of copies and bibliogr. notes with distinction of issues, for 192 items, 1796–1828.

Rev: J. W. Carter Pub Wkly 135:1160–1 '39.

4610 —— Cancels in sir Walter Scott's Life of Napoleon. Edinburgh Bib Soc Trans 3pt2:137–51 '54.

Collation of first 2 ed., 1827, with bibliogr. notes.

4611 **Dyson, G.,** 1956: no.115.

4612 **Todd, William Burton.** Scott's Vision of Don Roderick, 1811. Bk Coll 14no4:544 '65.

Distinction, with collation and bibliogr. notes, of 2 ed.

SCOURFIELD, SIR JOHN HENRY, 1808–1876

4615 **Vaughan, Herbert M.** Sir John Henry Scourfield, baronet, and his writings. Welsh Bib Soc J 3:33–8 Ja '26.

'Bibliography' (p.37–8): checklist of 5 works, with notes.

SEAGER, JOHN, fl.1614–1656

4616 **Dredge, John Ingle,** 1889–99: no.886.

SEDLEY, SIR CHARLES, 1639?–1701

4617 **Pinto, Vivian de Sola,** *ed.* 'A bibliography of works by or ascribed to sir Charles Sedley' *in* The poetical and dramatic works of sir Charles Sedley. London, 1928. V.2, p.235–61.

TP transcrs., collations, locations of copies, and some bibliogr. notes on 43 early ed.

SELOUS, EDMUND, fl.1905–1931

4618 **Giffard, N. D.,** 1951: no.128.

SETTLE, ELKANAH, 1648–1724

4619 **Brown, Frank Clyde.** 'An account of Settle's works' *in* Elkanah Settle, his life and works. Chicago, Ill. [1910] p.[75]–133.

Annotated checklists with some locations of copies and bibliogr. notes *passim.*

4620 **Moss, William Edward.** Elkanah Settle, a postscript. Bk Coll Q 14:91–6 Ap/Je '34.

Notes on 11 of Settle's armorial bindings, with chronol. checklist of his eulogistical poems so bound.

4621 **Dunkin, Paul Shaner.** Issues of The fairy queen, 1692. Library ser4 26:297–304 Mr '46.

Quasifacsim. TP transcr., collation, and bibliogr. notes and locations of copies of operative adaptation of Midsummer Night's Dream, attrib. to Settle.

4621a **A list** of works in Guildhall library by or relating to Elkanah Settle, 1648–1724. Guildh Misc 2:418–23 Ag '67.

SHADRACH, AZARIAH, 1774–1844

4622 **Jones, E. D.** The works of Azariah Shadrach, an attempted bibliography. Welsh Bib Soc J 6:68–89 Jl '44.

Chronol. checklist of 21 items, with quasifacsim. TP transcrs.; no collations.

SHAFTESBURY, ANTHONY ASHLEY COOPER, 3D EARL, 1671–1713
See Cooper, Anthony Ashley, 3d earl of Shaftesbury.

SHAKESPEARE, WILLIAM, 1564–1616
Bibliographies of the works of Shakespeare are listed in a separate volume. Other items listed herein referring to him are noted in the Index.

SHARP, SIR CUTHBERT, 1781–1849

4623 **Hill, B. Rowland.** 'A sketch of the life of sir Cuthbert Sharp, with a bibliography of his writings' *in* Sunderland antiquarian society. Antiquities of Sunderland, edited by R. Hyslop. Sunderland, 1910. p.115–32.

'Bibliography' (p.124–31): checklist with some bibliogr. notes.

SHAW, GEORGE BERNARD, 1856–1950

4625 A **continuing** check-list of Shaviana. Shaw Bull 2n04– Ja– '58– .
Comp. by Charles A. Carpenter. (From 2n09 My '59, entitled Shaw R).

4626 **Keough, Lawrence C.** George Bernard Shaw, 1946–1955: a selected bibliography. Bull Bib 22:224–6 S/D '59; 23:20–4, 36–41 Ja/Ap, My/Ag '60.
Principally Shaviana.

4627 **Scott, Clement.** George Bernard Shaw. Eng Illus Mag new ser 29:438–40
Jl '03.
'Bibliography' (p.440).

4628 **Babington, Percy Lancelot.** The bibliography of G. B. Shaw: collation of
The heretics, with notes. Bkmns J 12n046:165 '25.
Addenda to Wells.

4629 **Wells, Geoffrey Harry.** A bibliography of the books and pamphlets of
George Bernard Shaw. Bkmns J 16n07–8:*1–16, 17–32* '27; 17n09: *33–46*
'29.

First pub. in parts as Supplements to Bkmns J 11n041–2, 12n043 '25 (*rf.* his Some additional notes. *ib.* 12n048:241–2 '25); this ed. rev. and issued as Supplements to Bkmns J.
TP transcrs., collations, and some bibliogr. notes on first ed., pamphlets, etc.; and
contribs. to works by others.

4630 **Broad, Charles Lewis** and **V. M. Broad.** A dictionary of plays and novels of
Bernard Shaw, with a bibliography of his works and of the literature con-
cerning him, with a record of the principal Shavian play productions.
London, A. & C. Black [1929] xi,230p. port. 23cm.

4631 **Holmes, sir Maurice Gerald.** Some bibliographical notes on the novels of
George Bernard Shaw, with some comments by Bernard Shaw. London,
Dulau [1929] 19[1]p. 16cm.
'Collations of the four published novels' (p.17–[20]).

4632 **National book league,** LONDON. Bernard Shaw; catalogue of an exhibition.
. . . [London] Published for the National book league by the C.U.P.
[1946] 53p. 21cm.

4633 **Loewenstein, Fritz Erwin.** The rehearsal copies of Bernard Shaw's plays,
a bibliographical study. London, Reinhardt & Evans, 1950. 36p. 24cm.
Chronol. table of 29 items, 1909–49, with some bibliogr. notes.

4634 **New York. Public library. Berg collection.** Bernard Shaw, 1856–1950; an
exhibition from the Berg collection: manuscripts, autograph letters, first
editions, by John D. Gordan. New York, New York public library, 1956.
51p. 26cm.
Repr. from N.Y. Pub Lib Bull 61:117–38, 192–207, 250–9 Mr–My '57.

SHAW, THOMAS EDWARD, formerly LAWRENCE, 1888–1935
See Lawrence, Thomas Edward, afterwards Shaw.

SHEARING, JOSEPH, *pseud.*
See Long, Gabrielle Margaret Vere (Campbell), 1888–1952.

SHELLEY, HARRIET (WESTBROOK), d.1816
4640 **Wise, Thomas James,** 1924: no.4652.

SHELLEY, PERCY BYSSHE, 1792–1822
4641 **Kooistra, J.** Shelley—bibliography, 1908–1922. Eng Stud 4:177–81 Ag '22.

4642 —— [Same]: Supplement. *ib.* 5:79–80 Ap '23.

4643 **Verkoren, L.** A note on the Shelley bibliography, 1908–22. Eng Stud 20:61 Ap '38.

4644 **White, William.** Fifteen years of Shelley scholarship, a bibliography, 1923–38. Eng Stud 21:8–11 F '39.
Includes modern ed.

4645 —— [Same]: Verkoren, L. and W. White. Additions. *ib.* 21:120 Je '39.

4646 **Raysor, Thomas Middleton,** *ed.* 1956: no.20/5.

4647 **London. Guildhall library.** Hand-list of manuscripts, letters, printed books, & personal relics of Percy Bysshe Shelley and his circle, exhibited. . . . London, Blades, East & Blades, 1893. 27p. 17cm.
Comp. by Charles Welch.

4648 **Slicer, Thomas Roberts.** 'An illustrated bibliography of the early writings of Percy Bysshe Shelley' *in* Percy Bysshe Shelley, an appreciation. New York, 1903. p.[55]–82.
Bibliogr. notes drawn largely from H. B. Forman's The Shelley library. London, 1886.

4649 **English association,** 1912: no.650.

4650 **Forman, Harry Buxton.** The library of the late H. Buxton Forman. [New York] 1920. 2v. in 1. facsims. 23cm.
Anderson galleries sale catalogue of 2,228 entries.

4651 **Granniss, Ruth Shepard.** A descriptive catalogue of the first editions in book form of the writings of Percy Bysshe Shelley, based on a memorial exhibition. . . . New York, Grolier club, 1923. xx,133p. facsims. (part fold). 24cm.

4652 **Wise, Thomas James.** A Shelley library, a catalogue of printed books, manuscripts, and autograph letters by Percy Bysshe Shelley, Harriet Shelley and Mary Wollestonecraft Shelley, collected by Thomas James Shelley. London, Ptd. for private circulation only, 1924. xvii,164[2]p. port., facsims. 27cm.
Bibliogr. catalogue substantially repr. from the Ashley library catalogue (no.342) of editiones principes and ana; no index.

4653 **Carlton, William Newnham Chattin.** Shelley's Adonais, 1821. Amer Coll 5:25–31 Oc '27.

4653a **Marsh, George L.** The early reviews of Shelley. Mod Philol 27:73–95 Ag '29.

Annoted chronol. checklist, 1810–26.

4654 **Texas. University. Library.** An account of an exhibition of books and manuscripts of Percy Bysshe Shelley, with something of their literary history, their present condition and their provenance. Austin, Tex., University of Texas, 1935. 40p. port. 22cm.

4655 **Taylor, Charles H.** 'Bibliographical descriptions' *in* The early collected editions of Shelley's Poems, a study in the history and transmission of the printed text. New Haven, 1958. p.89–101.

SHENSTONE, WILLIAM, 1714–1763

4660 **Williams, Iolo Aneurin,** 1924: no.633.

SHEPPARD, JOHN ('JACK'), 1702–1724

4460a **Ellis, Stuart Marsh.** 'Bibliography of Jack Sheppard' *in* Bleackley, Horace W. Jack Sheppard. Edinburgh, 1933. p.127–36.

Classified checklist of newspapers, tracts and biographies, plates, mss., later publications including romances, and ana.

SHERBURNE, SIR EDWARD, 1616–1702

4461 **Van Beeck, F. J.** 'A list of Sherburne's printed works' *in* The poems and translations of sir Edward Sherburne. . . . Assen, 1961. p.145.

Checklist, preceded by 'Bibliographical notes on the 1651 edition'; census of 19 copies, collation, and bibliogr. notes.

SHERIDAN, FRANCES (CHAMBERLAINE), 1724–1766

4662 **Russell, Norma Hull (Hodgson).** Some uncollected authors XXXVIII: Frances Sheridan, 1724–1766. Bk Coll 13no2:196–205 '64.

'Check-list of works by Frances Sheridan' (p.201–5): 13 items, with quasifacsim. TP transcrs., collations, locations of copies, and notes.

SHERIDAN, RICHARD BRINSLEY, 1751–1816

4663 **Anderson, John Parker,** *comp.* 'Bibliography' *in* Sanders, Lloyd C. The life of Richard Brinsley Sheridan. London [1891] p.[i]–xi at end.

4664 **Sichel, Walter Sydney,** *ed.* 'Bibliography of Sheridan's works, published and unpublished' *in* Sheridan. . . . London, 1909. V.2, p.445–59.

4665 **Williams, Iolo Aneurin,** 1924: no.633.

4666 **Rhodes, Raymond Crompton.** Some aspects of Sheridan bibliography. Library ser4 9:233–61 D '28.

'Select bibliographical summary of early editions of Sheridan's plays and poems' (p.260–1).

4667 ——, *ed.* [Bibliographies] *in* The plays & poems of Richard Brinsley Sheridan. Oxford, 1928. 3v.

Checklists after separate works, recording 'every discoverable early edition of the plays and poems'.

4668 —— 'Bibliography' *in* Harlequin Sheridan, the man and the legends. . . . Oxford, 1933. p.283–98.

4669 **Shuttleworth, Bertram.** Early editions of The school for scandal. Theat Notebk 6:4–7 Oc/D '51; 8:23 Oc/D '53.

SHIEL, MATTHEW PHIPPS, 1865–1947

4675 **Gawsworth, John,** *pseud.* [1932]: no.686.

4676 **Morse, Albert Reynolds.** The works of M. P. Shiel, a study in bibliography. . . . Los Angeles, Fantasy publishing co., 1948. xix,170p. illus., ports., facsims. 23cm.

Discursive bio-bibliogr., with 'The personal library of M. P. Shiel' (p.20–3); 'Check list of the various editions of the novels of M. P. Shiel' (p.24–8); 'The collations' (p.29–120); miscellaneous works, mss.; and collaborations.

SHIRLEY, JAMES, 1596–1666

4677 **Nason, Arthur Huntington.** 'Annotated bibliography' *in* James Shirley, dramatist, a biographical and critical study. New York, 1915. p.401–59.

Chronol. checklist of works and ana.

4677a **Stevenson, Allan H.** Shirley's publishers: the partnership of Crooke and Cooke. Library ser4 25:140–51 D/Mr '44/5.

'Plays published by Shirley during his years in Ireland' (p.144).

SHIRLEY, JOHN, fl.1680–1702

4678 **Magaw, Barbara Louise.** The work of John Shirley, an early hack writer. Pa Bib Soc Am 56:332–43 '62.

Chronol. checklist of 20 items, 1681–9.

SHORTER, DORA (SIGERSON), d.1918

4679 **Somerville, Edith Anna Œnone.** Bibliography of Dora Sigerson. Stud 7:144–5 Mr '18.

4680 **[Wise, Thomas James]** The books of Dora Sigerson Shorter (mrs. Clement Shorter). Edinburgh, Ptd. for private circulation, 1924. 7p. 24cm. Covertitle.

Repr. from Ashley library catalogue (no.342). TP transcr. collations, and some bibliogr. notes on works and ana, 1883–1928.

SHOWER, JOHN, 1657–1715

4681 **Dredge, John Ingle,** 1889–99: no.886.

SICKERT, WALTER RICHARD, 1860–1942

4682 **Fawcett, T. C.,** 1961: no.120.

SIDNEY, SIR PHILIP, 1554–1586

4683 **Sommer, H. Oskar,** *ed.* [Bibliographical introduction] *in* The countess of Pembroke's Arcadia, written by sir Philip Sidney. London, 1891. p.[1]–45.
TP facsims. and locations of copies.

4684 **Tannenbaum, Samuel Aaron.** Sir Philip Sidney, a concise bibliography. New York, 1941. ix,69p. 23cm. (Elizabethan bibliographies, no.23)
Classified chronol checklist of works and ana; 1,335 items.

4685 **Riding, J.,** 1948: no.190.

4686 **Oxford. University. Bodleian library.** Sir Philip Sidney, 1554–1586; list of exhibits. . . . [Oxford] 1954. lv.(unpaged) 18cm. Covertitle. (Duplicated typescript)

4687 **Jensen, Bent Juel-.** Some uncollected authors xxxiv: sir Philip Sidney 1554–1586. Bk Coll 11no4:468–79 '62.
'Checklist of editions of Arcadia to 1739' (p.469–79): quasifacsim. TP transcrs., collations, extensive locations of copies, and bibliogr. notes on 15 items.

4688 —— [Same]: *ib.* 12no2:196–201 '63.
Lists miscellaneous works (items 16–28) and addenda and corrigenda to first part.

4689 —— Sidney's Arcadia, London, 1599: a distinguished ghost. *ib.* 16no1:80 '67.

4689a —— Sir Philip Sidney's Arcadia, 1638: an unrecorded issue. Library ser5 22:67–9 Mr '67.

SIMPSON, PERCY, 1865–1962

4690 **A list** of the published writings of Percy Simpson. Oxford, Clarendon pr., 1950. 29p. port. 22cm.
Chronol. checklist, ed. by F. P. Wilson.
Rev: TLS 12 Ja '51:26; G. Tillottson R Eng Stud new ser 2:299 '51; C. J. Sisson Mod Lang R 46:298 '51.

SITWELL, DAME EDITH, 1887–1964

4691 **Rosenberg, Lois D.** Edith Sitwell, a critical bibliography, 1915–1950. Bull Bib 21:40–3 D '53; 21:57–60 Ap '54.

4692 **Gawsworth, John,** *pseud.* [1932]: no.686.

SITWELL FAMILY

4693 **Balston, Thomas.** Sitwelliana, 1915–27, being a handlist of works by Edith, Osbert, and Sacheverell Sitwell. . . . London, Duckworth, 1928. x,24p. 19cm.

4694 **Fifoot, Erik Richard S.** A bibliography of Edith, Osbert, and Sacheverell Sitwell. London, R. Hart-Davis, 1963. 394p. 21cm. (Soho bibliographies, XI)

Classified arrangement of original works; contribs. to books; contribs. to periodicals; unpub. books, translations, musical settings, recordings, of each author separately, with quasifacsim. TP transcrs., collations, and some bibliogr. notes. Based on London university School of librarianship and archives bibliography (*see* no.122).

Rev: TLS 25 Oc '63:876; Pa Bib Soc Am 58:340 '64.

SKEAT, WALTER WILLIAM, 1835–1912

4694a **Skeat, Walter William.** 'Bibliography' *in* Student's pastime. Oxford, 1896. p.[lxxix]–lxxxiv.

Chronol. checklist, rev. and enl. from N&Q ser8 2:241–2 S '92.

4694b —— Bibliography: Walter W. Skeat. N&Q ser11 2:61–2 Jl '10.

SKEFFINGTON, FRANCIS SHEEHY, fl.1916

4695 **O'Hegarty, Patrick Sarsfield,** 1936: no.4109.

SKELTON, JOHN, 1460?–1529

4696 **Whitmee, D. E.,** 1939: no.230.

SLEZER, JOHN, d.1717

4697 **Cameron, James.** A bibliography of Slezer's Theatrum Scotiæ; with an analytical table of the plates by W. Johnston. Edinburgh Bib Soc Proc 3pt3:141–7 Mr '99.

Chronol. list, with collations and notes, of ed. from 1693 to 1874.

SMART, CHRISTOPHER, 1722–1771

4698 **Gray, George John.** A bibliography of the writings of Christopher Smart. ... Bib Soc Trans 6pt2:269–303 Oc/Mr '01/2.

Chronol. checklist of 57 items, 1740–51, with discursive bibliogr. notes, and some locations of copies.

4698a **Jones, Claude Edward.** Christopher Smart, Richard Rolt and The universal visiter. Library ser4 18:212–14 S '37.

Checklist of periodical contribs.

4699 **Brittain, Robert E.** Christopher Smart in the magazines. Library ser4 21:320–36 D/Mr '40/1.

Chronol. checklist of periodical pubs., 1746–1818, with some bibliogr. notes (p.325–36).

SMILES, SAMUEL, 1812–1904

4705 **Sharp, William.** Samuel Smiles, LL.D. Eng Illus Mag new ser 30:292–4 D '03.
'Bibliography' (p.294): checklist of works; works ed. by; and ana.

SMITH, ADAM, 1723–1790

4706 **Franklin, Burt** and **F. G. M. Cordasco.** Adam Smith, a bibliographical checklist; an international record of critical writings and scholarship relating to Smith and Smithian theory, 1876–1950. New York, 1950. 63p. facsim. 23cm. (Burt Franklin bibliographical series, III)

4707 **Harvard. University. Graduate school of business administration. Baker library. Kress library of business and economics.** The Vanderblue memorial collection of Smithiana; an essay by Charles J. Bullock . . . and a catalogue of the collection. Boston, Mass., Baker library, Harvard graduate school of business administration [1939] xiv,68p. port., facsims. 28cm.
Classified short-title catalogue with some bibliogr. notes; no index.

SMITH, ERNEST BRAMAH, 1868–1942
See Bramah, Ernest, pseud,

SMITH, GEORGE CHARLES MOORE, 1858–1940

4708 **A bibliography** of the writings of G. C. Moore Smith. Cambridge, Ptd. for the subscribers at the University pr., 1928. 60p. port. 24cm.
Chronol. checklist, 1895–1928.

SMITH, GOLDWIN, 1823–1910

4709 **Cooper, John James.** Goldwin Smith, D.C.L., a brief account of his life and writings. Reading [Poynder, 1921] 14p. 21cm.
Chronol. checklist, 1845–1909 (p.10–14).

SMITH, JAMES, 1775–1839

4710 **Boyle, Andrew,** *ed.* 'Bibliography' *in* Rejected addresses; or, The new theatrum poetarum. London, 1929. p.177–[82]
Discursive descrs., and collations of early ed.

SMITH, LLOYD LOGAN PEARSALL, 1865–1946

4711 **Bibliographies** of modern authors. Logan Pearsall Smith. Lond Merc 3no16:435–6 F '21.
Chronol. checklist of verse; and prose, 1908–20.

SMITH, PHILIP HENRY PYE-, 1839–1914

4712 **Winston, J. H. E.** . . . Bibliography of the published writings, 1866–1910, of Philip Henry Pye-Smith. [London] 1915. 12p. port. 21cm. (Bibliographies of Guy's men, no.5)
Chronol. checklist.

SMITH, SYDNEY, 1771–1845

4713 **Halpern, Sheldon.** Sydney Smith in the Edinburgh review: a new list. N.Y. Pub Lib Bull 66:589–602 N '62.

Annotated checklist, 1802–28.

4714 **Schneider, Duane B.** Sydney Smith in America to 1900: two check lists. N.Y. Pub Lib Bull 70:538–43 Oc '66.

'A check list of Sydney Smith's works in America to 1900' (p.538–40): chronol. checklist of 26 items, 1809–93; 'A check list of works in America to 1900 about Sydney Smith (p.540–3).

SMOLLETT, TOBIAS GEORGE, 1721–1771

4715 **Cordasco, Francesco G. M.** Smollett criticism, 1770–1924; a bibliography enumerative and annotative. New York, Long Island U.P., 1948. vii,28p. 24cm. ([Eighteenth century bibliographical pamphlets, no.2])

4716 —— Smollett criticism, 1925–1945, a compilation. New York Long Island U.P., 1947. 9p. 24cm. ([Eighteenth century bibliographical pamphlets, no.1])

4717 —— Smollett and the translation of the Don Quixote, a critical bibliography. N&Q 193:383–4 S '48.

Checklist of works, 1755–1926, relating to this question.

4717a **Bouce, P. G.** Smollett criticism, 1770–1924: corrections and additions. N&Q 212:184–7 My '67.

4718 **[Anderson, John Parker]** *comp.* 'Bibliography' *in* Hannay, David. Life of Tobias George Smollett. London, 1887. p.[i]–x at end.

Classified checklist of works and ana, with 'Chronological list of works' (p.x).

4719 **[Isaacs, J. H.]** *comp.* 'Bibliography of Humphry Clinker' *in* Humphry Clinker . . . illustrated by George Cruikshank. London, 1895. p.[vii]–viii.

4720 ——, *ed.* 'A list of Smollett's works, with dates of first issues and bibliographical notes' *in* Roderick Random, by Tobias Smollett. London, 1895. p.[ix]–xii.

'Bibliography of Roderick Random' (p.[xiii]–xv).

4721 **Joliat, Eugène.** 'Bibliographie des traductions de Smollett' *in* Smollett et la France. Paris, 1935. p.[255]–69.

4722 **Cordasco, Francesco G. M.** 'Bibliography' *in* Letters of Tobias Smollett: a supplement to the Noyes collection, with a bibliography of editions of the collected works. Madrid, 1950. p.45–6.

4723 **Newman, Franklin B.** A consideration of the bibliographical problems connected with the first edition of Humphry Clinker. Pa Bib Soc Am 44:340–71 '50.

Distinction of 4 ed., with quasifacsim. TP transcrs., collations, bibliogr. notes including facsims. and points.

4724 **Roper, Derek.** Smollett's four gentlemen: the first contributors to the Critical review. R Eng Stud new ser 10:38–44 F '59.

'Works reviewed by Smollett in the Critical review, 1756' (p.41–3); 'Annotations to volumes I and II of the Critical review in the University of Oregon library' (p.43–4).

SMYTH, AMELIA GILLESPIE, fl.1826–1875

4730 **Strout, Alan Lang.** The anonymous works of mrs. A. Gillespie Smyth. Library ser5 10:208–9 S '55.

Checklist of contribs. to Blackwood's magazine, 1826–9.

SMYTH, RICHARD, fl.1593–1610

4731 **Dredge, John Ingle,** 1889–99: no.886.

SNOW, CHARLES PERCY, BARON SNOW, 1905–

4732 **Stone, Bernard,** *comp.* 'Bibliography' *in* Greacen, Robert. The world of C. P. Snow. [Lowestoft] Scorpion pr. [1962] p.41–64.

Classified checklist of books; contribs. to books; to scientific journals; to periodicals; a selection of contributions to newspapers; dramatisations and broadcasts; ana; a selection of periodical and newspaper criticisms and reviews; and ephemera.

SOMERVILLE, EDITH ANNA ŒNONE, 1858–1949

4733 **Hudson, Elizabeth.** A bibliography of the first editions of the works of E. Œ. Somerville and Martin Ross. . . . New York, Sporting gallery & bookshop, 1942. x,79p. facsims. 20cm.

Chronol. arrangement of early ed.; magazine contribs., etc.; miscellaneous; and coll. ed., with TP transcrs., collations, some locations of copies, and bibliogr. notes; no index.

4734 **Vaughan, Robert,** *comp.* 'The first editions of Edith Œnone Somerville and Violet Florence Martin; a bibliography' *in* Cummins, Geraldine. Dr. E. Œ. Somerville, a biography. London [1952] p.[243]–71.

Chronol. list, 1885–1949, with quasifacsim. TP transcrs., collations, and bibliogr. notes.

SOUTAR, WILLIAM, 1898–1943

4735 **Aitken, William Russell.** William Soutar; bibliographical notes and a checklist. Biblioth 1no2:3–14 '57.

'William Soutar, a chronological checklist' (p.9–14): classified checklist of early ed. and some periodical contribs., and ana.

SOUTHEY, ROBERT, 1774–1843

4736 **Houtchens, Carolyn Washburn** and **L. H. Houtchens,** *ed.* [1966]: no.2017.

4737 **Haller, William.** 'Appendix A: Works of Robert Southey' *in* The early life of Robert Southey, 1774–1803. New York, 1917. p.313–28.

4738 **Zeitlin, Jacob Israel.** Southey's contributions to The critical review. N&Q ser12 4:35–6, 66–7, 94–6, 122–5 F–My '18.

Checklist of 24 items (p.124–5).

4739 **New York. Public library.** First and rare editions of Southey in the library. N.Y. Pub Lib Bull 26:1–5 Ja '22.

Chronol. checklist, comp. by L. Nelson Nichols.

4740 **Curry, Kenneth.** Southey's contributions to the Annual review. Bull Bib 16:195–7 S/D '39.
Checklist by author of book reviewed.

4741 **Bristol. Public libraries.** Robert Southey, 1774–1843; poet and man of letters; lecture and exhibition to commemorate the centenary of his death. [Bristol] 1943. 11p. 19cm.
'Works by and dealing with Robert Southey . . .' (p.5–10).

4742 **Simmons, Jack.** 'List of Southey's works' *in* Southey. London, 1945. p.226–9.
Chronol. checklist of 66 items, 1792–1929.

SOUTHWELL, ROBERT, 1561?–1595

4745 **Janelle, Pierre.** 'Bibliography' *in* Robert Southwell the writer; a study in religious inspiration. New York, 1935. p.[306]–23.
Classified chronol. checklist of works, and direct sources, and ana; with quasifacsim. TP transcrs., locations of copies, and some bibliogr. notes.

4746 **Oxford. University. Bodleian library** [1935]: no.4282.

4747 **Macdonald, James Harold.** The poems and prose writings of Robert Southwell, S.J.; a bibliographical study. Oxford, Ptd. for presentation to members of the Roxburghe club, 1937. xix,161p. facsims. 30cm.
Classified chronol. list of works; manuscripts; attrib. works; and ana; with quasifacsim. TP transcrs., and facsims., collations, locations of copies, and bibliogr. notes and refs.; no index.

SPARROW, ANTHONY, 1612–1685

4748 **Dredge, John Ingle,** 1889–99: no.886.

SPENCE, THOMAS, 1750–1814

4749 **Rudkin, O. D.** Select bibliographies, no. 34. The writings of Thomas Spence. Bull Brit Lib Pol Sci 34:27–34 My '26.
Classified checklist of works.

SPENCER, HERBERT, 1820–1903

4750 **Turnbull, H. G. D.** Herbert Spencer. Eng Illus Mag new ser 29:88, 90 '02.
'Bibliography' (p.88, 90): chronol. checklist.

SPENDER, STEPHEN HAROLD, 1909–

4751 **Texas. University. Humanities research center.** Stephen Spender, 1928–1959; notes for an account of his writings. Austin, 1959. 26p. facsim. 22cm.
Covertitle. (Not seen)

SPENSER, EDMUND, 1552?–1599

4752 **Carpenter, Frederic Ives.** A reference guide to Edmund Spenser. Chicago, Ill., University of Chicago pr.; Cambridge, C.U.P., 1923. (Repr. 1950) vi,333p. 25cm.

4753 **Parrott, Alice.** A critical bibliography of Spenser from 1923–1928. Stud Philol 25:468–90 Oc '28.

4754 **Stephens, Robert F.** A check list of masters' theses on Edmund Spenser. Charlottesville, Va., Bibliographical society of the University of Virginia, 1950. 16p. 17cm. Covertitle.

4755 **McNeir, Waldo Forest** and **F. Provost.** Annotated bibliography of Edmund Spenser, 1937–1960. Pittsburgh, Pa., Duquesne U.P.; Louvain, Editions E. Nauwelaerts, 1962. xxi,255p. 27cm.

4756 **Grolier club,** NEW YORK. Catalogue of an exhibition of the original editionsof the works of Edmund Spenser. . . . [New York, DeVinne pr., 1899] 19cm. 18cm.

4757 **Johnson, Francis Rarick.** A critical bibliography of the works of Edmund Spenser printed before 1700. Baltimore, Johns Hopkins pr., 1933. xiv,61p. facsims. 27cm.

Chronol. bibliogr. with TP transcrs. and facsims., collations, locations of copies, and bibliogr. notes and refs.

Rev: TLS 22 F '34:132; *rf.* F. R. Johnson *ib.* 8 Mr '34:168; W. Fischer Anglia Beibl 45:45–6 F '34; W. L. Renwick Mod Lang R 29:448 '34; A. G. van Kranendonk Eng Stud 16:112–14 '34; C. Slade Sat R Lit 10:497 '34; H. Stein Bk Coll Q 14:79 '34; A. Brandl Archiv 166:103–5 '34; I. A. Williams Lond Merc 29:449 '34; D. Hamer R Eng Stud 11:479–82 '35; C. B. Millican J Eng Germ Philol 34:449–51 '35; H. S. V. Jones Mod Lang N 50:206–7 '35; J. Hoops Eng Studien 74:362–5 '40.

SPRAT, BP. THOMAS, 1635–1713

4758 **Jones, Harold Whitmore** and **A. Whitworth.** Thomas Sprat, 1635–1713, bishop of Rochester; checklist of his works and those of allied writers. [London, Queen Mary college] 1952. [36]p. 26cm. (Duplicated typescript)

Classified chronol. checklist of works; periodical contribs.; doubtful works; and ana; 61 items.

SQUIRE, SIR JOHN COLLINGS, 1884–1958

4759 **Bibliographies** of modern authors. John Collings Squire. Lond Merc 2n09:346–7 Jl '20.

Chronol. checklist of verse and prose, 1909–20.

4760 **Williams, Iolo Aneurin.** Bibliographies of modern authors, no.4. John Collings Squire and James Stephens. London, L. Chaundy, 1922. 13p. 15cm.

For Squire, checklist of English first ed. of verse; prose; and parodies, based on previous item; for Stephens, checklist of English first ed. of prose; and verse, based on list in Lond Merc, 1921: *see* no.4778.

STANHOPE, PHILIP DORMER, 4TH EARL OF CHESTERFIELD, 1694–1773

4761 **Gulick, Sidney Lewis.** A Chesterfield bibliography to 1800. Pa Bib Soc Am 29:1–114 '35.

Classified arrangement of 'books by or about lord Chesterfield from . . . 1773) to 1800', with TP transcrs., collations, locations of copies, and bibliogr. notes.
Rev: TLS 1 F '36:100; R. W. C[hapman] Library ser4 17:120–1 '36.

4762 **Todd, William Burton.** The number, order, and authorship of the Hanover pamphlets attributed to Chesterfield. Pa Bib Soc Am 44:224–38 '50.

Quasifacsim. TP transcrs., collations, locations of copies, and bibliogr. notes with distinction of impressions complementing Gulick.

4763 **Price, Cecil.** The Edinburgh edition of Chesterfield's Letters to his son. Library ser5 5:271–2 Mr '51.

Descr. of 1775 ed. by C. Macfarquhar, supplementing Gulick.

STANLEY, ARTHUR PENRHYN, 1815–1881

4766 **Prothero, Rowland Edmund, baron Ernle,** and **G. G. Bradley.** 'Appendix . . . list of Stanley's publications . . .' *in* The life and correspondence of Arthur Penrhyn Stanley. London, 1893. p.[575]–82. (Also pub. New York, 1894)

Classified list of works and periodical contribs.

STANLEY, THOMAS, 1625–1678

4767 **Flower, Margaret Cameron Coss.** Thomas Stanley, 1625–1678; a bibliography of his writings in prose and verse, 1647–1743. Cambridge Bib Soc Trans 1pt2:139–72 '50.

Quasifacsim. TP transcrs., collations, locations of copies, and bibliogr. notes on 68 items.

STANSBY, CHARLES WALTER, 1886–1945
See Williams, Charles, pseud.

STARK, FREYA MADELINE (MRS. STEWART HENRY PEROWNE), 1893–
4768 **McLorn, M. E. R.,** 1957: no.163.

STARKEY, JAMES SULLIVAN, 1879–
See O'Sullivan, Seamas, pseud.

STATHAM, HENRY HEATHCOTE, 1839–1924
4769 **Statham, M. H.,** 1957: no.209.

STEELE, SIR RICHARD, 1672–1729
4770 **Aitken, George Atherton.** 'Bibliography' *in* The life of Richard Steele. London, 1889. V.2, p.387–428.
Classified checklist of collections; single works; selections; and ana.

4771 **Blanchard, Rae,** *ed.* 'Bibliography' *in* The Christian hero, by Richard Steele. London, 1932. p.[89]–101.
Repr. from Library ser4 10:61–72 Je '29.
Quasifacsim. TP transcrs., collations, locations of copies, and some bibliogr. notes on 22 ed., 1701–1820.

4772 ——, *ed.* 'Pamphlets and papers attributed to Steele' *in* Tracts and pamphlets by Richard Steele. Baltimore, 1944. p.634–5.

4773 ——, *ed.* 'The Englishman, a bibliographical list' *in* The Englishman, a political journal by Richard Steele. Oxford, 1955. p.xvii–xx.
Descr., and locations of copies, of early ed. of first 2 series.

4774 ——, *ed.* 'Bibliographical list' *in* Richard Steele's periodical journalism, 1714–16. Oxford, 1959. p.318–24.
Checklist of early ed. of The lover and the reader; Town-talk; and Chit-chat; with locations of copies and some bibliogr. notes.

STEINGASS, FRANCIS JOSEPH, 1825–1903
4775 **Wright, Thomas.** 'Bibliography of F. Steingass' *in* The life of sir Richard Burton. London, 1906. V.2, p.xi at end.
Chronol. checklist of 5 items, 1882–98.

STEPHEN, SIR JAMES FITZJAMES, 1829–1894
4776 **Stephen, sir Leslie.** 'Bibliographical note' *in* The life of sir James Fitzjames Stephen. . . . London, 1895. p.[483]–6.
Checklist of books and periodical contribs.

STEPHEN, SIR LESLIE, 1832–1904
4777 **Gosse, sir Edmund William.** Sir Leslie Stephen. Eng Illus Mag new ser 30:182–4, 186 N '03.

STEPHENS, JAMES, 1882–1950
4778 **Bibliographies** of modern authors. James Stephens. Lond Merc 4n020:193 Je '21.

4779 **Williams, Iolo Aneurin,** 1922: no.4760.

4780 **Saul, George Brandon.** James Stephens' contributions to The Irish review. Pa Bib Soc Am 46:398–9 '52.

Chronol. checklist, 1911–14, with some bibliogr. notes.

4781 —— 'Crutches towards Stephens, a tentative James Stephens check list' *in* Stephens, Yeats, and other Irish concerns. New York, 1954. p.42–5.

Repr. from N.Y. Pub Lib Bull 57:175–81 Ap '53; 58:94–7 F '54.

Chronol. checklist of works and ana; 'A descriptive account of James Stephens' contributions to Sinn Féin' (p.30–6).

4782 **Black, Hester Mary.** A check-list of the first editions of works by James Stephens and George Moore. Trinity Coll Dublin Ann Bull 4–11 '55.

4783 **Bramsbäck, Birgit.** James Stephens, a literary and bibliographical study. Uppsala, A–B Lundequista bokhandeln [etc.] 1959. 209p. port., facsims. 23cm.

'Part II: Printed sources': classified chronol. checklist of separate pubs.; contribs. to books; contribs. to periodicals and newspapers; and ana.

4784 **McFate, Patricia.** The publication of James Stephens' short stories in The nation. Pa Bib Soc Am 58:476–7 '64.

Supplements Bramsbäck.

4785 **Pyle, Hilary A.** 'Bibliography' *in* James Stephens, his work and an account of his life. London [1965] p.183–91.

Classified chronol. checklist of pubs.; periodical contribs.; criticism by; BBC broadcasts by; and ana.

STEPHENS, WILLIAM, 1692?–1731
4786 **Dredge, John Ingle,** 1889–99: no.886.

STERNE, LAURENCE, 1713–1768
4787 **Thurley, R. L.,** 1939: no.222.

4788 **Cordasco, Francesco G. M.** Laurence Sterne, a list of critical studies from 1896 to 1946. New York, Long Island U.P., 1948. 13p. 24cm. (Eighteenth century bibliographical pamphlets, no.4)

4789 **Hartley, Lodwick Charles.** Laurence Sterne in the twentieth century; an essay and a bibliography of Sternean studies, 1900–1965. Chapel Hill, University of North Carolina pr. [1966] x,189p. 24cm.

'Bibliography' (p.[75]–180).

Rev: H. H. Campbell Pa Bib Soc Am 60:383–8 '66.

4790 **Cross, Wilbur Lucius.** 'A descriptive bibliography of Sterne's manuscripts and published works' *in* The life and times of Laurence Sterne. New York, 1909. p.524–37.

4791 —— [Same]: New ed. New Haven, 1925. V.2, p.[265]–98.

4792 —— [**Same**]: 3d ed., with alterations and additions. New Haven, 1929. p.[596]–618.

Chronol. arrangement of early ed., 1741–1923, with TP transcrs., and some facsims., and some bibliogr. notes.

4793 **Birley, P.**, 1939: no.85.

4794 **Oates, John Claud Trewhard.** Notes on the bibliography of Sterne. Cambridge Bib Soc Trans 2pt2:155–69 '55.

TP facsims., collations, and bibliogr. notes with distinction of issues, and locations of copies examined.

4794a **Fluchère, Henri Auguste E.** 'Bibliographie' *in* Laurence Sterne, de l'homme à l'œuvre. Paris, 1961. p.[655]–93.

Classified checklist of works and ana. Trans. with title: Laurence Sterne from Tristram to Yorick. London, 1965. The bibliogr. (p.449–50) is abbreviated.

STEVENSON, ROBERT LOUIS, 1850–1894

4795 **Wood, Arnold.** Robert Louis Stevenson; first editions and some early pamphlets in the library of Arnold Wood. New York, Privately ptd., 1898. [27]l. illus., facsims. 17cm.

Collection sold in 1946: *see* no.4810.

4796 **Williamson, George Millar.** Catalogue of a collection of the books of Robert Louis Stevenson in the library of George M. Williamson. . . . Jamaica, N.Y., 1901. [96]p. port., facsims. 26cm. (Not seen)

4797 **Prideaux, William Francis.** A bibliography of the works of Robert Louis Stevenson. London, F. Hollings; New York, Scribners, 1903. xvi,300p. port., facsims. 23cm.

See no.4805.

4798 **Keogh, Andrew,** 1910: no.662.

4799 **Harvard university. Library. Widener collection.** A catalogue of the books and manuscripts of Robert Louis Stevenson in the library of the late Harry Elkins Widener, with a memoir by A. S. W. Rosenbach. Philadelphia, Privately ptd., 1913. xi,266p. facsims. 29cm.

Collection bequeathed to Harvard university.

4800 **Slater, John Herbert.** Robert Louis Stevenson, a bibliography of his complete works. London, G. Bell, 1914. vii,45p. 20cm.

4801 **Gerhardt, C. and co., bksllrs.,** NEW YORK. . . . Robert Louis Stevenson; catalogue. . . . New York [1915] 36p. 21cm. Covertitle.

4802 **Grolier club,** NEW YORK. First editions of the works of Robert Louis Stevenson 1850–1894, and other Stevensoniana exhibited at the Grolier club. New York, 1915. xxiii,87p. facsims.(1 col). 24cm.

4803 —— [**Same**]: [Anr. issue, with slightly different title.] vi,74p. 18cm.

4804 **Hill, Walter M.** Robert Louis Stevenson; catalogue of a remarkable collection of first editions. . . . Chicago, 1916. 88p. illus., facsims. 24cm.

4805 **Prideaux, William Francis.** A bibliography of the works of Robert Louis Stevenson. New and rev. ed., ed. and supplemented by mrs. Luther S. Livingston. London, F. Hollings, 1917. viii,400p. illus., port., facsims. 23cm.

Classified chronol. arrangement of works and ana, with TP transcrs., collations, and bibliogr. notes.

4806 **Colgate, Henry A.** The Stevenson library of Henry A. Colgate . . . to be sold by auction. . . . New York, Anderson galleries, 1928. 58p. illus., facsims. 23cm.

4807 **Literary anniversary club of San Francisco.** Robert Louis Stevenson; catalogue of the Stevenson exhibition . . . displayed in the San Francisco public library. . . . [n.p., San Francisco] 1932. 22p. illus. 18cm.

4808 **West, William.** English and American first editions, including the remarkable collection of R. L. Stevenson writings. . . . New York, Parke-Bernet galleries, 1943. 77p. facsims. 25cm.

4809 **A Stevenson** exhibition. Colby Lib Q ser1 9:139–41 Ja '45.

Checklists of limited ed.

4810 **Wood, Arnold.** Unrestricted auction sale . . . including the Arnold Wood collection of Robert Louis Stevenson . . . Van Brink galleries. . . . New Rochelle, N.Y. [1946] [16]l. 23cm.

4811 **Osborne, Charles Glidden.** Catalogue of . . . collection of the writings of Robert Louis Stevenson . . . sold by auction by messrs. Sotheby. . . . [London, 1949] 2pts. illus., facsims. 25cm.

Sold on 9 My '49 and 14 N '49.

4812 **Edinburgh. Public libraries.** Robert Louis Stevenson, 1850–1894; catalogue of the Stevenson collection in the Edinburgh room. . . . [Edinburgh] Public libraries committee, 1950. 36p. illus. 23cm.

4813 **Yale university. Library.** A Stevenson library; catalogue of a collection of writings by and about Robert Louis Stevenson formed by Edwin J. Beinecke, compiled by George Leslie McKay. New Haven, 1951–64. 6v. illus., ports., facsims. 26cm.

Partial contents: v.1–2 Printed books, pamphlets, broadsides, etc.—6. Addenda & corrigenda.

STODDON, SAMUEL, d.1705

4815 **Dredge, John Ingle,** 1889–99: no.886.

STOKES, WILLIAM, 1804–1878

4816 **Stokes, sir William.** 'Bibliography' *in* William Stokes, his life and works, by his son. London, 1898. p.243–7.
Classified checklist of books, articles, lectures and addresses.

STRACHEY, GILES LYTTON, 1880–1932

4817 **Kallich, Martin.** Lytton Strachey; an annotated bibliography of writings about him. Eng Fict Transit 5no3:1–77 '62.

4818 **Sanders, Charles Richard.** 'A chronological check list of Lytton Strachey's writings' *in* Lytton Strachey; his mind and art. New Haven; London, 1957. p.355–66.
Books and periodical contribs., 1901–38, expanded from Mod Philol 44:189–92 F '47.

STRODE, WILLIAM, 1602–1644

4819 **Dredge, John Ingle,** 1889–99: no.886.

STRONG, LEONARD ALFRED GEORGE, 1896–1958

4820 **Gawsworth, John,** *pseud.* [1933]: no.687.

STRYPE, JOHN, 1643–1737

4821 **Wire, A. P.** 'A bibliography of works by John Strype' *in* John Strype, F.S.A., the Leyton antiquary and historian. Leyton [1902] p.13–15.
Checklist.

STUBBS, BP. WILLIAM, 1825–1901

4822 **Shaw, William Arthur,** 1903: no.2918.

STURT, JOHN, fl.1809–1820

4823 **Hazen, Allen Tracy.** J. Sturt, facsimilist. Library ser4 25:72–9 Je/S '44.
Checklist of 17 items (p.75–9) with bibliogr. notes; *rf.* Hugh Macdonald *ib.* ser4 26:307–8 Mr '46.

SUCKLING, SIR JOHN, 1609–1641

4824 **Yeo, C. M.,** 1948: no.239.

SUMMERS, ALPHONSE MONTAGUE JOSEPH-MARY AUGUSTUS, 1880–1948

4825 **Smith, Timothy d'Arch.** A bibliography of the works of Montague Summers. London, N. Vane, 1964. 164p. illus., port., facsims. 23cm.
Classified bibliogr. of separate and contrib. works, with quasifacsim. TP transcrs., collations, bibliogr. notes, with chronol. conspectus (p.137–48).
Rev: TLS 23 Jl '64:656; Pa Bib Soc Am 59:85–6 '65.

SURREY, HENRY HOWARD, EARL OF, 1517?–1547
See Howard, Henry, earl of Surrey.

SWIFT, JONATHAN, 1667–1745

4826 **Landa, Louis A.** and **J. E. Tobin.** . . . Jonathan Swift; a list of critical studies published from 1895 to 1945. . . . New York, Cosmopolitan science and art service, 1945. 62p. 19cm. (Eighteenth century bibliographical pamphlets [2])

4826a **Lamont, Claire.** 'A checklist of critical and biographical writings on Jonathan Swift, 1945–65' *in* Jeffares, A. N., *ed.* Fair liberty was all his cry . . . London; New York, 1967. p.[356]–91.

4826b **Stathis, James J.** A bibliography of Swift studies, 1945–1965. Nashville, Vanderbilt U.P., 1967. xi,110p. 24cm.

4827 **Jackson, W. Spencer,** *comp.* 'Bibliography of the writings of Jonathan Swift' *in* Scott, Temple, *ed.* The prose works of Jonathan Swift. London, 1908. V.12, p.[107]–241.

4828 **Hubbard, Lucius Lee.** Contributions towards a bibliography of Gulliver's travels, to establish the number and order of issue of the Motte editions of 1726 and 1727, their relative accuracy and the source of the changes made in the Faulkner edition of 1735; with a list of editions in a private collection and twenty-five plates. Chicago, W. M. Hill, 1922. xiii,189p. illus., facsims. 22cm.

'List of editions of Gulliver's tales, mainly from a private collection' (p.[125]–89) followed by 25 facsims.

4829 **Eddy, William Alfred.** 'Gulliveriana; a chronological list of all the imitations of Gulliver's travels, of the 18th century' *in* Gulliver's travels, a critical study. Princeton; London, 1923. p.[201]–3.

4830 **Williams, sir Harold,** *ed.* 'Collations and notes' *in* Gulliver's travels by Jonathan Swift. London, 1926. p.[lxxxiii]–cii.

4831 **White, Newport Benjamin.** Bibliography of dean Swift. TLS 9 Je '27:408. Addenda to Jackson: no.4827.

4832 **Dobell, Percy John.** A catalogue of xviiith century verse and a catalogue of books by and relating to dr. Jonathan Swift. London [P. J. & A. E. Dobell] 1933. 168, 29p. 24cm.

Reissue in lv. of Dobell's catalogues no.99, 102, 122, 128, 133, and 105.

4833 **Davis, Herbert John,** *ed.* 'Collations' *in* The drapier's letters to the people of Ireland . . . by Jonathan Swift. Oxford, 1935. p.lxxxi–xcv.

See also 'Other pamphlets and broadsides in prose concerning Wood's coinage' (p.[352]–73); 'Verse written by, or attributed to, the Drapier, etc.' (p.[374]–83);' Imitations of the Drapier's letters' (p.[384]–7).

4834 **Dublin. University. Trinity college. Library.** Catalogue of the exhibition held in the library . . . to commemorate the bicentenary of the death of Jonathan Swift. Dublin, Ptd. at the University pr. by Ponsonby and Gibbs, 1945. 16p. 17cm.

4835 **Teerink, Herman.** A bibliography of the writings in prose and verse of Jonathan Swift, D.D. The Hague, M. Nijhoff, 1937. xi,434p. 26cm.

See no.4842.

4835a **Rothschild, Nathaniel Mayer Victor, baron Rothschild.** The publication of the first Drapier letter. Library ser4 19:107–15 Je '38.

'Appendix A' (p.122–13): quasifacsim. TP transcrs., collations, bibliogr. notes and locations of copies for 6 early ed., supplementing Davis.

4836 **Cambridge. University. Library.** A catalogue of printed books and manuscripts by Jonathan Swift, D.D., exhibited in the Old schools . . . to commemorate the 200th anniversary of his death. . . . Cambridge, C.U.P., 1945. 44p. 18cm. Covertitle.

Comp. by John D. Hayward largely from the collections of lord Rothschild and sir Harold Williams.

4837 **Wiley, Autrey Nell.** Jonathan Swift, 1667–1745; an exhibition of printed books at the University of Texas. . . . [Austin, University of Texas pr., 1945] 48p. 26cm.

4838 **Craig, Maurice James,** *comp.* 'Short catalogue of the exhibition held in the Royal college of physicians in Ireland . . .' *in* Dublin. St.Patrick's hospital. The legacy of Swift, a bi-centenary record . . . [Dublin] 1948. p.49–70.

4839 **Teerink, Herman.** Swift's Discourse . . . contests . . . Athens and Rome, 1701. Library ser5 4:201–5 '49.

4840 **Todd, William Burton.** Another attribution to Swift. Pa Bib Soc Am 45:82–3 '51.

Descr. of 2 issues of Taste, an essay, 1732, 1739.

4841 **Smith, David Nichol,** *comp.* 'List of editions' *in* Guthkelch, Adolph C. L. and D. N. Smith, *ed.* A tale of a tub . . by Jonathan Swift. 2d ed. Oxford, 1958. p.lxv–lxxvii. (First ed. 1920)

4842 **Teerink, Herman.** A bibliography of the writings of Jonathan Swift. 2d ed., rev. and corr. Ed. by Arthur H. Scouten. Philadelphia, University of Pennsylvania pr. [1964] xviii,453p. illus., facsims. 26cm.

Substantially rearranged classified chronol. bibliogr. first pub. 1937 of works to 1814; biography and criticism, 1709–1895, with 'Table of location of Teerink numbers' (p. xi–xvi); quasifacsim. TP transcrs., collations, locations of copies and bibliogr. notes; title index only.

Rev: D. P. French Bks Abroad 38:317 '64; Bull Bib 24:61 '64; D. F. Foxon Bk Coll 13:379–80 '64; TLS 27 My '65:424; H. Davis Library ser5 22:75–9 '67.

4843 **Weedon, Margaret J. P.** An uncancelled copy of the first collected edition of Swift's Poems. Library ser5 22:44–56 Mr. '67.

Discursive descr., with 'Summary table of cancellations' (p.46–7).

SWINBURNE, ALGERNON CHARLES, 1837–1909

4845 **Faverty, Frederic Everett,** *ed.* 1956: no.2016.

4846 **Wise, Thomas James.** 'A bibliographical list of the scarcer works and uncollected writings of Algernon Charles Swinburne' *in* Nicoll, sir William
R. and T. J. Wise. Literary anecdotes of the nineteenth century. London,
1895–6. V.2 (1896), p.291–374.

4847 —— [Same]: London, Ptd. only for private subscribers, 1897. 112p. illus.,
facsims. 22cm.

4848 **Powell, F. York.** Algernon Charles Swinburne. Eng Illus Mag new ser
29:84, 90, 213–14 Ap,My '03.
'Bibliography' (p.84, 90, 213–14).

4849 **Thomson, Joseph Charles.** Bibliographical list of the writings of Algernon
Charles Swinburne. Wimbledon, J. Thomson, 1905. 48p. 20cm.

4850 **Vaughan, Charles Edward.** Bibliographies of Swinburne, Morris and
Rossetti. [London] 1914. 12p. 25cm. (English association. Pamphlet, no.
29)

4851 **Gosse, sir Edmund William.** A catalogue of the works of Algernon Charles
Swinburne in the library of mr. Edmund Gosse. London, Privately ptd.
at the Chiswick pr., 1919. 17p. 17cm.

4852 **Wise, Thomas James.** A bibliography of the writings in prose and verse of
Algernon Charles Swinburne. London, Ptd. for private circulation only
by R. Clay, 1919–20. 2v. illus., ports., facsims. 23cm.

4853 **Livingston, Flora Virginia (Milner).** Swinburne's proof sheets and American
first editions; bibliographical data relating to a few of the publications
of Algernon Charles Swinburne, with notes on the priority of certain
claimants to the distinction of editio princeps. Cambridge, Mass.,
Privately ptd., 1920. 30[2]p. facsims. 22cm.

4854 **Butler, Edward K.** A catalogue of first editions of the works of Algernon
Charles Swinburne in the library of Edward K. Butler. Boston, Privately
ptd., 1921. 25p. port., facsims. 25cm.

4855 **[Danielson, Henry]** Privately printed works of Swinburne. Bkmns J
4n093:244–5 '21.
Chronol. table of works classified by publisher, with brief bibliogr. details, including no.
of copies ptd., comp. from Wise (no.2852).

4856 **Wise, Thomas James.** A Swinburne library; a catalogue of printed books,
manuscripts, and autograph letters by Algernon Charles Swinburne,
collected by Thomas James Wise. London, Ptd. for private circulation
only, 1925. xiv,295[2]p. illus., ports., facsims. 26cm.

4857 ——, *comp.* A bibliography of the writings in prose and verse of Algernon Charles Swinburne *in* Gosse, sir Edmund W. and T. J. Wise, *ed.* The complete works of . . . Swinburne. London; New York, 1927. V.20 (xii,573p.)

Rev. ed. without facsims. of no.4852. Classified chronol. arrangement of editiones principes; periodical contribs.; coll. ed.; ana; works wrongly attrib. to Swinburne; with TP transcrs., collations, and bibliogr. notes.

4858 **Brooklyn. Public library.** Atalanta in Calydon, by Algernon Charles Swinburne, an exhibition containing books and manuscript material relating to Atalanta and to other Swinburne writings including Swinburneiana, from the collection of Evelyn & Lowell Kerr. . . . Brooklyn, N.Y., 1965. 31p. illus., facsims. 21cm.

SYMONDS, JOHN ADDINGTON, 1840–1893

4859 **Babington, Percy Lancelot.** Bibliography of the writings of John Addington Symonds. London, J. Castle, 1925. xi,244p. facsim. 23cm.

Classified chronol. arrangement of editiones principes; books ed. or contrib. to; periodical contribs.; later ed.; American issues; European translations; and ana, with TP transcrs., collations, and bibliogr. notes.

Rev: TLS 24 D '25:900; A. W. P[ollard] Library ser4 6:397–9 '26.

SYMONS, ARTHUR, 1865–1945

4860 **Danielson, Henry,** 1921: no.680.

4861 **Welby, Thomas Earl.** 'Bibliographical note' *in* Arthur Symons, a critical study. London, 1925. p.141–[8]

Classified checklist of works; trans. by; works ed. or introduced by; and ana.

4862 **Scarlett, O. W.,** 1958: no.194.

SYNGE, JOHN MILLINGTON, 1871–1909

4863 **Bourgeois, Maurice.** 'General bibliography. (i) Synge's works' *in* John Millington Synge and the Irish theatre. London, 1913. p.251–96.

4864 **MacManus, Michael Joseph.** A bibliography of books written by John Millington Synge. Dublin, Ptd. for the author by A. Thom, 1930. 7l. 24cm.

Repr. from Dublin Mag new ser 5:47–51 Oc/D '30.

4865 **O'Hegarty, Patrick Sarsfield.** Some notes on the bibliography of J. M. Synge, supplemental to Bourgeois and MacManus. Dublin Mag new ser 17:56–8 Ja/Mr '42.

O'Hegarty's collection is now in the University of Kansas library.

4866 **Mulcahy, B.,** 1951: no.176.

4867 **Black, Hester Mary.** A check list of first editions of works by John Millington Synge and George William Russell. Trinity Coll Dublin Ann Bull 4–9 '56.

4868 **Dysinger, Robert E.** The John Millington Synge collection at Colby college: a check list. Colby Lib Q ser4 9:166–72 F '57; additions 10:192–4 My '57.

4869 Dublin. University. Trinity college. Library. John Millington Synge, 1871–1909; a catalogue of an exhibition held at Trinity college library, Dublin, on the occasion of the fiftieth anniversary of his death. Dublin, Friends of the library of Trinity college, 1959. 38p.+2p. addenda sheet. facsims. 22cm.

Classified catalogue of 96 items, including books and periodical contribs., with quasi-facsim. TP transcrs. and facsims., collations, and bibliogr. notes; comp. by Ian S. MacPhail.

4870 MacPhail, Ian Shaw. John Millington Synge: some bibliographical notes. Irish Bk 1no1:3–10 '60.

Discussion of bibliogr. problems in mounting Trinity college exhibition.

TALFOURD, SIR THOMAS NOON, 1795–1854

4875 **Coles, William A.**, 1958: no.4259.

TARGETT, JAMES HENRY, d.1913

4876 **Wale, William.** . . . Bibliography of the published writings of James Henry Targett. [London] 1913. 8p. port. 21cm.

Repr. with add. from Guy's Hosp Gaz 1913; chronol. checklist.

TAYLOR, BP. JEREMY, 1613–1667

4877 **Hardy, Robert Gathorne-,** *comp.* 'A bibliography of Jeremy Taylor' *in* Smith, L. Logan P., *ed.* The golden grove; selected passages from the sermons and writings of Jeremy Taylor. Oxford, 1930. p.[297]–330. (Repr. Oxford, 1955)

Classified arrangement of 43 authentic books; first ed. contrib. to; attrib. works; obituary pamphlets; and ana, with quasifacsim. TP transcrs., collations, and some bibliogr. notes.

4878 **Stranks, Charles James.** 'Taylor's works' *in* The life and writings of Jeremy Taylor. London, 1952. p.[297]–300.

TAYLOR, JOHN, 1578–1653

4879 **Johnston, William.** A bibliography of the thumb bibles of John Taylor the water poet. Aberdeen, Ptd. at the University pr., 1910. 13p. facsims. 26cm.

Repr. from Edinburgh Bib Soc Pub 9:73–85 '10.

4880 **Stone, Wilbur Macey.** 'An attempt toward a list of editions' *in* The thumb bible of John Taylor. Brookline, Mass., 1928. p.48–68. (Not seen)

Repr. from Am Coll 5:46–59 '28.

TAYLOR, THOMAS, 1758–1835

4881 **Axon, William Edward Armytage.** Thomas Taylor the platonist, a biographical and bibliographical sketch. London, For private circulation, 1890. 15p. 22cm.

Repr. from Library 2:245–50, 292–300 Jl, Ag '90. [Checklist] (p.10–14).

4882 **Balch, Ruth.** Thomas Taylor the platonist, 1758–1835: list of original works and translations compiled for use in the Newberry library. Chicago, 1917. 34p. 27cm. (Duplicated typescript)

Chronol. checklist, 1780–1917.

TAYLOR FAMILY

4883 **Watkins, D. G.**, 1936: no.226.

4884 **Harris, G. Edward.** Contributions towards a bibliography of the Taylors of Ongar and Stanford Rivers. London, C. Lockwood, 1965. xii,65p. facsims. 23cm.

TP transcrs., collations and bibliogr. notes on early ed., principally of children's literature.

Rev: TLS 14 Oc '65:928; Pa Bib Soc Am 59:468 '65.

TEMPLE, SIR WILLIAM, 1628–1699

4884a **Woodbridge, Homer Edwards.** 'Bibliography' *in* Sir William Temple, the man and his work. New York, 1940. p.334–44.
Classified checklist of works and ana.

TENNIEL, SIR JOHN, 1820–1914

4884b **F., C.** Tenniel's book-illustrations. N&Q ser12 4:237–8 S '18.
Chronol. checklist of 36 items, 1845–81.

TENNYSON, ALFRED, 1ST BARON TENNYSON, 1809–1892

4885 **Brooklyn. Public library.** Alfred Tennyson, 1809–1892; a list of books with references to periodicals in the Brooklyn public library. Brooklyn, N.Y. 1909. 19p. 16cm.

4886 **Faverty, Frederic Everett,** *ed.* 1956: no.2016.

4887 **[Shepherd, Richard Herne]** The bibliography of Tennyson; a bibliographical list of the published and privately-printed works of Alfred (lord) Tennyson . . . by the author of Tennysoniana. London, 1896. vii,88p. 19cm.

4888 **Grolier club,** NEW YORK. A chronological list of the works of Alfred, lord Tennyson . . . exhibited at the Grolier club. [New York] 1897. 24p. 19cm.

4889 **Collins, John Churton,** *ed.* 'Bibliography of the Poems of 1842' *in* The early poems of Alfred lord Tennyson. London, 1900. p.315–17.

4890 **[Livingston, Luther Samuel]** Bibliography of the first editions in book form of the works of Alfred, lord Tennyson; the description of a set brought together . . . with notes referring to items not included in the set. New York, Dodd, Mead, 1901. ix,95p. illus., port., facsim. 25cm.
The collection is now in the Pierpont Morgan library, N.Y.

4891 **Thomson, Joseph Charles.** Bibliography of the writings of Alfred lord Tennyson. Wimbledon, J. Thomson; New York, G. E. Stechert, 1905. (Repr. London, H. Pordes, 1967) 72p. 17cm.

4892 **[Wise, Thomas James]** A bibliography of the writings of Alfred, lord Tennyson. London, Ptd. for private circulation, 1908. 2v. port., facsims. 24cm.
TP transcrs. and facsims., collations, and bibliogr. notes on editiones principes; periodical contribs.; ptd. issues; coll. ed.; and ana; no index.

4893 **Fine art society,** LONDON. Tennyson centenary exhibition: catalogue. London, 1909. 43p. 17cm.

4894 **Bowden, Marjorie Moreland.** 'Bibliography' *in* Tennyson in France. [Manchester] 1930. p.155–7.
Checklists of 'English texts of Tennyson published in France' (p.155–6); 'Translations of Tennyson' (p.156–7).

4895 **Adkins, Nelson Frederick.** Tennyson's Charge of the heavy brigade; a bibliography. N&Q 167:189 S '34; *rf.* Olybrius *ib.*167:266 Oc '34.
Wise addendum.

4896 **Eidson, John Olin.** 'American editions of Tennyson's Poems, 1827–1858' *in* Tennyson in America; his reputation and influence from 1827 to 1858. Athens [Ga.] 1943. p.[153]–62.
Classified checklist of complete poems and individual works, with some locations of copies and bibliogr. notes. See also 'Tennyson items in American literary annuals and gift books, 1827–1858' (p.[163]–6); 'Reviews of Tennyson's poems in American magazines and newspapers, 1827–1858' (p.[167]–82).

4897 **Texas. University. Library.** An exhibition of manuscripts and printed books at the University of Texas ... Alfred, lord Tennyson, 1809–1892. By Fannie E. Ratchford. Austin, Tex., 1944. 20p. 23cm.

4897a **B., A. C.** Extant copies of Tennyson's Timbuctoo, 1829. Bk Coll 7no3:296 '58.
Checklist of 6 copies with bibliogr. notes.

4898 **Virginia. University. Library.** The Tennyson collection presented to the University of Virginia in honor of Edgar Finley Shannon, jr. Charlottesville, Va., University of Virginia pr. [1961] 52p. facsims. 24cm.
Based on the Templeton Crocker collection.

4899 **Collins, Rowland L.** Tennyson's original issue of Poems, reviews, etc., 1842–1886: a compilation by Henry van Dyke. Princeton Univ Lib Chron 24no1:39–50 '63.
Account of Van Dyke collection in Princeton library, with 'First publications of poems in periodicals' (p.47).

4900 **Lincoln. City libraries, museum, and art gallery.** Tennyson collection, Usher gallery, Lincoln, with foreword and annotations by sir Charles Tennyson. Lincoln, 1963. 34p. illus., ports. 25cm.

4901 **Paden, W. D.** Tennyson's The lover's tale, R. H. Shepherd, and T. J. Wise. Stud Bib 18:111–45 '65.
Extended discussion, with descrs. of 4 issues and locations of copies.

THACKERAY, WILLIAM MAKEPEACE, 1811–1863

4905 **Brooklyn. Public library.** William Makepeace Thackeray, 1811–1863; a list of books and of references to periodicals in the Brooklyn public library. Brooklyn, N.Y., 1911. 51p. 16cm.

4906 **Stevenson, Lionel,** *ed.* 1964: no.1705.

4907 **Anderson, John Parker,** *comp.* 'Bibliography' *in* Merivale, Herman and F. T. Marzials. Life of W. M. Thackeray. London, 1891. p.[i]–xxii at end.

4908 **Williams, W. J.,** *comp.* 'Bibliography of the works of W. M. Thackeray' *in* The biographical edition of the works of William Makepeace Thackeray. London, 1898–9. V.13 (1899), p.721–43.

4909 **Melville, Lewis,** *pseud.* 'Bibliography' *in* The life of William Makepeace Thackeray. Chicago, 1899. V.2, p.[295]–345.
See no.4912.

4910 **Spielmann, Marion Harry.** 'Bibliography of Thackeray's contributions to Punch' *in* The hitherto unidentified contributions of W. M. Thackeray to Punch . . .' London, 1899. p.[281]–306.

4911 **[Dickson, Frederick Stoever]** *comp.* 'A bibliography of William Makepeace Thackeray in the United States' *in* Wilson, James G. Thackeray in the United States, 1852–3, 1855–6. London, 1904. V.2, p.[223]–403.

4912 **Melville, Lewis,** *pseud.* 'The bibliography of William Makepeace Thackeray' *in* William Makepeace Thackeray, a biography. London, 1910. V.2, p.[143]–376. (First bib. 1899)
Chronol. checklist of 1,277 items, 1828–1908, with some TP facsims. and bibliogr. notes.

4913 **Grolier club,** NEW YORK. Catalogue of an exhibition commemorating the hundredth anniversary of the birth of William Makepeace Thackeray . . . [New York, DeVinne pr., 1912] viii,105p. 18cm.

4914 —— **[Same]:** New York, Grolier club, 1912. xii,141p. ports., facsims. 24cm.

4915 **Van Duzer, Henry Sayre.** A Thackeray library; first editions and first publications . . . forming a complete Thackeray bibliography. New York, Privately ptd., 1919. xiii,198p. illus.(part col.)ports.(1 col.) facsims. 28cm.

4916 —— **[Same]:** [Reissued, with a new introduction by Lionel Stevenson] Port Washington, N.Y., Kennikat pr., 1965. 198p. illus., ports., facsims. 24cm.

4917 **McCutcheon, George Barr** [1926]: no.3074.

4918 **Elwin, Malcolm.** 'Bibliography: Published books . . . Novels in numbers. Contributions to newspapers and periodicals. Contributions to almanacks, annuals, etc.' *in* Thackeray, a personality. London [1932] p.372–92.

4919 **Gulliver, Harold Strong.** 'Additions, etc. to Thackeray bibliography' *in* Thackeray's literary apprenticeship, a study of the early newspaper and magazine work of William Makepeace Thackeray. . . . Valdosta [Ga.] 1934. p.255–8.

4920 **Thrall, Miriam Mulford H.** 'Bibliography of Thackeray' *in* Rebellious Fraser's, Nol Yorke's magazine in the days of Maginn, Thackeray, and Carlyle. New York, 1934. p.294–8.
Checklist of contribs. to Fraser's magazine.

4921 **[Parrish, Morris Longstreth]** Catalogue of an exhibition of the works of William Makepeace Thackeray; together with books, articles and catalogues referring to Thackeray, held at the Library company of Philadelphia. . . . Philadelphia, Privately ptd., 1940. [95]p. 22cm.
Chronol. catalogue comp. from copies at Dormy house.

4922 **New York. Public library. Berg collection.** William Makepeace Thackeray; an exhibition from the Berg collection; first editions, manuscripts, autograph letters and drawings, in celebration of the one-hundredth anniversary of Vanity fair, by John D. Gordan. New York, 1947. 39p. 26cm.

4923 **Winegarner, Lela.** Thackeray's contributions to the British and foreign review. J Eng Germ Philol 47:237–45 Jl '48.

4924 **Ray, Gordon Norton.** Thackeray and Punch; 44 newly identified contributions. TLS 1 Ja '49:16.
From 4 N 1848 to 23 S '54 in v.15–27.

4925 **White, Edward M.** Thackeray's contributions to Fraser's magazine. Stud Bib 19:67–84 '66.
Chronol. annotated checklist of 'disallowed contributions' and 'Thackeray's contributions to Fraser's' (p.78–84).

THOMAS, DYLAN MARLAIS, 1914–1953

4930 **Huff, William Howard.** Dylan Thomas, a bibliography. Evanston, Ill., Northwestern university library, Reference dept., 1953. 26p. 28cm.

4931 ——, *comp.* 'Bibliography' *in* Olson, Elder. The poetry of Dylan Thomas. [Chicago, 1954] p.102–46.

4932 **Rolph, John Alexander.** Dylan Thomas, a bibliography. London, J. M. Dent; New York, New directions [1956] xix,108p. illus., ports., facsims. 23cm.
Classified arrangement of books and pamphlets; periodical contribs.; contribs. to books; trans. of; and gramophone recordings; with quasifacsim. TP transcrs. and facsims., collations, and bibliogr. notes.
Rev: C. Woolf Bk Coll 5:287–91 '56; G. D. McDonald Pa Bib Soc Am 51:98–100 '57; W. White Bull Bib 22:32 '57; Listener 57:395 '57.

4933 **St. Bonaventure university,** ST. BONAVENTURE, N.Y. **Friedsam library.** Checklist of Dylan Thomas, 1914–1953; memorabilia from the collection of dr. T. E. Hanley, Bradford, Pennsylvania . . . [n.p.] 1956. [6]l. (Not seen)

4934 **Todd, William Burton.** The bibliography of Dylan Thomas. Bk Coll 6no1:71–3 '57.
Rolph addenda and corrigenda.

4935 **Sanesi, Roberto.** 'Bibliografia' *in* Dylan Thomas. Milano, 1960. p.175–9.

4936 **Smith, Timothy d'Arch.** The second edition of Dylan Thomas's 18 Poems. Bk Coll 13no3:351–2 '64.
Descr. and points in Rolphs item B2.

THOMAS, ERNEST CHESTER, 1850–1892

4939 **Tedder, H. R.** In memoriam Ernest Chester Thomas. Library 4:73–80 Mr '92.
'. . . titles of books, either written, edited, or translated by Thomas, with a list of his contributions to periodicals and other publications' (p.79–80).

THOMAS, PHILIP EDWARD, 1878–1917

4940 **Bibliographies** of modern authors. (Philip) Edward Thomas. Lond Merc. 2no12:740–1 Oc '20.

4941 **Murphy, Gwendolen.** Bibliographies of modern authors, no.2. Edward Thomas. Lond Merc 16:71–5, 193–8, 526–30 My,Je,S '27; 17:76 N '27.

4942 **Eckert, Robert Paul.** Edward Thomas, soldier-poet of his race. Am Bk Coll 4no2:66–9 Ag '33.

4943 —— Edward Thomas, a biography and a bibliography. London, J. M. Dent [1937] xxi,328p. ports., facsims. 22cm.

'Part ii: bibliographical' (p.[183]–289): classified arrangement of books; books contrib. to or ed. by; periodical contribs; and ana; with TP transcrs., collations and bibliogr. notes on principal ed.

Rev: TLS 10 Jl '37:513; W. R. Benét Sat R Lit 16:11 '37.

THOMPSON, FRANCIS JOSEPH, 1859–1907

4945 **Stonehill, Charles Archibald** [1925]: no.682.

4946 **Boston college,** BOSTON, MASS. **Library.** An account of books and manuscripts of Francis Thompson, edited by Terence L. Connolly. Chestnut Hill, Boston college [1937] ix,79p. port. 24cm.

Based on the collection of Seymour Adelman, now in the library.

4947 **Connolly, Terence Leo,** *ed.* 'Bibliographies' *in* Poems of Francis Thompson. Rev. ed. New York, 1941. p.[559]–73. (First pub. 1932)

4948 ——, *ed.* 'An essay towards a bibliography of Francis Thompson's uncollected book reviews and literary criticism contributed to periodicals' *in* Literary criticisms of Francis Thompson, newly discovered and collected. New York, 1948. p.563–96.

See no.4950.

4949 **Harris public library,** PRESTON. Catalogue of manuscripts, letters, and books in the Harris public library, Preston, based on the collection presented by J. H. Spencer in 1950. [Preston, 1950] 77p. 30cm. (Duplicated typescript)

See no.4952.

4950 **Connolly, Terence Leo,** *ed.* 'A revised essay toward a bibliography of Francis Thompson's book reviews and literary criticisms contributed to periodicals' *in* The real Robert Louis Stevenson and other critical essays by Francis Thompson. New York, 1959. p.353–98.

4951 **Pope, Myrtle Pihlman.** A critical bibliography of works by and about Francis Thompson. New York, New York public library, 1959. 37p. 26cm.

Repr. from N.Y. Pub Lib Bull 62:571–6 D '58; 63:40–9, 155–61, 195–204 Ja–Ap '59.

Annotated classified checklist of works and ana.

4952 **Harris public library,** PRESTON. . . . Catalogue of Francis Thompson collection presented to the Harris public library, . . . by mr. J. H. Spencer . . . 1950, with a supplementary list of Thompsoniana. . . . Preston [1959?] 23p. 18cm.

At head of title: Francis Thompson centenary, 1859–1959.

THOMPSON, SIR HENRY, 1820–1904

4955 **Spencer, E. M.,** 1957: no.205.

THOMPSON, HUGH, 1860–1920

4956 **Spielmann, Marion Harry** and **W. C. Jerrold.** 'Bibliography of Hugh Thomson's printed work' *in* Hugh Thomson; his art, his letters, his humour and his charm. London, 1931. p.237–54.
Classified checklist of works and ana; 189 items.

THOMSON, JAMES, 1700–1748

4957 **Wells, John Edwin.** Thomson's Spring: early editions true and false. Library ser4 22:223–43 Mr '42.
Discursive checklist of separate and coll. issues to 1760, with bibliogr. notes.

4958 **Rogers, F.,** 1952: no.192.

4958a **Francis, T. R.** Some Dublin editions of James Thomson's Tancred and Sigismunda. Bk Coll 7no2:190 '58.
Checklist of 4 items, 1745–8.

4959 —— James Thomson's Tancred and Sigismunda. Bk Coll 8no2:181–2 '59.
TP transcrs. and collations of 6 early ed.

4960 **Stratman, Carl Joseph.** Tancred and Sigismunda. Bk Coll 9no2:188 '60.
Adds 8 unrecorded ed. to previous item.

4961 **Hopkinson, Cecil** and **C. B. Oldman.** 'A check-list of the various issues and editions of Thomson's Original Scottish airs' *in* Egerer, Joel W. A bibliography of Robert Burns. Edinburgh, 1964. p.361–4.
Repr. from Edinburgh Bib Soc Trans 2pt1:14–16 '38.

THOMSON, SIR ST.CLAIR, 1859–1943

4965 **King, S. E. A.,** 1950: no.153.

TICKELL, RICHARD, 1751–1793

4966 **Butterfield, Lyman Henry,** *ed.* Anticipation by Richard Tickell, reprinted from the first edition, London, 1778, with . . . a bibliography of Tickell's writings. . . . New York, 1942. (Not seen)

TICKELL, THOMAS, 1686–1740

4967 **Butt, John Everett.** Notes for a bibliography of Thomas Tickell. Bod Q Rec 5:299–302 D '28.
Discursive checklist.

4968 **Tickell, Richard Eustace,** *ed.* 'Bibliography of Thomas Tickell's writings' *in* Thomas Tickell and the eighteenth century poets. . . . London, 1931. p.187–97.
Checklist of coll.; separate; and unpub. works.

TOLAND, JOHN, 1670–1722

4969 **Heinemann, F. H.** Prolegomena to a Toland bibliography. N&Q 185:182–6 S '43.
Classified checklist supplementing DNB.

4970 **Dieneman, W.**, 1953: no.109.

TONE, THEOBALD WOLFE, 1763–1798

4971 **MacManus, Michael Joseph.** A bibliography of Theobald Wolfe Tone. Dublin, Privately ptd. by A. Thom, 1940. 15p. 25cm.
Repr. from Dublin Mag new ser 15:52–64 Jl/S '40.
Chronol. checklist of 18 early ed., 1790–1826, with TP transcrs., collations, and some bibliogr. notes.
Rev: TLS 26 Oc '40:548.

TOWNSHEND, LETITIA JANE DOROTHEA (BAKER), fl.1892–1927

4972 **Morgan, N.**, 1950: no.173.

TOWNSHEND, RICHARD BAXTER, 1846–1923

4973 **Morgan, N.**, 1950: no.173.

TOYNBEE, ARNOLD JOSEPH, 1889–

4974 **Greenslade, Rush.** Arnold Joseph Toynbee, a checklist. Twent Cent Lit 2:92–104 Jl '56.
Chronol. classified checklist.

4975 **Popper, Monica.** A bibliography of the works in English of Arnold Toynbee, 1910–1954. London, Royal institute of international affairs, 1955. iii,59l. 30 cm. (Duplicated typescript)
Chronol. checklist of 296 items.

TOZER, HENRY, 1602–1650

4976 **Dredge, John Ingle,** 1889–99: no.886.

TRENCH, FREDERIC HERBERT, 1865–1923

4977 **Bibliographies** of modern authors. Frederic Herbert Trench. Lond Merc 4no19:87 My '21.
Chronol. checklist of verse and drama; and prose, 1900–19.

TRESCOT, THOMAS, 1612–1684

4978 **Dredge, John Ingle,** 1889–99: no.886.

TREVES, SIR FREDERICK, 1853–1923

4979 **Pinnock, C. L.**, 1952: no.184.

TROLLOPE, ANTHONY, 1815–1882

4980 **Stevenson, Lionel,** *ed.*, 1964: no.1705.

4981 **Lavington, Margaret.** 'A bibliography of the first editions of the works of Anthony Trollope' *in* Escott, Thomas H. S. Anthony Trollope . . . London; New York, 1913. p.[309]–36.

4982 **Sadleir, Michael Thomas Hervey,** 1922: no.1706.

4983 **Irwin, Mary Leslie.** Anthony Trollope; a bibliography. New York, H. W. Wilson; London, I. Pitman, 1926. 97p. front. 20cm.

Rev. from Bull Bib 12:71–3, 92–6 My/D '24; 12:114–16, 150–5 Ja/Ap, S/D '25.

4984 **Sadleir, Michael Thomas Hervey.** 'Bibliography of Anthony Trollope' *in* Trollope, a commentary. London, 1927. p.412–15. (2d ed., 1928, 1933; new ed., rev., 1945)

4985 —— Trollope, a bibliography; an analysis of the history and structure of the works of Anthony Trollope and a general survey of the effect of original publishing conditions on a book's subsequent rarity. London, Constable, 1928. (Repr. London, Dawsons, 1964) xv,321p. illus., port., facsims. 23cm.

4986 —— [Same]: Addenda and corrigenda, 1934. . . . London, 1934. 10p. 23cm.

Classified bibliogr. of early ed., periodical, etc. contribs.; and coll. ed., with quasifacsim. TP transcrs., collations, and bibliogr. notes. The Sadleir Trollopeiana passed via M. L. Parrish to Princeton university library.

Rev: TLS 8 N '28:817; Life & Letters 1:632–3 '28; I. A. Williams Lond Merc 19:82–8 '28; G.M.T. Sat R Lit 5:964 '29; F. W. Knickerbocker Sewanee R 37:114–20 '29; A. W. P[ollard] Library ser4 9:418–21 '29; TLS 30 Jl '64:672.

TROLLOPE, FRANCES (MILTON), 1780–1863

4990 **Sadleir, Michael Thomas Hervey.** 'Bibliography of Frances Trollope' *in* Trollope, a commentary. London, 1927. p.403–5. (2d ed., 1928, 1933; new ed., rev., 1945)

Chronol. checklist, 1832–56.

TRUSSELL, JOHN, fl.1595–1642

4990a **Shaaber, Matthias A.** The first rape of faire Hellen, by John Trussell. Sh Q 8n04:407–20 '57.

Quasifacsim. TP transcr., collation, bibliogr. notes and refs, with locations of copies. (Text repr. p.421–48).

TURNER, DAWSON, 1775–1858

4991 **Dawson, Warren Royal.** A bibliography of the printed works of Dawson Turner. Cambridge Bib Soc Trans 3pt3:232–56 '61.

Chronol. checklist of 78 items, 1800–53, with some bibliogr. notes; enl. from preliminary bibliogr. in Norfolk Archæol 26:59–72 '35.

Rev: J. Horden Library ser5 18:230–1 '63.

TURNER, WILLIAM, d.1568

4992 **Stearn, William Thomas,** *comp.* 'A list of the writings of William Turner . . .' *in* William Turner Libellus de re herbaria . . . facsimiles with introductory matter by James Britten, B. Daydon Jackson, and W. T. Stearn. London, 1965. p.27–35.

Checklist of 41 items, 1537–57.

TYNDALE, WILLIAM, d.1536

4993 **Gloucester. Public library.** A list of the material available in the public library . . . concerning William Tyndale. . . . [n.p., Gloucester, n.d., 1936] 15p. 19cm.

VANCOUVER, GEORGE, 1758–1798

4994 **Richmond, Surrey. Public library.** A list of books, prints, maps, &c. relating to captain George Vancouver . . . contained in the Vancouver collection. Richmond [1936] 9l. (Duplicated typescript) (Not seen)

VAUGHAN, HENRY, 1622–1695

4995 **Martin, Leonard Cyril,** *ed.* 'List of original editions with bibliographical notes' *in* The works of Henry Vaughan. Oxford, 1914. V.1, p.[xi]–xiii.

Checklist of 9 items, 1646–79.

4996 **Marilla, Esmond Linworth.** A comprehensive bibliography of Henry Vaughan. [University, Ala., University of Alabamba pr., 1948] 44p. 23cm.

Classified chronol. checklist of early and modern ed.; and ana; no index.

VENNING, RALPH, 1620–1673

4997 **Dredge, John Ingle,** 1889–99: no.886.

VERGILIUS, POLYDORUS, d.1555

4998 **Ferguson, John.** Hand list of editions of Polydore Vergil's De inventoribus rerum; compiled and arranged from a bibliography in manuscript by the late professor John Ferguson.... New Haven, Conn., Historical library, Yale university school of medicine, 1944. 15l. 28cm. Covertitle. (Duplicated typescript)

Ed. by John F. Fulton and C. H. Peters; chronol. checklist of 116 items including trans., from 1499, with locations of copies.

VERSTEGAN, RICHARD, c.1550–1641

4999 **Rombauts, Edward.** 'Werkjes ten Onrechte aam Verstegan toegeschreven' *in* Richard Vertstegan, een Polemist der contra-Reformatie. Brussels, 1933. p.310–19.

5000 **Petti, Anthony G.** A bibliography of the writings of Richard Verstegan, *c.*1550–1641. Recus Hist 7:82–103 Ap '63.

Classified checklist of canonical; lost; doubtful; and misascribed works; and works ptd. or ed. by; based on University of London School of librarianship and archives, bibliogr., 1957; with locations of copies, some bibliogr. notes and refs.

VERULAM, FRANCIS BACON, BARON, AND VISCOUNT ST.ALBAN, 1561–1626
See Bacon, Francis, baron Verulam and viscount St.Alban.

VINER, CHARLES, 1679–1756

5001 **Gibson, Strickland** and **sir W. Holdsworth.** Charles Viner's General abridgment of law and equity. Oxford Bib Soc Proc 2pt4:227–325 '30.

'Collation of Viner's Abridgment' (p.311–16): quasifacsim. TP transcrs., collations, locations of copies, and bibliogr. notes.

VOLUSENE, FLORENCE, 1504?–1547?

5002 **Smith, Dominic Baker-.** Florence Wilson, two early works. Biblioth 4no6:228–9 '65.

TP transcr. and collations of 2 psalm commentaries, 1531, 1532.

WALE, SAMUEL, 1721?–1786

5003 **Hammelmann, H. A.** Eighteenth century English illustrators: Samuel Wale, R.A. Bk Coll 1no2:150–65 '52.

'Books illustrated by Samuel Wale' (p.156–65): chronol. checklist, 1748–77, with some facsims. and bibliogr. notes.

WALEY, ARTHUR DAVID, 1889–1966

5003a **Johns, Francis A.** A bibliography of Arthur Waley. New Brunswick, Rutgers U.P.; London, Allen & Unwin, 1968. 187p. (Not seen)
Rev: TLS 2 My '68:464.

WALKER, ANTHONY, 1726–1765

5004 **Hammelmann, H. A.** Eighteenth century English illustrators: Anthony Walker. Bk Coll 3no2:87–102 '54.

'Books illustrated by Anthony Walker' (p.94–102): chronol. checklist, 1749–82, with some facsims. and bibliogr. notes.

WALLACE, ALFRED RUSSEL, 1823–1913

5005 **Chesterton, Gilbert Keith.** Alfred Russel Wallace. Eng Illus Mag new ser 30:420–2 Ja '04.

'Bibliography' (p.422): checklist of works; prefaces, introductions by; and ana.

WALLER, EDMUND, 1606–1687

5006 **Chew, Beverly C.** 'The first edition of Waller's Poems' *in* Essays and verses about books. New York, 1926. p.47–57.

Repr. from Bibliographer 1no7:296–9 Oc '02; TP facsims., collations, and bibliogr. notes on the 4 1645 ed.

WALPOLE, HORACE, 4TH EARL OF ORFORD, 1717–1797

See also under Presses and printing.

5007 **Hazen, Allen Tracy.** A bibliography of Horace Walpole. New Haven, Yale U.P.; London, G. Cumberlege, O.U.P., 1948. 189p. facsims. 27cm.

Classified arrangement of books by; books contrib. to; periodical contribs., etc.; books dedicated to; and apocrypha; with TP facsims., collations, locations of and notes on copies, and bibliogr. notes.

Rev: K. J. Holzknecht Pa Bib Soc Am 42:339–40 '48; W. H. Bond Lib Q 18:293 '48; W. A. Jackson 28:409 '49; R. W. Ketton-Cremer R Eng Stud new ser 1:172–4 '50.

WALPOLE, SIR HUGH SEYMOUR, 1884–1941

5008 **Danielson, Henry.** Bibliographies of modern authors, no.10. Hugh Walpole. Bkmns J 1no18–20:354, 369, 382 '20.

TP transcrs., collations and bibliogr. notes on 12 first ed., 1909–19.

5008a ——, 1921: no.680.

WALTON, IZAAK, 1593–1683

5009 **[Allibone, Samuel Austin]** The Waltonian collection. New York, Ptd. for the trustees, 1893. 56p. 25cm. (Contributions to a catalogue of the Lenox library, no.7) (Not seen)

'Books upon angling, birds, fishes, hunting, etc. in the Lenox library.'

5010 **Grolier club,** NEW YORK. Chronological hand-list of various editions of the Complete angler by Izaak Walton and Charles Cotton; with a supplement embracing other writings of Walton and Cotton, etc., 1593–1893. . . . [New York, 1893] 26p. 28cm.

5011 **Wood, Arnold.** A bibliography of The complete angler of Izaak Walton and Charles Cotton; being a chronologically arranged list of the several editions and reprints. . . . New York, C. Scribner's, 1900. 204p. port., facsims. 26cm.

Chronol. arrangement of ed. to 1900, with TP facsims., collations, and bibliogr. notes. 'Index of imprints' only.

5012 **Butt, John Everett.** A bibliography of Izaak Walton's Lives. Oxford Bib Soc Proc 2pt4:327–40 '30.

Chronol. checklist of 18 items, 1640–86, with quasifacsim. TP transcrs., collations, some locations of copies and bibliogr. notes.

5013 **Oliver, Peter.** A new chronicle of The compleat angler. New York, Paisley pr.; London, Williams & Norgate, 1936. xv,301p. port., facsims. 25cm.

Chronol. bibliogr. of 284 items, 1653–1935, with locations of copies.

WALWYN, WILLIAM, fl.1649

5015 **Wolfe, Don Marion.** [Chronological checklist, with locations of copies] *in* Milton in the puritan revolution. New York, 1941. (Repr. London, 1963) p.481–3.

WARD, SIR ADOLPHUS WILLIAM, 1837–1924

5016 **[Bartholomew, Augustus Theodore]** *comp.* 'A short bibliography of the writings of the late master of Peterhouse' *in* In memoriam Adolphus William Ward, master of Peterhouse, 1900–1924. Cambridge, 1924. p.[xxi]–xxvi.

5017 **Bartholomew, Augustus Theodore.** A bibliography of sir Adolphus William Ward, 1837–1924. . . . Cambridge, C.U.P., 1926. xxxiv,99p. port. 23cm.

Chronol. checklist, 1860–1924.

Rev: Library ser4 7:433 Mr '27.

WARD, EDWARD, 1667–1731

5018 **Jones, Claude Edward.** Short-title checklist of works attributed to Edward Ward, 1667–1731. N&Q 190:135–9 Ap '46.

234 items.

5019 **Troyer, Howard William.** 'A bibliography of the writings of Edward Ward' *in* Ned Ward of Grubstreet, a study of sub-literary London in the eighteenth century. Cambridge, Mass., 1946. p.[231]–82. (Repr. 1968)

Title checklist of works and doubtful attribs., with TP transcrs., collations, locations of copies, and some bibliogr. notes.

5020 **Cameron, William James.** Bibliography of Ned Ward, 1667–1731. N&Q 198:284–6 Jl '53.

Additions to Troyer.

5021 **Ward, S. H.** Bibliography of Edward Ward. N&Q 198:436–8 Oc '53.

WARD, MARY AUGUSTA (ARNOLD), MRS. HUMPHRY WARD, 1851–1920

5022 **Chesterton, Gilbert Keith.** Mrs. Humphry Ward. Eng Illus Mag new ser 31:293–5, 299–300 Je '04.

'Bibliography' (p.294, 299–300): checklist of works, translations, prefaces, and ductions; plays; and ana.

5023 **Keogh, Andrew,** 1910: no.662.

WARD, JAMES, fl.1892–1915

5024 **[Ward, James]** List of books relating to the history, bibliography, and genealogy of Nottinghamshire, published under the direction of James Ward, Nottingham, 1892–1903. Nottingham, 1904. 22p. illus., 16cm.

5025 [——] Catalogue of books relating to the history, bibliography, and genealogy of Nottinghamshire, published by James Ward. Nottingham, Cooke
& Vowles, 1913. 28p. 17cm.

WARTON, JOSEPH, 1722–1800

5026 **Partridge, Eric Honeywood,** ed. 'Works by the Wartons' in The three
Wartons; a choice of their verse. . . . London, 1927. p.19–23.

5027 **MacClintock, William Darnall.** 'A list of Warton's literary works' in
Joseph Warton's Essay on Pope, a history of the five editions. Chapel Hill;
London, 1933. p.72–4.
Chronol. checklist, 1739–97.

WARTON, THOMAS, 1688?–1745

5028 **Partridge, Eric Honeywood,** ed., 1927: no.5026.

WARTON, THOMAS, 1728–1790

5029 **Rinaker, Clarissa.** 'Bibliography' in Thomas Warton, a biographical and
critical study. [Urbana] 1916. p.233–8.
Classified checklist of early ed. of works; periodical contribs.; and ana.

5030 **Partridge, Eric Honeywood,** ed., 1927: no.5026.

WATSON, SIR JOHN WILLIAM, 1858–1935

5031 **Forman, Harry Buxton.** William Watson. Eng Illus Mag new ser 29:541–3,
548 Ag '03.
'Bibliography' (p.542, 548).

5032 **[Lane, John]** comp. 'A chronological list of mr. William Watson's works,
with contents of each volume' in Spender, J. A., ed. The poems of William
Watson. London, 1905. V.2, p.[i]–xxi at end.

5033 **Woolf, Cecil.** Some uncollected authors XII: sir William Watson. Bk Coll
5n04:375–80 '56.
'Check-list of first editions' (p.377–80): chronol. checklist of 53 items, 1880–1941, with
some bibliogr. notes.

5034 —— [Same]: Colbeck, Norman. Additions and corrections. ib. 6n01:66–7
'57.

5035 —— [Same]: Swayze, Walter E. ib. 6n03–4:285–6, 402 '57.

WATT, ROBERT, 1774–1819

5036 **Finlayson, James.** 'Dr. Robert Watt's published works and papers' in An
account of the life and works of dr. Robert Watt, author of the Bibliotheca britannica. London, 1897. p.42–4.

5037 **Cordasco, Francesco G. M.** A bibliography of Robert Watt . . . with a facsimile edition of his catalogue of medical books. . . . New York, W. F. Kelleher, 1950. 27p., facsim., 68[4]p. port. 23cm.

Checklist of works and ana (p. 23–7).

Rev: TLS 27 Oc '50:682.

WATTS, ISAAC, 1674–1748

5038 **Rogal, Samuel J.** A checklist of works by and about Isaac Watts, 1674–1748. N.Y. Pub Lib Bull 71no4:207–15 Ap '67.

Principally ana.

5038a **Stone, Wilbur Macey.** The divine and moral songs of Isaac Watts; an essay and a tentative list of editions. New York, Privately ptd. for the Triptych, 1918. 93p. port., facsims. 24cm.

'Bibliographical notes and lists of editions' (p.[39]–93): checklist of British and American ed., with locations of copies.

5039 **Stoke Newington. Public libraries.** Bi-centenary [of] dr. Isaac Watts, 1674–1748; catalogue of exhibition. . . . Stoke Newington, Stoke Newington central library, 1948. 31p. 20cm. Covertitle.

WATTS-DUNTON, WALTER THEODORE, 1832–1914
See Dunton, Walter Theodore Watts-.

WAUGH, EVELYN ARTHUR ST.JOHN, 1903–1966

5040 **Kosok, Heinz.** Evelyn Waugh, a checklist of criticism. Twent Cent Lit 12:211–15 Ja '66.

5041 **Doyle, Paul A.** Evelyn Waugh, a bibliography, 1926–1956. Bull Bib 22:57–62 My/Ag '57.

Classified chronol. checklist.

5042 **Linck, Charles E.** Works of Evelyn Waugh, 1910 to 1930. Twent Cent Lit 10:19–25 Ap '64.

Chronol. checklist.

WEBB, BEATRICE (POTTER), LADY PASSFIELD, 1858–1943

5045 **Tawney, Richard Henry.** Beatrice Webb, 1858–1943. Proc Brit Acad 29: 285–311 '43.

'List of works' (p.309–11): checklist of own works, works with Sidney Webb, and by Sidney Webb alone.

WEBB, MARY GLADYS, 1881–1927

5046 **Tolfree, M. P. G.,** 1956: no.223.

5047 **Sanders, Charles.** Mary Webb, an annotated bibliography of works about her. Eng Lit Transit 9no3:119–36 '66.

WEBB, SIDNEY JAMES, BARON PASSFIELD, 1859–1947

5048 **Tawney, Richard Henry,** 1943: no.5045.

WEBBER, FRANCIS, 1707–1771

5049 **Dredge, John Ingle,** 1889–99: no.886.

WEBSTER, JOHN, 1580?–1625?

5050 **Sampson, Martin Wright,** ed. 'Bibliography. 1. Texts' in The white devil and The duchess of Malfy. Boston [1904] p.[402]–5.

5051 **Lucas, Frank Laurence,** ed. 'Selected bibliography' in The complete works of John Webster. London, 1927. V.1, p.1–13. (Repr. New York, O.U.P., 1932)

5052 **Tannenbaum, Samuel Aaron.** John Webster, a concise bibliography. New York, 1941. x,38p. 23cm. (Elizabethan bibliographies, no.19)

Classified chronol. checklist of works and ana; 629 items.

WEDGWOOD, CICELY VERONICA, 1910–

5053 **Curle, Richard Henry Parnell.** The Richard Curle collection of the works of Cicely Veronica Wedgwood. Beaminster, J. S. Cox, Toucan pr., 1961. 19p. 13cm.

Discursive classified checklist.

WELLS, HERBERT GEORGE, 1866–1946

5053a **Costa, Richard Haner.** H. G. Wells's Tono-Bungay: review of new studies. Eng Lit Transit 10no2:89–96 '67.

5054 **Lankester, E. Ray.** H. G. Wells. Eng Illus Mag new ser 31:614–17 S '04.

'Bibliography' (p.617).

5055 **Chappell, Fred A.** A bibliography of H. G. Wells. Chicago, Covici-McGee, 1924. xviii,51p. 20cm.

5056 **Wells, Geoffrey Harry.** A bibliography of the works of H. G. Wells, 1893–1925. . . . London, G. Routledge, 1925. xiii,72p. 26cm.

5057 —— 'The bibliography' *in* The works of H. G. Wells, 1887–1925; a bibliography, dictionary and subject-index. London, 1926. p.1–86.

Classified chronol. arrangement of early ed.; misc. pubs. translations; and ana, with TP transcrs., collations, and some bibliogr. notes; no index.

5058 **Ray, Gordon Norton.** H. G. Well's contributions to the Saturday review. Library ser5 16:29–36 Mr '61.

Checklist of 111 items supplementing Wells (no.5057): p.32–6.

5059 **Ealing. Public library.** H. G. Wells, 1866–1946; a centenary booklist, compiled by James W. Thirsk. Ealing, 1966. 15p. 19cm. (Duplicated typescript)

WESLEY, CHARLES, 1707–1788
See under Wesley, John, 1703–1791.

WESLEY, JOHN, 1703–1791

5065 **Green, Richard.** The works of John and Charles Wesley; a bibliography containing an exact account of all the publications issued by the brothers Wesley, arranged in chronological order, with a list of the early editions and descriptive and illustrative notes. London, C. H. Kelly, 1896. 291p. 23cm.

5066 —— [Same]: Cheap ed. London, C. H. Kelly, 1899. 291p. 23cm.

5067 —— [Same]: 2d ed., rev. London, Methodist publishing house, 1906. viii,291p. 23cm.

Annotated chronol. checklist of 417 items, 1733–91, with some bibliogr. notes and account of later ed.

5068 **Melbourne. University. Queen's college. Library.** Catalogue of Wesleyana. . . . [Melbourne, 1926] 15p. 21cm.

5069 **Baker, Frank.** . . . A union catalogue of the publications of John and Charles Wesley. Durham, N.C., Divinity school, Duke university, 1966. 230p. 27cm. (Duplicated typescript)

At head of title: The Oxford edition of Wesley's works.
Arranged after Green, with extensive locations.

WEST, DAME REBECCA, *pseud. of* CICILY ISABEL FAIRFIELD, 1892–

5070 **Hutchinson, George Evelyn.** A preliminary list of the writings of Rebecca West, 1912–1951. New Haven, Yale university library, 1957. iv,102p. 18cm.

Classified chronol. checklist of early ed. and contribs., with quasifacsim. TP transcrs., collations, and bibliogr. notes; no index.

WEST, VICTORIA MARY SACKVILLE- (LADY V. M. NICOLSON), 1892–1962

5071 **Boochever, Florence.** A selected list of writings by and about V. Sackville West. Bull Bib 16:93–4, 113–15 Ja/Ap, My/Ag '38.

Annotated classified checklist.

5072 **Wines, J. M.,** 1958: no.235.

WETENHALL, EDWARD, 1636–1713

5073 **Dredge, John Ingle,** 1889–99: no.886.

WEYMAN, STANLEY JOHN, 1855–1928

5074 **Robertson, C. Grant.** Stanley Weyman. Eng Illus Mag new ser 31:507–10 Ag '04.

'Bibliography' (p.508, 510): checklist of works, 1883–1903; plays; and ana.

WHATELY, RICHARD, 1787–1863

5075 **Kane, Peter E.** Richard Whately in the United States, a partial bibliography. Bull Bib 23:87–8 Ja/Ap '61.
Title checklist of American ed.

WHISTLER, REGINALD JOHN, 1905–1944

5076 **Englefield, William Alexander Devereux.** Check list of Rex Whistler bookwrappers. Bk Coll Q 17:64–9 Ap/Je '35.
Chronol. checklist, 1927–35.

WHITE, GILBERT, 1720–1793

5077 **Watt, Hugh Boyd.** A list of the bibliographies of the writings of Gilbert White. Selbourne Mag 20:198–201 N '09.

5078 **Sherborn, C. Davies,** *comp.* 'Bibliography' *in* Sharpe, Richard B., *ed.* The natural history . . . of Selborne, by Gilbert White. London, 1900. V.2, p.[347]–64.

5079 **Gilbert White fellowship.** Catalogue of exhibition commemorating the bicentenary of Gilbert White. . . . Rev. issue, with preface. [London?] 1920. 12p. 20cm.

5080 **Martin, Edward Alfred.** A bibliography of Gilbert White, the naturalist & antiquarian of Selborne. . . . London, Halton, 1934. viii,188p. illus., plates., port. 22cm.
'Enlarged & revised ed'; first pub [1897]. Discursive checklist of ed. to 1929, arranged by editors, with some bibliogr. notes.
Rev: TLS 14 Je '34:421.

5081 **Ealing. Public library.** Selborne society library; a catalogue of Mss., books, and periodicals devoted to Gilbert White and natural history. [Ealing] Ealing reference library, 1958. 34p. 21cm. (Duplicated typescript)

WHITE, HENRY KIRKE, 1785–1806

5085 **[Godfrey, John Thomas]** *ed.* Catalogue of portraits, engravings, books, letters & manuscripts relating to Henry Kirke White exhibited . . . Nottingham, 1906. [Nottingham, 1906] 14p. illus., port. 17cm.

WHITE, WILLIAM HALE, 1831–1913
See Rutherford, Mark, pseud.

WHITEFIELD, GEORGE, 1714–1770

5086 **Austin, Roland.** Bibliography of the works of George Whitefield. Wesley Hist Soc Proc 10:169–84, 211–23 S,D '16.
Classified chronol. checklist of general works; sermons; and coll. sermons, with some bibliogr. notes; 133 items.

WHITEHEAD, ALFRED NORTH, 1861–1947

5087 **Lowe, Victor** and **R. C. Baldwin,** *comp.* 'Bibliography of the writings of Alfred North Whitehead to November, 1941, with selected reviews' *in* Schilpp, Paul A., *ed.* The philosophy of Alfred North Whitehead. Evanston, 1941. p.[701]–25.

5088 —— [Same]: '. . . to January 3, 1951 . . .' *in* Schilpp, Paul A., *ed*. The philosophy of Alfred North Whitehead. [2d ed.] New York [1951] p.745–78.
'Addenda' (p.773–8); chronol. checklist, 1879–1951.

5089 **Parker, Franklin.** Alfred North Whitehead, 1861–1947, a partial bibliography. Bull Bib 23:90–3 Ja/Ap '61.
Classified checklist of works and ana.

WHITEING, RICHARD, 1840–1928

5090 **Harris, Wendell V.** A selective annotated bibliography of writings about Richard Whiteing. Eng Lit Transit 8no1:44–8 '65.

WHITFORD, RICHARD, fl.1495–1555?

5091 **Evans, Albert Owen.** 'List of Richard Whitford's works' *in* Thomas à Kempis and Wales. Carmarthen, 1932. p.28–9.
Repr. from Welsh Bib Soc J 4:5–32 Mr '32; chronol. checklist, 1507–58.

WHYTE-MELVILLE, GEORGE JOHN, 1821–1878
See Melville, George John Whyte-.

WIDNALL, SAMUEL PAGE, 1825–1894

5092 **Dickins, Bruce.** Samuel Page Widnall and his press at Grantchester, 1871–1892. Cambridge Bib Soc Trans 2pt5:366–72 '58.
Checklist of 7 items, with quasifacsim. TP transcrs., collations, and locations of copies.

5093 —— [Same]: Addenda. *ib*. 3pt1:95 '59; Further addenda. 3pt2:176–8 '60.

WILBERFORCE, WILLIAM, 1759–1833

5094 **Hull. Public libraries.** William Wilberforce, 1759–1833; a catalogue of the books and pamphlets on William Wilberforce and slavery in the Reference library of Kingston upon Hull public libraries . . . Kingston upon Hull, Central library, 1959. 36p. port. 23cm. (Not seen)

WILDE, JANE FRANCESCA (ELGEE), LADY, 1826–1896

5095 **Coleman, James.** Bibliography of lady Wilde, née Jane Francesca Elgee. Irish Bk Lover 20:60 My/Je '32.
Classified checklist with bibliogr. notes and locations of copies

WILDE, OSCAR FINGAL O'FLAHERTIE WILLS, 1856–1900

5096 **R., W.** Notes for a bibliography of Oscar Wilde. Bks and Bkplates 5pt3: 170–83 '04/5.

5097 **Mason, Stuart,** *pseud., comp*. 'List of published writings of Oscar Wilde' *in* Gide, André. Oscar Wilde, a study; from the French. . . . Oxford, 1905. p.[93]–110.

5098 —— A bibliography of the poems of Oscar Wilde, giving particulars as to the original publication of each poem. . . . London, F. G. Richards, 1907. 147p. illus., port., facsims. 18cm.

5099 —— Bibliography of Oscar Wilde. [Edinburgh] Privately ptd. for the author, 1908. 21p. 24cm.

5100 —— Bibliography of Oscar Wilde. London, T. W. Laurie [1914] xxxix, 605p. illus., ports., facsims. 22cm.

Classified checklist of periodical contribs. by title of journal; chronol. arrangement of books; coll. ed.; pirated ed.; and selections; and ana; with TP transcrs. and extensive facsims., collations, and bibliogr. notes; 695 items. *See* no.5105.

5101 **Stetson, John Batterson.** . . . The Oscar Wilde collection . . . to be sold . . . April 23. . . . New York, Anderson galleries, 1920. 72p. facsims. 23cm.

423 entries.

5102 **Clark, William Andrews.** The library of William Andrews Clark, jr. Wilde and Wildeiana, collated and compiled by Robert Ernest Cowan [and others] San Francisco, Ptd. by J. H. Nash, 1922–31. 5v. ports. 27cm.

5103 **Dulau & co., bksllrs.,** LONDON. A collection of original manuscripts, letters, & books of Oscar Wilde . . . and unpublished letters, poems & plays formerly in the possession of Robert Ross, C. S. Millard (Stuart Mason) and the younger son of Oscar Wilde. London [1928] xi,139p. illus., facsims. 26cm.

5104 **Dublin. University. Trinity college. Library.** Catalogue of an exhibition of books and manuscripts in commemoration of the centenary of the birth of Oscar Wilde, 1954. Dublin, Ptd. by the Dublin U.P., Trinity college [1954] 24p. port. 23cm.

5105 **Mason, Stuart,** *pseud.* Bibliography of Oscar Wilde, by Stuart Mason (Christopher Millard). New ed., introd. by Timothy d'Arch Smith. London, B. Rota [1967] [6]xxxix,605p. illus., facsims. 22cm.

See no.5100.

Rev: TLS 11 My '67; Pa Bib Soc Am 61:292 '67.

WILKINS, JOHN, 1614–1672

5110 **Lord, H. M.,** 1957: no.159.

WILKS, SIR SAMUEL, 1824–1911

5111 **Wale, William.** . . . Bibliography of the published writings of sir Samuel Wilks. [London] 1911. 28p. port. 21cm.

Chronol. checklist, repr. with add. from Guy's Hosp Gaz '11.

WILLIAMS, CHARLES, *pseud. of* CHARLES WALTER STANSBY, 1886–1945

5111a **Dawson, Lawrence R.** A checklist of reviews by Charles Williams. Pa Bib Soc Am 55:100–17 '61.

Chronol. checklist of 280 items, 1918–45, with indexes.

WILLIAMS, DAVID, 1738–1816

5112 **Williams, David.** A bibliography of the printed works of David Williams, 1738–1816. Nat Lib Wales J 10no2:121–36 '57.

Annotated checklist of 35 items, 1771–1810, with locations of copies and some bibliogr. notes.

WILLIAMS, SIR IFOR, 1881–1965

5113 **Davies, A. M. E.,** 1960; no.106.

WILLIAMS, JOSHUA, 1813–1881

5114 **Moys, Elizabeth M.** Mr. Joshua Williams, Q.C., his life and writings. Law Lib J 51:117–24 My '58.

'Bibliography' (p. 122–4): classified checklist of books and periodical contribs.

WILLIAMS, RALPH VAUGHAN, 1872–1958

5115 **Starbuck, P. R.,** 1962: no.208.

WILLIAMS, THOMAS, 1769–c.1848

5116 **W., W. [William Williams?]** A Montgomeryshire worthy. Welsh Bib Soc J 2:318–19 Ag '23

Checklist of 8 works.

WILLIAMS, THOMAS HUDSON-, 1873–1961

5116a **Williams, A. Hudson-.** T. Hudson-Williams, 1873–1961: a bibliography. Welsh Bib Soc J 9no4:211–18 Ap '65.

Chronol. checklist, 1897–1964.

WILLIAMSON, HENRY, 1897–

5117 **Girvan, I. Waveney.** The first editions of Henry Williamson. Bkmn 78:160 My '30.

5118 —— A bibliography and critical survey of the works of Henry Williamson. . . . Chipping Camden, Alcuin pr., 1932. 56p. 23cm.

Chronol. checklist of early ed. and contribs. to books, with quasifacsim. TP transcrs., collations, and bibliogr. notes; no index.

Rev: TLS 21 Ja '32:45; Bk Coll Q 5:111–12 '32.

WILLIS, THOMAS, 1621–1675

5120 **Wing, H. J. R.,** 1962: no.236.

WILMOT, JOHN, 2D EARL OF ROCHESTER, 1647–1680

5121 **Prinz, Johannes.** 'Bibliography of the works of the earl of Rochester' *in* John Wilmot, earl of Rochester; his life and writings. . . . Leipzig, 1927. p.[305]–443.
Classified checklist of works and ana, with TP transcrs., and facsims., locations of copies, and some bibliogr. notes.

5122 **Gray, Philip Hayward.** Rochester's Poems on several occasions; new light on the dated and undated editions, 1680. Library ser4 19:185–97 S '38.
'Bibliography' (p.196–7) with TP facsims.

5123 **Pinto, Vivian de Sola** and **D. Dale.** The 1680 'Antwerp' edition of Rochester's Poems. Library ser4 20:105–6 Je '39.

5124 **Thorpe, James,** *ed.* 'Census of copies and editions' *in* Rochester's Poems on several occasions. Princeton, N.J., 1950. p.[153]–9.
The Introduction (p.[ix]–xxxviii) affords the fullest available discussion of the different ed. and variants.

5125 **Todd, William Burton.** The 1680 editions of Rochester's Poems with notes on earlier texts. Pa Bib Soc Am 47:43–58 '53.
'Check-list of separate texts in the British museum and Bodleian libraries' (p.50–6).

WILSON, FLORENCE, 1504?–1547?
See Volusene, Florence.

WILSON, JOHN, 1785–1854
See North, Christopher, pseud.

WILSON, JOHN DOVER, 1881–

5130 **[Butt, John Everett** and **J. C. Maxwell]** 13 July, 1961; a list of his published writings presented to John Dover Wilson on his 80th birthday. Cambridge, C.U.P., 1961. 32p. 18cm.
Classified chronol. checklist of 223 entries.
Rev: F. P. Wilson Library ser5 17:330–1 '62.

WINSTANLEY, GERRARD, fl.1648–1652

5130a **Abram, W. A.** Gerrard Winstanley the leveller. Palatine Notebk 3:104–10 My '83.
Discursive checklist.

5130b **Axon, Ernest.** Gerrard Winstanley the leveller. N&Q ser8 12:185–6 S '97.
Addenda to Abram.

5131 **Berens, Lewis H.** 'Complete list of Digger publications' *in* The Digger movement in the days of the commonwealth. London, 1906. p.255–6.
Chronol. checklist.

5132 **Wolfe, Don Marion.** [Chronological checklist with locations of copies] *in* Milton in the puritan revolution. New York, 1941. p.483–5. (Repr. London, 1963)

WISE, THOMAS JAMES, 1859–1937

5133 **S., W. B.** Thomas James Wise. N&Q ser12 7:392–4 N '20.
Classified checklist of works with which Wise was associated.

5133a **Carter, John Waynflete** and **G. Pollard.** 'Dossiers' *in* An enquiry into the nature of certain nineteenth century pamphlets. London; New York, 1934. p.[153]–360.
Checklist by author, with bibliogr. notes and discussion of Wise forgeries, etc.

5134 **Baughman, Roland.** Some victorian forged rarities. Huntington Lib Bull 9:91–117 Ap '36.
'Huntington library copies of books questioned by Carter and Pollard' (p.[102]–17): checklist of 54 items, with bibliogr. notes.

5135 **Partington, Wilfrid George.** 'The bibliography of the bibliographer; a record of his compilations, privately printed publications, edited works, forgeries, piracies, etc.' *in* Forging ahead; the true story of the upward progress of Thomas James Wise. . . . New York [1939] p.285–304.
See no.5138.

5136 **Ratchford, Fannie Elizabeth,** *ed.* 'List of the nineteenth-century forgeries in the Wrenn library, with the dates they were acquired and the prices Wrenn paid Wise' *in* Wise, Thomas J. Letters of Thomas J. Wise to John Henry Wrenn; a further inquiry. . . . New York, 1944. p.578–83.

5137 **Texas. University. Library.** Certain nineteenth century forgeries; an exhibition of books and letters . . . described by Fannie E. Ratchford. [Austin, Tex., 1946] 57p. 24cm.

5138 **Partington, Wilfrid George.** 'The bibliography of the bibliographer; a record of his compilations, privately-printed publications, edited works, forgeries, piracies, etc.' *in* Thomas J. Wise in the original cloth; the life and record of the forger of nineteenth-century pamphlets. London [1947] p.323–46.
Enl. ed. of no.5135.

5139 **Foxon, David Fairweather.** Thomas J. Wise and the pre-restoration drama; a study in theft and sophistication. London, Bibliographical society, 1959. viii,41p. 25cm.
Author checklist of 41 BM copies of plays mutilated by Wise, with collations, and bibliogr. notes and refs.; no index. 'Other made-up Ashley plays' (p.37–41): 27 items. *See also* no.512.
Rev: TLS 5 Je '59:344; M. Linton Theat Notebk 14:31 '59; G. Pollard Bk Coll 8:319–23 '59.

5140 **Texas. University. Humanities research center.** Various extraordinary books procured by Thomas J. Wise, and now displayed on All fools day in observance of the centenary of his birth. [Austin, Tex.] 1959. 18p. 24cm.
Introduction by William B. Todd; annotated classified short-title catalogue, with some bibliogr. notes.

5141 **Todd, William Burton,** *ed.* 'A handlist of Thomas J. Wise' *in* Thomas J. Wise centenary studies; essays by John Carter, Graham Pollard, William B. Todd. Austin, 1959. p.[80]–122.

Also pub. as Suppl to Texas Q 2no4 '59.

Checklist by author of 453 Wisean pubs., with some bibliogr. notes and refs.

5142 **Foxon, David Fairweather** and **W. B. Todd.** Thomas J. Wise and the pre-restoration drama; a supplement. Library ser5 16:287–93 D '61.

Checklist of copies made up with leaves removed from BM copies, supplementing no. 5139.

5143 **Garrett, Kathleen Isabella.** The artist and the author: an unidentified edition of a Cruikshank pamphlet. Guildh Misc 2:170–2 Oc '62.

Descr., and census of copies.

5144 **London. Guildhall library.** A handlist of books in Guildhall library associated with Thomas J. Wise. Guildh Misc 2:165–9 Oc '62.

Author checklist comp. by K. I. Garrett; *see also* no.5146.

5145 **Manchester. Public libraries.** Wise after the event; a catalogue of books, pamphlets, manuscripts and letters relating to Thomas James Wise, displayed . . . in Manchester central library. . . . Edited by G. E. Haslam. Manchester, 1964. xii,98p. 18cm.

Complete exhibition of forgeries, based on collection of Maurice P. Pariser, sold by Sotheby's, 1968.

5146 **London. Guildhall library.** Additional items in Guildhall library associated with Thomas J. Wise. Guildh Misc 2:305–6 S '65.

WISEMAN, CARD. NICHOLAS PATRICK STEPHEN, 1802–1865

5150 **Guibert, J.** 'Bibliographie de Wiseman' *in* Le réveil du catholicisme en Angleterre au XIXe siècle. Paris, 1907. p.[352]–64.

Classified chronol. checklist of works and ana.

WITHER, GEORGE, 1588–1667

5151 **Axon, William Edward Armytage,** 1895: no.910a.

5151a **Sidgwick, Frank,** *ed.* 'Bibliography of George Wither's early poetical works' *in* The poetry of George Wither. London, 1902. V.1, p.xlvii–lvi.

Checklist, with quasifacsim. TP transcrs.

WODEHOUSE, PELHAM GRENVILLE, 1881–

5152 **Checklist** bibliographies of modern authors. P. G. Wodehouse. Bk Trade J 68:17–19 Ag '36.

Chronol. checklist of early ed., 1902–36; collaborations; and plays and libretti, with notes on bindings.

5153 **Usborne, Richard Alexander.** [Classified chronological checklist of books, plays and films] *in* Wodehouse at work, a study of the books and characters. . . . London [1961] p.[213]–17.

WODROW, ROBERT, 1679–1734

5154 **Couper, William James.** Robert Wodrow. [Edinburgh] Reprinted from the Records of the Scottish church history society, 1928. 24p. 19cm.

'. . . list of Wodrow's printed writings' (p.15–20): annotated chronol. checklist.

WOODHEAD, ABRAHAM, 1609–1678

5155 **Brown, John Buchanan-.** The first publication of Abraham Woodhead's translation of st. Teresa. Library ser5 21:234–40 S '66.

Quasifacsim. TP transcrs., collations, bibliogr. notes and refs., with distinction of issues, for Wing T754–5.

WOODWARD, PHILIP, C.1557–1610

5156 **Russell, G. H.** Philip Woodward, elizabethan pamphleteer and translator. Library ser5 4:14–24 Je '49.

'Appendix' (p.23–4): quasifacsim. TP transcrs. of works discussed.

WOOLF, ADELINE VIRGINIA, 1882–1941

5157 **Beebe, Maurice.** Criticism of Virginia Woolf, a selected checklist, with an index to studies of separate works. Mod Fict Stud 2:36–45 F '56.

5158 **Kirkpatrick, Brownlee Jean.** A bibliography of Virginia Woolf. London, R. Hart-Davis, 1957. xii,180p. illus., port., facsims. 23cm. (Soho bibliographies, IX)

Classified arrangement of books; trans.; periodical contribs.; foreign ed.; etc.; with TP transcrs., collations and bibliogr. notes. Based on London university School of librarianship and archives bibliogr.: *see* no.154.

Rev: TLS 20 D '57:780; J. D. Gordan Library ser5 13:303–4 '57; C. Woolf Bk Coll 7:204, 207–8 '57.

5159 —— [Same]: Rev. ed. London, R. Hart-Davis, 1967. xii,212p. port., facsims. 22cm.

WORDSWORTH, WILLIAM, 1770–1850

5160 **Logan, James Venable.** Wordsworthian criticism; a guide and bibliography. Columbus, Ohio state university, 1947. xii,304p. 24cm.

'Bibliography' (p.157–275). *See* no.5165.

5161 **Gocking, W. E.,** 1952: no.129.

5162 **Raysor, Thomas Middleton,** *ed.*, 1956: no.2015.

5163 **Maxwell, James C.** Wordsworth in the Supplement to the Cambridge bibliography of English literature. N&Q 203:70–1 F '58.

Supplements CBEL for 1934–54.

5164 **Swayze, Walter E.** Early Wordsworthian biography; books and articles containing material on the life and character of William Wordsworth that appeared before the publication of the official Memoirs by Christopher Wordsworth in 1851. N.Y. Pub Lib Bull 64:169–95 Ap '60.

'Annotated list' (p.182–95).

5165 **Logan, James Venable.** Wordsworthian criticism, a guide and bibliography. [2d ed.] Columbus, Ohio state U.P., 1961. (First pub. 1947) xiv,304p. 23cm.

'Bibliography' (p.[155]–376).

5165a **Henley, Elton F.** A check list of masters' theses in the United States on William Wordsworth. Charlottesville, Va., Bibliographical society of the University of Virginia [1962] i,29[12]p. 17cm. (Duplicated typescript)

5166 **Henley, Elton F. and D. H. Stam.** Wordsworthian criticism, 1945–1964; an annotated bibliography. Rev. ed. New York, New York public library, 1965. (First pub. 1960) 107p. 26cm.

5167 **Dove cottage, AMBLESIDE. Local committee of management.** The official catalogue of Dove cottage, Grasmere, the home of Wordsworth . . . and of De Quincey. . . . Ambleside, G. Middleton, 1911. 39p. 15cm.

5168 **English association,** 1912: no.650.

5169 **Wise, Thomas James.** A bibliography of the writings in prose and verse of William Wordsworth. London, Ptd. for private circulation only by R. Clay, 1916. xv,268p. facsims. 23cm.

5170 **St.John, Cynthia (Morgan).** Collection of Wordsworthiana made by the late mrs. Cynthia Morgan St.John. . . . [Ithaca, N.Y., 1920] 30p. 25cm.

See no.5172.

5171 **Wise, Thomas James.** Two Lake poets; a catalogue of printed books, manuscripts and autograph letters by William Wordsworth and Samuel Taylor Coleridge, collected by Thomas James Wise. London, Ptd. for private circulation only, 1927. (Repr. London, Dawsons, 1965) xxi,135p. port., facsims. 26cm.

Bibliogr. catalogue of early ed. and ana; Wordsworth: p.1–48; Coleridge: p.51–135. No index.

5172 **Cornell university. Library.** The Wordsworth collection formed by Cynthia Morgan St.John and given to Cornell university by Victor Emanuel; a catalogue compiled by Leslie Nathan Broughton. Ithaca, N.Y., 1931. xii,124p. ports. 24cm.

See no.5176.

5173 **Patton, Cornelius Howard.** The Amherst Wordsworth collection; a descriptive bibliography. [Amherst, Mass.] Trustees of Amherst college, 1936. x,304p. 25cm.

Annotated classified catalogue of works and ana, with 'Other Wordsworth collections: check-list of books and manuscripts' (p.273–90) listing early ed. in 9 British and 9 American collections.

5174 **Cornell university. Library.** The Cornell Wordsworth collection; a brief account together with a catalogue of the exhibition held in the University library on the occasion of the centenary of Wordsworth's death. New York, Cornell U.P., 1950. 42p. port., facsims. 24cm.

Comp. by Robert C. Bald.

5175 **New York. Public library. Berg collection.** William Wordsworth, 1770–1850; an exhibition. By John D. Gordan. New York, New York public library, 1950. 31p. 26cm.

Repr. from N.Y. Pub Lib Bull 54:333–48, 384–96 Jl, Ag '50.

5176 **Cornell university. Library.** The Cornell Wordsworth collection; a catalogue of books and manuscripts presented to the University by mr. Victor Emanuel, Cornell, 1919. Compiled by George Harris Healey. Ithaca, N.Y., Cornell U.P., 1957. xiii,458p. facsims. 27cm.

Classified bibliogr. catalogue of 3,206 entries, with TP facsims.

5177 **Barnes, Jack C.** A bibliography of Wordsworth in American periodicals through 1825. Pa Bib Soc Am 52:205–19 '58.

Classified checklist of works and ana.

5178 **Wisconsin. University. Library.** The Arthur Beatty Wordsworth collection; given by Hamilton Beatty. . . . Madison, Wisc., University of Wisconsin, Memorial library, 1960. 16p. 23cm.

5179 **Woof, R. S.** Wordsworth's poetry and Stuart's newspapers, 1797–1803. Stud Bib 15:149–89 '62.

[Annotated chronol. checklist of contribs to the Morning post, and The courier, 1797–1814] (p.159–89)

WOTTON, SIR HENRY, 1568-1639

5185 **Smith, Lloyd Logan Pearsall,** *ed.* 'Prose works, poems and letters of sir Henry Wotton' *in* The life and letters of sir Henry Wotton. Oxford, 1907. V.2, p.[412]–54.
Checklist, principally of manuscripts.

WRANGHAM, FRANCIS, 1769-1842

5186 **Sadleir, Michael Thomas Hervey.** 'Wrangham's works, dated and provisionally datable' *in* Archdeacon Francis Wrangham, 1769–1842. [Oxford] 1937. p.61–95.
Chronol. checklist of 77 items, 1786–1842, with some TP facsims., and bibliogr. notes, followed by checklist of attribs. (p.95–7) and ana (p.97–9).

5187 —— [Same]: Supplement. Library ser4 19:422–61 Mr '39.
Mainly biographical.

WRIGHT, SIR ALMROTH EDWARD, 1861-1947

5188 **Colebrook, Leonard.** Bibliography of the published writings of sir Almroth E. Wright. London, W. Heinemann, 1952. 32p. port. 25cm.
Chronol. annotated checklist of 144 items, 1904–17; no index.

WRIGHT, THOMAS, 1561-1623

5189 **Rogers, David Morrison.** A bibliography of the published works of Thomas Wright, 1561–1623. Biog Stud 1no4:262–80 '52.
Annotated checklist of 14 items, with locations of copies.

WYATT, SIR THOMAS, 1503?-1542

5190 **Doughty, D. W.,** 1939: no.110.

WYCHERLEY, WILLIAM, 1640?-1716

5191 **Bibliographical** notes. Bk Hndbk 1no3:183 '47.
Checklist, with bibliogr. notes.

WYCLIFFE, JOHN, d.1384

5192 **British museum.** . . . Wycliffe exhibition in the King's library, arranged by E. M. Thompson. London, Ptd. by order of the trustees, 1884. xix,68p. 22cm.

5193 **Shirley, Walter Waddington.** Shirley's catalogue of the extant Latin works of John Wyclif. Rev. by Johann Loserth. London, Wyclif society [1924] 19p. 21cm. Covertitle.
Classified checklist of 100 items.

WYLSHMAN, WALTER, 1572-1636

5194 **Dredge, John Ingle,** 1889–99: no.886.

WYNNE, ELLIS, 1671-1734

5195 **Williams, William.** Gweledigaetheu y Bardd Cwsc; a bibliography. Welsh Bib Soc J 4:199–208 Jl '34.
'List of editions [of The visions of the sleeping bard]' (p.205–8): 39 items, with TP facsim.

WYNTOUN, ANDREW OF, 1350–1420?

5196 **Geddie, William,** 1912: no.2034.

YEATS, JACK BUTLER, 1871–1957

5197 **MacC[arvill], E.** Jack B. Yeats, his books. Dublin Mag new ser 20:47–52 Jl/S '45.

Chronol. checklist of 17 books written and illus. by Yeats, 1901–44, with TP transcrs., collations, and some bibliogr. notes.

YEATS, WILLIAM BUTLER, 1865–1939

5198 **Sidgwick, Frank.** William Butler Yeats. Eng Illus Mag new ser 29:286–8 Je '03.

'Bibliography' (p.288).

5199 **[Wade, Allan]** *comp.* 'Bibliography' *in* The collected works of William Butler Yeats. Stratford-on-Avon, 1908. V.8, p.[197]–287.

Includes 'American editions, compiled by John Quinn' (p. [280]–7).

5200 **Bibliographies** of modern authors. William Butler Yeats. Lond Merc 2n08:220–1 Je '20.

5201 **Symons, Alphonse James Albert.** A bibliography of the first editions of books by William Butler Yeats. London, First edition club, 1924. viii,46p. 21cm.

5202 **O'Hegarty, Patrick Sarsfield.** Notes on the bibliography of W. B. Yeats. Dublin Mag new ser 14:61–5 Oc/D '39; 15:37–42 Ja/Mr '40.

The O'Hegarty collection of Yeats, Synge, and lady Gregory is now in the University of Kansas library.

5203 **Roth, William M.** A catalogue of English and American first editions of William Butler Yeats . . . prepared for an exhibition of his works held in the Yale university library. . . . New Haven, 1939. 104p. 24cm.

5204 **Wade, Allan.** A bibliography of the writings of William Butler Yeats. London, R. Hart-Davis, 1951. 390p. port., facsims. 22cm. (Soho bibliographies, 1)

See no.5207.

5205 **Dublin. University. Trinity college. Library.** W. B. Yeats, manuscripts and printed books exhibited in the library . . . catalogue compiled by R. O. Dougan. Dublin, Ptd. for the Friends of the library of Trinity college, Dublin [1956] 50p. 22cm.

5206 **Kansas. University. Libraries.** William Butler Yeats; a catalogue of an exhibition from the P. S. O'Hegarty collection in the University of Kansas library, by Hester M. Black. Lawrence, 1958. 41p. facsim. 24cm.

5207 **Wade, Allan.** A bibliography of the writings of W. B. Yeats. [2d ed., rev.] London, R. Hart-Davis, 1958. 449p. port., facsims. 23cm. (Soho bibliographies, 1)

Classified bibliogr. of works and trans. to date, and 'The Cuala press, first called the Dun Emer press' (p.399–405); with quasifacsim. TP transcrs., collations, and bibliogr. notes. The Wade collection is now in the University of Indiana library.

5208 **Skelton, Robin** and **Ann Saddlemyer,** *ed.* 'Books and manuscripts' *in* The world of W. B. Yeats, essays in perspective; a symposium and catalogue . . . on the occasion of the W. B. Yeats centenary festival . . . University of Victoria. . . . Victoria, B.C. [1965] p.70–8, 177–88, 266–76.

5209 **Maxwell, Desmond Ernest Stewart** and **S. B. Bushriu,** *ed.* 'A select bibliography' *in* W. B. Yeats, centenary essays on the art of W. B. Yeats. [Ibadan] 1965. p.227–41.

5209a **Wesleyan university. Olin library.** William Butler Yeats, 1865–1965; a catalogue of his works and associated items. . . . Catalogue by Michael J. Durkan. Middletown, 1965. 92p. 21cm.

YONGE, CHARLOTTE MARY, 1823–1901

5210 **Laski, Marghanita** and **K. M. Tillotson,** *comp.* 'Bibliography' in Battis-combe, Esther G. and M. Laski, *ed.* A chaplet for Charlotte Yonge. . . . London [1965] p.204–[16]

Classified alphabetical checklist of works; trans.; contribs. to books; and ana, with some bibliogr. notes.

YOUNG, ANDREW JOHN, 1885–

5211 **Clark, Leonard,** *ed.* 'Checklist of the writings of Andrew Young' *in* Andrew Young, prospect of a poet. London, 1957. p.109–12.

Chronol. checklist, 1911–56, with some bibliogr. notes.

YOUNG, ARTHUR, 1741–1820

5212 **Anderson, John Parker,** *comp.* 'Bibliography of Arthur Young' *in* Hutton, A. W., *ed.* Arthur Young's Tour in Ireland, 1776–1779. London, 1892. V.2, p.[349]–74.

Classified checklist of works; trans. of; ana; and contribs. to Annals of agriculture.

5213 **Amery, George Douglas.** The writings of Arthur Young. J Roy Agric Soc Eng 85:1–31 '24.

'List of the editions and issues of the works of Arthur Young' (p.16–21): chronol. checklist, 1758–1898, with locations of copies; 'Arthur Young's contributions to the Annals of agriculture' (p.21–31).

5213a —— 'List of the editions and issues of Arthur Young' *in* Fussell, George E. More old English farming books. . . . London [1950] p.154–65.

Chronol. checklist, 1758–1898, with some locations of copies.

YOUNG, EDWARD, 1683–1765

5214 **Cordasco, Francesco G. M.** Edward Young, a handlist of critical notices & studies. New York, B. Franklin for Long Island U.P., 1950. 9p. 24cm. (Eighteenth century bibliographical pamphlets, no.11)

5215 **Kind, John Louis.** 'Bibliography of German translations, editions, reviews, and notices' *in* Edward Young in Germany. New York, 1906. p.134–80.

5216 **Pettit, Henry J.** A checklist of Young's Night-thoughts in America. Pa Bib Soc Am 42:150–6 '48.

'Night-thoughts': 92 items; 'Works': items 93–108.

5217 **Templeman, William Darby.** Additions to the check-list of Young's Night-thoughts in America. Pa Bib Soc Am 43:348–9 '49.

5218 **Pettit, Henry J.** Further additions to the check-list of Young's Night-thoughts in America. Pa Bib Soc Am 44:192–5 '50.

'Night-thoughts': items 109–42; 'Works': items 143–5, with locations of copies, and 'A finding-list of items in sections I and II' (p.194–5).

5219 —— A bibliography of Young's Night thoughts. Boulder, Col., University of Colorado pr., 1954. 52p. facsims. 26cm.

Quasifacsim. TP transcrs. and facsims., collations, and bibliogr. notes on early ed., 1742–62.

Rev: A. D. McKillop Philol Q 34:330 '55; R. W. Chapman Library ser5 10:139–40 '55.

INDEX

THE Index records the names of authors, compilers, editors, and publishers of the items entered in the Bibliography, together with subjects, in a single alphabetical sequence. Name references and the references pertaining to them, are in roman type. If an item number under a name entry is enclosed by parentheses, that item is a reference in the Bibliography. The entry for Dredge gives an example of this.

Subject entries are in SMALL CAPITALS. Under the main subject headings, the numbers printed in **bold** face refer to the entries under the same heading in the main arrangement of the Bibliography.

Since this index is quite brief, it is not expected that the arrangement of name and subject entries will be obscure. However, it should be noted that, because it is desirable to keep divided headings under the main entry, the general practice of placing subject headings after name (author, compiler, etc.) headings has been followed. Hence, 'London' followed by various divided entries for publishers, institutions, etc., then LONDON the subject, with its subject divisions. 'Chesterton, G. K.', the compiler of a bibliography, is followed by CHESTERTON, G. K., the subject of a bibliography.

Such prefixes as 'bp., archbp., sir, ld.' have been ignored in the filing order. Titles of books and periodicals are in *italics*, or *ITALIC SMALL CAPITALS* if they are the subjects of bibliographical lists. The heading BOOKS has been used to provide a division by period or subject for items entered in the Bibliography under headings not divided by period.

No special authority is claimed for the names and dates in the Bibliography and Index. These have been taken from standard sources (*D.N.B.*, *Who was Who*, *Who's Who*, *The Oxford Companion*, and the like), but where they differ from those authorities, it is because more correct information has come readily to hand, often in the bibliographical items listed in the Bibliography.

Abbatt, William. 1436
Abbey, John Roland. 1750–1 1753
ABBOT, archbp. George, 1562–1633. **2300**
ABBOT, John, 1588–1650? **2301**
Abbott, Claude Colleer. 2949
Abbott, Thomas Kingsmill. 425
Abbott, Wilbur Cortez. 2921
Abdul-Muizz, Mohammed *see* Muizz, Mohammed Abdul-.
À Beckett, Arthur William. 3180
Abel, Lola L. 70
ABERCROMBIE, Lascelles, 1881–1938. **2302–3**
Aberdeen. University. Library. 454–5 711–12 1180 1505 1961
ABERDEEN, Aber. **982–5**
— Universities. 981 **984–5**
ABERDEENSHIRE. **980–5**

Abertay historical society. 1006
Aberystwyth. National library of Wales *see* Wales. National library, Aberystwyth.
ABERYSTWYTH, Cardiganshire. **962**
Abrahams, Aleck. 2925
Abram, W. A. 5130a
Abstracts of English studies. 25
ACCOUNTING. **2080–5**
ACHILL, CO. Mayo. **1106**
ACHILL PRESS. **1240**
ACKERMANN, Rudolph, 1764–1834. 1738–9
ACTON, John Emerich Edward Dalberg, 1st baron Acton, 1834–1902. **2304**
Adam, Robert Borthwick. 397–8 3839 3841
Adams, H. M. 1519 1523
Adams, John Couch. 329
Adams, R. E. 71 (2468)

ADAMS, Sarah Fuller (Flower), 1805-1848. **2305**

ADDISON, Joseph, 1672-1719. **2306-7**

Adelman, Seymour. 2542 4946

Adkins, Nelson Frederick. 4895

Æ, *pseud. of* George William Russell, 1867-1935. **2308-12**

AGRICULTURE *see also* GARDENING. **2090-8**

AIKIN, Anna Lætitia (mrs. Barbauld), 1743-1825. **2313**

AINSWORTH, William Harrison, 1805-1882. 672 **2314-15**

Aitken, George Atherton. 2330 4439 4770

Aitken, William Russell. 969 3425 3538 4091 4735

AKENSIDE, Mark, 1721-1770. **2316**

Albu, K. M. 72 (4142-3)

ALCHEMY. **2100-a**

ALCOCK, Deborah, fl.1866-1910. **2317**

Aldeburgh festival of music and the arts, 7th., 1954. 2903

Alden, John Eliot. 540 603-4 609 735 2771

Alderman, William E. 2880a

ALDINGTON, Richard, 1892-1962. **2318-19**

Aldis, Harry Gidney. 716 1323

ALDISS, Brian Wilson, 1925- . **2320**

Aldred, Thomas. 1662 1666 1670

Alexander, Elizabeth H. 3284-5 4595

Alexander, Mary. 2565 2785

Alexander Turnbull library, Wellington, N.Z. 578 585 1997 3953

Alice Meynell centenary tribute. 4212

ALKEN, Henry, fl.1816-1831. 1738

ALL THE YEAR ROUND. 3061 3096

Allan, D. J. 3295

Allardyce, Mabel D. 712

Allen, Don Cameron. 576

Allen, Reginald. 3433

ALLEN, card. William, 1532-1594. **2321**

Allford, J. M. 73 (4060)

Allibone, Samuel Austin. 5009

Allingham, Helen. 2322

ALLINGHAM, William, 1824-1889. **2322-3**

Allison, Antony Francis. 535 548 2257 2264 3279 3396 3739

Allison, William Talbot. 4227

Allnutt, William Henry. 866-7

Allum, M. P. 4030

Almack, Edward. 2762

ALMANACS AND PROGNOSTICATIONS. **1425-30**

ALNWICK, Northumb. **926a**

Altschul, Frank. 4202

Alston, Robin Carfrae. (1582) 1730 (1731) 2203-4 (2282) (2283a)

Altick, Richard Daniel. 5 657

Ambleside. Dove cottage *see* Dove cottage, Ambleside.

American antiquarian society. 1893

— Library. Isaiah Thomas collection. 1466

American art association, New York. 395 401 671 1744 3074 3077 3082 3586

American bible society. 1495

American book collector. 275

AMERICAN LITERATURE *see* FOREIGN BOOKS PUBLISHED IN ENGLISH—United States.

Amery, George Douglas. 5213-a

Ames foundation *see* Harvard university. Ames foundation.

Amherst, William Amhurst Tyssen-, 1st baron Amherst of Hackney. 385

Amherst college. Library. 5173

Amory, Harcourt. 2727

An Leabharlann. 276

ANATOMY. 2221 2228

Anders, H. 2039a

ANDERSEN, Hans Christian, 1805-1875. 802

Anderson, A. 2098

Anderson, Alan. 3501

Anderson, John. 1026-8 2677

Anderson, John Parker. 855 2365 2898a 3247 4220 4541 4542 4598 4663 4718 4907 5212

Anderson, Peter John. 711 984-5 1001 1935a 1961 3856 4054-6 4102-4

Anderson, Robert Bowie. 2211

Anderson auction co., New York. 384 388-9 1740

Anderson galleries, New York. 393-4 396 398 400-1 518 665 671 3082 4649 4806 5101

Anderton, Basil. 926 2458

Andrew, R. V. 2851

Andrews, C. S. 3774

Andrews, Charles Edward. 2532

Andrews, John Harwood. 1818

ANGELSEY. **961**

ANGLIA, EAST *see* EAST ANGLIA.

ANGLIÆ NOTITIÆ. 74

ANGLING. **2101-2**

ANGLO-INDIAN LITERATURE. 333 1664

ANGLO-IRISH LITERATURE. 3 1719 2035

ANGLO-LATIN LITERATURE. 346 1443 1607 1727-8 1983 1986a 3729 5193

ANGLO-SAXON *see* PRINTING IN ANGLO-SAXON.

Angus, I. 4373

Angus, William Craibe. 2631-2

ANNALS OF AGRICULTURE. 5212-13

Annals of English literature. (348) 364

ANNAN, Dumf. **995**

ANNUAL ANTHOLOGY. 1903b

Annual bibliography of English language and literature. 26

ANNUAL REVIEW. 4740

ANNUALS. 1927b

ANONYMA AND PSEUDONYMA. **1435-42**

ANSELM, st., 1033-1109. **2324**

ANSTEY, Christopher, 1724-1805. **2325-6**

ANSTEY, F., *pseud. of* Thomas Anstey Guthrie, 1856-1934. **2327-8**

O o

PRINTED IN GREAT BRITAIN
AT THE UNIVERSITY PRESS, OXFORD
BY VIVIAN RIDLER
PRINTER TO THE UNIVERSITY